LIFE AND CULTURE
IN THE ANCIENT NEAR EAST

LIFE AND CULTURE IN THE ANCIENT NEAR EAST

Editors

Richard E. Averbeck
Mark W. Chavalas
David B. Weisberg

CDL Press
Bethesda, Md.

LIBRARY OF CONGRESS CATALOGING-IN-PUBLICATION DATA

Life and culture in the ancient Near East / editors, Richard E. Averbeck, Mark W. Chavalas, David B. Weisberg.
p. cm.
Includes bibliographical references.
ISBN 1-883053-73-0
1. Middle East—Civilization—To 622. 2. Middle East—Social life and customs. I. Averbeck, Richard E. II. Chavalas, Mark W. III. Weisberg, David B.

DS54.L54 2003
939'.4–dc21 2002072883

The cover design by Duy-Khuong Van.

The drawing separating some articles is of a board for the Egyptian game of Mehen, from the article by Alfred J. Hoerth.

TABLE OF CONTENTS

— The Levant —

— Egypt —

— The New Testament World —

— SPECIAL SUBJECTS —

INTRODUCTION

At the joint meeting of the American Oriental Society Middle West, the Society of Biblical Literature Midwest, and the American Schools of Oriental Research Midwest, held at Marquette University, February 15–17, 1998, it was decided that the theme of the next conference was to be "Everyday Life in the Ancient Near East." The next meeting was held at Hebrew Union College in Cincinnati, Ohio, February 14–16, 1999. We would like to express our sincere appreciation to the administration and staff of Hebrew Union College for the fine hospitality and generosity at the conference. Special thanks go to President Sheldon Zimmerman, Dean Kenneth Ehrlich, and Judy Greer and her staff.

Because of the enthusiastic participation and high quality of papers on everyday life, we decided to publish them in the present format. We thank all the participants for their work at the conference and for their contributions to the present volume. There were, of course, many places, times, and subjects of interest that were not represented at the conference. This was unavoidable. We have been fortunate, however, that other highly qualified scholars have been willing to step forward to fill some of these gaps. They include: Alfred J. Hoerth (games), Stephan J. Joubert (the poor), Wilfred G.E. Watson (Ugarit), and Edwin M. Yamauchi (athletics). We thank each of these men for their important contributions to the volume.

Scholars interpret "everyday/daily life" in various ways, so it was expected that there would be a variety of approaches to the topic at the conference. This is natural and, in fact, provided for a variety of kinds of essays. This will come through in the present volume. We have arranged the essays primarily according to geography, moving from the northeast to the southwest, from Mesopotamia, to Hatti, to Syria, to Palestine, and finally to Egypt. Following that there are essays on the New Testament world and then some special subjects: use of animals, a special calendrical practice, games, and athletics. The following is a brief summary of each of the essays.

Dan Snell begins his paper on daily in ancient Sumer with an examination of "the concept of daily life as it arose apparently in the last century in the context of Romantic interest in the exotic." He then turns his attention to the peculiarities of the institution of slavery as reflected in the Sumerian proverb collections and other similar kinds of literature.

The article by Richard Averbeck shows how certain kinds of Sumerian literary compositions can also contribute to our understanding of daily life in ancient Sumer. He defines "daily life" as "quotidian life: the everyday concerns common to all regular people in every place at all times." The myth known as *Enki and the World Order* provides an important point of departure for understanding the main principles and patterns of daily life in Sumer.

The essay by Samuel Greengus on "Biblical and Mesopotamian Law: An Amorite Connection?" explores the possibility of a connection between the Bible and earlier Mesopotamian law collections through the Amorites. He focuses his attention on the talionic laws ('an eye for an eye, tooth for tooth...") and the laws of debt slavery.

David Weisberg offers a brief sketch of "Everyday Life in the Neo-Babylonian Period." He is especially concerned with the integration of material and non-material features of Babylonian culture. Both contribute significantly to the discussion.

Harry Hoffner provides a very valuable overview of the private life and exploitation of resources by the Hittites, based largely on textual rather than archaeological evidence. This article serves as an expansion on previous work done in his 1974 book on *Food Production in Hittite Asia Minor*.

The article by Wilfred G.E. Watson is a fine survey of what we know about life and culture in ancient Ugarit from both documents and material remains. He reviews all the previous work done and organizes the results in the following categories: climate, resources, buildings and building materials, the inhabitants, family, schools and scribes, crafts and trade, farming and agriculture, army and navy, calendar, religion, medicine and magic, music and entertainment, and death and burial.

In his essay on the physical house, family household, urban context, and status of a homeowner named Puzurum at Terqa in northern Syria (1700–1500 B.C.E.), Mark Chavalas combines all the archaeological, comparative, and textual resources available (some cuneiform texts were found in the house). He concludes that this man was "an independent householder, purchaser and seller of real estate (fields, and possibly gardens), a debtor, and possibly a slave owner."

Jan Gallagher suggests in her article on "An Extraordinary Everyday for Emar's Diviner" that the diviner, in fact, fulfilled multiple functions, not just the performance of divination procedures. He was a major local character who, among other things, served as the master scribe and liaison to the Hittite overlords of Emar.

Carol Meyers' approach in "Everyday Life in Biblical Israel: Women's Social Networks" is, in her words, "to ignore the urban elite and instead focus on the agrarian families, or peasant farmers,... to reconstruct the social relationships, rather than the physical realities of everyday life." She is particularly interested in the extra-familial social networks established and maintained by women, and their function in village life in ancient (biblical) Israel.

In her treatment of "sisterhood" stories (relationships between women in the Hebrew Bible), Beverly Bow argues that "the patriarchal message is that women cannot or should not band together" under normal conditions, although there are a few instances where such cooperation between women "serves a patriarchal purpose."

Peter Feinman focuses on "boy meets girl" stories and the various elements of them: the eligibility of the parties involved, how the meeting is managed, how is it made legitimate or sanctified. Aside from the basic social necessity of such meetings, they also carry significance for social dramas and even political messages.

Anson Rainey's essay deals with two "Aspects of Life in Ancient Israel" in the first temple period: (1) the estates of landed aristocracy worked by stewards and peasants, who were responsible to make regular deliveries to their overlords from the produce of these estates, as reflected in "fiscal bullae" that were used as labels for these shipments and the Samaria ostraca, and (2) corvée labor imposed on the remnants of the pre-Israelite population of the land as well as the Israelite tribes themselves in Solomonic days.

Lawson Younger's paper "'Give Us Our Daily Bread': Everyday Life for the Israelite Deportees" is an investigation of "the various filtering processes used by the Assyrians that determined deportee status," specifically, the Samarians taken into captivity from 734 to 716 B.C.E. He examines "the personal impact of these extraditions on the people of the northern kingdom."

The article by Robert Miller breaks new methodological ground in the archaeological study of the farming economy of Iron Age Israel. He starts with climate and "environmental zones" as a basis for "mapping production schemes" in the various regions and combines with that flora and faunal remains known from archaeological excavations. He adds to this a comparison with analogous environmental zones throughout the world.

The article by Jennie Ebeling on "ground stone tools in Bronze and Iron Age Palestine" goes beyond the normal "form = function equations" to include study of the different wear patterns caused by the processing of different kinds of materials (e.g., animal hide versus corn). She also presents an overview of the kinds of ground stone tools excavated in Palestine.

James Hoffmeier's essay deals with "Everyday Life in Ancient Egypt." Selecting his material from the plethora of evidence about daily life from the Old Kingdom through Roman times, he examined four sources of evidence: (1) tomb paintings and reliefs, (2) models of workers, (3) surviving tools and equipment, and (4) written sources, which, when taken together, supply a fairly comprehensive picture of daily life.

Bruce Malina's "Daily Life in the New Testament Period" provides us with a look at the Roman aristocratic empire based on a ruralized society, which was shaped by kinship ties and their associated political, economic, and religious units. Power, violence, and patronage were primary features of the empire in city and village. He describes the distinctive "daily rhythm of life in the region" for elites as opposed to non-elites.

The essay by Stephan Joubert contributes to the discussion of "reciprocity and the poor among the first followers of Jesus in Jerusalem." He points out that the cultural pattern of benefaction, in which the benefactor and beneficiary were bound to a long-term relationship of reciprocity, was overturned in the early Jerusalem Christian community in favor of humanitarian giving based on the notion that Christ himself would eventually reward the benefactor. This, in turn, led to the centralization of efforts in Jerusalem to care for the poor as well as collections from churches elsewhere in the Roman world for the Jerusalem Christians during times of famine in Judah.

Ritva Williams develops the early church authority of bishops as brokers of heavenly goods and blessings according to Ignatius' letter to the Ephesians, associating it with the brokerage system of the Greco-Roman cultural world. According to this pattern of authority, the local congregation is like a household where the owner (Christ) is absent and a steward is in charge (the bishop). This is the historical basis of the Episcopal form of Christian organization.

In his essay on "Methods and Daily Life" Gerald Klingbeil develops an understanding of "The Use of Animals in Daily Life in a Multi-disciplinary Framework." He warns against a too narrow approach that would separate archaeology from textual and iconographic sources and hopes that, in the future, these various kinds of sources will be used in combination to develop more well-rounded reconstructions of ancient life.

Leo Depuydt investigates the ancient calendrical practice of the Second Feast Day of the Diaspora (*Yom Tov Sheni Shel Galuyyot*). The purpose of the double celebration was to be sure that the Jews celebrated the feast on the proper day even if they miscalculated the date on which the Sanhedrin announced the New Moon.

The study of "Games People Played" by Alfred Hoerth deals with board games in the ancient Near East, from Egypt to Mesopotamia, Cyprus to Iran, and in Syria-Palestine, from the third to the first millennium B.C.E. He treats four games (Mehen, Senet, Tau, and Hounds and Jackals) and offers a specific set of rules for Tau and Hounds and Jackals.

Edwin Yamauchi's essay on "Athletics in the Ancient Near East" surveys the evidence for athletic games and contests in Mesopotamia, Anatolia, Syria-Palestine, Egypt, and Crete. Wrestling seems especially widespread and popular, but other athletic activities are also known: running, boxing, fencing, stick fighting, archery, and "bull-jumping" (leaping on the back of a rampaging bull, only in Crete as far as we know).

Richard E. Averbeck
Mark W. Chavalas
David B. Weisberg
October, 2002

Mesopotamia

THE ORDINARITY OF THE PECULIAR INSTITUTION

Daniel C. Snell*
The University of Oklahoma

This essay examines the concept of daily life as it arose apparently in the last century in the context of Romantic interest in the exotic, perhaps as a function of the manipulation of time in industrializing societies. We shall briefly examine what the term "daily life" has meant in the historiography of the Ancient Near East, concluding that there is no generally accepted definition. We shall then look for "daily life" among the Sumerian proverb texts from Early Dynastic and Early Old Babylonian times.

I must confess that my 1997 Yale University Press book was, right up to the last moment, titled *A Social and Economic History of the Ancient Near East*. But the Press and I agreed that that was pretty dry—of course, that was when the scintillating exposition of why we lack an economic theory was still Chapter One instead of an obscure appendix, as now. The Press suggested we call the book *Daily Life in the Ancient Near East*. I bristled at this on the assumption that "daily life" was a definable genre that I had definitely not set out to write. Could I accept the title without the "daily?" Sure, and we took the revolutionary step of not even having a subtitle. Who could object? Life, as the Sumerian Proverbs say, is life![1]

And yet perhaps I have been naive. Possibly my book has been received as if it were a Daily Life, so that at some level I have written a lie. Or, to put a better face on it, unintentionally I may have written a Daily Life on the assumption that Daily Life was a well-known and oft-produced something else, a recognized genre full of precedents. But I was wrong.

When I survey Mesopotamian Daily Lives, I find a wild variety of topics covered. Contenau's 1966 (in English) effort contains the big divisions: General Information, King and State, Mesopotamian Thought, and Religious Life. The jacket blurb assures us, "M. Contenau covers every

---

* My thanks go to Richard Averbeck, Mark Chavalas, David Weisberg, and Gordon Young for suggestions for this paper.

1 Ti-la ti-la! Alster (1997) 195, 11.71, or, with Alster there: "To live is to live." See Snell (1997).

conceivable aspect of Mesopotamian life." Saggs' 1965 effort also ranges broadly; his chapters include "A Forgotten Civilisation," "Kingdoms Rise and Fall," "Life at an Amorite Court," "The Scribe in Babylonian Society," "Running an [Assyrian] Empire," "Ancient Crafts and Industries," "Law," "Nebachadnezzer's Babylon," and "Religion." Here, clearly, this scholar has "plopped down" in three interesting times and places: Mari, Assyria of the Empire, and the Neo-Babylonian period. Horst Klengel avoids the temptation of breadth by concentrating on Hammurapi and his reign, discussing political events, society, Hammurapi and his efforts, and, finally, his laws. Martin Stol, writing in 1995 on "Private Life"—which I would argue is something rather different—speaks of the phases of life, the identification (of individuals), the family, marriage, man and woman, pregnancy and childbirth, childlessness, education, sexuality, old age, widows, work and subsistence, food, the house, and entertainment. Karen Nemet-Nejat's 1998 effort begins with a historical overview, and then turns to writing, the sciences, city life and country life, private life, recreation, religion, government, the economy, and the legacy.

A survey of books with Daily Life titles dealing with other areas shows that there is no standard content. Several books even include political background to provide some context to the everyday. I wonder if the study of the use of time, the consideration of what is usual, is not by definition a hallmark of the genre. But how do we decide what is usual? Not being participant-observers, we cannot know with any certainty. Or can we be guided by repetition? If it happens more than once, perhaps it is usual, and if it is usual, perhaps it is "daily." If so, logically we would seek the repeated action. To my mind that would appear to exclude politics and war since such events are not exactly repeatable, although there might be Daily Lives of politicians and warriors—I have run across the 1894 volume by Frédéric Masson, *Napoleon at Home; The Daily Life of the Emperor at the Tuileries* and Henry (Baron) Snell's (no relation) *Daily Life in Parliament* from 1930. Can we then not define the content of Daily Life? Perhaps not, except to say that a Daily Life that strays far from the study of the usual is probably not fulfilling expectations. But the silly variety of things in Daily Lives may show that really there are no expectations.

To me, this is astonishing and important because it indicates that we have here a major category of thinking about time and the past that apparently has not found systematic treatment. I am particularly amazed that the *Annales* school, with its massive volumes on Everyday Life in various ages, has not managed to be coherent, as far as I can see, about what it might be that they are studying. We have a theory for everything but "daily life," for what we might call "ordinarity."

There is a French series called *La Vie Quotidienne,* in which various professions of the nineteenth century are studied. And there is an American series called *The Writer's Guide to Everyday Life in...* by Writer's Digest Books. I have not studied each of these, alack, but the one I have studied has no reflection at all about what the subject might entail. A search of the OCLC catalogue showed 2,111 entries in July, 1998, under the category Daily Life, and Worldcat had 2,170 in January, 1999. I was amazed to see the announcement of a multidisciplinary Center for the Ethnography of Everyday Life at the University of Michigan, Ann Arbor. There the focus is "in the area of the ethnography of work and family transitions among middle class Americans, with the category 'middle class' somewhat broadly construed." A solicitation for fellowship applications from that center required "a Ph.D. or equivalent degree in Anthropology, Economics, Psychology, Sociology, Organizational Behavior or related field," but not, apparently, History though the advertisement appeared in the American Historical Association's newsletter (*Perspectives,* December, 1998, p. 69). This center may advance someone's preconceived paradigm. We study what we know to be normal or everyday, in a certain class, place, and time, and we find, presumably, what we knew we would find. I am all for reinforcing helpful paradigms of knowledge, but I fear incoherence or at least tautology.

In German the term *das Alltag* has become, since World War II, a rallying cry for younger historians wanting to study not the great movements of politics but the activities and, to an extent, the possible culpability of ordinary citizens, especially during the Third Reich. This study of the "little people" has tried to integrate Nazi life with politics, and it has angered many in the historical establishment. As its champion, Alf Lüdtke writes, "Quite obviously a large number of 'general historians' are still convinced that historians of everyday life are interested only in colorful supplements, anecdotal materials—the tinsel and trivia of the historical process," which they term "intellectual oatmeal."[2] Clearly passions have been aroused by these concerns, which perhaps parallel the United States' interest in social history broadly conceived. It is clear that a concern for the "little people" is a major focus of historical study nowadays for all periods and places.

Is that all we mean by "Daily Life?" Maybe so, but if you will permit me a short trip into the nineteenth century, I may be able to sort out some of the strands of thought that lead to our use of the term "Daily Life," and these, in turn, may help define what we mean—or what we ought to mean—by the study of Daily Life.

2 Lüdtke (1995) 12.

The earliest book I could find with a title utilizing "Everyday Life" or "Daily Life" was written in 1837.[3] (I am willing to admit I may not have found the very earliest reference, but it seems to me that it is very likely that we will not find such a work much older than that.) So, no Daily Life before 1837. What are the implications? It was a high Romantic period, when researchers were looking for the spirit of the folk, to be found not necessarily among the high and mighty but at the hearths and in the mouths of the lowly and simple. Is it possible that before that there was no concern for everyday life, or simply no high culture, no scholarly concern for it?

E.P. Thompson's problem of industrial time also evolves in that era: factories cannot operate efficiently unless the workers all arrive at the same time. Thompson saw that preindustrial task orientation precluded much "demarcation between 'work' and 'life'."[4] Thus there was little occasion to see time as separable into ordinary and extraordinary, as had existed in a

---

3 (Sir) John Gardner Wilkinson, (1797–1875) *Manners and customs of the ancient Egyptians, including their private life, government, laws, art, manufactures, religion, and early history; derived from a comparison of the paintings, sculptures, and monuments still existing with the accounts of ancient customs.* 3 volumes, (London: J. Murray, 1837). Compare also Jacob Abbott, *Every day duty: illustrated by sketches of childish character and conduct,* (London: A. Bell, 1837) and David Boswell Reid, *Rudiments of Chemistry: with illustrations of the chemical phenomena of daily life,* (Edinburgh: Chambers, 1836). Something was in the air!

To be fair, the use of "daily" and "everyday" in English goes back earlier in the literature of devotion and spiritual formation, including William Penn's 1682 *No Cross, No Crown. A discourse shewing the nature and discipline of the holy cross of Christ, and that the denyal of self and daily bearing of Christ's cross is the alone way to the rest and kingdom of God: to which are added living and dying testimonies of divers persons of fame and learning in favor of this treatise,* (London: Clark). And this usage may in turn go back to the Lord's Prayer's "daily," ἐπιούσιον, really "sufficient for the day." But we are interested here in the idea that the daily lives of former persons might have been markedly different from ours and thus worth chronicling.

The derivation from devotional literature is also connected to travel literature, developed as Europeans were increasingly in contact with new peoples of different customs. Compare John James Blunt (1794–1855), *Vestiges of ancient manners and customs, discoverable in modern Italy and Sicily,* (London: J. Murray, 1923). The very earliest example I could find that appears to be relevant combines the catechetical with the historical interest in a modern and Romantic way, but long before these other works: Abbé Claude Fleury (1640–1723), *Moeurs des Israélites,* (Paris: Veuve G. Clouzier, 1681), but translated into English only in 1802 as *A Short History of the Ancient Israelites: with an account of their manners, customs, laws, polity, religion, sects, arts and trades, division of time, wars, captivities, &c...* (Liverpool: J. Nuttal for W. Baynes, 1802).

4 Thompson (1967).

preindustrial world. In contrast, with industrial time, Thompson argues, "Time is now currency: it is not passed but spent."[5] The concept of "time-thrift" to which we are all now addicted, arises in the industrializing context.[6] It may be that as time was being commodified at the beginning of the eighteenth century, some persons were drawn to consider what things had been like before industrialization, in a form of nostalgia.[7]

It is the quest for the quaint that may be the key to defining a category "Daily Life." Antiquarianism predates this phenomenon and may feed directly into it. The British Society of Antiquaries was founded in 1707, but it only launched its journal in 1779.[8] People collecting old objects and genealogical trivia derive intellectually from the late medieval collectors of cabinets or oddities. But neither they nor the antiquaries apparently wrote Daily Lives.

The transition between collecting trivia and trying to explore daily lives may be marked by Sir Walter Scott. In the preface to his first novel, *Waverly*, he speaks of his desire to make concrete the researches of an earlier antiquary, whose literary remains he had worked through.[9] His career had begun with collecting old poetry and reworking it for modern taste. In his novel, purely a fiction in its title character, he is concerned with the 1745 rebellion in Scotland and touches historical persons, including the incoherent but utterly charming prince who led and lost the revolution. Oddly for a novelist, but sensibly for an antiquary, Scott included extensive footnotes exploring the histories of the places, persons, and customs mentioned. And the motive for all this may emerge from what he has his title character, an Englishman, say in reply to a highland leader who asks if he has come among them to prepare the highlanders for the impending revolt. Scott writes, "Waverly, surprised and somewhat startled at this question from such a character, answered he had no motive in visiting him but curiosity to see his extraordinary place of residence," which was a cave.[10] It is this curiosity about the extraordinary that appears to impel us to daily life.

---

5 *Ibid.*, 61.

6 *Ibid.*, 83.

7 The word *nostalgia* at first meaning homesickness is first found in English in 1770, though the longing for the past supposedly only appears in 1920, relying on *The Oxford English Dictionary*, (Oxford: Clarendon, 1971), volume N, 219, and Supplement (1987), 1254.

8 Hargreaves (1997).

9 Scott (1982) 10.

10 Scott (1982) 161.

Waverly has been criticized for having a non-entity as its hero. He really is a cipher, not joining the rebellion until the charming prince directly asks him to, and then weaseling out of responsibility for participation when it fails. But such criticism ignores Scott's real purpose, which was to illustrate a now vanishing style of life, common "sixty years since," as Scott repeatedly says.

There may be no expectations in terms of content because we do not know what will appear strange and worthy of comment by a modern writer, but I believe there are expectations in terms of mood. One wants to feel while reading a Daily Life as if one could understand what it was to live in the place and time being studied. Through fiction there may be ways of creating such an illusion, but Daily Life does not usually permit itself fiction; this seems to be one thing not usually allowed! How is this feeling achieved in Daily Lives? I believe successful Daily Lives have, if they are not wholly organized around them, anecdotes—telling demonstrably true stories that reinforce the feeling, sometimes fallaciously, that we are much like the people in the studied context. This may be oatmeal, but it can be nutritious.

I want, nonetheless, to find some daily life, or something that is likely to seem like daily life, in older Mesopotamian sources. To do that I have turned to Alster's magnificent recent edition of the Sumerian proverb collections, which lured me in with many promises. Alster is adamant that the sayings "belong to the speech of daily life."[11] He argues that the mythopoeic approach to life perhaps seen in other literary texts "was not the normal attitude toward daily life," which instead we see reflected in the texts he edits.[12] Most appear to come from the Isin-Larsa period, and yet there are clear connections to the Instructions of Šuruppak and to the Early Dynastic Proverb collection, which I will also consider here.[13] Because of these lines of connection it is reasonable to view this material as a unity. But we ought not to assume that all of it goes back to Early Dynastic times, or that everything was still current in the Early Old Babylonian Period. Still, this is a span of six hundred years, at least, and meanings might change even if sayings persisted.

---

11 Alster (1997) xiii.

12 Alster (1997) xviii.

13 In what follows, the following works will be used: Alster (1997; 1991/2; 1974). If sayings are from the Early Dynastic Period around 2400 B.C.E., that will be indicated; otherwise they may be assumed to be from the Old Babylonian period, around 1800 B.C.E.

There is controversy about how literary such Sumerian collections were, but Alster thinks that they express the language of daily life, if only because he cannot explain why some are in the Emesal, the "thin" dialect of Sumerian, and some are not. If there was no motivation from content for the language choice, perhaps the dialect was merely a feature of how the sayings were said when they were said. And by the Old Babylonian period, when the language was presumably dead or dying, the things had become fossilized on clay in whatever dialect was the original.

In surveying this material I have limited myself to studying sayings that deal with slaves because of my interest in dependent persons, and I seek to tease out what the sayings might imply about daily treatment and activities of slaves. Naturally the question of how you evaluate treatment of slaves is a vexing one, and it is not my interest here to say whether one or another aspect of the lives of slaves in the period was mild or not.[14]

As Alster makes clear, the point of view in most of this material was that of the "household-owner."[15] Alster notes that "proverbs are extremely conservative; they promulgate the *status quo*. They do not question the validity of the existing social order. Those at the bottom of the social scale are told to stay there."[16]

The gender division expressed in the material is stark. I have not counted the several repeated sayings, but of the 55 sayings dealing with slaves, only 15 refer to males, while 45, or 81%, refer to female slaves. Does this reflect the demographics of slavery? Perhaps, but it may also be the case that slave-girls inspired more proverbial sayings because of their roles in the household, where the master class observed them and interacted with them more than with males. But the males were probably domestic servants too and not field hands. Why do they not catch the imagination? A sinister answer might be the right one, one linked to master-slave sex.

There are five subject areas in which slaves are mentioned: (1) food; (2) work and laziness; (3) the low status of the slave; (4) sex; (5) and advice on dealing with slaves. The numbers of sayings for each topic are as follows, along with the percentage of all sayings about slaves these topics represent:

---

14 On this question see the American examples of Genovese (1969).

15 Alster (1997) xviii.

16 Alster (1997) xxiv.

Category	*Number*	*Percentage*
Food	3	5%
Work	21	38%
Status	13	24%
Sex	8	14%
Advice	4	7%
Unclassified	6	11%

Clearly the concentration is on the large category of sayings concerning work, with sayings about low status also of importance; sayings about sex are fewer in number. Within each category we will proceed in chronological order, with Early Dynastic evidence, if any, first.

FOOD

> Although the pea-flour of the home-born slaves is mixed with honey and fine oil, there is no end to their lamentations.[17]
>
> Fat meat is good. Meat with sheep fat is good. What shall I give the slave girl (to eat)?[18] Let her eat the ham of a pig![19]

Presumably the slave girl was not given the "good stuff," but at least she did get some meat.

> A slave of a lamentation singer keeps howling in the streets, My food ration, it is large in bulk, but its weight is small. Let me tell about the bulkiness of my food ration. (It is) a lance (that) penetrates the city quarters.[20]

The thrust of these sayings is that slaves were always complaining that they were not given enough to eat or that, perhaps, they had enough but not of the quality they wanted. The slave holder proverbialists found this complaint completely unjustified—there was honey in the pea-flour! The concentration of this subject in two collections may indicate that this was not a major concern to proverbialists.

---

17 Alster (1997) 14 saying 1.47.

18 Alster (1997) 37 1.190, in Emesal.

19 Alster (1997) 38 1.191.

20 Alster (1997) 66, 21.105.

Work

> A sleeping slave neglects things.[21]
>
> Collect like a slave girl, eat like a queen.[22]
>
> My son, collect like a slave girl, eat like a queen, thus shall it be indeed![23]

That is, you need to work very hard to get your food together, or your work done, but when it comes to dining, you ought to be most genteel. Or perhaps the saying recommends hard work with the reward being very fine fare. All depends on the context in which the saying was invoked.

> Build like a lord, walk like a slave; build like a slave, walk like a lord![24]
>
> ...A freeborn man cannot avoid corvée work.[25]
>
> A slave girl is one who opens the door,
>
> A slave girl from the palace is inconsiderate (?).
>
> A slave from the palace devours its good will.[26]
>
> A slave girl carried her ransom money with her. She [lost?] thirty minas.[27]
>
> You grind with the pestle like a fearful slave girl.[28]

This saying just uses the slave girl as an image, but it clearly shows that the slave girl was expected to be anxious and unsure of her status.

> The slave girl, who neglected to fill the container, grumbled, It does not fill to the top, it does not fill? the middle.[29]

So, because of neglectful laziness, the slave girl did not do the required work and blamed it on the container she was to fill.

---

21 Alster (1991/92) Early Dynastic p. 14, 21 line 84.

22 Alster (1974) 42–43 line 137.

23 Alster (1974) 42–43 line 138.

24 Alster (1997) 71 saying 2.137.

25 Alster (1997) 74 2.157b= p. 147 6.5b: dumu-gi$_7$ du-lum la-ba-an-tag$_4$-tag$_4$.

26 Alster (1997) 87 3.37: "inconsiderate" is za-ra dug$_4$-dug$_4$, which is equated with *muštālu* "giving bad advice" or *muštarriḫu* "vainglorious," Alster (1997), II, 381.

27 Alster (1997) I, 88 3.38.

28 Alster (1997) I, 88 3.39.

29 Alster (1997) I, 88 3.40.

> After (the lady) had left the house and (the slave girl) had entered from the street, (away from) her lady the slave girl sat down at a banquet.[30]

We say, "When the cat's away, the mice will play," and here there is expressed the mistrust of the slave by her absent mistress.

> If there is a dispute at the mill, a slave girl reveals(?) what she has stolen.[31]
>
> To a slave girl who has not been purchased, the upper millstone...You toss like a millstone torn out (of its joint?).[32]
>
> A runaway slave girl sleeps badly.[33]

Really? As Alster points out, only in the view of the slave holder, though one could imagine that she would need to be vigilant against people who might identify her as a slave and detain her for her master or for their own use.[34] The legal material makes clear that harboring slaves, with or without their consent, was a major concern.[35]

> A released weaver (equals) two slave girls. A released *ungur*-worker equals three slaves.[36]

This may mean that ex-slaves made better workers than did slaves. The word for release is du$_8$, not usual for the manumitted,[37] and they may not have been quite slaves before release. But obviously free workers did much more work than did slaves,[38] an accurate perception echoed in other societies with slaves. Recall Adam Smith:

> A person who can acquire no property, can have no other interest but to eat as much, and to labor as little as possible. Whatever work he does

---

30 Alster (1997) I, 88 3.41.

31 Alster (1997) I, 89 3.42.

32 Alster (1997) I, 89 3.45.

33 Alster (1997) I, 94 3.79.

34 Alster (1997) I, xxiii; see II, 385.

35 See Snell (2001) chapter 3, on harboring; relevant legal texts include Lipit-Ištar paragraph 12, Ešnunna 50, Hammurapi 16 and 19, Hittite Laws 24, and, concerning harboring a free person, Middle Assyrian Laws 24.

36 Alster (1997) I, 110–11 3.183.

37 Which was /a-/ ma-ar-gi$_8$-ni ì-gá-ar, Falkenstein (1956–57) II, 30:2, pp. 49–50, and I, p. 93 n. 1.

38 Wuhong (1998) suggests, partly on the basis of this saying that the íl-people of Pre-Sargonic texts were released slaves.

> beyond what is sufficient to purchase his own maintenance, can be squeezed out of him by violence only, and not by any interest of his own.[39]

Another saying goes,

> (To say) Let me…, let me…,…destroyed, is characteristic of the slave girl of a *lukur*-priestess.[40]
>
> This is how the slave girl speaks: It has been carried away.[41]

Presumably the slave girl could not perform the required work because of circumstances beyond her control.

> The dirt was not apparent to the slave girl. To her lady it kept increasing.[42]

Oh, no! The slave girl could not even perceive the cleaning problem, but the freeborn lady could.

"The Lazy Slave Girl"

> (1) Now, should the work not please the slave girl, (2) should the slave girl's children not… (3) should barley not be eaten with the donkeys, (4) should their owner not drive them to run, (5) should fresh water not be drawn from the deep well, (6) should herbs not be grown at the side of the well, (7) a "nest" of lice will settle in the woolen cloth (?) (8) the loincloth will be used for drinking as if it were flowing water, (9) he whose heels were split (?) would accept shoes, (10) he who was clad only in a loincloth would accept a woolen cloth, (11) you, slave girl, when the lord has succumbed, when the lady has succumbed, and you roam the streets (12) you, slave, the fact that the lord is gone, you slave girl, the fact that the lady is gone, (13) the state of things that used to be yours, (14) you will never compare the affairs of former days to this, (15) but you will have to compare the future order to this.[43]

The gist of this is that the slave girl may not like her work now, but she will be worse off when the lord and lady are dead. Then she will recollect fondly of how things had been, presumably because, as a result of the division of the inheritance, the heirs may completely neglect to take care of the slaves, turning them loose in the streets.

---

39 Smith (1937) 365.

40 Alster (1997) I, 162 7.88.

41 Alster (1997) I, 192 11.23.

42 Alster (1997) I, 247 19 D 10.

43 Alster (1997) I, 256–57 21 A 16 in Emesal.

> If an unreliable slave girl...a sale cannot be obtained.[44]
>
> The male servant because the lord is gone, the female servant, because the lord is gone...[45]

As the American song goes, "Jimmy Crack corn, and I don't care—Massa's gone away."

Many of these sayings about work show that the much discussed, derided, and racialized "Sambo" image is actually quite old.[46] The slaves *were* unreliable workers because it was in their interest to slow work down, and, for them, complaint was a weak but persistent weapon.

LOW STATUS

> The thief is indeed a lion, the receiver(?) is indeed a slave.[47]
>
> A forsaken slave girl's child receives beer.[48]
>
> A slave girl's "coarse" bread and milk is a slave girl's property?[49]

That is, that is all she has.

> A leftover garment, the inheritance share of a slave girl's child, was thrown away. It became chaff.[50]

This saying stresses the pathetic nature of slave families; the inheritance, while not legally unthinkable, was worthless.

> What is the slave girl's dream? What is the servant's prayer?[51]

I do not know, but the sensible answer, not supplied in the contextless collection, is freedom. Servant here is not clearly slave, but an odd word.[52]

---

44 Alster (1997) I, 302 YBC 8713:5.

45 Alster (1997) I, 303 CBS 3805.

46 O'Neil (1998) noted that there were several contradictory stereotypes of slaves.

47 Alster (1974) site of Adab, Early Dynastic pp. 21–23, II:13 geme$_2$, and pp. 36–37, line 34, sag.

48 Alster (1991/2) Early Dynastic, lines 185–86.

49 Alster (1991/2) Early Dynastic 187.

50 Alster (1997) 115 4.43.

51 Alster (1997) 116 4.51, in Emesal.

52 e-re-sì-ki-in; see Alster (1997) II, 398.

> My mother, who was [not given her] dowry, is treated as if she were my slave girl.[53]
>
> He whose speech is humble, his wife is a slave girl.[54]
>
> When the lord's spouse has succumbed, the female servant is dead.
> When the lord has succumbed, the male servant is dead.[55]

Is this to be taken literally or merely socially, in the sense that a new master may not recognize the privileged or relatively honored position of a long-term slave?

> I, a slave girl, I have no authority over my lady. My husband, [let me pluck!][56]

That is, we move down the food chain to attack those lower than us, and the slave girl's husband qualified, whether himself a slave or free. This was translated into Akkadian, so it had a long life.[57]

> A slave girl wanders restlessly(?) around when it is getting dark at midnight.[58]
>
> It was not dear to her. She is the slave girl of a...[59]
>
> It is a slave girl's tears...it is a slave girl's child.[60]
>
> A home-born slave was treated with contempt. He wept. He had chaff in his hands. He showed his teeth (in anger).[61]

The one born at home could presumably expect more consideration than someone bought and brought into the house. But proverbialists imagined him being dishonored too, and they knew he would be angry, protective of his prerogatives.

---

53 Alster (1997) I, 116 4.54.

54 Alster (1997) 159 7.44 in Emesal.

55 Alster (1997) 180 9. A 14.

56 Alster (1997) 247 19 D 11.

57 "Let me pluck" is *lu-ub-qú-ma-am*.

58 Alster (1997) 254 21 A 6, in Emesal.

59 Alster (1997) 255 21 A 9.

60 Alster (1997) 285–86 28.10:10.

61 Alster (1997) 313 *UET* 6/2 279.

SEX

> Do not have sexual intercourse with your slave girl, she will call you: Traitor! (?)[62]

This saying makes it into the Old Babylonian version too, where the pun zu-ur "to your" and "traitor?" is more explicit:[63]

> Old Babylonian: geme$_2$-zu-úr gìš na-an-dù zu-úr šu-m[u]-ri-in-ša$_4$
>
> Early Dynastic: geme$_2$-zu$_5$(AZU) SAL+gìš na-e zú-ur$_5$ šè-mu-š[a$_4$]

Why will she call you a traitor? Presumably because with a slave girl, the free man is not usually setting up a permanent relationship, so when the man married or simply went back to his wife, she would feel powerlessly abused. Shades, for us, of Sally Hemings, but did she feel Tom was a traitor?[64]

> A slave girl is a man's property.[65]
>
> A slave girl guards a (pouch?).[66]
>
> When you go to the slave girl, she will throw it back to you.[67]

Perhaps this is in the same vein as the previously discussed passage.

> Your slave girl who has been brought down from the mountains, she brings pleasure, but she also brings damage.[68]

The saying epitomizes the ambivalence of men who held slaves; the women enslaved presumably felt even more negative!

> The voluptuous slave girl (says), Let Iškur…split the 'good place' like a cucumber.[69]

---

62 Alster (1974) Early Dynastic p. 12, vi 6–7.

63 Cf. Alster (1997) 37, 54, and Alster (1997) 87 and 111 to line 230 on the meaning, derived from this context.

64 On her before the recent notoriety, see Stanton (1998); since, see Lewis and Onuf (1999).

65 Alster (1991/2) Early Dynastic, 111.

66 Alster (1991/2) Early Dynastic, 161 and p. 30.

67 Alster (1974) Old Babylonian, 37 line 60.

68 Alster (1974) 198–99: geme$_2$-zu(?) ḫur-sag-ta ši-im-ta-an-tùm, šag$_5$-ga ši-im-ta-an-túm, ḫul ši-in-ga-àm-ta-an-tùm.

69 Alster (1997) I, 87 3.36.

This is not in detail particularly clear, but the general thrust—if I may be forgiven the pun—is obvious.

> He who sleeps with a slave girl..., a male...what the slave girl has stolen, what the lady...with a man, the one does not reveal to the other.[70]
>
> When I...my vulva...is worthy of slavery.[71]

The reality of sex with female slaves is obvious, but the ambivalence is unexpected, to me at least. The moralists are clear about this issue, but the fact that they stress it shows that it was an issue. The slave girl brings pleasure, but also damage.

ADVICE

> Do not buy a prostitute, it is horrible(?).[72]
> Do not buy a free man,[73] it is miserable.[74]

This "free man" may have been of a low rank in society. And yet it must have happened.

> Do not buy a slave girl from the palace, the house will be too dependent on it (?).[75]

Here it is interesting that the problem is seen as a political, not a personal one. It does not matter what she was doing for the palace, but rather what our relation to power will be.

And finally we have this amazing set of reflections on the proper behavior for the slave procurer:

> After you have brought down a foreign slave from the mountains, After you have brought a man from his unknown place, My son, even

---

70 Alster (1997) I, 89 3.43.

71 Alster (1997) I, 256 21 A 13; here I correct Alster's otherwise flawless English: slavery for slavehood.

72 Alster (1974) Early Dynastic, 15 II 3 D = Old Babylonian 159, and compare the discussion, pp. 102–3.

73 Dumu-gi$_7$. This is defined in Falkenstein (1956–57) III 103 as "bedingt frei, Paramonar," that is, "conditionally free, freedman with continuing obligations" with both gi$_7$ and gi attested in the word; see Alster (1974) 105–4.

74 Alster (1974) Old Babylonian, 161.

75 Alster (1974) 162, b: gìri KU-bi-šè é gál-gál-la-àm , and pp. 104–5: "to be at the place of the feet."

> to the place where the sun rises, He will pour water for your house, and walk in front of you, Not having a house, he does not go to his house. Not having a city, he does not go to his city. He does not favor it more than you, he does not appreciate it more than you. My son, toward the East, do not travel alone. A countryman does not enslave you.[76] When you are among known persons you can rely on (?) a man. Do not pile up a mountain in the mountains. Fate is a slippery bank that makes a man slide.[77]

This is a saga, unique in Mesopotamia, of slave capture. We go and capture him in the east, and now he does not appreciate city life. And we are advised that we free slave holders ought not to travel alone, exposing ourselves to similar enslavement. It could happen to us, and there are no guarantees. This is an extraordinary witness to what must have been an ordinary process of enslavement. It accords with the idea that the barbarian east and north may have been major sources of slaves.[78]

Let me note negatively that issues concerning slaves that do show up in legal material do not find expression in the mouths of the folk as recorded in these sayings. There is no talk of manumission and, except for the "released" workers, there are no freedmen. This absence does not argue that they were not important but rather that the proverbialists' interest was not engaged about those matters.

Do these notes on sayings from at least two different periods really give us a feel for daily life in its monotony and strangeness? Since we could not define it, I suppose we may be satisfied, and yet I find myself unsatisfied about Daily Life. The solution is certainly more self-awareness about what we wish to accomplish and more involvement of our audience in our task.

---

76 lú.zu.a-zu sag šu UD? ba-ra-ak-e.

77 Alster (1974) 43–45, lines 163–76, and p. 106.

78 Compare Paquette (1998) and the idea of "victim societies" of Jack Goody, explored by James (1988).

Note there are also several sayings concerning slaves the subjects of which I find difficult to classify:

A slave girl makes...? of lapis lazuli. (Alster [1991/2] Early Dynastic 188).

The master...his servant... (Alster [1997] 200 12 B 3)

...a daughter is a man's favored (?) female servant(?). (Alster [1997] 245 129 C 7)

The slave girls took out a harp. The Queen of Heaven remained seated in the lowest dike. (Alster [1997] 255, 21 A 10, in Emesal).

She is a slave girl of a... (Alster [1997] 298 *TIM* 9, 18 rev. 7).

A slave girl should not...a slave girl. (Alster [1997] 319 *UET* 6/2 321).

What I mean by that may derive from my pleasure in reading some books with my daughter, books produced to market expensive dolls, the American Girl Series, which brings readers into the daily lives and problems of fictitious girls from particular times and places. They each end with a historical chapter on objects and problems discussed in the books. The brilliant entrepreneuse who devised the dolls and the series recently wrote, "It is the simple details of everyday life—the clothing our ancestors wore, the furniture they sat on, the dishes and decorations they used in their kitchens and parlors—that breathe life into history and inspire the imagination."[79] I note that Mattel Toys recently bought her operation for $750 million; she got something right. My daughter and I have read of a fictional girl who lived in pre-Revolutionary Williamsburg, Virginia, and confronted the issue of Tory sympathizers among the Americans, though her father was, predictably, on the eventually winning side. My daughter wants to go to Williamsburg now. I want a Daily Life that arouses such enthusiasm for Mesopotamia. That may be harder than scholarship, or at least a bit different.

Would such a Daily Life read in part as follows?

> "I will kill him! I will scream!" she said firmly in the quiet, dim courtyard.
>
> "I don't have to suffer this way. That idiot told me we'd be together always. There would never come a day of separation since, after all, he owned me. He owned me. And I believed him. I believed him, and now look at me!"
>
> She almost yelled, but she did not. The courtyard surrounded by mudbrick was small, and several other slaves were asleep in it, and their owners were sleeping in rooms around the court.
>
> The old man sat up and grabbed at her hand and pulled her down to the ground, hissing at her to be quieter. She slumped to his side. In the weak light of the new moon he saw her fine regular features. How like her mother she looked, almost regal in her anger. Her mother too had been frequently angry—slaves often were, he thought. This girl was the one child of theirs who had lived, but her life had become a burden for her tonight. And, given the duties that had been performed by her mother, the old man did not really know if she were even his child, but he had taken care of her when the mother died, and he had no hint that she had ever thought about the ambiguity of her birth.

---

79 Rowland (1999).

"Daddy," she moaned to him, "Why can't I kill him?"

"What happened?" the old man asked.

"He stopped wanting me. He got me pregnant and now he stopped wanting me, said he'd sell me as soon as he could. He's negotiating with his uncle, you know, to get a cousin as a younger wife."

"You knew this would happen," the old man said.

"No, no, I thought...I thought we would be happy together, that I would be his hot-limbed wife.[80] He'd recognize the baby, who'd be free, and so would I. But he's sweeping us out the door, as if we never existed, as if I never gave in to him." She was just a girl, still in her teens, and this had been her first love.

"He is heartless," said the old man, "but he thinks he can do better than the likes of us for family."

"He won't get anybody prettier," she shot back proudly.

"No," said the old man. "Or smarter. Those cousins are known for their dullness. But you must remember he may not want someone smart or beautiful, and still a slave."

"But he wanted me before!" She was near tears, but in anger.

It was a winter night, and the wind was cold. He had dragged a blanket around him; she shivered in her shift. He drew her to him and whispered, "There is a way."

She drew back from him a little, putting her hand on his chest as if to hold him in focus. "There is?" she asked.

"You were born here, and your mother too, house-born slaves if ever there were such, but I was not. You must listen carefully; I can recite to you the route I was brought in on. It is long and difficult, but it is not impassable. When you have retraced my steps from long ago, you must seek out my nephews. My older brother might be dead by now, I don't know. But there were nephews born before I was captured. They will take you in." He continued, giving a detailed account of how she must go, at what landmarks she would need to turn.

The two were illiterate, and their memories were used to retaining details; she paid very close attention and seemed to grow more excited as he retraced his journey in his memory.

"But I won't know the language of your nephews," she lamely complained.

"No, but they will know my name, and my name will be enough."

Then they moved quietly to get her a sack and fill it with parched grain, which would last. He let her out the gate and returned to lie

---

80 Compare Alster (1997) 30, 1.147.

down in his place, not sleeping until the sun was up, and it was almost time for the day's work to begin.

She avoided inhabited places as she followed canals north and east; she moved by night and slept—contentedly—during the day. But the days were short and the nights were long. Within ten days she was in the foothills and began to walk by day since there were fewer villages. And now she began to see the large trees her father had told her she would. She was amazed at their height, unknown in her river-valley life.

She passed the last landmark, a large odd-shaped stone that appeared from a distance to have a hole through it, but when you got closer, you saw it was two stones standing near each other. And there in the alpine village, very much colder than down in the plain, everyone seemed to have heard of her father, even though she could not understand what they said about him until she had lived there for several months, with, apparently, the widow of one of the nephews.

When the baby was born, the young mother named it after her father; such was the custom of the village.

But that was a very long time ago.

This is not exactly fiction, but an imaginative recreation of incidents reflected in the proverbial sayings. Daily? I don't know, but life…

BIBLIOGRAPHY

Alster, Bendt (1974) *The Instructions of Šuruppak.* Copenhagen. (1991/2) Early Dynastic Proverbs and other Contributions to the Study of Literary Texts from Abū Salābīkh. *Archiv für Orientforschung* 38–39: 1–51. (1997) *Proverbs of Ancient Sumer,* 2 volumes. Bethesda, Md. **Contenau, Georges** (1966) *Everyday Life in Babylon and Assyria.* New York. **Falkenstein, Adam** (1956–57) *Die neusumerische Gerichtsurkunden,* 3 volumes. Munich. **Finkelman, Paul and Joseph C. Miller** (1998) *The Macmillan Encyclopedia of World Slavery* 2 volumes. New York. **Genovese, Eugene D.** (1969) The Treatment of Slaves in Different Countries: Problems in the Applications of Comparative Method. In *Slavery in the New World. A Reader in Comparative History,* edited by Laura Foner and Eugene D. Genovese, 202–10. Englewood Cliffs, N.J. **Hargreaves, A.S.** (1997) Antiquaries, Society of. In *The Oxford Companion to British History,* edited by John Cannon, 38. Oxford. **James, Wendy** (1988) Perceptions from an African Slaving Frontier. In *Slavery and Other Forms of Unfree Labor,* edited by Léonie Archer, 130–41. London and New York. **Klengel, Horst** (1992) *König Hammurapi und der Alltag Babylons.* Darmstadt. **Lewis, Jan, and Peter S. Onuf** (1999) *Sally Hemings and Thomas Jefferson: History, Memory, and Civic Culture.* Charlottesville, Va. **Lüdtke, Alf** (1995) *The History of Everyday Life: Reconstructing*

Historical Experiences and Ways of Life. Princeton, N.J. **Nemet-Nejat, Karen** (1998) *Daily Life in Ancient Mesopotamia*. Westport, Conn. **O'Neil, Patrick** (1998) Stereotypes, Slavish. In Finkelman and Miller, 2, 879–81. **Paquette, Robert L.** (1998) Enslavement, Methods of. In Finkelman and Miller, 1, 303–12. **Rowland, Pleasant** (1999) *American Girl 1999 Winter Catalogue*, p. 2. **Saggs, H.W.F.** (1965) *Everyday Life in Babylonia and Assyria*. New York. **Scott, Walter** (1982) *Waverly*. London. **Smith, Adam** (1937) *An Inquiry into the Nature and Causes of the Wealth of Nations*. New York. **Snell, Daniel C.** (1997) *Life in the Ancient Near East*. New Haven and London. (2001) Flight and Freedom in the Ancient Near East. Leiden. **Stanton, Lucia C.** (1998) Hemings, Sally. In Finkelman and Miller, 1, 390–91. **Stol, Marten** (1995) Private Life. In *Civilizations of the Ancient Near East*, edited by Jack M. Sasson, I: 485–501. New York. **Thompson, E.P.** (1967) Time, Work-Discipline, and Industrial Capitalism. *Past and Present* 38: 56–97. **Yuhong, Wu** (1998) Un-il$_2$ 'the released slaves, serfs.' *N.A.B.U.* 1998: 4:104, p. 95.

DAILY LIFE AND CULTURE IN "ENKI AND THE WORLD ORDER" AND OTHER SUMERIAN LITERARY COMPOSITIONS

Richard E. Averbeck
Trinity Evangelical Divinity School

Thirty years ago Samuel Noah Kramer published an article in which he selected sections from various kinds of Sumerian literary compositions that he believed gave insight into specific aspects of Mesopotamian society, and "daily life" in particular.[1] For social justice and morality he drew upon Gudea's two-cylinder temple building hymn, the divine hymn *Enlil in the Ekur*, and the Sumerian law codes, especially the poetic prologues. He used the Shulgi hymns to gain insight into the proper qualities and duties of a king, including the support of social justice and morality in the society. The myth *Inanna and Enki* was his basis for discussing the fundamental sociological and cultural elements of Sumerian civilization (e.g., kingship, priesthood, virtues, crafts, wisdom, the musical arts). For social morality and political theory he cited the lamentations over the destruction of Sumer and some of its cities. Finally, he used wisdom compositions to support his idea that there was a high regard for the working people and their welfare in ancient Sumer.

I will make use of some of these same compositions as well as others in my investigation of "quotidian life" in ancient Sumer—the everyday concerns common to all regular people in every place at all times. There are, however, some methodological issues that need clarification before going any further.

First, it is important to remain cautious about how one draws implications from literary texts. It is all too easy to overstep the boundaries of sound methodology. One cannot determine from literary compositions that a society is characterized by "the drive for superiority and pre-eminence with ... great stress on competition and success."[2] All societies struggle with social tension, contention, and competition. Moreover, religious

[1] Kramer (1971). See Kramer (1963) 249–68 for a summary of his previous work on this subject.

[2] Kramer (1963) 249.

and/or literary sources often concern themselves with the social and moral issues that are of concern to all people and societies everywhere at all times. Raising such concerns does not suggest that the people group involved has an abnormally troublesome problem with such matters. It could, in fact, mean just the opposite in the sense that they are especially sensitive to such issues. Furthermore, a literary/religious text might show special concern for social harmony on special solemn occasions without implying that the society is extremely rancorous during normal days. Such a text may well just be emphasizing that the regular legal concerns and squabbles that arise among all peoples ancient and modern must be set aside on that particular occasion.

Second, it is obvious that the ideologies, perspectives, and even the literary techniques of these kinds of compositions have the potential to distort what they appear to say or reflect about "how things really were" in ancient Sumer. For example, even the language of geography in such texts can be metaphorical, that is, used in figurative ways.[3]

Third, one needs to resist accepting and depending on interpretations of literary compositions that are based on supposed historical, political, cosmological, or other kinds of correspondences that are less than obvious on the surface of the text. Mythological texts in particular lend themselves to the imagination not only of the ancient writer(s) but also the modern reader(s).[4]

Fourth, since the approach to daily life in Sumerian literary compositions that I am taking here is based largely on mythological texts (although not limited to them), it is important to clarify the nature of myth. As Anna Maria G. Capomacchia has recently put it:

> through its myth every civilization founds its own historical dimension, connecting it with the events of mythical time, which give it a permanent sacred guarantee.
>
> All the elements connected, in myth, with historical events, and thus giving reality a certain order in its historical dimension, must be examined carefully; as carefully must be examined mythical geography, a cultural characterization of true geography. There is a "different" geographical dimension, in mythical time, that, just because of its being "different," reaches the aim of culturally defining the otherwise purely geographical reality. In the same way, also, historical reality is

---

3 Michalowski (1986).

4 For a good summary of some of these proposals and trenchant arguments against them see Cooper (2001).

> defined through the mythical dimension, where cultural characters, institutions, and historical events are sacrally established, as are the relationships, peaceful and not with neighboring countries, which likewise receive in the myth a specific characterization.[5]

There are myths that do the things referred to above, not only with historical and geographical reality, but also cultural, social, economic, vocational, moral, and other related aspects of human experience or perceptions of it. This kind of myth, in particular, is much more than fiction, even if it has fictional elements in it.[6] It consists of imaginative stories that are, in fact, based on reality and/or history, and, therefore, reflects foundational understandings of the world that are important to the culture of the composer and those who read his compositions or hear them read. There is a natural correspondence between fiction, myth, and history because all three manifest themselves primarily in story form, even though they are different kinds of stories.

Over the last sixty years or so a rather large body of scholarly literature about mythology has arisen in the fields of cultural anthropology, philosophy, and literary studies.[7] According to this literature, a well-founded approach to myth will distinguish between "analogical" and "rational-instrumental" ways of thinking and writing. On the one hand, in their administrative and economic texts the ancient Sumerians show that they were capable of careful rational-instrumental ("scientific" empirical) thinking. This was necessary for them to accomplish such feats as irrigation agriculture. Their mythology, on the other hand, consists largely of "analogical thinking" about what is perceived by the writer(s) as reality, specifically historical, natural, geographical, cultural, economic, or social reality.

Myth reflects upon the human world by describing or imaging creative analogies between the circumstances and experiences of human beings in the world and beliefs about the world of the gods. In the process, therefore, myth naturally contemplates and describes the idealized perception and understanding that the writer has of her or his world. What is important for us here is that one side of the analogy arose from the author's knowledge and experience of the historical, natural, geographical, cultural, economic, vocational, or social reality in which he or she lived. This is not writing out of pure imagination, even though one's religious and/or literary imagina-

---

5 Capomacchia (2001) 91–92.

6 Doty (1986) 7–8.

7 A convenient and recent summary of this scholarship is Douglas (1999) 15–65.

tion could be fully exercised in myth. The mythical analogical character of the story does not eliminate the fact that the realities upon which the story is based did exist and were important to the ancient people. Yes, there is fiction here, but not *just* fiction.

Enki and the World Order

One of the clearest examples of mythological analogical thinking is the Sumerian myth *Enki and the World Order* (EWO).[8] Here, the analogical nature of certain portions of the text is readily apparent to anyone, and the analogies reflect directly on issues of quotidian life. In fact, it begins with the author's opening praise of Enki, the god of Eridu, the god of the underground waters, fertility, and productivity, whose brother, Enlil, the chief god of Sumer, commissioned to make rulers and common people alike happy, prosperous, and secure in Sumer (ll. 1–60).[9]

EWO is a long and relatively well-preserved composition (*ca.* 472 lines), although there are some tantalizing lacunae in the story. It divides naturally into four major sections: (1) the opening third-person praise to Enki (ll. 1–60); (2) two first-person praises in which Enki praises himself (ll. 61–139), the first about Enlil's commission of Enki and the gift of the *me*'s and nam-tar (the various cultural components that made up the core of Sumerian culture and the power to determine destinies, respectively; lines 61–85), and the second in which Enki proposes to undertake a journey through Sumer on his barge, in order to fulfill the commission (ll. 86–139); (3) the long central section of the composition, in which Enki journeys on his barge through the land, decreeing the destiny of the Sumerian world, beginning with Sumer as a whole—and especially Ur, from there to the surrounding regions of Magan, Meluḫḫa, and Dilmun, and then back to the Sumerian homeland itself, where he assigns specific deities to take charge

---

8 Kramer and Maier (1989) 38–56 refers to it as *Enki and Inanna: The Organization of the Earth and Its Cultural Processes*. There is no up-to-date critical edition of this composition now available, although Benito (1969) is still useful. Jerrold Cooper informs me that he plans to produce such an edition. For the time being, however, there is a very good and handy composite transliteration available from Oxford through The Electronic Text Corpus of Sumerian Literature (abbrev. ETCSL; http://www-etcsl.orient.ox.ac.uk), based on the work of M. Civil, J. Krecher, H. Behrens, and B. Jagersma. The following discussion is based on the transliteration and translation in ETCSL compared with the translation and notes by Kramer in Kramer and Maier (1989) 38–56, and my own work on this composition using these and a few other primary and secondary text resources.

9 Vanstiphout (1997e) 118–20.

of the functions of various regions and elements of the Sumerian world (ll. 140–386); and (4) Inanna's complaint to Enki that he had not assigned her any special functional powers in his decreeing of destinies, and Enki's response to her complaint (ll. 387–471).

THE TWELVE CYCLES

A main concern of EWO was the restoration, or perhaps better, the proper maintenance of world order in Sumer. The Sumerians were constantly fighting erosion (physical alluvial erosion), or its converse, silting up (and the corresponding need for the ongoing dredging out of rivers, canals, etc.), or other kinds of socio-cultural economic "erosion" of their civilization and its resources. Vigilance was necessary to maintain the efficiency and prosperity of the land and its economy.

In the third section (ll. 140–386), Enki, having established Sumer in relation to its surrounding regions and/or peoples, turns his attention to the proper development and maintenance of the Sumerian homeland (ll. 250–386).[10] Enki himself initiates the various forces of nature and cultural

---

10 Horowitz (1998) 142–43 treats this section of EWO as a creation account of cosmic geography. Of course, there are several different accounts of creation in Sumerian literature, and he attempts to coordinate this one with the others, to some degree at least. In this regard, it is important to realize that myths such as this are analogical thinking about the world as it exists. So even if there are competing views, they are really only different analogies for how the world works based on differing views of the pantheon or the diversity of other competing concerns.

Vanstiphout (1997e) 121–22 suggests that this composition is not really a creation account, but instead refers to Enki's organizing of the world in order to realize the full potential of the land of Sumer. Perhaps we should even step back behind cause and effect and think of EWO as a cosmology rather than a cosmogony, or even as a description of how the Sumerian world functioned rather than an explanation of how it came to function that way. It uses analogy to reflect upon the world order and how that world order connects to the world of the gods, which, of course, was of great concern to the Sumerians in their understanding of the world order and their worship and service of the gods. Cosmogony and cosmology are not mutually exclusive in mythological compositions; each can presume or imply the other.

However, there are two lines near the end of this composition that suggest another more defined interpretation (ll. 451–52). Perhaps the primary concern of EWO was the restoration of world order in Sumer, or the reflex of that, namely, the need to maintain that world order against erosion, whether it be physical alluvial erosion or other kinds of socio-cultural erosion of their civilization and its resources. The first half of lines 451–52 refer explicitly to Enlil's heart overflowing to bring abundance to Sumer, and the second half says: "the country (of Sumer) is indeed restored (Sum. gi_4) to its place," referring to its proper condition and position of prosperity.

phenomena necessary to make Sumer a prosperous place, and then puts one of the Anunna-gods in charge of each component. Although the text is somewhat broken in places, it appears that there are twelve cycles of initiation and assignment.

It is important to observe that, after detailing the twelve cycles, the text comes to a turning point where Inanna raises a complaint in the first person that she had not been put in charge of anything. In the main body of her complaint, she recites the functions of five of her sister goddesses (ll. 387–421), only one of which (Nanše) had been mentioned in the unbroken sections of the previous twelve-fold cycle (ll. 285–308). The fact that only Nanše had been mentioned previously suggests that the author did not conceive of his twelve cycles as a complete record of Enki's decrees down to the last detail. Rather, they establish a comprehensive context for everything that was important to life in Sumer, without developing every possible component of it.

Turning now to the twelve-fold cycle itself, according to the account, first, Enki ejaculates to fill the Tigris and Euphrates with the flow of life-giving water, predicting that this would cause there to be sweet wine and abundant barley. He puts "Enbilulu, the inspector of rivers," in charge of this (ll. 250–73). The fragmentary second cycle refers to the marsh regions and its abundance of reeds, fish, and fowl. Such marsh regions arose naturally in the environment created by the two rivers (ll. 274–284). Third, he places the goddess Nanše in charge of the area near the sea in the south (the Persian Gulf) and the surging waters of the deep in the delta region (ll. 285–308). These first three cycles, therefore, appear to move through the land from north to south, in terms of the supply of water and the abundance that naturally comes with it. Note that there is no lack of correspondence to the real geography of the land here, although it is certainly fictional on another level.

The next three cycles begin with Enki initiating rain and putting "the canal inspector of heaven and earth, Iškur" (the god of rain and storm) in charge of its maintenance. Of course, canals were essential to the irrigation agriculture of Sumer and rainfall was important to maintaining the water supply in the canals (ll. 309–17). Fifth, Enki makes "the farmer of Enlil, Enkimdu" responsible for the working of the fields with plows and yokes of oxen (ll. 318–25). Sixth, he puts the agricultural fertility goddess, Ašnan, in charge of the various crops: barley, chickpeas, lentils, and so on (ll. 326–34).

The seventh and eighth cycles relate to the building of houses and other edifices. It involves the fabrication of bricks with hoe and brick mold, over which Enki places Kulla (ll. 335–40), and the laying of bricks to make foundations according to a plan, lined up with strings, under the supervision of "Mušdama, Enlil's master builder" (ll. 341–48).

Up to this point all the cycles relate to the resources and activities of the river basin, where irrigation and the agriculture associated with it took place along with the building of houses and cities.

With cycles nine and ten, Enki moves from the river basin to the plain, where ecology, vocations, and lifestyles are of a different nature altogether. Here, the text seems to make a distinction between two regions. The first is the highland plain (an-edin) of the hinterland and, perhaps also, the regions north and east of the Tigris river, over which Enki places the god "Šakkan, king of the foothills (ḫur-sag)" (ll. 349–57). The second is the (lowland) plain (edin), probably that between the two rivers or at least close by them, which Enki assigns to Dumuzi, "the dragon of heaven," the spouse of Inanna (goddess of sexual fertility) (ll. 358–67). The highland plains were places of grass and herbs fed on by wild animals such as ibex and wild goats. The lowland plains were also a place of grass and herbs but here the focus was on domesticated sheep and cattle, sheepfolds and cattlepens, fat and cream.

The eleventh cycle tells us that Enki organized the whole region by establishing boundaries between the various cities of Sumer, providing dwellings (i.e., temples) for the Anunna-gods, and dividing the agricultural land among them. He then put Utu, the sun-god, god of the underworld, and the divine judge, in charge of the order he had established (ll. 368–80). Finally, the twelfth cycle relates that Enki established the textile industry as the task of women, placing the goddess "Uttu, the dependable woman, the silent one" in charge (ll. 381–86).

These twelve cycles develop the various foundational components of land and society in which the Sumerians lived. It is not my goal here to develop a complete picture of daily quotidian life in ancient Sumer. This was not the purpose of the composition. Moreover, if my understanding of Inanna's complaint is correct, much is left out that was probably assumed to fit within the larger framework provided by the twelve cycles.

From the perspective of the Sumerian literary corpus, EWO provides perhaps the most natural point of departure for gaining a comprehensive view of the Sumerian world order.[11] We can fill out much of the detail by

---

11 A comprehensive picture of the overall shape of the Sumerian "world order" is the primary concern of EWO, but there are also certain passages in other Sumerian literary compositions that reflect something of the same pattern to one degree or another. For example, consider *Nanna-Suen's Journey to Nippur* (ETCSL 1.5.1, cf. Ferrara [1973]) ll. 331–48; *Lamentation over the Destruction of Sumer and Ur* (see ETCSL

making reference to other available texts of various sorts as well as the results and publications of non-textual archaeological, environmental, and geographical investigations.

Cycles 1–4: Flow and Fecundity of Rivers and Canals

EWO reflects the fundamental fact that the culture and economy of ancient Sumer was largely agrarian. As others have observed, the twelve cycles of world order within the Sumerian homeland begin with that which is basic to agriculture—water supply and its management.[12] Nevertheless, there is also the natural produce of animals and plants in the rivers themselves, and in the lakes and marshlands along their courses.

The first cycle mentions wine, barley, and the abundance that comes forth from the irrigated ground of the river valley alluvium. Cycles 2 and 3 focus on the marshes, reed beds, and produce from the sea to the south (the Persian Gulf). Thus, beginning in the north and moving southward, the first three cycles recount how the god Enki activated the natural ecosystem of the southern part of the Tigris and Euphrates alluvial basin that made up the Sumerian homeland. Cycle 4 rounds this off with rainwater, another important element in the natural ecological and agricultural system.

CYCLE 1: THE TIGRIS AND EUPHRATES (EWO 250–73)

In the first cycle, Enki turns his attention away from the regions surrounding Sumer, and looks toward the two rivers that were the basis of ecology, economy, and civilization in Sumer. Like a wild bull, he ejaculates to fill the Tigris with the flow of life-giving water,[13] which cause there to be,

---

2.2.3, cf. Michalowski [1989]) ll. 493–518; *The Death of Ur-Namma* (Ur-Namma A) ll. 22–30 (see ETCSL 2.4.1.1, cf. Kramer [1991]; *Ninurta's Journey to Eridu* (Ninurta B) ll. 8–28 (ETCSL 4.27.02, cf. Reisman [1971]; see also *Ninurta F* (ETCSL 4.27.06).

12 Vanstiphout (1997e) 118 and n. 6, and 129–31 rightly emphasizes the importance of water in this composition. Following Thorkild Jacobsen, however, he argues that even those cycles of the twelve that do not explicitly refer to water, nevertheless, focus on fertility and, therefore, allude to the sexuality of water/semen, etc. It seems to me that we do not need to go so far with it. Fertility is certainly a primary concern in this text, water is essential for fertility, and in this first cycle the sexuality of Enki is the mythological basis of the fertility of the land, but that does not mean we need to shape everything in this text into the mold of sexuality of people, animals, or even the gods.

13 Cooper (1989) has examined this element of the story in some detail and relates it to the sexuality of the Inanna-Dumuzi love poetry. He concludes that the rationale for it is to be found "in Enki's role as the ultimate source of fresh water

among other things, sweet wine and abundant barley, thus supplying food for the people, plenty for the Ekur (Enlil's temple at Nippur), and prosperity for the palace. Enki places "Enbilulu, the inspector of rivers/canals" in charge of maintaining the river system as a whole, but some of the associated ecosystems that derive from the two rivers are treated in the following cycles, and other gods are made responsible for them.

The Tigris receives most of the attention here, more than the Euphrates, although both are involved. This is significant in light of the fact that scholars have long considered the Euphrates to be the most manageable source of water for Sumerian agriculture, and argued that the Tigris was more of a hindrance than a help to Sumerian irrigation of the alluvium. Recent studies have shown, however, that the Tigris was more significant in watering certain regions of Sumer than scholars had realized, especially in the far south regions of Umma and Lagaš.[14]

In any case, the rivers were the lifeline of ancient Sumer and, at the same time, a major threat to the civilization that they spawned. The alluvial plain south of Baghdad has a negligible slope (Baghdad, at 410 km from Basrah, is only about 33 m above sea level). This results in extremely unstable water courses very sensitive to the pressures of the yearly flood and to sedimentation. Also, the flood comes practically at the same time as the cereal harvest, in April/May. Not only the flood comes at an inopportune time for the plants growth, but it also menaces the crops themselves. Flood control has always been the central concern of farmer and king alike in the history of southern Mesopotamia.[15]

Since the flood as well as the harvest were in the spring of year (April/May), the goal was to control the flood and drain off excess waters so that

---

irrigation, the fecundation that is the very basis of Babylonia's agricultural economy."

14 Steinkeller (2001a with the additions in 2001b), following Heimpel (1987) and (1990), corrects the long-standing misconception that the watering of the Sumerian heartland was accomplished largely by the Euphrates, with the Tigris not much involved. See the latter view in Jacobsen (1960) 175 n. 2 with (1982) 63, Adams (1981) 6–7, 244, and accepted most recently by Verhoeven (1998) 198 n. 131. Steinkeller points out that literary and other texts have long been known to connect the Umma /Lagaš region with the irrigating and fertilizing waters of the Tigris. See esp. the very helpful maps in Steinkeller (2001a) 40 and 50, and the summaries of his conclusions on pp. 40–41, 48–49, 55–56, and 64–65. The importance of both rivers is reflected here in EWO, but regarding the Tigris specifically, and its importance to the Lagaš region, see also, for example, the well-known prologue to Gudea's temple hymn in Gudea Cyl. A col. i ll. 5–9.

15 Civil (1994) 68, cf. also 110.

it did not destroy the harvest, while, at the same time, capture the flood waters and channel them so as to flood fields where and when this was appropriate for the irrigation for the next year's agricultural cycle. This "was one of the major activities in Mesopotamian life,"[16] employing immense amounts of labor to keep the large-scale irrigation system intact, especially through communal efforts during the seasons when the actual fieldwork was minimal.[17] It involved two main types of work: (1) earth moving, which included digging and/or dredging out canals and ditches, as well as piling the filler to make levees and dikes, and (2) the gathering, binding up, and mixing of reeds from the marshes with sand/earth to reinforce the dikes and levees, and especially to prevent destruction during the annual time of the flood.[18]

After sowing the crop in September/October, came the removal of the remaining clods and then four irrigations over the winter months (November to February/March) as the crops grew and matured for the harvest in March/April/May (cf. cycles 5 and 6 below).[19] The amount of human labor needed to carry on large-scale irrigation of this kind was immense, thus accounting for much of the daily quotidian life of many of the common people in ancient Sumer.[20] However, because irrigation resulted in "relatively high agricultural productivity, ... large surpluses thus could be mobilized above the needs of the primary producers," so that

> relatively high population density was attainable even at a fairly simple, only slowly improving level of technique. At least equally important, considerable proportions of the population could be maintained in specialized pursuits rather than agriculture itself.[21]

So with irrigation came urbanization and specialized occupations, thereby increasing variation in the daily quotidian lives of various groups of people in the society, including the construction of housing complexes

---

16 Civil (1994) 29 ll. 2–4, and commentary pp. 68–69, with Jacobsen (1982) 57–58.

17 See also the helpful summary in Eyre (1995) 180–82, 185.

18 Civil (1994) 115, 121–22.

19 Civil (1994) 31 ll. 67–73, and commentary pp. 88–89, with Jacobsen (1982) 59–61. It is not clear if there was a fifth irrigation, which would have been the first of five, immediately after the sowing of the crop; Civil (1994) 31 ll. 61–63, and commentary pp. 86–88. See Roaf (1990) 127 for a picture of canal lines that remain on the Mesopotamian landscape even today.

20 For a full discussion of the kinds of work involved in irrigation, see Civil (1994) 109–35 and the remarks on cycle 5 below.

21 Adams (1981) 243.

and administrative buildings (cf. cycles 7–8 below). All of this, along with the combination of the need to organize labor to control the annual flood and, at the same time, the need to maintain access to the irregular, unpredictable, and sometimes scarce supply of water for agriculture, brought with it the need for "political consolidation."[22] Thus, in ancient Sumer, irrigation and urbanization were necessary companions.[23]

CYCLE 2: MARSHES AND REED BEDS (EWO 274–84)

The second cycle is relatively broken and obscure. The general subject is the lagoons, marshes, and reed beds that teemed with fish and waterfowl. These arose naturally in the environment created by the two rivers, especially in the far southern delta region near the Gulf, but also at various places along the meandering courses of the Tigris and Euphrates. The line that mentions the deity whom Enki placed in charge of this part of the Sumerian world order is not readable, but he or she is said to be adept at netting fish and snaring birds, and was one who loved fish.

Of course, the way of life associated with this environment would be quite different from that of the irrigation agriculture discussed above.[24] The life of the fisherman or fowler in a river culture is very distinctive, and some of its features have remained the same from ancient times until now:

> Although the positions of the lakes have shifted over the years, ... it is likely that there were always marsh dwellers who supported themselves by fishing.... The canoes in use today are almost identical to models found in the Royal Cemetery at Ur, and reed boats like those depicted on the Assyrian reliefs (c. 700 BCE) are still used in the marshes.[25]

Also, the significance of reed beds should not be overlooked:

> Reed matting is used in the roofs of traditional mud-brick houses, but reeds are also typical of the buildings of the marshes. Thick pillars of bundles of reeds form the supports for houses made entirely of reeds,

---

22 Adams (1981) 243. He further states, "In the largest sense, Mesopotamian cities can be viewed as an adaptation to this perennial problem of periodic, unpredictable shortages" of water (244).

23 Adams (1981) 242–52.

24 See the beautiful picture of a marsh of reeds in Roaf (1990) 40–41 and the explanation and description on p. 42, where he writes: "The still waters of the lakes with their plentiful supplies of fish, provide an alternative way of life to the farming communities found elsewhere in the Near East."

25 Roaf (1990) 51 pictures and text (cf. also pp. 122–23).

very similar to those depicted on cylinder seals and on stone reliefs of the Uruk period more than 5,000 years ago.[26]

Reed matting was used also on the floors and elsewhere in housing, and as binding material betwixt and between multiple courses of mud bricks in structures such as temples and ziggurats, sometimes leaving residue or even their imprint in the bricks for us to observe even today in excavations (see cycles 7 and 8 below for the making of mud bricks for construction of buildings).[27] Moreover, large amounts of reeds were mixed with earth/sand to reinforce dikes and levees (see the remarks on cycle 1 above).

Other Sumerian literary compositions that can be used to fill out the literary presentation of life and nature in the marshes include *The Disputation between Bird and Fish*,[28] *The Heron and the Turtle*,[29] *The Home of the Fish*,[30] and *Nanše and the Birds*.[31] The first two of these are of special interest because, like EWO, they are devoted to Enki (i.e., among other things, the dispute is presented to Enki for his decision). This makes perfectly good sense in light of the fact that Enki was the main deity of the southern city of Eridu, and the god in charge of ground water.

The Disputation between Bird and Fish, in fact, is reminiscent of EWO in that it begins with long past decrees of Enki, when he founded dwelling places, life-giving waters, the Tigris and Euphrates, smaller streams and ditches, pens and stalls with shepherd and herdsman, cities and villages, "and so made mankind thrive; a king he gave them for shepherd."[32] Then he moved on to marshes, "growing there reeds young and old; ... ponds and large lakes he made birds and fishes teem; ... he gave all kinds of living creatures as their sustenance, ... and so placed the abundance of the gods in their charge."[33] After fashioning the bird and the fish, Enki filled the canebrake with them and established the rules of their existence. But the fish became afraid of the bird, which sometimes fed on fish eggs and even on the fish themselves. Thus, the fish raised a dispute against the bird, and eventually sought out and destroyed its nest. The bird retaliated by snatch-

---

26 Roaf (1990) 51 pictures and text.

27 Moorey (1999) 361–62.

28 ETCSL 5.3.5 and Vanstiphout (1997a).

29 ETCSL 5.9.2 and Gragg (1997).

30 ETCSL 5.9.1 and Civil (1961).

31 ETCSL 4.14.3.

32 Vanstiphout (1997a) 581 ll. 3–12.

33 Vanstiphout (1997a) 581 ll. 13–16.

ing the fish out of the water with its claws. Finally, they went to Enki for a decision, resulting in the bird being declared victorious over the fish.[34] The important point is the environmental bond between birds and fish. As this second cycle of EWO also reflects, both are associated with the marshes, although the birds also had a place in the fields and cities, even in the temples.

The Heron and the Turtle, however, begins with a detailed description of the major marsh regions of ancient Sumer and the various kinds of reeds that grew there. Again, we must not overlook the significance of reeds, not only for the habitat of fish and birds, but also for human purposes. The villain here is the turtle, who keeps attacking the heron's nest and smashing her eggs. Again, the dispute is brought to Enki, but in this instance the text is too broken to allow us to know the decision.

Unlike *The Disputation between Bird and Fish* and *The Heron and the Turtle*, the two compositions *The Home of the Fish* and *Nanše and the Birds* are devoted to Nanše, the goddess of Sirara, in the southern part of the Lagaš district, near the Gulf. Her close association with Enki in the management of fish and birds is evident from references to her as "the child born in Eridu" and "the child of Enki" in *The Nanše Hymn*.[35] *The Home of the Fish* and *Nanše and the Birds* give us further information about the various kinds of birds and fish in the marshes, amid the reed beds, as well as those from the sea. That brings us to the third cycle.

CYCLE 3: THE SOUTHERN SEA (EWO 285–308)

Nanše is not the deity Enki placed in charge of the fish and birds in cycle two (see above), and this feature is not mentioned here in the third cycle either. However, in her complaint to Enki later in EWO, Inanna points to the fact that Nanše had been made "produce inspector of the sea" and was, therefore, responsible for bringing fine fish and birds to Enlil in Nippur (ll. 420–21). The third cycle recounts how Enki constructed "a holy shrine" (èš-kù, ll. 285 and 289), "a shrine in the sea" (a-ab-ba èš, l. 286), and placed Nanše in charge.

The surging waters of the deep and the waters from the Tigris and Euphrates meet in the delta region. It is this confluence of the world of the rivers of Sumer with that of the sea that accounts for the description of this shrine in terms of the awesomeness of the sea and its waves.[36] Reference is

---

34 Vanstiphout (1997a) 581–84.

35 See, e.g., Heimpel (1997) 526–27 ll. 8 and 61 (cf. ETCSL 4.14.1).

36 The sea is on the fringe of Sumer, so it is associated with the "deep" (Sum. engur

also made to "the pelican of the sea" (u_5^mušen^-a-ab-ba). In *Nanše and the Birds* Nanše is closely associated with the pelican, perhaps because it is such a large and majestic bird, and can be either a fresh water or a salt water bird (ll. 1–22).[37] From that shrine Nanše is in charge of the sea and its inundations, as well as inducing sexual intercourse.[38] In fact, it has been suggested that perhaps it is the sea itself that is the shrine referred to in these lines.[39]

The mention of filling the temple of Enlil in Nippur "with all sorts of goods" (l. 299) and the fact that Enki placed Nanše in charge of the sea brings us back to the issue of trade.[40] Dilmun, Magan, and Meluḫḫa are mentioned earlier in EWO as sources for needed raw materials and luxurious goods of various sorts that were not native to Sumer (see ll. 123–30, 219–47).[41] As a major doorway into Sumer from the south, the Persian Gulf was

---

= Akk. *apsû*), which may refer to, among other things, the swamp regions in the far southeastern corner of Sumer, below Sirara, and the open sea beyond, as well as the "deep cosmic waters" below the surface of the earth and the sea, and even the underworld itself; see Horowitz (1998) 334–47, esp. the citation of EWO ll. 302–7 on p. 341 and the summary on p. 344.

37 See ETCSL 5.9.1 and Civil (1961).

38 Perhaps sexual intercourse is mentioned here because of the close association between it and water/semen (see note 12 above).

39 Kramer and Maier (1989) 220 n. 84.

40 This is the only cycle in which constellations are mentioned, specifically, the "Field" and the "Chariot" constellations (ll. 288–89). This is puzzling (Kramer and Maier [1989] 49 and 220 n. 85), but perhaps it refers to directional guides for those who traveled the sea, or something of that sort. Moreover, according to ll. 301 and 307, Nanše is "the one who sets sail…in the holy shrine" and Enki is put here in charge of "the broad width of the sea."

41 Moorey (1999) xxi places all these regions to the south and east of Sumer: Dilmun is the coastal region of northeastern Saudi Arabia along the coast of the Persian Gulf; Magan is further to the southeast along the same coastline, but beyond the straits between the Persian Gulf and the Gulf of Oman, leading into the Arabian Sea; and Meluḫḫa is still further east, along the coast of Pakistan and western India, the so-called pre-Aryan Harappan Civilization of the Indus valley (cf. also the collection of data and helpful discussion in Potts [1995] 1453–59).

A recent discussion in Michaux-Colombot (2001) concludes that these geographical terms can be "vague metaphors," and that: (1) Magan may have referred generally to "the North Arabian corridor linking Mesopotamia to Canaan and Egypt" along the inland Gerrah-Petra-Suez route, and would have also provided access to western Mediterranean trading partners; (2) Dilmun, probably southeast of Sumer along the Persian Gulf on the Arabian side, may have shared "the whole Arabian peninsula, including Oman and Yemen" with Magan; and (3) Meluḫḫa, the black country, could refer to the region from Suez to the mining areas of Madja

a natural course for such trade, whether near, along the coast of the Persian Gulf further to the south, Dilmun, or far, even farther down the southern coastline into the Gulf of Oman and beyond, perhaps Magan. Meluḫḫa is especially difficult. It could be along the northern coast into Pakistan and India, or around the Arabian Peninsula to the south, all the way to Egypt/ Ethiopia via the Red Sea, or both (i.e., it is beyond Magan in any direction?).

Although native agriculture was foundational, and other natural produce that could be (nurtured and) gathered from land and river, as well as the sea in the south, were significant in ancient Sumer, trade also had an affect on quotidian life there. The latter would be important not only for those who were directly involved in trading, but also those who worked with the products brought from afar or benefitted from them in some way. The products traded for included mainly metals, stones, and timber. The native resources used to trade for them were largely "manufactured goods, most notably textiles."[42] The third cycle, therefore, reflects on the abundance that came to Enlil's temple, the Ekur in Nippur (ll. 299–300), from the south, including perhaps both native and foreign produce and other material resources not indigenous to Sumer.

CYCLE 4: RAIN AND STORM (EWO 299–308)

Iškur is the god of wind and storm and, as such, was the one Enki placed in charge of rain and lightening storms. Nature is somewhat hard to predict and manage. Rain could not be relied upon as a steady source of water for the crops, but it could sometimes be useful as a source of water. It is said that by this means Enki "turned the mounds into fields," which suggests that, like the yearly flood, rain was important for making the land and soil ready for cultivation. Thus, Iškur is called "the man of abundance" (l. 316).

Iškur is also referred to here as "the canal inspector of heaven and earth" (l. 315), in contrast to "Enbilulu, the inspector of rivers/canals" (l. 272), who was in charge of maintaining the river system that was the basis of irrigation (see cycle 1 above). The distinction is important. The former is

---

in the desert on the Egyptian side of the Red Sea, and down the southern corridor through Sudan and Ethiopia to link with a so-called "Indian thalassocracy," which extended along the Arabian coastline all the way to India in the far East.

42 See Moorey (1999) 5 and the literature cited there, as well as the extensive discussion of the various crafts and industries throughout his book: stoneworking (both common and ornamental stones); bone, ivory, and shell; ceramics and glass; metalworking; and building crafts.

in charge of the rains that come from the sky, so he is said to do in both heaven and earth that which the latter does by means of the waterways on the ground.

As Adams has observed, today, as in ancient Sumer:

> the amount of rainfall is, with rare exceptions, quite inadequate to produce a winter crop and is better regarded as only an occasional supplement to irrigation....
>
> Heavy showers can be expected at any time from November through much of May, but they may not occur before December or even January and may be almost completely suspended for as much as two or three months during the growing cycle.[43]

Therefore, "it seems incontestable that agriculture was introduced into lower Mesopotamia only on the basis of irrigation."[44] No doubt, in some years rainfall was more helpful than in others, so the irrigation regimen to be discussed in more detail below (cycle 5) was perhaps more variable than *The Farmer's Instructions* would lead us to believe.[45] Nevertheless, the fact that rainfall is presented as the last element of water supply in this description of the Sumerian world order suggests that even here it is viewed as secondary to river water irrigation.

Cycles 5–6: Farmers and Crops

Cycles 5–6 describe Enki's activation of agriculture, both the work of farmers (cycle 5) and the crops they cultivated (cycle 6). Of course, all of this depended on the natural ecological system generated by the rivers and rain of cycles 1–4, discussed above. Moreover, agriculture required the support of a large work force to construct and maintain the irrigation system of canals, ditches, and dikes, as well as to perform the labor of actually working the soil, planting the crops, watering them, harvesting, storing, and processing the produce.

---

43 Adams (1981) 12.

44 Adams (1981) 13.

45 Civil (1994) 4 warns that the *The Farmer's Instructions* is somewhat idealized, or at least lay out the ideal pattern without taking into consideration all the variations in circumstances and resources that would have warranted, on occasion, a change in the pattern. For example, if there was a heavy rain at the time of one of the four normal irrigations, no doubt the irrigation would be cancelled or at least delayed.

Since the seasonal patterns determined much about daily quotidian life in ancient Sumer, it will help to pay special attention here to the debate poem *The Disputation between Summer and Winter*.[46] The growing season in Sumer was during the winter months, not the summer, because the latter was too hot and dry for cereal crops to survive and produce. According to this disputation poem, summer, on the one hand, was for bringing in the harvest, storing it in barns, sending out laborers and oxen to work and eventually sow the fields for the next winter's growing season, building houses, walls, and temples in cities and villages (see, e.g., ll. 20–22, 61–68, 157–182). Winter, on the other hand, was for early flooding of the fields, which brought bounty to Sumer in the form of the irrigation of the grain crops, gardens, and orchards, as well as the supplying of water for the pastures of domesticated and wild animals by rainfall (ll. 23–61, 189–243).

The disputation ends with Enlil granting victory to Winter because he is the "director" of "the life-giving waters from the midst of the mountains" (l. 305); he is "the farmer of the gods" (ll. 306, 317). The important point for us here is the correspondence of cycles 1–4 above with winter, and the correspondence of cycles 5–8 below with summer. So the cycles in EWO appear to flow in logical order not only geographically (see the remarks on cycles 1–4 above) but also temporally—beginning with winter and continuing through summer. One can also discern from this dispute other common practical concerns of the people in the winter (cold and damp) versus the summer (hot and dry).

CYCLE 5: FIELDS AND FARMERS, DIKES AND IRRIGATION DITCHES (EWO 318–25)

The previous cycles have been concerned with the annual flood of the Tigris and Euphrates that brought the life-giving irrigation waters to Sumer from the mountains (cycle 1), the produce of the rivers and the seas (cycles 2–3), and the water of winter rains (cycle 4). The fifth cycle is about the work of the farmer that Enki initiated and then put under the control of "the farmer of Enlil, Enkimdu," also known as the one responsible for "dikes/levees and irrigation ditches."[47] Farmers were responsible for the

46 ETCSL 5.3.3 and Vanstiphout (1997d). Interestingly, in this composition Enlil, not Enki, ejaculates and impregnates the foothills (ḫur-sag) with Summer (Emeš) and Winter (Enten), ll. 12–15.

47 Civil (1994) 109–12 affirms that these are the correct interpretations of these terms. Moreover, the digging or dredging of ditches and the building up of dikes or levees go together, since the earth dug up from irrigation ditches was naturally used

actual irrigation of the crops in their fields and, therefore, also the maintenance of the ditches, dikes, and levees in a process of digging out the ditches and using that soil to build up the dikes and levees (see the remarks on cycle 1 above).

The first watering was, of course, that of the annual spring flood. This is where *The Farmer's Instructions* begins (see ll.1–4 and the remarks on cycle 1 above).[48] The places on which the flood-waters stood temporarily after the flood were the areas on which the silt was deposited. The farmers were also to release the irrigation water at certain times during the growing season. According to *The Farmer's Instructions* (ll. 67–73) this occurred at least four times during the winter growing season up to the time of harvest in the spring:

(First watering):	(67) When the plants overflow the narrow furrow bottoms,
	(68) water them with the "water of the first seed."
(Second watering):	(69) When the plants form (like) a reed mat, water them.
(Third watering):	(70) Water the plants in heading.
	(71) When the plants are fully formed, do not water them, they would become infected with rust.
(Fourth watering):	(72) When the barley is right for husking, water it.
	(73) It will provide a yield increase of one *sila* per *ban*.[49]

There is some uncertainty about how all this worked. For example, it is not clear from *The Farmer's Instructions*, or from any other source, whether irrigation was accomplished by running the water on the raised furrows, where the crop was planted, or simply by flooding the whole field so that the water would run between the furrows.[50] Also, this composition is not at all clear about whether or not there was a watering immediately after the

---

to build up the dikes along the banks of those ditches. The same principle applies to the larger canals that brought the water from the rivers or lakes to the fields.

48 Civil (1994) 29.

49 The translation is according to Civil (1994) 31, but the explicit numeration given here is added. See also note 19 above. For details of the means and methods of irrigation see Civil (1994) 109–40, and for a very helpful overview see Eyre (1995) 180–83 and the literature cited on p. 188.

50 Civil (1994) 103 n. 70 on ll. 55–56.

sowing of the crop.[51] On practical grounds, it seems most likely that the soil may well have been watered after planting to allow for the seeds to germinate and flourish, especially if the fall rains were relatively light.

In addition to dikes and irrigation ditches, Enkimdu was put in charge of all the farm implements. Plows, yokes, and oxen are given special attention in the fifth cycle. There was basically one kind of plow, but depending on the plowshare attached to its frame, it could be used, first, to break up the soil so that it could be properly worked into a seedbed, and later in the year as a seeder-plow for sowing the crop.[52] According to *The Farmer's Instructions*, however, other implements used by the farmer were, for example, hoes of various kinds to work the soil (see cycles 7–8 below for the various uses of the hoe), the whip to drive the oxen, harrows, mauls to break up lumps of dirt, wagons to carry the sheaves to the threshing floor, and threshing sledges.

In *The Disputation between the Hoe and the Plow*,[53] the plow proclaims its importance, although the hoe wins the dispute (ll. 196–98). The plow views itself as the exalted farmer, who is responsible for and credited with the harvest at harvest festivals (ll. 20–54). The hoe responds with the following points: it comes to the field before the plow, is essential to the irrigation of the field (which the plow is not), it takes six oxen to pull it and four people to run it, it keeps on breaking,[54] it works only for four months as opposed to the twelve months for the hoe, and is awkward to handle in transport (ll. 85–118). Because there was so much stress on the plow due to the resistance of the soil and the force of the pulling oxen, it was susceptible to all sorts of

---

51 Civil (1994) 87–88, commentary on lines 62f and 67f. Eyre (1995) 182 suggests that the water was run between the furrows so that it reached nearly to the top of the furrows. As it soaked down into the soil, the water would leach the salt out of the soil of the furrow, creating "a suitable microenvironment in the vital rooting zone. Successful germination and seedling growth could then take place in a field that was otherwise too saline for cultivation." For more on soil salinity and water management, see cycle 6 below.

52 Civil (1994) 169. See also the cylinder seal impression in Roaf (1990) 128 picturing a yoked ox pulling a seeder-plow with the farmer holding the plow and following along behind (*ca.* 2200 B.C.E.; cf. also Salonen [1968] 37–106 and Tafeln II–XII). For more on the plow, its parts and its functions, see the commentary on ll. 15, 20–31, 41–63 in Civil (1994).

53 ETCSL 5.3.1 and Vanstiphout (1997c). The lineation used here is that of Vanstiphout.

54 See also *The Farmer's Instructions*, which call for having a second plow at hand for each plow; Civil (1994) 29 l. 25 and the commentary pp. 74–75.

breakdowns, which were no doubt a frustration to the farmer in ancient times as they are today. Farming is hard work, and it is dependent upon getting the work done on a time schedule to match the seasons and the conditions: "When your field work becomes excessive, you should not neglect your work, so no one has to tell anyone: 'Do your field work!'"[55] *The Farmer's Instructions* walk step by step through the agricultural year, from the annual flood in the spring to preparation of the fields by hoeing, plowing, harrowing, sowing, maintaining the furrows, irrigation, harvesting, threshing, winnowing, and distributing and storing the produce.[56] One can gain from this a rather clear impression of the kind of work farming was and, therefore, something about the cycle of daily life of the farmer through the year. The data we have suggests that during the Sumerian Ur III period (*ca.* 2112–2004 B.C.E.) a peasant farmer (i.e., the one who was responsible to actually work the field) and his family would work perhaps about 15 acres of land. Groups of them may have worked together as well, perhaps under one head farmer. They would do this under the supervision of a local administrator, who was under the supervision of higher officials, all the way up to the ruler and/or the temple (i.e., the deity). The farmers themselves would receive a portion of the crop as payment for the work they performed, as did everyone else up the hierarchy. At least in some instances, there may have been mid-level farmers who worked the land, although having other workers under them.[57]

The Farmer's Instructions make note of four occasions during the growing season during which the farmer was to perform certain rites (sizkúr). The first was "after the seedlings break open the ground," and these rites were "against mice" and other such rodent pests that might chew up the young plants (ll. 64–65). The other three sets of rites were performed during the harvest season. The second occasion was daily rites during the time when the grain was being cut down and bound into sheaves in the fields (l. 87). The third set of rites was performed after the threshing of the grain by oxen dragging threshing sledges over the grain on the threshing floor, when the grain was spread out on the threshing floor, before it was cleaned through winnowing (ll. 100–1). The fourth occasion on which rites were to

---

55 *The Farmer's Instructions*, Civil (1994) 31 ll. 35–37.

56 Civil (1994) 1–3 provides a brief overview of this pattern of work throughout the year, and his text edition and commentary discusses most of the issues in considerable detail. I will not repeat it here. For a brief but clear explanation of these processes and their timing, see Eyre (1995) 181–82.

57 See Eyre (1995) 186–88.

be performed was in the evening and night after the grain had been winnowed and piled up on the threshing floor (ll. 105–6).[58] The important point here is that religious rites were not just for the temples, but also for the fields and for concerns of daily life and productivity in the world of the common farmer. They worked hard, and along the way depended on the support of the gods in their work.

CYCLE 6: CROPS AND FERTILITY (EWO 326–34)

In the sixth cycle Enki activates the cultivated field and the barley cereal crop, along with chickpeas, lentils, and other garden varieties. In this way Enki and Enlil brings prosperity to the people in the form of piles of grain. Enki puts all this under the charge of the goddess Ašnan, "the good bread of all the earth." She is described as having dappled head and body (l. 331), her face covered with syrup/honey, the mistress who induces sexual intercourse, the strength of the land (of Sumer), and the life of the black-headed ones (i.e., the Sumerians). This, of course, is the culmination of the work of the farmer in cycle 5 above, but is also dependent on the fertility of the soil, which, in turn, depends on the silt deposit of the annual flood and the management of the water supply from rivers and rain (cycles 1–4 above).

One of the main soil problems facing the Sumerian farmer was the salinity of the soil. The annual flood brought various minerals with it, including salt. The chemical nature of salt is such that it absorbs water. The salinity of the soil created competition with the plants for the available water in the soil.[59] In general, we can perhaps reconstruct three complementary practices that had some effect on making such soil productive. First, the water of the spring flood was redirected so that it covered the fields that had been left fallow from the previous year. This would not only soften the soil so that it could be worked, but leached the salts from the topsoil down into the subsoil.[60] Second, the farmers probably irrigated the

---

58 See Civil (1994) 31–33 and comments on ll. 64–65, 87, and 106, especially p. 92 on "rites of the field" in general, and the special importance of the "sizkúr-rites of the threshing floor" that required a sheep, not just flour, dates, and beer like the other rural rites. We have no further information about how the rites were performed, who performed them, or what words may have been recited.

59 See the helpful explanation in Jacobsen (1982) 5–8.

60 See Eyre (1995) 181 and note especially Jacobsen (1982) 60–61: "if relatively large amounts [of water] are used the danger of a rapidly rising watertable may be incurred and excessive irrigation can then wet the soil through and create condi-

newly sown crops by flooding the field so that it filled up the space between the raised furrows where the seeds were planted. As the water soaked down into the soil it leached the salts down with it into the subsoil. Third, and this is the most important point for us here, as the primary cereal crop they planted more barley than anything else because it is most resistant to salt. This was especially so as the salinity in the soil increased over time. Wheat, various emmers (including emmer wheat), onions, and pulses (peas and chick-peas) were also grown, but in lesser amounts partly because they are less resistant to salt. We also have records of other lesser crops: garlic, flax, beans, lentils, and sesame. All these are known from Sumerian times, whether early or late, or both; but barley was always predominant.[61] This gives us a relatively clear picture not only of the major crops, but also, of course, of the agriculturally produced part of the diet of the ancient Sumerians.[62]

Cycles 7–8: Brick-making and Building

Enki initiated the making of bricks and the construction of buildings to house the people and their leaders, political (palaces) and religious (temples). This is the subject of cycles 7–8. As we have already observed, irrigation agriculture brought with it not only high levels of production so that more people could be fed, but also required a large labor force. Therefore, irrigation and urbanization naturally developed side by side in ancient Sumer. Moreover, concentration of population and political organization in cities provided protection from natural disasters through diversification of resources and, at the same time, empowered them to compete with other urban centers for the limited natural resources available, including water.[63]

---

tions under which capillary action brings the saline waters below to the surface. If, on the other hand, irrigation waters are used too sparingly, …no necessary surplus will be available to leach amounts of salts deposited by previous irrigations down below the root-zone and the soil may then over the years increase in salt content to points where harmful concentrations are reached."

61 Jacobsen (1982) 15.

62 For the preparation of foods from these and other plant food sources, such as orchard trees, see Renfrew (1995). Although they are not mentioned in EWO, other food sources include, for example, those of trees and shrubs: olives, grapes, figs, sycamore figs, pomegranates, and dates, depending on the climate and other factors in various regions. See the very useful description of regions and their peculiar crops in ancient Sumer, and their association with certain deities in Jacobsen (1970) 16–38.

63 Adams (1981) 242–43, 248–52.

It is interesting that there is no reference to the hoe as a farming implement in cycle 5, especially since we know that it was used extensively in fieldwork. Perhaps this is because the hoe, unlike the plow, was also essential to mixing clay for making bricks, so it was reserved for this part of the world order in EWO. The literary compositions *The Disputation between the Hoe and the Plow*[64] and *The Song of the Hoe*[65] are especially relevant here. In the disputation, the hoe won even though it was simpler and less impressive than the plow, and associated with the poor (ll. 1–5, 59–61, 65–198). Although it could draw furrows in the field and was, therefore, highly valued, the plow did not compare to the hoe because it could not dam up water, put dirt into basket, make bricks (see the remarks on cycle 7 below), lay foundations, build a house (see the remarks on cycle 8 below), strengthen the base of a wall, or put a roof on a man's house (ll. 9–19). These fundamental abilities were essential for the irrigation of the cultivated fields and the maintenance of swamps for the fish and birds (ll. 70–82). Obviously, the point is that the hoe can do these things and not the plow, so we get a clear picture of some of the things that the hoe would be used for in the work of farmers, boatmen, and gardeners, and for builders of city walls, regular houses, palaces, and temples (ll. 83–160). Thus, by means of the hoe the common farmhand, the boatman, and the gardener can support his wife and children (ll. 134–40, 143, 152). *The Song of the Hoe* reflects further upon the significance of the hoe by proclaiming its importance in the creation of the world and humankind and in building temples, its relationships with the various gods, and its relevance to all aspects of Sumerian life.[66]

CYCLE 7: HOES, BRICK MOLDS, AND BRICKS (EWO 335–40)

EWO specifically emphasizes the importance of the hoe along with the brick mold in the fabrication of clay bricks (cycle 7) for construction purposes (cycle 8). In line 339 the meaning of the verb is not certain, but it is clear enough that Enki puts the deity Kulla in charge of supplying bricks to the land of Sumer: "Kulla, who … bricks in the land" (l. 339).

The first line refers to the "great prince" (Enki) binding the head of the hoe to the handle with a string/sinew (l. 335).[67] The handle was apparently

64 ETCSL 5.3.1 and Vanstiphout (1997c). The lineation used here is that of Vanstiphout.

65 ETCSL 5.5.4 and Farber (1997).

66 Farber (1997).

67 *The Disputation between the Hoe and the Plow* begins with a similar expression: al-

made of wood with one or more "teeth" made of wood or some other material. *The Disputation between the Hoe and the Plow* (ll. 2–4) describes it this way: "Hoe, made from poplar, with a tooth of ash; Hoe, made from Tamarisk, with a tooth of sea-thorn; Hoe, double-toothed, four-toothed."[68] The regular hoe would have the blade(s) (i.e., its tooth or teeth) set at 90º to the handle, but there were many different kinds of hoes, some of which set the blade on the same plane as the handle, more like a pickax.[69]

In *The Disputation between the Hoe and the Plow*, the hoe is not ashamed of its smallness, humble estate, or dwelling by the river bank (ll. 65–69), because of its importance place in Enlil's temple and its usefulness in almost every aspect of Sumerian life (ll. 70–188). No doubt, everyone in Sumer was familiar with the hoe and its various uses. One of its most important uses was in the making bricks, so alongside the hoe in this cycle is the brick mold. This was a rectangular wooden frame with no top or bottom that would be placed on the ground and filled with clay. The frames usually were singular, but could also be made in sets of two or three. Binding material was added to the clay mix to prevent the cracking of the brick. This could be straw, dung, pulverized sherds, or some other matter. The hoe was used to mix the clay for making the bricks. Brickfields were located near cultivated fields and their watercourses, since large amounts of water were needed for mixing the clay.

Once the clay had been properly pressed into shape in the brick mold and the excess clay cleaned off the top, the brick mold itself would be lifted up and off the brick so that the brick could be left to dry, perhaps only a day or two if the sun was hot, but sometimes for much longer periods of time.[70] The bricks were made in various shapes and types through the millennia.[71] The flat rectangular-shaped brick became standardized virtually every-

---

e sa lá-e "Hoe, tied up with string"; ETCSL 5.3.1 l. 1 and Vanstiphout (1997c) 578. According to Salonen (1968) 141, this refers to the binding of the head of the hoe to the handle when it is not attached in another way, e.g., with a nail, but the interpretation remains "somewhat uncertain"; Sjöberg (1998) 141, 18.4 and the references there.

68 Vanstiphout (1997c) 578. For the various references to the hoe in its various uses in building, agriculture, etc., and in its numerous combinations with other terms, see Sjöberg (1998) 136–43.

69 Civil (1994) 71–72 comment on ll. 10 and 12, and pp. 149–51. Kramer and Maier (1989) 51 translate here in EWO "pickax."

70 See Moorey (1999) 305 and the pictures and explanation in Roaf (1990) 31.

71 Moorey (1999) 304, 306–9.

where during the last quarter of the third millennium B.C.E.,[72] but in first 600 years of the third millennium (Early Dynastic I–III) the plano-convex brick was popular in Sumer (flat on the bottom but convex shaped on the top, perhaps because the excess clay was not cleaned off the top of the mold).[73]

The preferred time for brick-making was May/June, when there was plenty of water and straw available from the recent spring flood and the harvest, respectively. This would be the same time when the first plowing of the fields for the next season of farming occurred. Since the brickfields were in close proximity to the cultivated fields, we may speculate that labor was sometimes shared between them. There was work to be done on the soil, of course, but different seasons called for different occupations with the soil and perhaps also other kinds of projects for the same people or other members of the family, for example, making bricks. Similarly, July and August would be natural months for building, the bricks having already been made and dried, and the weather being suitable for dry hard ground on which to build and good conditions for the work of construction.[74] That brings us to the next cycle, which is concerned with the construction of brick buildings.

CYCLE 8: FOUNDATIONS AND BUILDINGS (EWO 341–48)

The eighth cycle is concerned with using the bricks of cycle 7 in the construction of buildings. According to the text, in addition to proper performance of purification rituals (šu-luḫ), this involved the stretching of strings to guide the laying of foundation bricks straight according to the plan of the house, and then actually laying of the foundations and the rest of the bricks. Enki put all this under the supervision of "Mušdama, Enlil's master builder," whose foundations are laid so that they do not sag, whose houses are properly built so that they do not collapse, and whose vaults reach high into the sky like the rainbow. From these lines we learn of the major concerns of builders, and even some of the dangers that come with inadequate building procedures.[75]

---

72 See Roaf (1990) 106–7 for a good view of the standard rectangular brick of Ur-Nammu's ziggurat at Ur and the manner of its laying in courses (*ca.* 2100 B.C.E.).

73 See the explanation and illustration of the shape of these bricks and the patterns used in laying them in Moorey (1999) 307–8.

74 Moorey (1999) 304–5.

75 For a meticulous discussion of building procedures, see Moorey (1999) 302–62, which includes the making of various kinds of bricks (see above, cycle 7), proce-

We have some good sources for some of the (purification) rituals associated with laying foundations and planning houses, especially from the Gudea cylinders.[76] Gudea was a very important ruler of ancient Lagaš (ca. 2150–2125 B.C.E.). Gudea cylinders A and B record a very long hymnic narrative poem recounting the construction and dedication of the Eninnu-temple, which Gudea built for the chief god of Lagaš, Ningirsu, and his spouse, Baba. Certain formulas structure the text and reflect the ritual nature of the composition overall.[77] We cannot treat all of these ritual procedures in detail here, but there were dream revelation and incubation rituals (Gudea Cyl. A i 12–14, vii 24–viii 13, xx 5–8), other kinds of prayers, offerings, and musical worship, including prayer offerings (A ii 7–9, B i 12–ii 6, ii 11–13, xiii 14–17 and following, xviii 18–xix 1), divinations by extispicy (inspection of the entrails of a sacrificial animal) and other means (A xii 14–19), various kinds of purifications during the construction and dedication of the temple (A xiii 12–13, B iii 13–27, v 20–vi 10), and especially the rituals associated with the making of the first brick.

Unfortunately, the interpretation of some of the terms and ritual procedures are not certain, but the basic pattern for making the first brick for Gudea's temple is relatively clear. First, there was divinatory preparation by means of extispicy—examining the entrails of a sacrificial animal, a he-goat (Gudea Cyl. A xiii 16–19). Depending on how one interprets certain terms,[78] the divination was perhaps for the shed (pisan or dá) of the brick mold and the clay pit (KA-al),[79] or, alternately, the brick mold itself and the hoe.[80] In any case, this is all associated with the shining forth of the emblem

---

dures for laying them in mundane and decorative ways, wall painting, plasters and mortars, the use of bitumen, various kinds of stone and wood (for roofing, walls, columns, doors, and interior decorations), and reeds (see in the remarks on cycle 2 above).

76 See Averbeck (1987) and now esp. Averbeck (2000) for treatments of this text. See also Jacobsen (1987) 386–444

77 See Averbeck (2000) 418 and the literature cited there.

78 Sjöberg (1998) 143 renders this and the following passages as a whole, but leaves these particular terms untranslated as "meaning unknown."

79 Jacobsen (1987) 405 and Edzard (1997) 77.

80 See Averbeck (2000) 424–25 and the philological discussion there (cf. also the important discussion in Salonen [1972] 102–4). If this interpretation is correct, it would correspond to the pairing of the hoe and the brick mold here in EWO. Perhaps it is also significant that cycle 7 begins with a reference to Enki as "the great prince" (nun-gal), and in the first and second steps in the making and placing of the first brick in Gudea cylinder A refer to the "princely" way in which the emblem of

of the *anzu*-bird in a "princely" way as the standard of Ningirsu (Gudea Cyl. A xiii 20–23).

The same problems plague our understanding of the second step as well, but in the sequence of the composition this comes after the gathering of laborers, provisions, and raw materials, and after the surveying and laying out of the sacred area. When the time finally comes, it is clear that in this instance that the rites accompany the actual fabrication of the brick (Gudea Cyl. A xviii 17–28). The rites themselves include the libation of water, the sounding of musical instruments, the hoeing of honey, butter, "princely oil," and essences from various kinds of trees into the clay mix. Gudea himself performed these rites and continued by taking up the carrying basket and putting the clay into the brick mold, while oils and perfumes were being sprinkled all around.

Since the brick needed to dry and harden at least to some degree, some time elapsed—perhaps only a day—before the third step could be performed (Gudea Cyl. A xix 1). The third step in making the first brick involved striking the brick mold so that it fell out into the sunlight, anointing it with perfumes and oils, lifting up the brick and parading it around like a shining crown so all the people could see it, and finally placing the brick properly where the temple was to be built (Gudea Cyl. A xix 2–19).[81]

There is good reason to believe that ritual procedures also accompanied the construction of ordinary houses.[82] So once again we have important information on the some of the major concerns in the daily life not only of those involved in construction, but also those for whom houses were built. They would be concerned about proper building procedures so that the foundation would stay solid and the house would not collapse, but they would also be concerned about ritual (purification) procedures that called upon the gods for favor and protection.

Cycles 9–10: Plains and Pastures, Herds and Flocks

Up to this point all the cycles relate to the resources and activities of the river basin and its alluvium, where fishing and fowling, as well as irrigation and the agriculture associated with it, took place, along with the building of houses and cities. We will return to cities and industries in cycles 11–12, but for now the text turns to the plains and pastures where various wild

---

the *anzu*-bird shone forth in the preparations for making the brick, and the use of "princely" oil in the actual fabrication of the brick.

81 Averbeck (2000) 427.

82 Moorey (1999) 305 and Ellis (1968) 19.

and domesticated animals are the focus of attention. Even though ecology, vocations, and lifestyles were different here, this was still an important part of the Sumerian homeland and its economy. To be sure, there were distant nomadic pastoralists who were not considered to be part of that homeland and Sumerian culture proper, namely, the Martu. But that does not mean that no pastoral activities were engaged in within Sumer itself. On the contrary, it is a well-known fact that there was a symbiosis of sorts between the practices of animal husbandry and farming, and among pastoralists, farmers, and cities.[83] Sometimes this even included Martu tribal groups and their herdsmen.

EWO distinguishes between the "lofty, mighty, upland" (uru_{16}), "plain, steppe" (edin), also referred to as the "highland plain" (an-edin-na) where ibex and wild goats pastured (cycle 9),[84] as opposed to the "(lowland) plain" (edin) of sheepfolds and cattlepens (cycle 10). According to the description given, the former was a place of undomesticated wild animals wandering and grazing, whereas the latter was where domesticated animals likewise grazed but could also be contained in pens and sheepfolds. Both were fertile places of grasses, herbs, and copulation, but the lower plain regions needed to be managed more directly because they were in closer proximity to the agricultural lands of the river basins and canal irrigation systems and, therefore, more within the bureaucratic administrative reach of the city-states. This was the case especially during the Ur III period. But the importance of animal husbandry was well established long before that according to archaeological remains and written records from earlier in the third millennium.

CYCLE 9: THE HIGHLAND PLAINS (EWO 349–57)

The highland plains were a place of animals that could perhaps be managed to some degree, but at least according to this cycle of EWO, they were largely roamed by wild animals that multiplied and fed on the grasses and herbs of the foothill meadows (contrast the cattlepens and sheepfolds of cycle 10 below). Enki placed the god "Šakkan, king of the foothills (ḫur-sag)," "the king of the countryside (edin)" in charge because, as the text puts it, he was muscular, like a lion, hefty and burly. Analogically, it is apparent that those who inhabited these regions would need to be vigorous and have the skills to hunt down wild animals for their own subsistence and as part of their service to state and temple.

---

83 Adams (1981) 11, 250.

84 *The Disputation between Summer and Winter* also refers to the "high plain/ steppe" (an-edin-na) as a place of "deer and buck" (l. 52); Vanstiphout (1997d) 585.

The temples of the city-state centers were supplied with deer and other wild game probably brought in largely from these highland regions, along with birds and fish from the rivers and marshes. The temple administrative texts keep records of fishers and fowlers, but there must have also been those who brought wild game from the highland plains.[85] Obviously, the lifestyle of those who lived there would have been vastly different from that of those involved in irrigation agriculture, and even quite different from the pastoralists who lived and grazed their herds and flocks in the lowland plains amid or just beyond the reach of the developed tracts of irrigated farmland of the Tigris and Euphrates alluvium (again, see cycle 10 below).

The references to the "foothills," "the holy crown of the upland plain," and the "lapis lazuli beard and headdress of the highland plains" appear to be "poetic images for the verdant vegetation of the steppe."[86] The term for "foothills," (ḫur-sag) in particular, often refers to the slopes of the eastern mountains (beyond the Tigris to the north and east, visible from the Sumerian plains), where there was "luxuriant vegetation, ... wondrously fresh green pastures ..., contrasting so markedly with the barren Mesopotamian plain."[87] This suggests that perhaps the "highland plain" here refers not only to the higher parts of the plain between the two rivers but also to the foothills of the mountains to the east and north, the so-called pastoral corridor approaching the piedmont of the Taurus-Zagros mountain ranges.[88] It is clear that the latter also supplied pasture for the herdsmen of certain nomadic pastoral tribal groups that were so significant in the economy of the Ur III state.

CYCLE 10: THE LOWLAND PLAINS (EWO 358–67)

Enki charged Dumuzi, the dragon of heaven, the spouse of Inanna (goddess of sexual fertility), "a friend of An," with the care of the lowland plains. Like the highland plains, this too was a region where grass and herbs provided pasture, but here the focus is on domesticated sheep and cattle, sheepfolds and cattlepens, fat and cream. The reference to Inanna, Dumuzi's spouse, recalls the many myths and love poems about the marriage and sexual relationship between the two of them in the Sumerian

---

85 Robertson (1995) 446.

86 Kramer and Maier (1989) 220 n. 99.

87 See Jacobsen (1970) 118 and the literature cited there.

88 Adams (1981) 135.

repertoire of literary compositions.[89] The text refers specifically to her as "the lady of the great *me*'s, the one who calls for copulation in the squares of Kulaba" (ll. 364–65). The connection to fertility and reproduction among the herds and flocks, the prosperity of the plains (l. 361), is unmistakable.

Sheep and cattle were certainly a source of meat, but the emphasis here seems to be on fat and cream (dairy) production (l. 359), which was an important part of the Sumerian diet. Such foods brought balance to the regular fare of staple grains produced by irrigation agriculture, even "luxury to the dining places of the gods" (l. 360). The subject of the Sumerian composition *The Herdsman and the Farmer* is Inanna's preference for the farmer (Enkimdu) rather than the shepherd (Dumuzi) as the one whom she should marry.[90] Although the text is severely broken in places, there are perhaps somewhat caricatured depictions of the life and lifestyle of the shepherd and the farmer. The shepherd (Dumuzi) has fine butter and milk, as well as an abundance of wool, and the farmer (Enkimdu) has colorful flax and dappled grain. The farmer is associated with dikes and canals. He has black and white garments, but the shepherd has the black and white ewes from which the wool was obtained to make the garments. The farmer has beer and beans, but the shepherd has milk and cheese. At one point the text refers to the shepherd pasturing his flock on the riverbank, eating the stubble of the farmer's crops, and drinking from the canal.

The latter mixture of realms and contacts between the shepherd and the farmer reflects the interchange between them that would have been common in ancient Sumer. Yes, they competed for resources, but they also relied on the sources and resources of each other. In reality, even the farmers had livestock to manage, partly as work animals, and perhaps also to supplement their agricultural produce (especially milk, butter, cheese, and other dairy products). For example, *The Farmer's Instructions* mention that "at the time the field emerges from the water" after the spring flood, the farmer should "not let the cattle herds trample it (anymore)."[91] Thus, at certain other times cattle were allowed to wander and feed on the cultivated fields. Pasturing them in this way would not only feed the cattle, but also help keep the weeds down, assist with the preparation of the soil, provide natural fertilization by means of animal dung, and even thin out the young barley crop to prevent "lodging" when it came to maturity.[92]

89 See Sefati (1985), the special selections in Sefati (1995), and Jacobsen (1987) 1–98.

90 ETCSL 4.08.33.

91 Civil (1994) 29 l. 7, with commentary on pp. 70 and 145.

92 Civil (1994) 145, Eyre (1995) 181, and Schwartz (1995) 250. If grain crops are

In addition to the farm herds, there were extensive networks of pastoralists in ancient Sumer. These functioned largely on the lowland plains, which were on the eastern periphery of Sumer and in the hinterlands of the core river basin region, respectively. At least in certain times and places, the lowland plains constituted dimorphic zones where sedentary agricultural life and nomadic grazing of herds could co-exist and, in fact, be mutually beneficial.[93] After all, the alluvial zone of irrigation agriculture was relatively narrow, so there was room for pastoral activity not only in the open ranges of the hinterland but also in the fallow fields and along the banks of the rivers of the alluvium itself.[94] Because their livestock was moveable, the pastoralists tended toward a nomadic lifestyle, sometimes rather far ranging, even if they were closely linked with certain rural villages or large urban centers by family (tribal based) or through trade or production agreements.[95] However, the relationships between pastoralists and agriculturists had to be managed properly, since they also competed with each other for some resources (i.e., water and land). Sometimes hostilities broke out between pastoralists and agriculturists and their urban centers over needed goods and resources, especially during times of climatic or environmental stress.[96]

The highland plains or steppes of Sumer's eastern periphery was also a region for pastoral nomadism in a less dimorphic sense. The Third Dynasty of Ur developed a massive system of administration at Drehem (Puzriš-Dagan, near Nippur) to manage the large numbers of animals, especially cattle, sheep, and goats, collected from the pastoralists in all regions controlled by the state. These were used to supply various state institutions and especially the temples. The animals were a major resource not only for sacrifices to the gods and for meat to be consumed, but also for dairy products of various kinds, as well as leather and wool for processing into textiles (for the latter see cycle 12 below).[97]

---

planted and grow too densely populated, upon ripening the heavy heads of grain can cause the plants to bend over and flatten out into the mud as if in waves of sheets under the effects of heavy rains and/or strong winds. This is called "lodging."

93 Schwartz (1995) 250.

94 See Adams (1981) 135–36 and the literature cited there, especially the work of M.B. Rowton, and the adjustments made to his work by Adams himself on these pages.

95 Adams (1981) 135, 250; Hesse (1995) 209–11.

96 Schwartz (1995) 254.

97 Adams (1981) 147–48; Hesse (1995) 210; and Robertson (1995) 446–47.

Cycles 11–12: Cities and Industries

> At the end of the fourth and beginning of the third millennium the Mesopotamian countryside was shaped by the process of urbanization/ruralization. In the large city-states dependent workers on the great estates of temples and palaces supplied produce both for internal consumption and for exchange. In the countryside nearby villages became parts of city-states that were vying for the best land and water, but some land was owned in traditional ways. More distant from the city-states and in less fertile areas, nomads or villagers who were nomadic for part of the year tended to flocks and were inclined to resist control by city-states.[98]

Norman Yoffee follows this summary description of the situation as it was at the end of the fourth and beginning of the third millennium with a further summary of developments through the third millennium and beyond. During the third millennium there were trends toward: (1) political centralization as the city-states competed with each other (see cycle 11), eventually ending with Ur becoming the center of the Ur III state and everything else the periphery from the perspective of the Sumerian homeland and its organized institutions; (2) stratification and specialization of Mesopotamian economy and society; (3) administrative sophistication, including the standardization of measures and careful keeping of records; (4) the binding of private individuals to the larger bureaucracy of the state on various levels in diverse ways, depending on occupation and labor management principles; and (5) finally, rather extensive trade relations based on agricultural surpluses and especially textiles, made possible through the massive organization of largely female labor (see cycle 12).

The twelve cycles of EWO recount how Enki established and provided for the proper maintenance of the major elements of the Sumerian world order that contributed to this evolving state of affairs. The last two cycles focus specifically on urban organization and industry in the Sumerian homeland. Cycle 11 is especially concerned with the problem of demarcating and maintaining the proper boundaries between the city-states, a problem that would be adjudicated by Utu, the sun-god and judge among the gods. Cycle 12 is concerned with the making of textiles, a largely female industry with a female deity in charge. The fact that textiles were so important as a trade commodity for ancient Sumer renders the special mention of king and palace here understandable.

---

[98] Yoffee (1995) 1398.

CYCLE 11: CITIES AND BOUNDARIES, DWELLINGS AND FIELDS

According to cycle 11, Enki had pleased Enlil with many possessions and made Nippur glad, so he organized the whole region by establishing boundaries between the various cities of Sumer, providing dwellings (i.e., temples) for the Anunna-gods, and dividing the agricultural land among them into fields.[99] He put Utu, the sun-god, god of the underworld, and the divine judge, in charge of heaven and earth, and the order he had established in it. Since he was the divine judge, Utu was responsible for making judgments among the gods so, in the end, conflicts between cities were to be resolved by him.

Cities were political centers and centers of trade and commerce, as well as "seats of the gods."[100] Furthermore, "if ancient Sumer ... was the 'heartland of cities'..., then its temples were the 'hearts' of those cities."[101] Temple economy was a primary factor in the overall economy of the Sumerian city-states. Since EWO focuses on the gods in relation to all the primary factors of ecology, economy, and technology in ancient Sumer, it naturally emphasizes the cities as temple centers in relation to those phenomena here in cycle 11. However, even though there were large temple "estates" that controlled and absorbed significant parts of the resources, goods, and wealth, that does not mean that ancient Mesopotamia was made up of "temple-states" in which virtually everything was under the control of the temples.[102] On the contrary, scholars have come to realize over the past forty to fifty years that there were also substantial private and communal sectors of the economy.[103]

In Sumer the cities were located within the alluvium and the watercourses flowed through them. In terms of city planning, the temples were located on the edge of the city, not at the center, and always at the point of highest elevation, whether by virtue of the terrain or through the construction of raised temple platforms or ziggurats, or both. Where palaces have been found, they were not on raised platforms, and they were separated

---

99 See Kramer (1963) 123, 172, 286 on the Anunna-gods and their significance in EWO.

100 Stone (1995) 235).

101 Robertson (1995) 443, playing off the title of Adams (1981), *Heartland of Cities*.

102 This may have been true at the beginning, of the fourth millennium B.C.E. (Stone [1995] 236), but during the third millennium other institutions also controlled and contributed to city-state political, economic, and commercial enterprises.

103 Robertson (1995) 443–44.

from the temple complex either by distance or by a wall or canal. Canals, streets, and walls divided the city into sectors. Canals and streets also provided means of transport between different parts of the city. Fortified walls surrounded the major cities, enclosing the settlement mound as well as some non-settled areas (perhaps for growing fruits and vegetables). Aside from temple and palace sectors, there were also residential zones where both elites and commoners lived, and where one would also find various kinds of workshops. Much of the manufacturing was carried on in the residential areas.[104]

As for the temples, they were organized as households of the major deities, the Anunna-gods mentioned here, perhaps referring in this context especially to those put in charge of the various ecological, societal, and technological phenomena mentioned in these 12 cycles. Compare, for example, the establishment of the various offices and supplies of the household of Ningirsu in Gudea cylinder B. The overall importance of these divine households, however, also lent to them the character of "corporations." They were responsible for a large portion of the resources of the community and, therefore, much of the administration and support of the labor force available to the community. There were "upper-level managers" referred to as "elders," who were, in turn, headed by a top administrator with the title of šanga or šabra.

The elders were the heads of certain functions or industries: archivists, field surveyors, managers of grain storage, workers and/or soldiers, scribes who kept charge of the numbers and distribution of plow animals, foremen of the ox drivers, treasurers, and constables, among others. They kept charge of work details and their management, especially the work of agriculture and the irrigation projects so essential to it. Many of the laborers themselves were actually sharecroppers, assigned to certain plots of land, who received a portion of the produce of their plot(s) for their work (see further the remarks on cycles 5 and 6 above). Sometimes these same workers would receive rations for serving on other kinds of work details. There were also those who were completely dependent on the temple household, probably mostly those who were destitute (e.g., widows and other women with no means of support, orphans) or handicapped in some way. There were also prisoners of war and captives. Such dependents were supported completely by temple rations.[105]

---

104 Stone (1995) 236–43.

105 Robertson (1995) 444–47.

CYCLE 12: THE TEXTILE INDUSTRY

The twelfth cycle relates that Enki also established the textile industry and placed the goddess "Uttu, the dependable woman, the silent one" in charge. This description of Uttu corresponds to the fact that female dependents of various kinds were especially important in the fabrication of textiles in the temple workshops,[106] as well as in the palace industrial offices.[107] Textiles were, in fact, one of the most important trade commodities for ancient Sumer, so the mention of this industry after the establishment and management of cities in cycle 11 is logical.

The Disputation between the Ewe and the Wheat is a good literary source for a depiction of some of the benefits that accrue from the Ewe's production of wool, even though in the end Wheat turns out to be the winner of the dispute.[108] After all is said and done, wheat is the staple food and those who did not have it in ancient Sumer had to obtain it in some way from those who did (ll. 189–90). The fact remains, however, that this shows how pastoral goods were essential to daily life, not just in terms of hides and dairy products, but for the wool that was produced so abundantly and used to make fabric for clothing of all sorts. Agricultural activity was not the only major economic activity in ancient Sumer. The sheepfolds of the lowland plains in cycle 10 anticipate this textile industry as much as the cities of cycle 11 do. There were hundreds of thousands of sheep that were sheared for their wool each year in the Lagaš city-state alone during the last century or two of the third millennium.

Regarding daily life in particular, the institutions of city and industry in cycles 11–12 present us with whole sets of diverse kinds of occupations and circumstances of people's lives in the cities of ancient Sumer. There were the administrative elites who managed those under them and were responsible for their productivity; there were foremen who actually guided the work in process; and there were the workers. The means of subsistence and lifestyle that came along with these levels of society were distinctive. As far as the common people were concerned, some were artisans, others were sharecroppers, some were pastoralists, some were laborers who were supported at least partially by rations from the royal and temple institutions, others were (temple) dependents supported totally by (sometimes reduced) rations, and so on.

---

106 Robertson (1995) 447.

107 See Adams (1981) 148 and Bier (1995) 1570, and the literature cited there. Bier (1995) explains the various procedures of textile fabrication.

108 Vanstiphout (1997b).

Conclusion

The goal of this essay has been to determine what we might be able to discern from Sumerian literary compositions about the recurring "daily (quotidian) life" concerns of various elements of the population of ancient Sumer. The myth *Enki and the World Order* has occupied most of our attention because it programmatically sets forth the fundamental environmental, ecological, technological, economic, agricultural, architectural, pastoral, and industrial occupations and conditions that were the foundations of life. To be sure, there are problems with taking literary texts at face value as representations of realia and real lives. In light of that, this essay has also taken other sources of information into consideration, including modern studies of topology, environment, and climate in the alluvium, archaeological discoveries of various kinds of realia, from bricks to plows, etc., ancient art, and studies of not only other literary texts but also economic and administrative archival documents from different times and places in Sumer.

Enki and the World Order is well named in that it provides a literary analogical picture of the basic framework of the ancient Sumerian world order. No claim can be made here to completeness, neither in terms of the topics covered nor in the treatment of them. The goal has been simply to follow the lead of the twelve cycles of Enki's action outlined above as foundational to the lives of people. Other things not included in the twelve cycles are also important. We know that these cycles were not viewed as presenting a complete picture, because in Inanna's complaint that follows five goddesses are mentioned along with the element(s) of culture over which Enki had placed them. Only one of them is mentioned in the twelve cycles (i.e., Nanše). The other four include giving birth to children, jewelry, metal working, and scribal practice.

The twelve cycles discussed here provide a very helpful outline of the primary framework of life and culture in ancient Sumer. It begins with the lifeline of ancient Sumer, the watercourses of the Tigris and Euphrates rivers, the swamps and lakes that arose in connection with them, all the way down to the sea in the south, and even the importance of rainfall (cycles 1–4). In turn, these rivers provided for the possibility of irrigation agriculture, which involved the work of digging canals and ditches, working the soil and planting crops with plows and teams of oxen, and the growth and harvesting of barley, lentils, and other crops (cycles 5–6). The making of bricks and use of them in the construction of buildings, domestic and otherwise, fills out the basic foundations of city life in ancient Sumer (cycles 7–8). Enki's work then turns to the highland and lowland plains, the places of wild game and pastoral activity—the place of the shepherd as opposed to the farmer (cycles 9–10).

Finally, the prosperity that came with the combination of all these resources brought with it the need to demarcate the boundaries between the various city-states in the alluvium (cycle 11) and establish the textile industry, which was foundational to the development of trade (cycle 12). The latter was actually based on the pastoral resources of the plains that extended beyond the agricultural alluvium. This is the picture of the ancient Sumerian homeland as *Enki and the World Order* paints it. It should be taken seriously as it stands. It provides a very helpful point of departure for the study of life and culture in ancient Sumer from the viewpoint of the ancient Sumerians themselves, or at least from one point of view in ancient Sumer.

BIBLIOGRAPHY

Adams, R. McC. (1981) *Heartland of Cities: Surveys of Ancient Settlement and Land Use on the Central Floodplain of the Euphrates.* Chicago. **Averbeck, R. E.** (1987) *A Preliminary Study of Ritual and Structure in the Cylinders of Gudea.* Dissertation Dropsie College/Annenberg Research Institute. University Microfilms International. Ann Arbor, Mich. (2000) The Cylinders of Gudea. In W.W. Hallo and K.L. Younger, eds., *The Context of Scripture.* II. *Monumental Compositions from the Biblical World,* 417–33. Leiden. **Benito, C.A.** (1969) "Enki and Ninmaḫ" and "Enki and the World Order." Dissertation University of Pennsylvania. University Microfilms International. Ann Arbor, Mich. **Bier, C.** (1995) Textile Arts in Ancient Western Asia. In J.M. Sasson, ed., *Civilizations of the Ancient Near East.* Volume 3, 1567–88. New York. **Capomacchia, A.M.G.** (2001) Heroic Dimension and Historical Perspective in the Ancient Near East. In T. Abusch, P. Beaulieu, J. Huehnergard, P. Machinist, and P. Steinkeller, eds., *Historiography in the Cuneiform World.* Proceedings of the XLVe Rencontre Assyriologique Internationale. Part I, 91–97. Bethesda, Md. **Civil, M.** (1961) The Home of the Fish: A New Sumerian Literary Composition. *Iraq* 23: 154–75, plate 66. (1994) *The Farmer's Instructions: A Sumerian Agricultural Manual.* Aula Orientalis – Supplementa 5. Barcelona. **Cooper, J.** (1989) Enki's Member: Eros and Irrigation in Sumerian Literature. In H. Behrens, D. Loding, and M. T. Roth, eds., *DUMU-E$_2$-DUB-BA-A: Studies in Honor of Åke W. Sjöberg,* 87–89. Philadelphia. (2001) Literature and History: The Historical and Political Referents of Sumerian Literary Texts. In T. Abusch, P. Beaulieu, J. Huehnergard, P. Machinist, and P. Steinkeller, eds., *Historiography in the Cuneiform World.* Proceedings of the XLVe Rencontre Assyriologique Internationale. Part I, 131–47. Bethesda, Md. **Doty, W.G.** (1986) *Mythography: The Study of Myths and Rituals.* Alabama. **Douglas, M.** (1999) *Leviticus as Literature.* Oxford. **Edzard, D.O.** (1997) *Gudea and His Dynasty.* The Royal Inscriptions of Mesopotamia, Early

Periods, Volume 3/1. Toronto. **Eyre, C.J.** (1995) The Agricultural Cycle, Farming, and Water Management in the Ancient Near East. In J.M. Sasson, ed., *Civilizations of the Ancient Near East*, Volume 1, 175–89. New York. **Farber (-Flügge), G.** (1997) The Song of the Hoe. In W.W. Hallo and K.L. Younger, eds., *The Context of Scripture. I. Canonical Compositions from the Biblical World*, 511–13. Leiden. **Ferrara, A.J.** (1973) *Nanna-Suen's Journey to Nippur*. Studia Pohl Series Major 2. Rome. **George, A.R.** (1993) *House Most High: The Temples of Ancient Mesopotamia*. Mesopotamian Civilizations 5. Winona Lake, Ind. **Gragg, G.B.** (1997) The Heron and the Turtle. In W.W. Hallo and K.L. Younger, *The Context of Scripture. I. Canonical Compositions from the Biblical World*, 571–73. Leiden. **Heimpel, W.** (1987) The Natural History of the Tigris according to the Sumerian Literary Composition Lugal. *Journal of Near Eastern Studies* 46: 309–17. (1990) Ein zweiter Schritt zur Rehabilitierung der Rolle des Tigris in Sumer. *Zeitschrift für Assyriologie* 91: 204–13. (1997) To Nanshe. In W.W. Hallo and K.L. Younger, eds., *The Context of Scripture. I. Canonical Compositions from the Biblical World*, 526–531. Leiden. **Hesse, B.** (1995) Animal Husbandry and Human Diet in the Ancient Near East. In J.M. Sasson, ed., *Civilizations of the Ancient Near East*, Volume 1, 203–22. New York. **Horowitz, W.** (1998) *Mesopotamian Cosmic Geography*. Mesopotamian Civilizations 8. Winona Lake, Ind. **Jacobsen, T.** (1960) The Waters of Ur. *Iraq* 22: 174–85. (1970) *Toward the Image of Tammuz and Other Essays on Mesopotamian History and Culture*. Edited by W.L. Moran. Cambridge, Mass. (1982) *Salinity and Irrigation Agriculture in Antiquity*. Bibliotheca Mesopotamica 14. Malibu, Calif. (1987) *The Harps That Once... Sumerian Poetry in Translation*. New Haven. **Kramer, S.N.** (1963) *The Sumerians: Their History, Culture, and Character*. Chicago. (1971) Aspects of Mesopotamian Society. Evidence from the Sumerian Literary Sources. In H. Klengel, ed., *Beiträge zur Sozialen Struktur des Alten Vorderasien*. Sonderdruck aus Schriften zur Geschichte und Kultur des Alten Orients 1, 1–13. Berlin. (1991) The Death of Ur-Nammu and His Descent to the Netherworld. In M. Mori, H. Ogawa, and M. Yoshikawa, eds. *Near Eastern Studies. Dedicated to H.I.H. Prince Takahito Mikasa on the Occasion of His Seventy-Fifth Birthday*, 193–214. Wiesbaden. **Kramer, S.N. and Maier, J.** (1989) *Myths of Enki, The Crafty God*. Oxford. **Michalowski, P.** (1986) Mental Maps and Ideology: Reflections on Subartu. In H. Weiss, ed., *The Origins of Cities in Dry-Farming Syria and Mesopotamia in the Third Millennium B.C.*, 129–56. Guilford, Conn. (1989) *The Lamentation over the Destruction of Sumer and Ur*. Mesopotamian Civilizations 2. Winona Lake, Ind. **Michaux-Colombot, D.** (2001) Magan and Meluḫḫa: A Reappraisal through the Historiography of Thalassocratic Powers. In T. Abusch, P. Beaulieu, J. Huehnergard, P. Machinist, and P. Steinkeller, eds., *Historiography in the Cuneiform World*. Proceedings of the XLV[e] Rencontre Assyriologique Internationale, Part I, 329–55. Bethesda, Md. **Moorey, P.R.S.** (1999) *Ancient Mesopotamian Materials and Industries: The Archaeological Evidence*. Winona Lake, Ind. **Potts, D.T.** (1995) Distant Shores: Ancient Near Eastern Trade with South Asia and Northeast Africa. In J.M. Sasson, ed., *Civilizations of the Ancient Near East*, Volume 3, 1451–63. New York.

Reisman, D. (1971) Ninurta's Journey to Eridu. *Journal of Cuneiform Studies* 24: 3–10. **Renfrew, J.M.** (1995) Vegetables in the Ancient Near Eastern Diet. In J.M. Sasson, ed., *Civilizations of the Ancient Near East,* Volume 1, 191–202. New York. **Roaf, M.** (1990) *Cultural Atlas of Mesopotamia and the Ancient Near East.* Oxford. **Robertson, J.F.** (1995) The Social and Economic Organization of Ancient Mesopotamian Temples. In J.M. Sasson, ed., *Civilizations of the Ancient Near East,* Volume 1, 443–54. New York. **Salonen, A.** (1968) *Agricultura Mesopotamica.* Helsinki. (1972) *Die Ziegeleien im Alten Mesopotamien.* Helsinki. **Schwartz, G.M.** (1995) Pastoral Nomadism in Ancient Western Asia. In J.M. Sasson, ed., *Civilizations of the Ancient Near East,* Volume 1, 249–58. New York. **Sefati, Y.** (1985) *Love Songs in Sumerian Literature: Critical Edition of the Dumuzi-Inanna Songs.* Bar-Ilan Studies in Near Eastern Languages and Culture. Publications of the Samuel N. Kramer Institute of Assyriology. Ramat-Gan. **Sjöberg, Å.W.** (1998) *The Sumerian Dictionary of the University of Pennsylvania Museum,* Volume A, Part III. Philadelphia. **Steinkeller, P.** (2001a) New Light on the Hydrology and Topography of Southern Babylonia in the Third Millennium. *Zeitschrift fur Assyriologie* 91: 22–84. (2001b) Addenda to <<New Light on the Hydrology and Topography of Southern Babylonia in the Third Millennium>> *ZA* 91 (2001) 22–84. *N.A.B.U.* nº 3: 62. **Stone, E.** (1995) The Development of Cities in Ancient Mesopotamia. In J.M. Sasson, ed., *Civilizations of the Ancient Near East,* Volume 1, 235–48. New York. **Vanstiphout, H.** (1997a) The Disputation between the Bird and Fish. In W.W. Hallo and K.L. Younger, eds., *The Context of Scripture.* I. *Canonical Compositions from the Biblical World,* 581–84. Leiden. (1997b) The Disputation between Ewe and Wheat. In W.W. Hallo and K.L. Younger, eds., *The Context of Scripture.* I. *Canonical Compositions from the Biblical World,* 575–78. Leiden. (1997c) The Disputation between the Hoe and the Plow. In W.W. Hallo and K.L. Younger, eds., *The Context of Scripture.* I. *Canonical Compositions from the Biblical World,* 578–81. Leiden. (1997d) The Disputation between Summer and Winter. In W.W. Hallo and K.L. Younger, eds., *The Context of Scripture.* I. *Canonical Compositions from the Biblical World,* 584–88. Leiden. (1997e) Why Did Enki Organize the World? In I.L. Finkel and M.J. Geller, eds., *Sumerian Gods and Their Representations.* Cuneiform Monographs 7, 117–34. Groningen. **Verhoeven, K.** (1998) Geomorphological Research in the Mesopotamian Flood Plain. In H. Basche and M. Tanet, eds., *Changing Watercourses in Babylonia: Toward a Reconstruction of the Ancient Environment in Lower Mesopotamia,* volume 1. Mesopotamian History and Environment Series II, Memoirs V, 159–245. Ghent and Chicago. **Yoffee, N.** (1995) The Economy of Ancient Western Asia. In J.M. Sasson, ed., *Civilizations of the Ancient Near East,* Volume 3, 1387–99. New York.

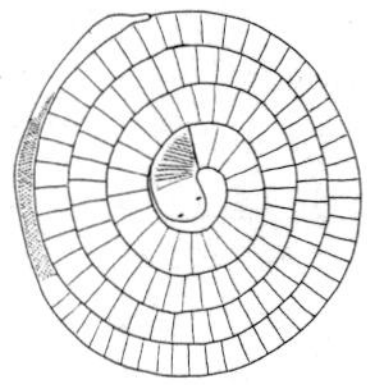

BIBLICAL AND MESOPOTAMIAN LAW: AN AMORITE CONNECTION?

Samuel Greengus
Hebrew Union College – Jewish Institute of Religion

Laws and adjudication are familiar features of everyday life in ancient, as well as in modern, times; they are present in general social consciousness and, at times, also in personal experience. Some features of law and adjudication are mentioned in the Bible; but an overwhelmingly more massive amount of information is preserved in the ancient cuneiform documents. The collective data represent numerous communities and cover a span of centuries. Yet, even so, they often exhibit unities that endure and transcend the boundaries of time and space. These unities and continuities invite our attention and deserve investigation.

We know that there are striking similarities between groups of laws appearing both in the Bible and in earlier Mesopotamian law collections, especially in the "Covenant Code" (Exod 21–23) and in the book of Deuteronomy (especially chapters 19–25). But there remains a persistent problem in how to explain why these similarities exist, inasmuch as the two cultures are separated by so much time and such great physical distance. One response is the theory that the Israelites adopted the legal institutions of their Canaanite neighbors, who, in turn, either borrowed or shared a legal culture and practice in common with the peoples of Mesopotamia.[1] This "Canaanite" theory appears to be a reasonable explanation, but then also loses credibility because there is absolutely no evidence for the mediating Canaanite laws and legal culture.

ABBREVIATIONS: AbB: Altbabylonische Briefe in Umschrift und Übersetzung (13 = van Soldt [1994]); *AHw*: Akkadisches Handwörterbuch. Von Soden (1965–81); BIN: Babylonian Inscriptions in the Collection of J. B. Nies (7 = Alexander [1943]); HL: Hittite Laws. Cited according to Hoffner (1997); LE: Laws of Eshnunna. Cited according to Goetze (1956); LH: Laws of Hammurapi. Cited according to Driver and Miles (1952–56); MAL: Middle Assyrian Laws. Cited according to Driver and Miles (1935); MARI: *Mari-Annales de Recherches Interdisciplinaires*; SEM: *Sumerian Epics and Myths*. Chiera (1934).

1 For a discussion of this position and some earlier literature, see Greengus (1991) 149–51.

There is, however, another version of this theory, which looks for connection through the Amorites. This theory has the advantage because we are able to place the Amorites in proximity both to ancient Mesopotamia and to ancient Israel. In Mesopotamia, the Amorites are known to us primarily through their West Semitic personal names, which stand out in documents written in Sumerian and Akkadian, beginning in the Ur III period (after 2100 B.C.E.) and continuing to the fall of Babylon (in 1600 B.C.E.). Amorite individuals are, in ancient times, often further identified by the label MAR.TU or *Amurrû*. The Amorites appear to have been divided into a number of tribes, and whereas some parts of them are semi-nomadic, others are found residing in cities and towns. By the time of Hammurapi (*c.* 1792–1750 B.C.E.), we find Amorite dynasties ruling most of the lands lying between the Syrian coast and the Persian Gulf; these include the kingdoms of Aleppo, Tirqa, Mari, Assur, Eshnunna, Babylon, Larsa, and Uruk.[2] Hammurapi and other rulers in his dynasty, at times, use the title "king of the Amorites," and the commanding officers of the Babylonian army bear the title "chief of the Amorites."[3] Zimri-Lim, king of Mari, is sometimes addressed also as the "king of the Akkadians and the Amorites," and this distinction is retained in the Edict of Ammiṣaduqa, which divides the population into "Akkadians" and "Amorites."[4] This division suggests that the Amorites maintained some ethnic and, perhaps, social distinctiveness throughout the period, even after gaining dominant political power.[5]

---

[2] Most of the identifications are based upon the personal names of the rulers. But there is also evidence from royal titles, even when the rulers bear Akkadian PNs, e.g., LUGAL *Amnanum* (an Amorite tribe) born by kings of Uruk; cf. Seux (1967) 421.

[3] For the titles, LUGAL MAR.TU, LUGAL DAGAN KUR MAR.TU, AD.DA KUR MAR.TU, cf. Seux (1967) 384–85, 423. For the titles *rabi* (GAL) *Amurrîm* and PA MAR.TU see *CAD* A/2 93–95. A list of military titles and citations may be found in Voth (1981) 117–38, 225–30. Cf. further AbB 13 nos. 37, 38, 60, 87, 170 and Abrahami (1998).

[4] For Mari, see Durand (1992) 113 in the unpublished letter A.489. Durand also cites, for Zimri-Lim, the title "king of the Ḫaneans"; and for Yaḫdun-Lim, "king of Mari and the land of the Benē Simal." Cf. also the title "king of Mari and the land of the Ḫaneans," which is given to Zimri-Lim in M.6435+M.8987, the treaty between him and Hammurapi of Babylon against Elam; see Charpin and Durand (1986) 148. For Ammiṣaduqa's edict, see Kraus (1984) 174–75 (par. 9).

[5] For the Amorites, their names and geographic distribution, see Gelb *et al.* (1980) and literature cited there. A good summary of known facts can be found in Whiting (1995).

The Amorites, as an identifiable group, disappeared in Babylonia after the fall of Babylon but continued to rule in Syria throughout the second millennium. They are recorded in the Bible as having strong powers in Palestine during the patriarchal and early Israelite periods.[6] Because of their long history, marked by sustained contact with Babylonia and Assyria, the Amorites can be seen as maintaining cultural links in and, perhaps, even between east and west. So when we find similarities between the laws of the Bible and of Babylonia, it is an attractive idea to suggest that the Amorites were in some way responsible for these shared traditions.

Yet how could this sharing come about? We know very little about Amorite culture. Since no documents written in Amorite have been found, many scholars assume that the Amorites abandoned all their native culture when they settled down in Mesopotamia and elsewhere. The Sumerian *Myth of Martu* describes the Amorites as hardy barbarians: "He is a tent-dweller, [buffeted by] wind and rain, [who knows not] offerings, he digs up *truffles* in the highlands, knows not how to bend the knee, eats uncooked meat, has no house in his lifetime, is not brought to burial when he dies."[7] In line with this depiction, it is suggested that the Amorites adopted and, subsequently, exported Babylonian laws to the west. The suggestion of an east-to-west cultural tide finds support in the fact that cuneiform documents were written in Palestine during the Old Babylonian and Middle Babylonian periods, which correspond to the Middle and Late Bronze periods in Palestine. There are some letters and more than a few scribal school texts; these reflect the use of Akkadian as the medium of international communication in an age before the development of alphabetic writing. So one could argue that the laws came to the west along with other scribal learning.

However, when we look for evidence that could demonstrate the penetration of Akkadian language into everyday life and culture of Palestine, we find surprisingly few documents. There are a couple of administrative documents known: one at Hazor and another at Hebron, and two

---

6 Cf., e.g., Gen 14:13; 15:16, 21; Exod 22:23; Num 13:29; 21; Josh 5:11; 7:7; 10:5; Judg 1:34–36; 11:22–23; 1 Sam 7:14; Amos 3:9–10. For discussion of the Amorites in Syria-Palestine and additional references, see Singer (1991) 137–41, 179–88. A helpful, supplementary study is Singer (1991a).

7 For this passage (SEM 58 iv 24–29 = lines 133–38 in Kramer's edition), see Kramer (1990). Line 135 is translated in *PSD* B 10a and partly in *CAD* K 133b. J. Klein, in notes appended to Kramer's article (Kramer [1990] 25–27), calls attention to similar characterizations made by the Sumerians about the Subarians; see Hallo (1982) lines 24–27. The ancient, literary descriptions of the Amorites (those cited here and some others) are also discussed by Buccellati (1966) 330–32.

legal documents: one at Hazor and a second from Shechem.[8] No Akkadian legal compositions or "codes" have ever turned up in the west. There was, moreover, especially in Palestine, a marked decline in the linguistic quality of Akkadian learning during the Late Bronze or Amarna period.[9] For all these reasons, one may wonder how the Amorites, a people who never wrote their own language, could have managed successfully to teach another people (i.e., the Canaanites or Hebrews) the laws of a third foreign nation (i.e., the Babylonians).[10]

The Amorite connection, however, might become a more plausible theory if we are willing to assume that there might be features in both the Babylonian and Israelite laws that are Amorite in origin. The similarities in their laws would thus emerge from a dynamic process of cultural sharing and interaction that went beyond the scholastic level. Is it possible that the Amorites could have retained and passed on some cultural ideas of their own? If they indeed did so, then we could search for Amorite "influences" upon both the Babylonian and biblical law systems. This concept would view the Amorites acting as agents, transferring their *own* cultural institutions and we might thereby explain *some*, although not all the similarities between Mesopotamian and biblical laws. The idea is not so far-fetched. There is some evidence for the retention of native Amorite cultural expressions at the highest levels of Mesopotamian society. A royal letter from Eshnunna, for example, describes the custom of bringing and presenting valuable gifts (gold, silver, copper utensils, garments, and a slave) at the funeral of an Amorite chieftain.[11] Then there is also the custom of slaugh-

---

[8] For references see the following note.

[9] I have discussed these arguments as well as the cuneiform administrative and legal documents found in Palestine (giving references to earlier studies) in Greengus (1997). The decline of Akkadian literacy during the Amarna period has also been noted by P. Artzi, who, nevertheless, still maintains that this poor level was sufficient to support cultural transfer. He states: "In spite of the fact that Canaan in the Amarna period and thereafter suffered a decline in its level of cuneiform literacy, some degree of activity was continued in this area by local scribes. It is due to this literary and cultural continuity that subsequent Israelite culture and civilization was significantly influenced by Mesopotamian culture and civilization, through Western mediation." See Artzi (1990) 155.

[10] The role of the Amorites as agents of cultural transfer has been championed by Mendenhall (1992). However, I have previously questioned the alleged cultural transfer of cuneiform law to the west via non-Babylonians and even scribes, in Greengus (1994) 83–87.

[11] This custom is described in Whiting (1987) nos. 11, 15.

tering a donkey foal or a puppy in treaty-making rituals that took place among the Amorite rulers of the Old Babylonian period.[12] In the Mari documents one finds references to the spoken use of Amorite language, along with the retention of Amorite vocabulary, especially in the socio-political realm. Changes in the writing of cuneiform signs and in the shape of tablets also occur in the Old Babylonian period and may perhaps be due to their influence. Suggestions have been made also for their cultural impact in the areas of literature, music, prophecy, and professions, such as horticulture and medicine.[13] These are only some examples, but perhaps already sufficient to show us that aspects of Amorite culture could be preserved and expressed within the larger Mesopotamian civilization.

The Amorites and Talion

The idea of Amorite influence upon the laws has, in fact, been put forth by W.G. Lambert, who suggests that talionic punishments, which are found both in the Laws of Hammurapi and in the Hebrew Bible, are Amorite institutions that were taken over both by the Babylonians and the Hebrews.[14] Talion finds its clearest statement in the Bible and is mandated for homicide, as well as for battery and wounding. The Bible in its formulation includes "life for life" alongside "an eye for an eye, tooth for a tooth," continuing with hand, foot, burn, wound, and stripe.[15] Capital punishment for homicide is, of course, not limited to Israel or to Mesopotamia; so it is, therefore, not in homicide, but with talion for battery and wounding,

---

12 See *ḫayaram qatālum/dâkum*, *CAD* Ḫ 118–19 plus discussion of Charpin (1990). For *mērānum u ḫassum* see *CAD* Ḫ 128. *AHw* 339b corrects *ḫassum* to *ḫazzum* "goat"; cf. *CAD* Ḫ 83b sub *ḫanzum*. The slaying of a puppy is found in Hittite rituals; see Collins (1990). Collins calls attention to a possible biblical reference, Isa 66:3–4. Durand (1992) 114–20 comments on the political importance of this intra-ethnic rite.

13 Durand (1992) 121–27. On p. 125 Durand mentions a small unpublished tablet (M.9777) that is written in "a language clearly Semitic although not Akkadian"; we must wait to find out if this is an actual Amorite text. See also Malamat (1997), where previous literature is cited. Cf. also, Malamat (1999).

14 Lambert (1982) made this same argument some years earlier in Lambert (1965); see especially pp. 288–89. This same idea also appears in a brief comment made by Loewenstamm (1957), who, in turn, credits B. Mazar. Frymer-Kensky (1980) also presents the idea of West Semitic influence, crediting both Lambert and Loewenstamm.

15 This is the formulation in Exod 21:23–25. Lev 24:19–20 has this sequence of bodily injuries: broken bone, eye, tooth; homicide is dealt with separately in 24:17, 21. Deut 19:21 has life for life, eye for eye, followed by tooth, hand, and foot for foot.

that we find our unique parallels with Mesopotamian laws. Our comparative discussion of talion will, therefore, focus on non-fatal physical injuries where, in Mesopotamia, the earlier "codes," such as those of Ur-Nammu, Lipit-Ishtar, and Eshnunna, require pecuniary sanctions for wounding; but the later Laws of Hammurapi applies talionic sanctions for these same injuries.[16]

In cases dealing with bodily injuries causing the loss of a limb, nose, or tooth, the Ur-Nammu (perhaps, better Shulgi) Laws §§ 18–22 impose monetary penalties.[17] This earlier pattern continues in Eshnunna Laws §§ 42–43, which deal with injury and loss of nose, ear, eye, tooth, and finger. But Hammurapi Laws §§ 196–97 impose talionic reprisal for causing the loss of an eye or breaking a bone of persons in the highest social class (while continuing with monetary compensation for the same injuries that are sustained by commoners or slaves in §§ 198–201).

A.S. Diamond, an historian of law, has argued that, in the progress of law through history, one may discern lines of development that correlate with the increasing power of central governments along with other changes, such as the waning importance for kinship groups, economic development, and a fall in the status of women relative to that of men. At such points in history, says Diamond, one encounters an increase in capital punishment (including mutilation) and its wider application to offenses that earlier were seen as private and capable of being settled by pecuniary settlement. These offenses may include homicide, battery, adultery, and theft. As part of this societal change, talion—that is to say, the rule of "an eye for an eye and a tooth for a tooth"—makes its appearance and signals a replacement of earlier pecuniary sanctions. Diamond finds evidence for this pattern of increased corporal punishment in medieval English law as well as in Mesopotamia. According to Diamond, these different and separate civilizations should not be evaluated in terms of their absolute chronologies but, rather, in terms of their relative position on the ladder of governmental, social, and economic development.[18]

---

16 Although our focus here is talionic reprisal for non-fatal injuries, I should point out, in connection with homicide, an implied parallel to the biblical formulation, "life for a life," which appears in an Old Babylonian letter containing the instruction of King Rimsin of Larsa to his officials: "because he (the slave) threw the young lad into the furnace, you (now) cast the slave into the furnace"; the letter is BIN 7 10 treated by Driver (1957/58).

17 The attribution of the Ur-Nammu laws to Shulgi is supported by evidence presented by Kramer (1983).

18 A.S. Diamond (1971) 70–103. Cf. also his earlier article, Diamond (1957).

Diamond considers the well-known passages expressing the talion rule in Exod 21:23–25, Lev 24:19–20, and Deut 19:21 to be interpolations into the biblical text, presumably added in the time of the monarchy, when the power of central government was first established. He reads these biblical passages in a literal fashion but argues that "the vogue of the talionic idea is short-lived; it was in practice unknown in later Jewish law, where there was much debate as to the meaning of the rule and as to whether it had ever been literally applied."[19] He finds evidence of a partial retreat from talion in the statement of Josephus (*Antiquities* IV, 280), who says that the injured victim has the choice of accepting money in place of exacting talionic retribution "for the law makes the sufferer the judge of the value of what he has suffered, and permits him to estimate it, unless he be more severe." Philo, however, read the law in a literal fashion (*De spec. leg.* III, 181–82). Later Jewish interpreters (e.g., Bab. Baba Qamma 83b) retreated totally from talion and argued against the plain reading of the text to say that the option of physical retaliation should never be taken literally nor could such remedies be made available to an injured victim. For the rabbis, only monetary compensation was allowed in the cases of non-fatal wounding and injury.[20]

Lambert, perhaps because he wished to forge a stronger link between *lex talionis* and the Amorites, rejects Diamond's explanation of its origins as "methodologically unsound." He characterizes talion as a kind of primeval law of the desert.[21] Lambert offers no proof for this characterization nor does he comment on the changes in English law. In his favor, it could be pointed out that although English law increased the use the corporal punishments, it did not fully embrace talionic reprisal as a total concept.[22]

---

19 Diamond (1971) 150–51.

20 Some rabbinical authorities, albeit in guarded language, continued to voice recognition that the received, i.e., oral tradition, went against the plain wording of the biblical text; so, for example Abraham Ibn Ezra on Exod 21:24 and Maimonides, *Guide* III, 41. See further Weiss Halivini (1991) 85–87, 200 and n. 75, which adds the commentary of R. Abraham, the son of Maimonides, on Exod 21:24 and the passage in the *Guide*.

21 Lambert (1980) 69 states: "Dieses „Aug um Auge, Zahn um Zahn" war vermutlich ein amoritischer Rechtsgrundsatz, besser geeignet für die Bedingungen der Wüste als für das städtische Leben."

22 This is the position taken by Pollock and Maitland (1898) 2: 489 n. 2, where they state: "Long ago King Alfred...had copied the Hebraic rule from Exodus, but without intending to enforce it. When crude retaliation appears in a medieval code, the influence of the Bible may always be suspected. What we may call characteristic punishment, e.g., castration for adultery, or loss of a hand for forgery, is a very

And as for the primeval nature of talion, one might argue this from customs of physical retaliation, addressed by the Qur'an, that were still being practiced in tribal Arabia at the time of Muhammad.[23]

B.S. Jackson follows Diamond in seeing these talionic formulations as later additions to Hebrew law, but attributes their adoption not so much to the power of the crown but more to the role of "aristocratic circles" which arose as a result of increasing social stratification. He finds support for his idea in the punishment sustained by Adonibezek in Judg 1:7, who accepts his physical mutilation as a sign of divine punishment for the seventy kings whom he had mutilated in the same way.[24] Jackson looks for support to the Laws of Hammurapi (§§ 196–201, cited above), where talionic punishments are required only if both the offender and the injured victim belong to the highest social class, not when the victim is a slave or commoner. He further wants to argue—but allows that he is not able to prove—that talion is a foreign import into Hebrew law.[25]

Social class, to be sure, is a factor in determining the levels of punishment for offenses elsewhere in the ancient laws. In Mesopotamia, in the oft-repeated classic case involving a man who strikes a pregnant women and causes her death as well as that of her foetus, the offender, too, must die if the woman belonged to the highest social class. This is the rule in the Laws of Lipit-Ishtar and Hammurapi. But if the victim was a commoner or slave, only monetary penalties were imposed.[26] This pattern is again found in the

---

different thing." Diamond (1971) 99 n. 1, in turn, although admitting that talionic sanctions were not regularly used in England, attacks their assertion, saying: "The authors (i.e., Pollock and Maitland) were here blinded by contemporary German racial theory, and crowd these sentences with misapprehension."

23 See Schacht (1979). He states that the institution was based on the customs of pagan times and confirms that it included retaliation for non-fatal injuries as well as for homicide. (I thank Prof. Daniel C. Snell for pointing out this reference.) That talion, the taking of "an eye for an eye," survives even today was reported in an article on Saudi Arabia appearing in the *Economist* 359 no. 8226 (June 16–22, 2001) 46: "Nowhere else are the qiṣaṣ, or retaliatory punishments allowed under Islam, applied with such punctilio: last August, an Egyptian worker's eye was surgically removed at the insistence of a man who lost the use of his own eye after the Egyptian had thrown acid in his face."

24 Jackson (1973) 298–301.

25 Otto (1991) agrees that talion was a foreign element but goes on to argue that the replacement of physical retaliation by compensation already took place in biblical times, when the Pentateuch was being redacted.

26 Cf. UM 55-21-71, iii, 7′–13′ in Civil (1965); LH §§ 210, 212, 214. A similar case appears in the later MAL A § 50.

case of the doctor whose ministrations result in his patient dying or losing an eye. The doctor will lose his hand if his patient was a free person but pays compensation if his patient was a slave.[27] Another case exhibiting this same social difference is that of the negligent builder who, if the house collapses, will lose his life if the house-owner dies or the life of his son if the house-owner's son dies. But if his negligence causes the death of a slave (or loss of property), only monetary compensation is required.[28] We again find this distinction between free person and slave operating in the case of the distrainee who is mistreated and dies while being held in the house of a creditor.[29]

The determination of punishment according to social status appears in the Bible as well, albeit in more limited fashion. In the case of the negligent owner of an ox known to be dangerous, if the ox gores a free person, the penalty ranges from monetary compensation to death; but if the victim was a slave, a set monetary amount is prescribed; there is no talk of death penalty for the owner of an ox killing a slave.[30] Non-fatal bodily injury inflicted by a master upon his slave that results in loss of eye or tooth is satisfied with compensation rather than with talionic reprisal, which would be the case if the victim was a free person. Compensation is extended through the manumission of that slave (Exod 21:26–27).[31] The Bible does not tell us what would happen if a person injured a slave belonging to another master. This case, however, does appear in later rabbinic law, which offers only compensation and which thereby restricts manumission to the case involving one's own slaves.[32]

---

27 LH §§ 218–20.

28 LH §§ 229–31.

29 LH § 116; a similar case is found in LE § 23–24.

30 Exod 21:29–32.

31 Schacht (1979) 180 notes that in Arabia there could be no valid action of retaliation for non-fatal injuries between a free person and a slave; thus compensation was the only remedy in such cases. Joseph Bekhor Shor, in his commentary on Exod 21:26 (see Nebo [1994]), argues that the slave must be manumitted because he lacks independent legal status to receive and keep compensation, since anything that he holds legally belongs to his master, who injured him. This reasoning may explain why the rabbis did not extend the benefit of immediate manumission to injured (Hebrew) slaves who were originally free; see note 39 below.

32 The case of injuring another's slave might have been expected in the transition from Exod 21:25 to 21:26. This case is found outside of the Bible in LH § 199 and in HL §§ 8, 14, VI, VIIB, XIII. In rabbinic laws, m. B. Qam. 8:3 supplies these "missing cases" where one who injures another's non-Hebrew or Hebrew slave must pay

So where does our data lead us with respect to a suggested Amorite derivation for talion? In my own view, the hypothesis will be enhanced if we can accommodate both an historic semi-nomadic background on the one hand and the obvious favoring of higher social class in the laws on the other. This could happen if we understand that the Amorites became the higher social class in Babylonia and introduced their traditional talionic laws for their own benefit as conquerors and rulers.[33] The situation for ancient Israel is less clear. Jackson's idea that the Israelite kings and nobles adopted the privileges formerly held by the indigenous ruling classes—perhaps the Amorites or their successors—is an attractive explanation. But if, with Lambert, we also maintain that talion is a characteristic feature of semi-nomadic tribal life, then we would look for less cultural distance between Israelites and Amorites in holding onto practices of talionic reprisal; talion would then be a cultural feature shared by both peoples.[34] In either case—Lambert or Jackson—we are able to assume that it was because of the Amorites that the Babylonians embraced talion.

Treatment of Debt Slaves

Once we open up the possibility of Amorite influence upon the laws of both Babylonia and Israel, we may then begin to look for other situations, especially when laws are found only in these two systems. We cannot simply assume that all similarities between Babylonia and Israel are borrowed from the Amorites, since there is also the enormous cultural debt owed to the Sumerians and Sumerian law. But laws unique to Babylonia and Israel may be potential candidates for consideration, and the case for them becomes stronger if we can link a unique set of laws in some way to our concept of Amorite culture.

---

compensation. (The case of injuring another's Hebrew slave is further discussed in b. B. Qam. 96a, 87a.)

33 Lambert (1982) 312 appears to agree with this idea when he states: "the Amorite ruling classes were not barbarians or country bumpkins, immediately cowed by the brilliance of Sumero-Akkadian culture. For one thing, they were the rulers."

34 Talion is known also in ancient Assyria, where it coexisted with compensation in capital cases; for discussion see Greengus (1994) 70–71. In *MAL* A § 52 we find an echo of biblical formulations in the expression *miḫṣi kī miḫṣi*, "blow for blow." Lewy (1961) 33 noted that the presence of Amorites in Assyria, as well as in Babylonia. Assyrian society and culture continued many features that we associate with semi-nomadic peoples, e.g., the persistence of blood feud and tribal identity. Cf. Grayson (1992) 751, 753.

We may find a second possible set in the laws dealing with debt slaves, i.e., fellow citizens who descended into poverty and were forced to give themselves or members of their families into servitude in order to satisfy their debts. The Babylonian law is LH § 117, which requires the release of a free man or woman who became a debt slave after three years of service. This law has long puzzled scholars because there is no evidence showing that it was put into practice. Scholars have thus imagined it to be "utopian" in character and have suggested that Hammurapi was required to abandon this measure aimed at giving individual relief and, in its place, rely only upon intermittent royal proclamations of debt release, i.e., the *mīšarum* acts, which addressed all such debtors at once in a kind of "class action."[35] F.R. Kraus has called attention to the close similarity in language and phrasing that appears in LH § 117 and § 20 of Ammiṣaduqa's edict of debt release.[36] The similarity in language is perhaps not surprising since these two measures were alternative responses to the same, recurring type of social and economic problems.

There is a textual issue that must also be addressed in the interpretation of LH § 117. This paragraph lists a variety of ways in which the free individual could fall into debt slavery; the terms used are *ana kaspim nadānum*, *ana kiššatim*, and Ammiṣaduqa's Edict § 20 adds a third, *ana manzazānim*. These may be translated: "sale (for debt), bondage for (penalty), and being held for pledge."[37] Although these terms are well known, a question has arisen with respect to the term for sale (*ana kaspim nadānum*). The same expression is used for permanent sale; yet, at least in the law paragraph LH § 117, one might argue that the sale *ab initio* was intended to be a temporary one only since manumission would occur after three years. Some scholars have, therefore, argued that only the rights to the debtor's labor were being sold; but perhaps they are seeking a level of distinction that was not, in ancient times, present in the language.[38]

---

35 See Hallo (1995) 88. Hallo argues that LH § 117, "however well intentioned ...may have proved unworkable in practice." See further, similar arguments given by Chirichigno (1993) 60, 72.

36 Kraus (1984) 265; for other scholars who have commented upon this similarity, see Chirichigno (1993) 89.

37 See Westbrook (1996). For *kiššatum*, see also Kraus (1984) 266–76; for *mazazānum*, *CAD* M/1 232–33.

38 For discussion of *ana kaspim nadānum*, see Chirichigno (1993) 68–69. Cf. also Fleischman (1990), who argues that the purpose of LH § 117 was to abrogate what would otherwise be a permanent sale. The Hebrew verb מכר, which appears in Exod 21:7, Deut 15:12, etc., could be subject to a similar analysis with respect to

The biblical law parallel to LH § 117 appears in two places: Deut 15:12–18 and Exod 21:2–5. These are the cases of Hebrew debt slaves who are to be freed after six years of service. There are a number of textual issues that have arisen, but that will not deter us from making the comparison between the various laws. We will deal with the textual issues only briefly. The context of debt slavery appears certain in Deut 15, where this law occurs in a larger unit discussing poverty and the lending of money. But the terms עבד and עברי, which occur in both passages, have generated a great deal of discussion, especially for Exod 21, where the debt slave is not further characterized as אחיך, "your brother" as he is in Deut 15. Scholars have, moreover, pondered the retention of what appears to be an archaic term, i.e., "Hebrew," and have further debated whether Exod 21:2–5 and the other slave laws presented in Exod 21 are laws pertaining to debt slaves or perhaps, at times, also to chattel slaves.[39] The biblical formulations, at least to modern readers, are not as transparent as the Akkadian ones, where it is clear when we are dealing with a free person who, because of debt, falls into a condition of slavery. The biblical term עבד by contrast, in Deut 15 and Exod 21–22, is applied without distinction, to chattel slaves and also to debt slaves who can be freed or redeemed. The term עברי appears to have been added to denote a fellow Israelite; but here, too, there has been much discussion, because some have linked this term to Akkadian *ḫabiru/ḫapiru*, which seems to describe a social class rather than an ethnic group.[40]

The biblical laws also differ from LH § 117 in requiring six years of service rather than just three. Cardellini has suggested that the number seven emerged through an association with the sabbatical fallow year, the development of the institution of the Sabbath, and the Exodus narratives

---

permanent versus temporary sale; but, to my knowledge, no one has argued for any such distinction in the uses of the Hebrew verb. There seems to have been no such distinction, to judge from Lev 25:14–16, where a time limitation needed to be explicitly added to the sale.

39 This question is well discussed by Chirichigno (1993) 148–85; see especially after p. 178. Rabbinic interpretation of these passages generally assumes that chattel slaves are the focus of Exod 21:20–26, 32 and, in fact, interprets these passages as uniquely directed toward the non-Hebrew slave who suffers irreparable injury at the hands of his master. Cf. t. Qidd. 1.6 (Lieberman [1973] 4:278), which follows *Mekilta de Rabbi Ishmael* (Lauterbach [1935] 3: 7–9, 58–67, 73–74).

40 Cf. Chirichigno (1993) 200–18. The laws dealing with debt slavery in Lev. 25:39–44 eschew the term עבד, which is applied only to chattel slaves. This law passage, which releases the slave only in the Jubilee year, has no parallel in Mesopotamia and, therefore, must be kept separate in our discussion.

celebrating freedom from slavery.[41] Some scholars, medieval and modern, have attempted to connect the seventh year in Deut 15:12 (and Exod 21:2) with the sabbatical release mentioned in Deut 15:1–3 (and elsewhere); they have argued that the seventh year of release from slavery was intended to be the regular sabbatical or fallow year.[42] But most scholars have taken the seven years to be a personal computation made individually for every slave; they then usually explain Deut 15:1–3 as releasing debts or pledged assets belonging to debtors who were not (yet) enslaved.[43]

Textual issues aside, we do find a shared concern for impoverished and enslaved free citizens as a strong theme in the biblical and Mesopotamian legal traditions. The practice of debt release is found among many ancient peoples, including the Sumerians and the Anatolian rulers of Kanesh during the Old Assyrian period.[44] The concept was, thus, not limited to Mesopotamia and ancient Israel. Nevertheless, it is true that the institution found a rich expression in these two cultures. When we look to explain the reasons for this shared value and its reception, we discover that some scholars have looked to tribal or semi-nomadic origins—and the Amorites —as a possible explanation. The *mīšarum* and *andurārum* traditions of general debt release are, in fact, widely practiced in areas where the Amorites and other tribal groups had settled. Our richest evidence is from Old Babylonian documents from kings ruling in Babylonia, the Diyala area, where the term *mīšarum* is most frequently used. The related institution of *andurārum* is found in the Mari region and, slightly later, in Syria at Alalakh; it occurs also in Assyrian documents dating from the Old through Neo-Assyrian periods.[45]

---

41 Cardellini (1981) 367–68.

42 For modern scholars holding this view, see Chirichigno (1993) 284–85. The medieval scholar is Joseph Bekhor Shor in his commentary on Exod 21:2; see Nebo (1994) 137. Nebo points out that Bekhor Shor's interpretation is supported by the Targum of Jonathan ben Uziel. There is also a discussion on this point in Lockshin (1997) 227 n. 9.

43 For discussion, see Chirichigno(1993) 263–75; Wright (1992). Weinfeld (1972) 283–84 argues that Deut 15:2–3 is a reinterpretation of the original fallow year concept.

44 Among the Sumerians, debt releases were proclaimed by Enmetena and Uruinimgina, and later by the kings of Isin writing in Sumerian and perhaps, therefore, also continuing a Sumerian tradition. Cf. Edzard (1976); the earlier passages are also presented in Cooper (1986) 58, 67, 73. For Ur-Nammu (now ascribed to Shulgi), see Finkelstein (1969). For debt release at Isin and at Kanesh, see Kraus (1984) 16–30, 104–5.

45 For citations, see Kraus (1984) 16–110. Additional Mari evidence can be found

In speaking of debt releases, J. Lewy, years ago, made the following observation:

> As was mentioned..., the Old Babylonian testimonies to the habit of "establishing" general releases in favor of indebted citizens come from those kingdoms in the eastern half of the Fertile crescent which saw a large influx of Amorites and were ruled by dynasties of Amorite descent. In view of the eminent role the Amorites played also in Palestine...this fact suggests that, in the last analysis, the biblical legislation relating to the "proclaiming" of releases reflects and perpetuates the influence which the Amorite states of the Holy Land and their institutions exerted upon the tribes of Israel prior to their unification under monarchs.[46]

More recently, Weinfeld has written in a similar vein:

> It seems to be no coincidence that these [Old Babylonian] documents were discovered among the Hana tribes, which retained the institution of tribal property. Furthermore, it can be assumed that the *mīšarum* tradition of the Amorite dynasty drew upon the Amorite nomadic background, which it shares with Israel.[47]

Writing from a totally different angle, trying to explain the disappearance of what he calls "the *ḫabiru/ḫapiru* movement," Lemche adds a further idea:

> The possibility exists that the ideological foundations of the new states which arose during the Iron Age, not least in W. Asia, promoted a better understanding of social responsibility among the leading class, since many of the states were founded on the basis of former tribal societies. It may be that the egalitarian ideology of these tribal societies lived on, although it cannot be assumed that debt slavery disappeared in the Iron Age. To the contrary, debt slavery was very much in evidence, but it was perhaps softened by an ideology which proclaimed brotherhood among all members of the new states.[48]

---

in Charpin (1990). Old Assyrian passages are given in Kraus (1984) 103–5. For the Middle Assyrian period there is so far only the indirect evidence found at Nuzi, an area that was under Assyrian control; for some references, cf. *CAD* A/2 116b. For the more numerous Neo-Assyrian occurrences, see Radner (1997) 70.

46 Lewy (1958) 29.

47 Weinfeld (1995) 91–92.

48 Lemche (1992) 9.

We appear to have before us the ingredients for a hypothesis that links these unique biblical and Mesopotamian laws to the Amorites, resting upon the notion that the Israelites and other ancient neighbors, in response to their tribal backgrounds, retained a particular sympathy to a cultural legacy of debt release and social equality. But the laws of individual release in LH § 117, with its parallels in Exod 21:2–5 and Deut 15:12–18, stand out in a discussion of Amorite cultural influence for a number of reasons. First, because of their unique character, they are found in the law collections and have a clear link to the Amorites through Hammurapi and his dynasty. Second, because, both in Mesopotamia and in Israel, these laws of individual release were in ancient times replaced by other remedies offered by the state or central authorities. This replacement occurred at different epochs but at similar points in the social history of each society—apparently, when the remedy of individual release was seen as unworkable or when memories and practices of tribal-based institutions had perhaps begun to fade. Third, as already noted, the use of state-based releases of debt was not limited to the Amorite dynasties alone. Thus, although the Amorite cultural heritage may, indeed, have fostered appreciation of the notion of debt release overall, the institution of state-based releases of debt is not unique to the Amorites.

LH § 117 and its parallels in Exod 21:2–5 and Deut 15:12–18 thus appear to be our most likely link to actual Amorite practices. Their release of debt slaves after a fixed term of service does not appear to depend upon a central government or authority for implementation. It is a transaction between the individual parties. The giving of release can be seen as impelled by the social expectations and pressures of the group, particularly in communities where there existed little or no feelings of inherent social inequality between persons. The fixed years of service are a kind of "bankruptcy" measure, giving something back to the creditor but also releasing the debtor from perpetual bondage and eventually restoring him to full membership within the community.

The *mīšarum* and *andurārum* traditions appear to draw upon similar feelings of social equality, but such releases cannot be implemented by individuals or small communities acting on their own. They depend, rather, upon the initiative of a central governmental authority, eliminating the equity held by all creditors without regard to factors of time or personal circumstance. These releases "drop down from heaven" so to speak; they are unpredictable and bear no relationship to any economic cycle. We may perhaps, therefore, properly view them as royal actions designed to gain favor with the masses of the populace, while placing the real costs upon the smaller group of wealthy citizens. There was, predictably, resistance to such debt release; we know this very well from Jer 34: 8–22 and Neh 5:1–13. So too, there is evidence of resistance in Babylonia, where creditors violated the royal releases,[49] and at Mari, Alalakh, and Assyria, where creditors prepared documents that contained clauses committing the parties to ignore any future cancellation of debts.[50] In view of their history, therefore, we would view the *mīšarum* and *andurārum* traditions as supported by ideals connected with a semi-nomadic past, but emerging in response to the political needs of sedentary and urbanized populations.

The biblical system of universal debt release occurring according to a fixed time schedule, either every seven years as in Deut 15:1–3 or after forty-nine years as in Lev 25, may have arisen to "fix" the problem of unpredictability and also to sever any connection of dependency between the releases and the exercise of royal powers. The evidence for implementation of these measures is scanty and these passages are generally dated late, even post-exilic. But some have argued for connection to Israel's tribal origins, because, here again, the sentiments they express for restoring economic equilibrium go back to older times.[51] However, the fixed heptadic patterns of these biblical releases find no parallels in ancient Near Eastern sources—legal or non-legal; these laws, therefore, cannot be considered in our present discussion of Amorite connections. They appear to be uniquely Israelite.

Conclusions

The assumptions and arguments we have presented lead us at this time to offer two examples of laws that could be linked to the Amorites: debt release and talion. Are there any more? And what of other laws in the Bible

---

49 Kraus (1984) 16–85 includes discussion of many Old Babylonian documents recording judgments of redress following failures of creditors to abide by the royal releases.

50 For Old Babylonian documents from Ḫana containing exemption clauses, see *CAD* A/2 (*sub andurāru*) 116a and N/2 (*sub nazbu*). For Mari and Tirqa, see further Charpin (1990) 253 n. 3, 261–63. For Alalakh, see references collected in *CAD* D 109 (*sub darāru*). Some of these passages are treated by Kraus (1984) 99–101, 105–7. The Neo-Assyrian documents do not ignore releases, but, instead, require the seller to return money to the buyer if a release should occur subsequent to the sale; for references, see Radner (1997) 70.

51 For the late dating of these passages, see the discussion in Chirichigno (1993) 317–28, 357. Weinfeld (1995) 177, on the other hand, argues for an earlier tradition going back to the pre-monarchial period. For additional bibliography on the views of other scholars, see Wright (1992a).

and in the Mesopotamian collections that, because of similarity, may be compared with one another, like the "goring ox" or "injuring a woman and her foetus?" Can these laws also be Amorite in origin? Perhaps our lesson here is not to try to explain all similarities using one hypothesis only. Or, perhaps other cases like these could be linked with the Amorites if we could find arguments and rationales like the ones presented here. There is, obviously, still a lot more to think about and perhaps more work will reveal whether or not more facets of the native Amorite culture can be persuasively resurrected.

BIBLIOGRAPHY

Abrahami, P. (1998) A propos des généraux (gal mar-tu) de la Mésopotamie du Nord à l'époque du règne de Zimri-Lim. *Nouvelles Assyriologiques Brèves et Utilitaires*: no. 31. **Alexander, J.B.** (1943) *Early Babylonian Letters and Economic Texts*. New Haven. **Artzi, P.** (1990) The Library of the Amarna Archive. In J. Klein and A. Skaist, eds., *Bar-Ilan Studies in Assyriology Dedicated to Pinhas Artzi*, 139–156. Ramat Gan. **Buccellati, G.** (1966) *The Amorites of the Ur III Period*. Naples. **Cardellini, I.** (1981) *Die biblischen „Sklaven"-Gesetze im Lichte des keilschriftlichen Sklavenrechts: Ein Beitrag zur Tradition, Überlieferung und Redaktion der alttestamentlichen Rechtstexte.* Bonner Biblische Beiträge 55. Bonn. **Charpin, D.** (1990) L'andurārum à Mari. MARI 6: 253–270. (1990a) Une alliance contre l'Elam et le rituel du *lipit napištim*. In *Mélanges Jean Perrot*, 109–18. Paris **Charpin, D, and Durand, J.-M.** (1986) Fils de Sim'al: Les origines tribales des rois de Mari. *Revue d'assyriologie et d'archéologie orientale* 80: 141–83. **Chiera, E.** (1934) *Sumerian Epics and Myths*. Oriental Institute Publications 15. Chicago. **Chirichigno, G.C.** (1993) *Debt-Slavery in Israel and the Ancient Near East*. Journal for the Study of the Old Testament Supplement Series 141. Sheffield. **Civil, M.** (1965) New Sumerian Law Fragments. In *Studies in Honor of Benno Landsberger on his Seventy-Fifth Birthday April 21, 1965*, 1–10. Assyriological Studies 16. Chicago. **Collins, B.J.** (1990) The Puppy in Hittite Ritual. *Journal of Cuneiform Studies* 42: 211–22. **Cooper, J.** (1986) *Sumerian and Akkadian Royal Inscriptions I, Presargonic Inscriptions*. Translation Series 1. New Haven. **Diamond, A.S.** (1957) An Eye for an Eye. *Iraq* 19: 151–55. (1971) *Primitive Law, Past and Present*. London. **Driver, G. R.** (1957/58) *Ana utūnim nadû*. *Archiv für Orientforschung* 18: 129. **Driver, G.R. and J.C. Miles** (1935) *The Assyrian Laws*. Oxford. Reprint edition 1975. (1952–56) *The Babylonian Laws*. 2 vols. Oxford. **Durand, J.-M.** (1992) Unité et diversités au Proche-Orient à l'époque amorrite. In D. Charpin and F. Joannès, eds., *La circulation des biens, des personnes at des idées dans le Proche-Orient ancien Actes de la XXXVIIIe RAI (Paris, 8–10 juillet 1991)*, 97–128. Paris. **Edzard, D.O.** (1976) Sociale Reformen im Zweistromland bis ca. 1600 v. Chr.: Realität oder Literarischer Topos? In J. Harmatta and G. Komoróczy, eds., *Wirtschaft und Gesellschaft im Altern Vorderasien*, 145–56. Budapest. **Finkelstein,**

J.J. (1969) The Laws of Urnammu. *Journal of Cuneiform Studies* 22: 66–82. **Fleischman, J.** (1990) The Authority of the Paterfamilias According to CH 117. In J. Klein and A. Skaist, eds., *Bar-Ilan Studies in Assyriology Dedicated to Pinhas Artzi*, 249–53. Ramat Gan. **Frymer-Kensky, T.** (1980) Tit for Tat: The Principle of Equal Retribution in Near Eastern and Biblical Law. *Biblical Archeologist* Fall:230–34. **Gelb, I.J., J. Bartels, S.-M. Vance, R.M. Whiting** (1980) *Computer Aided Analysis of Amorite*. Assyriological Studies 21. Chicago. **Goetze, A.** (1956) *The Laws of Eshnunna*. The Annual of the American Schools of Research 31. New Haven. **Grayson, A.K.** (1992) History and Culture of Assyria. In D.N. Freedman, ed., *Anchor Bible Dictionary* 4:732–35. New York. **Greengus, S.** (1991) Filling Gaps: Laws Found in Babylonia and in the Mishna but Absent in the Hebrew Bible. *Maarav* 7:149–71. (1994) Some Issues Relating to the Comparability of Laws and the Coherence of the Legal Tradition. In B.M. Levinson, ed., *Theory and Method in Biblical and Cuneiform Law*, 61–87. Journal for the Study of the Old Testament Supplement Series 181. Sheffield. (1997) The Selling of Slaves: Laws Missing from the Hebrew Bible? *Zeitschrift für altorientalische und biblische Rechtsgeschichte* 3: 1–11. **Hallo, W.W.** (1982) The Royal Correspondence of Larsa: II. The Appeal to Utu. In G. van Driel, Th. J.H. Krispin, M. Stol, V.R. Veenhof, eds., *Zikir Šumim. Assyriological Studies Presented to F. R. Kraus on the Occasion of his Seventieth Birthday*, 95–109. Leiden (1995) Slave Release in the Biblical World in the Light of a New Text. In Z. Zevit, S. Gitin, and M. Sokoloff, eds., *Solving Riddles and Untying Knots: Biblical, Epigraphic, and Semitic Studies in Honor of Jonas C. Greenfield*. 79–93. Winona Lake, Ind. **Hoffner, H.A.** (1997) *The Laws of the Hittites: A Critical Edition*. Documenta et Monumenta Orientis Antiqui 23. Leiden. **Jackson, B.S.** (1973) The Problem of Exod xxxi 22–25 (Ius Talionis) *Vetus Testamentum* 23:273–304. **Joseph Bekhor Shor.** See Nebo (1994). **Kramer, S.N.** (1983) The Ur-Nammu Law Code: Who was its Author? *Orientalia* NS 52: 453–56. (1990) The Marriage of Martu. In J. Klein and A. Skaist, eds., *Bar-Ilan Studies in Assyriology Dedicated to Pinhas Artzi*, 11–27. Ramat Gan. **Kraus, F.R.** (1984) *Königliche Verfügungen in altbabylonischer Zeit*. Studia et Documenta ad Iura Orientis Antiqui Pertinentia 11. Leiden. **Kwasman, T. and S. Parpola** (1991) *Legal Transactions of the Royal Court of Nineveh, Part I: Tiglath-Pileser III through Esarhaddon*. State Archives of Assyria 6. Helsinki. **Lambert, W.G.** (1965) A New Look at the Babylonian Background of Genesis. *Journal of Theological Studies* NS 16: 287–300. (1980) Babylonien und Israel. In H.R. Balz, S.G. Hall et al., eds., *Theologisches Realenzyklopädie* 5: 67–79. Berlin. (1982) Interchange of Ideas Between Southern Mesopotamia and Syria-Palestine as Seen in Literature. In H.J. Nissen and J. Renger, eds., *Mesopotamien und sein Nachbarn*, 311–16. Rencontre Assyriologique Internationale 25. Berlin. **Lauterbach, J.Z.** (1935) *Mekilta de Rabbi Ishmael*. 3 vols. Philadelphia. **Lemche, N.P.** (1992) Ḫabiru/Ḫapiru. In D.N. Freedman, ed., *Anchor Bible Dictionary*, 3: 6–10. New York. **Lewy, J.** (1958) The Biblical Institution of Deror in the Light of Akkadian Documents. *Eretz Israel* 15: 21–31. (1961) Amurritica. *Hebrew Union College Annual* 32: 31–74. **Lieberman, S.** (1973) *The Tosefta*. 4 vols. New York. **Lockshin, M.I.** (1997) *Rashbam's Commentary on Exodus: An Annotated Trans-*

lation. Brown Judaica Studies 310. Atlanta. **Loewenstamm, S.** (1957) Review of *The Laws of Eshnunna* by A. Goetze. *Israel Exploration Journal* 7: 194. **Malamat, A.** (1997) The Cultural Impact of the West (Syria-Palestine) on Mesopotamia in the Old Babylonian Period. *Altorientalische Forschungen* 24: 310–19. (1999) The Flow of Cultural Influences from Syria and the Land of Israel to Mesopotamia in the Old Babylonian Period. In R. Chazan, W.W. Hallo, L. Schiffman, eds., *Ki Baruch Hu. Ancient Near Eastern, Biblical, and Judaic Studies in Honor of Baruch B. Levine,* 35–41 (Hebrew). Winona Lake, Ind. **Mendenhall, G.** (1992) Amorites. In D.N. Freedman, ed., *The Anchor Bible Dictionary* 1: 99–202. New York. **Nebo, Y.** (1994) *Commentaries of Joseph Bekhor Shor on the Torah.* Jerusalem. **Otto, E.** (1991) Die Geschichte der Talion im alten Orient und Israel. In D.R. Daniels *et al.*, eds., *Ernten, was man sät. Festschrift für Klaus Koch zu seinem 65. Geburtstag,* 101–30. Neukirchen-Vluyn. **Pollock, F. and F.W. Maitland** (1898) *The History of English Law.* 2 vols. Cambridge. 2nd ed. reprint 1952. **Radner, K.** (1997) *Die Neuassyrischen Privatrechtsurkunden als Quelle für Mensch und Umwelt.* State Archives of Assyria Studies 6. Helsinki. **Schacht, J.** (1979) Kiṣāṣ. In H.A.R. Gibb, J.H. Kramers, E. Lèvi-Provençal, J. Schacht, eds., *The Encyclopaedia of Islam.* 5: 177–80. Leiden. **Seux, M.-J.** (1967) *Épithètes Royales Akkadiennes et Sumeriennes.* Paris. **Singer, I.** (1991) A Concise History of Amurru. In S. Izre'el, *Amurru Akkadian: A Linguistic Study.* 2 vols. Harvard Semitic Series 41. Atlanta. 2: 135–95 (Appendix III). (1991a) The Land of Amurru in the Šaušgamua Treaty. *Iraq* 53: 69–74. **van Soldt, W.H.** (1994) Letters in the British Museum, Part 2. Altbabylonische Briefe in Umschrift und Übersetzung 13. Leiden. **von Soden, W.** (1965–81) Akkadisches Handwörterbuch. 3 vols. Wiesbaden. I (1965): A–L; II (1972): M–S; III (1981): Ṣ–Z. **Voth, S.M.** (1981) Analysis of Military Titles and Functions in Published Texts of the Old Babylonian Period. Ph.D. diss., Hebrew Union College-Jewish Institute of Religion. Cincinnati. **Weinfeld, M.** (1972) *Deuteronomy and the Deuteronomic School.* Oxford. (1995) *Social Justice in Ancient Israel and in the Ancient Near East.* Jerusalem and Minneapolis. **Weiss Halivini, D.** (1991) *Peshat and Derash. Plain and Applied Meaning in Rabbinic Exegesis.* Oxford. **Westbrook, R.** (1996) Zíz.da/*kiššatim. Wiener Zeitschrift für die Kunde des Morgenlandes* 86: 449–59. **Whiting, R.M., Jr.** (1987) *Old Babylonian Letters from Tell Asmar.* Assyriological Studies 22. Chicago. (1995) Amorite Tribes and Nations of Second-Millennium Western Asia. In J.M. Sasson et al., eds., *Civilizations of the Ancient Near East.* 4 vols. 2: 1231–42. New York. **Wright, C.J.H.** (1992) Sabbatical Year. In D.N. Freedman, ed., *The Anchor Bible Dictionary* 5: 857–61. New York. (1992a) Jubilee, Year of. In D.N. Freedman, ed., *The Anchor Bible Dictionary* 3: 1025–30. New York.

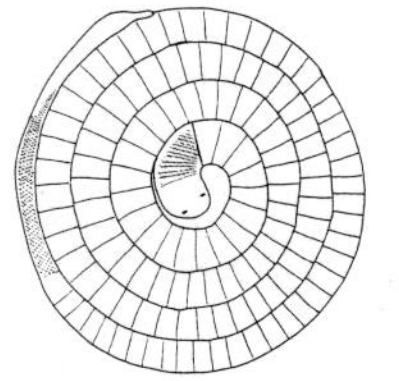

EVERYDAY LIFE IN THE NEO-BABYLONIAN PERIOD

THE INTEGRATION OF MATERIAL AND NON-MATERIAL CULTURE *

David B. Weisberg
Hebrew Union College – Jewish Institute of Religion

1. *Major Themes and Recent Works*

The theme of this essay is best exemplified in the works of many scholars who have made important contributions in many aspects of the field.[1] The present author has given a critique of the background of the period under discussion in "The Neo-Babylonian Empire"[2] under the following headings:

Chronology of the Neo-Babylonian Dynasty;
The Downfall of Assyria and the Rise of Babylonia;
The Golden Age of Babylon;
Trade and Material Culture;
Religion;
Polytheism and Politics;
Language, Literature and Calendar;
Family and Society;
Achaemenid Conquerors; and
The Legacy of Babylon.

Daily life is not a new theme in Assyriology, witness for example, Georges Contenau's *La vie quotidienne à Babylon et Assyrie*, published in

* I wish to thank W. W. Hallo and Getzel Cohen for their generous scholarly help, and Arnona Rudavsky for her help in locating research materials. The friendly encouragement of Richard Averbeck has benefitted the article very much. I am indebted to HUC students Christopher Morgan, Christian Rata and Angela Roskop for their helpful comments as well as Jeffrey Cooley, Tiffany Grantham, Ronald Hardin, N. Blake Hearson and In Seh Lee, who contributed important ideas on this topic. For recent Hebrew Union College Neo-Babylonian dissertations, see, in Bibliography B.T. Arnold, S. Fudge, J. Shao and P. Wright. Note also the related work of D. Redford.

1 See our remarks below and see Bibliography.

2 Weisberg (1996).

Paris in 1950. Other fields have been active, too. Note some ways people have phrased this topic:

Daily Life in	*Ancient Mesopotamia*	Nemet-Nejat	1998
Life in	*the Ancient Near East*	Snell	1997
A Day in the Life of	*Ancient Athens*	Deighton	1995
Everyday Life in	*Babylon and Assyria*	Contenau	1966
Life in	*Ancient Athens*	Tucker	1906

Many writers focusing upon our theme have employed the term "material culture" as complement to "non-material" elements of the civilization, such as literature, art, and religion.

Archaeology gives us many of the clues we are seeking about material culture, especially what one might call "New archaeology"—looking at small finds.[3] Assyriology, of course, concentrates mostly upon written sources, by and large, and, in this case, from clay tablets from the Neo-Babylonian period.

In this study our objective is to (1) look briefly at some features of the material culture, the "everyday life" ("Alltagsleben") of the Neo-Babylonian period and (2) features of non-material culture. We hope for the prospect of integrating more successfully our abundant social and economic data from this period with non-material aspects of Neo-Babylonian society.

In discussing the topic of "Everyday Life in…" or "Life in…" (as per above) we are harking back to a theme that became popular during the heyday of Communism and materialism.[4] Though we are not arguing for a direct cause and effect relationship between the perspectives of Communism and the interest in the scholarship dealing with daily life, we pose the following question: Could it be that though Marxist historians were not necessarily interested in the "nitty-gritty'" of daily life (but rather essentially in class-struggle), their focus upon materialism was one of the factors that piqued a general interest in daily life? Thus the notion has remained in our heads that what is "real" is "counting beans" but what has to do with non-material culture is of less substance. Despite the fall of Communism

---

3 Stager (1985); Moorey (1999).

4 Cp. Childe (1967) 8, preface by Grahame Clark: "A …point to remember is that he [Childe] made no secret of his interest in Marxism. He found it useful to suppose that societies at each phase of social evolution rested on definite productive forces which shaped their lives, which harboured contradictions that in due course compelled the emergence of new productive forces and a new cycle of social evolution."

and the discrediting of much of Marxist historiography, the notion may not have given way.

Dan Snell[5] and Karen Nemet-Nejat[6] have recently published works on everyday life.

Snell's book contains much valuable information, as well as careful reflection and theorization on society. His effort at surveying life in the Ancient Near East from the social and economic perspective is a success, covering a remarkable three millennia. As for the Neo-Babylonian period, one reviewer maintains:

> The narrative is entertaining and easy to follow, yet the later chapters dealing with the Assyrian Empire, Chaldean and Persian domination, and relations with the classical Greek world are considerably less informative than those dealing with the rise of the Sumerians and Amorites... His primary area of specialization is early Mesopotamian economic history, and this too is reflected in a treatment of Assyrian, Chaldean and Persian economic life that is a good deal less detailed than where focused on the third and second millennia.[7]

Karen Nemet-Nejat's well-done work offers a close look at certain topics in greater detail, such as mathematics, a subject on which the author has written before. She approaches the field from the perspective of a Neo-Babylonian scholar, as can be seen by her treatment of religion, slavery, crafts and labor, and others.

2. *Perspectives on Neo-Babylonian Material Culture*

P.R.S. Moorey (1999) provides a recent comprehensive archaeological "synthesis of the major industries and technologies of the ancient Near East... the author covers a chronological range that traces the first (prehistoric) use of the material and/or technology through to its later methods of manufacture in the Late Iron Age."[8] There is thus much valuable material for the student of the Neo-Babylonian period.

From the perspective of Neo-Babylonian textual evidence, there are still a great many unknowns, despite the fact that the Neo-Babylonian period is the second best-attested period in Mesopotamian antiquity.[9]

---

5 Snell (1997).

6 Nemet-Nejat (1998).

7 Sack (1998).

8 Lamberg-Karlovsky (1997).

9 Cp., for example, the index of Weisberg (forthcoming).

An innovative probe into "material culture," including, but not limited to, Neo-Babylonian civilization, was undertaken by Oppenheim, in his volume *Ancient Mesopotamia*. Oppenheim organized his survey into what he called "Three vistas: plants-animals-[and] minerals." In his section on plants,[10] Oppenheim divided the theme into "[plants grown] in gardens and [plants grown] in fields,"[11] the former being an older source of food than the latter. He reflected:

> If we knew about the relationship between the acreage used for fields and gardens in Mesopotamia, we would have better insight into the economic and social texture than that offered us by many hundreds of documents.[12]

This problem was remedied with the publication of texts bearing upon fields and field plans by Nemet-Nejat.[13]

The date palm provided the most essential subsistence throughout this area.[14] Coming next in importance, as reflected in our textual evidence, are barley and various types of emmer and emmer wheat. These were stored in a massive pile of barley called the *karû*.

Hartman and Oppenheim have studied beer and brewing techniques, as reflected in an important text "inscribed in typical Neo-Babylonian script,... written somewhere in southern Mesopotamia during the fifth or fourth century B.C."[15] Further on the subject of "alcoholic beverages," note the following novel feature introduced in the period under discussion here:

> As a rare example of an innovation in Mesopotamian food technology, we discover in Neo-Babylonian texts references to a beer, or better, an alcoholic drink, made of dates, a practice not mentioned before this period.[16]

Paul-Alain Beaulieu edited a document from the administration of Ekur, the Enlil sanctuary, that supplies new information about the Nippur temples and their brewers. He notes:

---

10 Oppenheim (1977) 311–15; see Renfrew (1973) for a valuable discussion on the cereals, pulses, legumes, flax, and fruits of the Near East.

11 Oppenheim (1977) 311.

12 Oppenheim (1977) 312.

13 Nemet-Nejat (1982).

14 Cocquerillat (1968).

15 Hartman and Oppenheim (1950) 1.

16 Oppenheim (1977) 315.

> prosopographical interconnections with other dated documents from Nippur" would date this material from "the first half of the Neo-Babylonian dynasty.[17]

This information augments that from the Eanna-temple of Uruk and elsewhere previously known.

In the comprehensive picture of domestic animals[18] we note the centrality of sheep, goats, and cows and the significance of dairy products made from them that could be processed into cheese.

We note the importance of hair, skins, and wool and the employment of horses for warfare and commerce, and bulls for pulling the plow. Examining Neo-Babylonian economic documents from the cattle industry available to him at the mid-twentieth century, M. San Nicolò examined many aspects of this as reflected in temple transactions.[19]

In the category of usage of animal products we can think of tanning and weaving. Landsberger sorted out the problem of colors and fabrics in his article on that subject, bringing much important material from Middle- and Late Babylonian texts.[20]

As for minerals, such features as stone-working for tools and weapons, work on beads, amulets and pendants, and cylinder seals have been studied from an archaeological and lexical point of view.[21]

Oppenheim described the importance of the chamber oven, the use of iron, copper, and bronze. His insights into glass-making were, of course, a result of his own research on this topic.[22] He then cited the widespread "three main uses of clay in Mesopotamia—pottery, clay tablets, and bricks."[23]

3. *Perspectives on Neo-Babylonian Non-Material Culture*

It should not cause surprise that the material side of Neo-Babylonian culture has been more thoroughly investigated than the non-material side. It is easier to access and study objects from the material culture that can be

---

17 Beaulieu (1995) 96.

18 Clutton-Brock (1981) discusses aspects of domestication of animals, geography and nomenclature with much material on the Ancient Near East.

19 San Nicolò (1948).

20 Landsberger (1967).

21 See Moorey (1999) chapters 1, 5 and 6; Gibson and Biggs (1977).

22 Oppenheim (1970). See Moorey (1999) 189ff.

23 Oppenheim (1977) 324.

held in one's hand than to gain entree to the subtleties of non-material culture. Nevertheless, it is possible to learn a lot about the non-material aspects of Neo-Babylonian culture from several important sources. First, one might mention the surviving literary compositions.

> The poems, hymns and prayers of the Neo-Babylonian period reflect a broad benevolence, universalism and spirituality that are characteristic of our own religious faith.[24]

Another aspect of religious life that is possible to "read" rather clearly is that of names people gave their children.

> The personal names reflect individual prayers, often requesting divine protection and sometimes asking for the restoration of lost family members.[25]

The workings of the temples can be understood both from archaeological and philological materials.

> The precincts of the temple contained both cultic rooms and various auxiliary chambers and areas that housed numerous economic activities.[26]

One of the problems involved in the combination of material culture with "Persönliche Frömmigkeit" is that Babylonian (and Assyrian) religion as we know it is essentially "royal" and does not involve "collective responsibility."[27] The individual has not much to do except watch from a distance. One does not get the impression that the individual had much to do with religion. Perhaps in the case of a sick child one would need to get an exorcism performed or the like—then there was the involvement of the individual. But otherwise, not. The cult that we know of is the cult of "official" religion.

---

24 Weisberg (1996) 226. See also Foster (1993) vol. 2—incorporating, in Foster's words, "The Mature Period" (1500–1000 B.C.) and "The Late Period" (1000–100 B.C.) of Akkadian literature, is a masterly collection of late works. On p. 905 is one of my favorites—late, though Assyrian and not Babylonian—perhaps the most deeply moving personal poem from ancient Mesopotamia, telling about a woman's tragic death in childbirth. It is translated also in Reiner (1985), where it is entitled "An Assyrian Elegy."

25 Weisberg (1996) 226. Knut Tallqvist (1905) is still the basic source for Neo-Babylonian personal names.

26 Weisberg (1996) 228. A recent work that collects and studies cuneiform material dealing with temples is George (1993).

27 See Shao (1989).

Personal religion intersects with official religion at the festivals that we know of in the Neo-Babylonian period. Nevertheless, one does not see a heavy connection between the private person and the public, official structures.[28]

Thorkild Jacobsen had the notion that there was an evolution from the third to the second to the first millennia. He described the life and culture of the Neo-Babylonian period in the following terms:

> A world, barely livable before, had now collapsed and become rank jungle.[29]

But it is our feeling that the personal religious fervor expressed in the examples quoted above, such as in personal names, hymns and prayers, and visits and donations to the temples tell a different story.

Looking for examples of personal piety leads us to Leo Oppenheim's comments in a chapter on particular cases of non-literary genres:

> At times, personal requests and all sorts of incidentals are added [to letters answering queries of the king]. The scholar ends the report with his name, in the same abrupt and matter-of-fact way he began. (Here Oppenheim's note [68 on p. 382] reads: "For a unique [because private] reference to astrological matters, see the Neo-Babylonian letter UET 4 168.")[30]

Much important work on Everyday life in the Neo-Babylonian period has been accomplished in recent decades. Many scholars have emphasized the integration of material and non-material culture. We feel their example is worth following.[31]

---

28 See Cohen (1993) 391–99, 427–53.

29 Jacobsen (1976) 226.

30 Oppenheim (1977) 279, "Patterns in Non-Literary Texts."

31 Cp. Snell (1997) ix: "Eckart Otto in a brief essay has suggested that the interest in the field among Christian biblicists derives from their sense that today faith and daily life are separated in people's lives, and to study ancient Israel's society may be a way for them to see how faith and daily life were once integrated and perhaps could be again."

BIBLIOGRAPHY

Albertz, Rainer (1978) Persönliche Frömmigkeit und offizielle Religion. *Calwer Theologische Monographien* 9. Stuttgart. **Arnold, B.T.** (1985) Babylonian Letters from the Kuyunjik Collection. Seventh Century Uruk in Light of New Epistolary Evidence. Ph.D. Dissertation, Hebrew Union College, Cincinnati, Ohio. **Beaulieu, Paul-Alain** (1995) The Brewers of Nippur. *Journal of Cuneiform Studies* 47, 85–96. **Childe, V. Gordon** (1967) *What Happened in History*. Rev. ed. Baltimore. **Clutton-Brock, Juliet** (1981) *Domesticated Animals from Early Times*. Austin and London. **Cocquerillat, Denise** (1968) Palmeraies et Cultures de l'Eanna d'Uruk (559–520). *Ausgrabungen der Deutschen Forschungsgemeinschaft in Uruk-Warka* Band 8. Berlin. **Cohen, Mark E.** (1993) *The Cultic Calendars of the Ancient Near East*. Bethesda, Md. **Contenau, Georges** (1950) *La vie quotidienne à Babylon et Assyrie*. Paris. (1966) *Everyday Life in Babylon and Assyria*. New York. **Foster, Benjamin R.** (1993) *Before the Muses. An Anthology of Akkadian Literature*. Two Volumes, Bethesda, Md. **Fudge, Sarah** (2000) The Lure of the Past. Ancient Man's Interest in His History. With Translations of the Neo-Babylonian Texts of the Carlos Museum. Ph.D. Dissertation, Hebrew Union College, Cincinnati, Ohio. **George, A.R.** (1993) *House Most High. The Temples of Ancient Mesopotamia*. Winona Lake, Ind. **Gibson, McGuire and Robert D. Biggs** (1977) Seals and Sealing in the Ancient Near East. *Bibliotheca Mesopotamica* 6. Malibu, Calif. **Hallo, W.W.** (1968) Individual Prayer in Sumerian: The Continuity of a Tradition. *Journal of the American Oriental Society* 88, 71–89. **Hallo, W.W. and W.K. Simpson** (1998) *The Ancient Near East. A History*. 2nd edition. Fort Worth, Tx. **Hartman, Louis F., and A.L. Oppenheim** (1950) On Beer and Brewing Techniques in Ancient Mesopotamia According to the XXIIIrd Tablet of the Series ḪAR.ra = *ḫubullu*. *Supplement to the Journal of the American Oriental Society* 10. **Jacobsen, Thorkild** (1976) *The Treasures of Darkness*. New Haven. **Lamberg-Karlovsky, C.C.** (1997) Our Past Matters: Materials and Industries of the Ancient Near East. *Journal of the American Oriental Society* 117, 87–102. **Landsberger, Benno** (1967) Über Farben im Sumerisch-Akkadischen. *Journal of Cuneiform Studies* 21, Special Volume Honoring Professor Albrecht Goetze, 139–73. **Moorey, P.R.S.** (1999 [reprinted from Oxford University Press (1994)]) *Ancient Mesopotamian Materials and Industries. The Archaeological Evidence*. Winona Lake, Ind. **Nemet-Nejat, Karen Rhea** (1982) Late Babylonian Field Plans in the British Museum. *Studia Pohl, Series Maior* 11, Rome. (1998) Daily Life in Ancient Mesopotamia. In *Daily Life through History*. Westport, Conn. **Oppenheim, A.L.** (1970) *Glass and Glassmaking in Ancient Mesopotamia*. New York. (1977) *Ancient Mesopotamia*. 2nd edition, Erica Reiner, ed. Chicago. **Otto, Eckart** (1981) Sozialgeschichte Israels. Probleme und Perspektiven. Ein Diskussionspapier. *Biblische Notizen. Beiträge zur exegetischen Diskussion*. Heft 15 [Bamberg], 87–92. **Redford, Douglas W.** (1998) Quest for the Crown Jewel: The Centrality of Egypt in the Foreign Policy of Esarhaddon. Ph.D. Dissertation, Hebrew Union College, Cincinnati, Ohio. **Reiner, Erica** (1985) *Your Thwarts in Pieces, Your Mooring Rope Cut*. Ann

Arbor: University of Michigan. **Renfrew, Jane M.** (1973) *Palaeoethnobotany. The Prehistoric Food Plants of the Near East and Europe.* New York. **Robbins, Ellen** (1996) Tabular Sacrifice Records and the Cultic Calendar of Neo-Babylonian Uruk. *Journal of Cuneiform Studies* 48, 61–87. **Sack, Ronald H.** (1998) Review of Daniel Snell, *Life in the Ancient Near East.* In *Journal of the American Oriental Society* 118, pp. 601–2. **San Nicolò, M.** (1948) Materialien zur Viehwirtschaft in den neubabylonischen Tempeln. I, *Orientalia* NS 17, 273–293; II, (1949) *Orientalia* NS 18, pp. 288–306; III, (1951) *Orientalia* NS 20, pp. 129–150; IV, (1954) *Orientalia* NS 23, 351–82; V, (1956) *Orientalia* NS 25, 24–38. **Setness, Daniel Edward** (1984) Pantheon, Piety and Religious Beliefs in the Neo-Babylonian Royal Inscriptions. Ph.D. Dissertation. Columbia University. New York. **Shao, Joseph T.** (1989) A Study of Akkadian Royal Hymns and Prayers. Ph.D. Dissertation, Hebrew Union College, Cincinnati, Oh. **Snell, Daniel C.** (1997) *Life in the Ancient Near East.* New Haven. **Stager, Lawrence** (1985) The Archaeology of the Family in Ancient Israel. *Bulletin of the American Schools of Oriental Research* 260, 1–35. **Tallqvist, Knut L.** (1905) Neubabylonisches Namenbuch. *Acta Societatis Scientiarum Fennicae.* Helsingførs. **Weisberg, David B.** (1996) The Neo-Babylonian Empire. In *Royal Cities of the Biblical World,* Joan Goodnick Westenholz, ed. Jerusalem, 221–33. (Forthcoming) The Oriental Institute Neo-Babylonian Texts. *Oriental Institute Publications.* **Wright, Paul H.** (1994) The City of Larsa in the Neo-Babylonian and Achaemenid Periods. A Study of Urban and Intercity Relations in Antiquity. Ph.D. Dissertation, Hebrew Union College, Cincinnati, Oh.

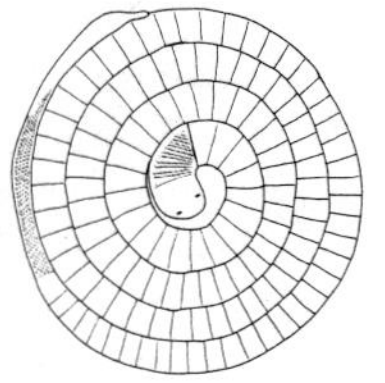

Anatolia

DAILY LIFE AMONG THE HITTITES

H. A. Hoffner*
Oriental Institute

CLIMATE AND GEOGRAPHY

The Hittite heartland is a relatively high-altitude tableland with mountains nearby. Today it has cold winters with lots of snow and hot, dry summers. Oliver Gurney once wrote:

> The plateau of Asia Minor is in a sense a continuation of the Russian steppe, and its climate is hard. Bitter winds from the north bring heavy falls of snow during the winter months, and after the brief but delightful spring the country is scorched during the summer by a relentless sun. The rain-clouds spend themselves for the most part on the slopes of Taurus or on the hillsides bordering the Black Sea. Thus the central plateau is a parched steppe-land, and it is only in the river-valleys that enough water and shelter can be found for human habitation.[1]

The climate pattern 3500 years ago was not greatly different.

The area was thickly forested in Hittite times, but over the centuries, the ancient forests have fallen prey to human exploitation and the ravages inflicted by goat grazing.[2]

---

* It is a daunting task to give even a somewhat satisfactory overview of the subject of daily life within a single chapter of a book. The task is made even more difficult when our sources of knowledge are as sparse as they are for the Hittites, and when the author is not an archaeologist or one trained in the technical sciences such as mineralogy, palaeo-zoology, or palaeo-botany. My only claim to familiarity with the subject is a book I wrote twenty-six years ago on food production among the Hittites, which was based almost exclusively on textual evidence (Hoffner [1974]).

In order to cover the subject in the space allotted me I shall adopt the expedient of enlarging upon a few of the basic publications on major aspects of the topic with apologies to their authors and editors. Among these publications are the general surveys of Hittite civilization by Goetze, Gurney, and MacQueen, and the few essays in Sasson (1995).

1 Gurney (1990) 65.

2 For a very thorough discussion of the subject see Ünal (1985) 423–25.

Natural Resources

Flora

Trees and timber were plentiful. The van Zeist and Bottema map reproduced in Allan Gilbert's survey article "The Flora and Fauna of the Ancient Near East"[3] shows forest and woodland covering all but the highest areas of central Anatolia four thousand years ago. Gilbert notes that as one moves to the Syrian and Anatolian maquis, "the oak-pistachio association remains dominant, [but] myrtle...becomes common, and Aleppo pine ... is replaced by the closely related and more cold-tolerant *Pinus brutia*."[4]

Regarding the Euxinian district in the Pontic Mountains of northern Anatolia he notes that:

> The climate...resembles that of southeastern Europe, with summer rainfall and annual precipitation exceeding 1,000 millimeters (40 inches). ... The coastal Eu-Euxinian belt is the most humid, and it supports a forest of beech (*Fagus orientalis*) and Pontic rhododendron (*Rhododendron ponticum*), now much degraded through agriculture and timbering. In the drier hills of the Upper or Sub-Euxinian belt, communities of hornbeam (*Carpinus betulus*) and several species of oak (*Quercus hartwissiana, Q. cerris, Q. frainetto*) are accompanied by coniferous associations of European pine (*Pinus sylvestris*), fir (*Abies nordmanniana*), and spruce (*Picea*). Heading off into central Anatolia is the Xero-Euxinian steppe forest, which contains Euxinian oaks and black pine dispersed throughout an Irano-Turanian steppe flora that may have invaded the Anatolian Plateau after human destruction of the original forest.[5]

Hittite texts contain over twenty terms for trees and shrubs and an additional fifteen logograms for the same.[6] Just how many varieties of trees grew in the Hittite heartland is uncertain. But of those mentioned in the texts it is clear that they included both conifers and deciduous trees. Among the deciduous trees were several varieties of oak.[7] Among the conifers were juniper, fir, and pine.[8]

---

3 Sasson (1995) 155.

4 Sasson (1995) 156.

5 Sasson (1995) 158.

6 Hoffner (1967) 91. A larger list of all words bearing the GIŠ "wood" determinative is given in Reichert (1963) 125f.

7 Hittite *allantaru* probably refers to a variety of oak; cf. Hoffner (1974) 57, Hoffner (1966) 390f.

8 Probably included in the terms *eya(n), irimpi* "cedar," *paini* and *BURĀŠU*

Fruit trees were present in great variety. Those written with Sumerian or Akkadian logograms can be more nearly identified than those written in Hittite. They include the grape vine (^{GIŠ}GEŠTIN),[9] the olive (^{GIŠ}*SERDU*), the fig (^{GIŠ}PÈŠ),[10] the apple (^{GIŠ}ḪAŠḪUR), the "mountain apple" (^{GIŠ}ḪAŠḪUR.KUR.RA), and other Sumero-Akkadian tree names whose botanical identification in Hatti is not clear: the ^{GIŠ}ŠENNUR (Akk. *šallūru*) and the ^{GIŠ}ŠINIG (Akk. *bīnu*, possibly "tamarisk"). The fruit of the pomegranate (^{GIŠ}NU.ÚR.MA, Akk. *nurmû*) is mentioned in ritual texts, but no text refers to the tree or its cultivation.[11] The date (^{GIŠ}ZÚ.LUM.MA, Akk. *suluppu*), mentioned rarely in texts, was certainly imported from warmer and drier climates.[12]

Of vegetables and condiments often mentioned in food preparation we may include lentils (GÚ.TUR), chickpeas (GÚ.GAL), beans (GÚ.GAL.GAL), bitter vetch (GÚ.ŠEŠ), cucumbers (ÚKUŠ), leeks (GA.RAS^{SAR}), onions (*wašḫar*, Sum. SUM), garlic (*šuppiwašḫar*, Sum. SUM.SIKIL^{SAR}), coriander (ŠE.LÚ^{SAR}), bitter garlic (*AZANNU*), asa foetida (Ú.NU.LUḪ.ḪA), garden cress (ZÀ.AḪ.LI^{SAR}, Hitt. *marašḫanḫaš*), lettuce (*ḫazzuwani*), and the onion-like plant *ANDAḪŠU*.

Approximately seven syllabically written (i.e., Hittite) terms for cereals are presently known. From cereal remains found in excavations it is likely that several varieties of wheat (tr. aestivum, emmer, and einkorn) and of barley were cultivated, but precisely which are to be associated with which terms in the texts has yet to be determined. The most common term for wheat, Hittite *ḫattar* (written usually with the Sum. ZÍZ), probably represents tr. aestivum, common bread wheat. Emmer wheat was written with the Akkadian *kunāšu* and with one of the syllabic Hittite spellings. The generic term for "cereal" or "grain" (*ḫalkiš*), as in Akkadian, was also a term for "barley."

Barley was processed into beer, was used to make some cooked porridges and breads for human consumption, and was used as horse fodder.

"juniper," *šuinila-* "fir."

9 Hoffner (1974) 39–41, 113; cf. also del Monte (1995a); Gorny (1995).

10 A list of the holdings of a Hittite family mentions that on their property was a vineyard, olive trees, and fig trees (KBo 5.7 rev. 38).

11 Gurney ([1990] 66) translated ^{GIŠ}ḪAŠḪUR.KUR.RA "mountain-apple" as "pomegranate" in a list of fruit trees on a Hittite estate. But that translation is almost certainly incorrect. Imparati in Sasson (1995) 584 claims the pomegranate was cultivated in Hatti, but gives no supporting evidence. MacQueen (1986) 98 ("possibly pears and pomegranates were grown") doesn't give his evidence. They are mentioned in the texts as fruits to be consumed, but not as trees to be harvested.

12 Imparati in Sasson (1995) 584 rightly doubts it was grown locally.

Wheat was used almost exclusively to bake breads, or its flour was sprinkled into cooked dishes. Parched grain[13] eaten as a dry food like popcorn or roasted nuts has not yet been unequivocally identified in the published texts, although it is quite possible that it is what is called *taršan mallan* in the cult inventory texts.[14]

Some varieties of nuts are mentioned, such as pistachio and almond. Sesame or linseed (ŠE.GIŠ.Ì) was used both as a seed and for its oil.

Fauna

Among the wild animals mentioned in the texts are bears, wolves, foxes, hares, several types of great cats (lions, panthers, leopards), several varieties of deer, wild boar, gazelles, mountain goats, wild oxen or buffalo, bees, birds, fish, and several types of reptiles.[15] Through limited hunting and fishing the meat of several kinds of wild animals were included in the Hittite diet. Birds, fish, and hares would have required the least effort and risk to catch. The meat of all three of these is mentioned in texts as being dried for delayed consumption.[16] No text describes hunting for birds. But there is a Hittite letter found at Alalakh that tells how an official sent a shipment of birds to the king, only to discover that when they reached him, they had spoiled and could not be eaten.[17] Animal remains (i.e., bones) found on Hittite sites indicate that the most commonly eaten wild animal was the deer.[18]

Domesticated animals included sheep and goats, cattle and water buffalo, swine, horses, donkeys, mules, and dogs. Animal remains found in Hittite sites indicate the presence of chickens, but no term found in the texts has yet been proposed for the chicken. The chicken came to the Near East from India. It was known as a foreign bird (Sum. dar-me-luḫ-ḫa, "the francolin of Meluḫḫa") in the Ur III period, but was kept domestically only in much later periods.[19] Other birds actually kept domestically might

---

13 Compare Akk. *qalītu*, Sum. ŠE.SA.A, *CAD* Q 59f. and BibHebr. *qālî*.

14 Cf. Hoffner (1974) 139f. Compare also *ḫādan mallan* "dried milled (grain)" KBo 16.78 i 8′.

15 For a comprehensive study of wild animals in Hittite texts, see the unpublished doctoral dissertation of Collins (1989).

16 KUB 30.32 rev. 10–12 cited in a footnote 26.

17 Alalakh Tablet 125, lines 3–15.

18 Boessneck and von den Driesch (1981), Ünal (1985).

19 Heimpel (1975) and Salonen (1973) 154ff. Landsberger suggested the Achaemenid period as the earliest time in which the bird was widespread in Mesopotamia.

include the duck (MUŠEN.GAL). Otherwise, the texts mention wild birds occasionally hunted and their meat eaten (the partridge and quail). Of these animals only cattle, sheep, goats, and possibly chicken were killed for their meat. The texts contain no mention of eggs, although it is reasonable to assume, if they kept chickens, that they harvested their eggs for food. And since milk was used to produce cheese, it is clear that this too came from the domesticated animals. But whether it was cow's or goat's milk is not yet known.

Water Sources

The sources of water for drinking, watering animals, irrigating fields, and washing were three: rivers, springs, and collected rainwater.

The principal river in the Hittite heartland was the Maraššanta, which corresponds to the modern Kizil Irmak, the classical Halys River. Other rivers were the Zuliya and Kummesmaha in the north. Since these were hardly navigable in their upper courses, they were not used for travel and transport, but did supply water for the abovementioned uses.

Springs were everywhere treated with religious veneration. Shrines and fountains were built. With very few exceptions springs and rivers were conceived as female, rather than male, deities. But the other principal water source, the sky, was conceived as male.

Exploiting the Resources

The people exploited this particular combination of natural resources both for food production and for the construction of habitations and protection against enemies.

For Food Production

Christopher J. Eyre has well expressed the central role of farming in the ancient Near East when he wrote:

> The states of the ancient Near East were essentially agrarian. The vast majority of their populations were farmers. Their political systems were based on control of farming. Their ideology was that of the farmer's world. Their mythology focused on the order of the annual farming cycle and fear of the disorder that threatens to break in and destroy this world—the natural forces of flood, storm, and drought and the wild men living outside the bounds of the fields.[20]

---

20 Sasson (1995) 175f.

The main botanical food products were cereals, vegetables, fruits, nuts, and wine[21] from vineyards.

In 1986 J. G. MacQueen wrote that "The main crops were emmer-wheat and barley; but peas, beans, onions, flax, figs, olives, grapes, apples and possibly pears and pomegranates were also grown."[22] But in 1974, basing myself on Old Assyrian and Hittite terminology for the Anatolian cereals, I had already proposed that the most frequently occurring term for wheat in Hittite texts, ZÍZ, did not refer to emmer-wheat, as it is generally translated by Hittitologists, but rather to bread wheat.[23] Subsequent textual evidence from Maşat texts (where ZÍZ and Akk. *kunāšu* "emmer" denote separate cereal types),[24] as well as statistical analysis of cereal remains from Hittite sites, has supported this view. The picture that emerges is that emmer was not the type of wheat most commonly cultivated by the Hittites. Texts employ a general term for "grain" (Hittite *ḫalki-*, Sumerogram ŠE) that is also used for "barley," terms for bread or club wheat (ZÍZ or *ḫattar*) and emmer-wheat (Akk. *kunāšu*), two other terms (*kar-aš* and *kant*) for wheat, and two more (*šeppit* and *ewan*) for barley.

Vegetables were cooked, the finished cooked dishes being described with a Sumerogram that denotes stew or soup (TU_7, Akk. *ummaru*).

As noted above, a number of fruit frees were cultivated in the Hittite heartland: apples (Hitt. *šamallu*, Sum. ḪAŠḪUR), "mountain-apples" (ḪAŠḪUR.KUR.RA, perhaps apricot), figs, olives, dates, tamarisks, pomegranates, and pears. There is little textual evidence for cooking fruits, although it stands to reason that in order to preserve them for winter consumption they were either cooked or dried. Raisins are often mentioned in the ritual texts, as are dried figs. Certain breads or pastries seem to have contained fruits, which were in this manner certainly cooked. All kinds of meat was dried.[25]

That olives were eaten for their meat is extremely probable, since their oil plays a prominent role in the texts, and the meat would hardly have been wasted. Nevertheless, it is striking that no text mentions eating olives. Old Hittite magic ritual incantations single out the main characteristic of an

---

21 Hoffner (1974) 113, Gorny (1995).

22 MacQueen (1986) 98.

23 Hoffner (1974) 60.

24 HKM 109:1–4. See also del Monte (1995b).

25 Cf. Hoffner (1967) 33 notes 38–40; KUB 30.32 rev. 10 ^{UZU}ÚR UDU *ŠĀBULU* "dried cuts of mutton," ibid. 11–12 mentions dried meat of hares, birds, and fishes. KUB 39.61 i 11 also mentions ^{UZU}ÚR UDU ḪÁD.DU.A "dried cuts of mutton."

olive: it holds oil in its heart.[26] Along with other aromatic woods, olive wood was sometimes burned to fumigate and thereby ritually purify a house.[27]

That the "honey" (Hitt. *milit,* Luwian *mallit,* Sum. LÀL) mentioned in Hittite texts was not vegetable syrup but real bee-honey is clear from the mention in the laws §§91–92 of stealing bees from a beekeeper's swarm.[28] The bee figures prominently as a positive force in the Old Anatolian myths of the so-called "vanishing god" type.[29] Honey was used as a sweetening agent and was cited in metaphors as the standard of sweetness. Wax (Sum. DUḪ.LÀL) was used to seal vessels and thus preserve the flavor and odor of their contents, and in rituals was applied to parts of the body in order to purify them from evil and uncleanness. Its propensity to melt under heat was exploited in analogic magic to induce evils to likewise melt and disappear. This analogy was rendered even more vivid by making wax or mutton fat figures of evil entities and melting them while pronouncing the spell.

Milk and cheese were used in a variety of ways for food. Milk was consumed both "sweet" ($GA.KU_7$) and "sour" (GA *EMṢU*), the latter being perhaps something like the "clabber" consumed in rural areas of the United States.[30] Cheese was sometimes an ingredient in breads.[31] We have no idea how large a single cheese might be. But the value of a cheese can be estimated by noting that in the Hittite laws two cheeses cost the same amount as a full-grown sheep, a bottle of lard, a bottle of honey, 150 liters of wheat, 200 liters of barley, one shaggy sheepskin, two lambs, four goat kids, or the meat of two yearling oxen.[32] Cheeses were a stock component of the diet. An Old Hittite text listing provisions for a trip mentions among the foodstuffs: high quality lard, five cheeses, five rennets, and 250 liters of wheat flour.[33]

Of the equids, horses would be used by the wealthier class for drawing chariots, donkeys and mules for carrying loads. Mules were the most

---

26 KUB 17.10 ii 19–20, translated in Hoffner (1998) 16 §13.

27 KUB 33.67 iv 1–6, edited in Beckman (1983) 74f. as text Fa.

28 Hoffner (1974) 123, (1997b) 90f., 196.

29 Hoffner (1998) 14–22.

30 Cf. Hoffner (1993); Ryder (1993); Hesse (1995).

31 Hoffner (1974) 121–23.

32 See the table of prices in Hoffner (1997b) 7–10.

33 KBo 22.1:7–12, edited in Archi (1979).

expensive single domestic animal. This was undoubtedly because they could not reproduce themselves and they are extremely sure-footed in mountainous areas.

Sheep were raised for milk, meat, fat, and wool. Cattle were raised for milk, meat, hides and horns, and of course to draw plows, wagons, and vehicles for human transport. Although for most people meat was a rare part of the diet, every family at one time or another had to slaughter a domestic animal: either a cow, a sheep, a goat, or a pig. Those who could afford to do so fattened the animals that they intended to slaughter for meat.[34]

Hunting was no longer in Hittite times a main avenue for procuring food. Hunting is mentioned only as a sport of kings and in mythological narratives. Meat was too expensive to form a regular part of the diet of all but the very wealthy. When it was eaten, it could be the product of hunting wild game or the occasional slaughter of a domestic animal: a cow, a sheep, a goat, or a pig. Animal bones recovered from excavation attest to the following animals being killed for their meat: red deer, roe deer, cattle, sheep, goats, wild goats, wild sheep, swine, wild boar, badger, weasel, bear, lion, leopard, hare, tortoise, mollusks, various types of ducks, and fishes (including carp and shark!).[35]

Salt was valuable both as a preservative and to flavor food. It was obtained from outcroppings on the faces of cliffs.[36] The fat of slaughtered sheep and pigs was used to season food. One of the most popular of sweet pastries (NINDA.Ì.E.DÉ.A, Akk. *mersu*) was made from a combination of honey, flour, and mutton fat.

Since only a very large family unit could consume the entire meat from a cow, and sometimes not even an entire sheep, means were employed to preserve the meat, usually by drying it. The adjective *ḫādan* "dried" is applied to the meat of pigs, sheep, birds, and fish. Other foodstuffs that were dried included flour (ZÌ.DA), and fruits ([GIŠ]*INBI*).

---

34 A fattened animal was called *warkant-*, the Sumerogram for which was NIGA (the ŠE-sign).

35 See the discussions in Boessneck and von den Driesch (1981); Ünal (1985); Hesse 1995.

36 Watkins (1997).

For Building

Hittite houses had foundations of field stones and upper courses of timber-reinforced unbaked mud brick.[37] Roofs were flat, composed of brushwood and dried mud supported by timber beams. The mud was periodically renewed to keep rain from entering the house through cracks. Windows, where they existed, were small openings high on the walls and probably covered with fabrics or shutters in winter to keep out the cold. Floors were either of beaten earth or paved with pebbles or flagstones. Each house had an indoor hearth (Hittite *ḫaššaš*, Sum. GUNNI) or oven for cooking. And some had stone sinks connected to drains. Clay bathtubs used for indoor bathing have been recovered, some even with seats. It is likely that all but the wealthy ate and slept on the floor without benefit of wooden beds, tables, and chairs. Chests were used to store household linens and other objects. Ceramic objects were plentiful: vases of all sizes and shapes, pitchers, bowls, cups, flasks. Among the wealthy these objects were often zoomorphic: in the shapes of lions, bull, ducks, or eagles.

Domestic tools consisted of spindle whorls, loom weights, rakes, and shovels.

The typical Hittite house had a courtyard, but rather than being centrally placed was more like a front yard used for domestic purposes.[38] There was often an upper story entered from the courtyard by a ladder. Gutters carried rainwater away from the foundations of the walls.

Houses were grouped into larger blocks, often with common party walls and surrounded by streets. Attention was paid to overall town-planning.[39] The streets were laid out as straight as the terrain allowed and were covered with a surface of coarse gravel. To permit building on sloping terrain, systems of terracing were necessary, and much thought was given to drainage and water disposal. The large drainage channels that ran down the middle of main streets were roofed with stone slabs and fed by clay pipes running from houses on either side.[40]

The larger public buildings, such as the great temple complex in Ḫattuša, had storage chambers on the periphery in which all kinds of items could be stored. Large *pithos* vessels contained both foodstuffs and other

---

37 Darga (1971), Naumann (1971), Darga (1985), Boysan-Dietrich (1987), Neve (1993).

38 MacQueen (1986) 80.

39 MacQueen (1986) 79.

40 MacQueen (1986) figure 52.

articles. Large pits in the ground lined with straw to repel rodents have been found on the Büyük Kaya in Ḫattuša.[41] These are undoubtedly to be equated with similar storage pits mentioned in Hittite texts, which are denoted by the Sumerogram ÉSAG.[42]

CLOTHING MANUFACTURE

Materials

Garments were made of wool or linen. Weavers are mentioned in the texts. Leather (KUŠ) was used to make belts (Hitt. *išḫuzzi*), although often a cloth sash served the same purpose.

Styles

As in all cultures the wearer's gender was marked by his clothing.[43] Some garments might be worn by either sex, but there were several that were gender-specific. The short kilt seen on reliefs worn by warrior gods[44] was male-specific, as was the sleeved tunic of varied length. Belts or sashes are listed among the typically male attire. The vertical downward extension of the belt or sash shown in the relief depicting warrior gods or human acrobats[45] may have passed between the legs and gone up the opposite side to join the belt on the other side, thus keeping the man's kilt down in position during strenuous activity. Women[46] and goddesses[47] were dressed from head to foot in a long mantle under which they wore a thin garment. Gender-specificity was especially true of headwear. There was a kind of scarf (*kureššar*) worn by women of all classes. Women were veiled only after marriage. Hittite male footwear had a distinctive appearance, the toes of the shoes being turned up. On the other hand, men and women alike wore jewelry: earrings,[48] necklaces, bracelets, and rings.

---

41 Seeher (1997) and (2000).

42 Hoffner (1974) 34–37 (using the older reading ARÀḪ instead of the more correct ÉSAG).

43 For a general survey of Hittite clothing terms and a classification of gender-specific articles, see Goetze (1955).

44 Akurgal (1962) figures 44, 47, 50, 64, 65.

45 Akurgal (1962) figure 93.

46 Özgüç (1988) plates G, J, and K; Akurgal (1962) figure 101.

47 Akurgal (1962) figure 77.

48 Earrings on males are shown in Akurgal (1962), figures 71, 78, 82, 86, 92–93.

Personal Appearance

Hittite adult males were clean-shaven. This feature doubtless set them apart visually from men in the cultures to the east and southeast. Occasionally a god portrayed on a relief will be bearded.

Since adult males shown on reliefs and relief vases wear headdresses, it is difficult to say what the normal hair length was. The King Šuppiluliuma, shown in Chamber 2 of the Southern Citadel at Hattuša, may have a pigtail protruding from under his helmet, which would indicate longer hair.

Priests may have had shaven heads, since ritual texts imply that filth that might pollute the gods was to be found in the hair and under the fingernails. The same may well have been the case with cooks in the royal kitchen.

SANITATION AND PERSONAL HYGIENE

Personal cleanliness was primarily the concern of people who daily had to be in the presence of the king or of the gods or who prepared their food. Such persons would be the cooks and courtiers in the palace and temples. Texts exist that give elaborate instructions about safeguards against defiling king or god. Severe penalties, sometimes death, were meted out to royal or temple servants who violated these rules.

But even private servants were expected to be clean and free of obnoxious odors when attending their masters. One text expresses it this way: "Are the mind of man and god somehow different? No. Is this what concerns us? No. Their attitude is one and the same. When a servant stands before his master, he is washed. He wears clean clothes. He serves his master food and drink. And since his master eats and drinks, he is relaxed in spirit and favorably inclined to his servant."[49]

Latrines and Waste Products of Human Life

Outdoor latrines were the rule, but for wealthier persons and for the convenience of all during bitter cold seasons chamber pots were used.[50]

Bathing

We have no idea how often an ordinary citizen bathed. Temple personnel whose daily tasks required closer contact with the gods' cult statues and

---

49 KUB 13.4 i 21–26. See a slightly different translation in Hallo and Younger (1997) 217.

50 The Hittite term for such a chamber pot is *kalti*.

altars were supposed to bathe daily, and were especially cautioned to bathe after sexual intercourse.

Meal Times

Non-wealthy families probably ate only twice a day: once before beginning work and again after the labor of the day was over. Wealthier individuals may have had more frequent meal times. The texts use an Akkadogram to designate the principal meal of the day (*naptānu rabû* "big meal"). We have no menus to indicate even for royalty precisely what they ate. But a few texts of analogous nature have been used to extrapolate.

TRANSPORTATION AND VEHICLES

The principal mode of transportation was walking. Loads were moved on donkey-back or on carts or wagons. One could also ride on a donkey or mule. Horses were principally used to draw chariots. Kings and high officials rode in chariots or were carried on litters.

BASIC SOCIAL NEEDS

Kinship Groups, Mutual Protection, Natural Allies and Friends

Families were cohesive social units, not just because of shared affection, but because mutual loyalty between members of nuclear and extended family groups gave financial security and protection.

Family Life

Although royal women, such as queens, exercised considerable independence of their husbands, as a rule Hittite society was patriarchal, and inheritance was patrilineal. In some cases, however, when a husband died, the widow could control her children by the threat of disinheriting.

To gain a spouse and children and thus form one's own nuclear family was a great achievement. It was often occasion for thanksgiving to the gods. Nor were husbands, even prominent members of the royal family, particularly shy about expressing their affection for their wives.

Of course, among wealthier men who could afford to support multiple wives and children or who had large estates where multiple children could profitably work polygamy was common. But lower classes were characterized—so far as our limited documentation allows us to say—by monogamy. As in other cultures of the ancient Near East, Hittite husbands took a second wife only if the first one was unable to provide him with children.

What we know about the composition of an individual nuclear family is gained from lists of "households" of semi-free status donated by the crown to the service of a particular deity,[51] or from land-deeds. Since the "normal working unit" of deportees assigned to domestic labor was ten, Imparati reasons that this was also "the average size of a functioning domestic unit, including parents, three or four children, and servants."[52] A typical middle-class family is described in a land-deed as follows:

> Estate of Tiwatapara:
> 1 man, Tiwatapara;
> 1 boy, Hartuwanduli;
> 1 woman, Azziya;
> 2 girls, Anitti and Santawiya;
> (total) 5 persons;
> 2 oxen,
> 22 …,[53]
> 6 draft-oxen …,
> [18] sheep—among the ewes 2 female lambs, and among the rams 2 male lambs;
> 18 goats—among the (female) goats 4 kids, and among the he-goats 1 kid;
> (total) 36 small cattle;
> 1 complex of buildings;
> As pasture for oxen one acre of meadow in the town Parkalla.
> 3½ acres of vineyard, and in it
> 40 apple-trees, 42 'mountain-apple' trees in the town Hanzusra, belonging to the estate of Hantapi.[54]

Marriage

We lack such important marriage and family records as marriage or adoption contracts. What knowledge we have is derived from incidental information provided in the Hittite laws and in other documents chronicling the lives and affairs of royal and upper-class individuals.

As mentioned above, betrothal often took place early in the life of a Hittite girl. Whether marriages were also arranged in advance for sons while they were still little boys we cannot say. In the case of the prince who eventually gained the throne under the name Hattušili III, he apparently had no pre-arranged marriage, and as an adult entered into a marriage agreement with an influential priest in the land of Kizzuwatna, directed—

---

51 So in the so-called "Vow of Puduḫepa" text.

52 Imparati (1995) 571.

53 The text reads "22 sheep (UDU)" here, which contradicts what follows.

54 Translation quoted with adaptations from Gurney (1990) 66.

so he claimed—by an oracular word from a deity.[55] The Hittite laws give us a picture of the stages in marriage arrangements, which included (1) initial non-written agreement between the prospective husband or his parents and the bride's parents, (2) formal betrothal, and (3) the consummation of the marital union. At both of the first two stages gifts were exchanged: the prospective husband giving in stage two (betrothal) a payment that may be called a "bride price" (*kušata*), and the bride's parents giving at stage three a dowry (Hittite *iwaru*). The size of these would naturally depend upon the relative wealth of the givers. If the agreement was broken by either party, his payment would be forfeit (law §30). If the bride's parents accepted the *kušata* and then reneged on the marriage, they had to repay double (law §29). It does not appear that the consent of the bride-to-be was required. After stage one the young woman was "promised," but after stage two she was legally "bound."

The woman's "dowry" (Hittite *iwaru*) was in actuality her inheritance share from her parents, for henceforth she would leave her own family and become a member of her husband's family. The opposite situation was a rarity, but is attested both in the laws and in one of the Old Hittite myths.[56] A son from a family too poor to provide a suitable bride price might, in exchange for a *kušata* given to his parents by the bride's family, enter her family and lose all formal connection with his own, being in effect adopted by his wife's parents. If he was a free man and his wife a slave, the children of their union would derive free status from him. Thus an unfree man who had sufficient financial resources could purchase the freedom of his grandchildren by paying a *kušata* for such an "in-living" husband for his daughter (laws §§27 and 36). An added benefit to the arrangement for the bride's parents was that, if their daughter predeceased her "in-living" husband, her dowry remained in her parents' possession and could not be claimed by her husband (§27).

Like the ancient Israelites and Assyrians, the Hittites knew the custom of what has been called "levirate marriage." If a man predeceased his wife, his brother took her to wife. And if the brother predeceased her as well, first

---

55 KUB 1.1 iii 2, edited by Otten (1981), with a recent English translation in Hallo and Younger (1997) 199ff.

56 The documentation in the laws can be studied conveniently in one of the recent English translations, for example Hoffner (1997a). More detailed, scientific treatment can be found in the recent new edition of the text (Hoffner [1997b]). The relevant Old Hittite myth, that named for the giant serpent Illuyanka, is translated in Hoffner (1998) 12–13. See already the observations of Güterbock (1961) 152, reprinted in Hoffner (1997c) 53.

his father and then his nephew took her (law §193). Law §192 raises an even more intriguing possibility, which—if it proves correct—shows even more vividly the economic, rather than sentimental, motivation behind the levirate. That law has been read to provide that when a man predeceased his wife, the wife took her husband's share. But an improved collated reading suggests it rather provides that when a man dies, his business partner shall take his wife![57] This long and involved series of "heirs" to the wife illustrates how important it was to keep the woman, her children, and her dowry in the family of her deceased husband.

No text describes a wedding. But some scholars have seen a depiction of its activities in the famous Old Hittite relief vase from Inandik,[58] which even shows in its upper right-hand register a scene of sexual intercourse.[59] A larger consensus of scholars have agreed that on the Bitik vase[60] we see a tender scene between husband and wife on their wedding night, where the groom offers her a cup of wine and lifts her veil for the first time.[61]

Trade or Occupation

Food, clothing, shelter, and protection from danger are the primary requirements of the individual. Family in the form of parents, siblings, spouse, and children is the focus of primary social needs. Work provides both a means of obtaining food, clothing, shelter, and protection. But it also can provide a sense of worth and identity.

When individuals are identified in Hittite texts, it is either by a personal name, by a name plus a patronymic, by a name plus an occupational title, or simply by the occupational title alone. For most of the common people their occupation would be determined by that of their parents. A son would pursue the trade of his father. In the higher ranks of society, where the father's occupation was a royal appointment, it was by no means assured that the man's sons would ever occupy the position. But a father could also pay a master of a craft to take his son on as an apprentice. One of the laws describes such a situation: "If anyone gives his son for training either as a carpenter or a smith, a weaver, a leather-worker or a fuller, he shall pay 6 shekels as (the fee) for the training. If the teacher makes (the

57 Hoffner (1997b) 152, 225f.

58 Özgüç (1988) 175 (fold-out drawing), plates F–M.

59 Özgüç (1988), discussed in Haas (1994) 523ff.

60 Akurgal (1962) 63 (color plate).

61 Bittel (1976) 143 and 145, figures 140 and 144.

student) an expert, (the student's parent) shall give to (the teacher) one person" (law §200b).[62]

While some craftsmen were indentured to the service of palace or temple, others lived in independent households, where they served the needs of their own households and accepted outside work for a fee. Examples of such service for fee are given in the laws. A table of prices, many of them for finished goods, the products of a trade, are given, ranging from 30 shekels for a fine garment, 25 for a trained augur, 20 for a blue wool garment, 12.5 for a copper box weighing 1.5 minas, 10 for a trained potter, smith, carpenter, leather worker, fuller or weaver, 5 for a large bolt of linen, 4 for a hide of an ox, all the way down to a tenth of a shekel for a copper ax weighing one mina. The persons trained in a craft whose prices are given in the above-mentioned laws are obviously slaves whose masters have had them trained.

Entertainment

Another essential social need that the Hittites recognized was entertainment. Music was an obvious and elemental form of entertainment.

The texts actually tell us very little about entertainment for the general public, although we can safely extrapolate from what was provided for the royal family and for the gods. Texts mention that singing and playing musical instruments were regular and indispensable parts of the agenda at festivals. Among the musical instruments are drums, cymbals, harps, lyres, flutes, and horns.[63] Relief scenes from Alaca[64] and Inandik[65] show musicians playing these instruments.

Evidence for the existence in Hatti of children's toys is very meager and controversial.

Various athletic contests were popular to spectators. The texts describing such contests performed for the benefit of the gods include boxing, wrestling, stone throwing, foot racing, archery, and chariot racing.[66] Both

---

62 Hoffner (1997b) 158–59. KBo 22.66 iv 15′–19′, inadvertently printed on p. 160 with "unplaced fragments," obviously belongs on p. 159 as the third text witness to §200b.

63 See Boehmer (1988) de Martino (1988), Badalì (1989), (1991), Boehmer (1992), Özgüç (1992), Klinger (1993), de Martino (1995), Güterbock (1995), Polomé (1996), de Martino (1997), Dinçol (1998).

64 Akurgal (1962) plate 93 upper.

65 Özgüç (1988) plates I–K.

66 For Hittite athletic contests to entertain the gods, see Ehelolf (1925), Carter (1988), Puhvel (1988), Haas (1989), de Martino (1995).

texts and relief sculptures attest to the performance of jugglers, acrobats,[67] and sword swallowers.[68] Related to acrobats, but not strictly identical, were dancers—some who whirled about much in the manner of the later Turkish dervishes. Rope climbing may also have been a sport.[69] There is evidence in the texts for mock battles[70] and ritual drama—occasionally the performer bowed to the audience,[71] and in some athletic contests indication is given that the audience applauded or cheered the winner.[72] Recently two Old Hittite relief vases similar to those found at Bitik and Inandik were recovered by staff of the Çorum Museum at a site near Sungurlu, north of Boghazköy. Both were broken, but with all pieces intact. One is medium-sized, the other large like the Inandik. The pieces are now in the Çorum museum, where the vases are being restored. When restored they show scenes of Hittite bull-leaping strongly reminiscent of scenes on Minoan frescoes.[73] Mention of bull-leaping may in fact be found in certain broken passages of Hittite texts.[74]

In some of the religious festivals actors donned masks or other forms of costume to mimic animals such as the wolf, the bear, and the dog.[75] Some scholars believe that there was an official (^{LÚ}ALAN.ZU_9) who served in temple and palace to entertain through humor.[76] It is probably misleading to call him a "jester," but his role was definitely to amuse and entertain. He

67 Özgüç (1988) plate K 4.

68 Bittel (1976) 193 figure 218 ("Gauklerszene"), Akurgal (1962) 93. "Gaukler" ("juggler, acrobat" in Akk.) is *mubabbilu(m)* (*AHw* 665a). Sword swallowing and balancing on ladders as entertainment in festivals are now attested in texts as well; cf. KUB 60.56:2′–10′, and Ünal (1988), Gurney (1994).

69 Ünal (1988).

70 KUB 17.35 iii 9–14; comments in Ehelolf (1925). See also Goetze (1957) 163.

71 In several cases to the god's cult statue, which was the principal audience (KUB 17.35 iii 14, KBo 23.55 i 22–23).

72 See Hoffner (1978) and later *CHD* P 81 sub mng. a 2′.

73 See Sipạhi (2001) and Yildirim (2001).

74 The possibility that Hittite bull-leaping contests were referred to in KBo 23.55: 26′ EGIR=*ŠU*[=*ma* ......] GU_4.MAḪ.ḪI.A *tarpa tianzi* was first noted by Hoffner (1978) before the discovery of the relief vase, then afterwards on the basis of the broken context of KUB 35.132+ iii 1–9 by Güterbock (forthcoming in Fs. Hoffner).

75 Jakob-Rost (1966), de Martino (1995) 2667.

76 The ^{LÚ}ALAN.ZU_9 (Akk. *aluzinnu*), cf. Güterbock (1964b), (1964a); de Martino (1984), Güterbock (1989). In Akkadian compare not only the *aluzinnu*, but the *muṣiḫḫu*.

does not entertain through funny sayings, but through burlesque actions. In one festival two ALAN.ZU_9's squat naked in a vat of beer, while someone pours beer three times over their backs.[77] In another festival the chief ALAN.ZU_9 hits the chief cook over the head three times with a club in "Coyote and Roadrunner"-cartoon style,[78] and in another festival fragment the chief cook pours hot coals over the head of the ALAN.ZU_9.[79] What goes around comes around! These actions can hardly have been intended for anything other than humor.

THE FUNDAMENTAL RITES OF PASSAGE

A Hittite's identity was maintained through national loyalty, ethnicity, language, gender, profession, parentage, and individual name. Some of these markers were inherited at birth without any choice by the individual. Although parents gave children names, many people acquired sobriquets, not unlike our "nicknames." A person was born of a certain race, color, and gender. Language was acquired from one's parents, although in ancient Hatti there may have been as many as eight languages used in the royal bureaucracy. If you were of one of the upper classes, you would likely acquire at least one additional language.

Birth

A woman in labor sat on a birth stool and was attended by another woman.[80] Often it could be the woman's mother who aided her. At other times it was a professional, a midwife. We have no information about midwives' fees, but like the physicians of the day they must have had a rate. Manuals of Babylonian origin, cataloguing omens associated with birth that indicated likely futures for the child, were translated into Hittite for the use of the royal court.[81] We have no way of knowing if similar superstitions about events attending birth that foreshadowed the newborn's destiny were held by the general public. It is not at all unlikely.

---

77 KUB 2.3 ii 11–27.

78 KUB 20.11 ii 12–13.

79 KUB 60.21: 6.

80 The standard work on birth rituals is Beckman (1983). Other useful studies of aspects of birth in Hatti are: Hoffner (1968), Beckman (1978), Pringle (1983), Zinko (1995).

81 Riemschneider (1970).

Puberty

When a female child reached puberty, she was ready for marriage. She may have been betrothed to a future husband when she was only a small child.[82] We know almost nothing about what rites may have accompanied the onset of puberty among Hittite boys and girls. A tantalizing hint is provided by a ceremony designed for a Hittite prince, which Hans Güterbock once suggested was a kind of puberty rite.[83] During the ceremonies that stretched over several days the prince was entertained at several banquets in a special kind of house or inn. At one banquet his dinner companions were twelve priests. At another they were twelve prostitutes. After the last-mentioned banquet the prince retired to a chamber in the house, where he was ritually consecrated and made to lie down on a bed. On each side of his head two loaves of bread were placed, and on each side of his feet two loaves were placed. After this, beer was poured in a circle around him, and the twelve prostitutes who had been his banquet companions were brought in. At this suspenseful point the text reaches the end of the tablet, and the next tablet in the composition has not yet been found. It doesn't take much imagination, however, to reconstruct what followed. Now this is a particular case, one involving a prince, perhaps even the crown prince. We must therefore exercise caution in generalizing it to the ordinary rank and file. Yet it is difficult to avoid the conclusion that this is an elaborate and much more expensive counterpart to simple puberty rites that may have existed among the general population.

Death and Burial

The final rite of passage is death. We will conclude our survey of "daily life" with a summary of proceedings attending the death of a Hittite. Death was a reality from which ancient Hittites, unlike many of us today, were not shielded. Parents or grandparents died in the same room in which the children slept. Many of us are familiar with the expression from the Book of Genesis "he slept with his fathers." Such an expression, regardless of the details of its interpretation, clearly associates death with family cohesiveness. Physical cohesiveness in death is sometimes ensured by communal burial. In Ugarit, as elsewhere, family members could be interred in the very house in which the surviving members lived. When this was not the case, the physical remains of the deceased were deposited in an area where

---

82 Balkan (1986).

83 Güterbock (1969).

those of other deceased ancestors still lay. In the Hittite laws one of the requirements laid upon a person held to be responsible for the killing of a Hittite citizen while the latter was away from his home city was that he bring the body home for burial.[84] And an Old Hittite song, often hailed as the earliest bit of Indo-European poetry, sung by soldiers anticipating possible death on the battlefield, contains the refrain "bury me together with my mother."[85] The same song may, with the repeated mention of "the clothes of Neša," allude to the burial shroud. Family cohesiveness in death is also indicated by the attested euphemism for death "the day of your father and mother," often abbreviated "the day of your mother."[86]

It is still not known what the proportion of cremation to non-cremation interments was in the Hittite population at large. Formal state rituals show that, at least in the New Hittite period, members of the royal family were invariably cremated, and excavations at Osmankayasi, on the northern outskirts of Hattuša, show that cremation was practiced much more widely than just in the royal family.[87] Since we have no direct textual evidence for the funerary rites of an ordinary citizen, we are left to extrapolate from the royal funerals.[88]

The burial rite was also a rite of passage, since the Hittites did not believe in the cessation of conscious existence at the moment of physical death. Oracular inquiries as to what might be causing the spirit of a dead person to trouble the living illustrate how important it was to continue to appease the personalities of the dead. At least among the royal family, and perhaps also in the general population, some tangible representation of the deceased ancestors was retained and venerated. When the imperial capital was transferred from Hattuša to Tarhuntassa during the reign of Muwa-

---

84 Hoffner (1997a) laws 1–5; Hoffner (1997b) 17–20, 166–67.

85 KBo 3.40:14–15, see discussion in Watkins (1969) 240f.

86 *annaš* UD-*za* "the day of the mother" KUB 5.3 + 18.52 i 45, *ŠA* AMA=*ŠU*=*wa*=*šši* UD.KAM-*za* KUB 39.49:26; *ŠA* AMA=*KA* UD-*az ari* KUB 21.1 + 19.6 i 64 (Muw. II treaty with Alakšandu). It is said of a person who lives longer than expected that "the day of his father and mother is long for him" (KUB 26.1 iii 14–15). On Hittite terminology for life, death, and longevity, see Hoffner (1987).

87 For photos of interments of bones and of incinerated remains, see Goetze (1957), Tafel 12, photos 22 and 23.

88 These were first systematically edited by Otten (1958). Subsequent partial treatments of the subject are: Christmann-Franck (1971), Stefanini (1974), Börker-Klähn (1995), Gonnet (1995), van den Hout (1995). A new edition is planned by van den Hout.

talli II, it was said that the images of the gods and of the deceased ancestors were carried to the new capital.[89]

Just what kind of conscious existence the dead had—pleasurable or not—is more difficult to determine. In the case of deceased royalty the wording of the funerary ritual implies that the king will enjoy in the afterlife the activities of daily life, including agricultural ones that in his lifetime he may never have pursued, such as plowing.[90] A fragment of a composition whose nature and full context cannot yet be determined describes the dead as experiencing a gloomy existence, eating mud clods and drinking filthy water.[91] The similarity of this picture to that conveyed in certain Mesopotamian literary texts raises the currently unanswerable question of whether this is a fragment of a Mesopotamian literary text translated into Hittite, and therefore not necessarily representative of native Hittite conceptions.

The end, then, of "daily life" for the Hittite was an existence over which a large question mark was placed. No one prepared for death, as if no action prior to death could in any way determine whether the afterlife would be pleasant. Hittite daily life was spent focused on the matters at hand, not the future.

BIBLIOGRAPHY

Akurgal, Ekrem (1962) *The Art of the Hittites*. London. **Archi, Alfonso** (1979) L'humanité des hittites. In *Florilegium Anatolicum. Mélanges offerts à Emmanuel Laroche*, 37–48. **Badalì, Enrico** (1989) Beziehungen zwischen Musik und kultischen Rufen innerhalb der hethitischen Feste. In *XXIII. Deutscher Orientalistentag vom 16. bis 20. September 1985 in Würzburg. Ausgewählte Vorträge*, 282–92. (1991)*Strumenti musicali, musici e musica nella celebrazione delle feste ittite*. Texte der Hethiter 14. Heidelberg. **Balkan, Kemal** (1986) Betrothal of girls during childhood in Ancient Assyria and Anatolia. In *Kaniššuwar: A Tribute to Hans G. Güterbock on his Seventy-fifth Birthday, May 27, 1983*. Assyriological Studies 23: 1–11. **Beckman, Gary M.** (1978) *Hittite Birth Rituals: An Introduction*. Sources from the ancient Near East; v. 1, fasc. 4. Malibu. (1983) *Hittite Birth Rituals*. Studien zu den Boğazköy-Texten 29. Wiesbaden. **Bittel, Kurt** (1976) *Die Hethiter. Die Kunst Anatoliens vom Ende des 3. bis zum Anfang des 1. Jahrtausends vor Christus*. München. **Boehmer, Rainer Michael** (1988) Früheste Abbil-

89 KUB 1.1+ ii 52–53, translated recently into English in Hallo and Younger (1997) 201 (translated here as "the gods of Hatti and the manes").

90 Otten (1958) 48, 78, 80. See also Haas (1995).

91 Hoffner (1988).

dungen von Lautenspielern in der althethitischen Glyptik. In *Documentum Asiae Minoris Antiquae*, 51–58. (1992) Von zwei Musikanten gespielte Leiern. In *Hittite and Other Anatolian and Near Eastern Studies in Honour of Sedat Alp*. Anadolu Medeniyetlerini Araşirma ve Tanitma Vakfi Yayinlari—Sayi 1: 67–68. **Boessneck, Joachim, and Angela von den Driesch** (1981) *Reste von Haus- und Jagdtieren aus der Unterstadt von Boğazköy-Ḫattuša*. Boğazköy-Ḫattuša 11. Berlin. **Börker-Klähn, Jutta** (1995) Auf der Suche nach einer Nekropole: Ḫattuša. *Studi Micenei ed Egeo-Anatolici* Fascicolo 35: 69–92. **Boysan-Dietrich, Nilüfer** (1987) *Das hethitische Lehmhaus aus der Sicht der Keilschriftquellen*. Texte der Hethiter 12. Heidelberg. **Carter, Charles W.** (1988) Athletic Contests in Hittite Religious Festivals. *Journal of Near Eastern Studies* 47: 185–87. **Christmann-Franck, Lisbeth** (1971) Le rituel des funérailles royales hittites. *Revue hittite et asianique* 71: 61–84. **Collins, Billie Jean** (1989) The Representation of Wild Animals in Hittite Texts. Ph. D. Dissertation, Yale University. **Darga, Mühibbe** (1971) Die Architektur der hethitischen Städte und Befestigungsanlagen. *Revue hittite et asianique* 29: 17–60. (1985) *Hitit Mimarlığı, I-Yapı Sanatı*. Istanbul. **de Martino, Stefano** (1984) Il ^{LÚ}ALAN.ZÚ come 'mimo' e come 'attore' nei testi ittiti. *Studi micenei ed egeo-anatolici* 24: 132–48. (1988) Il lessico musicale ittita: usi e valori di alcuni verbi. *Hethitica* 9: 5–16. (1995) Music, Dance, and Processions in Hittite Anatolia. In *Civilizations of the Ancient Near East*, 2661–70. (1997) Musik. A. III. Bei den Hethitern. In *Reallexikon der Assyriologie und Vorderasiatischen Archäologie, Band 8*, 483–88. **del Monte, Giuseppe F.** (1995a) Bier und Wein bei den Hethitern. In *Studio Historiae Ardens. Ancient Near Eastern Studies Presented to Philo H. J. Houwink ten Cate on the Occasion of his 65th Birthday*. Publications de l'Institut historique et archéologique néerlandais de Stamboul 74: 211–24. (1995b) I testi amministrativi da Maşat Höyük/Tapika. *Orientis Antiqui Miscellanea* 2: 89–138. **Dinçol, Belkıs** (1998) Beobachtungen über die Bedeutung des hethitischen Musikinstruments ^{GIŠ}*huhupal*. *Anatolica*: 1–5. **Ehelolf, Hans** (1925) Wettlauf und szenisches Spiel im hethitischen Ritual. *SPAW* 1925: 267–72. **Goetze, Albrecht** (1955) Hittite Dress. In *Corolla linguistica. Festschrift Ferdinand Sommer*. 48ff. (1957) *Kleinasien*. Handbuch der Altertumswissenschaft. Kulturgeschichte des Alten Orients. München. **Gonnet, Hatice** (1995) Le culte des ancêtres en Anatolie hittite au IIe mill. avant notre ère. *Anatolica* 21: 189–95. **Gorny, Ronald L.** (1995) Viticulture and Ancient Anatolia. In *The Origins and Ancient History of Wine*. Food and Nutrition in History and Anthropology Series 11: 133–74. **Gurney, Oliver R.** (1990) *The Hittites*. Baltimore. (1994) The Laddermen at Alaca Höyük. *Anatolian Studies* 44: 219–20. **Güterbock, Hans Gustav** (1961) Review of *Die hethitischen Gesetze* by J. Friedrich. *Journal of Cuneiform Studies* 15: 62–78. (1964a) Lexicographical Notes II. *Revue hittite et asianique* XXII/74: 95–113. (1964b) ^{LÚ}ALAN.KAxUD = ^{LÚ}ALAN.ZÚ = *aluzinnu*. *Revue hittite et asianique* fasc. 74: 95–97. (1989) Marginal Notes on Recent Hittitological Publications. *Journal of Near Eastern Studies* 48 (4): 307–11. (1995) Reflections on the Musical Instruments *arkammi, galgalturi* and *huhupal* in Hittite. In *Studio Historiae Ardens. Ancient Near Eastern Studies Presented to Philo H. J. Houwink ten Cate on the Occasion of his 65th Birthday*. Publications de l'Institut historique et archéologique néerlandais de Stamboul 74: 57–72. **Haas, Volkert** (1989) Kompositbogen und Bogenschiessen als Wettkampf im Alten Orient. *Nikephoros* 2: 27–41. (1994) *Geschichte der hethitischen Religion*. Handbuch der Orientalistik. 1. Abteilung. 15. Band. Leiden. (1995) Death and the Afterlife in Hittite Thought. In *Civilizations of the Ancient Near East*, 2021–30. **Hallo, William W., and K. Lawson Younger**, eds. (1997) *The Context of Scripture. Volume One: Canonical Compositions, Monumental Inscriptions and Archival Documents from the Biblical World*. Leiden. **Heimpel, Wolfgang** (1975) Huhn. In *Reallexikon der Assyriologie und Vorderasiatischen Archäologie. Band 4*, 487–88. **Hesse, Brian** (1995) Animal Husbandry and Human Diet in the Ancient Near East. In *Civilizations of the Ancient Near East*, 203–24. **Hoffner, Harry A., Jr.** (1966) Composite Nouns, Verbs, and Adjectives in Hittite. *Orientalia Nova Series* 35: 377ff. (1967) *An English-Hittite Glossary*. Revue Hittite et Asianique XXV/80. Paris. (1968) Birth and Namegiving in Hittite Texts. *Journal of Near Eastern Studies* 27: 198–203. (1974) *Alimenta Hethaeorum: Food Production in Hittite Asia Minor*. American Oriental Series 55. New Haven. (1978) Review of *Keilschrifttexte aus Boghazköy, Heft XXIII* by H. Otten and C. Rüster. *Bibliotheca Orientalis* 35: 246–48. (1987) Hittite Terms for the Life Span. In *Love & Death in the Ancient Near East* [*Festschrift for Marvin Pope*], 53–55. (1988) A Scene in the Realm of the Dead. In *A Scientific Humanist. Studies in Memory of Abraham Sachs*, 191–99. (1993) Milch(produkte). B. Bei den Hethitern. In *Reallexikon der Assyriologie und Vorderasiatischen Archäologie. Band 8*, 702–6. (1997a) The Hittite Laws. In *Law Collections from Mesopotamia and Asia Minor. Second Edition*. Writings from the Ancient World 6: 211–47. (1997b) *The Laws of the Hittites. A Critical Edition*. Documenta et Monumenta Orientis Antiqui, 23. Leiden. (1998) *Hittite Myths. Second Revised Edition*. Writings from the Ancient World 2. Atlanta. (1997c) ed., *Perspectives on Hittite Civilization: Selected Writings of Hans Gustav Güterbock*, Assyriological Studies 26. Chicago. **Imparati, Fiorella** (1995) Private Life Among the Hittites. In *Civilizations of the Ancient Near East*, 571–86. **Jakob-Rost, Liane** (1966) Zu einigen hethitischen Kultfunktionären. *Orientalia Nova Series* 35: 417–22. **Klinger, Jörg** (1993) Review of *Strumenti musicali, musici e musica nella celebrazione delle feste ittite* by E. Badalì. *Wiener Zeitschrift für die Kunde des Morgenlandes* 83: 276–84. **MacQueen, J.G.** (1986) *The Hittites and Their Contemporaries in Asia Minor*. Ancient Peoples and Places. London. **Naumann, Rudolf** (1971) *Architektur Kleinasiens von ihren Anfängen bis zum Ende der hethitischen Zeit*. Tübingen. **Neve, Peter J.** (1993) Ein Hethitisches Hausmodell aus Boğazköy-Hattuša. In *Nimet Özgüç'e armağan. Aspects of Art and Iconography: Anatolia and its Neighbors*, 439–44. **Otten, Heinrich** (1958) *Hethitische Totenrituale*. Deutsche Akademie der Wissenschaften zu Berlin, Institut für Orientforschung, Veröffentlichung Nr. 37. Berlin. (1981) *Die Apologie Hattusilis III.: Das Bild der Überlieferung*. Studien zu den Boğazköy-Texten. Heft 24. Wiesbaden. **Özgüç, Nimet** (1992) A Lute Player from Samsat. In *Hittite and Other Anatolian and Near Eastern Studies in Honour of Sedat Alp*. Anadolu Medeniyetlerini Araştirma ve Tanitma Vakfi Yayinlari—Sayi 1: 419–24. **Özgüç, Tahsin** (1988) *Inandiktepe. An Important Cult Center in the Old Hittite Period*. Atatürk kültur, dil ve tarih yüksek kurumu. Türk tarih kurumu yayinlari. V. Dizi. Sa. 43. Ankara. **Polomé, Edgar C.** (1996) Review of *Strumenti musicali, musici e musica nella celebrazione delle feste ittite, Texte der Hethiter, 14/1* by E. Badalì. *Journal of Indo-European Studies* 24: 150. **Pringle, J.** (1983) Hittite Birth Rituals. In *Images of Women in Antiquity*, 128–41. **Puhvel, Jaan** (1988) Hittite athletics as prefigurations of Ancient Greek games. In *The Archaeology of the Olympics*, 26–31. **Reichert, Pierre** (1963) Glossaire inverse de la langue hittite. *Revue hittite et asianique* 21 (fasc. 73): 59–145. **Riemschneider, Kaspar K.** (1970) *Babylonische Geburtsomina in hethitischer Übersetzung*. StBoT 9. Wiesbaden. **Ryder, M.L.** (1993) Sheep and Goat Husbandry with Particular Reference to Textile Fibre and Milk Production. In *Domestic Animals of Mesopotamia Part I*, 9–32. **Salonen, Armas** (1973) *Vögel und Vogelfang*. Helsinki. **Sasson, Jack M.**, ed. (1995) *Civilizations of the Ancient Near East*. 4 vols. New York. **Seeher, Jürgen** (1997) Die Ausgrabungen in Boğazköy-Ḫattuša 1996. *Archäologischer Anzeiger* 1997: 317–41. (2000) Getreidelagerung in unterirdischen Grossspeichern: Zur Methode und ihrer Anwendung im 2. Jahrtausend v. Chr. am Beispiel der Befunde in Ḫattuša. Studi Micenei ed Egeo-Anatolici 42: 261–301. **Sipahi, Tunç** (2001) Eine althethitische Reliefvase vom Hüseyindede Tepesi. Istanbuler Mitteilungen 51: 63–86. **Stefanini, Ruggero** (1974) Elisi greci ed elisi ittiti. *Paideia* 29: 257–67. **Ünal, Ahmet** (1985) Beiträge zum Fleischverbrauch in der hethitischen Küche: Philologische Anmerkungen zu einer Untersuchung von A. von den Driesch und J. Boessneck über die Tierknochenreste aus Bogazköy-Hattuša. *Orientalia Nova Series* NS 54: 419–38. (1988) Hittite Architect and a Rope-Climbing Ritual. *Belleten* 52 (205): 1469–1503. **van den Hout, Theo P. J.** (1995) An Image of the Dead? Some Remarks on the Second Day of the Hittite Royal Funerary Ritual. In *Atti del II congresso Internazionale di Hittitologia*. Studia Mediterranea 9: 195–212. **Watkins, Calvert** (1969) A Latin-Hittite Etymology. *Language* 45: 235–42. (1997) Luvo-Hittite *lapan(a)-*. In *Studies in Honor of Jaan Puhvel: Part One. Ancient Languages and Philology*. Journal of Indo-European Studies Monograph Series 20: 29–35. **Yildirim, Tayfun** (2001) Yörüklü/Hüseyindede: Eine neue hethitische Siedlung im Südwesten von Çorum. Istanbuler Mitteilungen 51: 43–62. **Zinko, Christian** (1995) Hethitische Geburtsrituale im Vergleich mit altindischen Ritualen. In *Atti del II Congresso Internazionale di Hittitologia*. Studia Mediterranea 9: 389–400.

Syria

DAILY LIFE IN ANCIENT UGARIT (SYRIA)

Wilfred G. E. Watson
University of Newcastle upon Tyne

1. *Previous Study*

The ancient city-state of Ugarit, on the mound of present-day Ras Shamra, is located in Northern Syria and flourished in the Late Bronze Age, between 1700 and 1190–1185 B.C.E. (see sections 3 and 4), though the tell on which it stands had been occupied since the Neolithic period (*c.* 7000 B.C.E.)[1] (fig. 1). The first comprehensive work on daily life in ancient Ugarit, by van Selms,[2] dealt with marriage, family, death, and inheritance. However, the method

Figure 1. The sondage trench (deepest layer = Neolithic period).

---

1 For guides to the site, cf. Saadé (1978); Burns (1992) 230–34.

2 Van Selms (1954).

he adopted was to derive conclusions concerning human relationships exclusively from the Ugaritic epics (*Baal, Keret, Aqhat,* etc.),[3] although well aware that this entailed assumptions of many kinds.[4] In two books on Ugarit, the chapters "Life in Ancient Ugarit"[5] and "Everyday Life in Ugarit"[6] provide some idea of what it was like to live in that city. However, in each case the scope of those chapters was limited by the size of the book.[7] Also, there is a brief section on "Daily Life" in the entry "Ugarit" in the *Anchor Bible Dictionary*.[8] This can be supplemented by the description of day-to-day living in the southern residential section of Ugarit.[9] The longest and most significant survey is provided by Vita's "The Society of Ugarit."[10] In addition, there are studies that deal with the religion of everyday life,[11] family religion,[12] and the army,[13] and some more general indications are provided elsewhere.[14] A study on the town of Ugarit has recently been published[15] and a survey of vineyards and wine is now available.[16] Note that the description given here[17] relies heavily on previous works and provides a broad outline;[18] the photographs were taken on site.[19]

---

[3] As indicated by the title of his book, *Marriage and Family Life in Ugaritic Literature*. For translations of these texts see Wyatt (1998).

[4] Particularly concerning the date of the mythological texts and whether what they said about gods and heroes could be transferred automatically to ordinary life.

[5] Craigie (1983) 26–43.

[6] Curtis (1985) 49–65.

[7] See also, very briefly, Drower (1975) 130–32.

[8] Yon (1992b) 705 § E.1.

[9] Callot (1994) 185–202.

[10] Vita (1999). See also Rainey (1975) and Aboud (1994).

[11] Del Olmo Lete (1999) 324–88.

[12] Van der Toorn (1996); Wyatt (1999) 567–79.

[13] Vita (1995); see the critique by Márquez Rowe (1997/98).

[14] Korpel (1990) 213–522; Courtois *et al.* (1979).

[15] Yon (1997c).

[16] Zamora (2000); see previously Heltzer (1990). See also "The Mysteries of Ugarit," Near Eastern Archaeology 63/4 (2000): 182–243.

[17] Here I wish to express my thanks to Dr. Juan-Pablo Vita for comments on an early draft and to Prof. Nicolas Wyatt, who kindly provided reference material. Naturally, the usual disclaimers apply.

[18] There is no space here to discuss historical changes during the lifetime of the city. For the later years, cf. Yon (1992c) and Caubet (1992).

2. *The Sources*

The two main types of sources, both from the archaeological excavation of the site, are written documents and material remains.

THE DOCUMENTS

Almost all the texts found on the site (and elsewhere)[20] are in the form of clay tablets inscribed with cuneiform writing. Most of them are written either in Ugaritic or in Akkadian, but there are also texts in Hurrian and Hittite, as well as some multilingual texts (chiefly vocabularies) and some objects with Egyptian hieroglyphic inscriptions.[21] The texts in Ugaritic are written in alphabetic cuneiform and belong to the genres: myth, religion, letters,[22] administrative documents (lists, official acts, and documents concerning trade), and equine medical texts. There are also school exercise tablets and legal texts. However, most descriptions of life in Ugarit, such as they are, have been based on the mythological texts. A great deal can be gleaned also from the many administrative texts, but their laconic style—many are simply lists—makes for some uncertainty. The Akkadian material includes legal texts of various kinds (treaties, land transfers), administrative documents, and lists of gods and goddesses, though a few texts of this kind are also written in Ugaritic.[23]

MATERIAL REMAINS

Reports of archaeological excavations are, of course, the primary source of information, although some of the earlier reports have to be read with caution and others remain unpublished.[24] We are fortunate to have

---

[19] They were taken by Jean and Jon Davies and by Nicolas Wyatt during visits to Syria. I am deeply indebted to them for supplying me with these illustrations.

[20] Although they provide no further information on everyday life in Ugarit, tablets have also been found at Ras Ibn Hani as well as at Hala Sultan Tekke (Cyprus), Beth Shemesh, Kamid el-Loz, Mount Tabor, Sarepta, Tell Nebi Mend, Tell Soukas, and Tell Ta'anak; cf. Bordreuil and Pardee (1989) 362–82. See in general Pardee (1997).

[21] See Yon (1992b) 699b.

[22] Very few were written by ordinary people; cf. Watson (1999b) 4–9.

[23] As yet, no reasons can be found for choice of either language, although copies of Mesopotamian literary texts are only in Akkadian. Cf. van Soldt (1999); Pardee (1992).

[24] For bibliography, cf. Cunchillos (1992) 14–16, 45–57. Firsthand reports are usually published in *AAAS*, *CRAIBL*, and *Syria*.

very detailed descriptions of the palace,[25] the center of the town,[26] of the domestic architecture of the southern part of Ugarit,[27] and of a single house,[28] which are of particular significance for our topic.[29] There is also a survey of oil presses in the region.[30] Finally, a brief appraisal of iconography, including sculpture, statuettes, pendants, cylinder seals, and ivory carvings, is available.[31]

3. *The Kingdom of Ugarit*

Ugarit lies about 10 km north of Latakia. The area of the kingdom comprises the town of Ugarit, Ras Ibn Hani (ancient name unknown),[32] the harbor Maḫadu (modern Minet el Beida),[33] and the surroundings, and covers some 2000 sq km. Its borders are the Mediterranean to the west, Jebel Aqra^{c} (called Mount Sapunu in Ugaritic, height 1800 m) to the north, the Alaouite Mountains to the east, and the region of the Jableh and Nahr as-Sinn river to the south. It was a coastal town, at the intersection of caravan trade routes from Anatolia to Egypt and from Mesopotamia to the Mediterranean. The terrain is largely flat, with a few small hills.[34] The area also had forests. There are two streams, Nahr Chbayyeb and Nahr ed-Delbeh, along the north and south sides of the tell respectively.[35] The mild climate favored the growing of crops and the raising of livestock. Forests supplied wood and stone was readily available. According to recent estimates, the kingdom had about 35,000 inhabitants, with approximately 6000–8000 living in the city.[36]

---

[25] Margueron (1995).

[26] Yon ed. (1987).

[27] Callot (1994); cf. also Courtois (1979).

[28] Callot (1983).

[29] See also the account in Baldacci (1996) 121–80.

[30] Callot (1984).

[31] Cornelius (1999), with illustrations and bibliography.

[32] Possibly either *Rēšu* or *Appu*, both meaning "Cape"; cf. Astour (1995) 68.

[33] See Saadé (1995); Yon (1994; 1997b).

[34] Heltzer (1976) 2; Saadé (1978) 33–37.

[35] Yon (1992a) 23; (1997a) 255.

[36] Liverani (1982) 251–52; (1979b) 1319–20. Heltzer (1976) 103–12 suggests that 25000 people lived in the 150 or so villages. These figures have been accepted by Yon (1992a) 19 and Vita (1999) 455. The figure 7635 calculated by Garr (1987) 41–43 is probably incorrect according to Yon (1992a) 20–21 and Callot (1994) 199.

The site was inhabited intermittently from about 6500 B.C.E. to about 1600 B.C.E. and then continuously until the destruction of the town by the Sea Peoples in 1190/1185 B.C.E.[37] After that date the inhabitants were forced to leave the town and live in inland villages, as indicated by the fact that many Ugaritic village names survive in modern toponyms.[38]

The city contains many wells[39] (fig. 2), and dams had been built across the rivers Nahr Chbayyeb and Nahr ed-Delbeh, which, together with a system of canals, helped to preserve the underground water supply.[40] A bridge across the Nahr Chbayyeb led to a stone quarry and a road from the southern plain came over this bridge through the main commercial entrance and into the town.[41]

Ras Ibn Hani is 4.5 km southwest of Ugarit and 8 km north of Latakia. It is here that the kings of Ugarit built a secondary palace, called "Palais ougaritique nord" or "Petit Palais."[42] In spite of being so close to the sea it does not seem to have been used as a harbor, as was Minet el-Beida.[43] Instead, workshops for using precious stones and ivory, for producing clay objects, and for treating metals such as copper, bronze, and lead have been found.[44]

---

37 Besides squatters immediately after the destruction by the Sea Peoples, there was habitation of the site during the fifth to fourth centuries B.C.E. and traces of occupation in the first century B.C.E. (Yon [1992b] 698b–99a; Yon [1992c]).

38 Yon (1992c) 113. She also notes (119) that even though the city was pillaged, the surviving population probably fled away from the coast to live in rural villages. In fact, Caubet (1992) has shown that secondary sites along the Syrian Littoral both south and north of the Kingdom of Ugarit (notably Ras Ibn Hani and Ras Bassit) were later reoccupied.

39 Calvet and Geyer (1995).

40 Margueron (1999–2000) 398, following Calvet and Geyer (1992) 75.

41 Yon (1992a) 23; (1995).

42 Bounni (1982). According to Bounni, Lagarce, and Lagarce (1998), the palace had such luxuries as banqueting halls, bathrooms, and even toilets.

43 On these two sites, see the summary in Curtis (1999) 21–26; also Lagarce and Lagarce (1995).

44 Bounni, Lagarce, and Lagarce (1998).

Figure 2. One of the many well caps.

4. *The Town of Ugarit*[45]

The main public buildings are the two temples (to the gods Baal and Dagan)[46] and the very extensive palace[47] (figs. 3–7). Most of the city was composed of private houses closely crowded together, many of them semi-detached. There seems to have been no overall plan: streets followed the contours and were irregular, leading sometimes into tiny plazas, sometimes into dead-end alleys, and there were very few open spaces. The basic architectural unit is the "island," which was composed of dwellings, places for work, such as an oil-press, shops, and meeting places. Houses were built of stone, wooden beams, and earth or clay (pisé). Little brick or bitumen was used (figs. 8–11). Since the ground floor courtyards were dark and cramped, most activities were carried out on the next floor or on the flat roof.[48] Every house had a roof-roller to be used especially after rain.[49]

Since three-quarters of the tell have not yet been excavated, these facts are provisional only. There was ample provision for water, even for ordinary city-dwellers, in the form of wells, aqueducts, and stone reservoirs for

---

45 See, in general, Yon (1997c).

46 Identifications based on finding stelae of these gods in the vicinity. Near these temples is a small residential quarter connected with the House of the High Priest; see Yon (1992b) 702. On these see Werner (1994) 135–36.

47 Singer (1999) 629–30: "In its heyday, the palace of Ugarit, covering an area of nearly 7000 m^2 … was no doubt one of the most spectacular edifices in the Levant."

48 Yon (1992a) 27–29.

49 Elliot (1991).

Figure 3. The royal palace of Ugarit.

Figure 4. Entry into palace courtyard.

Figure 5. Palace courtyard (detail).

Figure 6. Part of the palace.

Figure 7. Palace fortifications with postern gate.

drainage cesspools[50] (figs. 12–16). One house even yielded a clepsydra or small perforated jar used to administer a shower.[51]

Ancient Ugarit was a bustling center of international trade, a seaport, and an administrative center. This means that it would have been full of people on their way to and from work, market traders selling all kinds of goods, not to mention merchants, travellers, sailors, servants, errand-boys, and, of course, those connected with the pursuit of leisure (innkeepers, prostitutes, entertainers). There was also a great deal of cultural activity connected with the temples and schools. And everywhere there would be animals: donkeys as beasts of burden, livestock, dogs, and poultry.

50 Yon (1992b) 705a; Calvet and Geyer 1987; Margueron (1999–5100) 397–98.

51 Lombard (1987).

Figure 8. Part of the residential quarter.

Figure 9. A street in the residential quarter.
The steps belong to a two-story house.

Figure 10. Houses in the residential quarter.

Figure 11. Houses in the residential quarter.

The two temples were built high above the promontory and in the best position to guide ships into harbor and also allow signals to be made to ships or to the palace at Ras Ibn Hani, which acted as a lookout post.[52]

5. *The People of Ugarit*

The inhabitants of Ugarit (or "Ugaritians") were divided into four classes.[53] The two principal classes were the royal servicemen (*bnš mlk*, lit.

---

52 Yon (1992c) 116; Frost (1991) 355.

53 It seems that the variations in tomb construction (some of which were very elaborate) reflect social stratification (Salles [1995] 175). For personal names as indicating social class or ethnic origin, see Hess (1999) 499–514.

Figure 12. Sewer.

Figures. 13 and 14. Gutters.

Figures 15 and 16. Gutters.

"people of the king") or palace employees, divided according to profession, and free citizens, for whom the term "son of Ugarit" (*mār Ugarit*) was used.[54] "This two-part division is apparent everywhere in the palace administration, which always distinguishes between guilds on the one hand and the towns and villages on the other."[55] A third category was composed of men and women who had become "servants" because of debt. "Servants formed part of a property ... and thus could be transferred and exchanged for other servants. For the state they carried out agricultural tasks on the royal farms." However, this status could be changed by

[54] Liverani (1975); Vargyas (1988). Vargyas (1988) 115–16 notes that the aristocracy was based not on noble birth but on profession.

[55] Hoftijzer and van Soldt (1998) 333.

marriage (in the case of women) or by replacing oneself with another servant.[56] Slaves were at a much lower level.[57]

From the archaeological evidence Callot[58] notes that, compared to the rest of the kingdom, the situation in the capital was somewhat artificial as it was so closely linked to the royal palace in terms of administration and economy. Furthermore, it is incorrect to divide the population of Ugarit into two classes, namely city dwellers, dependent on the palace, and country dwellers, who produced food.[59] Instead, it is true to say that the town dwellers also produced food and many houses included quarters for domestic animals. Food was not brought in from the countryside and stored in the palace as there was simply not enough storage space for large quantities. Instead, local produce was on sale in daily or weekly markets that were held in plazas in various parts of the town. More importantly, as Callot also points out,[60] citizens, irrespective of social class, produced their own food. However, all but the very rich lived on the bread line.

Besides native Ugaritians there was a considerable number of foreigners: Hurrians, Hittites, Cypriots, and Egyptians, as well as other ill-defined groups such as the *ḫapirū*.[61] Also, from the south, Tyrians, Sidonians, etc. Of these, perhaps the best integrated seems to have been the Hurrians, as shown by documents written only in Hurrian using the local (Ugaritic) alphabet, by bilingual documents (especially in connection with religion),[62] and by personal names.[63] The many loanwords in Ugaritic[64] indicate that foreigners used their own languages to some extent in daily transactions.

---

56 Vita (1999) 467.

57 Vargyas (1988). One document states that a slave could marry and have patrimony (Boyer [1955] 299); however, it is not clear whether the woman in question was a slave or, in fact, a servant. Several legal texts deal with emancipation (Márquez Rowe [1999] 401).

58 Callot (1994) 196–97.

59 This was argued by Liverani (1975), although he is probably correct in stating that the villages provided the town with a reservoir of manpower on which it drew, e.g., for the army (see section 10).

60 Callot (1994) 202.

61 See in general Vargyas (1995).

62 For a contrary view, see Sanmartín (1999–2000).

63 Vita (1999) 456–63. However, see Sanmartín (1999–2000) 123.

64 Watson (1995, 1996, 1998, 1999a).

6. *The Family*

Based on the documents, the average household was composed of four adults (husband and wife, one or two sons, and/or a daughter or daughter-in-law) plus dependents (children, elders, slaves, workmen). Occasionally brothers lived together in the same household.[65] The family was patriarchal, since lists give names under the husband's or father's name and the father was financially responsible for the family, which could be sold into slavery if debt was incurred.[66]

Marriage was a contract[67] that included a dowry, though much remains obscure and little is known of the wedding ceremony.[68] "When the groom (or his family) presented the *terḫatu* to the bride's family, she was not yet fully his wife... but instead had gained the status of *kallatu*"[69] ("fiancée"). This money remained the wife's property if the marriage did not take place or ended due to widowhood or separation.[70] Divorce (by the husband) was possible, not always because of the wife's infertility, and there may have been polygamy, especially among the rich.[71]

According to the literary texts, the duties of a model son were (1) to set up a stela; (2) to protect the ancestral grave; (3) to drive away defamers; (4) to assist one's father when inebriated; (5) to perform liturgical duty in the temple; and (6) to repair the roof and launder clothes.[72]

With regard to inheritance, the texts from Ugarit are probably modelled on Babylonian customs.[73] For example, in one document (in Akkadian) the father bequeaths one *ikû*[74] of his land to the eldest son and then divides up his house and (remaining) land between the two sons. In another, three sons are involved.[75] A woman could inherit family goods

---

65 Garr (1987) 34.

66 Rainey (1965) 12. The average price of a slave was 33 shekels (Heltzer [1999] 445).

67 Boyer (1955).

68 See Vita (1999) 475–76 for a possible scenario.

69 Vita (1999) 476.

70 Vita (1999) 476.

71 Callot (1994) 199.

72 KTU 1.17 i 25–33 and parallel passages; cf. Husser (1997); Wyatt (1998) 255–59 for this passage.

73 Davies (1993) 188–89.

74 A unit of measurement for area.

75 There are (at least) two other tablets; see Davies (1993) 188–89.

(within marriage), although in one case at least she could be passed over in favor of an adoptee.[76]

In fact, adoption in Ugarit was rather widespread,[77] and both adults and children were adopted, as sons or brothers, in the presence of the king, other authorities, or witnesses. Such adoptions were financial in nature (involving property or money) and undertaken for various reasons "such as a widow looking for financial security, the keeping of patrimony within the same family, or both at once." "Adoptions into brotherhood, perhaps by their very nature, could result in more equitable conditions between the two parties."[78]

7. *Schools and Scribes*

The scribes, many of whose names are known, probably belonged to guilds. They learned first to write Ugaritic and then other languages, particularly Akkadian and Hurrian, although ultimately their training was based on Mesopotamian culture.[79] They were bilingual and/or biscriptal[80] in Akkadian and Ugaritic. The Ugaritic scribes were largely copyists[81] and copied the mythological texts from a written original, which had been dictated.[82] Exercise tablets have been found, notably in the form of abecedaries. Schooling most probably took place in private houses since no single building identifiable as a school has been found.[83] However, the Library of the High Priest was, "in reality, a training school for scribes as well as being the main center for the preservation of the literary texts."[84] "Scribes usually studied in one 'school' only," although they could go to other teachers. Teachers were also peripatetic, but there is not enough evidence for more detailed conclusions.[85] Within the scribal guilds there

---

76 Vita (1999) 481; as he says, "the position of the woman as heiress of the paternal goods is not so clear, although it can be supposed that ... she could be named as heiress by her father."

77 Boyer (1955) 302–4.

78 Vita (1999) 479–80; Rainey (1965) 15–16.

79 For an amusing exercise letter, see Pardee (1992) 712, on KTU 5.10.

80 To use van Soldt's term (1995a) 186.

81 Horwitz (1979) 391 n. 10.

82 Horwitz (1974) 77, n. 6.

83 Yon (1992b) 705b.

84 Rainey (1969) 127.

85 Van Soldt (1995a) 181.

was a hierarchy and the sons of scribes usually followed the professions of their fathers and after their schooling ended up working in administration.[86] A scribe could be a public notary, a keeper of records, or a secretary, and could also plead on someone's behalf.[87] The *md* or "expert," was a street scribe and mathematician.[88]

8. *Crafts and Trade*

In the city of Ugarit many crafts were practiced and the craftsmen were organized into guilds.[89] Metals such as gold, tin, silver, bronze, and copper were imported, worked by skilled craftsmen, and then exported. Gems and precious stones were also carved. The manufacture of textiles and dyeing was a major industry.[90] Installations for treating textiles have been found[91] and fullers (*kbs/ś*) and weavers (*mḫṣ*) were employed, although the working of textiles was also a cottage industry. Heaps of murex shells, used in huge quantities for the expensive process of producing purple dye, were found at Minet el-Beida.[92] The widespread presence of pottery of all kinds indicates that there were potters (*yṣr*, Akk. *yaṣiruma* and *paḫḫaru*), although no workshop has yet been found.[93] Weapons of many kinds were produced: bows, arrowheads and arrows, lances, javelins, and, of course, war chariots. Tanners prepared leather used in the equipment for horses and chariots as well as for making quivers and cuirasses.[94] Craftsmen (*ḥrṣ*) built houses, carts, wagons, and chariots, boats and ships, as well as equipment such as oars, masts, and ropes.[95] Other professionals were employed by the palace, including fowlers, tailors, acrobats, jesters, seal-cutters, singers, cymbalists, cooks, and barbers.

---

[86] Van Soldt (1995a) 180–82.

[87] Rainey (1969) 139–43.

[88] Sanmartín (1989) 337–41.

[89] For a more detailed description, see Vita (1999) 484–92.

[90] Heltzer (1999) 446–47; van Soldt (1990).

[91] Callot (1994) 190.

[92] However, this tradition probably originated in Crete, before 1750 B.C.E. (Stieglitz [1994]).

[93] Callot (1994) 189. One may have been found near Minet el-Beida; cf. Curtis (1999) 21.

[94] Vita (1995) 78; (1999) 491.

[95] See, in general, Sanmartín (1995).

Due to its excellent connections by sea and overland, trade at Ugarit was very important.[96] Trading was both by barter and currency exchange[97] and was the prerogative of the *tamkārs* (Ug. *mkrm*, Akk. *tamkāru*), "who were the royal commercial agents of Ugarit and its neighboring countries, although they sometimes managed their own commercial operations, too."[98] For this purpose the weights and measures used were adapted to the country of the particular trading partner[99]—it is not clear which system was used internally. Prices are known for such commodities as wheat, barley, olive oil, wine, honey, dried figs, raisins, and cheese, as well as for cattle, donkeys, mules, textiles, and even slaves. The commercial value of metals (gold, silver, tin, copper, and bronze) can be determined, but the prices of some manufactured objects, such as cups and alabaster vessels, remain unknown.[100] Other items of trade included luxury goods such as herbs, spices, and ointments.

9. *Farming and Agriculture*

The term for an estate or royal farm[101] is *gt*, literally "fief."[102] "However, agriculture and animal husbandry are also fully part of life in the most urbanized center of the kingdom, the capital Ugarit, as is evident from finds ... of silos for cereal, sickles, and installations for making oil and keeping animals."[103] "The Ugaritic consonantal texts do not provide detailed information on the breeding, herding and keeping of ovine herds. Simple references to the personnel in charge are given, as well as to the number of such animals that a family could own and the market price they could fetch."[104] Shepherds (*r*ᶜ*ym*), who could have an assistant who kept

---

[96] See Cornelius (1981). "Ugarit... had trade relations with all the major cities and states of the ancient Near East, viz. Alalakh, Aleppo, Carchemish, Emar, Kadesh, Tyre, Byblos, Amurru, Babylonia, Assyria, Egypt, Anatolia, Alashiya, Crete and Palestine" (p. 26).

[97] Stieglitz (1979) 15.

[98] Heltzer (1999) 440.

[99] Heltzer (1999) 448.

[100] Heltzer (1999) 446–48.

[101] On which see Liverani (1979a).

[102] Michaux-Colombot (1997); Heltzer (1999) 425–27; DLU, 152b–53a. The equivalent in Akk. is *dimtu*, "tower."

[103] Vita (1999) 484, following Callot (1994) 190–96, 201–2.

[104] Del Olmo Lete (1993) 191.

watch (*śǵr*), were fundamental to an economy that was based on farming.[105] Other professions connected with farming were the *nqd*, "herdsman" and the *gzz*, "shearer." "An individual could possess small flocks of seven, eight or ten sheep up to middle size ones of some thirty or sixty head. The Ugaritic texts reflect in this way a modest peasant society and give in general a very credible image of the organization and standard level of the agricultural economy."[106] The animals in question were *ṣin* "sheep and goats," *ṯat* "ewe," *imr* "lamb," *kr* "lamb," *ᶜgl dt šnt* "yearling calf," *llu* "sucking (lamb or kid)," and *š*, "ram." The *mru*, a fattened animal, was evidently reared for food. Apart from meat and offal, animal products included milk (chiefly from goats) and butter (*ḫmat*). Also, wool and items such as hair, hide, and horns were used for clothing, tools, and weapons. A head of cattle was worth 1 or 1½ silver shekels, cheaper than in surrounding markets.[107] There seems to have been a tax on grazing (*maqqadu*).[108] Tools listed include: sickle (*ḫrmṯt*), adze (*nit*), pick (*krk*), scythe (*mᶜṣd*), and hammer (*mqb*).[109] The two most important products were wine, consumed locally or exported, and olive oil, used for consumption, lamps, and perfumes. Oil presses in the form of tables with a groove have been found.[110] Many of the city's inhabitants had land that they farmed. Grain, the staple food, was made into flour (*pḫd*) or stored in silos and, of course, exported.[111] Much of the food was used by the palace and some, of course, by the temple. Salt, from coastal salt-pans, was another export.[112]

10. *Army and Navy*

The considerable army was composed of regular soldiers, conscripts as need arose, and quite probably mercenaries. Estimates on the numbers of men involved vary.[113] The term *ḫrd*, Akk. *ḫurādu*, "seems to designate the

---

[105] See del Olmo Lete (1993) 191.

[106] Del Olmo Lete (1993) 193

[107] Heltzer (1978) 21–86, 100, 112; del Olmo Lete (1993) 193.

[108] Márquez Rowe (1995).

[109] Sanmartín (1987).

[110] Callot (1994) 191–96.

[111] Vita (1999) 491.

[112] Drower (1975) 5.

[113] The figures given by Vita (1999) 493, based to some extent on Heltzer (1982), indicate about 5000.

groups of soldiers or civilians... that were recruited from the villages and socio-professional categories, and that performed military as well as civil services for the king."[114] Citizens, including foreigners (KTU 3.7 lists Egyptians) were obliged to perform *ilku*-service (Ug. *unṯ*), either as professionals ("guards") or as members of a village. Possibly the *ilku*-service was military conscription; e.g., KTU 4.63 lists two recruits, one equipped with "a bow and shield," the other only with a bow.[115] Archers served both in war chariots and as light infantry and could carry lances and swords. Reference to cuirasses and helmets suggests heavy infantry as well and there may have been cavalry. More elite, perhaps, were the "royal guard" and the "king's lancers."[116] There was no dedicated navy, but ships (probably commandeered) could be used for military purposes such as troop transportation and engagements at sea.[117]

11. *The Calendar*

At Ugarit a lunar calendar was followed and nearly all the month names and their sequence are known:[118]

	Alphabetic Ugaritic	*Syllabic spelling*	*Modern equivalent*	*Meaning: "the month of ..."*
1	*riš yn*	[unknown]	Sept./Oct.	first wine
2	*nql*	[unknown]	Oct./Nov.	cultivation (?) / the sickle (?)
3	*mgmr*	*magmaru*	Nov./Dec.	[unknown]
4	*pgrm*	*pagrūma*	Dec./Jan.	the dead/ funeral offerings

114 Márquez Rowe *apud* van Soldt (1995b) 486.

115 Márquez Rowe (1993).

116 Vita (1999) 494–95.

117 Vita (1999) 497–98. For illustrations of such ships, see Wachsmann (1998) 49–50.

118 Where known, the syllabic spelling is given in brackets. The meanings are largely conjectural: *ḫyr* may mean "donkey," cf. Cohen, M. (1993) 374–75, hence perhaps "Donkey Festival" or it may be a Hurrian word. "Ashtabi" is a Hurrian deity.

5	*ibᶜlt*	*ʾibᶜalatu*	Jan./Feb.	ritual acts (?)
6	*ḫyr*	*ḫiyāru*	Feb./Mar.	the dead / the donkey
7	*ḥlt*	*ḥalatu*	Mar./Apr.	the phoenix (?)
8	*gn*	*gūnu*	Apr./May	the garden
9	*iṯb*	*išibu*	May/June	Ashtabi
10	*dbḥn*	[*dubuḥana*]	June/July	sacrifice
11	[unknown]	[unknown]	July/Aug.	[unknown]
12	*iṯṯbnm*	[unknown]	Aug./Sep.	Ashtabi (?); cf. month 9

Some of these names were also used in neighboring countries and at other periods, but this calendar is specifically Ugaritic.[119] The liturgical calendar is indicated by some religious texts and the seven-day week was used along with other divisions of time.[120] One text at least is astrological,[121] and an almanac, modelled on Babylonian texts, has been found listing favorable and unfavorable days for various activities.[122]

12. *Religion in Everyday Life*

There were four temples in Ugarit: besides the temples of Baal and Dagan on the acropolis (figs. 17–18), there was the Hurrian temple (in the palace complex) and the Temple of the Rhytons.[123] The cult personnel included priests (*khnm*), under one or more High Priests (*rb khnm*), who belonged to an association (*dr khnm*, "circle of priests") and who could own land (*šd*).[124]

---

119 Olivier (1971); (1972); de Jong and van Soldt (1987–88) 70–71; Arnaud (1993); Cohen, M. (1993) 377–83; Vita (1998) 50–52; Stieglitz (1999).

120 Details in del Olmo Lete (1999) 24–27; cf. also del Olmo Lete and Sanmartín (1998) 186–92.

121 KTU 1.78, which may refer to an eclipse. For a survey, see Wyatt (1998) 366–67.

122 Arnaud (1993).

123 Yon (1996). The "Temple of the Rhytons," which may have been dedicated to El, was found in a residential area and may be a sanctuary rather than a temple; cf. de Tarragon (1995); Mallet (1987); Werner (1994) 89–90.

124 Del Olmo Lete and Sanmartín (1998) 177; see also Lipiński (1988).

There were also consecrated or holy men (*qdšm*) who performed various duties in the cult,[125] singers (*šrm*), and "water-drawers of the sanctuary" (*šib mqdš*), as well as unskilled workmen (*bᶜlm*).

The ordinary people must have seen the public spectacle of religious rituals and ceremonies and to some extent may have taken part in them, though little is known. Just as little is known about popular religion,[126] although the incantation against the evil eye[127] and a single (public) prayer (KTU 1.119: 26–34) provide some indications. Votive gifts of anchors have been found (fig. 19), presumably from sailors or their families grateful for a safe return.[128] Popular religion is also apparent from letters,[129] although perhaps the closest we can come to personal piety is in the proper names.[130] The fact that tombs were built under many (but by no means all)[131] of the houses may indicate an ancestor cult (see 15).[132]

13. *Medicine and Magic*

Little is known about medical practice. KTU 1.114 may be a cure for a hangover. Apotropaic magic features in KTU 1.124[133] and in the cure for Keret (KTU 1.16 v 23–34). The omens based on deformed births (KTU 1.103+1.145; KTU 1.140) and the models of livers and lungs (cf. also KTU 1.78) evidently owe much to Babylonian tradition.[134] Even so, they do indicate some interest in and perhaps knowledge of anatomy. The hippiatric texts (KTU 1.71; KTU 1.72; KTU 1.85; KTU 1.97) describe specific symptoms of horses, for which remedies are prescribed, e.g., grain and bitter almond pulverized together, to be inserted into the nostrils. It is

---

125 Including "sacrifice, divination and singing" Dijkstra (1999–2000).

126 If one can speak of popular *versus* official religion; cf. Xella (1999).

127 Ford (1998), with further references.

128 More than half of the 43 anchors found at Ugarit and Minet el-Beida were in or near the Temple of Baal, the weather-god; cf. Frost (1991); Wyatt (1999) 583; Wachsmann (1998) 273.

129 Cunchillos-Ilarri (1989) 193–234.

130 Ribichini and Xella (1991).

131 Salles (1995) 175.

132 Vita (1999) 482–83.

133 Del Olmo Lete (1999) 313–14.

134 See generally Dietrich and Loretz (1990); del Olmo Lete (1999).

significant that no magic occurs in these texts.[135] On the other hand, the incantations against snakebite (KTU 1.82,[136] KTU 1.100 and KTU 1.107) contain no medical prescriptions. In KTU 1.107 it would seem that an apprentice snake-charmer is bitten by a snake and the gods are asked for a cure.[137] Other incantations involve necromancy[138] or at least invocation of the dead.[139]

14. *Music and Entertainment*

The musicians were singers and players and, of course, sometimes the player accompanied him/herself (e.g., in KTU 1.101: 18–22 || KTU 1.3).[140] There is a reference to a "chorister with a lovely voice," singers and songstresses (*šr, šrt*), and guilds of singers. There was a wide range of musical instruments, including cymbals (*mṣltm*), a hand-drum (*tp*), a reed instrument (*ṯlb*), perhaps a type of flute, clappers or castanets (*mrqdm*),[141] a lyre (*knr*), and a bull-headed lyre (*rimt*).[142] It is possible that these musical instruments were used for accompaniment since they co-occur with verbs for "sing" (*bd, šr*).[143] One of the most interesting finds was a tablet with a Hurrian musical score, which has been the subject of much discussion. In fact it would seem that the Hurrians had particular expertise in music as most of the syllabic texts in Hurrian concern music and Hurrian singers were known at Mari and Hattuša.[144]

Apart from hunting and fishing, which, besides being necessary, were also sports, there is no doubt that people played simple games, using counters and small gaming pieces, several of which have been found. One house in the southern residential zone may even have been a tavern.[145] Jesters, acrobats, and, no doubt, dancers were employed by the palace.

---

135 Cohen, C. H. (1996).

136 Del Olmo Lete (1999) 373–79.

137 Wyatt (1998) 391–94.

138 Tropper (1989).

139 Spronk (1999) 282–84.

140 Cf. Wyatt (1998) 390.

141 Clappers or castanets have been found at Ugarit; see Caubet (1999) 15–16.

142 Or perhaps the sound-box of a lyre.

143 Koitabashi (1998) 376–77.

144 Salvini (1995) 94–96.

145 Callot (1994) 198.

Figure 17. Temple of Dagan.

Figure 18. Temple of Baal.

Figure 19. Composite sea-anchor.

15. *Death and Burial*

Family tombs were usually located underneath houses or courtyards and had vaulted ceilings[146] (figs. 20–21). "A staircase would lead down into the funerary vault, which was paved and whose walls contained niches or 'windows'."[147] Most tombs had been robbed before modern excavators examined them. But some contained furniture and other items, presumably provisions for the dead (indicating belief in an afterlife)[148] (fig. 22), and so far one coffin has been found.[149] However, "contrary to a widely held opinion, there are no archaeological traces of a regular cult of the dead in a domestic context."[150] In addition, "it is likely that most common people were buried in still undiscovered cemeteries outside the city."[151] Evidence for mourning rituals comes only from the literary texts.[152] Inscribed stelae were sometimes erected to commemorate the dead.

16. *Future Discoveries*

There are many details of ordinary life that remain unknown or uncertain. For example, the names of stars or constellations or the names of the days of the week. As in Phoenicia, there appear to have been no written laws or law codes,[153] unlike the traditions of Anatolia (the Hittites) and Mesopotamia. Further excavation and the publication of finds will surely provide new information,[154] but because so much must have been written on

---

[146] The architecture of these tombs is not Mycenaean, as supposed by Shaeffer (1939) 67–68, 92, but local (Salles [1995] 173; Caubet and Matoian [1995] 101–2).

[147] Curtis (1999) 17.

[148] Curtis (1999) 17. There is no archaeological evidence that libations were made to the dead, as Virolleaud, the first excavator of Ras Shamra, had proposed; see Pitard (1994); Salles (1995) 180–81.

[149] Margueron (1977) and plates VII and X (with photograph of the sarcophagus).

[150] Van der Toorn (1996) 161.

[151] Spronk (1986) 142.

[152] KTU 1.6 i 2–8; KTU 1.15 vi 11–25; etc.; see, in general, Salles (1995).

[153] However, there is case law; for maritime law at Ugarit, see Wachsmann (1998) 323–25.

[154] Additional tablets are found almost every year, for example 66 in Ugaritic and 234 in Akkadian in 1994, according to Malbran-Labat (1995) 103, all unpublished. A descriptive catalogue of 113 texts found in the "House of Urtenu" since 1971 is provided by Bordreuil and Pardee (1999–2000).

Figures. 20 and 21. Tombs under houses.

perishable material[155] and because the site was plundered even in antiquity, there will always be data that can never be recovered.

Figure 22. Family vault.

[155] See e.g., Millard (1995).

Bibliography

Aboud, J. (1994) *Die Rolle des Königs und seiner Familie nach den Texten von Ugarit.* Forschungen zur Anthropologie und Religionsgeschichte 27. Münster. **Arnaud, D.** (1993) Jours et mois d'Ougarit. *Studi Micenei ed Egeo-anatolici* 32: 123–29. **Astour, M.C.** (1995) La topographie du royaume d'Ugarit. In RSO 11: 55–71. **Baldacci, M.** (1996) *La scoperta di Ugarit. La città-stato ai primordi della Bibbia.* Casale Monferrato. **Bordreuil, P. and D. Pardee** (1989) *La Trouvaille épigraphique de l'Ougarit.* RSO 5. Paris. (1999–2000) Catalogue raisonné des textes ougaritiques de la Maison d'Ourtenu. *Aula Orientalis* 17–18: 23–38. **Bounni, A.** (1982) Un deuxième palais ougaritique à Ras Ibn Hani. *La Syrie au bronze récent.* Paris, 23–27. **Bounni, A., É. Lagarce, and J. Lagarce** (1998) *Ras Ibn Hani, I. Le palais Nord du Bronze Recent. Fouilles 1979–1995, synthèse préliminaire.* Bibliothèque Archéologique et Historique 151. Beirut Damascus Amman. **Boyer, G.** (1955) Étude juridique. In J. Nougayrol, *Palais royal d'Ugarit. Textes accadiens et hourrites des archives est, ouest et centrales.* Mission de Ras Shamra 6, 281–308. Paris. **Burns, R.** (1992) *Monuments of Syria. An Historical Guide.* London and New York. **Callot, O.** (1983) *Une maison à Ougarit. Etudes d'architecture domestique.* RSO 1. Paris. (1984) *Huileries antiques de Syrie du Nord.* Bibliothèque archéologique et historique 118. Paris. (1994) *La tranchée «Ville Sud». Études d'architecture domestique.* RSO 10. Paris. **Calvet, Y. and B. Geyer** (1987) L'eau dans l'habitat. In RSO 3, 129–56. (1992) *Barrages antiques de Syrie.* Lyons. (1995) Environnement et ressources en eau dans la région d'Ougarit. In RSO 11: 169–82. **Caubet, A.** (1992) Reoccupation of the Syrian Coast after the Destruction of the "Crisis Years." In W.A. Ward and M.S. Joukowsky, eds., *The Crisis Years: The 12th Century* B.C. *From Beyond the Danube to the Tigris,* 123–31. Dubuque, Iowa. (1999) Chantres et devins: deux cas de pratiques de la musique à Ougarit. In M. Kropp and A. Wagner, eds., *'Schnittpunkt' Ugarit.* Nordostafrikanisch/ Westasiatische Studien 2, 9–30. Frankfurt am Main. **Caubet, A. and V. Matoian** (1995) Ougarit et l'Égée. In RSO 11: 99–112. **Cohen, C.H.** (1996) The Ugaritic Hippiatric Texts. Revised Composite Text, Translation and Commentary. *UF* 28: 101–54. **Cohen, M.** (1993) *Cultic Calendars of the Ancient Near East.* Bethesda, Md. **Cornelius, I.** (1981) A Bird's Eye View of Trade in Ancient Ugarit. *Journal of Northwest Semitic Languages and Literatures* 9: 13–31. (1999) The Iconography of Ugarit. In HUS: 586–602. **Courtois, J. C.** (1979) L'architecture domestique à Ugarit au Bronze Récent. *Ugarit-Forschungen* 11: 105–34. **Courtois, J.C. *et al.*** (1979) Ras Shamra. *Dictionnaire de la Bible Supplément* 9, Paris, cols. 1124–1466. **Craigie, P. C.** (1983) *Ugarit and the Old Testament.* Grand Rapids, Mich. **Cunchillos, J-L.** (1992) *Manual de estudios ugaríticos.* Madrid. **Cunchillos-Ilarri, J.-L.** (1989) *Estudios de epistolografía ugarítica.* Institución San Jerónimo para la investigación bíblica. Fuentes de la ciencia bíblica 3. Valencia. **Curtis, A.** (1985) *Ugarit (Ras Shamra).* Cities of the Biblical World. Cambridge. (1999) Ras Shamra, Minet el-Beida and Ras Ibn Hani: The Material Sources. In HUS: 5–27. **Davies, E.W.** (1993) The Inheritance of the First-born in Israel and the Ancient Near East. *Journal of Semitic Studies* 38: 175–91. **Dietrich, M. and O. Loretz**

(1990) *Mantik in Ugarit*. Abhandlungen zur Literatur Alt-Syrien-Palästinas und Mesopotamiens 3. Münster. **Dijkstra, M.** (1999–2000) The List of *qdšm* in KTU 4.412+ ii 8ff. *Aula Orientalis* 17–18: 81–89. **Drower, M.S.** (1975) Ugarit. In I.E.S. Edwards, C.J. Gadd and N.G.L. Hamond, eds., *The Cambridge Ancient History* 2/2, 130–60. Cambridge. **Elliot, C.** (1991) Ground Stone Industry. In RSO 6: 9–100. **Ford, J.N.** (1998) "Ninety-Nine by the Evil Eye and One from Natural Causes": KTU^2 1.96 in Its Near Eastern Context. *Ugarit-Forschungen* 30: 200–78. **Frost, H.** (1991) Anchors Sacred and Profane. Ugarit-Ras Shamra, 1986; the stone anchors revised and compared. In RSO 6: 355–410. **Garr, W.R.** (1987) A Population Estimate of Ancient Ugarit. *Bulletin of the American Schools of Oriental Research* 266: 31–43. **Heltzer, M.** (1976) *The Rural Community in Ancient Ugarit*. Wiesbaden. (1978) *Goods, Prices and the Organization of Trade in Ugarit* Wiesbaden. (1982) *The Internal Organization of the Kingdom of Ugarit*. Wiesbaden. (1990) Vineyards and Wine in Ugarit (Property and Distribution). *Ugarit-Forschungen* 22: 119–36. (1999) The Economy of Ugarit. In HUS: 423–54. **Hess, R.** (1999) The Onomastics of Ugarit. In HUS: 499–528. **Hoftijzer, J. and W.H. van Soldt** (1998) Texts from Ugarit Pertaining to Seafaring. In S. Wachsmann, *Seagoing Ships and Seamanship in the Bronze Age Levant*. College Station and London, 333–44. **Horwitz, W.J.** (1974) Some Possible Results of Rudimentary Scribal Training. *Ugarit-Forschungen* 6: 75–80. (1979) The Ugaritic Scribe. *Ugarit-Forschungen* 11: 389–94. **Husser, J.M.** (1997) Shapash psychopompe et le pseudo hymne au soleil (KTU 1.6 vi 42–53). *Ugarit-Forschungen* 29: 227–44. **de Jong, T. and W.H. van Soldt** (1987–88) Redating an Early Solar Eclipse Record (KTU 1.78) Implications for the Ugaritic Calendar and for the Secular Accelerations of the Earth and Moon. *Jaarbericht Ex Oriente Lux* 30: 65–77. **Koitabashi, M.** (1998) Music in the Texts from Ugarit. *Ugarit-Forschungen* 30: 363–96. **Korpel, M.C.A.** (1990) *A Rift in the Clouds. Ugaritic and Hebrew Descriptions of the Divine*. Münster. **Lagarce, J. and E. Lagarce** (1995) Ras Ibn Hani au Bronze Récent. Recherches et réflexions en cours. In RSO 11: 141–54. **Lipiński, E.** (1988) The Socio-Economic Condition of the Clergy in the Kingdom of Ugarit. In M. Heltzer, and E. Lipiński, eds., *Society and Economy in the Eastern Mediterranean (c. 1500–1000 B.C.). Proceedings of the International Symposium Held at the University of Haifa from the 28th of April to the 2nd of May 1985*. Orientalia Lovaniensia Analecta 23: 125–50. Leuven. **Liverani, M.** (1975) Communautés de village et palais royal dans la Syrie du IIème millénaire, *Journal of the Social and Economic History of the Orient* 18: 146–64. (1979a) Economia delle fattorie palatine ugaritiche. *Dialoghi di archeologia* NS 1: 57–72. (1979b) Ras Shamra, histoire, DBS 9: 1323–48. (1982) Ville et campagne dans le royaume d'Ugarit. Essai d'analyse économique. In Dandamayev, M.A. *et al.* eds., *Societies and Languages of the Ancient Near East. Studies in Honour of I. M. Diakonoff.* 250–58. Warminster. **Lombard, P.** (1987) Pneumatique d'Ougarit. Note sur une «clepsydre» du Bronze récent. In RSO 3, 351–56. **Malbran-Labat, F.** (1995) La découverte épigraphique de 1994 à Ougarit (les textes akkadiens). *Studi Micenei ed Egeo-Anatolici* 36: 103–11. **Mallet, J.** (1987) Le temple aux rhytons. In RSO 3, 213–48. **Margueron, J.-C.** (1977) Ras Shamra 1975 et 1976. Rapport préliminaire sur les campagnes d'autonne. *Syria* 54: 177–78. (1995) Le palais royal d'Ougarit. Premiers résultats d'une analyse systématique. In RSO 11: 183–202. (1999–2000) Égouts pour les eaux usées ou conduites de recuperation des eaux de pluie? *Aula Orientalis* 17–18: 393–405. **Márquez Rowe, I.** (1993) KTU 3.7 reconsidered. On the *ilku*-Service in Ugarit. *Aula Orientalis* 11: 250–52. (1995) More Evidence of the Grazing Tax in Ugarit. *Ugarit-Forschungen* 27: 317–31. (1997–98) Review of *El ejército de Ugarit* by J.-P. Vita. *Archiv für Orientforschung* 44–45: 369–76. (1999) The Legal Texts from Ugarit. In HUS: 309–422. **Michaux-Colombot, D.** (1997) Le *gat* de Gédéon, pressoir ou fief?. *Ugarit-Forschungen* 27: 579–89. **Millard, A.R.** (1995) The Last Tablets of Ugarit. In RSO 11: 119–24. **Olivier, J.P.L.** (1971) Notes on the Ugaritic Month Names. *Journal of Northwest Semitic Languages* 1: 39–45. (1972) Notes on the Ugaritic Month Names II. *Journal of Northwest Semitic Languages* 2: 53–59. **del Olmo Lete, G.** (1993) Sheep and Goats at Ugarit: Alphabetic Texts. *BSA* 7: 183–97. (1999) *Canaanite Religion according to the Liturgical Texts of Ugarit*. Translated by W.G.E. Watson. Bethesda Md. **del Olmo Lete, G. and J. Sanmartín** (1998) Kultisches in den keilalphabetischen Verwaltungs- und Wirtschaftstexten aus Ugarit. In M. Dietrich, and I. Kottsieper, eds., *"Und Mose schrieb dieses Lied auf." Studien zum Alten Testament and zum Alten Orient. Festschrift für Oswald Loretz zur Vollendung seines 70. Lebensjahres mit Beiträgen von Freunden, Schülern und Kollegen* (AOAT 250). 175–97. **Pardee, D.** (1992) Ugarit: Texts and Literature. *Anchor Bible Dictionary* 6: 706–21. (1997) Ugarit Inscriptions. In E.M. Meyers, ed., *The Oxford Encyclopaedia of Archaeology in the Near East* 5: 264–66. Oxford. **Pitard, W.** (1994) The 'Libation' Installations of the Tombs at Ugarit. *Biblical Archaeologist* 57: 20–37. **Rainey, A.F.** (1965) Family Relationships in Ugarit. *Orientalia* 34: 10–22 (1969) The Scribe at Ugarit. His Position and Influence, PIASH 3: 126–47. (1975) Institutions: Family, Civil and Military, RSP 2: 69–107. **Ribichini, S. and P. Xella** (1991) Problemi di onomastica ugaritica: il caso dei teofori. *Studi epigrafici sul Vicino Oriente antico* 8: 149–70. **Saadé, G.** (1978) *Ougarit. Métropole cananénne.* Beirut. (1995) Le port d'Ougarit. In RSO 11: 211–25. **Salles, J.-F.** (1995) Rituel mortuaire et rituel social à Ras Shamra/Ougarit. In S. Campbell and A. Green, eds., *The Archaeology of Death in the Ancient Near East*, 171–84. Oxford. **Salvini, M.** (1995) Ougarit et les Hourrites. In RSO 11: 89–97. **Sanmartín, J.** (1987) Herramientas agrícolas y burocracia en Ugarit. *Aula Orientalis* 5: 149–52. (1989) Glossen zum ugaritischen Lexikon (VI). *Ugarit-Forschungen* 21: 335–48. (1995) Das Handwerk in Ugarit. *Studi epigrafici e linguistici sul Vicino Oriente antico* 12: 169–90. (1999–2000) Sociedades y lenguas en el medio sirio-levantino del II milenio a.C.: Ugarit y lo hurrita. *Aula Orientalis* 17–18: 113–23. **Schloen, J. D.** (2001) *The House of the Father as Fact and Symbol. Patrimonialism in Ugarit and the Ancient Near East.* Studies in the Archaeology and History of the Levant 2. Winona Lake, Ind. **van Selms, A.** (1954) *Marriage & Family Life in Ugaritic Literature.* Pretoria Oriental Series 1. London. **van Soldt, W.H.** (1990) Fabrics and Dyes at Ugarit. *Ugarit-Forschungen* 22: 321–57. (1995a) Babylonian Lexical, Religious and Literary Texts and Scribal Education at Ugarit and Its Implications for the Alphabetic Literary Texts. In Dietrich, M. and Loretz, O., eds.,

Ugarit. Ein ostmediterranes Kulturzentrum im Alten Orient. Ergebnisse und Perspektiven der Forschung. Band I. Ugarit und seine altorientalische Umwelt. Abhandlungen zur Literatur Alt-Syriens Palstina 7. Münster, 171–212. (1995b) KTU 4.784:2. *Ugarit-Forschungen* 27: 485–86. (1995c) Ugarit: A Second Millennium Kingdom on the Mediterranean Coast. In J. M. Sasson, ed., *Civilizations of the Ancient Near East*, 2: 1255–66. New York. (1999) The Syllabic Akkadian Texts. In HUS: 28–45. **Spronk, K.** (1986) *Beatific Afterlife in Ancient Israel, and in the Ancient Near East.* Alter Orient und Altes Testament 219. Kevelaer and Neukirchen-Vluyn. (1999) The Incantations. In HUS: 270–86. **Stieglitz, R.R.** (1979) Commodity Prices in Ugarit. *Journal of the American Oriental Society* 99: 15–23. (1994) The Minoan Origin of Tyrian Purple. *Biblical Archeologist* 57: 46–54. (1999) The Phoenician-Punic Menology. In M. Lubetski, C. Gottlieb and S. Keller, eds., *Boundaries of the Ancient Near Eastern World. A Tribute to Cyrus H. Gordon.* Journal for the Study of the Old Testament Supplement Series 273: 211–21. Sheffield. **de Tarragon, J.-M.** (1995) Temples et pratiques rituelles. In RSO 11: 203–10. **van der Toorn, K.** (1996) *Family Religion in Babylonia, Syria and Israel. Continuity and Change in the Forms of Religious Life.* Studies in the History and Culture of the Ancient Near East 7. Leiden. **Tropper, J.** (1989) *Nekromantie, Totenbefragung im Alten Orient und im Alten Testament.* Alter Orient und Altes Testament 223. Kevelaer and Neukirchen-Vluyn. **Vargyas, P.** (1988) Stratification sociale à Ugarit. In M. Heltzer and E. Lipiński, eds., *Society and Economy in the Eastern Mediterranean (c. 1500–1000 B.C.).* Orientalia Lovaniensia Analecta 23, 111–23. Leuven, 111–23 (1995) Immigration into Ugarit. In K. van Lerberghe and A. Schoords, eds., *Immigration and Emigration with the Ancient Near East. Festschrift E. Lipinski.* Orientalia Lovaniensia Analecta 65: 395–402. Leuven. **Vita, J.-P.** (1995) *El ejército de Ugarit.* Banco de Datos Filológicos Noroccidentales, Monografías 1. Madrid. (1998) Datation et genres littéraires à Ougarit. In F. Briquel-Chatonnet and H. Lozachmeur, eds., *Proche-orient ancien temps vécu, temps pensé: Actes de la Table-Ronde du 15 novembre 1997 organisée par l'URA 1062 'Etudes Sémitiques'.* Antiquités sémitiques 3: 39–52. Paris. (1999) The Society of Ugarit. In HUS: 455–98. **Wachsmann, S.** (1998) *Seagoing Ships & Seamanship in the Bronze Age Levant.* College Station and London. **Watson, W.G.E.** (1995) Non-Semitic Words in the Ugaritic Lexicon. *Ugarit-Forschungen* 27: 533–58. (1996) Non-Semitic Words in the Ugaritic Lexicon (2). *Ugarit-Forschungen* 28: 701–19. (1998) Non-Semitic Words in the Ugaritic Lexicon (3). *Ugarit-Forschungen* 30: 751–60. (1999a) Non-Semitic Words in the Ugaritic Lexicon (4). *Ugarit-Forschungen* 31: 785–99. (1999b) "Message" in Myth and Missive: Ugaritic *tḥm*. *Journal of Northwest Semitic Languages* 25/2: 1–16. **Werner, P.** (1994) *Die Entwicklung der Sakralarchitektur in Nordsyrien und Südotkleinasien vom Neolithikum bis in das 1. Jt. v. Chr.* Münchener Universitäts-Schriften Philosophische Fakultät 12 / Münchener Vorderasiatische Studien 15. Vienna. **Wyatt, N.** (1998) *Religious Texts from Ugarit. The Words of Ilimilku and His Colleagues.* The Biblical Seminar 53. Sheffield. (1999) The Religion of Ugarit: An Overview. In HUS: 529–85. **Xella, P.** (1999) Die ugaritische Religion: Methodologische und kulturhistorische Betrachtungen. In M. Kropp and A. Wagner, eds., *'Schnittpunkt' Ugarit.* Nordostafrikanisch/Westasiatische Studien 2: 285–302. Frankfurt am Main. **Yon, M.** (1992a) Ugarit: The Urban Habitat, The Present State of the Archaeological Picture. *Bulletin of the American Schools of Oriental Research* 286: 19–34. (1992b) Ugarit. *Anchor Bible Dictionary* 6: 695–706. (1992c) The End of the Kingdom of Ugarit. In W.A. Ward and M.S. Joukowsky, eds., *The Crisis Years: The 12th Century B.C. From Beyond the Danube to the Tigris*, 111–22. Dubuque, Iowa. (1994) Minet el-Beida. In RLA 8: 213–15. (1995) La maison d'Ourtenu dans le Quartier Sud d'Ougarit (Fouilles 1994). *CRAIBL* 428–33. (1996) The Temple of the Rhytons at Ugarit. In N. Wyatt, W.G.E. Watson and J.B. Lloyd, eds., *Ugarit, Religion and Culture. Proceedings of the International Colloquium on Ugarit, Religion and Culture Edinburgh, July 1994. Essays Presented in Honour of Professor John C. L. Gibson*. Ugaritisch-biblische Literatur 12, 405–22. Münster. (1997a) Ugarit. In E.M. Meyers, ed., *The Oxford Encyclopaedia of Archaeology in the Near East* IV, 255–62. Oxford. (1997b) Ougarit et la port de Mahadou/Minet el-Beida. In S. Swiny *et al.*, eds., *Res Maritimae*. Cyprus and the Eastern Mediterranean from Prehistory to Late Antiquity. 357–69. Atlanta. (1997c) *La cité d'Ougarit sur le tell de Ras Shamra*. Paris. (Forthcoming) *The Royal City of Ugarit on the Tell of Ras Shamra*. Winona Lake, Ind. (= ET of 1997). **Zamora, J.-A.** (2000) *La vid y el vino en Ugarit*. Madrid.

Abbreviations

AAAS	*Annales Archéologiques Arabes Syriennes.*
BSA	Bulletin on Sumerian Agriculture, Cambridge.
CRAIBL	*Comptes Rendus de l'Académie des Inscriptions et Belles-Lettres.* Paris.
DLU	Del Olmo Lete, G. and J. Sanmartín, eds., *Diccionario de la lengua ugarítica.* Aula Orientalis Supplementa 7. vol. 1, 1996; Aula Orientalis Supplementa 8. vol. 2, 2000. Barcelona (Sabadell).
HUS	Watson, W.G.E, and N. Wyatt, eds., *Handbook of Ugaritic Studies.* Handbuch der Orientalistik I/39. Leiden 1999.
KTU	Dietrich, M., O. Loretz, and J. Sanmartín, *The Cuneiform Alphabetic Texts from Ugarit, Ras Ibn Hani and Other Places.* Abhandlungen zur Literatur Alt-Syrien-Palästinas und Mesopotamiens 8, Münster 1995.
PIASH	Proceedings of the Israel Academy of Sciences and Humanities, Jerusalem.
RLA	*Reallexikon der Assyriologie.*
RSO	Ras Shamra-Ougarit.
RSO 3	Yon, M. ed. *Le centre de la ville. 38e-44e campagnes (1978–1984).* RSO 3. Paris 1987.
RSO 6	Yon. M. et al. *Arts et Industries de la Pierre.* Paris 1991.
RSO 11	Yon, M., M. Sznycer, and P. Bordreuil, eds., *Le pays d'Ougarit autour de 1200 av. J.-C. Histoire et archéologie. Actes du Colloque International Paris, 28 juin–1er juillet 1993.* Paris 1995.
RSP 2	Fisher, L. R., ed., Ras Shamra Parallels. Analecta Orientalia 50; vol. 2. Rome 1975.

PUZURUM,
A HOMEOWNER FROM KHANA-PERIOD TERQA

Mark W. Chavalas*
University of Wisconsin - La Crosse

Traditionally, most excavators in Syro-Mesopotamia have concentrated their efforts on public or monumental architecture, with only an occasional interest in the more modest private or domestic remains.[1] Recently, however, the researcher of Syro-Mesopotamian civilization has become increasingly concerned with understanding and defining social structure, which has caused a greater interest in the study of domestic architecture.[2] Along with the study of cuneiform sources, one should be able to make some preliminary statements about the urban context and social status of the inhabitants of a particular residence.[3]

With this in mind, this paper will study the domestic units from Tell Ashara (ancient Terqa), in Syria, where epigraphic remains have been discovered in domestic units dated to the Late Old Babylonian or Khana period (c.1700–1500 B.C.E.).[4] Many of the contracts found therein mention a certain Puzurum as buyer, who will be the primary subject of this re-

---

* I would like to thank A. Podany for her helpful comments with an early draft of this paper. I would also like to thank the University of Wisconsin-La Crosse for a Small Research-Scholarship Grant that helped me complete this work, as well as the Co-Directors of the Joint Expedition to Terqa (1976–1987), G. Buccellati and M. Kelly-Buccellati for their generous access to the Terqa field notes and photographs.

1 In fact, the excavator of Bismaya (E.J. Banks) considered the domestic remains that he uncovered were "small, square, windowless boxes of clay, with a hole for the doorway" ([1912] 299).

2 E.g., see the recent studies by Aurenche (1981); Castel (1992); Veenhof (1996); Castel et al. (1997); Dezzi-Bardeschi (1998); and Battini-Villard (1999).

3 See C. Jansen (1986) 237.

4 For the Khana period at Terqa, see G. Buccellati (1988) 43–62; Podany (1991–93) 53–62, (1997) 417–32, forthcoming; and Rouault (1992) 247–56. For the Terqa preliminary reports, see G. Buccellati, and M. Kelly-Buccellati,1977) 1–43, (1978) 1–36, and (1983) 47–67; G. Buccellati et al. (1979); and Rouault (1997) 71–103.

search.[5] Domestic architecture from this area and period is notably lacking from other sites.[6] Thus, a study of archaeological evidence (house size, house layout, construction, urban context, and objects), comparisons with houses from other late third millennium B.C.E. and Old Babylonian period sites,[7] and cuneiform archival material (primarily contracts in this case) will be of great benefit. Terqa was probably the capital of the middle Euphrates region after the fall of Mari about 1750 B.C.E.; thus any study of its architectural and textual remains will be useful for reconstructing of the history of this period.

The extant size of the domestic units involved is not large, since only portions of eight rooms have been preserved. They are adjacent to a cliff overlooking the Euphrates at a point where the mound has eroded. The total length from street to cliff is 12 m. At least two separate houses have been articulated, which have been labeled Houses A and B. Contracts concerning Puzurum have been found in House A; four rooms of this house have survived, which are only 40 sq m in their total layout. Furthermore, only two of these rooms are complete in terms of their layout. Because of the nature of the deposits found in the rooms, we have been given a rare opportunity to reconstruct the stratigraphic history of the rooms. Excavation has revealed that a fire kept most of the architectural and artifactual material virtually intact and in relatively good condition, with no evidence of retrieval in antiquity of any of the items. Charred roof beams and impressions of matted reed roofing material were found in some of the rooms. A number of epigraphic remains, whole and fragmentary, primarily from House A, have been found, including tablets, envelopes, tags, bullae, and seal impressions. As most of the artifacts were unearthed in room A1, it has been designated an "archive" room, or attic. A number of unusual objects were found, including a Hittite stamp seal and silver crescent, both from A2, and cloves from A3.

HOUSE SIZE/LAYOUT

Although we do not know the precise size of Puzurum's house, there is a parallel from Haradum, an Old Babylonian site south of Terqa on the Euphrates.[8] Of the houses found there, House 2 shows the closest affinities

5 For the contracts found in the domestic units, see Rouault (1979) 1–12, and (1984). For the overall description of the houses, see M. Chavalas (1988).

6 But see McClellan (1997) 29–59 for extensive work in Late Bronze Age northern Syria.

7 See the expansive studies by Dezzi-Cardeschi (1998) and Battini-Villard (1999).

8 Kepinski and LeComte (1985) 48–60, (1992) 111–15, Fig. 34.

to Puzurum's house, and can serve as an example for a hypothetical reconstruction. House 2 at Haradum has a central courtyard and two sets of rooms flanking the long sides. The 3 eastern rooms are comparable in size and shape to rooms A1–A3 at Terqa. The two larger western rooms are probably living areas; we can project the same type of layout for Puzurum's house.

Battini-Villard's recent study of over 130 Ur III and Old Babylonian houses found that over half had a "central courtyard" layout. Only eight had a "central hall," while the remainder had no central courtyard.[9] Puzurum's house, according to our comparative reconstruction was of the first variety, a "central courtyard" house, or a "double-flanked house."[10] It also fits the "Central Room House," according to McClellan's plan (small rooms symmetrically on two long sides of a large room).[11]

The size of the house is usually measured by the total area of its interior roofed room space or by its outer dimensions, including the area of its walls.[12] The Haradum house is approximately 65 sq m, and so we can postulate a full size of about 65–85 sq m for Puzurum's house.[13] There are, of course, many variables to understanding house size and its relationship to social status. One must take into account historical processes and origins, physical environment, economic factors, regional polities, variations in household composition and size, and ideology.[14] Many of these factors cannot be known in the case of the Terqa house. In fact, McClellan has argued that "the function and wealth of houses are intimately connected with the articulation of the settlement itself within the larger regional polity."[15] Of course, it is believed that Terqa was the seat of the Khana kingdom in the late eighteenth century, when this house flourished.

One can postulate about how many people lived in Puzurum's house based upon archaeological and ethnographic studies, which have claimed approximately one inhabitant per seven to 10 sq m of living space.[16] Of

---

9 See the discussion in Battini-Villard (1999) 345–49.

10 Cf. Hill, in Delougaz (1967) 146–51.

11 McClellan (1997) 33–34; also see Dezzi-Bardeschi (1998) 19–31.

12 See McClellan (1997) 34.

13 House size is not always an indicator of wealth; Stone (1976) 284.

14 McClellan (1997) 36.

15 McClellan (1997) 44.

16 E.g., Naroll (1962) 587–89; Pfälzner (1996) 120; Kramer (1976) 125; cf. Woolley (1976) 10.

course, this does not take into account families of different socio-economic status. It is probably more appropriate to speak of persons per hectare, using the methods of "paleo-demography."[17] Scholars have argued for 100–200 persons[18] per hectare.[19] Although not all of the 65–85 proposed meters could have been used for living space, one could postulate that Puzurum lived within the confines of a small sized nuclear family. This corresponds to lists of deported families at Mari, which averaged about four to seven persons, depending upon the village.[20] We can then conclude that Puzurum did not conduct business at his own residence, based on the house size and the domestic nature of the extant rooms.

In Battini-Villard's study, over half of the central courtyard house types were predominantly 100–200 sq m in layout.[21] Only five percent of her study had house layouts of less than 100 sq m, the proposed size of Puzurum's house.

Excavators have estimated that the average size of what they have considered to be a Mesopotamian private house was about 200 sq m.[22] However, house sizes at Old Babylonian Ur appeared to have varied greatly, although one must realize that the published ground plans were in greatly reduced scales and cannot be used easily.[23] Van de Mieroop has shown that there was great variation in size at Old Babylonian Ur, from about 40 sq m to an excess of 120 m.[24] However, many portions of the larger houses were used for other functions (e.g., places of business), which would explain their greater size. Gelb claimed that most houses have been excavated in areas near temples and palaces, and were usually of more well-to-do owners, as opposed to those owners who lived in the outskirts, where fewer excavations have exposed more modest houses.[25] These

---

17 See Battini-Villard (1999) 385–401.

18 Wilkinson and Tucker (1995) 78.

19 Stone (1995b) 244; see the discussion by Postgate (1994) 47–65 and Battini-Villard (1999) 385–401.

20 Lion (1997) 109–18.

21 Battini-Villard (1999) 349–50.

22 Especially in work from the Early Dynastic III to Old Babylonian periods: Frankfort (1948) 396 n. 23, *idem* (1950) 103–4; Adams (1966) 98; and Heinrich and Siedl (1967) 24–45. Pallis (1956) 640–41 gives detailed dimensions of houses, ranging from 200–600 sq m.

23 See Van De Mieroop (1992) 38.

24 Van De Mieroop (1992) 223–25.

25 Gelb (1976) 197.

figures, however, do not compare favorably with the textual sources in this period, which give a much smaller estimate of house size, which is about 35–50 sq m. On the other hand, Stone has suggested that the Sumerian É.DÙ.A (usually Akkadian *bītum* when describing measurements) may have only been referring to roofed floor space, with unroofed areas, such as stables, walls, and courtyards, excluded from the measurements.[26] Henrickson has concluded that in the Diyala region a house size of 40–100 sq m was that of a nuclear family, and larger houses belonged either to wealthier families or showed a long lineage of ownership.[27] However, larger houses may have been internally subdivided with two or more nuclear families living in one unit. Stone holds that each house at Old Babylonian Nippur contained one nuclear family per living room.[28] Puzurum's proposed house size is smaller than the average size discerned by archaeologists, but larger than the 35–50 m mentioned in texts, although one must remember that his living room(s) is no longer extant. Although one cannot determine social status strictly from house size,[29] Puzurum's house size is certainly modest in nature.

CONSTRUCTION

All walls were constructed of sun-dried mud bricks and plastered with mud 2–4 cm thick, occasionally showing evidence of a white finish. Some walls exhibited up to three separate replasterings, while walls in the courtyard (A4) were repaired with sherds and mud packing. Many house walls showed evidence of the fire because the bricks were bright orange and over fired. Their thickness was approximately about 75–95 cm, probably a bit wider than the average Old Babylonian house wall.[30] The bonding relationships of the walls were of good quality, showing good workmanship. There was no visible means to ascend to another level, suggesting that the walls were not made to support a second story.

The floors were made of the typical beaten earth or clay, normally about 1–3 cm thick. The types of surfaces were actually diverse, including gypsum, fine clay, and charcoal, but most showed evidence of the burning. The floors from House A at Terqa are similar to those found at other Old

---

26 Stone (1981) 20.

27 Henrickson (1981) 54.

28 Stone (1981) 31; for the relationship between house layout and social status, see Meijer (1989) 221–35.

29 Again, McClellan (1997) 29–47.

30 Battini-Villard (1999) 364–65 and Dezzi-Bardeschi (1998) 289–335.

Babylonian period sites. However, some floors (possibly in a domestic context) in Area F at Terqa employed baked bricks. Some rooms at Ur and at Nippur were constructed with baked brick floors,[31] often occurring in rooms where water was employed for cooking or bathing.[32] The absence of drainage has been seen as an economic indicator of individuals of modest means.[33] Puzurum may not have had terracotta plumbing, as none came to light, which may be explained by the disclosure of remains of only domestic compartments. However, an extensive drainage/ hydraulic system was found in an earlier public building in Area F at Terqa, similar to drains from Isin during the same period.[34] A bathtub, however, was stored broken in A1 of Puzurum's house. Many houses at Ur, Isin, Nippur, and some at Nuzi contained some sort of drain, usually in a bathroom or courtyard, in order for rain water to drain off (perhaps there was a drain in the non-extant portion of A4).

Few permanent installations were found, most of which were found in the courtyard, A4. These included a rectangular bin that contained two tablets, two benches, and a hearth, similar to those found at Tell Fakhariyah[35] and Nuzi.[36] Seven burials were found, but six are associated with a re-occupation of the structure, as they were at a much higher level of elevation and did not respect the extant walls. Only one burial was associated with the contemporary living floor, a small bowl burial in A3 dug into the floor.

In sum, the materials used to make Puzurum's house appear to have been modest in nature, and comparable to those at other Old Babylonian period sites.

Room Function

Although rooms in Mesopotamian domestic units were traditionally multifunctional in nature,[37] some of the rooms in Puzurum's house, however, betrayed a single function.

---

31 Ur: Woolley and Mallowan (1976); Nippur: McCown et al. (1967).

32 Delougaz et al. (1967) 152–53.

33 Henrickson (1981) 63.

34 Hrouda (1977) Plan 6.

35 McEwan (1958).

36 Starr (1939).

37 The thesis of Castel (1992).

Six floors in room A1 were found, along with great amounts of fallen brick and three small permanent installations, including a hearth and benches. Other remains included baked bricks, large sherds, a bathtub, as well as the numerous epigraphic items. The variety of items, the broken or apparently discarded objects, and the haphazard scattering of items in this room suggest it as utilized for dead storage.

A2 had less fallen brick and roof material, but did contain most of the burials found in the re-occupation levels. The function of this room is more difficult to determine, but the items found within suggest an area of usable storage. Ceramic and stone items were significant, but fewer were broken or discarded, than in A1.

Nearly all of the items found in A3 were lying on the living floor of the room or leaning on another object that was on the floor. Forty-nine ceramic items were found, nearly all complete, as well as over 20 stone tools. The great number and variety of ceramic objects suggest a kitchen or pantry area. Most of the objects were found aligned along the west and south walls, away from the doorway.

The walls of A4 showed more wear on the inside than the walls of other rooms, which suggests that it was an exterior space. They also were repaired more often than walls of other rooms. It had relatively little evidence of burnt roofing material and fallen brick, except near the doorway connecting it to A1. A4 had at least ten floors or usage spaces, one of which having been repaired with small stones. Most of the permanent installations (including hearths) were found here, items that would have been used in an open or activity area. A smaller percentage of artifacts were also found in A4. All of the preceding suggest this room to be an open courtyard.

Objects

Objects comparable to those found in House A at Terqa have been found in cultic, domestic, military, and economic contexts at other Old Babylonian period sites. Many like items were found in well-to-do houses at Nuzi, temples at Mari, and tombs from various sites. However, the lack of many luxury items in Puzurum's house may suggest he lived in a modest household. The artifact corpus is made up of 657 recorded objects, both whole and fragmentary. Over two hundred of these were textual in nature, nearly all of which came from A1, labeled the "archive" room. However, because of the fragmentary nature of the textual remains, only fifteen whole tablets were found, as well as parts of texts and envelope fragments. Seals were found on many of the texts, clearly an indicator of economic activity in

Puzurum's household.[38] There were 166 ceramic items, including jars, platters, goblets, bowls, and pots, 165 stone objects, including numerous grinders and pestles, 18 bone objects, 8 shell objects, 13 metal objects, 19 unbaked clay objects, as well as a few other miscellaneous objects.

Cuneiform inventory lists of objects found at private residences at Mari and elsewhere show a drastic difference with our Terqa house. Many gold, bronze, and other specialized materials are described that are not found in the Puzurum house.[39] Obviously, this can be explained by the fact that the Terqa house was abandoned after the fire, and the most precious objects may have been taken. Thus, one cannot easily compare cuneiform lists of objects to archaeological realia.

URBAN CONTEXT

The spatial context of a building in the town would appear to be of primary importance to understanding the social status of the owners. Domestic architecture has often been found surrounding the public area, which was normally located in the center of town.[40] One may posit that in many cases the closer a private house was to a monumental building and to the center of town, the more important the owner was considered, although there are numerous exceptions to this idea. Houses near palaces in the Diyala were larger, but were not necessarily richer in luxury items.[41] R. Harris gleaned from the texts at Sippar that wealthier houses were facing "broad streets."[42] Conversely, many of the large private houses at Nuzi, including the house of the king's brother, were a distance from the center of town,[43] while houses at Nimrud that had a good view of the outer town were probably evidence of a wealthy sector. It has been argued that at Haradum, large houses in the center of town were due to the extension of the family unit, and not necessarily an indication of high social status.[44]

Puzurum's house was not near the center of town, but was about 20 m from the city wall, just across the street from the Temple of Ninkarrak, perhaps a relatively unimportant religious center at Terqa. The site of Terqa

38 Henrickson (1981) 69.

39 See Birot (1958) 77; Michel (1994) 285–90; and DeJong Ellis (1974) 136–37.

40 Lampl (1968) 13–23; Nauman (1953) 246–61.

41 Henrickson (1981) 75.

42 Harris (1975) 17.

43 Starr (1939).

44 Kepinski and Le Comte (1996) 195.

had been in existence for well over a millennium by this time, and land in the fortified town was at a premium. Thus, Puzurum did not have available room to expand his residence, and shared a party wall with at least one neighbor.

As only fragments of two houses were found at Terqa thus far that are from this period, it is not possible to make any statements concerning whether or not Puzurum's house was unique in nature or part of a tract of houses.

PUZURUM FROM TEXTUAL SOURCES

From the archaeological data, it appears that the family that occupied House A at Terqa consisted of modest homeowners. However, when complementing the archaeological sources with the epigraphic material, Puzurum does not seem to fit perfectly into any easily recognizable Old Babylonian period social category. Once again, the texts that were found in the domestic units consist of a number of different documents, including ten contracts, one administrative document, two name lists, and two documents concerning goods. Some of the contracts are contemporary with the reign of the Khana king Yadikh-abu, who is probably mentioned in a year date of Samsu-iluna of Babylon, dated to 1723 B.C.E.[45]

However, interpreting social status from the textual sources is not so simple a matter. Although research of cuneiform sources has continued for well over a century, there have been few attempts at a synthesis to understand the social structure of Mesopotamian society.[46] What were the prerequisites for class distinction in ancient Syro-Mesopotamia?[47] Did they emphasize property ownership, availability of certain resources and commodities, or membership in a clan or family organization? Many modern terms, such as "free" or "slave" had more fluid meanings in ancient societies, and will cause ambiguities for the modern researcher.[48] Legal, social, political, and economic criteria may well have overlapped and contradicted each other.[49] The epigraphic sources do not enlighten us

---

45 Rouault (1979) 4.

46 See Schneider (1920) and Deimel (1931) 71–113.

47 Diakonoff notes that many of the modern terms, such as "class" and "property," have not been well defined by Assyriologists, thus causing confusion ([1972] 41). Also cf. Murdock (1949) 87.

48 Renger (1979) 250; Foster (1982) 13; Adams (1966) 79.

49 Adams (1966) 103; Gelb (1967) 5.

with regard to this problem.[50] The texts contain information and designations for individuals, but take for granted that the reader understands these terms. Furthermore, land that was sold by individuals may have belonged to extended family groups.[51]

On the surface, it may seem relatively simple to define the structure of Old Babylonian society, and consequently Puzurum's place in it. The "Code" of Hammurapi divided male society into three convenient categories,[52] *awīlum*, so-called nobles,[53] landowners who were under no particular obligation to serve the palace or temple;[54] *muškēnum*, the peasant class who owned land, but only because of the grace of the crown,[55] and *wardum*, the slaves. This threefold division is clear and logical, but not strictly adhered to by the Babylonians themselves.[56] The terms *awīlum* and *muškēnum* have caused confusion for modern scholars. *Awīlum* may have denoted a social status only when paired with *muškēnum*.[57] The term *muškēnum* has been seen as a substantive, meaning commoner or plebian.[58] Diakonoff has considered the main difference between the two terms to be linked to owning inalienable and alienable land.[59] He cites a letter from Hammurapi to Šamaš-ḫazir as describing the land of an *awīlum* as *eqlum dūrum mātim innekem,* "perpetual land" or "land that cannot be taken away." Either an individual possessed the land by property rights or by a conditional land grant by the king in return for services rendered. In this

---

50 Oppenheim (1964) 76, (1967) 2; Adams (1982) 11.

51 Diakonoff (1985) 48, (1996) 55–57.

52 Woolley (1935) 127.

53 Kraus (1958) 151–52; the term has an ambiguous meaning; also cf. Driver and Miles (1952) 88.

54 In the Middle Assyrian period, the term *awīlu* could be applied also to slaves; see Driver and Miles (1975) 16 n. 3.

55 Scholars have had difficulty in defining the term. The following are some who have attempted: Kraus (1951) 30ff.; Driver and Miles (1952) 86ff., 409ff.; Goetze (1956) 49ff.; Speiser (1958) 19–28; Kraus (1958) 144–55; von Soden (1964) 133–41; Yaron (1969) 83ff.; Diakonoff (1971) 15–31; Kienast (1972) 99–103; Kraus (1973) 92–125; Adams (1982) 11ff.; Buccellati (1991) 91–100; and Stol (1997) 492–93.

56 Diakonoff (1987) 2.

57 Yaron ([1969] 86) understood the term *awīlum* at Eshnunna to be generic for "all men."

58 See Stol (1997) 492–93; contra Speiser (1958) 19.

59 Diakonoff (1971) 22.

case, a man who was not a *muškēnum* was *ina bītim ša ālim*.[60] Adams suggests that the *muškēnum* might have referred to the rural population.[61]

At nearby Mari, Durand has made it clear that the term *muškēnum* (coupled with *enšum* "poor") did not necessarily denote "the poor," but those citizens not attached to the palace.[62] In particular, the expression *muškēnum enšum* (poor *muškēnum*) implies that the *muškēnum* were not by definition, poor.[63] Whatever the case, the terms *awīlum* and *muškēnum* were not mutually exclusive, but had merging boundaries of definition.

Unfortunately, it is not certain whether these social classifications were used in the Khana kingdom at Terqa. G. Buccellati has postulated that during the Khana period the terms *awīlum* and *muškēnum* referred to two different types of individual land ownership: a *muškēnum* held real property as a family title for subsistence, an *awīlum* for "speculative purposes."[64] A *muškēnum* held no more than one piece of land, while an *awīlum* held several. The *muškēnum* had special homesteading rights, but his land could be repossessed.

Of course, it is not clear as to how this issue concerns Puzurum. In the contracts of Puzurum's archive, a recurrent phrase is *naṣbum ša lā baqrim u lā andurārim*, "property that is not subject to repossession, whether as a result of private claim or state intervention."[65] This phrase is formulaic and is not found in this form in the nearby Mari texts. The obscure term *naṣbum* here concerns a type of property, which is variously identified as a house, garden, tablet, field, or even an adopted son. In any case *naṣbum* property was inalienable property. *Andurārum* signified a remission of commercial debts of real estate only at Terqa, which indicates that under certain conditions sales of real estate may have been invalidated by a royal act (there is no evidence of Puzurum having any obligations to the palace or temple, although there is one text concerning his taking out a loan from the temple of Šamaš).

Within this framework, a *muškēnum* is understood as a homesteader, whose subsistence property enjoys special protections, even though his property is not specifically inalienable. An *awīlum*, on the other hand, is a

---

60 In the power of the community, not the crown; Diakonoff (1987) 51.

61 Adams (1982) 12, cf. von Soden (1964) 133–41.

62 Durand (1987) 21: see ARMT XXVI/2, 377: 11–13.

63 Also see Stol (1997) 492–93.

64 Buccellati (1991) 91–100.

65 See now, Chavalas (1997) 179–88.

"speculative landlord," who controlled real estate in the form of income, or *naṣbum* property. An individual such as Puzurum, who purchased a number of free fields, would then be categorized as an *awīlum* (if, in fact, this term was in use at Terqa). The fair amount of property exchange noted in the Puzurum contracts may remind one of a similar situation at contemporary Nippur, where Stone has postulated an abandonment of the city,[66] evidenced partly by a frequency of property transfers that could have been the result of overdue debts to the purchaser or from administrative pressure.

What was Puzurum's profession? He evidently did not conduct business at his residence (based upon the size of his house and courtyard). The fact that Puzurum borrowed money from a temple may show him to have been a modest businessman, and probably not a palace official or merchant. He was also most likely modest in wealth, based upon Gelb's model that the wealthier a person, the longer was the patronym listed with the person in question.[67] Van de Mieroop has ascertained at Old Babylonian period Ur that the three major domestic areas excavated within the walled city of Ur contained inhabitants with different occupations, one area with temple dependents, one with financiers, and one with landowners.[68] There is, of course, not enough data from Terqa to determine Puzurum's position in light of this.

What was the size of his family? Stone has proposed that there was one nuclear family per living room at Old Babylonian Nippur.[69] We do not have the living rooms for House A, but according to my reconstruction, it could have contained at the most two living rooms, while the extant rooms were predominantly used as storage compartments. This would mean that only Puzurum's immediate family lived there (although no adult sons are listed as witnesses in the contracts). How many people would have lived in Puzurum's house? If Puzurum's house was 65–85 sq m, as I have proposed, then it would have contained six to eight inhabitants, the size of a nuclear family.[70] Of course, extended families may have owned property, and so individual ownership is often hard to ascertain.[71] This also may explain

66 Stone (1976) 283–90.

67 Gelb (1979) 26.

68 Van De Mieroop (1992) 165–67.

69 Stone (1981) 19–34.

70 Again, Naroll (1962) 587–89.

71 Diakonoff (1996) 55–57.

why there were relatively few land transactions.[72] If, however, Puzurum owned other houses or plots of land, we might have to modify our estimation of his relative wealth. Did he then live in this house? He was probably gone by the time of the fire, since the documents were no longer in use.[73] One must remember that those landowners who had residence in the city left records of their transactions, and for this reason, may have been considered relatively wealthy.[74]

R. Harris has considered the possibility that when important personages appeared in documents as witnesses (in her case, judges), it may have been an indicator of the high position of one of the parties.[75] We can now investigate this in the case of the texts from Puzurum's house. In the texts from Puzurum's house, one judge is mentioned in *TFR* 1 13, 30 as the first witness,[76] and another in *TFR* 1 5,24, listed with the indemnities. In most cases, the witnesses in the archive of Puzurum were not of a special type. At Nippur, Stone has understood that witnesses represented some of the associates of the transacting parties.[77] In one document there is a certain Abi-Ḫel,[78] who is described as ŠU.I LUGAL, or "barber of the king," who was an executive officer.[79] There is also a certain Gimil-Ninkarrak[80] who is also mentioned in other Terqa texts as UGULA ŠU.I, or "overseer of the barbers.[81] Moreover, in *TFR* 1 1, Puzurum bought the field of a certain Ili-dumqi, IGI.GÁL, daughter of an *igigallatu* of Dagan. This is not normally seen as a particular vocation, but as a wise person.[82] It is possible that Ili-dumqi was a relative of Puzurum.[83] The last witness mentioned in *TFR* 13,

---

72 Van De Mieroop (1992) 170.

73 Buccellati, in Rouault (1984) xvii.

74 Van De Mieroop (1992) 171.

75 Harris (1975) 123.

76 Abbreviations for the tablet numbers are to be found in Rouault (1984). They are, TFR = Terqa Final Reports, and AO = Antiquités orientales.

77 Stone (1987) 17.

78 *TFR* 1,1 28.

79 Walther (1917) 177–78.

80 *TFR* 1 6,47.

81 Thureau-Dangin and Dhorme (1924) 272, 5, = AO 9052.

82 But cf. Wiseman (1953) 229, 1.

83 If we assume that kin desired to keep land in the family; cf. Kelly-Buccellati (1987) 139.

47 is Wa[rad]-k[u]bi, whose profession is listed as SIMUG (DÉ.A), or *nappāḫu*, metallurgist.[84] Also in *TFR* 1 3,11 was Samu-Dagana *sebi'um*, or innkeeper, who also often took care of tavern duties and sales.[85] The *sebi'um* was also often involved in credit transactions. Puzurum's field was near Napsi-Dagan, a *barû*-priest. Idin-Dagan (*TFR* 1 5,34) was an *arkû*, or a guarantor of another witness.[86] Finally, no palace officials were mentioned in the contracts.

SUMMARY

From the previous discussion, it is still not entirely apparent into what socio-economic category Puzurum fit, but he was most likely an *awīlum*, if that category was operative at Terqa. He was an independent property owner, owning a household and arable land outside of the city. According to Diakonoff's model,[87] Puzurum was a member of "a class of persons sharing property rights in the means of production and partaking in the process of production in their own interests." This group would have worked with its own soil or some other means of production. Klengel adds that independent householders, "were subject to the sovereign power of the ruler and forced by extra-economic coercion to perform certain public services."[88] Both the archaeological and textual data suggest the model of Puzurum as an independent householder, purchaser and seller of real estate (fields, and possibly gardens), a debtor, and possibly a slave owner.

---

84 See Dalley et al. (1976) 43.

85 Zimmern (1918–19) 166; Landsberger (1915) 504, idem (1915–16) 72 n.1; and Hartman and Oppenheim (1950) 12, 41 ns. 26–27.

86 Weidner (1952) 309, Oppenheim (1952) 138.

87 Diakonoff (1987) 3.

88 Klengel (1987) 160.

BIBLIOGRAPHY

Adams, R. (1966) *The Evolution of Urban Society: Early Mesopotamia and Prehistoric Mexico* (Chicago). (1982) Property Rights and Tenure in Mesopotamian Rural Communities. In N. Postgate et al., eds., *Societies and Languages of the Ancient Near East: Studies in Honour of I.M. Diakonoff*, 1–14. Warminster. **Aurenche, O.** (1981) *La maison orientale: l'architecture du Proche Orient ancien des origines au milieu du quartrième millénaire.* Paris. **Banks, E.J.** (1912) *Bismaya, or the Lost City of Adab.* New York. **Battini-Villard, L.** (1999) *L'Espace domestique en Mésopotamie de la IIIe dynastie d'Ur … l'époque paléo-babylonienne.* Oxford. **Birot, M.** (1958) *Tablettes d'époque babyloninne ancienne: Archives Royales de Mari: Textes.* Paris. **Buccellati, G.** (1988) The Kingdom and Period of Khana, *BASOR* 270: 43–61. (1991) A Note on the Muškēnum as a 'Homesteader.' In R. Ratner et al., eds., *Let Your Colleagues Praise You: Studies in Memory of Stanley Gevirtz.* Maarav 7: 91–100. **Buccellati, G., and M. Kelly-Buccellati** (1977) Terqa Preliminary Reports 1. General Introduction and the Stratigraphic Record of the First Two Seasons, *Syro-Mesopotamian Studies* 1/3: 1–43. (1978) Terqa Preliminary Reports 6. The Third Season: Introduction and the Stratigraphic Record, Syro-Mesopotamian Studies 2/6: 1–36. (1983) Terqa: The First Eight Seasons, *Annales archéologiques arabes syriennes* 33.2: 47–67. **Buccellati, G., et al.** (1979) *Terqa Preliminary Reports 10. The Fourth Season: Introduction and Stratigraphic Record.* Malibu. **Calvet, Y.** (1996) Maisons privées paléo-babyloniennes … Larsa: Remarques d'architecture, in K. Veenhof, ed., 1996: 197–209. **Castel, C.** (1992) *Habitat urbain néo-assyrien et néo-babylonien.* Paris. **Castel, C., al-Maqdassi, M., and F. Villeneuve, eds.** (1997) *Les maisons dans la Syrie antique du IIIe millénaire aux débuts de L'Islam: pratique et représentations de l'espace domestique: actes du colloque International, Damas, 27–30 Juin 1992.* Beruit. **Chavalas, M.** (1988) The House of Puzurum, (Ph.D. Diss., UCLA). (1997) Naṣbum in the Khana Contracts from Terqa. In G. Young, M. Chavalas, and R. Averbeck, eds., *Crossing Boundaries and Linking Horizons: Studies in Honor of Michael C. Astour on His 80th Birthday*, 179–88. Bethesda, Md. **Charpin, D.** (1986) *Le Clergé d'Ur au siScle d'Hammurabi: (XIXe–XVIIIe siècles av. J.-C.).* Geneva. **Dalley, S., et al.** (1976) *The Old Babylonian Tablets from Tell al Rimah.* London. **Dandamayev, M.** (1972) The Economic and Legal Character of the Slaves' Peculium in the Neo-Babylonian and Achaemenid Periods, *Comptes rendus: Rencontre assyriologique internationale* 18: 35–39. **Deimel, A.** (1931) Sumerische Templewirtschaft zur Zeit Urukaginas und seiner Vorgänger, *Analecta Orientalia* 2: 71–113. **DeJong Ellis, M.** (1974) The Division of Property at Tell Harmal, *JCS* 26: 133–53. **Delougaz, P., et al.** (1967) *Private Houses and Graves in the Diyala Region.* Chicago. **Dezzi-Bardeschi, C.** (1998) *Architettura domestica nella Mesopotamia settentrionale nel II millennio A.C.* Florence. **Diakonoff, I.** (1971) On the Structure of Old Babylonian Society. In H. Klengel, ed., *Beiträge zur socialen Struktur des alten Vorderasien, Schriften zur Geschichte und Kultur des alten Orients*, 15–31. Berlin. (1972) Socio-Economic Classes in Babylonia and the Babylonian Concept of Social Stratification,

Comptes rendus: Rencontre assyriologique internationale 18: 41–52. (1985) Extended Families in Old Babylonian Ur, *ZA* 75: 47–65. (1987) Slave Labour vs. Non Slave Labour: The Problem of Definition. In M. Powell, ed., *Labor in the Ancient Near East,* 1–3. New Haven. (1996) Extended Family Households in Mesopotamia (III–II Millennia B.C.), in K. Veenhof, ed., 1996: 55–59. **Driver, G. and J. Miles** (1975) *The Assyrian Laws.* 2nd edition. Darmstadt. (1952) *The Babylonian Laws,* Vol. I. Oxford. **Durand, J.-M.** (1991) Précurseurs syriens aux Protocoles néo-assyriens. In D. Charpin and F. Joannès, eds., *Marchands, Diplomates et empereurs: études sur la civilisation Mésopotamie offerte ... Paul Garelli,* 13–71. Paris. **Foster, B.** (1982) *Administration and Use of Institutional Land in Sargonic Sumer.* Copenhagen. **Franke, J.** (1987) Artifact Patterning and Functional Variability in the Urban Dwelling, Old Babylonian Nippur, Iraq. Ph.D. Diss., University of Chicago. **Frankfort, H.** (1948) *Kingship and the Gods: A Study of Ancient Near Eastern Religion as the Integration of Society and Nature.* Chicago. (1950) Town Planning in Ancient Mesopotamia, *Town Planning Review* 21: 95–115. **Gelb, I.** (1972) From Freedom to Slavery, *Comptes rendus: Rencontre assyriologique internationale* 18: 81–92. (1976) Quantitative Evaluation of Slavery and Serfdom. In B. Eichler, ed., *Kramer Anniversary Volume: Cuneiform Studies in Honor of Samuel Noah Kramer,* 195–208. Kevelaer. (1979) Household and Family in Early Mesopotamia. In E. Lipinski, ed., *State and Temple Economy in the Ancient Near East,* 1–97. Leuven. **Goetze, A.** (1956) *The Laws of Eshnunna.* New Haven. **Harris, R.** (1975) *Ancient Sippar: A Demographic Study of an Old Babylonian City, 1894–1595 B.C.* Istanbul. **Hartman, L. and A. Oppenheim** (1950) *On Beer and Brewing Techniques in Ancient Mesopotamia.* JAOS Supplement 10. **Heinrich, E. and V. Seidl** (1967) Grundrisszeichnungen aus dem alten Orient, *MDOG* 98: 24–45. **Henrickson, E.** (1981) Non-Religious Residential Settlement Patterning in the Late Early Dynastic of the Diyala Region, *Mesopotamia* XVI: 43–140. **Hill, H., Th. Jacobsen, and Ph. Delougaz** (1990) *Old Babylonian Public Buildings in the Diyala Region.* Chicago. **Huot., J.-L., et al.** (1989) *Larsa, travaux de 1985.* Paris. **Hrouda, B.** (1977) *Isin-Ishan Bahriyat I: Die Ergebnisse des Ausgrabungen, 1973–74.* Munich. (1987) *Isin-Isan Bahriyat III: Die Ergebnisse der Ausgrabungen 1983–1984.* Munich. (1992) *Isin-Isan Bahriyat IV: Die Ergebnisse der Ausgrabungen 1986–1989.* Munich. **Jansen, C.** (1996) When the House Is on Fire and the Children Are Gone, in K. Veenhof, ed., 1996: 237–46. **Kalla, G.** (1996) Das altbabylonische Wohnhaus und seine Struktur nach philologischen Quellen, in K. Veenhof, ed., 1996: 247–56. **Keinast, B.** (1972) Zu Muškēnum = Maulā, *Comptes rendus, Rencontre assyriologique internationale* 18: 99–103. **Kelly-Buccellati, M.** (1986) Sealing Practices at Terqa. In M. Kelly-Buccellati, ed., *Insight Through Images: Studies in Honor of Edith Porada,* 133–42. Malibu. **Kepinski, C., and O. LeComte** (1985) Haradum/Harada: Une forteresse sur l'Euphrate, *Archéologia* 205: 46–55. (1996) Spatial Occupation of a New Town Haradum (Iraqi Middle Euphrates, 18th–17th Centuries B.C.). In K. Veenhof, ed., 1996: 191–96. **Kepinski, C., and O. LeComte, eds.** (1993) *Haradum I: Une Ville Nouvelle sur le Moyen-Euphrate.* Paris. **Klengel, H.** (1987) Non-Slave Labour in the Old Babylonian Period: The

Basic Outlines. In M. Powell, ed., *Labor in the Ancient Near East*, 159–66. New Haven. **Kramer C.** (1982) *Village Ethnoarchaeology: Rural Iran in Archaeological Perspective.* New York. **Kraus, F.** (1951) Nippur und Isin nach altbabylonischen Rechtsurkunden, *JCS* 3 (entire issue). (1958) *Ein Edikt des Königs Ammi-Saduqa von Babylon.* Leiden. (1973) *Vom mesopotamischen Menschen der altbabylonischen Zeit und seiner Welt: Eine Reihe Verlesungen.* Amsterdam. **Kupper, J.-R.** (1957) *Les nomades in Mésopotamie au temps des rois de Mari.* Paris. **Lampl, P.** (1968) *Cities and Planning in the Ancient Near East.* New York. **Landsberger, B.** (1915) Bemerkungen zur altbabylonischen Briefliteratur, *ZDMG* 69: 491–528. (1915–16) Zu den Frauenklassen des Kodex Hammurabi, *ZA* 30: 67–73. **Lion, B.** (1997) Les enfants des families déportées e Mésopotamie du nord ... Mari. In B. Lion, C. Michel, and P. Villard, eds., *Enfance et éducation dans le Proche-Orient ancien*, 109–18. Strasbourg. **McClellan, T.** (1997) Houses and Households in North Syria during the Late Bronze Age. In C. Castel et al., eds., 1997: 29–59. **McCown, D. et al.** (1967) *Nippur I: The Temple of Enlil, Scribal Quarter, and Surroundings.* Chicago. **McEwan, C.** (1958) *Soundings at Tell Fakhariyah.* Chicago. **Mallowan, M.** (1966) *Nimrud and Its Remains*, 3 Vols. New York. **Meijer, D.** (1989) Ground Plans and Archaeologists: on Similarities and Comparisons. In O. Haex et al., eds., *To the Euphrates and Beyond: Archaeological Studies in Honour of Maurits van Loon*, 221–36. Rotterdam. **de Meyer, L., et al.** (1971) *Tell ed-Der I.* Leuven. (1978) *Tell ed-Der II* (Leuven: Peeters). (1984) *Tell ed-Der IV* (Leuven: Peeters). **Michel, C.** (1994) Une maison sous scellés dans le karum, *NABU* 3: 285–90. **Miglus, P.** (1996) Die räumliche Organisation des altbabylonischen Hofhauses. In K. Veenhof, ed., 1996:211–20. **Murdock, G.** (1949) *Social Structure* (New York: Macmillan & Co.). **Naroll, R.** (1962) Floor Area and Settlement Population, *American Anthropologist* 27: 587–89. **Naumann, R.** (1953) Das Hausmodell vom Tell Halaf und die nach unten verjüngten Säulen Nordsyriens, *Jahrbuch für kleinasiatische Forschung* 4: 246–61. **Oppenheim, A.L.** (1952) The Archives of the Palace of Mari: A Review Article, *JNES* 11: 128–39. (1964) *Ancient Mesopotamia: Portrait of a Dead Civilization.* Chicago. (1967) A New Look at the Structure of Mesopotamian Society, *JESHO* 10: 1–16. **Pallis, S.** (1956) *The Antiquity of Iraq: A Handbook of Assyriology.* Copenhagen. **Pfälzner, P.** (1996) Activity Areas and the Social Organisation of Third Millennium B.C. Households. In K. Veenhof, ed., 1996: 117–27. **Podany, A.** (1991–93) A Middle Babylonian Date for the Hana Kingdom, *JCS* 43–45: 53–62. (1997) Some Shared Traditions between Hana and the Kassites. In G. Young, M. Chavalas, and R. Averbeck, eds., *Crossing Boundaries and Linking Horizons: Studies in Honor of Michael C. Astour on His 80th Birthday*, 417–32. Bethesda, Md. (2002) *The Land of Hana: Kings, Chronology, and Scribal Tradition.* Bethesda, Md. **Postgate, N.** (1994) How Many Sumerians Per Hectare: Probing the Anatomy of an Early City, *Cambridge Archaeological Journal* 4: 47–65. **Renger, J.** (1979) Interaction of Temple, Palace, and 'Private Enterprise' in the Old Babylonian Economy. In E. Lipinski, ed., *State and Temple Economy in the Ancient Near East*, 249–55. Leuven. **Rouault, O.** (1979) Terqa Preliminary Reports 7. Les Documents épigraphiques de la troisième saison, *Syro-Mesopotamian Studies* 2/7: 1–12. (1984) *Terqa Final Reports 1. L'archive de Puzurum.* Malibu. (1992) Cultures locales et influences extérieures: La Cas de Terqa, *Studi Micenei ed Egeo-Anatolici* XXX: 247–56. **Rouault, O. et al.** (1997) Terqa: rapport préliminaire (1987–1989), *MARI* 8: 71–103. **Schiel, V.** (1902) *Une saison de fouilles ... Sippar.* Le Caire. **Schneider, A.** (1920) *Die Anfänge der Kulturwirtschaft: Die sumerische Tempelstadt.* Essen. **von Soden, W.** (1964) Muškēnum und die Mawālī des frühen Islam, *ZA* 56: 133–41. **Speiser, E.** (1958) The Muškēnum, *Orientalia* 27: 19–28. **Starr, R.** (1939) *Nuzi: Report on the Excavations at Yorgan Tepe Near Kirkuk, Iraq*, 2 Vols. Cambridge, Mass. **Stol, M.** (1997) Muškēnu, *RlA* 8: 492–93. **Stone, E.** (1976) Economic Crisis and Social Upheaval in Old Babylonian Nippur. In L. Levine, and T. Cuyler-Young, eds., *Mountains and Lowlands: Essays in the Archaeology of Greater Mesopotamia*, 267–90. Malibu. (1981) Texts, Architecture, and Ethnographic Analysis: Patterns of Residence in Old Babylonian Nippur, *Iraq* 43: 19–34. (1987) *Nippur Neighborhoods.* Chicago. (1995) The Development of Cities in Ancient Mesopotamia. In J. Sasson, ed., *Civilizations of the Ancient Near East*, vol. I, 235–48. New York. (1996) Houses, Households, and Neighborhoods in the Old Babylonian Period: The Role of Extended Families. In K. Veenhof, ed., 1996: 229–35. **Thureau-Dangin, and F., Dhorme** (1924) Cinq jours de fouilles ... 'Asharah, *Syria* 5: 265–93. **Van De Mieroop, M.** (1992) Berliner Beiträge zum Vorderen Orient 12. Berlin. **Veenhof, K.R., ed.** (1996) *Houses and Households in Ancient Mesopotamia: Papers Read at the 40th Rencontre Assyriologique Internationale, Leiden, 5–8 July, 1993.* Leiden. **Walther, A.** (1917) *Das altbabylonische Gerichtswesen.* Leipzig. **Weidner, E.** (1952) Vier neue Inschriften, *AfO* 16: 307–10. **Wilkinson, T., and I. Tucker** (1995) *Settlement Patterns in the North Jazira, Iraq.* Warminster. **Wiseman, D.** (1953) *The Alalakh Tablets.* London. **Woolley, C.** (1935) *Abraham: Recent Discoveries and Hebrew Origins.* London. **Woolley, C., and M. Mallowan** (1976) *The Old Babylonian Period: Ur Excavations VII.* London. **Yaron, R.** (1969) *The Laws of Eshnunna.* Jerusalem. **Zettler, R.** (1991) Nippur and the Third Dynasty of Ur: Area TB. In P. Michalowski et al., eds., *Velles Paraules: Ancient Near Eastern Studies in Honor of Miguel Civil on the Occasion of His Sixty-Fifth Birthday*, 251–82. Barcelona. **Zimmern, H.** (1918–19) Der Schenkenliebeszauber Berl. VAT 9728 (Assur) = Lond. K.3464+ Par. n. 3554 (Nineve), *ZA* 32: 164–84.

AN EXTRAORDINARY EVERYDAY FOR EMAR'S DIVINER

Jan Gallagher
Cincinnati, Ohio

Emar was a town located at the great bend of the Euphrates River in Syria in the middle of the second millennium B.C.E. The excavations of 1972–76 provided a huge surprise to the French salvage team called in by the Syrian government. They expected to find evidence from the middle of the *third* millennium, since Ebla documents indicated that Emar had been well established by then.[1] At the very least they expected evidence of an early second-millennium town, as indicated by Mari records.[2] But their findings at the lowest level of the excavation dated to the middle of the second millennium, specifically to the fourteenth and thirteenth centuries.

The archaeologists found an artificially constructed town at the top of a small hill. The site was a promontory about halfway up and jutting out from the cliff behind it to the west; and it was separated from that cliff by a wadi that had been artificially dug out to make the separation even greater.[3]

There *had* to have been an old Emar. By the time it was decided that the old town had been down at the river's edge, the waters were starting to back up from the new dam downriver at Tabqa—this was July of 1973, and the newly forming Lake Assad soon flooded at least another thousand years of history.[4]

The town that was found was an engineering marvel, well beyond the resources of river-plain commercial shippers. Emarites were transshippers of land- and water-borne goods from all directions, into all directions. The old town down on the riverbank was threatened annually by the flooding

1 Archi (1990) 24–29.

2 Margueron (1995) 127.

3 Margueron (1995) 129. In Margueron (1977) 44 he had credited Paul Sanlaville with asserting that the western ravine was artificial, that natural erosion could not have cut it.

4 Margueron (1990) 105.

of the Euphrates, which occasionally caused a shift in the river's course.[5] So who built this new town? The commercial functioning of Emar must have been important enough to somebody to expend the time and effort to maintain it.

By the fourteenth century B.C.E. the Hittites from Anatolia were reestablishing their control in northern Syria and wanted to use this town at the southeastern corner of their new empire as a buffer against military pressure from the east and for the economic advantages Emar would bring. It was the Hittites who built the new town, which involved constructing terraces along that hillside, a practice unknown to the river-plain Emarites, but known in Ḫattuša in Anatolia.[6] Also, some, but not all, of the architecture of the new Emar is thought to be in Hittite style.

In a general overview of the 1970s finds at Emar, textual and nontextual, one finds a great deal more cooperation between conqueror and conquered than one would expect. The Emarites allowed the Hittites to do for them what they probably could not have accomplished by themselves: preserve their city's life from flood destruction. The Hittites apparently felt they could gain more by peaceful means than by harsh ones, so they let the Emarites continue to run their own commercial affairs. The Hittites needed some of those goods that passed through the docks of Emar.

The Hittites and the Emarites made a good team. The Hittites were adaptors, borrowers, too. They were wise enough to rule politically with a loose rein, and to leave Emar alone culturally and economically for the most part. The Hittites were smart enough to recognize a kindred type of practicality in Emar. Both groups practiced a political and diplomatic opportunism that enabled them to borrow what would be most advantageous for each. Both groups were able and willing to adjust to a realistic balance of military/political power with economic necessity. The result was an apparently amicable accommodation that worked to everyone's advantage.

There was, most likely, one person in Emar—perhaps better: one at a time—who fostered, perhaps even coordinated, the cooperative spirit. Behind the scenes, quietly, this one person was possibly the most powerful man in Emar. Scholars have labeled him the "diviner," and that convention is adequate for the sake of convenience and brevity. However, I suggest that divining was third or fourth down on the list of his functions. The diviner was most likely the local liaison between the city and the Hittite

---

5 Geyer (1990) 110.

6 Margueron (1980) 289.

overlords, and he certainly led in the maintenance of Emar's economic, commercial functioning by his ability to read and write and by his teaching of those skills.

The diviner-scribe controlled communications, with everyone, in every direction. He fostered, enabled, facilitated communication; or he monopolized it. He could even have prevented communication. He was political propagandist, arbiter of style, the king's secretary, and more.

Several hundreds[7] of tablets and fragments were discovered in a building near the center of the new town. The archaeologists labeled this building M1. It is categorized as a temple because it is built in the same megaron-style as the two major temples of Emar located in the southwestern part of the city, a style thought to be indigenous to northern Syria.[8]

This particular M1 building, following the basic architectural pattern, differs from the other temples slightly in three respects. First, the orientation of M1 is toward the northeast rather than the east.[9] This could be due to a topographical feature of the built-up site that excavation has not yet disclosed. Or, it could indicate that M1 was not so important religiously as to require an eastern orientation. It could mean that M1 was not considered sacred space at all or perhaps directional orientation of sacred space was not a high priority for Emarites.

Second, there is more to the edifice than simply the cella and its open terrace at the back end of the building. A smaller edifice of three rooms side by side was built against the eastern wall of M1. There was probably no access to these rooms from inside the sanctuary itself. Apparently there was a second story over the three-room annex. Perhaps the additional rooms constituted the diviner's living quarters, his omen-seeking laboratory, and/or his school and library. It was in this annex that the Emar archives were discovered, possibly having fallen from the second story.[10] Clay tablets stored on wooden shelves met a similar fate in Ebla.

The third difference between M1 and the other temples is that M1, unlike the other temples, appears to have been dedicated to not just one

---

7 The number varies with the writer of the report, but that is not to say that the writers cannot count. Broken fragments, estimates, categorization of tablets, are all causes for variation. There is also the problem of numbering duplicates of the same text, and how to count a tablet that contains two or more separate texts or partial texts on it. Daniel Fleming (1992) 51 counted Arnaud's lists in *Emar* VI and arrived at 1821 numbered tablets gathered into 793 numbered texts.

8 Margueron (1995) 132.

9 Margueron (1995) 132.

10 Margueron (1995) 132.

god, but to "all" the gods of Emar. It has thus been informally dubbed the Pantheon.[11]

The diviner could conceivably have used the sanctuary too for some of his secular functions, perhaps as a kind of chapel with small shrines, or diplomatic consulate space for the transport workers passing through Emar, with the diviner functioning as a kind of chaplain or diplomat.[12]

The diviner "belonged" to the entire city of Emar and was not associated, as a priest, with only one god. He may have been a priest, but I suggest that the performance of worship and sacrificial rituals was not part of this particular priest's functions; he rather functioned as something of a "theological administrator" for the city, an "overseer of public spirit."[13]

As diviner, he performed the operations producing omens for the benefit of the local king or any other element of local government. As diviner, his status was only quasi-religious. The power potential of a diviner was great; there was no one who could check on the quality of a diviner's work, unless one of his students became insubordinate.

I suggest that Emar's diviner was responsible to the Hittite king at Carchemish, if he was actually responsible to anyone. Publicly he was probably considered to be accountable to the local king, but I think his real authority and power were his own, with the permission or actual encouragement of the Hittite overlords.

One Emarite diviner, Zu-Bala, was apparently in independent or autonomous communication with a religious official in Carchemish named Aal-Šimegi regarding a priest's installation at Emar in the service of the god Ninkur.[14] Also, the Hittite Great King residing in Ḫattuša was known to intervene directly in Emarite affairs at least once, when Muršili II released the diviner Iadi-Baal from paying taxes or doing corvée work.[15]

Emar's diviners over at least the 150 years of the new city's existence probably came from one blood family. There is evidence that a grandfather and grandson held the office. This would strengthen an argument for the

---

11 Margueron (1995) 132. "All" meant "70" according to one Emar text, that is, a round number indicating completeness, or "all."

12 I am indebted to Professor Isaac Jerusalmi of Hebrew Union College for the consul idea and the possible connection to a group of small religious shrines.

13 "[S]on titre de 'devin' rend trop modestement compte du rôle essential qui fut le sein: être le chef de la religion émariote et plus généralement surveiller l'esprit public" (Arnaud [1980] 378).

14 Arnaud (1985) I, 268; text 74106b. Beckman (1996) 6.

15 Arnaud (n.d. [Hethitica VIII]) 12.

independence and the autonomous functioning of any one diviner; methods of exerting such quiet power are far more easily—and quietly—passed on through a loyal blood family than through people who are not related to each other. This would be an example of the stereotype of "blood thicker than water."

It is possible that the diviner was considered by the ruling Hittites to be on the same level of authority as the local king, simply having different areas of responsibility and jurisdiction. The Emarite local king might publicly hold authority over civil government functions, matters of defense, foreign (Hittite) workers, and other "international" relations; and the diviner would have authority in the "humanities" and "social sciences," such as health, medicine, omen-determined philosophy, religion, and education.

It is even possible to imagine the diviner as a "check and balance" to the local king, a mild reminder by the ruling Hittites to the local king not to consider rebelling against Hittite domination.[16] It should be remembered that one of a diviner's jobs was to forecast success or failure of a king's military expeditions. By that reasoning, Emar's diviner would have had a great degree of control over any military activities of Emar's local king. The diviner's patron was more likely a secular/civil authority than a religious one. It is quite possible that the patron was the Carchemish king, and not the local king.

Emar's diviner most likely was Emar's master scribe also. The performance of functions proper to a master scribe must certainly have taken up more time than any other of his functions.

The hundreds of tablets and fragments of tablets found in the M1 annex are of different types: private records, public rituals, festival programs, literary works, administrative records; and it should be kept in mind that we do not know what else might have been there. The private records could be those of the blood family of the diviner, particularly if the annex happened to be the diviner's personal quarters.

It is also possible that new family residences, on the terraces running up the hill, were smaller than the old houses on the river plain. Therefore, M1 could have been a public repository of private documents that several families could no longer keep in their own homes.

---

16 Beckman (1992) 46 could be considered as support for the idea that the diviner may have been a local "plant." Beckman thought that the Hittite garrisons assigned to vassal kingdoms functioned as much to keep an eye on the activities of the local ruler as to protect his life.

Perhaps the records of land and slave sales and purchases, marriages, divorces, adoptions, unusual inheritances, disinheritances, loans, and other family and civil matters were used as *Vorlagen* for the scribes-in-training who were beyond copying lists and phrases and were ready to practice writing out facsimiles of real documents.[17]

Some of the records could be temple records: receipts of objects and animals and foods for sacrifices or priestly support. We simply have no way of knowing the origin, owner, or degree of completeness of the record collection in M1.

Many tablets, both personal and municipal, might need to be available for future reference; M1 could thus be termed a reference library.

Some texts appeared in M1 in multiple copies. For instance, Arnaud collated six different tablets or fragments for the enthronement of the *entu*-priestess, four for the *zukru*-festival, and nineteen for one joint *kissu* text.[18] Two major reasons for copying texts would have been to fill out the personal library of someone[19] or to practice language learning of vocabulary and syntax.[20] Both reasons, but the latter particularly, lead to the further conclusion that the archaeologists at Emar had found a scribal school, or at least a storage room of a scribal school, in the annex of M1.

The question can be raised: why should a town no larger than seven hundred by one thousand meters, approximately one-half by three-quarters of a mile (or three-eighths of a square mile) have an entire scribal school? One scribe, yes, perhaps a few scribes working the temples, the legal courts, the local market, and the docks at riverside. They could have been imported—scholars have noted the moving around of specialists such as scribes, physicians, diviners, and teachers as far back as Sumerian times.[21] Here, Emar appears to be more cosmopolitan than its size would

---

17 The civil tablets in M1 could also be those practice tablets, although this is less likely than the *Vorlage* possibility for this particular category of tablet. Practice tablets are useful for only a relatively short time, yet they take up much space. They would be destroyed, or wetted down, smoothed over, and reused—unless the destruction of Emar happened too quickly, and practice tablets just ended up in the heap with authentic records.

18 Arnaud (1986) 326, 350, and 379. For the *zukru*-festival, see most recently Fleming (2000).

19 Oppenheim (1977) 243.

20 Hallo (1992) 75 suggests that the presence of duplicates is one criterion for labeling certain tablets as school texts.

21 Beckman (1983) 107, 108–9, 112, 113–14; Arnaud (1987) 212; Kramer (1979) 258; Zaccagnini (1983) 245–64 *passim*.

lead one to expect. Emar's world extended far beyond its city limits, and the town prepared itself, generation after generation, to participate in that world. Importation of scribes from outside was not satisfactory; Emar apparently preferred to train its own.

Emar's need for an educated cadre was greater than Emar's size might indicate. The scope and level of education required at Emar were also greater than would be expected; a simple elementary learning of reading, writing, and arithmetic in the local language would not suffice. Emar needed people who could read, write, and count in all the languages represented on the docks at riverside, people who could move easily among several measuring systems and their varied technical terminology, people who could feed and pay the imported construction workers, people who could effect communication between ruler and ruled in civil, judicial, local governmental, and international matters. Dealing with foreigners and foreign languages was not just one part of Emar's functioning as a city; such dealings constituted almost all of Emar's municipal life.

By the time of our new town on the hill, Akkadian had become or was becoming the major language of international communication, and scribal schools appeared from Egypt up to Anatolia to handle the necessary language training (which would automatically include Sumerian as well).[22]

The schools were patterned after the original é-dub-ba-a of Sumer. Some think these schools gave way by the early sixteenth century to training by individual guilds or groups of common interest, something on the order of labor unions training their own. But at Emar, schools probably continued to function in the Mesopotamian pattern until the very end of the town, around 1200 B.C.E.

The "tablet house" was geared to training for practical life, but it was not limited to using only practical works in its curriculum. Future scribes needed to learn how to write legal documents for both local and international use. Land sales and purchases had to be recorded as security for future inheritance rights in a family. Marriage contracts and divorce documents had to be recorded for protection of the rights of the parties involved. Adoptions had to be recorded for the impact they would have on inheritance or disinheritance. Land surveys to determine boundaries had to be recorded. Correspondence of political or economic nature was necessary. Divination of omens represented a large portion of the tablets and fragments found in M1. Writing down in detail the findings of divination was equivalent to composing a medical textbook for future diviners.

---

22 Hallo (1992) 75.

The most important use of writing at Emar was certainly the keeping of records of the mercantile activities that sustained the town. Goods from Mesopotamia moving up the rivers or alongside them, by land or water, to the Mediterranean or to Anatolia, or down to lower Syria and Palestine, passed through Emar. Goods from across the Mediterranean Sea or from Anatolia, or from lower Syria and Palestine moved through Emar on their way down the rivers to Mesopotamia. Emar was a crossroads town; it facilitated the movement of goods. Emar was not the terminal point of the movement of goods; it effected and facilitated the transshipment of goods, or functioned as a stopover point.

Even if the vocabulary of all the languages represented by this movement of goods was reduced to Akkadian plus Sumerian, the merchants and other interested parties would still have to be able to move facilely from one measuring system and its terminology to another in order to write out the records of receipts and shipments for the clients at both ends of the road, and for Emar's own profit.

The school at Emar, then, had to teach many subjects to the students to prepare them to take their places in Emar's society, government, and work force.

Learning the languages began with vocabulary lists, at least bilingual. The syllabaries were in dictionary-like, and columnar, format.[23] Another style was topical lists: gods, animals, names of artisans, any specialized vocabulary, such as a list of foodstuffs—beer, wine, and their ingredients, mustard, garlic, onion, cinnamon, oils—or the technical jargon of any occupation.[24] The students copied and recopied the lists until they knew the words in all the necessary languages and how to form them in cuneiform on clay.

There were exercises in legal phraseology and formulas; epistolary formulas, such as greetings, salutation and closing forms; special diplomatic or mercantile phraseology. The students had to learn mathematics, including fractions and reciprocals, accounting, calculation of volume, and payroll. They had to learn surveying and its terminology, how to divide property and define the limits of fields. Then, of course, there was the possibility of hymn-writing on commission.[25]

---

23 Landsberger (1957–58) 328–41 *passim*.

24 Sjöberg (1976) 162–63, 166; Weisberg (1967) 55, 61, 67; Landsberger (1957–58) *passim*.

25 Sjöberg (1976) 168–69 thinks hymns were ordered by the royal court to be written by the school.

Syntax could be learned only from connected prose or poetry; therefore, literary texts in the relevant languages were certainly transported to Emar to be used as *Vorlagen* for this aspect of language learning and scribal training. Some fragments of Gilgameš, some wisdom literature from Mesopotamia, and some incantations against demons have been found at Emar.[26]

Copying "literary" texts served as an exercise in handwriting too. For example, in the *kissu* of Dagan a student scribe messed up royally. He tried for a few lines to make corrections, failed, and ended up just doodling. Another text, the *kissu* of Ninkur, showed a scribal cursus with an upward-bending flourish at the end of some of his lines, as if he knew the language and writing well enough to play and develop his own style of handwriting.

The festivals of Emar are generally considered to be indigenous to Syrian Emar, at least in their final forms. They were originally written down in order to preserve the importance of the festivals to the community life of the city, or to preserve the memory of the proper sequence of events within each festival, to ensure that the complicated offerings were not mixed up, to ensure that all the gods were remembered. The impetus to write down public rituals probably came from the Hittites, with whom it was common practice. According to Arnaud, this type of writing was rare in the Semitic Near East and, for the most part, was later than the time of Emar.[27]

I suggest that one festival, the *zukru*, originated after the Hittites rebuilt Emar in the second half of the fourteenth century, without an oral background, and that it reflects a covenant or treaty celebration of some kind. The *entu* and *maš'artu* installation festivals may have been older and may have had an oral background.

It is possible that Emar's diviner-scribe, with a sense of humor, composed a series of texts in mock-epic style for the writing practice of his mid-level scribal students. The *kissu* texts, brief and relatively informal as they are, are miniature festival texts. I suggest that they were composed in Emar specifically for the purpose of providing scribal students with practice texts. They are brief, to hold a student's attention. They could be considered tongue-in-cheek, for instance, by endowing a chair with royal or divine status. The place where a king sits takes on the king's royalty. The *kissu* texts contain the same language elements as the longer texts: lists of foodstuffs, containers, animals, numbers and math problems, all woven

---

26 Pitard (1996) 19.

27 Arnaud (1980) 379.

into a connected, narrative-like structure. A student could have more "fun" with such a text than copying out dull lists of these items. One thinks of such students as being beyond the copying of lists but not quite ready to tackle the long and complicated *entu* or *zukru* texts, of young students with a limited attention span, but not children.

Some of the master scribe's (the diviner's) students might never reach this point; perhaps they learned their letters and all the math they needed and went early to work on the docks, keeping Emar functioning profitably. But the diviner taught them too.

In sum, the diviner of Emar carries today far too modest a title, so modest as to be misleading. He was much more than that. He was a priest and international chaplain; he was a diviner and author of medical texts; he was a diplomat without portfolio and liaison between his people and his foreign overlords. He was schoolmaster and author, molder of young minds. The quality of his training was reflected in the quality of the work performed by his students on the docks. If they messed up, Emar stood to lose at the economic level.

Many of his functions were performed on an "on-call" or "as needed" basis. He probably held regular classes for the students, but I think there was no other "everyday" for him.

On the other hand, an educated guess is that the diviner would have been content with that title. He did not need public acknowledgment of the power he held. By not drawing attention to his many functions and the importance of them all to the very existence of his town, he could better perform them all, quietly and behind the scenes, determining, shaping, and controlling all of the town's communications.

BIBLIOGRAPHY

Archi, A. (1990) Imâr au IIIeme millénaire d'après les archives d'Ebla. *Mari. Annales de recherches interdisciplinaires* 6: 21–38. **Arnaud, D.** (1980) La bibliothèque d'un devin Syrien à Meskéné-Emar (Syrie). In *Comtes Rendus des Séances de l'Académie des Inscriptions et Belles-Lettres*, pp. 375–88, n.p. (1985) *Recherches au pays d'Astata, Emar VI.1: textes sumériens et accadiens, planches.* Paris. (1986) *Emar VI.3: textes sumériens et accadiens, texte.* Paris. (1987) *Emar VI.4: textes de la bibliothèque, transcriptions et traductions.* Paris. (n.d.) Les Hittites sur le moyen-Euphrate: protecteurs et indigènes. *Hethitica* VIII: 9–27. Leuven. **Beckman, G.** (1983) Mesopotamians and Mesopotamian Learning at Hattuša. *JCS* 35: 97–114. (1992) Hittite Administration in Syria in the Light of the Texts from Hattuša, Ugarit and Emar. In Mark W. Chavalas and John L. Hayes, ed., *New Horizons in the Study of Ancient Syria*, pp. 40–49. Bibliotheca Mesopotamica 25. Malibu. (1996) Emar and Its Archives. In Mark W. Chavalas, ed., *Emar: The History, Religion, and Culture of a Syrian Town in the Late Bronze Age*, pp. 1–12. Bethesda, Md. **Fleming, D.** (2000) *Time at Emar: The Cultic Calendar and the Rituals from the Diviner's House.* Winona Lake, Ind. (1992) The Rituals from Emar: Evolution of an Indigenous Tradition in Second-Millennium Syria. In Mark W. Chavalas and John L. Hayes, eds., *New Horizons in the Study of Ancient Syria*, pp. 51–62. Bibliotheca Mesopotamica 25. Malibu. **Geyer, B.** (1990) Une ville aujourd'hui engloutie: Emar. *Mari. Annales de recherches interdisciplinaires* 6: 107–19. **Hallo, W.W.** (1992) The Syrian Contribution to Cuneiform Literature. In Mark W. Chavalas and John L. Hayes, eds., *New Horizons in the Study of Ancient Syria*, pp. 69–88. Bibliotheca Mesopotamica 25. Malibu. **Kramer, S.N.** (1979) Sumerian Literature, a General Survey. In G. Ernest Wright, ed., *The Bible and the Ancient Near East*, pp. 249–66. Winona Lake. **Landsberger, B.** (1957–58) Practical Vocabulary of Assur. *AfO* 18: 328–41. **Margueron, J.-C.** (1977) Un exemple d'urbanisme volontaire à l'époque du Bronze Récent en Syrie. *Ktèma* 2: 33–48. (1980) Emar: un exemple d'implantation hittite en terre syrienne. In J.-C. Margueron, ed., *Le Moyen Euphrate: Zone de contacts et d'échanges*, pp. 285–312. Leiden. (1990) Imar et Emar: Une recherche qui se prolonge… (Histoire d'une problématique). *Mari. Annales de recherches interdisciplinaires* 6: 103–6. (1995) Emar, Capital of Astata in the Fourteenth Century BCE. *BA* 58: 126–38. **Oppenheim, A. L.** (1977) *Ancient Mesopotamia: Portrait of a Dead Civilization.* Rev. ed. Erica Reiner. Chicago. **Pitard, W.** (1996) The Archaeology of Emar. In Mark W. Chavalas, ed., *Emar: The History, Religion, and Culture of a Syrian Town in the Late Bronze Age*, pp. 13–23. Bethesda, Md. **Sjöberg, Å.** (1976) The Old Babylonian Eduba. In *Sumerological Studies in Honor of Thorkild Jacobsen*, pp. 159–79. Assyriological Studies 20. Chicago. **Weisberg, D.** (1967) *Guild Structure and Political Allegiance in Early Achaemenid Mesopotamia.* New Haven. **Zaccagnini, C.** (1983) Patterns of Mobility among Ancient Near Eastern Craftsmen. *JNES* 42: 245–64.

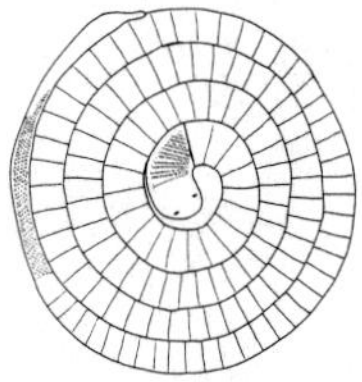

The Levant

Everyday Life in Biblical Israel: Women's Social Networks

Carol Meyers
Duke University

An advertisement in *Archaeology* magazine caught my eye as I began to prepare for the conference on "Daily Life in the Ancient Near East" and to think about what was meant by "daily life." The ad announced a new book series called *What Life Was Like*. Claiming to be the "first world history of everyday lives," the series would "re-create the experiences of everyday life ... offering ... a journey to the past that's more personal, more alive, and less like history [sic] than you ever thought possible." Deciding to examine a volume in this grandly heralded series, I sent away for a copy of a book on ancient Egypt called *What Life Was Like on the Banks of the Nile*. Two things about the book were, as expected, readily apparent. First, it was lavishly illustrated. Second, it dealt largely with the lives of the elite. Indeed, there was a disclaimer, saying how unfortunate it was that "the people at the bottom of the human pyramid [!], the shepherds, the cattle-drivers, and the peasant farmers, left no traces of how they lived" and so couldn't be included in this volume. This book meant to attract the general reader glibly dismissed the general population of Egyptian antiquity.

And what does a book about daily life of the elite depict? Again, as expected, it shows what people ate and wore, what they used for weapons and tools, where they lived, where they worshipped, and where they were buried. It gives the impression that daily life consisted only of activities and not of relationships, as if daily life revolved around *things* and not around *people*. Looking at this book, and at other such examples of the "daily life" genre, strengthened my resolve, in considering everyday life in biblical Israel, to ignore the urban elite and instead focus on the agrarian families, or peasant farmers, that probably constituted the vast majority of the population of biblical Israel throughout its existence, from the pre-monarchic era to the exile and beyond.

Note: This essay is adapted from part of a longer study (Meyers 1999a), published in a festschrift for Edward F. Campbell, Jr. A related piece (Meyers [1999c]) appears in a volume in the *Feminist Companion to the Bible* series.

In focusing on farm families rather than elites, this study will depart from traditional daily-life genres in another way: it will try to reconstruct the social relationships, rather than the physical realities of everyday life. Everyday life for people everywhere certainly means the use of items and structures of material culture. Because those items and structures are recoverable through archaeology, the reconstruction of daily life naturally looks first at where people lived and how they secured the basic necessities of life. But, everyday life also involves a series of interactions among people. The social relations of daily life—how, with whom, and why people interacted with each other—are not directly visible in the archaeological record. However, reasonable hypotheses about those interactions can be suggested by considering archaeological data, scattered clues in ancient texts, and comparative data provided by ethnography.

The terrain of social interactions is vast. It will be narrowed here in two ways. First, it will consider *informal social networks* (rather than formal ones) of two kinds: cooperative social interactions among neighboring family groups—families inhabiting the same village or towns; and cooperative interactions among kin-related households in neighboring settlements. Second, because women are often overlooked in considerations of Israelite, or any, society, it will focus on *women's* informal cooperative associations, or networks, in Israelite agrarian communities.[1] Doing so will perhaps help to redress the balance, that is, to give visibility to women along with men. Furthermore, reconstructing women's roles means acknowledging the important but usually unrecognized contributions of women, economically and socially, to their own households and also to the communities in which they lived. The fact that the social and economic contributions of women are usually unrecognized is a function of assumptions about male dominance in society and deserves some discussion.

---

1 "Agrarian communities" denotes not only small villages and hamlets but also larger settlements called *ᶜārîm* ("cities") in the Hebrew Bible. In the Iron Age, many of the latter did not actually have the functions and features associated with the urban life of their Bronze Age precursors; most had no public buildings and were little more than fortified villages (or "residential cities") inhabited by farming families that worked the surrounding lands. See Frick (1997) 14–19 and Fritz (1997) 19–25. Given this distinction between residential cities and true urban centers, it has been estimated that only a tiny minority of people in agricultural societies—never more than 10% and perhaps as little as 5%—lived in truly urban settings. See Lenski (1984) 199–200.

Theoretical Considerations

Assumptions that men dominate the communal life of traditional as well as contemporary societies are common. Social scientists who examine human cultures, both ancient and modern, tend to give most of their attention to formal associations formed by men for military, economic, religious, and political purposes. Indeed, in many cases men's public organizations in the premodern world—armies, guilds, priesthoods, bureaucracies—are the only extra-domestic associations to be recognized by observers and scholars. The result has been that the varied, and often powerful informal, extra-domestic connections formed by women have largely gone unnoticed. The contributions of women's groups to the social, political, religious and economic aspects of their communities have thereby been rendered invisible or, at best, trivialized. Certainly such is the case for ancient Israel. To be sure, in recent years, feminist biblical scholarship has drawn attention to formal women's activities, such as those of professional mourners, singers and dancers, prophets, health care practitioners (midwives and sorcerers/witches), and wise women.[2] Yet the existence of informal groups of women interacting on a daily basis in informal networks has hitherto been overlooked.

Why is this so? One part of the reason for this, of course, is that the major source of information about Israelite society, the Hebrew Bible, is itself relatively silent about women's daily activities and relationships; using it as the only source of information about how women interacted with each other entails blindness to many significant areas of women's behavior patterns.[3] However, overlooking Israelite women's daily interactions, because of their invisibility in the Hebrew Bible, is only part of the problem. The failure to take note of women's informal groups in biblical Israel is probably part of a wider androcentric bias, a bias that exaggerates the juridical and political spheres by focusing on formal or national structures in which men are the major participants and that ignores or discounts female activities in informal and local settings. Western ideological constructions are also implicated. Contemporary patriarchal notions of gender and gender roles in the West originated, to a great extent, in the changes in family life brought about by the industrial revolution. The stay-at-home full-time wife-and-mother pattern, which emerged with the industrial revolution and contributed powerfully to the family's success in mak-

---

2 For example, see Brenner (1985) 33–38, 46–59, 67–77; Brenner and Van Dijk-Hemmes (1993) 48–52, 62–71, 83–86; Meyers (1999a; 1999b).

3 Cf. Allen and Barber (1976) 3.

ing the transition to industrialization, also created distorting preconceptions about women's roles. The radical functional shifts in family life in the West in the nineteenth century were accompanied by ideological shifts that reinforced the reconfiguration of the family and that took away the opportunity or need for women's economic productivity, except in the poorest sectors of society. A woman's role, limited to the reconfigured family, became that of non-producing housewife and mother. The home became "private," and the Cult of Domesticity effectively kept most women out of the "public" sphere. Child rearing and housekeeping were the woman's household domain; and religion in America and on the continent contributed to the development and maintenance of the ideology of this distinct woman's sphere.[4]

The power of such ideas permeated critical biblical scholarship as it emerged in the nineteenth century. Biblical women were invariably compared to biblical men and inevitably pronounced subordinate and inferior possessions of men. For example, in his classic work on the institutions of *Ancient Israel*, De Vaux remarks that a wife addressed her husband "as a slave addressed his master, or a subject his king" and that any participation in public affairs was highly exceptional.[5] Male biblical scholars, reading the text with their own presuppositions and perhaps with their own claims to authority at stake, saw women through distorting interpretive lenses. Even feminist biblical scholarship, which in its early stages sought to rescue women mentioned in the Hebrew Bible from obscurity,[6] also tended to think of women primarily in "wife-mother" terms, which are difficult to separate from their western connotations of the separation of the public from the private, and which usually imply the absence of an economic role. In her pioneer article on "Images of Women in the Old Testament," for example, Bird claims that "Central to most [references in the historical and prophetic books] ... and underlying all are the images of wife and mother (or wife-mother) ... .These two images defined most women's lives," with women in legal texts, if mentioned at all, being dependent and usually infirm.[7]

Thus there are two factors—the relative paucity of information about women in the Hebrew Bible, and also the modern ideological creation of the idea of women's separate domestic sphere—that have influenced

4 So Rudy (1997) 15–44.

5 De Vaux (odp 1958; Eng ed. 1961) 39; see also Baab (1962) 865.

6 Bellis (2000) 27–28.

7 Bird (1974) 69, 56.

consideration of Israelite gender roles and made it difficult to see women as other than subservient wife-mothers. Public figures such as Deborah and Miriam are regularly noted; yet they appear as exceptions that prove the rule that women's daily lives consisted of activities in their immediate households under the authority of men. The legitimacy of such claims, which ironically have been made by both the supporters and the critics of biblical patriarchy, must be contested, because now we have new ways of examining Israelite society and reconstructing women's roles. Social scientists in the last third of the twentieth century have extensively investigated the lives of women in traditional societies. Motivated by the second wave of American feminism in the 1960s and 1970s, they have looked at women in their own right, not simply as adjuncts to males. This ethnography of the last few decades has provided new data and perspectives on women in marginal agrarian societies, like that of ancient Israel, where 90% or more of the population resided in agrarian households.[8]

These advances in social science research have caused radical revisions in general notions about women's status in premodern farming households. The conventional wisdom that saw women as passive and powerless in virtually all pre-industrial cultures is now known to be deeply flawed. That idea is not borne out by newer studies of such societies, which rely on information gathered from within households and from female as well as male informants, rather than on the biased information about women's roles given by male informants to earlier generations of social or cultural anthropologists.[9] What has emerged is a radically different picture. The work patterns and authority structures that characterize the reality of daily life in premodern societies are rarely hierarchical along gender lines, even if such hierarchies do exist in certain political, religious, or jural aspects of the society.[10] A rich assortment of recent studies of the family and household in traditional societies is especially cognizant of the range of women's contributions to and also control of household economic functions.[11] Such information helps, as one researcher has put it, to "strip

---

8 See note 1.

9 In her article reviewing the impact of the women's movement on anthropology, Quinn (1977) highlights the biases and distortions of traditional male-oriented ethnography and its readiness to see gender asymmetry as signifying male privilege, dominance, or superior status.

10 A pioneering piece on this subject, based on fieldwork in rural Greece, is by Friedl (1967). See also Cronin (1977) and Rogers (1975).

11 E.g., in Biblical Studies, Burnette-Bletsch (1998).

away ideological blinders to women's actual economic contributions"[12] at the household level and beyond. Traditional views of female dependency on males have been overturned by studies that reveal the breadth and complexity of women's work in traditional agrarian societies and thus of male dependence on female productivity.

Just as important, the newer ethnographies examine the articulation of the household with wider community functions. They have discovered that the modern conceptual separation between domestic and public spheres[13] cannot hold up to nuanced evaluations of women's extra-domestic activities. The two domains, it is now understood, are not necessarily separate.[14] Public and private are not two distinct kinds of social realms, the first society-wide and the second consisting only of small family units. Rather, in most premodern, village-based societies, the lines between such hypothetical spheres are blurred. Needs or issues arising in family units are dealt with by the larger community. Thus, the private *is* the public when the interests of individual households are reflected in the collective actions of larger groups. In traditional societies, it is not an "either/or" matter of private vs. public; rather, many issues are "both/and." To put it another way, activities in the household or family are connected to and have implications for the broader social world. Women's daily domestic roles are not household-bound; and they often have consequences in the wider "public" community. Public and private are thus overlapping and integrated domains in many aspects of family and community life in traditional societies.

The contemporary western notion of public and private as discrete realms has negatively influenced evaluation of women's roles in premodern societies. When community and household are looked at as separate structures and are related hierarchically, public roles tend to be valued more than private ones. This has created a tendency to devalue women's unpaid housework in modern urban settings, which in turn has unconsciously and unfairly colored considerations of women's labor in traditional agrarian ones. Our western eyes often blind us to the possibility that women's productive labor, carried out in household units in premodern societies, can be valued as highly as men's leadership tasks in community-

---

12 March and Taqqu (1986) viii.

13 Classically expressed by Rosaldo (1974) and Sanday (1974).

14 Rosaldo herself (1980) questions the validity of some of the binary constructions of public/private as expressed in her earlier essay (1974). See also the essays in Helly and Reverby (1992) and in Sharistanian (1987).

wide structures. Similarly, greater male visibility in public life is not equivalent to higher male status in all aspects of daily life. The idea of a fixed relationship between genders—women subordinate, men superior—cannot be demonstrated for *all* gender interactions.[15] Indeed, status itself is not a unitary condition; it involves may variables, often causally independent of one another.

Recent studies of traditional societies thus are clearly important for recognizing and correcting the biases of western scholarship. More specifically, with respect to the focus of this study, they can also help identify women's daily interactions. They show how women in traditional societies connect with other women across family boundaries in ways that have consequences for community as well as domestic life. The existence and function of informal associations of women have been so well documented across cultures all over the globe that there can no longer be any doubt about their existence and also their significance. Indeed, relations forged by women outside of formal public structures, and usually overlooked by older investigations, are ubiquitous across cultures and are often essential to community life even when they are grounded in household activities.[16]

Women's informal alliances, designated "women's networks," are not some hypothetical web of acquaintances or sets of casual friendships among women.[17] Rather, informal as they are and even as invisible as they may be to an outside observer, women's networks actually function as institutions that provide critical social linkages. The tendency to relate "informal" with "unimportant" and "formal" with "important" does not do justice to the dynamics of informal cooperative alliances; and it occludes the way women's networks perform essential social and economic tasks and hence carry considerable weight.[18] Such networks function in two domains: first, they link women (and thus their families) to other communities; and second they provide connections among women (and their families) in neighboring households in the same community.

Women's Networks: Linking Communities

Considering women's inter-community alliances in ancient Israel depends on recognizing that marriages were usually parentally arranged and in-

---

15 Strathern (1977) 290.

16 March and Taqqu (1986) 16.

17 Maher (1976) 52–53.

18 Maher (1976) 52, 71.

volved patrilocal residence: the newly wed couples resided near or with the husband's family. Anthropologically informed studies of the incest prohibitions of Leviticus (18:7–9; 20:11–14, 17, 19–21) tell us that eligible spouses for a man had to come from beyond his residential family.[19] Because Israelite villages were generally small, with appropriate potential spouses few in number, seeking marriage partners from outside a man's village would have been common. This practice had the pragmatic function of creating alliances among families of neighboring villages. The resulting webs of kinship perhaps constitute the Israelite *mišpāḥâ*, which functioned as a "protective association of families."[20] These inter-village marital connections typically help maintain peace among contiguous settlements and increase the likelihood that related families would come to each other's assistance in times of economic or personal troubles.[21] Economic, social, and political matters thus become part of kinship interactions.[22] For Israelite villagers, the groundwork for inter-family and inter-village mutual aid would have been laid by their marital ties and supported by the ties, both fictional and real, created by the constructions of lineages (genealogies). The resulting cooperation and reciprocity among families is essential for the survival of family units in an uncertain agrarian world, such as that of the Israelites.

The actual mechanisms for maintaining ties with kin in nearby settlements were likely to have been women's networks. Women, ethnographers have demonstrated, are well situated to play such a role. Women typically retain connections with their natal family—with their parents (as long as they are alive), brothers, and others; and those relationships often prove vital to various aspects of their lives in their marital communities. That is, women are often the ones who effect cooperation between communities because they have affiliations with *two* descent groups, or communities. When a woman marries *into* a family, she acquires a marital affiliation,

---

[19] McClenney-Sadler (2000). Those taboos also served to regulate the intimacies and tensions of the complex families (that is, domestic groups larger than the nuclear family), that characterize agrarian households such as those of ancient Israel; see Meyers (1988) 135–36. The archaeological data that are evidence for complex families in biblical Israel are presented in Stager (1985) 17–22.

[20] The terminology is that proposed by Gottwald (1979) 257–84. Others might call this structure, based on descent structures that can be real and/or fictitious, a *lineage* or *clan*.

[21] Zonabend (1996) 25–39.

[22] Lévi-Strauss (1982) 174 suggests that traditional societies knew how to "disguise social and political manoeuvres under the cloak of kinship."

namely, the residential household of her husband; but she doesn't thereby lose her natal affiliation, that is, the family into which she was born.[23] Israelite patrilocal marriage customs therefore meant that Israelite women had two sets of family ties and were thus uniquely positioned to facilitate relationships between them.

The dynamics of mutual assistance among *mišpāḥôt* are not indicated in the Hebrew Bible, and thus it is not surprising that the role of Israelite women in activating such alliances is not specified. However, a number of texts do indicate the sine qua non of such assistance—that married women remained connected with their natal families. Discussion of the tragic narrative of the Levite's concubine in Judges 19 inevitably focuses on the sexual outrage and the violence. Yet the tale also reveals that, when marital difficulties arise, the unnamed secondary wife returns to her natal household (Judg 19:2). Also in Judges is the narrative of Abimelech, the son of Gideon. Abimelech is said to have returned to his mother's family in Shechem, indeed to his mother's whole clan, when he sought support for his political ambitions. Abimelech's unnamed mother provides the connection. Similarly, in 2 Samuel the fleeing Absalom seeks refuge with his mother's family (2 Sam 3:3; 13:37). And in a priestly law of Leviticus, a divorced or widowed woman returns to her natal family (Lev 22:13).

The ongoing relationship between women and their families of origin would not only have been a mechanism for creating solidarity and aid among nearby Israelite communities. It also would have been activated in order to arrange marriages for sons with young women from other villages. Mothers of eligible sons typically retain or obtain knowledge about eligible mates from their natal community. The formal negotiation of marriage arrangements may be done by men, but the information obtained from women's networks is often decisive in the selection of mates for offspring.[24]

Given the function of marital alliances in helping to secure aid for families in need, the traditional way of viewing the financial aspects of marriage arrangements must be contested. The brideprices or dowries involved in Israelite marriages should not be conceptualized as the buying or selling of brides, but rather as exchanges or gifts that contributed to or helped maintain connections between two family groups.[25] Such marriage customs as the *mōhar*, the money paid by a groom or his parents to his

---

23 Strathern (1972) viii–ix, 130.

24 March and Taqqu (1986) 39.

25 March and Taqqu (1986) 41.

wife's family, created mutual obligations, which in turn increased the likelihood that families connected in this way would provide economic or other assistance to each other. Crop disaster in one village, given the great variation in nearby ecosystems, would thereby be mitigated by aid from affines living in a neighboring village. Women's informal intercommunity networks, while not necessarily activated on a daily basis, were nonetheless ever-present alliances that contributed to group welfare and that gave women a sense of community and connectedness.

Women's Networks: The Residential Community

Although natal ties were surely important to Israelite women, most of their daily interactions were with women in their marital communities: the women in their husband's extended family household, and also the women in the larger residential community. Several biblical passages, notably in Ruth but also in several other books, provide evidence that such informal associations were part of community life.

The Book of Ruth is more of a folktale than the authentic record of an historical event, yet most critics agree that certain aspects of Israelite society are reflected in the plausible details of the narrative.[26] The author may have taken liberties with legal niceties and cultural expectations in order to serve plot development, characterization, and dramatic interest. Yet, because the narrative assumes audience familiarity with certain practices, the social customs and interactions in Ruth are likely to be authentic.

The discussion of female relationships in Ruth tend to focus on the interactions of the named women, especially Ruth and Naomi.[27] Whatever else can be said about their relationship, it is important here to consider it in anthropological terms, that is, as an instance of bonding between female members of a marital household. An incoming bride, in patrilocal societies, is typically in a precarious position as the newcomer in an established household.[28] Although Ruth's position vis-à-vis her mother-in-law may have departed from the norm, it nonetheless stands as an exemplar of how female members of a household can act conjointly to achieve results that will benefit the kin group.

---

26 E.g., Campbell (1975) 8–10; Sasson (1979) 228–30.

27 Examples of recent readings of Ruth appear in Brenner (1993) and Brenner (1999). See also one of the early feminist discussions of Ruth, as a "woman's story," in Trible (1978) 166–99, an expansion of Trible (1976).

28 For a brief consideration of the dynamics of the relationship of an Israelite wife to her mother-in-law, see Meyers (1997) 35–36.

The figures of Ruth and Naomi may be central to any study of the Book of Ruth, but the appearance and actions of unnamed women provide the most important data about women's networks. Note that the story of Ruth's sojourn in her mother-in-law's community, Bethlehem, is framed by the mention of women's groups. At the beginning of that sojourn, according to Ruth 1:19, "the whole town" is happily aware of Naomi's return with Ruth; it is "the women" of Bethlehem, however, who are specifically mentioned as the ones who greet the two women. At the end of the tale, in 4:17 (cf. 4:14) immediately before the genealogical appendix, the "women of the neighborhood" appear at the occasion of the birth of Ruth's son Obed, who will be an ancestor of King David. This group of women names the infant. Although women outnumber men as name-givers in the Hebrew Bible (by nearly 2 to 1), this is the only instance of a group of women naming a child.[29] In so doing, they signify solidarity with the new mother.

Viewed anthropologically, the references in Ruth to local women depict the behavior of women in informal groups. At the outset, when women join together to greet Ruth and Naomi, they are helping to establish them in Naomi's, and ultimately Ruth's, marital community. At the end, they participate in the ceremonial event, a naming, connected with an important life event, childbirth.[30] This is part of the way neighboring women assist each other, emotionally as well as physically; they attend childbirth, with or without the presence of a midwife, and then help to care for mother and newborn child.

If ethnography suggests the solidarity of the neighboring women in the Book of Ruth, so too does the Hebrew terminology. The word used in Ruth 4:17 for the group of women who participate in the naming ceremony, which the NRSV (*The Holy Bible*. New Revised Standard Version) translates "women of the neighborhood," is actually one word in Hebrew: *šĕkēnôt*, "neighbors," a feminine plural participle (absolute) of the verb *škn*, "to settle, dwell." This feminine form is found in only one other place in the Hebrew Bible: in Exod 3:22, where, in anticipation of the exodus, the women are instructed to collect valuables from their (female) Egyptian

[29] Mothers, more often than fathers, give names to newborns in the Hebrew Bible. In seventeen instances names are provided by men; in twenty-seven cases the name-givers are women. See the discussions of naming in Pardes (1992) and Bohmbach (2000b).

[30] The name-giving ceremony, occurring soon after the birth, may have been conducted by the midwife as part of her role. See the naming of Tamar's twins in Gen 38:27–30 and the discussion in Meyers (2000).

neighbors and from any women living in their (female) neighbors' houses. These items of movable wealth become "plunder" in the eyes of the narrator. Yet that exploitative outcome depends on the existence of the solidarity of women in residential proximity. Note that the Israelite women "ask" for the valuables: they don't steal them. The text assumes that the Egyptian women who are "neighbors" participate in a woman's network with a high enough degree of solidarity that the Egyptian women would accede to the request of the Israelite women. Indeed, the notion that neighboring women would have been part of a social network was apparently more powerful in this verse than the general biblical construction of Egyptians as "others" or enemy.[31]

The masculine form of "neighbor" is also found in the Bible in several passages where it probably represents instances of inclusive language, with the masculine word referring to both women and men. For example, in Exod 12:4, neighboring households are instructed to share a lamb for the Passover feast. All the family members are included in that designation of neighbors (cf. Exod 12:21), which indicates a shared festal occasion of the sort in which food preparation was probably carried out by the women in neighboring households working together. Similarly, Prov 27:10 proclaims the value of "friends" and of "neighbors" who live nearby, over distant kin; that is, associations, female or male, involving residential contiguity can be more important at times than kinship connections. Finally, 2 Kgs 4:3 tells of a widow receiving economic aid from "neighbors." The aid is in the form of household containers for the storage of oil; the masculine form "neighbors" likely includes the female members of the neighbors' families, for women are typically the ones who deal with domestic food supplies and their containers. All these instances of "neighbor," feminine and masculine, indicate the importance of networks of people sharing community space and similar lifestyles. Such associations based on residential proximity were vital to the economic and cultural life of the community in ways that are difficult for those of us living in the urban west, often never seeing or knowing our neighbors, to grasp.

Another Hebrew term indicating a female network derives from the root *rʿh*, "to associate with." The noun forms are sometimes translated "friend," which does not adequately convey the closeness of the relationship. Note that this word sometimes appears synonymously with "brother" or "sister," as several times in Proverbs (Prov 17:7; and compare Ps 69:9 [8] with Ps 88:9 [8]). Note also that the verse in the Decalogue (Exod

---

31 An astute analysis of Egypt's prominent function as "other," as part of constructing Israel's identity in the Pentateuch, is found in Griefenhagen (1998).

20:16; Deut 5:20) about bearing false witness uses *rēa*ᶜ, "friend" (NRSV, "neighbor"), whereas an equivalent Deuteronomic law about bearing false witness (Deut 19:18–19) has *ʾāḥ* "brother." A friend, in other words, can be the equivalent of a sibling.[32] Indeed, a good friend can be even better than a sibling; several sayings in biblical wisdom literature (Prov 18:24; 27:10) elevate the solidarity of close friendship over that of close kinship. All told, the overlapping notions of "friend" and "neighbor"—people strongly connected to each other —reflect the intimacy that develops among people with whom one is in frequent daily contact.

Several biblical uses of feminine noun forms of *rᶜh (rēᶜâ, raᶜyâ, rĕᶜût)* indeed seem to designate such intimate relationships. The companions of Jephthah's daughter (in Judg 11:37, 38) and of the princess in Psalm 45 (v. 14 [15 in Heb]) are designated by this term, which we might today render "support group."[33] In addition, Exod 11:2, a reprise of Exod 3:22 (discussed above), in which women asked their "neighbors" (*šĕkēnôt*) for silver and gold, has God telling Moses that every man and woman should ask his or her Egyptian male and female neighbor, *rēᶜa,* and *rēᶜût* respectively, for those precious items. The intimacy of such friends or companions is clear from the way the male lover in the Song of Songs repeatedly calls his beloved *raᶜyātî* "my friend" (1:9, 15; 2:2, 10, 13; 4:1, 7; 5:2; 6:4.), appropriately translated "my love" in the NRSV.

These textual glimpses of women's groups of friends and neighbors in residential proximity evoke questions about how such groups functioned. What were their specific activities, other than the ones revealed in these few texts? Again, ethnographic data are invaluable in attempting to answer such questions. Informal women's networks in residential communities have been observed in may traditional societies; and their importance is greatest in societies existing at the subsistence level,[34] as was often the case in Israelite villages.

Women's networks in small agricultural communities function in several important social and economic ways. The nature of women's daily routines in ancient Israel would have been dictated by the division of labor by gender. Women and men each had certain prescribed, gender-specific tasks as well as some that they shared.[35] Most of women's regular tasks involved food preparation (transforming raw products, such as grain,

---

32 See Ringgren (1974) 191–93.

33 For a discussion of Jephthah's companions, see Bohmbach (2000a).

34 March and Taqqu (1986) 20, 58.

35 The nature of farm family life and the concomitant division of productive labor by age and gender is described in Meyers (1988) 139–49, (1997), and (1998²).

olives, and grapes, into bread, oil, and wine), textile production, and some horticultural work.[36] Because of the spatial organization of Iron Age villages, with domestic clusters adjoining each other,[37] Israelite women probably had more access to each other as they went about their daily activities than men did to other men. Many repetitive household activities performed by women would have been done in each other's company. Indeed, a recent archaeological discovery from Tel Dor indicates that such daily contact apparently involved cooperative labor.[38] An Iron I installation, made of mud brick and covered with mud plaster, has now been interpreted as a communal trough in which women kneaded bread dough together. This interpretation is based on terracotta models, known from the Aegean, of several women bent over a common trough. It is also supported by the existence of evidence for women's joint bread-making in later periods.[39]

Such regular and intimate contact, in kneading dough and in doing other tasks, either jointly or in each other's company, creates familiarity and interdependence. The sharing of tasks means the sharing of problems and experiences, all of which contribute to a sense of identity. Familiarity and identity in turn foster solidarity among the women in daily contact with each other—these would be the "women of the neighborhood" and other close "friends" or "neighbors" mentioned or alluded to in the Hebrew Bible.

This solidarity meant more than simply providing companionship and making repetitive tasks less onerous; it also had important functional value. Regular female contact across households means that women's groups are information-sharing groups. Women quickly become aware if there are acute labor needs in an individual household because of the

---

36 This heavy load of female productive labor is given the unfortunate label as being "outside the household" by Bird (1992) 995. Perhaps influenced by the idea of "household" as coterminous with "domicile," she fails to see productive tasks as *part* of the household economy, and she completely misses the informal supra-household activities of women. The concept of "household"—physically, economically, and demographically—is addressed in Meyers (1988) 122–38; (1997) 13–21; and forthcoming b.

37 Stager (1985) 17–22.

38 Stern, Berg, Gilboa, Sharon, and Zorn (1997) 47–56, figs. 11, 12.

39 Hirschfeld (1995) 274 relates the cooperative activity of women in the talmudic period to the archaeological recovery of Roman-Byzantine dwellings with shared courtyards and to the ethnographic evidence of traditional Palestinian villages in the Hebron hills. See also the statement of Rabban Gamaliel: "Three women knead together, bake it [bread] in one stove, one after another" (*Y Pesaḥ* 3,30b).

illness, absence, or death of one or more family members. Because of their solidarity, they rally to provide assistance, perhaps creating informal labor pools or other non-hierarchical structures for rotational mutual aid.[40] These adaptive procedures, which are ultimately beneficial to all households, in turn increase the solidarity among the women. The character and location of women's tasks, as distinct from men's—men's field work, which occupies a large percentage of male subsistence tasks tends to be more solitary—create social connections that can be critical to the viability of individual households.

Another significant aspect of informal women's networks in Israelite villages was undoubtedly their role in religious or ritual activities. Biblical texts depict males in the leadership roles and also in most of the secondary roles of national and public cultic life. Indeed, women's cultic roles seem quite restricted if one looks only at the national cult, as delineated in the Pentateuch and in scattered references in the Deuteronomic History. However, cultic life existed outside the arena of the official Jerusalem cultus in untold numbers of domestic rituals and village celebrations. Such activities, in which women participated and which they probably sometimes orchestrated, are often viewed as secondary or of less value than the formal public events. That notion, however, must be contested, based as it is upon some of the false assumptions about the domestic-public dichotomy noted above. Religious activity in household or village settings can represent the most accessible and most significant experience for the majority of people in isolated agrarian communities. For Israel, this would have been especially true following the centralization of the official cult in Jerusalem in the seventh century B.C.E.

Just what would have been the nature of women's cultic activity in Iron Age Israel? Again, ethnographic studies of traditional societies are extremely useful in reconstructing the religious live of Israelite households.[41] Women probably organized and took part in a variety of domestic and community ritual events. Some may have been connected with female biological processes, such as the childbirth and child-naming that appear at the end of the Ruth story, and may thus have excluded males. But most events centering on the life-cycle events, such as marriage and death, would have been gender-inclusive family or "neighborhood" events. Groups of village women probably developed traditions of sacral behaviors for which they, not the men, were experts. Women's roles in creating feasts, in maintaining shrines or tombs of ancestors, in tending household

---

40 March and Taqqu (1986) 54–59.

41 See Bird (1987).

shrines and household gods, and in making and paying vows are widely attested aspects of women's religious practice.[42] From the perspective of agricultural village women rather than that of male urban priests, women's ritual behaviors are extraordinarily meaningful in sacralizing their lives and in helping them feel that they are contributing to the well-being of their families and their community. Furthermore, if one is to look at traditional complex societies as "heterarchical" rather than hierarchical, that is, with multiple separate internal hierarchies rather than with one overall system,[43] then one can in fact see a segment of group activities dominated by women.

Ethnographic, archaeological, and textual data together point clearly to the importance of the informal networks of Israelite women. Although they maintained ties with their natal villages, most of women's productive lives were lived in their marital communities, where their connections with other women constituted a vital aspect of their daily lives and also contributed to the welfare of their own households and to the larger settlements in which they resided. The very informality of Israelite women's networks gave them great flexibility to respond in innovative, situation-specific ways to human needs. Women's alliances in agrarian communities were hardly casual affairs with little relevance to the overall processes of social existence.[44] Though rarely recognized as such, much like the so-called "voluntary associations" that have long been part of women's powerful but little-heralded extra-household lives in America,[45] they performed essential functions without which the economic survival and social stability of the communities would not have been possible. And like women's associations in America, the networks of Israelite women created an infrastructure that helped maintain the community. The ubiquitous existence of such infrastructures means that "women have always been agents in history."[46]

Women's Groups and Women's Lives

The value of women's networks for the lives of the women themselves was as important as were the social and economic benefits of such groups. To use current terminology, women's groups empower women. The informal

---

42 So Sered (1992). See also Meres (forthcoming a)

43 As argued by Ehrenreich, Crumley, and Levy (1995). See also Crumley (1987).

44 March and Taqqu (1986) 9–11.

45 See Evans (1989) 1, 2–3; cf Lambert (1995).

46 Lerner (1999).

associations of village women in ancient Israel, as well as their links with women in other settlements, would have constituted a more diffuse and thus more elusive form of female power than that of women in formal or professional groups (i.e., musicians, mourning women, and others).[47] And the power of informal women's groups certainly differed from the institutionalized power of men's formal and public groups. Yet women's informal associations, which now can be identified in virtually every human society,[48] were no less real and important than were the more visible public organizations of both women and men. The participation of women in such networks, which provided emotional and material assistance for others, gave them the sense that they could get something done—that they could control labor and resources, albeit on a small scale.

The solidarity of women in informal groups, in ancient Israel as elsewhere, was not simply a psychological or social strategy of defense devised by women in vulnerable circumstances, although female solidarity can indeed provide collective female power over abusive or controlling males. More important, the quasi-autonomy of women's networks empowered women by virtue of the positive contributions such alliances make to the overall social fabric. Furthermore, the effective agency of the networks meant that women were in fact participants in the "public" domain. Women became part of that domain by virtue of their informal linkages within communities and between communities, by virtue of the fact that the public and private were not discrete realms. In sum, the role of women in extra-household alliances and activities represents a real, albeit little-recognized, form of female power. It would have compensated for the asymmetry of gender power that otherwise seems to have prevailed in Israelite public life; and it can support the notion of heterarchical structures in Israelite society.

One other value for women of such informal networks lay in the leadership possibilities they provided. As for more formal groups, hierarchies exist within informal groups as within any components of heterarchies. Some women, based variously on seniority (and wisdom), on

---

47 The empowering social dynamics of formal women's groups, or "guilds," of professionals are discussed in Meyers (1999a) 166–70, 179–82.

48 The ubiquity of informal women's networks and the way they exert effective power in their communities may actually be characteristic of female primates in general, not only of humans. Primatologists, e.g., Wrangham (1980), have noted that many primate groups are "female-bonded," with the females exhibiting very close relationships with each other. According to Small (1993) 144, alliances formed along both kinship and non-kinship lines provide social power to the females in primate communities.

expertise (in certain household tasks), or on charisma (in organizing labor or commodity exchanges) emerge as leaders and thereby garner status and respect. In this way, the dynamics of women's informal groups expanded and enhanced many women's lives.

The participation of Israelite women in informal groups meant that they led more complex and probably more interesting lives than is generally assumed. In the process of contributing to the welfare of their households, their families near and far, and their communities, women's daily undertakings, as well as those associated with special events and with occasional crises, were replete with opportunities for self-expression and self-fulfillment.

BIBLIOGRAPHY

Allen, S. and D.L. Barber (1976) Sexual Division and Society. In D.L. Barber and S. Allen, eds., *Sexual Divisions and Society: Process and Change*, 1–24. Explorations in Sociology 6. London. **Baab, O.J.** (1962) Women. In G.A. Butrick, ed., *Interpreter's Dictionary of the Bible* 4: 864–67. Nashville, Tenn. **Bellis, A.O.** (2000) Feminist Biblical Scholarship. In C. Meyers, T. Craven, and R. Kraemer, eds., *Women in Scripture: A Dictionary of Named and Unnamed Women in the Hebrew Bible, the Apocryphal/Deuterocanonical Books, and the New Testament*, 26–34. Boston. **Bird, P.** (1974) Images of Women in the Old Testament. In R.R. Ruether, ed., *Religion and Sexism: Images of Women in the Jewish and Christian Tradition*, 41–88. New York. (1987) The Place of Women in the Israelite Cultus. In P.O. Miller, P.D. Hanson, and S.D. McBride, eds., *Ancient Israelite Religion: Essays in Honor of Frank Moore Cross*, 397–420. Philadelphia. (1992) Women (OT). In D.N. Freedman, ed., *Anchor Bible Dictionary* IV: 951–57. New York. **Bohmbach, K.** (2000a) Companions of Jephthah's Daughter (Judg 11:37–38). In C. Meyers, T. Craven, and R. Kraemer, eds., *Women in Scripture: A Dictionary of Named and Unnamed Women in the Hebrew Bible, the Apocryphal-Deuterocanonical Books, and the New Testament*. Boston. (2000b) Names and Naming in the Biblical World. In *ibid.* **Brenner, A.** (1985) *The Israelite Woman: Social Role and Literary Type in Biblical Narrative*. Journal for the Study of the Old Testament Supplement Series 21. Sheffield. (1993) *A Feminist Companion to Ruth*. A Feminist Companion to the Bible 3. Sheffield. (1999) *A Feminist Companion to Ruth and Esther*. A Feminist Companion to the Bible (Second Series) 3. Sheffield. **Brenner, A. and F. Van Dijk-Hemmes** (1993) *On Gendering Biblical Texts: Female and Male Voices in the Hebrew Bible*. Leiden. **Burnette-Bletsch, R.** (1998) *My Bone and My Flesh: The Agrarian Family in Biblical Law*. Ph. D. dissertation, Duke University. **Campbell, E.F., Jr.** (1975) *Ruth: A New Translation with Introduction and Commentary*. Anchor Bible 7. Garden City, N.Y. **Cronin, C.** (1977) Illusion and Reality in Sicily. In A. Shlegel, ed., *Sexual Stratification: A Cross-Cultural View*, 67–93. New York. **Crumley, C.** (1987) A Dialectical Critique of Hierarchy. In T. Paterson and C. Gailey, eds., *Power Relations and State Formations*, 155–59. Washington, D.C. **De Vaux, R.** (1961) *Ancient Israel: Its Life and Institutions,* trans. J. McHugh. New York. (French edition, 2 vols., 1958 and 1960.) **Ehrenreich, R., C. Crumley, and J.E. Levy**, eds. (1995) *Heterarchy and the Analysis of Complex Societies.* American Anthropological Association, Archaeological Papers 6. Arlington, Va. **Evans, S. M.** (1989) *Born for Liberty: A History of Women in America.* New York. **Frick, F.S.** (1997) Cities: An Overview. In E.M. Meyers, ed., *The Oxford Encyclopedia of Archaeology in the Near East* 2: 14–19. New York. **Friedl, E.** (1967) The Position of Women: Appearance and Reality. *Anthropological Quarterly* 40: 97–108. **Fritz, V.** (1997) Cities of the Bronze and Iron Ages. In E.M. Meyers, ed., *The Oxford Encyclopedia of Archaeology in the Near East* 2: 19–24. New York. **Gottwald, N.K.** (1979) *The Tribes of Yahweh: A Sociology of the Religion of Liberated Israel, 1250–1050 B.C.* Maryknoll, New York. **Griefenhagen, F.W.** (1998) *Egypt in the Symbolic Geography of the Pentateuch: Constructing Biblical Israel's Identity.* Ph.D. dissertation, Duke University. **Helly, D.O., and S. Reverby**, eds. (1992) *Gendered Domains: Rethinking Public and Private in Women's History.* Ithaca, N.Y. **Hirschfeld, Y.** (1995) *The Palestinian Dwelling in the Roman-Byzantine Period.* Jerusalem. **Lambert, C.** (1995) Leadership in a New Key. *Harvard Magazine* 97: 28–33. **Lenski, G.** (1984^2) *Power and Privilege: A Theory of Social Stratification.* Second edition. Chapel Hill, N.C. (First edition, 1966). **Lerner, Gerda** (1999) "Encounters with History: Lerner Learned the Importance of History and Asked Why Women Were Ignored. " Interview, Duke University. **Lévi-Strauss, C.** (1982) *The Way of Masks.* London. **McClenney-Sadler, M.** (2000) Women in Incest Regulations (Lev 18:7–18, 20; 20:11–14, 17, 19–21). In C. Meyers, T. Craven, and R. Kraemer, eds., *Women in Scripture: A Dictionary of Named and Unnamed Women in the Hebrew Bible, the Apocryphal/Deuterocanonical Books, and the New Testament.* Boston. **Maher, V.** (1976) Kin, Clients, and Accomplices: Relationships among Women in Morocco. In D.L. Barber and S. Allen, eds., *Sexual Divisions and Society: Process and Change.* Explorations in Sociology 6. London. **March, K.S. and R.L. Taqqu** (1986) *Women's Informal Associations in Developing Countries.* Women in Cross-Cultural Perspective. Boulder, Co. **Meyers, C.** (1988) *Discovering Eve: Ancient Israelite Women in Context.* New York. (1997) The Family in Early Israel. Chapter 1 in L. Perdue, C. Meyers, J. Blenkinsopp, and J.J. Collins, *Families in Ancient Israel*, 1–47. Louisville. (1998^2) Everyday Life: Women in the Period of the Hebrew Bible. In C.A. Newsom and S. Ringe, eds., *The Women's Bible Commentary*, 251–59. Second edition. Louisville (First edition, 1992). (1999a) Guilds and Gatherings: Women's Groups in Ancient Israel. In P.M. Williams, Jr., and T. Hiebert, eds., *Realia Dei: Essays in Honor of Edward F. Campbell, Jr.* Atlanta, Ga. (1999b) Mother to Muse: An Ethnoarchaeological Study of Women's Performance in Ancient Israel. In A. Brenner and J.W. Van Henten, eds., *Recycling Biblical Figures: NOSTER Conference 1997.* Leiden. (1999c) 'Women of the Neighborhood' (Ruth 4. 17): Informal Female Networks in Ancient Israel. In A. Brenner, *Ruth and Esther*, 110–27. A Feminist Companion to the Bible (Second Series) 3. Sheffield. (2000)

Midwife (Gen 35: 17; 38: 28). In C. Meyers, T. Craven, and R. Kraemer. *Women in Scripture: A Dictionary of the Named and Unnamed Women in the Hebrew Bible, the Apocryphal/Deuterocanonical Books, and the New Testament.* Boston. (forthcoming a) From Household to House of Yahweh: Women's Religious Culture in Ancient Israel. In A. Lemaire, ed., *VT Supplement,* Vol. 92. Basel Congress Volume. Leiden. (forthcoming b) Material Remains and Social Relationships: Women's Culture in Agrarian Households of the Iron Age. In W.G. Dever and S. Gitin, eds., *Symbiosis, Symbolism, and the Power of the Past: Canaan, Ancient Israel, and Their Neighbors from the Late Bronze Age through Roman Palestine.* **Pardes, I.** (1992) Beyond Genesis 3: The Politics of Maternal Naming. Chapter 3 in *Countertraditions in the Bible: A Feminist Approach,* 39–59. Cambridge, Massachusetts. **Quinn, N.** (1997) Anthropological Studies on Women's Status. *Annual Review of Anthropology* 6: 181–225. **Ringgren, H.** (1974) *ᶜāch; ᶜāchôth.* In H. Ringgren and G.J. Botterweck, eds., *Theological Dictionary of the Old Testament* (trans. John T. Willis) 1: 188–93. Grand Rapids, Mi. (German edition, 3 fascicles, 1970, 1971, 1972). **Rogers, S. C.** (1975) Female Forms of Power and the Myth of Male Dominance: A Model of Female/Male Interaction in Peasant Society. *American Ethnologist* 2: 741–54. **Rosaldo, M.Z.** (1974) Women, Culture, and Society: A Theoretical Overview. In M.Z. Rosaldo and L. Lamphere, eds., *Women, Culture, and Society,* 17–42. Stanford, Calif. (1980) The Use and Abuse of Anthropology: Reflections on Feminism and Cross-Cultural Understanding. *Signs* 5: 389–417. **Rudy, K.** (1997) Haven in a Heartless World: The Historical Roots of Gendered Theology. Chapter 2 of *Sex and the Church: Gender, Homosexuality, and the Transformation of Christian Ethics,* 15–44. Boston. **Sanday, P.R.** (1974) Female Status in the Public Domain. In M.Z. Rosaldo and L. Lamphere, eds., *Women, Culture, and Society,* 189–206. Stanford, Calif. **Sasson, J.** (1979) *Ruth: A New Translation with a Philological Commentary and a Formalist-Folklorist Interpretation.* Baltimore. **Sered, S.S.** (1992) *Women as Ritual Experts: The Religious Lives of Elderly Jewish Women in Jerusalem.* New York. **Sharistanian, J.**, ed. (1987) *Beyond the Public/Private Dichotomy: Contemporary Perspectives on Women's Public Lives.* Contributions to Women's Studies 78. Westport, Conn. **Small, M.F.** (1993) *Female Choices: Sexual Behavior of Female Primates.* Ithaca, N.Y. **Stager, L.E.** (1985) The Archaeology of the Family in Ancient Israel. *Bulletin of the American Schools of Oriental Research* 260: 1–36. **Strathern, M.** (1972) *Women in Between: Female Roles in a Male World.* Seminar Studies in Anthropology 2. London and New York. **Stern, E., J. Berg, A. Gilboa, I. Sharon, and J. Zorn** (1997) Tel Dor, 1994–1995: Preliminary Stratigraphic Report. *Israel Exploration Journal* 47: 29–56. **Trible, P.** (1976) Two Women in a Man's World. *Soundings* 59: 251–79. (1978) *God and the Rhetoric of Sexuality.* Philadelphia. **Wrangham, R.W.** (1980) An Ecological Model of Female-bonded Primate Groups. *Behaviour* 75: 262–300. **Zonabend, F.** (1996) An Anthropological Perspective on Kinship and the Family. In A. Burghière, C. Klapisch-Zuber, and F. Zonabend, eds., *Distant Worlds, Ancient Worlds* (trans. S.H. Tenison, R. Morris, A. Wilson), 25–39. *A History of the Family,* vol. I. Cambridge, Mass. (French edition, 1986).

SISTERHOOD?
WOMEN'S RELATIONSHIPS WITH WOMEN IN THE HEBREW BIBLE

Beverly Bow
Cleveland State University

Biblical depictions of women's relationships with other women advance the interests of patriarchy. The few stories in which such relationships appear generally present these relationships in one of two negative ways. Often the relationship itself is negative: the women are rivals in conflict with one another. When this is the case, the outcome of the story is positive —certainly for whatever male characters figure in the story, and usually also for the women involved, or at least for the primary female character. In stories where women get along with each other, they are frequently cooperating for an evil purpose—again a negative depiction of women's relationships. Here the outcome of the story tends to be negative for the women, although it generally remains positive for the men. The patriarchal message is that women cannot or should not band together. In the few exceptions where women's cooperation leads to a positive outcome, their cooperation serves a patriarchal purpose; thus the exceptions also advance patriarchy.

Antagonistic Relationships

SARAH AND HAGAR

The first instance of an antagonistic relationship between women to appear in the biblical narrative is the story of Sarah and Hagar in Genesis 16 and 21. For a brief moment there is seeming cooperation: Sarah is willing to share her husband's sexual favors with Hagar in order to obtain a child for herself. But Sarah's attempt to produce Abraham's heir is in conflict with YHWH's control over matters of fertility. Sarah knows that YHWH has made her barren (Gen 16:2), but she is not content to leave the matter to YHWH and takes things into her own hands by giving Hagar to Abraham. Her plan is doomed to failure. Almost immediately, Sarah loses control of the situation and the two women become bitter rivals. Hagar shows contempt for Sarah, and when Abraham refuses to take Sarah's side, Sarah treats Hagar so badly that Hagar runs away.

Although YHWH rescues Hagar from her precarious situation as a pregnant runaway slave woman alone in the wilderness and promises a positive future for the son she carries, the angel's message gives Hagar no hope that the conflict with Sarah will be resolved.[1] The angel addresses Hagar as Sarah's servant and commands her to return and submit to her mistress.

The text is silent about the relationship between Hagar and Sarah upon Hagar's return, mentioning only Abraham in recording Ishmael's birth,[2] but when the two women next appear together in Genesis 21 it is clear that the rivalry has not abated. At Isaac's weaning feast, some fifteen years after Ishmael's birth, Sarah demands that Abraham send away her rival and her son's rival for their father's inheritance. Sarah finally manages to get rid of the competition, but only because at this time it is also in accordance with YHWH's wishes.

Sarah and Hagar are antagonistic almost from the beginning and never reconcile. However, the outcome of the story of the women's rivalry is positive for both women. Sarah's son becomes Abraham's sole heir, both to his property (Gen 25:5) and to God's promises to Abraham (Gen 26:4). God rescues Hagar and Ishmael after their exile into the wilderness and remains with Ishmael as he grows up;[3] the reader later learns that God's promises about Ishmael's future are fulfilled (Gen 25:13–18). Hagar retains sole authority over her son, and she is the only woman in the Hebrew Bible to arrange her son's marriage.[4] The outcome is of course also positive for Abraham, whose two sons by the rival women both become progenitors of great nations.

RACHEL AND LEAH

The next antagonistic pair of women appears in Genesis 29–30. Rachel and Leah are sisters married to one man, and each wants what the other has. Jacob loves Rachel, and Leah wants him to love her also, as the names she chooses for her sons reflect. Rachel wants what Leah has: sons, which YHWH has given to Leah as compensation for the fact that Jacob does not love her (Gen 29:31).

---

1 Pace Jeansonne (1990) 45–46.

2 Pace Jeansonne (1990) 47.

3 Fuchs (1985a) 132 notes that Hagar's "best consolation" concerns her son, not herself.

4 Pace Jeansonne (1990) 51–52.

The sisters remain rivals throughout the story. They have a contest with their maids, giving them to Jacob to provide him with more sons. They have an altercation over some mandrakes, an incident that some commentators view as cooperation,[5] but that is too positive a word. Rather, they argue and finally strike a deal, each sister obtaining something she wants: Leah gets Jacob for the night, and Rachel gets a fertility plant.

It should be noted that none of the women's attempts to procure children for themselves is effective. Although Rachel calls the first of Bilhah's sons her own son when she names him, all four sons born to the two maids are remembered as sons of their birth mothers, not the sisters (Gen 46:18, 25). The mandrakes do not enable Rachel to conceive; some three years pass before she bears Joseph.[6]

The sisters' rivalry is not explicitly mentioned after the mandrakes incident, but there is no indication that it ever ended. It is true that they both side with Jacob against Laban when Jacob wants to return to Canaan, but each woman has reason to hate Laban for the position he put them in; their common hatred does not mean that they are no longer rivals. Further, Rachel's theft of Laban's *teraphim* may be seen as an attempt to appropriate symbolically the leadership of the family; she has a son now, but Leah is still the mother of Jacob's firstborn.[7]

Again, the eventual outcome of this story of rival women is positive. In a culture that reveres women for producing children, especially sons, Leah bears six sons and a daughter. It is not clear that Leah ever gets what she really wants: Jacob's love[8]—but he does give her an honorable burial in the same cave where Abraham, Sarah, Isaac, and Rebekah were buried (Gen 49:31). Rachel does get what she wants: she bears two sons, when YHWH determines that it is time, and her sons are Jacob's favorites. Jacob, of course, benefits the most: he has twelve sons, the progenitors of the twelve tribes.

---

5 Bellis (1994) 85.

6 For the view that the mandrakes worked, see Niditch (1981) 97–98; Westermann (1984) 476. For the view that they did not work, see von Rad (1972) 295; Brueggemann (1982) 254; Sarna (1989) 209.

7 Pardes (1992) 76–77. On the primacy of the firstborn son of an unloved wife, see Deut 21:15–17.

8 Cf. Jubilees' retelling of the story, which notes that Jacob loved Leah very much after Rachel died (Jubilees 36:21–24).

HANNAH AND PENINNAH

1 Samuel 1–2 relates the story of the rival wives of Elkanah. Their situation is reminiscent of Rachel and Leah's: Peninnah is unloved but fertile, and Hannah is loved but infertile. Peninnah repeatedly provokes Hannah about her barrenness. Hannah does nothing to promote the rivalry, but neither does she do anything to smooth her relationship with Peninnah. There is no indication that they ever learn to get along.

Again the outcome of the story is positive, at least for Hannah. (Peninnah drops out of the narrative after her provocation is twice noted.) Hannah's barrenness ends when YHWH "remembers" her: first she bears the great prophet Samuel, and later three more sons and two daughters (1 Sam 2:21).

TWO PROSTITUTES

A final story of rival mothers appears in 1 Kings 3:16–28. Two women present themselves to Solomon for his judgment in their dispute over one living son. The depiction of these mothers is especially negative: not only are they in contention, but they are identified as prostitutes.[9] The real mother is treated more sympathetically than the one who would rather see the baby dead than have her rival win,[10] but neither comes across as an ideal for motherhood. As prostitutes, the women are outside of patriarchal control, and there is an implicit message here about the dangers unmarried mothers pose to their children.[11]

Nevertheless, the story has a positive outcome, not only for the real mother (since the judgment is in her favor), but primarily for Solomon. The story serves as the first example of the "understanding mind" Solomon asked God for just prior to this incident (1 Kgs 3:9) and highlights his wisdom above anything else.

ESTHER

An example of rivalry between women who are not mothers is found in Esther 2. Esther competes against rival women in a beauty contest to win a position as queen of Persia. Esther has no close relationships with women. Her mother is dead, she was raised by a male relative, and she is befriended only by the eunuch in charge of the contestants. The only relationship she has with other women is competitive.

---

[9] Trible (1978) 31 sees this merely as identification, not judgment.

[10] Fuchs (1985a) 134.

[11] Fuchs (1985a) 131.

The consequence of Esther's rivalry with other women is positive for her. Aided by the men in her life, she prevails over the other contestants and becomes Ahasuerus's queen. Her position also provides great benefits for her cousin Mordecai, whose directions she continues to follow and who, arguably, overshadows Esther in the final chapters of the book.[12]

MIRIAM AND MOSES' WIFE

All the examples thus far have been stories of female rivalry that end positively for the primary women involved.[13] One last instance of contention between women has a positive outcome from a patriarchal perspective, though not for the women. In Numbers 12 Miriam and Aaron want a share of Moses' authority, to which they think they are entitled because YHWH speaks through all three of them (Num 12:2). Apparently unwilling or afraid to criticize Moses' authority directly, they make his marriage to a foreign wife their target (Num 12:1). Although both Aaron and Miriam are named, the verb used is a feminine singular form (*wattĕdabber Miryam wĕʾAharon*), which may suggest a particular animosity between the two women.[14]

The story does not end well for Miriam, who is stricken with leprosy and exiled for seven days. She does not speak again and is not even mentioned until her death is noted (Num 21:1). Aaron, on the other hand, is neither punished nor exiled, and he retains his position of leadership at Moses' side until he dies (Num 20:28). But the real winner here is Moses, whose authority is upheld by YHWH himself, who says that whereas other prophets receive visions, YHWH speaks with Moses alone, face to face (Num 12:6–8).

Cooperative Relationships

The other broad category of women's relationships consists of stories in which women cooperate to achieve some end or have otherwise amicable relationships. Since the cooperative women are actually conspiring to commit evil acts, the end result is negative. Even when women are amicable but not plotting evil, the story ends badly for the women.

---

12 See the discussion in Bellis (1994) 213–15.

13 Although there is hardly enough information to constitute a "story," one might also note Rebekah's disdain for her Hittite daughters-in-law, Esau's wives (Gen 26:34–35), which she uses to get Isaac to implement her plan to send Jacob away from Esau's rage (Gen 27:46).

14 Pardes (1992) 8--9.

LOT'S DAUGHTERS

The most familiar example of women's cooperation for an evil purpose is the story of Lot's daughters. Lot and his two daughters are the only survivors to escape the destruction of Sodom and Gomorroh. The sisters conspire together to get Lot drunk and sleep with him on two consecutive nights so that each of them can get pregnant. Their own words suggest justification for what they do: the older sister notes that "there is not a man on earth to come into us" (Gen 19:31), so they may believe that the destruction encompassed the whole world.[15] Or they may simply doubt that Lot will do anything now to provide them with husbands; he certainly showed little regard for their welfare in Sodom and failed to rescue their fiancés even though the angels specifically commanded him to do so.[16] As further justification, both sisters identify their motivation as the desire to "preserve offspring" (Gen 19:32, 34), which is, after all, in the words of one commentator, "their foremost duty within the framework of biblical patriarchy."[17] But while their behavior can be defended, the fact remains that they conspired to commit incest with their father, a universal taboo and specifically forbidden between father and daughter in Leviticus 18:17.

The narrative does not explicitly commend or condemn what Lot's daughters did, but there are indications of disapproval. First, justification for the incest appears only in the speech of the sisters and is not corroborated by the narrator.[18] In fact, the narrator has already defined the limited area of the destruction (Gen 19:24–25) and specifically mentioned one living man other than Lot, Abraham (Gen 19:27), so the reader knows that Lot is not the only man left on earth. Second, the sons the sisters bear are identified as the eponymous ancestors of the Moabites and Ammonites. These two peoples appear repeatedly as Israel's enemies during the conquest of Canaan,[19] the prophets speak against them,[20] and they are singled out as forbidden to the assembly of YHWH in Deut 23:3. In other words, the outcome of the sisters' collaboration is negative: it results in the creation of Israel's enemies.

---

15 Bellis (1994) 79; Pace Jeansonne (1990) 41.

16 Pace Jeansonne (1990) 38–39.

17 Fuchs (1985b) 140.

18 Cf. the suggestion by Pace Jeansonne (1990) 26 that the narrator's silence on Abraham's claim that Sarah is his half-sister leads the reader to doubt the truth of his words.

19 E.g., Judg 3:28; 10:9; 11:4; 1 Sam 11:11; 2 Sam 10:8; 2 Kgs 3:24; 2 Chr 20:1.

20 E.g., Isa 15–16; Jer 48–49; Ezek 21, 25.

TWO CANNIBAL MOTHERS

A second example of women collaborating to do evil is in 2 Kgs 6:26–31, where two mothers conspire to cannibalize their own sons. This is an extremely negative portrayal of women banding together. In her appeal to the king of Israel for justice, the one mother expresses no remorse for having eaten her own son; she just wants him to force the other mother to live up to the terms of their agreement and give up her son to be eaten also. No husbands are mentioned; as with the prostitutes in 1 Kings 3, there is an implicit message about the danger of motherhood outside the control of any man.

The outcome for the mothers is unknown; they disappear from the text. The incident focuses on the horror the news of the cannibalism elicits in the king of Israel, and the immediate aftermath is negative. Although he had formerly been on good terms with Elisha (2 Kgs 6:8–23), this abomination turns the king against the prophet (2 Kgs 6:31). Again women's cooperation leads to a negative result.

FEMALE WORSHIPPERS OF THE QUEEN OF HEAVEN

A third example of women's evil cooperation occurs in Jeremiah. Twice the prophet denounces groups of women who make cakes and pour out drink offerings to the queen of heaven, i.e., the Babylonian goddess Ishtar. In Jeremiah 7, the prophet is condemning the people of Judah for using the Temple as a refuge while continuing to commit apostasy, and he specifically mentions the women of Jerusalem and the towns of Judah who worship Ishtar in this manner (Jer 7:17–18). Jeremiah 44 refers to the same[21] or perhaps a different group of women who are again making offerings of cakes and libations to the queen of heaven. This time they are in Egypt, where the remnant left after the fall of Jerusalem to Babylon (Jer 39:1–3) have gone, against YHWH's command, taking Jeremiah with them (Jer 42:1–43:7). Although the prophet warns that disaster will result from their continuing apostasy (Jer 44:1–14), both the women and their husbands verbally reject Jeremiah's prophecy (Jer 44:15–19). The husbands justify their actions by saying that worshipping Ishtar brought them prosperity, while the women defiantly declare that they will persist in their offerings, citing their husbands' approval.

---

21 Jer 44:21 suggests that it is the same group, although it could be their descendants: "...the offerings you made ..., you and your ancestors." The Israelites' worship of gods other than YHWH was ongoing; see, e.g., Frymer-Kensky (1992) 153–61; Bright (1981) 332–37.

Although it is not the sins of the female worshippers of the queen of heaven alone that bring on the exile or prompt Jeremiah's prophecies of doom, this is another instance where women act together to do what is, in the biblical view, evil. There are few references in Jeremiah to women performing specific actions together other than these two, and none so detailed.[22] The women who worship Ishtar are singled out, and their cooperative efforts contribute to the general apostasy that leads to a disastrous outcome for the people.

DINAH

There are two examples of women in amicable relationships where they are not plotting evil, but things still turn out badly for the women. In Genesis 34, Jacob's daughter Dinah goes out on a friendly visit to the women of Shechem, with disastrous results. She is raped[23] (Gen 34:2) and held captive (Gen 34:26) while Shechem tries to arrange to marry her. Dinah's brothers massacre all the men of Shechem and the women whom Dinah wanted to befriend are taken along with all the other plunder.

The reactions of Dinah's family evidence little concern for her welfare. Her father hesitates to do anything when he hears what happened to his only daughter and shows no reaction, although he is elsewhere depicted as highly emotional (Gen 29:11; 37:34–35).[24] Even though the beginning of the chapter identifies Leah as Dinah's mother and the reader might expect to learn her reaction, her mother neither says nor does anything on her daughter's behalf.[25] Her brothers overreact,[26] and by killing the man she should have married according to biblical law in such situations (Deut 22: 28–29), they make their defiled sister unmarriageable. No one asks Dinah what she wants.

Things do, however, turn out well for the males of Dinah's family. Although Jacob fears that the incident will endanger his family by prompt-

---

22 YHWH calls for women to mourn (Jer 9:17–20), and to dance (Jer 31:13); in a vision Jeremiah has, the women of the royal household speak as they are being led into captivity (Jer 38:22).

23 Shechem "took (*wayyiqqaḥ*) her, he lay with (*wayyiškab*) her, and he violated her (*way*ᶜ*anneha*)."

24 Aschkenasy (1986) 126.

25 Biblical mothers often intervene on behalf of their sons, but are rarely even shown in relation to their daughters. See the discussion in Fuchs (1985a) 134–35.

26 For the view that Dinah's brothers exercised the only option available to get their sister back, see Aschkenasy (1986) 127.

ing retaliation from other cities in the area (Gen 34:30), God sees to it that the other local inhabitants are afraid to take any action against them (Gen 35:5). In addition, the men increase their wealth by taking all the possessions of the Shechemites.

JEPHTHAH'S DAUGHTER

The other story with a bad outcome for a woman who has an amicable relationship with other women is the story of Jephthah's daughter in Judges 11. Her female friends are mentioned only after her father's vow has condemned her to death, so the relationship does not in any way contribute to her fate. But the story still contains the familiar elements: friendly relationship among women, bad outcome for women. And even though the entire story can be interpreted as a warning against making rash vows like Jephthah's,[27] it depicts Jephthah himself as one who does not commit the serious offense of breaking a vow to YHWH, no matter how painful fulfilling it might be.

Exceptions

There are a few stories in which women cooperate and the outcome is positive for them. The most obvious example is in the book of Ruth, where the relationship between Ruth and Naomi is characterized by love and loyalty. Their cooperative efforts result in financial security for both women, as well as the honor for Ruth of bearing David's ancestor. The women in Moses' early life also cooperate with good results. The two midwives Shiphrah and Puah work together to thwart Pharaoh's command to kill Hebrew male babies, and God rewards them with families (Exod 1:21). Miriam and Jochebed together ensure Moses' safety; Jochebed not only gets to nurse her son who might otherwise have died, but she also is paid for it (Exod 2:9). In Numbers 27, Zelophehad's daughters come together as a group and successfully petition Moses and the other male leaders to be allowed to inherit their father's property.

However, in all these cases the women's cooperation serves a patriarchal purpose. Ruth needs to marry a kinsman of her dead husband because he died without producing an heir, so she and Naomi engineer Ruth's marriage to Boaz. Boaz himself acknowledges that the marriage has this purpose (Ruth 4:5, 10). The efforts of the midwives and Moses' sister and mother prevent the elimination of every Israelite male and, therefore, of

---

[27] On the story as a negative judgment against Jephthah, see Hackett (1985) 30. See also the discussions in Bellis (1994) 127–31; and Trible (1984) 93–116.

Israel: since the girls whom Pharaoh allowed to live would presumably have become slaves or wives to the Egyptians, eventually there would have been no separate people. Most especially, the actions of the women in Moses' early life mean the survival of the future savior of Israel. Zelophehad's daughters themselves cite the preservation of their father's name as the reason for their petition (Num 27:4). Later the men of Zelophehad's tribe impose a restriction on the daughters' inheritance that benefits the patriarchal tribal system: they must marry within the tribe so that a man's property remains in his tribe even when he has no sons to inherit it (Num 36:1–9).

In conclusion, when we look at all the instances in the Hebrew Bible in which women interact with other women, it is clear that "sisterhood" is not presented as a positive option for women. Biblical women seem predisposed to compete with each other rather than get along.[28] Sisterhood is even dangerous:[29] when women do band together, they are up to no good or the women come to a bad end. The only times women's relationships with other women are presented in a positive light, occur when they serve patriarchal purposes. The inescapable conclusion is that in the biblical perspective, sisterhood is antithetical to patriarchy.

BIBLIOGRAPHY

Aschkenasy, N. (1986) *Eve's Journey: Feminine Images in Hebraic Literary Tradition.* Philadelphia. **Bellis, A.O.** (1994) *Helpmates, Harlots, Heroes: Women's Stories in the Hebrew Bible.* Louisville. **Bright, J.** (1981) *A History of Israel.* Third edition. Philadelphia. (First edition, 1959). **Brueggemann, W.** (1982) *Genesis.* Interpretation: A Bible Commentary For Teaching and Preaching. Atlanta. **Frymer-Kensky, T.** (1992) *In the Wake of the Goddesses: Women, Culture, and the Biblical Transformation of Pagan Myth.* New York. **Fuchs, E.** (1985a) The Literary Characterization of Mothers and Sexual Politics in the Hebrew Bible. In A.Y. Collins, ed., *Feminist Perspectives on Biblical Scholarship,* 117–36. Chico, Calif.: Scholars. (1985b) Who Is Hiding the Truth? Deceptive Women and Biblical Androcentrism. In A.Y. Collins, ed., *Feminist Perspectives on Biblical Scholarship,* 137–44. Chico, Calif. **Hackett, J.** (1985) In the Days of Jael: Reclaiming the History of Women in Ancient Israel. In C. Atkinson et al., eds., *Immaculate and Powerful: The Female in Sacred Image and Social Reality,* 15–38. Boston. **Niditch, S.** (1981) *Underdogs and Tricksters: A Prelude to Biblical Folklore.* Philadelphia. **Pace**

---

[28] Cf. Fuchs (1985a) 131.

[29] Cf. Fuchs (1985a) 132.

Jeansonne, S. (1990) *The Women of Genesis from Sarah to Potiphar's Wife.* Minneapolis. **Pardes, I.** (1991) *Countertraditions in the Bible: A Feminist Approach.* Cambridge, Mass.: Harvard. **Sarna, N.** (1989) *Genesis. The JPS Torah Commentary.* Philadelphia. **Trible, P.** (1978) *God and the Rhetoric of Sexuality.* Philadelphia. (1984) *Texts of Terror.* Philadelphia. **Von Rad, G.** (1972) *Genesis: A Commentary.* The Old Testament Library. Second edition. Philadelphia. (First edition, 1961). **Westermann, C.** (1984) *Genesis 12–36: A Commentary.* Minneapolis.

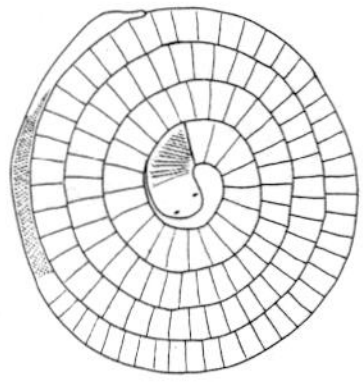

Boy Meets Girl: Stories of Eligibility and Encounter in Ancient Israel

Peter Feinman
Manhattanville College

> "As you start to translate the texts, which we did early on, you realize that these texts are written for mask theater....Characters had to be invested as soon as they walked on, especially because there were only two or three actors playing all the roles," said Peter Meineck, [artistic director of the Aquila Theater Company about the Greek classics on a collaborative project with the Lincoln Center, New York City]. The force of the masks onstage, for many scholars, has been something of a revelation.[1]

There is one important aspect of daily life in ancient times that deserves more attention in academic studies than it sometimes receives: boy meets girl. It is a simple and essential part of the social order—if it doesn't happen, the social order ceases; it doesn't get more basic than that. Indeed, the suggestion has been made that the communication between two unrelated males over the exchange of a woman is at the core of human language, communication, and culture.[2] Regardless of whether such claims are valid or not, the occurrence of this event certainly is critical to the continuity of human culture.

Given this importance, it should not be a surprise that there is a host of rules involving "boy meets girl" dealing with such issues as:

- When is one first eligible to participate in a boy-meets-girl encounter?
- What defines the eligibility of the other one, the one being met?
- How is the meeting legitimated or sanctified?

By answering these questions for a given society, one may gain insight into how those people choose to identify and define themselves. So how then in ancient times did boy meet girl:

1 Hedges (1999) E1 and 5.

2 Leach (1970) 35–43.

- Did the king send forth a prostitute as Gilgamesh did for Enkidu?
- Was the female abducted as Helen was for Paris?
- Were women raped as at the founding of Rome? or,
- Were they star-crossed lovers doomed to die like Romeo and Juliet?

But what about on a more prosaic level? What about the times that are not epic in nature? What about Joe Israel and Jane Judah, how did they meet?

To begin to resolve these issues about ancient Israel, the following methodology will be applied to the biblical narratives:

I. Identify the criteria for analysis to be employed when investigating a story;
II. Review in sequential order the biblical stories to determine:
  (a) if encounters of boy meets girl occur,
  (b) if any patterns or processes of development occur;
III. Propose a working hypothesis and suggest actions for future study.

The completion of these steps may enable us to develop some understanding of how Israelite society perceived itself and defined itself as uniquely Israelite.

During this process, one should keep in mind another aspect of daily life: the audience to the boy-meets-girl stories. As David Payne noted in his study of the story of Jonah: "I became increasingly convinced that it was vital to bear in mind the *audience* to which the book was addressed."[3] Payne recognized that the "study of the audience and of the audience reaction is a necessary prolegomenon to a discussion of the books message and purpose."[4] Thus any attempt in the present to understand the boy-meets-girl stories of the Hebrew Bible should attempt to understand what it meant to the original audiences, an admittedly difficult undertaking.

I. *Criteria for Analysis*

The criteria for analysis, as the phrase is being used here, refers to the diagnostic markers to be applied to a given individual story or pericope. These texts in question were created as an act of will. They do not exist without some conscious effort having been made to produce them. Even if it is only the ancient equivalent of putting pen to paper to record the words

---

3 Payne (1979) 4.

4 Payne (1979) 12.

heard, someone still had to have decided to do so. If that effort was to record the words thought by the individual author, then one needs to be aware that such thinking occurred within a given context that was part of the process of the creation of the text. It is precisely this world at the moment of creation that defines the *Sitz im Leben* of the story that most easily becomes lost over time: *Gulliver's Travels* is now a children's story.[5]

The transformation of *Gulliver's Travels* from political satire in eighteenth-century England to children's story in twentieth-century America is a reminder of the fate that can befall a story. When historical and/or

---

5 For a more recent example of this process, consider the Scopes Monkey Trial. The trial was an historic event that occurred in 1925. People at the time had the opportunity to follow the trial both in the contemporary written record via newspapers or, in part, orally, from live radio transmission. The way Americans of the 1930s were most familiar with this historic event was through the writings of Frederick Lewis Allen (1964) 162, 167–68, who had his own view of the events.

The cultural view shifted in the 1950s when *Inherit the Wind* was written and produced as a play, which opened in 1955 and then became a movie in 1960. The focus of Jerome Lawrence and Robert E. Lee, when writing the play, was to combat the McCarthy Era histrionics. They did so by revising the historical Scopes Trial so the historically real William Jennings Bryan morphed into the historically real Joe McCarthy, expressed through the fictional character of Matthew Brady. Indeed, by casting lovable Spencer Tracy in the fictional role based on the difficult Clarence Darrow (but meant to represent anti-McCarthy liberals), the artists were delivering a message in the present through the modern equivalent of the ancient masks of classical theater.

One fictional device employed in this process was the introduction of a love interest for the Scopes figure. Not only was a girl created by the artists, but she was made the daughter of the fire-breathing, fundamentalist minister of the backwards rural south. Thus, as the daughter struggled to choose between her duty to her father and following her heart, the audience was invited to root for her and make the same decision to embrace love and enlightenment that she had made. It would be a mistake to judge this boy-meets-girl encounter simply as a story of true love or in a genealogical sense. The boy-meets-girl story in this artistic creation is meant to reflect the social, cultural, religious, and political issues of the present of its creation.

In the decades since, the story has taken on a life of its own. This process continually challenges the efforts of anyone to create an accurate historical reconstruction based on its present performance. As a matter of fact, the movie has been listed as an aid to understanding the fundamentalist thinking of Bryan in the *National Standards for United States History* even though its dialogue exactly contradicts Bryan's stated views on the age of the earth. The story has become the taught historical truth far removed from its *Sitz im Leben*. Students may even think the girl was real.

For more on this subject see Larson (1997) 225–46; Numbers (1998) 76–91; Sandeen (1970) 266–69.

fictional figures are used to deliver political messages in the present, it presumes a familiarity of the audience with the characters of the stories.[6] This application may apply to someone telling a story in non-biblical times[7] or biblical times.[8] Indeed, certain times lend themselves to such stories

---

6 For example, the 1413 heresy trial of Sir John Oldcastle in the time of Henry V was transformed in the 1544 narrative by John Bale to the time of Henry VIII. Bale recognized the power of taking the words of the enemy and using them against their originators in the new account. The specific details of the efforts by the Protestants to be legitimated within the English religious and political world are secondary to the effort to use the legendary focus of English national pride, the reign of Henry V, to deliver a message about the contemporary reign of Henry VIII; see the analysis of Patterson (1996) 6–7, 21. Such a social drama served to legitimate the actions taken or contemplated in the present conflict.

> That powerful combination of Protestant bibles, English chronicles, and Sir John Oldcastle would reappear at the very end of the sixteenth century on the Elizabethan stage, as a group of playwrights set themselves to defend Oldcastle's reputation against the irreverence imputed to Shakespeare (Patterson [1996] 22).

An audience today might heartily enjoy the buffoonery of the unhistorical Sir John Falstaff of Shakespeare and wonder about his unhistorical Sir John Oldcastle of *Henry IV, Part I* without knowing about the pro-Oldcastle counter-plays being produced at the same time, the earlier revision by Bale, or the actual 1413 trial as suggested by Patterson (1996) 7–8. Fortunately, each of these different versions survives enabling the scholar more effectively to reconstruct the historical sequence of events. But if a comic figure like Sir John Falstaff is really part of the political process, how does one know if the figures in a boy-meets-girl story aren't also part of a political message, as occurred in *Inherit the Wind*: lo, the *Gulliver's Travels* syndrome.

7 The figure of Absalom, the biblical son of a king who sought the throne and failed, easily lends itself to appropriation in royal struggles. For example, in the 1681 poem of John Dryden, *Absalom and Achitopel*, the figure of Absalom represents James, the Protestant Duke of Monmouth and illegitimate son of Charles II, who was opposed by the legitimate heir, Catholic James, Duke of York according to Goldie (1996) 208. Again the specific details of the historical battle for the crown are not the concern here. While an audience at the time of the poem might be expected to readily understand the messages being delivered in the poem, what would happen in time when audiences were not familiar with either seventeenth-century English royal/religious politics or the biblical figures being used to represent that politics. Consider the information that must be available if an accurate historical reconstruction is to be completed. This story of boy-meets-girl and the issue of its sanctification in society was not simply a primer for everyday relations, but about a tense political battle of life-or-death repercussions in the present.

8 The attempt to determine how the audience would react to historical Jonah and the historical destruction of Nineveh is made by Hedges (1979) 4–7.

where everything is not what it seems and everything must be carefully scrutinized and dissected in order to fathom the true intention of the author.[9]

Authors as well as audiences take much for granted in storytelling when everything does not have to be spelled out or consciously remembered. The effort to determine what the author and audience take for granted is fraught with difficulty and subject to constant second-guessing. It becomes even more complicated as the audience changes over time.[10] As Robert Alter advises us:

> A coherent reading of any art work, whatever the medium, requires some detailed awareness of the grid of conventions upon which, and against which the individual work operates ... an elaborate set of tacit agreements between artist and audience about the ordering of the art work is at all times the enabling context in which the complex communication of art occurs.... One of the chief difficulties we encounter as modern readers in perceiving the artistry of biblical narrative is precisely that we have lost most of the keys to the conventions out of which it was shaped. The professional Bible scholars have not offered much help in this regard.[11]

This admonition serves as a necessary reminder of the challenge in attempting to enter into the world of another culture, a challenge further com-

---

9 England in the time of Protestants versus Catholics and the battle for the throne seems to have been a superb time for playwrights and poets delivering messages in the present through stories set in the English and biblical past. In addition to Goldie (1996) and Patterson (1996) previously cited, see also Wills (1995) on how the Gunpowder Plot of 1605 against the king was told in Shakespeare's *Macbeth*.

10 In ancient times this phenomenon has been documented in the epic tale of Gilgamesh, as his story changed from Sumerian to Akkadian to Old Babylonian (Amorite) times in the third and early second millennia B.C.E.; see Tigay (1982 and 1985). Authors themselves can be reinvented over time to reflect changing circumstances, as shown by Taylor (1989) of Shakespeare. Indeed, one of his most famous stories, the boy-meets-girl encounter of Romeo and Juliet, has been told cinematically seven times in the last century, and each film version reflects the time when it was produced. Anita Gates (1996) writes:

> Every generation, it seems, needs its own film version of Shakespeare's star-crossed lovers, now about 400 years old. And every generation, intentionally or not, puts its own mark on the story.

So stories of boy-meets-girl not only may have political significance for the time in which it is told, its retelling over time may provide a running commentary of social and cultural changes as well.

11 Alter (1981) 47.

plicated by its existence as a people speaking a different language thousands of years ago, thousands of miles away in a different social, technological, and historical context.

With this admonition in mind, one can now turn to the texts in question and the criteria for analysis to be applied in seeking to decipher their meaning.[12]

1. *Stage*: The identification of the stage on which the story occurs helps to determine the meaning of that stage to the original audience. For example, the "West" of the classic American Western movies automatically evoked certain images when those movies were first created, but has generated a different perception with the passage of time as people are removed from that original context.[13]
2. *Props*: The stage itself consists of a variety of props each with a carefully calibrated meaning instantly recognizable to the audience enveloped within its own cultural symbols. Such props do not need to be explained—their very existence immediately triggers a set of responses in the audience experiencing the artistic creation. For example, the setting and not rising sun, or the sun at "high noon" are staples of the American Western story.[14] In fact, they would be noticed by their absence as well as by their presence. Such props do not need to be explained with footnotes save to foreigners or if a culture forgets its own past.[15]

---

[12] Alter (1981) 48–49 uses the movies of the American West to illustrate the challenge in understanding a culture based on the chance findings of its films.

[13] The use of the Western landscape to deliver political messages in the present is perhaps best expressed by the contrast of the 1960 John Wayne movie *The Alamo* during the Cold War and the debunking 1971 movie *Doc* about Doc Holliday but really about cultural and political turmoil of the Vietnam era; see De Bruhl (1995) and Faragher (1995) 159.

[14] This metaphor of the rising and not setting sun has its most significant moment in American history at the signing of the Constitution when Ben Franklin compared the creation of the Constitution of the United States to a rising and not setting sun; Van Doren (1938) 754–55. Presumably, no American history scholar takes this reference to the motion of the sun literally.

[15] This phenomenon is responsible for the existence of footnotes to texts of *Gulliver's Travels* and may be compared to the use of glosses in biblical texts or the need for midrash.

As an example of this process, consider the Presidential Address of Paul Haupt at the annual conference of the American Oriental Society on April 16, 1914, entitled "Armageddon." In this speech Haupt (1915) 412 attempted to explain the meaning of that term as employed by Teddy Roosevelt in the 1912 presidential campaign

3. *Time*: Stories are set in a time known to the audience but not necessarily in the present of an audience. Until recently, such stories would be set primarily in time past or present and not time future.[16] Even so, that time past must be one that is recognizable in some way to the audience in the present, otherwise it would seem foreign, strange, and incomprehensible. For example, the American Western developed at a time when the frontier had been closed and that West was becoming a mythic memory. Yet the audience consisted of people who were the children and grandchildren of those pioneers or who believed in the American Dream represented by those figures in the past, whereas people today have become more removed from that time period and have a different perception of it.[17]
4. *Cast:* The characters of the story do not appear out of thin air.[18] The process of introduction within the text is not necessarily meant to

---

and suggested that proper nouns carry associative meanings to the audience beyond their literal significance not only today but in biblical times. Haupt (1915) 412 cited the example of "Waterloo" just as a later audience would be familiar with "Pearl Harbor" or the 1990s bequeathed its own share of proper noun personal names to the national vocabulary.

Interestingly, Haupt (1915) 413–14 goes on to refer to the recent sinking of the Titanic and the use of pseudo-mythic imagery to describe it. Therefore, he opines there was a need by biblical scholars to know oriental imagery and allegory. That icon itself would become the subject of a book by Biel (1996) that traced the cultural history of the Titanic disaster in twentieth-century America, showing how different peoples in different times used that one symbol as a metaphor for different objectives. The book was released just as the blockbuster movie was being filmed. One notes in *Titanic* the same pattern as with *Inherit the Wind*: the introduction of a fictional boy-meets-girl encounter in an historic event, where the woman has to chose between a male figure of authority (in this case, her fiancee) and the man she loves.

16 One could consider the origin of apocalyptic stories as being the ancient equivalent of cosmic galactic showdown science fiction stories popular in this present (including a movie entitled *Armageddon*). For information on this genre, see Cohn (1993) and Hanson (1985).

17 Other well-known examples in late twentieth-century America of this retrojection include the 1692 Salem Witch Trials being retold in 1953 by Arthur Miller as *The Crucible* about the McCarthy Era and the Korean War being used in the *Mash* movie and TV show for the Vietnam War. One can't help but wonder how successful the scholars of the future will be in understanding the *Sitz im Leben* of these stories.

18 Good characters often take on a life of their own. Their stories may be rewritten to reflect current circumstances or may be drastically revised until one can

provide a full biography, but is meant to provide the audience with sufficient information so it can make an informed decision about the members of the cast, their identities, their nature. For example, a character could ride onto the stage wearing a white hat or a black hat, wearing a badge or after being seen on a wanted poster.[19] Masks can have the same effect. From these directional clues immediately recognizable to the audience but which a foreigner might overlook or misunderstand, one can make relatively quick decisions about one's own attitudes toward the characters in this particular setting even before the action unfolds.

5. *Plot*: Stories often unfold according to basic type-scenes.[20] This means that within the diversity of the human experience, there are certain standard or stock concerns that play out across the spectrum of human cultures. For example, "boy-gets-girl," "cosmos and chaos," and (slapstick) humor are three of the staples of human storytelling either individually or in combination.[21] Authors have the option of starting with a base interest of concern to the larger culture, such as a threat to survival, but then can tell the story in a mythic, epic, legendary, historic, or annalistic manner, or by combining elements in an innovative way.
6. *Language*: Words themselves provide writers with the opportunity to express their own creative skills. Sometimes stock phrases may be employed like "Get out of town!" and the audience may be able to accurately anticipate other phrases to be used based on context already

---

hardly recognize the biblical original, such as with Enoch or Melchizedek; see Bergen and Stone (1998), Halpern-Amaru (1994), Kugel (1997), Nickelsburg (1981), Stone (1984) for rewriting in Greco-Roman times by Jews, Christians, and Samaritans of a host of stories. After all, which is easier to do: to redefine a known character, such as Eve, to fit contemporary feminist values or to create a new character who then has to be validated as authentic?

19 Moses appears as an Egyptian to the women of Midian in Exod 2:16–19, which helps set the stage for the change in identity that is about to occur. By contrast, the opening of a James Bond movie tends to have a certain familiarity and one knows the good guys from the bad guys fairly quickly; see Bennett and Woollacott (1987).

20 Alter (1981) 47–62.

21 In late twentieth-century America, perhaps the saga cycle that best combined these elements of boy-gets-girl, cosmos versus chaos, and humor were the Star Wars movies. Regardless of the technological element in producing such stories, one is right to ask if there has been any fundamental change in the DNA of the audience that would make such storytelling popular at this one point in time to the exclusion of other times and others people.

established through the stage, props, time, cast, and plot.[22] Still, no matter how trite the situation or obvious the context, some artists have the ability to make language soar in unsurpassed beauty, to create words that breathe a life and light to the story such that it becomes part of the canonical memory of the species, treasured forever.

7. *Performance*: In the current emphasis on the written word, one should not overlook the impact of the performed story.[23] How is it communicated? When is it performed: on New Year, a festival day, any day? Where is it performed: at the capital, at a sacred site, anywhere? Who performs in it: the king, sacred people, anyone? Everything from the costuming of the performers to their own individual identities and skills contributes to the message being delivered through a story.[24]

---

22 The "get-out-of-town" motif has been immensely popular in the films of the American West. An actual historical incident of such an occurrence, the showdown near, not in, the O.K. Corral, has been the subject of over two dozen Hollywood westerns with various degrees of commercial success. This rewriting of history or retelling of the story as with *Romeo and Juliet*, *Inherit the Wind*, and *Titanic*, reflects the ongoing attempt to understand the past in accordance with the world of the present. With the historical Earp, there was less of a need to create a fictional boy-meets-girl encounter, since the Jewish Josephine Marcus Earp was a story in her own right—in fact, there was a TV movie about her. She had been the ally of a rival of Earp's prior to her becoming associated with him, a real-life example of the fictional women in these three other plays and movies, switching sides to be with the men they loved. For more on the phenomenon of the retelling of the Earp story, see Barra (1998) and Faragher (1995).

23 According to Stricker (1955), the origin of the performed story or theater may be found with the threshing-floor, as supported by examples from Egypt, Israel, and Greece. This phenomenon of celebrating the harvest under the direction of the male figure of authority may itself have been a neolithic revision of paleolithic hunting rituals related to the obtaining of food suggests Burkert (1983) 42–44. In historic times in the Near East, Egypt was the scene of public performances by the king, as recounted in Blackman and Fairman (1942, 1943, 1944, 1949, 1950), Fairman (1935, 1958, and 1974), Frankfort (1978) 79–88 and 101–39, and Uphill (1965). Cross (1973) viii suggests that epic rather than the myth was featured in the ritual drama of the old Israelite cultus. Such a conjecture raises the issue of how the archaeologically attested (and unattested) Israelite and Judean kings of the Iron II period legitimated and validated their role before the people (see below).

24 In biblical studies, the issue of the performance of a story has been most ardently championed by the Myth and Ritual Schools of England and Scandinavia as expressed in Engnell (1967 and 1969), Hooke (1933 and 1958), Johnson (1955), Mowinckel (1962), and Segal (1998). These scholars stress the role of the king in reasserting order over chaos in the present parallel to the victory by the deity over chaos at the dawn of time. While Mesopotamia garners the bulk of their interest,

These criteria raise certain issues with regard to biblical scholarship. The natural and deeply ingrained tendency of biblical scholars at this point in time is to mentally divide the narrative text into pericopes, even authors according to the Documentary Hypothesis.[25] The natural and deeply ingrained tendency of biblical scholars is to view the story as literary text just as ivory tower scholars themselves experience texts individually and silently.[26] Should the model by which scholars encounter the biblical texts

---

Egyptian royal rituals, too, are included and hypotheses for the Israelite equivalent are proposed. See Snaith (1947) for an attempted reconstruction of the Jewish New Year festival. As noted above, the American Cross accepts the concept of such comparable rituals in Israelite tradition but refrains from accepting the king performing in the role of the deity. The issue of the chief priest (of YHWH) performing in such a role, with the king in the role of a human hero, does not appear to be one that he has seriously considered.

Perhaps by no coincidence whatsoever, the proponents of these royal rituals and dramas tend to come from countries where monarchy not only survives but thrives. For the Russian royal social drama, see Wortman (1995). The late twentieth-century phenomena of Princesses Grace and Diana attest to the immense appeal of such real-life stories to ordinary people, including those in non-royal America. Technology may be a factor in the extent and speed with which such stories are communicated, but on what basis would one conclude that people in the time of the archaeologically attested Iron II kings weren't interested in stories about their queens and queen mothers?

25 Biblical commentaries tend to be organized by biblical chapter or pericope as befitting their genre. This approach has contributed to what Knierim (1985) 126 refers to as the atomization of the text, which has become a concern to the discipline. Sometimes, scholars attempt to deal with a proposed narrative as a whole, such as the academic odd couple of Richard Friedman (1999) and John Van Seters (1992 and 1994).

26 The graduate seminar may not be representative of the way stories were experienced in ancient times. In the post-Napoleonic era of German scholarship, Ranke created the historical seminar whereby students applied the tools they had acquired to the technical problems of texts under the guidance of a mentor, notes Grafton (1997) 224. Then these nineteenth-century investigations led to "short, precise dissertations on source-criticism" Grafton (1997) 225. Such atomization became a staple of biblical scholarship as well.

One wonders as to the impact of this methodology on the conclusions about the meaning of biblical stories to the original audiences. If McNutt (1987) 50 is correct, then the winners of social dramas require cultural performances to legitimate their success. These social dramas as defined by Victor Turner (1974) 15–17 derive from conflicting groups and personages attempting to assert their paradigm and to deplete the one of their opponent. Based on Turner's analysis (1974) 23–59, there are dueling paradigms or ritual symbols expressed through dramas with history being written by the winner. Perhaps instead of atomizing

be imposed on the people of the past and if so, on what basis? The question is raised here precisely because it goes to the heart and soul of the way in which the message of the story is being communicated. There is a difference between reading a story alone, in private, and experiencing it publicly, surrounded by others.[27]

II. *Boy Meets Girl*

Now that the questions have been asked and the criteria for analysis have been proposed, the next step in the analysis is to review some examples from the biblical texts, starting at the beginning, and to see where it leads. Each story will not be reviewed in detail due to the constraints of space, but the salient details in relation to the encounter of boy-meets-girl, if one occurs, will be identified. In this process, one should approach the text as best one can, as if it had never been experienced before. Imagine being the proverbial ignorant juror with a blank slate *tabula rasa* mind. Or more commonly, imagine being part of a focus group asked to comment about a new product or show called "Biblical Boy Meets Girl: The Series." The challenge here is to put aside the scholarly constructs that condition one's response to a story and to bring to it the sense of experiencing the story for the first time, as a member of the general public.

ADAM AND EVE

> So the Lord God caused a deep sleep to fall upon the man, and he slept; then he took one of his ribs and closed up its place with flesh. And the rib that the Lord God had taken from the man he made into a woman and brought her to the man (Gen 2:21–22).[28]

The audience, as with science fiction or fantasy stories and movies, is likely to have recognized that this description of the creation of woman was not meant to recount standard operating procedure in daily life. All things considered, the creation of woman as detailed here probably was viewed

---

pericopes, one would be better off observing the storytelling at the holiday of Purim or for that matter, a professional wrestling match, to appreciate the audience's role in the process, as academically disdainful as such actions may be. But what happens if the writings of both the Federalists and the anti-Federalists survive and both are part of the social paradigm and both social dramas continue to be performed together?

27 For some biblical examples of public readings and/or audience participations, see Exod 24:3, Deut 27, Josh 24, 2 Kgs 22:10–11 and 23:1–4, 2 Chr 22:10–11 and 23:1–4, and Neh 8.

28 All translations are NRSV.

as more of a one-time occurrence in the beginning than as an ongoing or recurring event in the present. It is unlikely that in biblical times the male placed his hopes on a reoccurrence of this act as a way of meeting his intended. One would be hard pressed to conclude that the average Israelite male, upon hearing or reading this story, went to sleep at night thinking that he would get lucky and awaken with the woman who completed him.

However, a subsequent verse bears notice in regard to boy-meets-girl in the present of the audience:

> Therefore a man shall leave his father and his mother and cleave to his wife, and they shall be one (Gen 2:24).

Unlike the previous description, these actions were attainable in the present of the audience. I suggest that this verse, coming as it does following the creation of the first man and woman, may be considered to be the ideal standard for the Israelite culture, the way it is supposed to be, the way riding off into the sunset or Prince Charming on a white horse rescuing the damsel in distress have represented ideals in our own society. My working hypothesis is that the position of this verse in the text signals its importance in defining the official norm for the society of that text.

Nonetheless, this narrative leaves loosely defined some of the issues previously raised as questions that define a society.

(i) *When is one first eligible to participate in a boy-meets-girl encounter?*

The story does little to specify the age of the individual male participating in this relationship. One may deduce that a biological child is not involved. Clearly, there will be a change in the living conditions of the male in the aftermath of this event, so one might posit that a rite of passage for the adolescent turned adult is involved. While such an interpretation may be anthropologically sound, the story itself does not inherently cast the male character as a teenager as opposed to an adult. All things considered, one would have a lot of options in the casting of this role.

(ii) *What defines the eligibility of the other?*

Given the unique nature of the creation of the female, little is said about the traditional issues of endogamy or exogamy, which so concern ethnographers and anthropologists. Certainly, one may make the case that the woman is not from another tribe or people, but one could equally make the case that the issue is irrelevant to the story. The action by which the female was created was unique to this story and not to be repeated in the life of the individual male in the present audience; therefore, the question about eligibility would appear to be equally irrelevant. The story simply does not care; what counts is the action that the couple takes once boy does meet girl.

(iii) *How is the meeting legitimated or sanctified?*

According to Gen 2:24, the man is to leave his father and his mother and to cleave to the woman. Would the audience to this story conclude that the first man had complied with these conditions? If the man is to be defined as being in compliance, one would be obligated then to define YHWH, who provided the breath or spirit of life in Gen 2:7, as the father-figure and the earth, which provided the material for the body in the same verse, as the mother-figure. There simply are no other candidates available in this story.

The next question would be, were either of these candidates for father and mother physically present in the event the story was performed. In this particular pericope, YHWH has a speaking role whereas the ground does not. So if at minimum the role of YHWH the father needs to be cast, then who would perform in the role: the king, the high or chief priest, a professional storyteller, anyone? An off-stage voice seems unlikely given the dialogue, although certainly that remains an option to avoid the issue of casting. But once the selection is made for the deity, then what about the man? Suppose the role of YHWH the father was performed by the chief priest and the man was performed by the king—how would that influence the way one would interpret the meaning of the story?

These questions suggest a topic for future study. In the meantime, a working hypothesis may be proposed that Gen 2:24 has been stated by its author as the standard by which boy-meets-girl encounters in Israelite society are to be measured. Therefore, a sequential review of the subsequent stories of boy-meets-girl will then determine who is the first to meet this standard and identify those who do not.

CAIN AND ABEL

As far as Abel is concerned, the question is moot. Abel dies as an adult without knowing any boy-meets-girl encounter. His status as an adult lends credence to the interpretation that Gen 2:24 is not specifically intended as a rite of passage from adolescence to adulthood, otherwise one would have expected the adults Cain and Abel to have been married before the fatal encounter.

As for Cain, his story is different; he does know such an encounter: "Cain knew his wife" (Gen 4:17).

The story does not provide much information about this relationship. At first glance there might appear little to be gleaned from further analysis of it. However, it is equally possible that Cain's failure to comply with provisions expressed in Gen 2:24 were part of the message that the audience would have received given the juxtaposition of the two stories, especially if the same individual was performing in both roles of first man and Cain. Therefore, it is appropriate to answer the previously asked questions for this story.

(i) *When is one first eligible to participate in a boy-meets-girl encounter?*

Certainly one may suggest that only after one has taken life has one gained the right to produce life. However it hardly seems likely that the murder of a brother was intended as a positive step by which one gains the rights and privileges of adulthood. The story clearly portrays the actions of Cain in a negative light and adds little in terms of specifying an age when a male is eligible to meet a girl beyond the vague adulthood. As in the previous story, the issue does not appear to be relevant to the storyteller.

(ii) *What defines the eligibility of the other?*

No information whatsoever is provided about the origin of the woman who becomes the wife of Cain. Certainly there is nothing to suggest that she was the child of the first couple; there is nothing to suggest who her parents were. The traditional questions of eligibility based on ethnic, clan, or tribal designations appear irrelevant to this story. It should also be noted that due to the unusual circumstances of the story at the origin of the species, the normal rules of boy-meets-girl in present society may not be appropriate. The audience of the story may recognize that the governing laws in the present have been suspended for the duration of this story due to the obvious differences between the world of the story and the real world of the audience. Once again, the key issue for the story based on Gen 2:24 is the action of the male.

(iii) *How is the meeting legitimated or sanctified?*

According to the criteria of boy-meets-girl established in Gen 2:24, the male Cain is to leave his mother and father and cleave to his wife. Again, one may ask whether the audience would have considered Cain to have been in compliance with that boy-meets-girl standard. Whom does Cain leave?

> Then Cain went away from the presence of the Lord. (Gen 4:16).

Once again, the father-figure in the story who is left is YHWH. Although the introduction designates the man as the biological father (Gen 4:1), he has no role in the story beyond that initial procreation. The first man had left the presence of the Lord in the Garden, and now Cain the farmer, doing what the Lord intended for man to do, farm (Gen 2:5,15), leaves His presence as well, although the story itself is unclear about exactly where these actions of Cain and Abel transpire. It is reasonable to assume that the stage on which these actions occur was part of the message of the story, just as the American West has been in movies.

As for the mother of the story, the parallel with the opening story has not been maintained. In the opening of this story, a named woman bears two sons, both of whom she names herself. This introduction would make Eve the mother of all the living, as she is described in Gen 3:20, while diminishing the role of the human father; the father-figure in this story is still the deity YHWH, as it was in the first story. However, despite this effort to make Eve the mother of the story, after this introduction, she disappears from the story while the earth resumes the same role it had in the first scene. The statement that Eve is the mother of the living has not effectively been inserted into the narrative storyline where the woman then actually acts in that capacity.

When Cain leaves the presence of the Lord (the father), he also leaves the presence of the ground from which he has been cursed (the mother). Thus one may conclude that Cain has left the mother and the father as required by Gen 2:24 *and* that an unsuccessful attempt was made to put Eve in the mother role at the expense of the earth in this episode. Furthermore, his departure is the outgrowth of a curse, whereas Gen 2:24 states the departure in positive terms.

Cain's departure is for the land of Nod, presumably ground that has not cursed him. The proper noun Nod sometimes is translated as "Wandering" or so designated in a footnote to English Bibles, a reminder that the connotations of the word easily known to the original audience may be obscure to most readers today. Cain was going nowhere and only after he had left the presence of YHWH and the ground from which he had been cursed did he meet the nameless and indistinct woman to whom he would cleave: the departure and the cleaving are separate and unrelated actions without any cause and effect. All things considered, Cain appears more of an aberration to the social order proclaimed in Gen 2:24 than its fulfillment.

NOAH

In the story of Noah (separate from the genealogies), there is no mention of his father or mother. He does have a wife and family with married sons, but there is no mention of his life prior to his being married and no references to how he met the woman to whom he cleaved. Regardless of Noah's other virtues and heroic actions, the story itself reveals nothing about whether Noah had or had not complied with the boy-meets-girl conditions of Gen 2:24.

(i) *When is one first eligible to participate in a boy-meets-girl encounter?*
No information is provided here.

(ii) *What defines the eligibility of the other one?*
No information is provided here.

(iii) *How is the meeting legitimated or sanctified?*
No information is provided here.

One last note: if the same individual who performed in the role of the first man and Cain also played the role of Noah, then Noah, the tiller of the soil, may be said to be the *inclusio* who brings to completion the previous stories—the ground is no longer cursed, the burden of the work of man has been relieved, end of Act One.

ABRAHAM

With Abraham, a new sequence of stories begins:

> Now the Lord said to Abram, "Go from your country and your kindred and your father's house to the land that I will show you" (Gen 12: 1).

Continuing in the tradition of first man, Cain, and Noah, Abraham will depart from the land of his birth. This time the departure is not a curse but a blessing and is the harbinger not of cataclysmic disaster but divine promise. In contrast to the three earlier males in the narrative sequence, Abraham leaves the land of his origin with a specific purpose and toward a fixed destination (initially unnamed); he is neither cast out, cursed, nor a chance traveller on cosmic waters. If one were to cast the same person in the role of Abraham as in first man, Cain, and Noah, the continual unfolding of the human experience in this opening scene to Act Two would be dramatically apparent to the audience.

A change in the staging also has occurred. Presumably, the audience would also realize that the stage for the story is now closer to home, to the world of the present such that the suspension of the normal rules of boy-meets-girl in the initial sequence of stories may now be over: real-world rules now apply to the characters in the story, since the world of these figures is fully populated with diverse peoples with which one would interact just as the audience does in the present. These are not the stories of an isolated people unaware of the existence of many other peoples.

Would the audience regard Abraham as having been in compliance with the boy-meets-girl standards established in Gen 2:24? Abraham, like Noah, enters the narrative story already married and, unlike Noah, still living in the house of his father. His departure occurs subsequent to his marriage, perhaps by a considerable amount of time. Furthermore, neither his father nor mother is named in this story although the father previously had been named in a genealogical sequence. Thus little personal information has been provided and he would appear not to have fulfilled the conditions of Gen 2:24.

(i) *When is one first eligible to participate in a boy-meets-girl encounter?*

No information is provided.

(ii) *What defines the eligibility of the other one?*

In a genealogical reference prior to the narrative story, the wife of Abraham is named, but no information about her origins is provided nor are there any implications about how they had met. The narrative story itself is silent on such matters.

(iii) *How is the meeting legitimated or sanctified?*

No information about the meeting is provided, however, given the promise by YHWH to Abraham in Gen 12:2–3, one may conclude that he will become the ancestor of a great nation and infer that it will be through his still unnamed wife in the narrative story, indirectly sanctifying the relationship. With hindsight, we know, of course, that precisely this issue about who is the mother of his living people will be the focus of the bulk of the stories of the Abraham cycle.

Therefore it is appropriate to consider the other two women with whom Abraham is associated. For simplicity sake, this analysis will begin with Keturah, woman no. 3 (Gen 25:1). She appears abruptly out of nowhere and becomes the mother of six sons. No information is provided about her background and Abraham doesn't leave anyone or go anywhere to be with her. Indeed, she is not part of a story as much as she is part of a list. All things considered, her appearance in the text seems outside of the issue of compliance with Gen 2:24, although she certainly does appear to be the mother of a living people in the time of the audience.

By contrast, woman no. 2, Hagar, the Egyptian, is part of the narrative story (Gen 16 and 21:8–20). Since Sarah, woman no. 1, has remained barren, she offers her husband her servant woman as a surrogate to produce a child. The offer is accepted and action is successful. A son, later to be named Ishmael, is born. Although there is more information provided in the story of Hagar than there is in the listing of Keturah, the relationship still would not appear to fulfill the conditions of Gen 2:24. Abraham had left his father and mother long before he had undertaken this journey to the land YHWH would show him. He remains at home this time, since Hagar already resides within his household. Regardless of any other considerations about the role of Hagar within the biblical narrative, she does not assist Abraham in being in compliance with the boy-meets-girl conditions of Gen 2:24.

ISAAC (AND ISHMAEL)

With this story, there is now a named mother and father whom the son can leave. Perhaps now at last, the standard established way back in the opening story was to be fulfilled.

(i) *When is one first eligible to participate in a boy-meets-girl encounter?*

One notes again that the male in question is not portrayed as an adolescent, but as a single adult tending for himself; there is no rite of passage aspect to this first biblical story of a named adult male meeting a named adult female who are then to be married to each other.

(ii) *What defines the eligibility of the other one?*

Here, one also has some clear rules regarding the eligibility of the woman to be a wife:

> Abraham said to his servant, ... "you will not get a wife for my son from the daughters of the Canaanites, among whom I live, but will go to my country and to my kindred and get a wife for my son Isaac" (Gen 24:2).

A binding oath subsequently is entered into and the servant proceeds on his journey with some very clear guidelines.

(iii) *How is the meeting legitimated or sanctified?*

Abraham's charge to his servant clearly demonstrates approval on his side. Furthermore, as the story unfolds, it will be seen that a corresponding approval from the bride's family also is obtained.

However, it seems unlikely that the audience would have considered Isaac to have been in compliance with the boy-meets-girl provisions of Gen 2:24.

> Then Isaac brought her into his mother Sarah's tent. He took Rebekah, and she became his wife; and he loved her. So Isaac was comforted after his mother's death (Gen 24:67).

The long story of Isaac finding a wife concludes in what would seem to be a direct contradiction of the Gen 2:24 stipulations. Far from leaving his mother, her tent is still part of his household. He has left his father, but his mother's tent remains and Rebekah would appear to have replaced her to some extent. Leaving the psychology of the characters aside, the message about Isaac from the boy-meets-girl perspective of Gen 2:24 seems clear: he is being mocked, portrayed as a laughingstock for his failure to adhere to the provisions of Gen 2:24 and, indeed, for perverting them by being a "mama's boy."

The true travellers in the story are first the servant who locates the wife and second, Rebekah herself. The unnamed servant of Abraham is "the oldest of his house, who had charge of all that he had" (Gen 24:2), exactly as one might portray the firstborn son. So it is this surrogate son who is to leave the household of his father and mother to find a suitable wife for the biological son, thereby raising the issue of why the biological son couldn't go himself. Thus, in the opening of the story as in its conclusion, the role of the biological son has been diminished: he does not go forth to cleave unto a woman. The surrogate son leaves and returns with the surrogate mother for the mocked biological son who never goes forth or leaves the tent of his mother. Pity the actor who played that role!

In this story, it is possible that certain signals about boy-meets-girl in ancient Israel were being communicated even as the figure of Isaac was being mocked.

1. *Marriages could be arranged*: There is no sense in the story that what Abraham was attempting was in any way outside the norm; there is no sense in the story that the audience is expected to gasp in shock over this sequence of events; there is no sense of *OH MY GOD! HOW COULD YOU!* All in all, the tone is quite calm, suggesting that arranged marriages were a known quantity.
2. *Certain women were acceptable and certain were not*: Abraham specifies that the wife should not be a daughter of Canaan, but be a kindred woman from the homeland. The presumption is that the two conditions are connected, that Abraham would not say she could not be a Canaanite but an Egyptian was acceptable, as would be a Moabite or Ammonite. However, the charge was not made in the positive of choosing one's kin but in the negative of not marrying a Canaanite. So while the story clearly specifies the status of these two groups, it does leave open the question of other unnamed peoples.
3. *The watering hole provided a socially acceptable meeting place for strangers of the opposite sex*: Again, as with the arranged marriage, the meeting of the servant and Rebekah seems routine; there is no sense of the young unmarried girl recoiling in fear at the prospect of talking to a male stranger at the well—in contrast to the wife-sister stories where the fate of the woman is at stake and deception is the rule (see Gen 12, 20 and 26). Instead, there does seem to be a socially approved mechanism whereby a man and an unchaperoned unmarried young woman could "check each other out" at the watering hole. Indeed, it is likely that this

prop of pure clean socially productive water from the earth was chosen precisely for this purpose. No more blood from the ground! Life-sustaining water is now brought forth!

4. *The woman has a voice*: Not only for the first time is a woman named before being married, but she also has a voice in the story as well. In this particular case she appears to be genuinely supportive of the actions that are to follow and there is no sense that she is being coerced, quite the contrary. Furthermore, having such a voice seems perfectly normal within the context of the story and evidences no sense of violation of social norms. Presumably, she had the option to just say "No!" as well.
5. *The woman travels to the home of the man*: Whether this was the norm or not cannot be determined from this story. But unlike the Garden story, the emphasis here is not on the man leaving his mother and father, but on the woman leaving hers. In other words, to some extent there has been a role reversal with Rebekah being the one to fulfill the standard set for the man in Gen 2:24: she will leave the home of her father and mother and cleave to her husband. It is quite reasonable to suppose that this role reversal is part of the message of the story. The Isaac figure is mocked in the opening and conclusion of the story while in the interim it is the woman Rebekah who is the first figure in the biblical narrative to fulfill the provisions of Gen 2:24—except that she is a woman!

So, all in all, this story does not meet the ideal of Gen 2:24. In fact, despite its story of alliance between the Aramaeans and the Negevites, it represents a 180-degree reversal of the standard. Isaac doesn't go anywhere and he certainly doesn't leave his father and his mother; quite the contrary, as his wife is depicted at the end as replacing the mother in his life.

In the meantime, the other pre-Keturah son of Abraham already had married. Hagar the Egyptian had obtained a wife for her son Ishmael from the land of Egypt (Gen 21:21). To some extent, therefore, she has acted exactly as Abraham would for Isaac. She obtained a wife not from the local people but from the homeland, in his case Aram, in her case Egypt. True, she has to perform the work herself, having no servant and no details are provided, but the principle of marrying within one's ethnicity is maintained. Two parallel relationships have been established thus providing the audience the opportunity to chose sides if it was so inclined. In any event, Ishmael should not be considered to have been in compliance with the provisions of Gen 2:24.

ESAU

Then there is the story of Jacob and Rachel. However, before turning to the more well-known story of the marriage of Jacob, it is beneficial to consider the lesser-known marriages of his older brother Esau. The latter had his own abbreviated story to tell about his boy-meets-girl encounters.

> When Esau was forty years old, he married Judith daughter of Beeri the Hittite, and Basemath daughter of Elon the Hittite; and they made life bitter for Isaac and Rebekah (Gen 26:34–35).

This brief incident can be analyzed according to the same questions that have been applied to the previous boy-meets-girl encounters in the biblical narrative.

(i) *When is one first eligible to participate in a boy-meets-girl encounter?*

In this example there is no doubt that an adult male is involved. No matter how one chooses to interpret the biblical numbers, the idea that Esau was a teenager on the cusp of adulthood seems farfetched even though the Esau of the following story, the blessing of Jacob in Gen 27, appears to be an unmarried youth living at home. In any event, regardless of these other considerations, the male of the boy-meets-girl encounter here is portrayed as an adult.

(ii) *What defines the eligibility of the other one?*

The notice clearly emphasizes the Hittite ethnicity of the brides. No explanation is provided about the significance of this ethnicity. There is no pronouncement as Abraham had made about the Canaanites. The likelihood is that in this instance the audience automatically would have had a reaction to the Hittite ethnicity of not only one but both of the wives of Esau. This particular verse in itself (Gen 26:34) provides no clues about what that audience response would be expected to be.

The text does shed some light on that perception. The next phrase firmly establishes the impact of the marriage within the context of the story: the Hittite wives made life bitter for their in-laws. Again, however, no information is provided as to how this bitterness was engendered: by specific actions on the part of the wives or by their very existence as Hittites? It was acceptable to purchase a burial site from the Hittites, as Abraham had done (Gen 23), but would you want your son to marry a Hittite? It is reasonable to conclude that specific connotations to the ethnicity of the wives were part of the message of the passage without the narrator having to specify the cultural meaning of the term via footnotes or glosses. Anyone casting a play or a movie in late twentieth-century politically correct America would be very familiar with this phenomenon.

(iii) *How is the meeting legitimated or sanctified?*

This particular set of marriages would appear not to have been legitimated or sanctified in any way. Cain's problems had occurred because of what he had done when he had been single and not through the selection of a woman to be his wife, whatever her background. Similarly, the marriages of Abraham, Isaac, and Ishmael do not appear to have been met with disapproval by anyone. One could assert that Hagar forgot her place and became "uppity," as if she were not a surrogate but the real wife. But even when Sarah sought the banishment of Hagar and Ishmael, Abraham was very distressed until God alleviated his concerns with a divine promise (Gen 21:10–13). In this case, however, there is nothing positive said about the marriage of Esau and nothing in the narrative to suggest that anything good would come of it.

But Esau has a second and fairly brief boy-meets-girl encounter as well:

> Now Esau saw that Isaac had blessed Jacob and sent him away to Paddan-Aram to take a wife from there, and that as he blessed him he charged him, "You shall not marry one of the Canaanite women," and that Jacob obeyed his father and his mother and had gone to Paddan-Aram. So when Esau saw that the Canaanite women did not please his father Isaac, Esau went to Ishmael and took Mahalath daughter of Abraham's son Ishmael, and sister of Nebaioth, to be his wife in addition to the wives he had (Gen 28:6–9).

This passage goes right to the heart and soul of the effort to measure compliance with the provisions of Gen 2:24 in the boy-meets-girl encounters of the biblical narrative. There are three males to be considered here: Jacob, Ishmael, and Esau.

According to this author, Jacob was in the process of complying with the requirements of Gen 2:24. This commentator on the life of Jacob describes a man who had left his father and his mother with their blessing for the purpose of cleaving unto a woman who would be his wife. This description is a direct retelling of the Gen 2:24 standard located in the narrative in anticipation of Jacob fulfilling that standard. Furthermore, it occurs within a passage clearly intended to measure the actions of his brother Esau against him and therefore against the standards established in Gen 2:24 as well. Finally, the Abraham revision has been incorporated into the story standards, too. The Gen 2:24 requirements ignore the issue of ethnicity (in part due to the irrelevance at the time), whereas in the real world familiar to the audience, Abraham adds a provision against marriage to a Canaanite women. This passage, therefore, asserts that Jacob is in double compliance both with the strictures of Gen 2:24 and 24:3.

So, then, does Esau fulfill those provisions as well? The general reaction would appear to be, yes, Esau is in compliance but in a lesser way. Esau sees what has happened (Gen 28:6 and 8) and apparently has learned from these observations how he, the male son, was supposed to behave. It is almost as if he was being tutored in correct social protocol. According to this passage, Esau is a good student: since he cannot follow his brother to the brother of his mother to find a wife, he goes to the brother of his father in order to obtain one. There is no indication of Esau undertaking these actions with the overt blessings of his parents, but one presumes that these actions are in accordance with socially acceptable policy. Esau has learned how the boy-meets-girl encounter should be achieved and therefore leads his life accordingly.

A final note to the passage serves to remind the audience of the previous wives of Esau, although their ethnicity is not mentioned. These two Esau's are very different from each other, and one wonders if the second Esau has learned from the mistakes of the first Esau or if scenes from two plays now have been combined into one. In any event, these wives of Esau are not part of the story when Esau meets his brother with his own wives, upon Jacob's return to the land of Canaan (Gen 33).

The wives of Esau do appear again in the genealogies of Genesis 36 along with their children. That inclusion is a reminder of the importance of the grid of conventions. It raises the questions of what associations would have been made by the audience when these characters first appeared in the story line. Did the initial audience already have an awareness of who these people were in relation to the lands of Edom and Seir? Were they being informed about it for the first time in Genesis 36? Or was it something the initial audience knew but later audiences needed to have spelled out in greater detail since they had forgotten? Given the effort to identify the ethnicity of the wives of Esau, it is difficult to imagine that the original audience had no preconceived images of who such people were even without the information of Genesis 36.

The final male in this brief passage is Ishmael. When last seen, he was a loose end outside the main story line, seemingly dropped from the narrative. Suddenly, he reappears in a way that is socially constructive and beneficial. The figure of Ishmael in the wilderness, brother of Isaac, has been established as a counterpoint to Laban in Aram, brother of Rebekah. The Esau figure and the Ishmael figure enter into an alliance through the exchange of a socially acceptable woman, just as Jacob and Laban do. Hagar and Sarah both become the mother of a living people. How do those peoples relate to each other and what did it mean to audiences of the stories?

It seems unlikely that the ethnicities of the characters in these boy-meets-girl encounters are irrelevant to their message, a reminder that the determination of the grid of conventions is essential to understanding them.

This passage is an extremely carefully constructed one that seems fully conversant with previous stories and stories to come. It is a pro-Jacob, pro-Esau, and pro-Ishmael story that casts their boy-meets-girl encounters in a favorable light.

One last note. The passage identifies Mahalath as the daughter of Ishmael and sister of Nebaioth. The latter had been identified in a genealogy as the firstborn of Ishmael (Gen 25:13). Unlike in the genealogy, Nebaioth is the only son of Ishmael to be identified here in this passage and one presumes he is mentioned because his identification assists in the identification of the sister who marries Esau. In other words, just as the audience would be expected to react to the name Ishmael as part of the process of making a decision about the character of Mahalath, so too the name Nebaioth must have contributed to the positive way in which she was intended to be perceived, even though no record exists of what he did to warrant his mention. Mahalath is identified as the granddaughter of Abraham, daughter of Ishmael, and sister of Nebaioth in a single verse and the audience presumably is expected to have a positive reaction to the woman who is Esau's Rachel.

JACOB AND RACHEL

Now, at last, it is time to turn to the major boy-meets-girl story of the Pentateuch, the story of Jacob and Rachel. The existing narrative has already informed us in Gen 28:6–7 that Jacob is in compliance with the boy-meets-girl conditions of Gen 2:24, so there is little mystery in this regard. Jacob leaves the household of his mother and his father with their blessing to cleave to the woman who will be his wife and who is not Canaanite but from the family of his mother in the homeland in Aram. Nonetheless, the questions raised in the examples of boy-meets-girl encounters that do not fulfill the provisions of Gen 2:24 need to be asked and answered here.

(i) *When is one first eligible to participate in a boy-meets-girl encounter?*

Jacob, continuing in what appears to be a well-established tradition, is an adult. Certainly, one may discuss how mature an adult Jacob was in the narrative, especially if one was casting the story to be performed. Unlike the various other figures, the life of Jacob unfolds before the eyes of the audience in a long series of incidents stretching across decades. One feels as if one is watching this man from his origin in the womb to his attainment of patriarchal status for a people, a growth cycle not comparable to any of the figures previously encountered in the biblical narrative. The story of his departure to find a bride is not a presumed event or a narrative comment, but a vibrant and compelling tale that dominates his adulthood.

(ii) *What defines the eligibility of the other one?*

As previously noted, the narrative tells us that Jacob is going to the land of his mother's brother to marry there so as not to marry a Canaanite woman (Gen 28:6–7). This comment follows immediately from a passage in which Isaac directly communicates that message to Jacob:

> Then Isaac called Jacob and blessed him, and charged him, "You shall not marry one of the Canaanite women. Go at once to Paddan-Aram to the house of Bethuel, your mother's father; and take as wife from there one of the daughters of Laban, your mother's brother. May God Almighty bless you and make you fruitful and numerous, that you may become a company of peoples. May he give to you the blessing of Abraham, to you and to your offspring with you, so that you make take possession of the land where you now live as an alien—land that God gave to Abraham." Thus Isaac sent Jacob away; and he went to Paddan-Aram, to Laban son of Bethuel the Aramean, the brother of Rebekah, Jacob's and Esau's mother (Gen 28:1–5).

If the story was being performed, and if the same person performed in the roles as the first man, Cain, Noah in Act One, Abraham in Act Two, and now Jacob in Act Three, the change in scene to the real world of the audience may have become quite apparent. Jacob's departure is quite distinct from Abraham's, just as Abraham's was from his predecessors:

- Jacob is leaving at the request of his human father and not God, the father;
- Jacob is leaving for a specific and known destination, not an unknown land that will be shown to him;
- Jacob is leaving to marry, he is not already married;
- Jacob is the one who will fulfill the blessing of Abraham, with many offspring who will take possession of the land promised to Abraham; he is the real father of the people in the audience, the one with whom they can identify.

The words of Isaac in this passage, as in the editorial comment to follow, bespeak a thorough familiarity with previous incidents in the narrative and express a well-crafted speech and commentary on the roles of Jacob and Esau.

However, all is not quite as simple as it might seem. Despite this strong admonition to marry a good girl from back home and not a Canaanite woman, there is no such concern expressed in Gen 27:41–45, when Jacob is first preparing to leave. In these verses, the cause of Jacob's departure is the much more familiar one: fear of what the furious Esau, who has lost his birthright, might do if he ever "got his hands on" Jacob. The mother still advises Jacob to leave for the household of her brother, but only temporarily, until the rage of Esau is assuaged—the same rage Jacob fears in Gen 32–33, when he does return to face Esau. In this scenario, Jacob still leaves the household of his mother and father and marries, but the tenor is more of avoiding a negative than achieving a positive.

There is even a third consideration for the departure of Jacob. In between this passage of fleeing the fearsome brother seeking revenge and the passage of Isaac charging Jacob to fulfill the provisions of Gen 2:24, a long verse has Rebekah say to Isaac:

> "I am weary of my life because of the Hittite women [that Esau had married in Gen 26:34–35]. If Jacob marries one of the Hittite women such as these, one of the women of the land, what good will my life be to me?" (Gen 27:46).

Strong words indeed. Nonetheless, when Isaac does charge Jacob he refers solely to Canaanite women and not to Hittites. This switch raises the legitimate question of the identity of the people of the land, Canaanite or Hittite. It further raises the issue of what these terms meant to the audience.

> Abraham bought a burial site from a Hittite, Esau has married Hittites without having to travel anywhere, and Rebekah states that Hittites are the people of the land.
>
> By contrast, Abraham set forth for the land of Canaan and the Canaanites already were in the land (Gen 12:5–6), Abraham settled in the land of Canaan while Lot did not (Gen 13:11–12), and Abraham told his servant that his son is not to marry a Canaanite women from the land (Gen 24:4).

On what basis should the audience to this story decide who are the people of the land: the Canaanites or the Hittites? These two proper nouns flit through the story as already known quantities, almost as if there were separate and distinct audiences. The Hittites and the Canaanites are infrequent but critical participants in the biblical stories of boy-meets-girl. But even their brief appearances causes one to wonder how the current narrative sequence could be performed as a single story without insulting the intelligence of the audience regardless of the images connoted by those terms. One feels caught between dueling social dramas where both cultural paradigms have become part of the canonized ritual drama.

(iii) *How is the meeting legitimated or sanctified?*

On one level, the parents separately have sanctified and legitimated the marriage since Jacob is charged with leaving to marry a member of his mother's household. On a second level, the journey is validated by the dream at Bethel, the House of God, which Jacob has immediately upon leaving (Gen 28:10–22).

Then something new happens in the biblical stories of boy-meets-girl: the audience experiences the encounter of a male and a female before they are married to each other. Abraham is already married and Isaac meets Rebekah after she has been selected to be his wife. Only with Jacob does the future groom meet his future bride before any marriage has occurred or been arranged. Jacob, like a strutting male peacock, demonstrates his physical prowess to both the woman he desires and to an appreciative surrounding audience, much as male athletes continue to do to this very day. So despite the issue of arranged marriages, one should not overlook individual personal chemistry as a requisite for marriage. The story gives every indication that Rachel had the right to refuse Jacob. We are meant to feel the joy of the successful match.

But if such rejection was possible by the intended woman, it was even more so by the intended father-in-law. As the following incident in Genesis 29 makes abundantly clear, Jacob will have to earn the hand of his beloved. Again, the story introduces a new element to the boy-meets-girl encounter: the perspective groom must win the approval of both bride and father-in-law before the marriage is sanctified and legitimated. This is the first time in the narrative that this issue has been raised; undoubtedly it would not be the last. Perhaps the audience was familiar with this occurrence: the need of the groom to comply with an unreasonable request to placate the difficult father-in-law if true love was to be fulfilled.

Another wrinkle is then added to the process: the firstborn daughter must be married before the younger one (Gen 29:23–27). This custom appears to take Jacob by surprise and needs to be explained to him (and the audience). One cannot help but wonder if this action reflects the custom of the land or is intended as a narrative "curveball." The narrative portrays two women here: the woman as wife—Rachel, risking all to be with the man she loves—and the woman as dutiful daughter—Leah, who marries at the command of her father. Such, in fact, frequently is the dual reality of a woman's position in society as she struggles between following her heart or obeying the figure of authority. So if you were casting the story of Jacob and Rachel, would you cast two women for the roles of Rachel and Leah or one woman wearing a mask for the Leah role of social duty and with no mask for when her own feelings are expressed? Who would have played this role in ancient times and what message would it have delivered? Suppose the king was performing in the role of Jacob?

Jacob and Rachel fulfill the boy-meets-girl provisions of Gen 2:24 such that their story may be regarded as an *inclusio* to that initial story. To the author of this story, Jacob and Rachel are the ideal couple; they might just as well be singing the Song of Songs to each other. (About how many couples in the Hebrew Bible could one say that and be believed?) After a series of boy-meets-girl encounters of various types that fail to comply with, mock, shed no light at all on, or seem to approach fulfilling them without succeeding, at last the ideal couple takes center stage in the biblical narrative only to face two new challenges:

- the difficulty in entering into a covenant with the Aramaean (that is finally resolved in Gen 31:43–50);
- the difficulty in distinguishing between the woman who acts on the basis of love versus the woman who acts on the basis of duty to her father (which is implicitly resolved when Leah leaves Laban with Rachel and Jacob in the Gen 31 episode).

The Israelite, not the Aramaean, is now the master and the latter agrees to this new relationship; these ethnic considerations, too, are part of the message of this boy-meets-girl encounter.

III. *Conclusion*

One may readily observe that the boy-meets-girl encounter is one of the most common encounters in the biblical narrative once one leaves the primordial world of the beforetime and enters the real world of the present audience.[29] And this review has excluded such failed encounters as Pharaoh and Sarah (Gen 12:10–20), Abimelech and Sarah (Gen 20), and Abimelech and Rebekah (Gen 26) with their Egyptian and Philistine males (to say nothing of the rather unusual encounters of Gen 19:30–38).[30] At this

[29] See Ringgren (1987) on the marriage motif in Israelite religion.

[30] Unusual sexual encounters should not automatically be assumed to be about sex. For example, in the movie *Spartacus*, the female slave girl, Varinia, shuttles back and forth between Spartacus and Crassus with a frequency that defies human reason. Such transformations are reflective of the shifts in power between these two men, with sex serving as a metaphor for that power: the man who controls her sexually is the man who rules the people she represents. A similar expression of power occurs in the story of David, Absalom, and the royal concubines (2 Sam 16:20–22). Such actions should be a reminder of the importance of considering the political implications of sexual encounters where power politics is being fought through biological metaphors.

point, therefore, one must now return to the beginning to fulfill the conditions established in the introduction to this essay.

In the beginning of this analysis, certain criteria were proposed as diagnostic tools to be applied in an attempt to understand a story. Now that this initial review of stories has been accomplished from the statement of the standards for boy-meets-girl encounter in Gen 2:24 to their fulfillment with Jacob and Rachel, it is appropriate to look back on these stories and to identify the diagnostic markers that need to be understood if the message of the story is to be understood.

1. *Stage*: These stories of boy-meets-girl occur in the garden (first man),[31] at the well (the servant of Abraham and Jacob), in the more vague wilderness,[32] or at no designated location at all (Cain, Ishmael, Esau). Each of these stages may be presumed to have a meaning to the people experiencing the story in whatever form it is being communicated. Setting the stories in these locales is part of the stories' message just as is the *High Noon* street, the spring-break beach, Tara, or Rick's.
2. *Props*: These stories of boy-meets-girl contain props, such as a tree,[33] a tent,[34] and water in the wilderness[35] or from a well. The story of Jacob earning his right to the woman he loves involves sheep (and not the foreskins of the enemy as for David in I Sam 18:25–29).[36] As with the

[31] For the significance of the garden motif, see Lau (1981).

[32] For the significance of the wilderness motif, see Talmon (1987).

[33] For the significance of the tree motif, see Meyers (1976) 95–202.

[34] For the significance of the cosmic tent motif, see Clifford (1971).

[35] For the significance of water in the wilderness, see Propp (1983).

[36] For the significance of sheep as a motif, see Haupt (1905), Waters (1970), and Wright (1939). What is so striking in these analyses by all three scholars is how closely the shepherd and the king are intertwined in the storytelling and metaphors of the ancient Near East—except when it comes to the biblical patriarchs. One wonders if the original audiences of the biblical accounts would have been so quick to employ dictionary definition no. 1 of the census or business contract shepherd as one who tends biological sheep versus dictionary definition no. 2 of the epic shepherd as king. Of course, if the king was performing the role of Jacob who found true love, the answer would be obvious. Again this serves as a reminder of the need to understand the grid of conventions if the story is to be understood. Perhaps if the Rudolph Valentino/Lawrence of Arabia sheikh motif hadn't been so prevalent at the dawn of modern biblical scholarship, the nomadic ideal wouldn't have the strong hold it has had on biblical scholarship both in the Albright and German schools. For the patriarchal stories reflecting a non-nomadic setting, see Van Seters (1975) 13–38.

stage, one may presume that the selection of a given prop for the story was part of the message of the story.

3. *Time*: These stories of boy-meets-girl are markedly different based on the temporal setting. When the stories are set in the beforetime, the time before the world of the present existed, the time before the flood, the normal social rules appear suspended or irrelevant. Only after the full complement of peoples existed in the world as known to the audience did the rules of boy-meets-girl encounters enter in to the narrative. Then there were positive peoples (Aramaeans), negative peoples (Canaanites), and peoples who were both (Hittites). Stories that would not make sense in the world before the flood, become the typical story in the world after the flood.[37]
4. *Cast*: The casting of the characters in the story is an issue of enormous importance. During these narratives, one encounters:
   - unnamed common noun figures (the servant of Abraham, the wives of Cain and Noah);
   - a range of proper noun people with ethnic epithets;
   - proper noun individuals from having no story to tell (Keturah, the wives of Esau) to having a major story to tell (Jacob and Rachel).

The audience reaction to these characters is part of the message of the story. Are we to assume that these figures were previously unknown to the audience, that previously known figures were being elaborated on to reflect changing circumstances? For example, what did the name Jacob mean to a Canaanite audience and what are the implications of claiming that Jacob, and not Abraham, fulfilled the divine promise?[38] For that matter, what did Esau mean before he became Rome?

---

[37] For the significance of periodization in the stories, see Niditch (1985) 61. Periodization would an historical issue in Dan 2:39–45 and a cosmic one in Dan 7.

[38] Given the apparent zenith of Canaanite development during MB II c. 1650–1550, when West Semites ruled in Egypt, and, assuming an ethnic connection between the Canaanites and at least some of the Israelites who settled in the hill country beginning in the thirteenth century B.C.E., a logical question to be asked, therefore, is what was the legacy of Bronze Age Jacob's to the Iron Age Israelites of the same ethnicity and land? That legacy would be a factor in understanding the grid of conventions to the original audience of the Jacob stories. Redford (1992) 412 postulates an overlap between the biblical chain of events and the Hyksos-Jacob-Egypt legacy in secular history. Presumably, if the Canaanites who became Israelites brought their heroes in history with them, that legacy should be factored

5. *Plot*: The story of boy-meets-girl is one that is universal to the species and subject to infinite variations reflecting specific circumstances. The storylines here tend to be about adults older than Romeo and Juliet and more comparable to Rhett and Scarlet. And while one may relate to the universality of the love story between the latter, their Civil War story should be separated from its Depression production. The details of the plot tend to reflect the concerns of the present, whether retrojected into hoary antiquity or the recent past.[39] Jets, Sharks. Aramaeans, Israelites. Names change, but basic plot lines endure.

6. *Language*:[40] Many of these stories of boy-meets-girl are less stories than statements via genealogies or a narrative comment in the text. Isaac is mocked in one story, while it is the story of Jacob that receives the most extensive treatment. This analysis has focused more on the events that have transpired rather than the words used to express those events. One avenue for future study would be to attempt to determine if part of the reason for the seemingly contrary images being portrayed, the parallel sets of alliances, the dueling social dramas, is because different hands have penned those words.

---

into any attempt to reconstruct the grid of conventions for the prose of the Israelites. The fictional love interests added to the historic-based stories of *Inherit the Wind* and *Spartacus* served to cue the audience as to:

(i) the relative power of the competing males
(ii) the choice the audience was supposed to make.

Whereas these movies use one female figure in both the written story and the performed version, the biblical story may have used one actress and two written characters to accomplish the same: the Israelite audience was expected to choose the Canaanite hero Jacob just as Rachel had, or so may have been the original intent if this proposed grid of conventions is correct.

39 For an example of how twenty scholars retrojected their personal storylines of the present into the hoar antiquity of their medieval field of studies, see Cantor (1991). For an example of how an apparently legitimate academic change emerged out of political circumstances, see Farmer and Reventlow (1995) on nineteenth-century German national unification and the primacy of the Gospel of Mark over that of Matthew.

40 Gerstenberger (1985) 415 claims that there must have been an abundance of auditory devices at the disposal of the writer for use in both poetic and prose compositions. He continues (1985) 416–17 by noting the use of metaphors and symbols in poetic language without mentioning prose. Perhaps that omission should be reconsidered.

7. *Performance*: The issue of the performance of the story is perhaps the most critical of all the issues raised. If the academic model of the ivory tower or graduate seminar reading of a story or series of stories is retrojected as the norm for the original ancient audiences of the biblical texts, then the audience is effectively reduced to the individual or a class of scattered similar individuals. If the stories are presumed to be for the general public consumption, then an entirely different reading of them emerges. The issue then becomes not only what the name Jacob meant to the audience, but who was performing in the role of Jacob. It is precisely here where an essential difference between ancient Israel and its neighbors may be seen: if the king performed in the role of human heroes rather than a divine one. Such an occurrence would add a whole dimension to the effort to understand these stories.[41]

My intention here has been to raise questions for possible avenues of future study. I have done so by choosing a deliberately more public sense to these stories than is ordinarily done. This approach was even more evident during my presentation of the paper at the Midwest AOS/ASOR/SBL conference in February, 1999. The presentation took the form of a video using the different versions of the movie *State Fair* to illustrate boy-meets-girl encounters in a rural agricultural world of isolated farmsteads and annual gatherings with music, food, excitement and love, transpiring at the cosmic center Iowa (supplemented with scenes from *Field of Dreams*). It is a world not far removed from the Shiloh of Judg 21:19–22 or Baal Peor of Num 25:1–5 in many ways. Sacred time, sacred place, sacred story, sacred act: boy meets girl at the annual festival celebrating one's culture from high school prom to spring break to state fair.

---

[41] In modern times, there is a phenomenon known as "the invention of tradition," whereby people in the present create historic traditions from the past in order to meet some contemporary need. Examples from a variety of peoples have been portrayed by Hobsbawn and Ranger (1983) and Lowenthal (1985) while Zerubavel (1995) focuses on twentieth-century Israel's use of historical events from both the twentieth century and Roman times. Here is where the problem ensues: how does one distinguish between "rewritten histories" and "invented traditions"? In response to the McCarthy Era, the American 1950s witnessed the creation of *Inherit the Wind*, *The Crucible*, and *Spartacus*. These are all based on historical events rewritten for the present of their creation. They all then took on a life of their own, independent of their original *Sitz im Leben*, to the point where they can become the definitive interpreters of the past. They also are constantly revised in presentations by local communities to reflect the new present. This is what a storytelling species with a conscious awareness of time does.

The stories of boy-meets-girl are important not only for what they say about the social customs of the audience but for the political messages they deliver and the dueling social dramas or paradigms they illustrate. The latter is all the more important if it turns out that these stories were intended for a general audience and were being communicated by people in positions of authority. I hope through this paper to have sparked some thought not only about how boy met girl in ancient Israel, but how such stories may have been part of the way people in power communicated with the general public.

BIBLIOGRAPHY

Allen, Frederick Lewis (1964) *Only Yesterday: An Informal History of the 1920's.* New York. [First published 1931.] **Alter, Robert** (1981) *The Art of Biblical Narrative.* New York. **Barra, Allen** (1998) *Inventing Wyatt Earp: His Life and Many Legends.* New York. **Bennett, Tony, and Janet Woollacott** (1987) *Bond and Beyond: The Political Career of a Popular Hero.* London. **Bergen, Theodore A., and Michael E. Stone, eds.** (1998) *Biblical Figures Outside the Bible.* Harrisburg, Pa. **Biel, Steven** (1996) *Down with the Old Canoe: A Cultural History of the Titanic Disaster.* New York. **Blackman, A.M., and H.W. Fairman** (1942) The Myth of Horus at Edfu: II. *Journal of Egyptian Archaeology* 28: 32–38. (1943) The Myth of Horus at Edfu: II. *Journal of Egyptian Archaeology* 29: 2–36. (1944) The Myth of Horus at Edfu: II. *Journal of Egyptian Archaeology* 30: 5–22. (1949) The Significance of the Ceremony ḤWT BḤSW in the Temple of Horus at Edfu. *Journal of Egyptian Archaeology* 35: 98–112. (1950) The Significance of the Ceremony ḤWT BḤSW in the Temple of Horus at Edfu. *Journal of Egyptian Archaeology* 36: 63–81. **Burkert, Walter** (1983) *Homo Necans: The Anthropology of Ancient Greek Sacrificial Ritual and Myth.* Berkeley, Calif. **Cantor, Norman F.** (1991) *Inventing the Middle Ages: The Lives, Works, and Ideas of the Great Medievalists of the Twentieth Century.* New York. **Clifford, Richard** (1971) The Tent of El and the Israelite Tent of Meeting. *Catholic Biblical Quarterly* 33: 221–27. **Cohn, Norman** (1993) *Cosmos, Chaos and the World to Come: The Ancient Roots of Apocalyptic Faith.* New Haven. **Cross, Frank Moore** (1973) *Canaanite Myth and Hebrew Epic: Essays in the History of the Religion of Israel.* Cambridge, Mass. **De Bruhl, Marshall** (1995) The Alamo. In Mark Carnes, ed., *Past Imperfect: History According to the Movies,* 116–19. New York. **Engnell, Ivan** (1967) *Studies in Divine Kingship in the Ancient Near East.* Oxford. (1969) *A Rigid Scrutiny: Critical Essays on the Old Testament.* Nashville, Tenn. **Fairman, H.W.** (1935) The Myth of Horus at Edfu: I. *Journal of Egyptian Archaeology* 21: 26–36. (1958) The Kingship Rituals of Egypt. In S.H. Hooke, ed., *Myth, Ritual, and Kingship: Essays on the Theory and Practice of Kingship in the Ancient Near East and in Israel,* 74–104. Oxford. (1974) *The Triumph of Horus: An Ancient Egyptian Sacred Drama.* Los Angeles. **Faragher, John Mack**

(1995) The Tale of Wyatt Earp. In Mark Carnes, ed., *Past Imperfect: History According to the Movies*, 154–61. New York. **Farmer, William, and Henning Graf Reventlow, eds.** (1995) *Biblical Studies and the Shifting of Paradigms, 1850–1914*. Journal for the Study of the Old Testament Supplement 192. Sheffield. **Frankfort, Henri** (1978) *Kingship and the Gods: A Study of Ancient Near Eastern Religion as the Integration of Society and Nature*. Chicago. [First published 1948.] **Friedman, Richard Elliot** (1999) *The Hidden Book in the Bible: The Discovery of the First Prose Masterpiece*. New York. **Gates, Anita** (1996) One Juliet Has the Vapors, Another Packs a Gun. New York Times October 27: Arts and Leisure 13. **Gerstenberger, Erhard S.** (1985) The Lyrical Literature. In Douglas A. Knight and Gene M. Tucker, eds., *The Hebrew Bible and Its Modern Interpreters*. Atlanta, Ga. **Goldie, Mark** (1996) Contextualizing Dryden's Absalom: William Lawrence, the Laws of Marriage, and the Case for King Monmouth. In Donna B. Hamilton and Richard Strier, eds., *Religion, Literature, and Politics in Post-Reformation England, 1540–1688*, 208–30. Cambridge, UK. **Grafton, Anthony** (1997) *The Footnote *A Curious History*. Cambridge, Mass. **Halpern-Amaru, Betsy** (1994) *Rewriting the Bible: Land and Covenant in Postbiblical Jewish Literature*. Valley Forge, Pa. **Hanson, Paul D.** (1985) Apocalyptic Literature. In Douglas A. Knight and Gene M. Tucker, eds., *The Hebrew Bible and Its Modern Interpreters*, 465–88. Atlanta, Ga. **Haupt, Paul** (1905) The Poetic Form of Psalm XXIII. *American Journal of Semitic Languages and Literature* 21: 133–52. (1915) Armageddon. *Journal of the American Oriental Society* 34: 412–17. **Hobsbawm, Eric, and Terence Ranger, eds.** (1983) *The Invention of Tradition*. Cambridge, UK. **Hedges, Chris** (1999) Stealing Fire from Olympus: Staging the Greeks, with High-Voltage and Modern Energy. New York Times, December 1: E1 and 5. **Hooke, S.H., ed.** (1933) *Myth and Ritual: Essays on the Myth and Ritual of the Hebrews in Relation to the Culture Pattern of the Ancient East*. London. (1958) *Myth, Ritual, and Kingship: Essays on the Theory and Practice of Kingship in the Ancient Near East and in Israel*. Oxford. **Knierim, Rolf** (1985) Criticism of Literary Features, Form, Tradition, and Redaction. In Douglas A. Knight and Gene M. Tucker, eds., *The Hebrew Bible and Its Modern Interpreters*, 123–65. Atlanta, Ga. **Kugel, James L.** (1997) *The Bible as It Was*. Cambridge, Mass. **Johnson, Aubrey** (1955) *Sacral Kingship in Ancient Israel*. Cardif. **Larson, Edward J.** (1997) *Summer for the Gods: The Scopes Trial and America's Continuing Debate over Science and Religion*. New York. **Lau, Susan Carol** (1981) *Garden as a Symbol of Sacred Space*. Unpublished dissertation at the University of Pittsburgh. UMI, Ann Arbor. **Leach, Edmund** (1970) *Claude Lévi-Strauss*. New York. **Lowenthal, David** (1985) *The Past is a Foreign Country*. Cambridge, UK. **McNutt, Paula** (1987) Interpreting Israel's Folk Traditions. *Journal for the Study of the Old Testament* 39: 44–52. **Meyers, Carol** (1976) *The Tabernacle Menorah: A Synthetic Study of a Symbol from the Biblical Cult*. Missoula. **Mowinckel, Sigmund** (1962) *The Psalms in Israel's Worship: Volumes I and II*. New York. **Nickelsburg, George W.E.** (1981) *Jewish Literature Between the Bible and the Mishnah*. Philadelphia. **Niditch, Susan**

(1985) *Chaos to Cosmos: Studies in Biblical Patterns of Creation.* Atlanta, Ga. **Numbers, Ronald L.** (1998) *Darwinism Comes to America.* Cambridge, Mass. **Patterson, Annabel** (1996) Sir John Oldcastle as Symbol of Reformation Historiography. In Donna B. Hamilton and Richard Strier, eds., *Religion, Literature, and Politics in Post-Reformation England, 1540–1688,* 6–26. Cambridge, UK. **Payne, David** (1979) Jonah from the Perspective of Its Audience. *Journal for the Study of the Old Testament* 13: 3–12. **Propp, William Henry** (1987) *Water in the Wilderness: A Biblical Motif and Its Mythological Background.* Harvard Semitic Monographs 40. Atlanta, Ga. **Redford, Donald B.** (1992) *Egypt, Canaan, and Israel in Ancient Times.* Princeton, N.J. **Ringgren, Helmer** (1987) The Marriage Motif in Israelite Religion. In Patrick Miller, Paul Hanson, and S.D. McBride, eds., *Ancient Israelite Religion: Essays in Honor of Frank Moore Cross,* 421–27. Philadelphia. **Sandeen, Ernest R.** (1970) *The Roots of Fundamentalism: British and American Millenarianism 1800–1930.* Chicago. **Segal, Robert, ed.** (1998) *The Myth and Ritual Theory.* Oxford. **Snaith, Norman** (1947) *The Jewish New Year Festival: Its Origins and Development.* London. **Stone, Michael** (1984) *Jewish Writings of the Second Temple Period: Apocrypha, Pseudepigrapha, Qumran Sectarian Writings, Philo, and Josephus.* Compendia Rerum Iudaicarum ad Novum Testamentum Section Two. Philadelphia. **Stricker, B.H.** (1955) The Origin of the Greek Theatre. *Journal of Egyptian Archaeology* 41: 34–47. **Talmon, Shemaryahu** (1987) Har and Midbār: An Antithetical Pair of Biblical Motifs. In M. Mindlin, M.J. Geller, and J.E. Wansbrough, eds., *Figurative Language in the Ancient Near East,* 117–42. London. **Taylor, Gary** (1989) *Reinventing Shakespeare: A Cultural History from the Restoration to the Present.* New York. **Tigay, Jeffrey** (1982) *The Evolution of the Gilgamesh Epic.* Philadelphia. (1985) The Evolution of the Pentateuchal Narratives in the Light of the Evolution of the *Gilgamesh Epic.* In Jeffrey Tigay, ed., *Empirical Models for Biblical Criticism,* 21–52. Philadelphia. **Turner, Victor** (1974) *Dramas, Fields, and Metaphors: Symbolic Action in Human Society.* Ithaca, N.Y. **Uphill, Eric** (1965) The Egyptian Sed-Festival Rites. *Journal of Near Eastern Studies* 24: 365–83. **Van Doren, Carl** (1938) *Benjamin Franklin.* New York. **Van Seters, John** (1975) *Abraham in History and Tradition.* New Haven. (1992) *Prologue to History: The Yahwist as Historian in Genesis.* Louisville, Ky. (1994) *The Life of Moses: The Yahwist as Historian in Exodus-Numbers.* Louisville, Ky. **Waters, John** (1970) *The Political Development and Significance of the Shepherd-King Symbol in the Ancient Near East and in the Old Testament.* Unpublished dissertation at Boston University. UMI, Ann Arbor, Mich. **Wills, Garry** (1995) *Witches and Jesuits: Shakespeare's Macbeth.* New York. **Wortman, Richard S.** (1995) *Scenarios of Power: Myth and Ceremony in Russian Monarchy, Volume One.* Princeton, N.J. **Wright, George Ernest** (1939) The Good Shepherd. *Biblical Archaeologist* 2: 44–48. **Zerubavel, Yael** (1995) *Recovered Roots: Collective Memory and the Making of Israeli National Tradition.* Chicago.

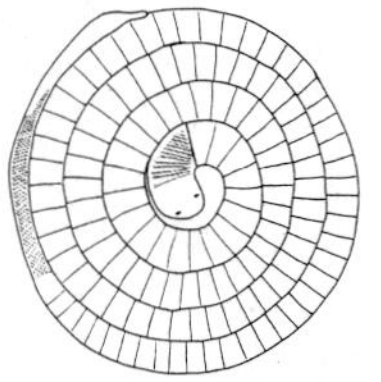

Aspects of Life in Ancient Israel

Anson Rainey
Tel Aviv University

The ensuing discussion concerns two aspects of life in the ancient society of Israel. Although they were recognized in some circles long ago, they are usually neglected in current sociological discussions about the kingdoms of Israel and Judah.[1] Nonetheless, both subjects are fundamental to the understanding of the social dynamics at play in the first-temple period.

The Landed Aristocracy in Ancient Israel

It was the late Isaac Mendelsohn[2] who first noted the parallel between the practices of the kings of Late Bronze Age Ugarit as reflected in the land grant documents discovered there[3] and the "Ordinance of the King" in 1 Samuel 8. The kings of Ugarit often assigned lands and possessions to loyal subjects frequently after appropriating such estates from other subjects who had apparently lost favor with the government.[4] Many of the same royal acts are ascribed to the authority of the king as depicted in this biblical passage. The focus here is on the transfer of real estate, including agricultural properties, from the citizenry to favored servants.

The King's Authority

The "Ordinance of the King" (1 Sam 8:11–17) is as follows:

He said, "These will be the ways of the king who will reign over you: he will take your sons and appoint them to his chariots and to be his horsemen, and to run before his chariots; and he will appoint for himself commanders of thousands and commanders of fifties, and some to plow his ground and to reap his harvest, and to make his

---

1 These aspects were discussed in Rainey (1962), (1967a–b), (1970a–b), (1979).

2 Mendelsohn (1956).

3 Nougayrol (1955).

4 Rainey (1967a).

> implements of war and the equipment of his chariots. He will take your daughters to be perfumers and cooks and bakers. **He will take the best of your fields and vineyards and olive orchards and give them to his courtiers.** He will take one-tenth of your grain and of your vineyards and give it to his officers and his courtiers. He will take your male and female slaves, and the best of your cattle and donkeys, and put them to his work. He will take one-tenth of your flocks, and you shall be his slaves.

The emphasized portion is a clear statement of royal practice as recognized in the Deuteronomistic history.

MERIBAAL'S ESTATE

An important illustration of this kingly prerogative is the handling of the Saulide estate by the newly appointed King David.[5] The monarch is depicted as assigning the "House of Saul" to Saul's grandson, the son of Jonathan (2 Sam 9:6–13):

> Mephibosheth son of Jonathan son of Saul came to David, and fell on his face and did obeisance. David said, "Mephibosheth!" He answered, "I am your servant."
>
> David said to him, "Do not be afraid, for I will show you kindness for the sake of your father Jonathan; **I will restore to you all the land of your grandfather Saul**, and you yourself shall eat at my table always." He did obeisance and said, "What is your servant, that you should look upon a dead dog such as I?"
>
> Then the king summoned Saul's servant Ziba, and said to him, "All that belonged to Saul and to all his house I have given to your master's grandson. **You and your sons and your servants shall till the land for him, and shall bring in the produce, so that your master's grandson may have food to eat;** but your master's grandson Mephibosheth shall always eat at my table."
>
> Now Ziba had fifteen sons and twenty servants.
>
> Then Ziba said to the king, "According to all that my lord the king commands his servant, so your servant will do." Mephibosheth ate at David's table, like one of the king's sons.
>
> Mephibosheth had a young son whose name was Mica. And all who lived in Ziba's house became Mephibosheth's servants. Mephibosheth lived in Jerusalem, for he always ate at the king's table. Now he was lame in both his feet.

---

5 Rainey (1967b) 39.

Ziba, the steward of Saul's estate, with his sons, was reaffirmed as manager of the estate and charged with delivering its produce to the new master, Meribaal (Mephibosheth), who would live in Jerusalem and eat at the king's table.

HEROD'S FOUNDING OF SEBASTIA

The custom of receiving land grants, i.e., agricultural estates, continued into the Roman period, as exemplified by Herod's generosity toward veterans who had served him.

> In the district of Samaria he built a town enclosed within magnificent walls...introduced into it six thousand colonists, and gave them allotments of highly productive land. (Jos. *War*, I, xxi, 2[403]; Thackeray 1927)

> ...he arranged to have settled in it many of those who had fought as his allies in war and many of the neighboring populations...and apportioned the near-by territory, which was the best in the country, among its inhabitants in order that they might find prosperity as soon as they came together to live there. (Jos. *Antiq*. XV, viii 5[296]; Marcus 1963)

The important point here is that the new settlers in Samaria were to live in the city but they were to be supported by the agricultural produce from the estates in the immediate vicinity which the king had awarded to them. It is obvious that there were stewards or peasants living on those estates who were responsible for regular deliveries to the owners.

ADMINISTRATIVE RECORDS

It stands to reason that when shipments were sent from the estates to the city where the owner was dwelling, there must have been some written notation to ensure that the goods reached the proper addressee. The inscription could have been an impression on a bulla of clay attached to the string holding the cover of a jar or vessel. Such "fiscal bullae" have shown up in various collections that have reached scholars via the antiquities market.[6] The formulae on these seal impressions usually have the year of the reign of the current ruler, the town from which the shipment is being sent, and the recipient, viz. the king, e.g.: "In the 26th year, (from) Eltolad,

---

6 Avigad and Sass (1997) 177–78, nos. 421, 422; Deutsch (1997) 137–43, nos. 97–102.

to the king."[7] It is possible also that many of the bullae bearing personal names were not just attached to papyrus letters but also to jars being sent to the person from his estate. However, the absence of a year date and a geographic designation makes this speculation somewhat tenuous.

Baruch Levine discerned that the administrative records dealing with the transfer of commodities can be divided into two classes.[8] Some texts are instructions about what must or should be issues; Levine designated them as "Prescriptive Texts." On the other hand, there are also records of transactions actually carried out; these are "Descriptive Texts." Examples of both types can be documented in the Bible and also in epigraphic finds.[9]

PRESCRIPTIVE TEXTS

There are instructions in the book of Leviticus about the dispersal of products offered at the temple. Certain portions were to go to the officiating priests for them to eat, usually within the scared precincts during their course of duty.[10]

> And the remainder from the *minḥa* is for Aharon and for his sons, most holy from the burnt offerings of the LORD. (Lev 2:3)
>
> And the remainder from it, Aharon and his sons will eat. (Lev 6:9a)

The orders issued to Elyashib, the responsible official at Arad,[11] also belong in this category, e.g., Arad No. 1 obv.:

> To Elyashib:
>
> And now give to the Kittiyim three b(aths) of wine and write the name of the day (date) and from the reserves of the best flour you will load two (measures) of flour to make for them bread; from the wine of the amphoras shall you give.

DESCRIPTIVE TEXTS

In this class, the "fiscal bullae" also record a shipment that is being or has been sent. The Samaria ostraca also include inscriptions of this nature. Their text probably arrived at the depot in Samaria either in the form of a

---

7 Avigad and Sass (1997) 177, no. 421.

8 Levine (1963, 1965).

9 Levine and Hallo (1967).

10 Rainey (1970b) 47.

11 Aharoni (1981) 12ff.

"fiscal bulla" or as an inscription on the side of the jar. The clerk in Samaria had to make a record of the shipment that arrived. This he did on small pot sherds, note pads. Later, most likely he entered the data on a papyrus ledger (or perhaps on a wax tablet). The chits, that is the sherds, were thrown away. The scribe used fragments of vessels broken at his place in Samaria; thus some of the Samaria ostraca are from the same vessel.[12]

The formulations on all the texts have the same general format, beginning with the (king's) regnal year and listing the recipient of the shipment. However, the remaining details divide the inscriptions into two groups. One type names the commodity being sent, a jar of either "old wine" or "purified oil." The other group ignores the commodity (apparently all of this group were for either wine or oil) but lists the sender of the shipment. Both groups give the name of the town from which the commodity was being sent, but the same group that omits the commodity adds the name of the clan district in which the town was located. The two groups are also distinguished by their respective dates. Those texts listing wine or oil are dated to "the ninth year" or "the tenth year" (the ordinal number being written out), whereas those that list the sender are from "the fifteenth year" (using Egyptian hieratic numerals).[13] The form of the letters is so similar in both groups of texts, that no chronological distinction can be made on the basis of paleography.[14] The relative date for the potsherds used as the writing material is the first quarter of the eighth century B.C.E.

It is sufficient here to cite one of the Samaria ostraca, in this case an example that contains a longer formula than usual (Samaria Ostraca No. 2):

In the ninth year
for *Gadyaw*
from *ʾAzzā(h)*
ʾAbî-Baʿal 2
ʾAḥaz 2
Šebaʿ 1
Meri-Baʿal 1

The year date is followed by the name of the recipient, *Gadyaw*, dependent on the preposition *lamed* (לגדיו), the town of origin, *ʾAzzā(h)*, dependent on the preposition *mi(n)* (מאזה), followed by the names of four senders,[15] each

12 Kaufman (1982) 232–33.

13 Aharoni (1979) 356–68.

14 Kaufman 1982) 233–34.

15 Cross (1975).

with the number of jars he has rendered. Unlike most of the ostraca from the ninth and tenth years, this one happens not to mention the commodity sent (whether wine or oil).

The roster of towns mentioned in these texts fills in a serious gap in our knowledge of the Manassehite territory in the hills of Samaria. The towns are generally not known from the Bible. On the other hand, Mazar, Cross, Aharoni, and Kaufman[16] have been able to identify many of these ancient toponyms with Arabic toponyms in the hills around Samaria. As mentioned above, the ostraca from the fifteenth year mention not only the name of the town from which the shipment was sent but also the name of the district in which it was located. These districts are named after eponyms in the genealogy of the tribe of Manasseh! They include some of the daughters of Zelophehad, whose inheritance along with the men was made a precedent case in biblical literature. The following table records the eponyms in the Manassehite genealogy and towns from the Samaria ostraca associated with them.

THE MANASSEH TERRITORY

The Genealogy of Manasseh

Num 26:28–34; 27:1–4(5–11); 36:10–12 (cf. 1–8); Josh 17:1–6; 1 Chron 7:14–19!!

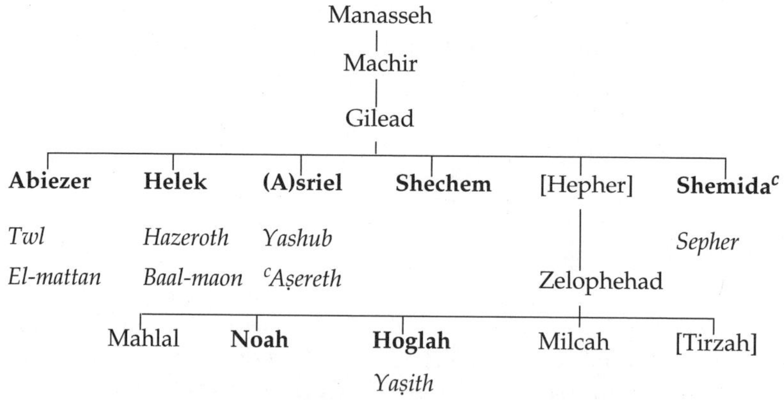

Bold: Clans appearing on Samaria ostraca.
Italics: Reconstructed place names appearing on Samaria ostraca.

16 Summarized by Aharoni (1979) 367–69.

It was possible for geographers to plot the general distribution of the clan districts in accordance with the identifiable towns as they appear on the map of Samaria. The distribution of the sites from which the shipments derived shows that the territory of Manasseh is involved with Samaria as the focal point. There were always a dozen or so people receiving wine or oil from their estates while they were in the capital of Samaria. The economic situation reminds us of Herod's arrangement mentioned above. But the shipments represented by the Samaria ostraca were evidently all coming to one central storage and distribution point. Perhaps these were dignitaries who "ate at the king's table."

It has been noted that some of the recipients got shipments from more than one town and from more than one district.[17] Besides receiving wine or oil from their family patrimony, they probably were supplied from other estates that had been allotted to them by the king (see the king's authority in 1 Samuel 8, discussed above). Since the texts must date to the first third of the eighth century B.C.E., one cannot help but be reminded of the strictures of the prophet Amos against the unlawful acquisition of properties:

> Thus said the LORD: For three transgressions of Israel, for four, I will not revoke it: because they have sold for silver those whose cause was just, and the needy for a pair of sandals.
>
> Ah, you who trample the heads of the poor into the dust of the ground, and make the humble walk a twisted course! Father and son go to the same girl, and thereby profane my holy name.
>
> They recline by every altar on garments taken in pledge, and drink in the house of their god wine bought with fines they imposed. (Amos 2:6–8)

So the Samaria ostraca reflect shipments to important people from their estates in the region of the Manassehite territory.[18]

---

17 Aharoni (1979) 365–66.

18 This interpretation was accepted immediately by Yohanan Aharoni and later by Andre Lemaire (1977) 67–81. However, there were—and perhaps still are—scholars who reject my view. This is due to the influence of the late Y. Yadin. Much of what Yadin proposed about the Samaria ostraca has subsequently been overturned: their date (mid-eighth century), their meaning (records of Menahem's collection for making his tribute payment to Tiglath-pilesar III), and the reading of the hieratic numerals—Yadin denied their Egyptian origin and insisted they indicated a year ten. But his interpretation of the *lamed* preposition as an indicator of the sender, not the recipient, of the shipments lingers on (Kaufman [1982] 235–37), especially in Israeli archaeological circles. Yadin compared the prepositional phrase on the Samaria ostraca with the prepositional phrases on private seals and

The Departments of Public Works in Ancient Israel

The second aspect of life in ancient Israel involves a socio-ethnic factor that is generally ignored today even though Old Testament studies have been so preoccupied with a "sociological" approach.

By the twelfth century B.C.E. the principle rival peoples in Palestine were becoming well established in their respective areas: the Canaanites continued to dwell in the northern valleys and plain, and the tribes of Israel in the hill country. The biblical tradition confirms that Israelites were unable to dislodge the Canaanites and Amorites in the lowland areas, for they had "chariots of iron" (Josh 15:63; 17:11–13). Judg 1:18–19 (LXX) confirms that Judah did not subdue the Philistines.

No tradition exists about the conquest of Shechem, whose situation may have been like Gezer's (Judg 1:19), a Canaanite population living in symbiosis with the Israelites. Jebus-Jerusalem, Gezer, and the Amorite towns that resisted the Danites were in the center of the country. Very early traditions reveal that the Ephraimites came into early contact with the indigenous population of the area where the Danites had been driven out (1 Chron 7:20–24; Judg 1:35). Some clans from Benjamin also migrated to the same area (1 Chron 8:12–13; 2 Sam 4:3–4).

Recent archaeological surveys in the hill country areas confirm the arrival of pastoralists who began their settlement along the fringes of the steppe land, east of the watershed. Gradually they expanded and established settlements in the areas of mixed agriculture and eventually moved into the western hill zones, where it became necessary to develop terraces and plant orchards and vineyards. Thus, originally pastoral groups became transformed into a thoroughly sedentary society with varied subsistence strategies.[19] The tribal groups that settled in Upper Galilee went through a

---

seal impressions and on the royal *lmlk* seal impressions. There, of course, the preposition designates the possessor. On the seals, it denotes the owner of the seal (Rainey [1966]). On the royal jars, it denotes the owner of the wine being produced at one of the four centers named.

The presence of the verbal form in the Arad letter actually confirms the function of the preposition as designating the recipient. Lev 2:3 is an excellent example from the Bible of a non-verbal clause indicating the recipient by the *lamed* preposition, for it deals with the disbursement of food stuffs employed in the temple ritual. There is no doubt that the priests were to receive the materials and to eat them themselves. There is a wonderful example of a non-verbal clause with two *lamed* prepositions, i.e., genitive and dative functions. It is Jehu's order to assemble the priests of Baal for a great "sacrifice" (2 Kgs 10:19): "for I have a great sacrifice **for** Baal."

[19] Finkelstein (1994) 160–62.

similar process; their material culture reflects a certain cultural affinity with the Phoenicians on the coast below.[20]

All this data confirm the new population revolution brought about in the twelfth and eleventh centuries. In the Late Bronze Age the main concentrations of population were in the plains; the hill country areas were largely uninhabited, providing refuge for *ᶜapîru* outlaws and for the *shosu*-pastoralists. The latter became more and more numerous and adopted sedentary ways of life, perhaps because of a decline in the overall Canaanite agricultural productivity.[21]

The dichotomy between Canaanites on the plains and Israelites in the hills characterizes the narratives throughout the books of Judges and Samuel.

Judg 1:27–35 lists the unconquered areas according to tribe. The main surviving Canaanite enclaves were in the Valley of Jezreel and along the Phoenician coast. The Asherites gained acceptance among the Phoenicians (Sidonians), apparently as client farmers for a society whose manpower was heavily committed to maritime activities (Judg 1:31–32).

Judg 1:27–35

> Manasseh did not drive out the inhabitants of Beth-shean and its villages, or Taanach and its villages, or the inhabitants of Dor and its villages, or the inhabitants of Megiddo and its villages; but the Canaanites continued to live in that land. When Israel grew strong they put the Canaanites to **forced labor**, but did not in fact drive them out.
>
> And Ephraim did not drive out the Canaanites who lived in Gezer; but the Canaanites lived among them in Gezer.
>
> Zebulun did not drive out the inhabitants of Kitron, or the inhabitants of Nahalol; but the Canaanites lived among them, and became subject to **forced labor**.
>
> Asher did not drive out the inhabitants of Acco, or the inhabitants of Sidon, or of Ahlab, or of Achzib, or of Helbah, or of Aphik, or of Rehob; but the **Asherites lived among the Canaanites**, the inhabitants of the land; for they did not drive them out.
>
> Naphtali did not drive out the inhabitants of Beth-shemesh, or the inhabitants of Beth-anath, but lived among the Canaanites, the inhabitants of the land; nevertheless the inhabitants of Beth-shemesh and of Beth-anath became subject to **forced labor** for them.

---

[20] Frankel (1994) 27–34.

[21] Stager (1985) 85.

> The Amorites pressed the Danites back into the hill country; they did not allow them to come down to the plain.
>
> The Amorites continued to live in Har-heres, in Aijalon, and in Shaalbim, but the hand of the house of Joseph rested heavily on them, and they became subject to **forced labor**.

In these passages the institution of *mas* (*ᶜôḇēḏ*) "forced labor" has been emphasized. It should be obvious that through the period of the Judges and till the end of Saul's reign, Israel did not have control over the Canaanite population in those unconquered towns. Israel did not have a political infrastructure that could facilitate the establishment of such an administrative institution as forced labor or corvée.

On the other hand, the newly established kingdom of Israel is depicted in the census ordered by David. The territory covered represents all the area directly under control of the monarchy in Jerusalem. Although the text of Joab's itinerary (2 Sam 24:5–7) is badly preserved in spots, the general course of the census can be discerned.

Joab began at Aroer on the traditional border with Moab (whenever Israel held the tableland). Then he progressed through the territory of Gad (in the western tableland itself according to Mesha's inscription) to Jazer and on through Gilead. The next stage of the journey is obscured by a textual corruption, *taḥtîm ḥōdšî*, but the best Greek version, viz. Θαβασων, albeit unclear, suggests that Bashan was the area visited. This makes sense since Joab went from there to Dan and on to "Jaan," a spelling of Ijon with metathesis. Next he moved across upper Galilee along the border with Sidon, past the "fortress of Tyre," probably the Usu known from Egyptian and Assyrian inscriptions (Hellenistic *Palaeotyrus*, "Old Tyre"). The next entry is the most tantalizing: "All the cities of the Hivvites and the Canaanites," in other words, all those towns that had initially been unconquered (Judg 1:27–35). Here we have the tacit admission that those elements of the pre-Israelite population who had maintained their social and political integrity up to now had finally succumbed to the new, united Israel. Specific details about how David subdued those Hivvite and Canaanite cities is not found in any ancient source.[22] The end result can be seen in the dispersal of Levitical settlements[23] and in the Solomonic commissioners' districts. The united monarchy reached its apogee after Solomon had ensured a steady flow of income from command of the world trade routes. This and a well-organized bureaucracy supported by the military estab-

---

[22] Alt (1939) 21–24 = (1953) I, 137–39.

[23] Aharoni et al. (1993) map 108.

lishment enabled him to harness the manpower now at his disposal. Besides the temple and the royal palace, Solomon built strong fortresses at key points throughout the realm; special mention is made in the Bible of Hazor, Megiddo, and Gezer (1 Kgs 9:15).

Albrecht Alt was the first to discern that the districts in this roster divide into two groups: those defined in terms of tribal entities and those defined in terms of the towns included in them.[24] The former were in hill country areas whereas the latter were generally in the plains. The list is presented below with distinctive headings (italics or bold) for each of the two categories.

1 Kgs 4:7–19

Solomon had twelve officials over all Israel, who provided food for the king and his household; each one had to make provision for one month in the year. These were their names:

First District — Mt. Ephraim
Ben-hur, in the hill country of Ephraim;

Second District — "Danite Territory"
Ben-deker, in Makaz, Shaalbim, Beth-shemesh, and Elon-beth-hanan;

Third District — Northern Sharon Plain
Ben-hesed, in Arubboth (to him belonged Socoh and all the land of Hepher);

Fourth District — Naphoth Dor
Ben-abinadab, in all Naphath-dor (he had Taphath, Solomon's daughter, as his wife);

Fifth District — Jezreel and Beth-shean Valleys
Baana son of Ahilud, in Taanach, Megiddo, and all Beth-shean, which is beside Zarethan below Jezreel, from Beth-shean to Abel-meholah, as far as the other side of Jokmeam;

Sixth District — Northern Gilead and Bashan
Ben-geber, in Ramoth-gilead (he had the villages of Jair son of Manasseh, which are in Gilead, and he had the region of Argob, which is in Bashan, sixty great cities with walls and bronze bars);

---

24 Alt (1913) = (1953) II, 76–89.

Seventh District — Eastern Jordan Valley
Ahinadab son of Iddo, in Mahanaim;

Eighth District — Naphtali
Ahimaaz, in Naphtali (he had taken Basemath, Solomon's daughter, as his wife);

Ninth District — Asher and Zebulon(?)
Baana son of Hushai, in Asher and Bealoth (=Zebulun?);

Tenth District — Issachar
Jehoshaphat son of Paruah, in Issachar;

Eleventh District — Benjamin
Shimei son of Ela, in Benjamin;

Twelfth District — Gilead (LXX GAD)
Geber son of Uri, in the land of Gilead, the country of King Sihon of the Amorites and of King Og of Bashan.

Thirteenth District
And there was one official in the land of Judah.

The thirteenth district commissioner, for Judah, seems to be either a literary embellishment or an afterthought. Judah was hardly included in the twelve-district system, since the heading to the roster specifically mentions twelve commissioners.

The list of initially unconquered towns in Judges 1 is probably based on this list of the Solomonic districts. One should also note that the geographical allotments in the book of Joshua are also based on the reality of the Solomonic roster even though the author of the book of Joshua sought to present a different picture, viz. a twelve-tribe system without any gaps between the tribal allotments. The few tribal borders that he does describe actually demarcate some of the "tribal" districts in Solomon's list.

What is usually ignored in commentaries on 1 Kings is that the ensuing references to Solomon's manpower organization reflect two branches of public labor conscription in accordance with the two types of districts in the preceding list.[25] Judges 1 stresses repeatedly that "when Israel became strong" the Canaanites were subjected to forced labor. This particular institution and its activities are defined in the following passage:

---

[25] Rainey (1970a).

1 Kgs 5:27–28

Press Gangs (*mas ᶜôḇēḏ*)

> King Solomon conscripted press gangs out of all Israel; the levy numbered thirty thousand men.
>
> He sent them to the Lebanon, ten thousand a month in shifts; they would be a month in the Lebanon and two months at home; Adoniram was in charge of the press gangs.

The clear intent of the context is that the newly subjected Canaanites and Hivvites were those required to spend one out of every three months in Lebanon, cutting and transporting the lumber needed by Solomon. The commissioners in charge of the districts in the plains, those districts defined by their towns (which correspond largely to the unconquered towns in Judges 1!), were responsible for carrying out those tasks.

The second government department is described in the ensuing text:

1 Kgs 5:29–31

Corvée (*nôśēᵓ sabbāl, sēḇel*)

> Solomon also had seventy thousand teamsters and eighty thousand stonecutters in the **hill country**, besides Solomon's three thousand three hundred officers who were over the work, exercising authority over the people who did the work.
>
> At the king's command, they quarried out great, costly stones in order to lay the foundation of the house with dressed stones.

The corvée was recruited from the Israelite tribes; they worked in the hill country in Israel, quarrying stone and transporting it to the building sites; they also provided the labor force for the actual construction (1 Kgs 5:15–17; 11:28). The quarries were naturally in the areas where the best building stone could be obtained, in the hill country areas. The former tribesmen did not have to go as far away as Lebanon to do their work. Their burden was undoubtedly onerous but not as humiliating as that imposed on the former Canaanites and Hivvites. Each department had its own cadre of commissioners and overseers. One of the most respected and brilliant of the commissioners working with the corvée was Jeroboam the son of Nebat.

1 Kgs 11:28

> The man Jeroboam was very able, and when Solomon saw that the young man was industrious he gave him charge over all the corvée of the house of Joseph.

When Solomon saw that Jeroboam was enjoying too much influence with his constituents, he sought to have him eliminated, so the young administrator fled to Egypt where he enjoyed political asylum (1 Kgs 11:4). At the confrontation between Rehoboam and the northern Israelites, he made the mistake of sending Adoniram, the commissioner in charge of the *mas ᶜôḇēḏ*, to try to browbeat the northerners into submission. They were so incensed that they stoned him to death (1 Kgs 12:18). Then they turned to the popular administrator who had been their supervisor in the *sēḇel* department and appointed him king.

The geographical analysis of the list of unconquered towns (Judges 1), the Davidic census (2 Samuel 24), and the Solomonic districts (1 Kings 4/5) reveals the dichotomy in the population of the Israelite united monarchy.

BIBLIOGRAPHY

Aharoni, Y. (1979) *The Land of the Bible.* Revised and enlarged edition, translated and edited by A.F. Rainey. Philadelphia. (1981) *Arad Inscriptions.* Jerusalem. **Aharoni, Y. and M. Avi Yohna.** (1993) *The Macmillan Bible Atlas.* Completely Revised Third Edition by A.F. Rainey and Z. Safarai. New York. **Alt, A.** (1913) Israels Gaue unter Salomo. *Beihefte zur Zeitschrift für die alttestamentliche Wissenschaft* Heft 13. (1939) Erwägungen über die Landnahme der Israeliten in Palästina. *Palästina Jahrbuch* 35: 8–63. (1953) *Kleine Schriften zur Geschichte des Volkes Israel.* 2 vols. Munich. **Cross, F.M.** (1975) Ammonite Ostraca from Heshbon: Heshbon Ostraca IV–VIII. *Andrews University Seminary Studies* 13: 1–20. **Deutsche, R.** (1997) *Messages from the Past, Hebrew Bullae from the Time of Isaiah through the Destruction of the First Temple, Shlomo Mousaieff Collection and an Up-to-Date Corpus.* (Hebrew). Tel Aviv. **Finkelstein, I.** (1994) The Emergence of Israel: A Phase in the Cyclic History of Canaan in the Third and Second Millennia BCE. Pp. 150–78. **Frankel, R.** (1994)Upper Galilee in the Late Bronze-Iron I Transition. In I. Finkelstein and N. Na'aman, eds. *From Nomadism to Monarchy, Archaeological and Historical Aspects of Early Israel*, 18–34. Jerusalem. **Kaufman T.** (1982) The Samaria Ostraca: An Early Witness to Hebrew Writing. *Biblical Archaeologist* 45: 229–39. **Lemaire, A.** (1977) *Inscriptions Hebraiques, Tome I, Les Ostraca.* Paris. **Levine B.** (1963) Ugaritic Descriptive Rituals. *Journal of Cuneiform Studies* 17: 105–11. (1965) The Descriptive Tabernacle Texts of the Pentateuch. *Journal of the American Oriental Society* 85: 307–18. (1974) *In the Presence of the Lord.* Leiden. **Levine, B. and W.W. Hallo** (1967) Offerings to the Temple Gates at Ur. *Hebrew Union College Annual* 38: 17–58. **Marcus, R.**, translator. (1963) *Josephus.* Vol. 8, *Jewish Antiquities*, Books XV–XVII. Completed and edited by A. Wikgren. The Loeb Classical Library. Cambridge, Mass. **Mendelsohn, I.** (1956) Samuel's Denunciation of Kingship in the Light of the Akkadian Texts from Ugarit. *Bulletin of the American Schools of Oriental Research* 143: 17–22. **Nougayrol, J.** (1955) *Le Palais royal d'Ugarit.* Vol. 3, Textes accadiens et hourrites des archives est, ouest et centrales. Vol. 6 of

Mission de Ras Shamra, C.F.A Schaeffer, ed. Paris. **Rainey, A.F.** (1962) Administration in Ugarit and the Samaria Ostraca. *Israel Exploration Journal* 12: 62–63. (1966) Private Seal-Impressions, A Note on Semantics. *Israel Exploration Journal* 16: 187–90. (1967a) The Land Grant System at Ugarit and Its Wider Near Eastern Setting. *Fourth World Congress of Jewish Studies, Papers.* I: 187–91. (1967b) The Samaria Ostraca in the Light of Fresh Evidence. *Palestine Exploration Quarterly* 99: 32–41. (1970a) Compulsory Labor Gangs in Ancient Israel. *Israel Exploration Journal* 20: 191–202. (1970b) Semantic Parallels to the Samaria Ostraca. *Palestine Exploration Quarterly* 102: 45–51. (1979) The *Sitz im Leben* of the Samaria Ostraca. *Tel Aviv* 6: 91–94. **Stager, L.E.** (1985) [Response]. Pp, 83–87 in *Biblical Archaeology Today. Proceedings of the International Congress on Biblical Archaeology, Jerusalem, April 1984.* Jerusalem. **Thackeray, H. St. J.**, translator. (1927) Josephus. Vol. 2, *The Jewish War*, Books I–III. The Loeb Classical Library. Cambridge, Mass.

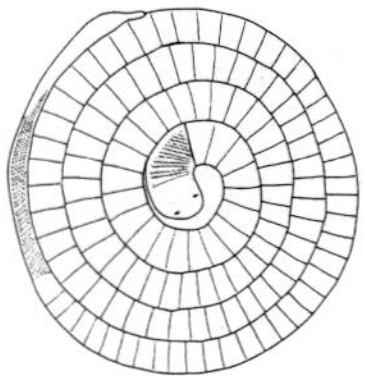

"GIVE US OUR DAILY BREAD"

EVERYDAY LIFE FOR THE ISRAELITE DEPORTEES

K. Lawson Younger, Jr.*

Trinity International University - Divinity School

The deportations of the Israelites were effected by three Assyrian kings (Tiglath-Pileser III, Shalmaneser V,[1] and Sargon II) from 734 to at least 716 B.C.E.[2] As I have argued and documented elsewhere, the deportations of Tiglath-Pileser III appear to have been uni-directional, whereas Sargon's was unquestionably the usual Assyrian bi-directional deportation.[3] The details of Shalmaneser's are unknown.

This paper will investigate the various filtering processes used by the Assyrians that determined deportee status, as well as the differences that the deportees' exile location made for their everyday lives. Based on Assyrian archival records, the paper will also examine the implications of these matters to ascertain the personal impact of these extraditions on the people of the northern kingdom. Finally, a more comprehensive understanding of the different levels of assimilation or acculturation to Assyria will be proposed.

The Israelite deportees were of two filtered types: (1) those who received preferred or at least reasonable treatment (a relatively small number), and (2) those who received hardship and bare subsistence[4] (the vast bulk of the deportees). This filtering process was most often determined

* A version of this paper was read at the ASOR Annual in Boston, November, 1999. I greatly appreciate the helpful comments made by its participants. I would like to thank Professors Peter Machinist of Harvard University and A.R. Millard of Liverpool University for their readings of the manuscript.

1 Shalmaneser V is credited with a deportation of Chaldeans from Bīt Adini (a place with this name that was located in Bīt Dakkuri according to Brinkman [1984] 43 and 15 with n. 59). The information concerning this deportation is found in the Aššur ostracon (*KAI* 233 15).

2 On the issues surrounding the fall of Samaria, see Younger (1999).

3 Younger (1998a) 201–27; Naʾaman (1993) 104–24.

4 Obviously, this is contrary to the *rab šāqê*'s propagandistic promises in 2 Kgs 18.

by the individual deportee's prior status and skills, especially as these matched the needs of the Assyrian administration. The personnel necessary to oversee the large scale deportations that were so characteristic of the Tiglath-Pileser to Sargon era must have been extensive. It must be remembered that Assyrian imperialism did not depend solely on violence, exploitation, and ruthless plunder, but also on a well-organized and well-functioning administrative apparatus that was capable of directing and controlling the peripheral regions of the empire.[5]

There is no direct evidence regarding when the filtering process took place, but the logistical demands on the transport of massive groups of people must have required that the filtering took place in the deportees' homeland. Hence, skilled workers needed in Dūr-Šarrukīn would not end up in the far reaches of the territory of the Medes.[6]

On the other hand, there is perhaps some evidence of this filtering process in some Assyrian reliefs. William Gallagher has recently collected evidence from Assyrian palace reliefs demonstrating that the Assyrian scribes interrogated prisoners and especially deportees for important information that could be useful in propaganda against Assyria's enemies.[7] In most of these scenes there are two scribes: one writing, the other interrogating the deportees. Although Gallagher's purpose in collecting the visual data is to explicate the *rab šāqê*'s speeches, some of the reliefs illustrate the likely time of interrogation that resulted in the filtering of the deportees.[8]

In any case, the emotional impact on individuals who were uprooted from their homes and forcibly moved great distances has been documented in recent psychological studies.[9] Even the later final deportation of the Judahites by the Babylonians as described in the book of Lamentations alludes to the immediate emotional impact on the individual. Although

---

5 See Pečírková (1987) 162–75.

6 Cf. the deportation of Jerusalem in 2 Kgs 24:14–16 = Jer 52:28.

7 Gallagher (1999) 187–89, and figs. 4–7. I wish to thank Dr. Gallagher for providing portions of his dissertation to me earlier, and for giving me advance notice of the publication of his important work.

8 See Gallagher (1999) figs. 4–7: Or.Dr. VI, 5 (a relief from Sennacherib's palace, Room XVII; Or.Dr. IV, 32 (Sennacherib's palace, Court LXIV, slab 3); Room 14 slabs 10–11 of Sargon's palace (relevant to the Israelite deportations); and Or.Dr. IV, 65. The last of these is particularly interesting because it pictures families being counted (and perhaps interrogated) as they are deported.

9 For some of the impact of post-traumatic stress disorder on deportees and refugees, see Dragoti (1996).

there is some evidence that nuclear families were kept intact during the deportation,[10] we know that this was not always the Assyrian policy (cf. the many reliefs where only men are pictured as being deported). Most certainly extended familial ties were severed. It should be remembered that part of the Assyrian army's pay was given in rape and plunder of the enemy's land and that this had already transpired *before* the long trek of these deportees to their destinations.[11]

According to 2 Kgs 17:6 and 18:11, the Israelites were deported to three locations: Halah or Ḫalaḫḫa,[12] Gozan or Guzāna (modern Tell Ḫalāf), and the cities of the Medes (see map). Extrabiblical material verifies the presence of Israelites at the first two locations, which were—after all—in Assyria proper.[13]

Those Who Received Preferred or At Least Reasonable Treatment (a relatively small number)

1. *Military Needs*

Assyria's population was insufficient to provide an army large enough for the needs of its expanding empire. Thus a large number of the people deported to Assyria proper were to relieve Assyrians of their domestic duties in order to serve in the military. Moreover, conscripts from the conquered countries or vassal states commonly filled the ranks.[14] This practice was particularly widespread during the reigns of Tiglath-Pileser

---

10 Cf. the relief of families being deported from Iran and the scene from the Lachish reliefs of Judahite families being deported. See Barnett, Bleibtreu, and Turner (1998) pls. 336–40, 393. See also *ANEP* no. 10 (Assurbanipal deporting Egyptian families); *ANEP* nos. 358–59 (Shalmaneser III deporting families from Ḫazazu).

11 Cf. the rape of an Arab woman (BM 124927). See Parpola and Watanabe (1988) 47 (fig. 14).

12 See Postgate (1972–75) 58.

13 According to Postgate's assessment ([1992] 251–52). However, Zadok has recently argued for an understanding of Assyria proper that, on onomastic grounds, distinguishes between the peripheral locations like Gozan and Harran and Assyria proper. See Zadok (1997) 215–16.

14 Oded (1979) 50. Reade, who describes the multi-national character of the Assyrian army as revealed in the Assyrian reliefs ([1972] 87–112, esp. pp. 101–8). See also Postgate (1989a) 1–10.

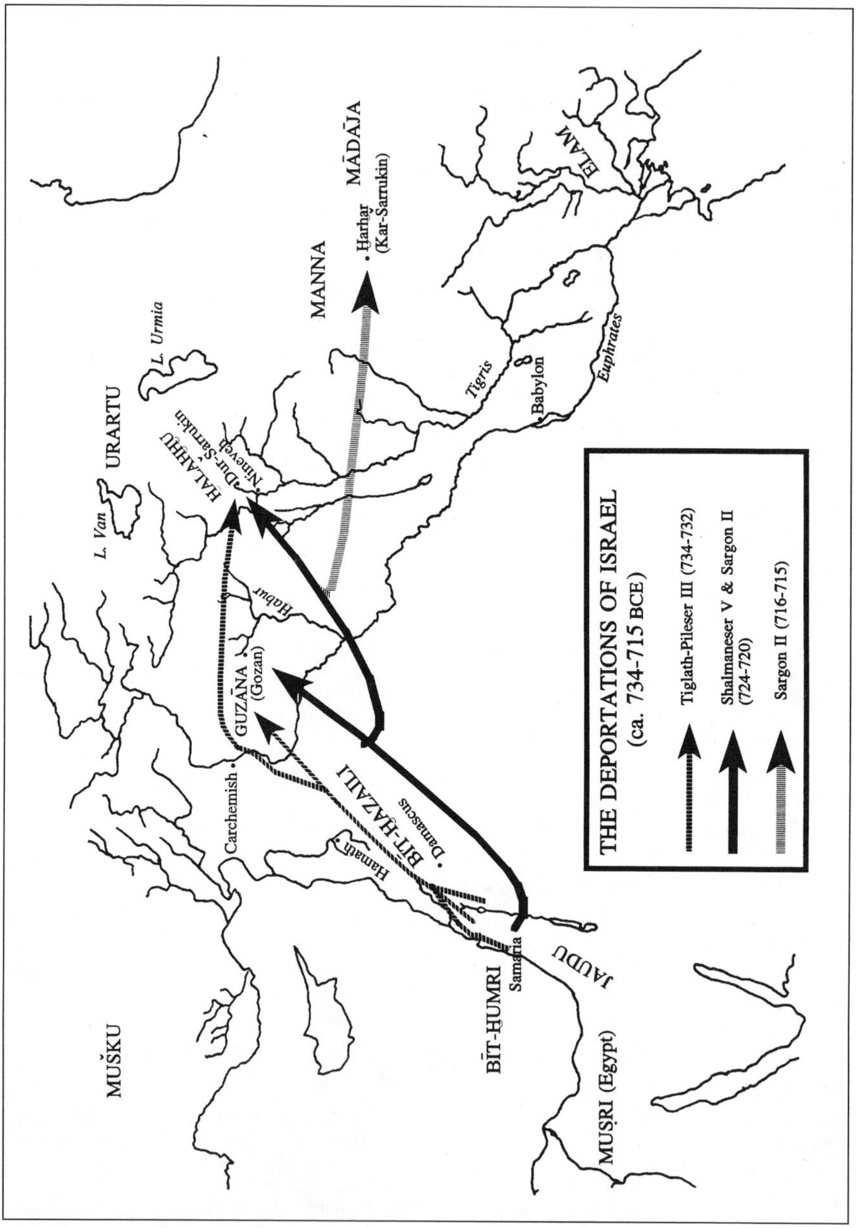
THE DEPORTATIONS OF ISRAEL
(ca. 734-715 BCE)
Tiglath-Pileser III (734-732)
Shalmaneser V & Sargon II (724-720)
Sargon II (716-715)
MUŠKU
URARTU
L. Van
L. Urmia
MANNA
MĀDĀJA
Ḫarhar
(Kar-Šarrukin)
HALAḪḪU
Nineveh
Dur-Šarrukin
Tigris
Babylon
Euphrates
ELAM
Ḫabur
GUZĀNA
(Gozan)
Carchemish
Hamath
Damascus
BĪT-ḪAZAILI
BĪT-ḪUMRI
Samaria
JAUDU
MUṢRI (Egypt)

III and Sargon II.[15] In fact, the onomastic evidence shows that "at least one-fifth" of Sargon's army bore West Semitic names.[16]

The Assyrian administrative documents called the "Horse Lists" identify a unit of Samarian charioteers (TFS 99).[17] While the identification of the Samarians in TFS 99 as deported Israelites has been questioned,[18] Sargon's inscriptions[19] clearly show that at least some (*sittūti*) of the Samarian chariot corps were treated favorably after the capture and annexation of the city in 720 B.C.E., being incorporated into the Assyrian army.[20] Some of the other defeated troops in this same campaign from Hamath and Philistia were incorporated into the Assyrian army.[21] For example, the Cyprus Stela

15 Oded (1979) 51.

16 Fales (1991) 104. For some possible references to Israelites among the West Semitic personal names found in other Assyrian documents, see Becking (1992) 66–93.

17 Dalley and Postgate (1984) 35–41.

18 Ephᶜal (1991) 41–42.

19 For example, "I settled the rest of them in the midst of Assyria ... I counted them as Assyrians" (Nimrud Prism D and E, iv 33–36). See Gadd (1954) 179–80, pls. xlv and xlvi; Tadmor (1958) 34. See also the Great "Summary" Inscription (lines 23–25): Fuchs (1994) 197; Winckler (1889) 100. It is not impossible that some of these Israelites were added to the Assyrian army by Tiglath-pileser III, though in his extant texts he does not mention adding Israelite charioteers, only Israelite auxiliary troops ([*ti*]-*il-lut* LÚ.[ERÍN(*ṣābē*) ...]) (Summary Inscription 4.16). See Tadmor (1994) 140–41.

20 Ephᶜal (1991) 42 correctly observes that only a few of the names can be considered undoubtedly Israelite. However, I do not accept his conclusion: "it seems preferable to associate most of the above-mentioned 'Samarians' with the foreigners who were transferred to the province of Samirina ... rather than with the Israelite exiles in Assyria." He bases this conclusion on the lack of Yahwistic names in the lists, even though he admits in a footnote (n. 38), that "for the sake of balance and completeness we should note that ... the northern, Israelite onomasticon (of which only a relatively small portion has survived) is not replete with Yahwistic names." Fales (1991) 104, n. 30 perceives the problem: "Ephᶜal's slightly circular reasoning fails to take into account the very concrete possibility that people may take on second names or entirely new names to adapt to new linguistic and societal settings—as e.g., many immigrants from Europe do in modern-day Israel. And moreover, since Sargon claims to have taken 27,290 people captive at Samaria and states that he added them to his army, one wonders where else would they have ended up, if not in the 'Samarian' contingent listed here!"

21 For the Hamathite troops, see Parker (1961) 15 and 40–41 (ND 2646). For the Philistines, see Parpola (1987) 155 (although they may have been added as a result of the later campaign of 716 B.C.E.).

indicates that "300 charioteers and 600 cavalry of Hamath" were enrolled in the Assyrian army.[22]

Scholars usually distinguish Israelites from other southern Levantines primarily by the use of the *Yhw* theophoric element. But this can be problematic.[23] Yahwistic names may occur in the onomastica of Hamath.[24] Several of these Hamathite names have Aramaic predicates, which also happens to be the case with a few of the names among the Samarian chariot contingent at Calah.[25] Based on that, it has been suggested that these names may reflect a Gileadite dialect.[26] Although very intriguing, there is simply not enough evidence to assert this "Gileadite" identification with any degree of confidence. Nevertheless, there seems to be little reason to doubt the identification of the Samarian charioteers as Israelite deportees—especially since they fall into the very small percentage (less than 2 percent according to Zadok) of personal names in Assyrian documents that occur with a gentilic designation.

---

22 *ARAB* 2 §183. Messerschmidt and Ungnad (1907) 29–36, VS I, 71, right side, 51ff.

23 Zadok (1997) 213. The use of theophorics for ethnic identifications must be done cautiously, since the same deity may be worshipped in a number of different countries. For example, the god Haldi was worshipped not only in Urartu, where he was the primary god, but also in a number of regions immediately to the northeast of Assyria. Thus one must be careful in ascribing a Haldi theophoric to only Urartians. This is now underscored by the very recent publication of the Bukān inscription from Mannea in which both Hadad and Haldi (but especially Haldi) are invoked in the curse formulae. See Ephʿal (1999) 116–21; Lemaire (1998) 15–30; (1997) 543–45; Sokoloff (1999) 105–15.

24 The most famous of these is the name of the king of Hamath, spelled *Ilu-biʾdi* and *Yau-biʾdi*, who led a coalition (including Samaria) in a losing cause against Sargon II in the battle of Qarqar in 720 B.C.E. Some scholars interpret the *Yau-* as a Yahwistic theophoric element. See Malamat (1963) 7; Cogan and Tadmor (1988) 166; with variation, Dalley (1990) 27, 31; Zevit (1991) 363–66. Other scholars are doubtful of a Yahwistic theophoric element in the name. See Lipiński (1971) 371–73. Another well-known but very enigmatic example, is Azriyau mentioned in Tiglath-pileser III's inscriptions. Although some scholars have argued that this Azriyau was Azariah of Judah (Tadmor [1961]; [1994] 273–76; Roberts [1985]), others have argued that this Azriyau was an otherwise unattested king of Hatarikka (biblical Hadrach), a Syrian state neighboring Hamath (Naʾaman [1995] 276–77; Weippert [1976–80] 205; and Hawkins [1976–80] 273). See also *PNA* 1:240; Younger (2002) 207–18.

25 Zadok (1997) 213.

26 To support this, Zadok cites as a possible example the Gileadite name *ʿAdrîʾēl*.

2. *Priests*

A wine list from Nimrud demonstrates how good it could be for some deportees. TFS 121 (lines 6–11) states that 2 *sūtus* or "seahs" (i.e., 20 *qas*) were given to a *raksūte*-soldier named Adad-būnī and three Samarian lamentation-priests, whereas only 3½ *qas* were assigned to three "Hittite" lamentation-priests, possibly along with one Abi-qamu. Since 2 *qas* might be considered the average daily ration for the general population,[27] and since 1 *qa* might be idiomatic for 1 loaf of bread,[28] the Samarian priests should be counted as part of the elite in the Assyrian daily-ration hierarchy: 4⅓ *qas* per Israelite lamentation-priest as compared to the 0.875 (⅞) *qas* per Hittite lamentation-priest.

It is also interesting to note that according to the tradition in 2 Kgs 17:24–41, it is a deported Samarian priest that is returned sometime later to the land in order to instruct the deportees from various nations now living in Samaria "the law of the god of the land." This priest returned and taught them how they should properly worship YHWH (2 Kgs 17:28).[29]

Finally, in connection with priests, a special group designated "singers" were deported and appear to have served in the Assyrian court (e.g., *ANEP* no. 205). It is not impossible that some Israelite priestly singers and musicians were attached to the Assyrian court.

3. *Administrative Positions*

TFS 99 mentions a person who appears to have risen to high administrative office in the Assyria empire. This individual is identified as a "Samarian" named Samaᶜ who was "a commander of teams" (*rab urâte* [written: LÚ.GAL *ú-rat*.MEŠ, TFS 99.1]) and who apparently, if this person in the horse lists is the same person by the same name found in economic and admin-

---

27 Fales (1990) 23–34, esp. p. 30.

28 Fales (1990) 29. 1 *qa* = 1 liter = 0.8 kg of grain.

29 Papyrus Amherst 63, an Aramaic text written in Demotic script, contains an interesting New Year's festival liturgy of some exiles imported to Upper Egypt, probably Syrene, from Bethel. These exiles came originally from places called *rš* and *ʾrš* in the papyrus. These place names should most likely be identified with lands between Babylonia and Elam known as Rashu and Arashu in Assyrian sources that Assurbanipal captured in his campaign against Elam, deporting its inhabitants to the Assyrian province of Samaria. According to Richard Steiner, there is reason to believe that most if not all of them wound up in Bethel, joining the foreign colonists settled there by earlier Assyrian kings. Their subsequent migration to Egypt may be recorded in the text's account of the arrival of soldiers from Judah and Samaria. See Steiner (1991) 362–63; (1995) 199–207; and (1997) 309–27.

istrative texts from Balawat and Nineveh,[30] had significant access and possible influence in the royal family of the Sargonids:

> From this evidence it is reasonable to suggest that Sama^c the Samarian commander of teams who served Sargon as a reliable, professional soldier in the royal army of Assyria, was a close friend of the king and had access to and perhaps influence over members of the royal family. As such he would have had opportunities to become closely acquainted with Sargon's vizier Nabu-belu-ukin who probably acted as the first commander of the Samarian unit. Whether or not Sama^c actually played a part in negotiating preferential treatment for Samaria, the evidence for his career is an indication of the important role played by Samarians in Nimrud and Nineveh in the late eighth and early seventh centuries.[31]

Another example of a high Assyrian official who was perhaps an Israelite is the *rab šāqê* in 2 Kgs 18. This *rab šāqê* appeared with two other Assyrian high court officials of the royal cabinet[32] (the *turtānu* "commander-in-chief" and the *rab ša-rēši* "chief eunuch") and spoke Hebrew to the people of Jerusalem during Sennacherib's attempt to overcome Jerusalem via propaganda.[33] As Cogan has suggested, this *rab šāqê* was very likely an Israelite.[34]

4. *Skilled Laborers*

Dūr-Šarrukīn, Sargon's new capital, was located in Ḫalaḫḫa. According to a pavement inscription (types 3, 4, 5),[35] Sargon states that Dūr-Šarrukin was built by enemy captives. There is little doubt that some of these deportees (in some instances perhaps used as skilled laborers) were Israelites, as one letter clearly demonstrates:

---

30 Dalley (1985) 40–41. See Parker (1963) 89–93 [BT 101 (dated 710 B.C.E.) and BT 112]; and Kwasman and Parpola (1991) nos. 37, 39, 40, 41 (= Kohler and Ungnad [1913] ARU 186, 554, 201, 59).

31 Dalley (1985) 41. She also notes: "Nadbi-Yau, *mukil appāti* 'rein-holder' in 709 BC according to ADD 234 was probably a Samarian; but we cannot be certain he was not a Hamathite" (p. 41, n. 67). But see the discussion of the *Yhw* theophoric above.

32 For the Assyrian cabinet, see Parpola (1995b) 379–401.

33 See Gallagher (1999) 169–216; (1994) 57–65; Machinist (1983) 729–34; (2000) and Cohen (1979) 32–48.

34 Cogan (1974) 97–98.

35 Fuchs (1994) 55–60. Also see the letter in Parpola (1987) letter 259.

> Concerning what the king, my lord, wrote to me: "provide all the Samarians in your hands with work in Dūr-Šarrukin," I subsequently sent your word to the sheikhs, saying: "collect your carpenters and potters; let them come and direct the deportees who are in Dūr-Šarrukin."[36]

However, not all the tasks in the building of the city seem to have deserved equal compensation. A fragmentary list of rations divides the laborers into two units: one entitled to a 2-*qa* ration of barley, the other entitled to only a 1-*qa* ration—the absolute minimal daily ration.[37]

5. *Merchants*

Recently a number of inscriptions from Tīl Barsip (Tel Aḫmar) have been published.[38] The hieroglyphic Luwian inscriptions may indicate that the Luwian name of the city was Masuwari.[39] Most of the Neo-Assyrian cuneiform documents from the site seem to come from a single archive of a man named Ḫanni. However, three other tablets attest a possible archive of a certain Ištar-dūri—hardly an Israelite name—but who is further identified as "the son of Samiraya" ("the Samarian") (written [I]15-BÀD DUMU [I]*sa-mir-a-a* [Tablet 13 24–25]).[40] Tablets 13, 18, and 20 appear to belong to this individual. In Tablet 13 he appears as a witness and in Tablet 20 he is the sealer and perhaps, therefore, also the creditor of a loan of silver. These tablets apparently date to the latter days of the reign of Assurbanipal and demonstrate two things. First, later generations of deportees adopted non-Israelite—specifically Assyrian—names. This reinforces the assertion that a certain "Assyrianization" (assimilation toward Assyrian) was at work, which is attested along "generational" lines (fathers vs. sons).[41] Second,

---

36 ABL 1065.1–10. On the building of Dūr-Šarrukīn, see Parpola (1995a) 47–77. See *COS* 3:248. Another Nimrud wine list (*NWL* 8 = ND 10047) that lists wine allocations to various professions and nationalities mentions 3 KUR.*Sa-me-ri-na-a-a* "3 Samarians" (r. 15). See most recently, Fales (1994) 373–74. See *COS* 3:279–80.

37 Fales and Postgate (1995) no. 20.

38 Dalley (1996–97) 108–17; and Bordreuil (1996–97) 100–7. For the earlier history of Tīl Barsip, see now Ikeda (1999) 271–302.

39 As previously suggested by Hawkins (1983) 131–36. On the basis of this Luwian name, Dalley suggests that the hitherto unidentified place Manṣuate in the Assyrian eponym chronicle for the year 796 is Tīl Barsip. Dalley (1996–97) 68–70.

40 Dalley [1996–97] 82–84 + plate 3 and figure 6.

41 The Israelites may have taken on second names or entirely new names to adapt to new linguistic and societal settings. See Fales (1991) 104–5.

some of the deportees could attain reasonably high social positions in their respective communities.

THOSE WHO RECEIVED HARDSHIP AND BARE SUBSISTENCE (THE BULK OF THE ISRAELITE DEPORTEES)[42]

1. *Agricultural Workers*

The Assyrian government organized much of its agricultural labor force—very frequently composed of deportees from Assyrian military campaigns—into "cohorts" (*kiṣru*), modelled along military lines. There were *kiṣru* of shepherds, oil-pressers, gardeners, etc.[43] Such organization provided the Assyrian hierarchy with clear control mechanisms for large numbers of workers.

a. Ḫalaḫḫa (Halah)

A letter (ADD 755) contains three West Semitic personal names that were possibly borne by Israelites.[44] The province of Ḫalaḫḫa had an agricultural function (either as lands owned by the king, the temples, or private individuals). A Neo-Assyrian letter shows that the inhabitants of Ḫalaḫḫa were obliged to perform *dullu*-duties—duties to work for the king. In Ḫalaḫḫa this entailed the digging and the upkeep of canals to improve the irrigation of the land and the delivery of straw (on the importance of straw see below).[45]

b. Guzāna (Gozan)

The area of Guzāna was an important agricultural part of Assyria proper, supplying rye, barley, and livestock to the Assyrian cities to the east. A legal document on the sale of slaves from 709 B.C.E. contains a number of West Semitic names, some of which are considered to be Israelite: *Pa-ka-ḫa, Na-ad-bi-ya-ú* and *Bi-in-di-qí-ri*.[46]

Like Ḫalaḫḫa, Guzāna could be considered part of Assyria's core, at least by the end of the eighth century B.C.E. But just because one lived in

42 See Parpola and Watanabe (1988) 40 (fig. 11) (the deportation and execution of rebels, Or. Dr. IV, 53).

43 Postgate (1995) 405.

44 Becking (1992) 62–63.

45 Postgate (1974b) 81, 83, 226–28.

46 Becking (1992) 65–66.

Assyria proper[47] did not mean that all was well. Although they are described by their Assyrian superintendent as "healthy persons" (ZI.MEŠ [š]*al-mu-te*), in an Assyrian letter the individual rations of deportees in Guzāna are mentioned: 1 *qa* of barley and 0.17 of a liter of oil per day—the "minimum-survival" nutritional dosage![48] It is very probable that some Israelites who were settled in Guzāna received this type of treatment.

Such a daily "minimum-survival" ration as 1 *qa* (i.e., roughly 1 liter), while supplying sufficient energy intake, would be accompanied by a marked nutritional imbalance over an extended period of time, especially manifesting deficiencies in vitamins A and C.[49] The insufficiency in the latter can cause scurvy, whereas lack in the former can cause blindness.[50]

It is very likely that a number of Israelites settled in Ḫalaḫḫa and Guzāna were assigned as farmers to lands owned by high state officials,[51] the Assyrian temples,[52] or the king himself. In fact, most of the families included in land grants from the Assyrian kings were likely to have been deportees, installed directly on state farms or temple lands on their arrival in Assyria. In many instances such land is likely to have been on the desert margins, and would have provided subsistence to its occupants only because the reserves of the state or other landowners accumulated from more favorable years and areas would have sufficed to see the "helots" through the periodic droughts.[53]

One letter (SAA 1.179 = K 889)[54] states that the Arabs of the area around the city of Ḫuzaza were not allowed to purchase iron from Bēl-liqbi, the

---

47 Concerning "Assyria proper," see Postgate (1992) 251–52.

48 See Fales (1990) 29; and Powell (1992) 904. For the letter, see Parpola (1987) letter 257. This is following Fales' interpretation of lines 12– r. 7.

49 Ellison (1981) 35–45. See also Younger (1998b) 121–32.

50 Technically, the deficiency of vitamin A is the main cause of xerophthalmia and keratomalacia—conditions that, if not halted, produce permanent blindness.

51 During the reign of Sargon, according to the Harran census, a group of Gambulaeans were assigned to plots of land belonging to high state officials. See Fales and Postgate (1995) nos. 219–20.

52 There was an estate of 4,000 hectares of land taken by Sargon for the new temple of Nabû at Dūr-Šarrukīn in Ḫalaḫḫa. See Fales (1973) no. 24, rev. 14 and Parpola (1987) 88 (ABL 480). As early as the reign of Adad-Nirari III the steward of the Aššur temple had owned large estates in the provinces of Aššur, Kurbail, and Guzāna. See Postgate (1969) no. 27.

53 Postgate (1989b) 152.

54 Parpola (1987) 140–41.

Assyrian official in charge at the city of Ṣūpat (Ṣobâ),[55] whereas the deportees (LÚ *ḫubti*) were allowed to. Bēl-liqbi sold only copper to the Arabs (lines 20–r. 2).

2. *Forced Laborers*

Sargon's building of Dūr-Šarrukīn appears to have put a great strain on the empire. The bulk of the unskilled labor was done by deportees. Sargon states in his annals: "At that time I erected with the enemy people, [my] booty, which Aššur, [Nabû] and Marduk had brought into submission, ... a city [and] I gave it the name [Dūr-šarru-ukīn]."[56]

As pointed out above, a fragmentary list of rations[57] divides the laborers into two units: one (apparently the skilled workers) entitled to a 2-*qa* ration of barley, the other (the unskilled laborers) entitled to only a 1-*qa* ration—the absolute minimal daily ration. The plight of the unskilled laborers must have been very grievous.

A text of Sennacherib narrates the efforts of some "earlier kings" to transport colossi to a new location.[58] The inscription very likely describes an incident that occurred during the reign of his father, Sargon.[59] Large trees were cut down "until they became a rarity"; ships were built with the wood; the colossi were transported across the Tebiltu River on these ships; and the ships sank under the load! The text notes the immense strain, toil and exhaustion of the work crews in bringing the project to completion. The entire project appears to have been too ambitious for the good of the empire. There was an acute shortage of straw for making bricks, which became so critical that Sargon resorted to death threats. Two letters threatened the governor of Calah with death if he did not deliver straw and reeds to Dūr-Šarrukīn by a certain date.[60] This kind of treatment for his high

55 For the most recent discussion of this toponym, see Charpin (1998) 79–92. Through the publication of a previously unpublished letter from Mari (M. 5423), he is able to demonstrate that the city of Ṣîbat was located in the Beqa Valley and that it is the same city attested with the form Ṣūpat/Ṣūpite in the Neo-Assyrian sources and Ṣobah in the Hebrew Bible. While Parpola ([1987] 238) proposed Ṣūpat = Homs?, Charpin argues that Forrer's earlier proposal (Ṣūpat = Baalbek) is more plausible (see Forrer [1920] 62).

56 Fuchs (1994) 339 (lines 424–26).

57 Fales and Postgate (1995) no. 20.

58 Frahm (1997) 81, lines 35–49.

59 See Frahm (1997) 81–84, comments to lines 46–47; and Gallagher (1999) 26. See also Fales (1993) 90–91.

60 Parpola (1987) 24 (ND 2408) and 25 (K 19673).

officials only underscores the kind of treatment that his unskilled labor force would have received.[61]

In 707 B.C.E., as Dūr-Šarrukīn was nearing completion, an epidemic (*mūtānu*) struck Assyria.[62] This epidemic may very well have had an impact on the labor force itself at the new capital since rank and file infantry were called upon to help complete the construction.[63] If any of these unskilled Israelite laborers survived to the completion of the new city in 706 B.C.E., many were probably moved to additional building sites, with perhaps some remaining to fulfill domestic labor requirements in the new city. However, this would have been short-lived. The very next year (705 B.C.E.), after the completion of his magnificent capital, Sargon was killed in battle. Dūr-Šarrukīn suddenly lost its significance. Sennacherib did not want to live in the accursed city and immediately began work on Nineveh, making it his new capital. Whatever laborers were involved in this project—there is, as yet, no evidence of Israelites being used here[64]— they did not fare any better than the laborers of Dūr-Šarrukīn. Sennacherib's palace wall reliefs depict the transport of his bull colossi with forced laborers being put under great exertion, some clearly exhausted, being driven by taskmasters with sticks.[65]

3. *Front Line / Border Towns / Forts*

Some Israelites of the second filtered type were deported to and suffered the hardships of living in a front-line region, described in 2 Kgs 17:6 and 18:11 as the "cities of the Medes" (*ʿry mdy*).[66] In the Assyrian sources, this would appear to be the area of Ḫarḫar and its neighboring townships (e.g., Kišessu). Sargon II captured the city of Ḫarḫar during his sixth campaign, renaming it Kār-Šarrukīn. In his seventh campaign he captured other towns, renaming them Kār-Nabû, Kār-Sîn, Kār-Adad and Kār-Ištar. The Israelites deported to Ḫarḫar could not have been deported before 716 B.C.E., simply because before that date Sargon had no "cities of the Medes"

---

61 Isa 14:16–17 may also underscore Sargon's labor policy.

62 See Grayson (1975) 76 (chronicle I ii 5).

63 Lanfranchi and Parpola (1990) 25–26. Note that the governor tells Sargon that only cavalrymen were at his disposal because the other men were working on the construction of Dūr-Šarrukīn.

64 Though Judahites from Sennacherib's third campaign (701 B.C.E.) were probably involved.

65 See Russell (1991) 94–116.

66 Concerning the textual variants, see Becking (1992) 48, n. 7.

within his provincial jurisdiction.[67] According to the Cyprus Stela, after the deportation of Ḫarḫar, people of other lands previously conquered by Sargon were settled there.[68] 2 Kgs 17:6 and 18:11 demonstrate clearly that the Israelites were one of those peoples.

It is important to remember that agricultural production was the heart of the Assyrian economy.[69] In order to accomplish the process of agricultural colonization,[70] a pattern of Assyrianization was developed. Thus following the initial campaigning of the Assyrian army, a network of forts and strongholds was established.[71] Around or between these garrisons, the Assyrians created new rural villages, populating them through mass deportations. The exiles were settled on unfamiliar, marginal or underutilized lands that were under strict Assyrian military control. The resulting immobility forced the deportees into the Assyrian socio-economic mold, where they were most susceptible to Assyrian census-takers, corvée-officers, taxation, and eventually acculturation.[72]

Moreover, the renaming of Ḫarḫar as Kār-Šarrukīn carried with it certain implications. The term *kāru*, of course, implies that Assyrian traders were installed in the city for trading purposes. Hence the city was a market for goods going in both directions.[73] Consequently, a few of the deported Israelites might have become involved in the commercial activities of this city.

Since, on occasion, deported soldiers were settled in border regions and at key places in conquered and vassal countries,[74] it is possible that

---

67 See Diakonoff (1991) 13. It is true that Tiglath-Pileser III fought the Medes earlier. But the only information concerning where he deported any Israelites is found in 1 Chr 5:26. This lacks mention of Media as a place to which he deported Israelites. Moreover, the verse is problematic and contains at least one corruption. See Younger (1998a) 207, n. 30. Sargon states in his annals concerning Ḫarḫar: "I conquered that city and carried off booty from it. I caused to enter there the peoples from the lands that I had conquered. I placed my eunuch as governor over them" (Fuchs [1994] 104 lines 97–98).

68 *ARAB* 2 §183. Messerschmidt and Ungnad (1907) 29–36.

69 Postgate (1979) 197; Grayson (1991) 142–61, esp. p. 213.

70 Liverani (1988) 88; Postgate (1974a) 237.

71 Parker (1997) 84.

72 Ibid.

73 An analogy on the other end of the empire would be Gaza, which Sargon claims to have made into an Assyrian *kāru*.

74 Oded (1979) 62–67.

some of these deported Israelites were soldiers, though probably mainly those of the rank and file rather than the elite specialized chariot forces, whose use would have been very limited in that particular mountainous region![75]

Other peoples deported to Ḫarḫar probably included Aramaeans, "pre-Iranians,"[76] people of Iranian tongues (e.g., Medes), and possibly Luwians from Carchemish. In such a situation, the only way to survive was to find a common language (obviously Assyrian or perhaps Aramaic[77] in this case), intermarry with everyone else, serve the Assyrian king loyally, perform the labor required, adapt other religious deities, and be receptive to other cultural practices.[78] That the Assyrians instructed some deportees in Assyrian or some common language can be seen in Sargon's Cylinder Inscription:

> The subject peoples of the four (quarters), (speaking in) foreign tongue(s), of divergent speech, the inhabitants of mountains and plains, all whom the light of the gods, the lord of all, shepherded, whom, by the command of Aššur, my lord, I had carried off (as booty) with my powerful scepter—I made them of one mouth and put them in its (i.e. Dūr-Šarrukin's) midst.[79]

While there was unquestionably influence by the West on Assyrian culture,[80] there should be little doubt concerning the Assyrianization of the deportees. It is not coincidental that in the wake of the annexation of large parts of Syria-Palestine and of widespread deportations during the reign of Sargon II, West Semitic names "enjoyed a peak of presence and of social

---

75 Cf. also the later garrison at Elephantine, whose soldiers were brought from the area of the former northern kingdom by the Saites as mercenaries to guard the border.

76 Following Naʾaman and Zadok's terminology ([1988] 40–41): "Pre-Iranian refers to the non-Iranian inhabitants of western Media: Ḫarḫar, Kishesim, and, probably Karalla and Uishdish … Of the pre-Iranian populations of the central Zagros area, only the Kassites can be specifically discerned as an ethno-linguistic group."

77 Especially now in light of the Bukān Aramaic inscription. See note 24 above for bibliography.

78 Irene Winter's study of receptivity in an adjacent region of the Zagros seems relevant to this point; see Winter (1977) 371–86.

79 Fuchs (1994) 44 (lines 72–73).

80 See Tadmor (1982) 449–70.

significance."[81] Subsequently, as Fales surmises, the importance of West Semitic names decreased somewhat, although the fresh arrival of new deportees (especially during the reign of Sennacherib) kept the "input" of the West Semitic onomastic component quite high. However the abundance of mixed names shows that a certain degree of Assyrianization was at work. In fact, it is evident that the direction of change was unilaterally toward Assyrian.[82] It is reasonable to assume that just as there were different Assyrian administrative policies for different regions or city-states, there were different policies of acculturation and assimilation throughout the vast Assyrian Empire.

BIBLIOGRAPHY

Barnett, R.D., E. Bleibtreu, and G. Turner (1998) *Sculptures from the Southwest Palace of Sennacherib at Nineveh.* London. **Becking, B.** (1992) *The Fall of Samaria: An Historical and Archaeological Study.* SHANE 2. Leiden. **Bordreuil, P.** (1996–97) The Aramaic Documents from Til Barsib. *Abr-Nahrain* 34: 100–7. **Brinkman, J.A.** (1984) *Prelude to Empire.* Philadelphia. **Charpin, D.** (1998) Toponymie amorrite et toponymie biblique: la ville de Ṣîbat/Ṣobah. *RA* 92: 79–92. **Cogan, M.** (1974) *Imperialism and Religion: Assyria, Judah and Israel in the Eighth and Seventh Centuries B.C.* SBLMS 19. Missoula. **Cogan, M., and H. Tadmor** (1988) *II Kings. A New Translation with Introduction and Commentary.* AB 11. Garden City, N.Y. **Cohen, Ch.** (1979) Neo-Assyrian Elements in the First Speech of the Biblical Rab-Shaqeh. *IOS* 9: 32–48. **Dalley, S.M.** (1985) Foreign Chariotry and Cavalry in the Armies of Tiglath-Pileser III and Sargon II. *Iraq* 47: 31–48. (1990) Yahweh in Hamath in the 8th Century B.C.: Cuneiform Material, and Historical Deductions. *VT* 40: 21–32. (1996–97) Neo-Assyrian Tablets from Til Barsib. *Abr-Nahrain* 34: 66–99. **Dalley, S.M., and J.N. Postgate** (1984) *The Tablets from Fort Shalmaneser.* CTN 3. Oxford. **Diakonoff, I.** (1991) *ʿry mdy* Cities of the Medes. In M. Cogan and I. Ephʿal, eds., *Ah, Assyria ...: Studies in Assyrian History and Ancient Near Eastern Historiography Presented to Hayim Tadmor.* 13–20. Scripta

[81] Fales (1991) 115. See also Millard (1983) 101–8; and (1972) 131–37.

[82] Fales (1991) 116. He concludes: "At the final count, we feel that if a partial 'Aramaization' of Assyrian culture may be said to take place in this time, at the same time, we must reckon with the opposite phenomenon occurring in *Namengebung* to some extent, i.e., a clearly discernible 'Assyrianization.' Or, to state it differently: it is conceivable that, hidden beneath unassuming Assyrian names, lay the bulk of conscious/unconscious contributors to the constitution of cultural links between Assyrian and Aramaic in the 8th and 7th BC." Zadok describes this situation as "an intensive Arameo-Assyrian linguistic and cultural interaction" (1997:212).

Hierosolymitana 33. Jerusalem. **Dragoti, E.** (1996)Ancient Crimes Return to Haunt Albania. *Psychology International* 7/4: 1–3. **Ellison, R.** (1981) Diet in Mesopotamia: The Evidence of the Barley Ration Texts (c. 3000–1400 BC). *Iraq* 43: 35–45. **Ephᶜal, I.** (1991) The Samarian(s) in the Assyrian Sources. In M. Cogan and I. Ephᶜal, eds., *Ah, Assyria ...: Studies in Assyrian History and Ancient Near Eastern Historiography Presented to Hayim Tadmor.* 36–45. Scripta Hierosolymitana 33. Jerusalem. (1999) The Bukān Aramaic Inscription: Historical Considerations. *IEJ* 49: 116–21. **Fales, F.M.** (1973) *Censimenti e catasti di epoca neo-assira.* Studi economicic e technologici 2. Rome. (1990) Grain Reserves, Daily Rations and the Size of the Assyrian Army: A Quantitative Study. *SAAB* 4: 23–34. (1991) West Semitic Names in the Assyrian Empire: Diffusion and Social Relevance. *Studi epigrafici e linguistici* 8: 99–117. (1993) River Transport in Neo-Assyrian Letters. In G. Zablocka and S. Zawadzki, eds., *Šulmu IV: Everyday Life in the Ancient Near East. Papers Presented at the International Conference Poznán, 19–22 September 1989.* 79–92. Seria Historia 182. Poznán. (1994) A Fresh Look at the Nimrud Wine Lists. In L. Milano, ed., *Drinking in Ancient Societies. History and Culture of Drinks in the Ancient Near East. Papers of a Symposium held in Rome, May 17–19 1990.* 361–80. HANES 6. Padova. **Fales, F.M., and J.N. Postgate** (1995) *Imperial Administrative Records, Part II. Provincial and Military Administration.* SAA 11. Helsinki. **Forrer, E.** (1920) *Die Provinzeinteilung des assyrischen Reiches.* Leipzig. **Frahm, E.** (1997) *Einleitung in die Sanherib-Inschriften.* AfO Beiheft 26. Vienna. **Fuchs, A.** (1994) *Die Inschriften Sargons II. aus Khorsabad.* Göttingen. **Gadd, C.J.** (1954) The Prism Inscriptions of Sargon. *Iraq* 16:179–82, pls. xlv and xlvi. **Gallagher, W.R.** (1994) Assyrian Deportation Propaganda. *SAAB* 8: 57–65. (1999) *Sennacherib's Campaign to Judah. New Studies.* SHCANE 18. Leiden-Boston-Köln. **Grayson, A.K.** (1975) *Assyrian and Babylonian Chronicles.* Locust Valley, N.Y. (1991) Assyria 668–635 BC: the Reign of Ashurbanipal. In J. Boardman, I.E.S. Edwards, N.G.L. Hammond and E. Sollberger, eds., *The Cambridge Ancient History.* 3/2: 142–61, Cambridge. **Hawkins, J.D.** (1976–80) Izrijau. *RlA* 5: 273. (1983) The Hittite name of Til Barsip, *AnSt* 33: 131–36. (1996–97) A New Luwian Inscription of Hamiyatas, King of Masuwari. *Abr-Nahrain* 34: 108–17. **Ikeda, Y.** (1999) Looking from Til Barsip on the Euphrates: Assyria and the West in Ninth and Eighth Centuries B.C. In K. Watanabe, ed., *Priests and Officials in the Ancient Near East. Papers of the Second Colloquium on the Ancient Near East—The City and its Life held at the Middle Eastern Culture Center in Japan (Mitaka, Tokyo).* 271–302. Heidelberg. **Kohler, J., and A. Ungnad** (1913) *Assyrische Rechtsurkunden in Umschrift und Übersetzung nebst einem Index der Personennamen und Rechtserläuterungen.* Leipzig. **Kwasman, T., and S. Parpola** (1991) *Legal Transactions of the Royal Court of Nineveh, Part 1. Tiglath-Pileser III through Esarhaddon.* SAA 6. Helsinki. **Lanfranchi, G.B., and S. Parpola** (1990) *The Correspondence of Sargon II, Part 2. Letters from the Northern and Northeastern Provinces.* SAA 5. Helsinki. **Lemaire, A.** (1998) Une inscription araméenne du VIIIᵉ s. av. J.-C. trouvée à Bukân. *Studia Iranica* 27: 15–30. (1997) Jérémie xxv 10b et la stèle araméenne de Bukân. *VT* 47: 543–45. **Lipiński, E.** (1971) An Israelite King of Hamath? *VT* 21: 371–73. **Liverani, M.**

(1988) The Growth of the Assyrian Empire in the Habur Middle Euphrates Area: A New Paradigm. *SAAB* 2: 81–98. **Machinist, P.** (1983) Assyria and Its Image in the First Isaiah. *JAOS* 103: 719–37. (2000) The *Rab Šāqēh* at the Wall of Jerusalem: Israelite Identity in the Face of the Assyrian "Other." *Hebrew Studies* 41: 151–68. **Malamat, A.** (1963) Aspects of Foreign Policies of David and Solomon. *JNES* 22: 1–17. **Messerschmidt, L., and A. Ungnad** (1907) *Vorderasiatische Schriftdenkmäler der königlichen Museen zu Berlin I.* Leipzig. **Millard, A.R.** (1972) Some Aramaic Epigraphs. *Iraq* 34: 131–37. (1983) Assyrian and Aramaeans. *Iraq* 45: 101–8. **Na'aman, N.** (1993) Population Changes in Palestine Following the Assyrian Deportations. *Tel Aviv* 20: 104–24. (1995) Tiglath-Pileser III's Campaigns Against Tyre and Israel (734–732 B.C.E.). *Tel Aviv* 22: 268–78. **Na'aman, N., and R. Zadok** (1988) Sargon's Deportations to Israel and Philistia. *JCS* 40: 36–46. **Oded, B.** (1979) *Mass Deportations and Deportees in the Neo-Assyrian Empire.* Wiesbaden. **Parker, B.** (1961) Administrative Tablets from the North-West Palace of Nimrud, *Iraq* 22: 15–67. (1963) Economic Tablets from the Temple of Mamu at Balawat. *Iraq* 25: 89–93. **Parker, B.J.** (1997) Garrisoning the Empire: Aspects of the Construction and Maintenance of Forts on the Assyrian Frontier. *Iraq* 59: 77–87. **Parpola, S.** (1987) *Correspondence of Sargon II, Part 1. Letters from Assyria and the West.* SAA 1. Helsinki. (1995a) The Construction of Dūr-Šarrukin in the Assyrian Royal Correspondence. In A. Caubet, ed., *Khorsabad, le palais de Sargon II, roi d'Assyrie. Actes du colloque organisé au musée du Louvre par le Service culturel les 21 et 22 janvier 1994.* 47–77. Louvre conférences et colloques. Paris. (1995b) The Assyrian Cabinet, In M. Dietrich and O. Loretz, eds., *Vom Alten Orient Zum Alten Testament. Festschrift für Wolfram Freiherrn von Soden zum 85. Geburtstag am 19. Juni 1993.* 379–401. AOAT. Neukirchen-Vluyn. **Parpola, S., and K. Watanabe** (1988) *Neo-Assyrian Treaties and Loyalty Oaths.* SAA 2. Helsinki. **Pečírková, J.** (1987) The Administrative Methods of Assyrian Imperialism. *ArOr* 55: 162–75. **Postgate, J. N.** (1969) *Neo-Assyrian Royal Grants and Decrees.* Studia Pohl: Series Maior 1. Rome. (1972–75) Ḫalaḫḫa. *RlA* 4: 58. (1974a) Some Remarks on Conditions in the Assyrian Countryside. *JESHO* 17: 225–43. (1974b) *Taxation and Conscription in the Assyrian Empire.* Studia Pohl, Series Maior 3. Rome. (1979) The Economic Structure of the Assyrian Empire, In M.T. Larsen, ed., *Power and Propaganda: A Symposium on Ancient Empires.* 193–222. Mesopotamia 7. Copenhagen. (1989a) Ancient Assyria —A Multi-Racial State, *Aram* 1: 1–10. (1989b) The Ownership and Exploitation of Land in Assyria in the 1st Millennium B.C. In M. Lebeau and P. Talon, eds., *Reflets des deux fleuves. volume de mélanges offerts à André Finet.* 141–52. Akkadica Supplementum 6. Leuven. (1992) The Land of Assur and the Yoke of Assur. *World Archaeology* 23: 147–263. (1995) Some Latter-Day Merchants of Aššur. In M. Dietrich and O. Loretz, eds., *Vom Alten Orient von Soden zum Alten Testament. Festschrift für Wolfram Freiherrn von Soden zum 85. Geburtstag am 19. Juni 1993.* 403–6. AOAT. Neukirchen-Vluyn. **Powell, M.A.** (1992) Weights and Measures. In *ABD* 6:897–908. **Reade, J.E.** (1972) The Neo-Assyrian Court and Army: Evidence from the Sculptures. *Iraq* 34: 87–112. **Roberts, J.M.M.** (1985) Amos 6.1–7. In J.T. Butler, E.W. Conrad, and B.C. Ollenburger, eds., *Understanding the*

Word: Essays in Honour of Bernhard W. Anderson. 155–66. JSOTSup 37. Sheffield. **Russell, J.M.** (1991) *Sennacherib's Palace without Rival at Nineveh*. Chicago and London. **Sokoloff, M.** (1999) The Old Aramaic Inscription from Bukān: A Revised Interpretation. *IEJ* 49: 105–15. **Steiner, R.C.** (1991) The Aramaic Text in Demotic Script: The Liturgy of a New Year's Festival Imported from Bethel to Syrene by Exiles from Rash. *JAOS* 111: 362–63. (1995) Papyrus Amherst 63: A New Source for the Language, Literature, Religion, and History of the Arameans. In M.J. Geller, J.C. Greenfield, and M.P. Weitzman, eds., *Studia Aramaica: New Sources and New Approaches*. 199–207. JSSSup 4; Oxford. (1997) The Aramaic Text in Demotic Script. *COS* 1:309–27. **Tadmor, H.** (1958) The Campaigns of Sargon II of Aššur: A Chronological-Historical Study. *JCS* 12:22–40, 77–100. (1961) Azriyau of Yaudi. *ScrHier* 8:232–71. (1982) The Aramaization of Assyria: Aspects of Western Impact. In H.-J. Nissen and E. Renger, eds., *Mesopotamien und seine Nachbarn*. 449–70. RAI 25. BBVO 1/2; Berlin. (1994) *The Inscriptions of Tiglath-Pileser III King of Assyria*. Jerusalem. **Weippert, M.** (1976–80) Israel und Juda. *RlA* 5: 205. **Winckler, H.** (1889) *Die Keilschrifttexte Sargons*. Leipzig. **Winter, I.J.** (1977) Perspective on the 'Local Style' of Hasanlu IVB: A Study in Receptivity. In L.D. Levine and T.C. Young, Jr., eds., *Mountains and Lowlands: Essays in the Archaeology of Greater Mesopotamia*. 371–86. Bibliotheca Mesopotamica 7. Malibu, Calif. **Younger, K.L. Jr.** (1998a) The Deportations of the Israelites. *JBL* 117/2: 201–27. (1998b) Two Comparative Notes on the Book of Ruth, *JANES* 26: 121–32. (1999) The Fall of Samaria in Light of Recent Research. *CBQ* 61: 461–82. (2002) Yahweh at Ashkelon and Calah? Yahwistic names in Neo-Assyrian. *VT* 52: 207–18. **Zadok, R.** (1997) The Ethnolinguistic Composition of Assyria Proper in the 9th–7th Centuries BC. In H. Waetzoldt and H. Hauptmann, eds., *Assyrien im Wandel der Zeiten*. 210–16. RAI 39. Heidelberger Studien zum alten Orient 6. Heidelberg. **Zevit, Z.** (1991) Yahweh Worship and Worshippers in 8th-Century Syria. *VT* 41: 363–66.

ABBREVIATIONS

ABC — A.K. Grayson. *Assyrian and Babylonian Chronicles*. Locust Valley, N.Y.: J. J. Augustin, 1975.

ABL — R.F. Harper. *Assyrian and Babylonian Letters*. London/Chicago, 1892–1914.

ADD — C.H.W. Johns. *Assyrian Deeds and Documents*. Cambridge: Cambridge University Press, 1898–1923.

ANEP[2] — J.B. Pritchard. *The Ancient Near East in Pictures Relating to the Old Testament*. 2nd Edition. Princeton: Princeton University Press, 1969.

ARAB — D.D. Luckenbill. *Ancient Records of Assyria and Babylonia*. 2 Vols. Chicago: University of Chicago Press, 1926–27.

ARU J. Kohler, and A. Ungnad. *Assyrische Rechtsurkunden in Umschrift und Übersetzung nebst einem Index der Personennamen und Rechtserläuterungen.* Leipzig: E. Pfeiffer, 1913.

BM British Museum.

COS W.W. Hallo and K.L. Younger, Jr., eds., *The Context of Scripture.* 3 Vols. Leiden, 1997–2002.

K Tablets in the Kouyunjik collection of the British Museum.

KAI H. Donner and W. Röllig. *Kanaanäische und aramäische Inschriften.* 3 Vols. Wiesbaden: Harrassowitz, 1962–64.

ND Field numbers of tablets excavated at Nimrud.

NWL J.V. Kinnier Wilson. *The Nimrud Wine Lists. A Study of Men and Administration at the Assyrian Capital in the Eighth Century B.C.* London, 1972.

PNA S. parpola, K. Radner, H. Baker, et al., eds., *The Prosopography of the Neo-Assyrian Empire.* Helsinki, 1998–.

RlA E. Ebeling, B. Meissner, et al., eds., *Reallexikon der Assyriologie.*

SAA State Archives of Assyria.

ScrHier *Scripta Hierosolymitana.*

TFS S. Dalley and J.N. Postgate. *The Tablets from Fort Shalmaneser.* CTN 3; Oxford: British School of Archaeology, 1984.

MODELING THE FARM COMMUNITY IN IRON I ISRAEL

Robert D. Miller, II
Mount St. Mary's Seminary

The goal of this paper is to reconstruct daily life and economy in ancient Israel. This will be done entirely apart from the biblical text, although surely the findings will have a great deal to say for biblical research. There have been many studies in the past that have attempted such archaeologically based environmental reconstructions, yet, as it will be shown, these are almost universally flawed. This paper will propose a new method for discovering ancient economies, and apply this method to Iron I Israel. The result will then be a reconstruction of ancient subsistence strategies and a model of the daily life of the Iron I community.

The entry point to reconstructing ancient economies has often been to describe the ancient environment around archaeological sites that could have been exploited for farming. These exploitable areas around sites are commonly called "catchment basins." Delimiting catchment areas is not very difficult. E.S. Higgs and Claudio Vita-Finzi at one time argued[1] that the mean catchment area is a 5 km radius around a site, but an analysis of closeness of nearest neighbor and cumulative area of terraces eventually led Vita-Finzi to a criterion of time more than one of distance.[2] Ethnographically, despite great technological and environmental differences, a one-hour radius appears accurate for agricultural sites, leaving sufficient hours for the day's activities after traveling to the outer boundary and back.[3]

Abbreviations used are: *BA (Biblical Archaeologist)*; *BAR* (*Biblical Archaeology Review*); BARInt (British Archaeological Reports International Series); *BASOR* (*Bulletin of the American Schools of Oriental Research*); *JAAR* (*Journal of the American Academy of Religion*); JSOTSup (Journal for the Study of the Old Testament Supplement Series); *PEQ* (*Palestine Exploration Quarterly*); SBLSP (Society of Biblical Literature Seminar Papers); *TA* (*Tel Aviv*).

1 Higgs and Vita-Finzi (1972) 31.

2 Vita-Finzi (1978) 26.

3 Jarman, Vita-Finzi, and Higgs (1972) 63; Vita-Finzi (1978) 26; and Peebles (1978) 404.

Based on calculations of walking time, David Hopkins concluded that this yields a 2 km radius around sites in the highlands of Palestine, 5 km in wadi valleys and plains.[4]

More difficult is estimating the ancient productivity potential of these catchment basins. The catchment basins of D. Webley for Palestine and Christopher Peebles for North America are simply based on soil type.[5] Webley calculates the percentage and total area within the catchment of each site that belongs to each soil zone,[6] thus solving the problem that sites often sit at the juncture of very different habitats[7] or at environmental anomalies in a general zone.[8] Webley's and Peebles's procedure, however, is much too simple. They fail to adequately take into consideration variations in precipitation, slope, and standing pre-cultivation vegetation. What is more important, soil depletion in Palestine since antiquity renders mapping of modern soil zones useless.

Other scholars have attempted more elaborate reconstructions of the productivity potential of various regions in highland Palestine.[9] Some of these still run into the problem of soil depletion, particularly those that rely on modern or nineteenth-century analogies for soil yields, as, for example, those of Frank Frick, James Flanagan, and some of Israel Finkelstein's work from the 1980s.[10] Certainly such analogies can be quite useful for understanding the dynamics of peasant farming in such regions, for consumption figures, and even for the yield profiles of different crops, as has been done by Steve Falconer,[11] who confirms the analogy figures against documents from Nuzi and Ugarit—but not for soil yields.

We must begin somewhere other than with the soil. Extensive studies have shown that climate, at least, has remained unchanged in Palestine since the Chalcolithic period.[12] This can enable the mapping of environ-

---

4 Hopkins (1985) 165.

5 Webley (1972) and Peebles (1978) 406.

6 Webley (1972) 178.

7 Jarman, Vita-Finzi, and Higgs (1972) 61; Higgs and Vita-Finzi (1972) 28.

8 Jarman, Vita-Finzi, and Higgs (1972) 61.

9 For example, Hopkins (1983) 188–91 and (1985); Frick (1985) 122; Finkelstein (1988a) and (1992a); and Dar (1992).

10 Examples include Frick (1985) 113, 120; (1987) 252–55; Finkelstein (1988a); (1988–89) 126; Flanagan (1988) 127; Hopkins (1997a) 30.

11 Falconer (1987) 73–74.

12 For the relevant data, see Danin (1985) 41; Davis (1984) 37–39; and references in Frick (1985) 101.

mental zones,[13] which is the preface to reconstructing and mapping production schemes. This serves not merely to come up with productivity potentials, but also provides a kind of *Alltagsgeschichte* of Iron I highland Palestine. Other evidence to be considered includes floral and faunal remains, not to reconstruct Iron I farming practices—because such remains are minimal and may be residual—but to reconstruct what fauna and flora occurred in different areas of ancient Palestine before the last millennium of erosion and over-grazing. Pollen samples from deep cores are thus also very useful. This skeleton of data can enable a reconstruction of the environmental zones *based on other analogous regions of the world*, and it is this that is novel in the approach proposed here.

To state this more clearly, the modern climate, rainfall, and so forth, can be applied to the ancient period. Elevation of various parts of Palestine is also obviously a constant. Elevation can be combined with rainfall, along with some minimal soil information: Cenomanian limestone has always eroded to *terra rosa* soil, and never did otherwise, for example. The combinations of these factors define distinct environmental zones—eighteen of them in ancient Hill Country Palestine—and these zones can be compared with analogous regions that exist today in the world (many of them in South Africa, California, and Chile). Those analogies can fill in the rest of the information needed to decide what subsistence strategies would have been most profitable in each zone, and that reconstructs the ancient daily life.

Table 1 illustrates eighteen regions of the north-central highlands, meaning that area south of the Jezreel valley and the passes connecting it to the coast, and north of Jerusalem.[14] Names of the regions are fairly arbitrary and imply neither assumptions about ancient toponyms nor modern political views. Each zone can be summarized as to probable ancient soil type, rainfall, standing vegetation, and potential economy. As it would be quite tedious to discuss each of the eighteen regions in turn and serve little purpose, Table 1 summarizes each. It should be noted that terms such as maquis, mattoral, scrub, and so forth, tend to be used very loosely and with varying meanings by Syro-Palestinian archaeologists.[15] Following Tomaselli,[16] these terms are here used very precisely with definitions explained

---

13 This was done in a more limited way by Fritz (1996) 94–95.

14 Flanagan (1988) 126–27 offers a mere three zones.

15 As with, for example, Flanagan (1988) 135.

16 Tomaselli (1981).

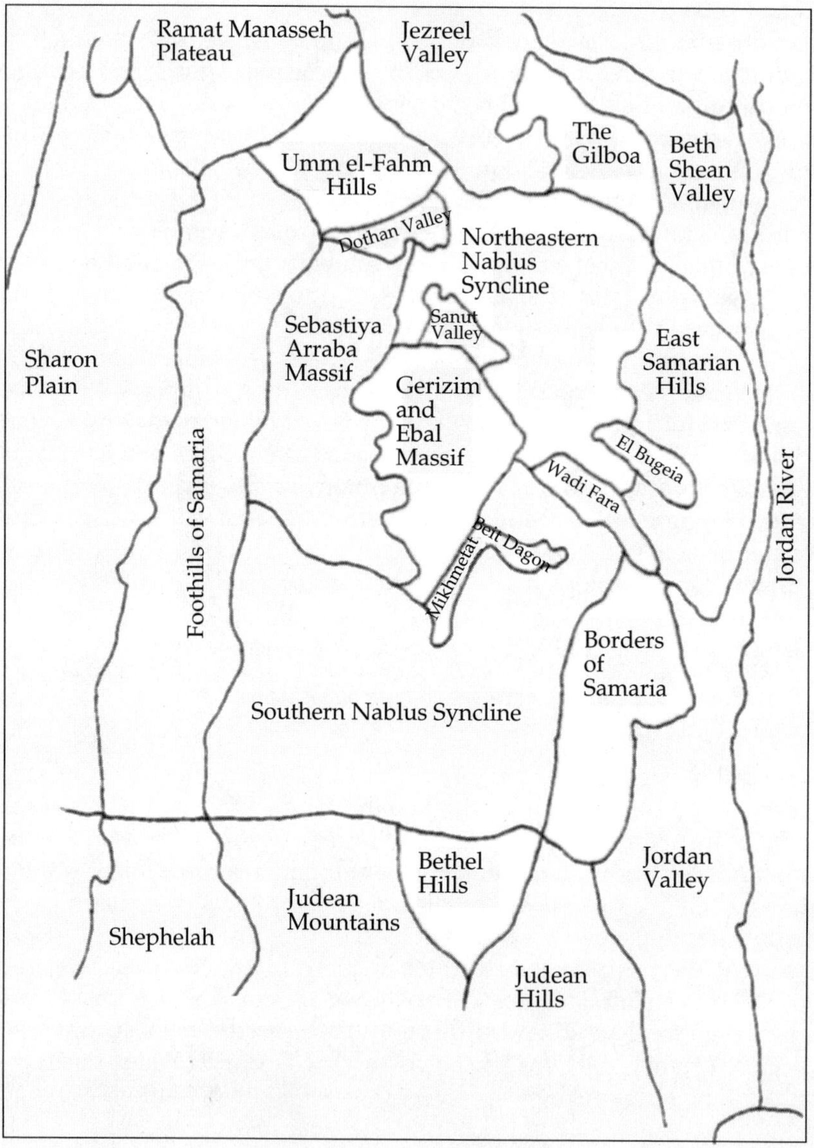

REGIONS OF THE HIGHLANDS

in Table 2. Although the descriptions of these regions are provided in Table 1, it will be useful to discuss a sample of three in order to illustrate the method.

The northwesternmost of these highland regions is the Umm el-Fahm hills, separated from the mountainous regions to the northwest by the Wadi Ara pass from Megiddo to the sea. This region had soils of Rendzina, Terra Rosa, and Mediterranean Brown Forest, although the modern predominance of the latter two would be the result of erosion.[17] The rainfall drops as low as 500 mm annually. This combination supported a three- to five-meter-tall thicket best-called "evergreen oak forest and maquis," a subtype of the middle-dense Garrigue scrub mattoral.[18] Thickest on western and eastern slopes where rainfall was less than 600 mm and elevation under 300 m,[19] this consisted of Kermesian (*Quercus calliprinos*) and Mt. Tabor (*Quercus ithaburensis*) oak, broomtree (*Retama raetam*), wormwood (*Artemisia*), wild olive (*Olea europaea)*—although its presence is debatable,[20] lilies, wild garlic and leeks, hyacinth, saffron, orchids, myrrh, peonies, and wild asparagus.[21] In the higher altitudes, balsam (*Styrax officinalis*) and terebinth[22] also would have been found.[23] The economy would have been equally divided between olive/vine horticulture and lentil (both *Lens esculenta* and *L. culinaris*), alfalfa (Karsena vetch, *Vicia ervilia*), fava bean ("broad beans," *Vicia faba*), and chickpea (*Cicer arietinum*) cultivation.[24] Red deer (*Cervus elaphus*) and hare (*Lepus sp.*) could have been hunted, and storax (from the balsam trees) and mastic incense exported.[25] Terebinth and oak timber could also have been exported to the Jezreel valley and coastal plain.[26]

---

17 Zohary (1962) 10; Rabinovitch-Vin (1983) 83.

18 Rabinovitch-Vin (1983) 75.

19 Rabinovitch-Vin (1983) 77; Steward and Webber (1981) 58–59.

20 By pollen count it was extremely rare in Iron I, as shown by Horowitz (1974) 409, but it has been found in archaeological contexts, for which see Van Zeist (1985) 203.

21 Dan (1988) 118; Quézel (1981) 91; Harel (1984) 70; and Rabinovitch-Vin (1983) 83.

22 Terebinth includes both *Pistacia lentiscus* and *P. palestina,* remains of which are found at Izbet Sartah according to Finkelstein (1985a) 154.

23 Dan (1988) 118; Steward and Webber (1981) 57, 59.

24 Aschmann (1973) 365.

25 The latter is the Eg. "*senetjer* from the Retenu route"; see Artzy (1994) 131. Regarding such exports, see Goffer (1996) 242.

26 Wright (1997) 363.

Immediately to the southwest lay the foothills of Samaria. Soil and rainfall replicate the conditions of the Umm el-Fahm hills, except the elevation is lower. The stand was again evergreen oak forest and maquis, thickest in the southern half of the foothills of Samaria. Due to the lower altitude, however, horticulture of wine and olives should have been the dominant industry where rain was under 600 mm.[27] Cultivation is possible for lentils, alfalfa (found at Izbet Sartah),[28] flax/linseed (*Linum*), fava beans, and chickpeas.[29] Grazing of goats and cattle, but not sheep, would have contributed to the economy in higher altitudes.[30] Additional casual sources would include figs (*Ficus carica*) and hunting of red deer and hare, along with the export of mastic incense and labdanum resin.[31]

Stretching across the center of the highlands from the southern edge of the Sebastiyya Arraba massif south to the Wadi esh-Shami, from about the longitude of modern Haris and Deir es-Sudan in the west as far east as the modern Allon Road, is the southern Nablus syncline. Soils were Rendzina and Grumsols, and rainfall is approximately 700 mm annually. The vegetation was transitional between the mixed Tabor oak forest shrublands of the Shephelah and the Aleppo pine forest.[32] The so-called Aleppo pine forest can grow up to ten meters high,[33] but it is highly unlikely that any Aleppo pines (*Pinus halepensis*) were present.[34] The forest of the southern Nablus syncline consisted of wild olive, *P. palestina* terebinth in the drier areas,[35] Kermesian oak in drier parts over 500 m elevation, Mt. Tabor oak and balsam above this altitude and on north-facing slopes below, except on Grumsols,[36] wild garlic, wild leeks, myrrh, broom tree, and boxthorn. The overall dominant economic factor would have been terrace-farming of

---

27 Bornstein (1993) 97; Quézel (1981) 91; Aschmann (1973) 365. Olive remains were found at Izbet Sartah, according to Finkelstein (1985a) 154.

28 Barley was also found, according to Finkelstein (1985a) 154.

29 Harel (1984) 70; note sickle blades at Izbet Sartah, as per Finkelstein (1985a) 94.

30 Webley (1972) 170; it seems from the faunal remains of Izbet Sartah that this was true for the lower altitudes as well, as seen in Finkelstein (1985a) esp. 150.

31 Goffer (1996) 242.

32 Tomaselli (1981) 99.

33 Rabinovitch-Vin (1983) 79.

34 Both pollen evidence and dendochronological evidence show this species to have been very rare in Iron I; see Liphschitz, Biger, and Mendel (1987–89) 141–50; Horowitz (1974) 409.

35 Quézel (1981) 91; Rabinovitch-Vin (1983) 77.

36 Steward and Webber (1981) 57, 59; Rabinovitch-Vin (1983) 75.

cereals: wheat (primarily durum wheat, *Triticum durum,* but also emmer, *T. dicoccum,* and *T. vulgare*), barley, lentils, alfalfa, peas, chickpeas, and fava beans.[37] This is confirmed by the presence of wheat, barley, lentils, and alfalfa in storage silos of Khirbet Seilun.[38] Cereal farming would have been especially dominant in the eastern half of the southern Nablus syncline, east of the longitude of modern Nablus. This half would have been free of olive horticulture, which would however have played a large role in the economy in the north central and southwestern areas.[39] An abundance of raisins from Khirbet Seilun suggests wine viticulture.[40] Caprovid grazing might have been substantial in the southwestern corner as well.[41] Supplementary strategies include nut and fig horticulture in the north-central area,[42] hunting of mountain gazelle (*Gazella gazella*) and red and fallow deer,[43] and export of storax incense and labdanum resin.[44]

Similar kinds of comparison and argumentation produce the schemes for the other zones, all of which are described in Table 1.

When looking at all this data, which in itself can be a tremendous resource for archaeologists and historians, one important observation is the complexity of the highland economies. It will certainly not be enough even to pull a given site out of one of the enumerated regions and read that as its subsistence strategy. Within each region there are variations dependent upon rainfall, altitude, position on the hillside (both directional and elevational), requiring *each site* individually to be identified according to these features before one could attempt a catchment basin analysis. This small-scale diversity contradicts an Annales School *longue durée* view of environmental factors and resultant economies being constant.

---

37 See Aschmann (1973) 365; Rabinovitch-Vin (1983) 79; Finkelstein (1988a); (1988–89) 135; (1995a) 353; Dar (1992); Borowski (1987); Zohary (1966–86) 2.222.

38 See Kislev (1993) 356–57.

39 Antoun (1972); Bornstein (1993) 97; Harel (1984) 70.

40 Kislev (1993) 356.

41 Harel (1984) 70. For example, see Hellwing, Sade, and Kishon (1993) 311). The amount of caprovid bones from Khirbet Seilun shown by Hellwing, Sade, and Kishon (1993) 311, 325 is confirmation; cattle were also found, but in a profile for cereal production traction, according to Rosen (1993) 366.

42 See Antoun (1972), as well as the fig remains from Khirbet Seilun cited by Kislev (1993) 357.

43 All were found at Khirbet Seilun, according to Hellwing, Sade, and Kishon (1993) 311.

44 Goffer (1996) 242.

Clearly, even where all factors are equal, there is often a choice of strategies, even a choice among such diverse strategies as cereal farming, grazing, and horticulture—and hunting, fishing, etc. A full study modeling the farming community[45] of Iron I Palestine is needed, but this is beyond the scope of this essay. What is needed is an ancient-period counterpart to G. Stanhill's 1978 "The Fellah's Farm," which incorporates not only productivity of the environmental zone, but human energy expenditure in gigajoules, percentages of men to women, manure from animals working in the fields as it impacts on fertilization, harvest-seed ratios, percentage of food coming from difficult-to-quantify sources such as eggs and milk, and much more. Such estimates as the method here proposed would produce, on the other hand, are based on resources alone, with the glaring omission of labor at least, and therefore explicitly not estimates of the amount of food actually produced.[46]

A rough sketch of Iron I farming practices, adding to this *Alltagsgeschichte*, might build on the following. Although cereals overall were on the decrease in Iron I,[47] wheats had to be the dominant field crop wherever possible. In the southern and northeastern Nablus syncline this would have been the case, using terracing technology.[48] Wheat was used for bread, beer, fodder, mulch, compost, woven straw, and possibly macaroni-type products.[49] The main wheat would have been durum, naked tetraploid, wheat (*Triticum durum*), although other constituents surely included emmer, hulled tetraploid (*T. dicoccum*) for porridge and fodder, and naked hexaploid dicoccoide (*T. vulgare*), as well.[50] As far as the microeconomics of a wheat-based farm, wheat produces 600 kg per hectare sown in a good year, but the produce can be as high as 1800 kg per hectare.[51]

---

45 What is termed in German *drübbel*, described by Aston (1985) 86.

46 See Feinman and Nicholas (1990) 79. For this reason, the various crop yields can be turned into comparable figures by converting them into units of human consumption (Feinman and Nicholas [1990] 79).

47 See the pollen data in Horowitz (1974) 409.

48 An example is the wheat remains from Khirbet Seilun noted by Kislev (1993) 356.

49 Said (1974) provides ethnographic examples.

50 See, *inter alia*, Borowski (1987) 89; Zohary (1966–86) 2.178; Kislev (1993) 356; Chernoff (1988) 383.

51 See Sweet (1957) 135; Rosen (1994) 347; Said (1974). Estimates vary about how much acreage people need to support themselves: Rosen (1994) 347 gives 0.3 ha per person based on 180 kg per year per person, the standard Greek grain ration yields

The second most important crop was barley.[52] Both six-rowed (*Hordeum vulgare*) and two-rowed (*H. distichon*) varieties were included.[53] In wheat-based economies, barley serves as fodder, is used in making beer, and is an additive to bread,[54] planted at a ratio of wheat to barley of five to one or six to one.[55] However, there were some cereal-farming areas of the highlands where wheat was not possible. And so on the Gilboa and in the Shephelah, barley became the dominant field crop[56] and was used for bread.[57] Barley's productivity is about 800 kg per hectare per year.[58]

The third-ranked crop in a wheat-based economy, presumably second-ranked in a barley area, is alfalfa.[59] This is specifically Karsena or "Camel" vetch (*Vicia ervilia*), and it is really a legume. It is used as fodder,[60] although in times of famine people will eat it. Archaeobotanical remains have been found at Tel Hefer, Afula, and Khirbet Seilun.[61]

The fourth-ranked crop is lentils (*Lens esculenta, L. culinaris*).[62] Although it ranks low in a wheat- or barley-based system, lentils can grow

---

0.67 ha per person based on 365 kg per year per person, as shown by Foxhall and Forbes (1982) 72–73. This is basically the same as the figures of Webley (1972) 178. Modern ethnographic figures yield 1.7 ha per person, according to Stanhill (1978) 442, roughly the same as Lutfiyya (1966) 189; see also Antoun (1972); and Falconer (1987) 77. Other figures thrown out are 2.2 ha per person, mentioned in Rosen (1993) 364, or even 93.3 ha per person [sic] from Glavanis (1989) 155. It must be remembered that 6000 kg per year will be consumed by the eight to twelve animals required to plow each 45 ha of land, according to Rosen (1994) 347. When this is subtracted, a 9 ha farm of a family of seven individuals produces 15.5 gigajoules of surplus food energy, as in the work of Stanhill (1978) 442.

52 Stanhill (1978).

53 Zohary (1966–86) 2.181; Rabinovitch-Vin (1983) 75; Borowski (1987) 91–92; Kislev (1993) 356.

54 Sweet (1957) 135.

55 Falconer (1987) 77.

56 Nevertheless, wheat remains were found at Tel Hefer, according to Chernoff (1988) 383.

57 See Turkowski (1969).

58 These are the calculations of Rosen (1994) 347.

59 Stanhill (1978).

60 See Turkowski (1969) 111; Sweet (1957) 135; Zohary (1966–86) 2.200.

61 The references are, respectively, Chernoff (1988) 383, Zaitscheck (1955) 71, and Kislev (1993) 356.

62 Kislev (1993) 356.

almost anywhere, and so may be the dominant crop.[63] Lentils can be used for bread, pottage, or fodder. So terraced lentil farming likely predominated in the regions of the Umm el-Fahm hills, Sebastiyya Arraba massif, Judean mountains, and Bethel hills.

Lesser field crops included fava ("broad," "horse") beans (*Vicia faba*), grown almost anywhere[64] and ground into a meal;[65] chickpeas ("Garbanzo" beans; *Cicer arietinum*), also cultivatable anywhere;[66] and millet, both broomcorn millet (*Panicum miliaceum*) and Italian pearl millet (*Setaria italica*), used for bread, porridge, and beer.[67] Although the latter could have been prevalent in the Judean mountains, some have argued that it was not found in Palestine until the Roman period.[68]

Ancient sources, such as the Samaria Ostraca,[69] suggest that animal husbandry served as a large part of the economy only in the desert fringe and summer pasture enclaves in the highland valleys.[70] Some have argued that in the hills above the valleys, the wild and bushy maquis vegetation prevented grazing.[71] On the other hand, there are many analogous maquis regions of the world where grazing is quite prevalent, especially for goats.[72] Faunal remains from Khirbet Seilun and et-Tell[73] show the importance of grazing in the economy. Thus one might presume grazing to have been a major part of the economies in the Dothan valley, the eastern part of the northeastern Nablus syncline, the Sanur valley, the Mikhmetat and Beit Dagon valleys, the Gilboa, the el-Bugeia and Wadi Farah valleys, the East Samarian hills, the steppe of Samaria, the Judean desert, and the Jordan valley.

---

63 Such cases are cited in Stanhill (1978).

64 One example is Afula; see Zaitscheck (1955) 72–74.

65 Zohary (1966–86) 2.194.

66 See Zohary (1972) 2.193; again, an example is Afula, as seen in Zaitscheck (1955) 72–74.

67 Zohary (1966–86) 2.301.

68 Turkowski (1969) 112.

69 See Zertal (1987) 199–200. The same can be gleaned from Ottoman tax records, as shown by Zertal (1987) 198.

70 This view is shared by Finkelstein (1988–89) 135 and (1995a) 353, and Zertal (1987) 197–98.

71 Zertal (1991) 32.

72 See the data in Wolf (1966) 32.

73 See, respectively, Hellwing, Sade, and Kishon (1993) 311, 325, and Callaway (1976) 30 and (1984) 60.

Non-field plant cultivation also played an important role in highland economic strategies, although these are normally considered "casual foods" rather than staples.[74] They are better termed "cash crops," as they depend on exchange for grain and animal products from nearby areas.[75] First among these is the viticulture of olives and the vine, which played an important role in the economies of the foothills of Samaria, Umm el-Fahm hills, Judean mountains, Gerizim and Ebal massif, and Bethel hills. Olives alone contributed in the southern and northeastern Nablus syncline, and the vine alone in the Sebastiyya Arraba massif. These are areas where raising grain was not worthwhile,[76] which also lacked pasture-lands.[77] One hectare could support 100 to 150 olive trees, capable of producing 500 to 1500 kg of oil per year.[78] Statistics for wine are more elusive, but wine was not the only use for grapes—fresh grapes, raisins, and grape molasses (Arab. *Dibs*) were also possible.[79] Other horticultural commodities included figs (*Ficus carica*) and apricots (*Prunus armeniaca*).

The importance of the above casual foods is debatable. Given the absence of proto-industrial installations needed to convert the produce into secondary products such as wine, oil, and dried fruits, some have argued that their importance in Iron I may have been marginal.[80] Yet often even where no installations are found, archaeobotanical remains of olives and grapes are found.[81] Additionally, it is simply no longer true that the installations did not exist in Iron I. At least five sites in the north-central highlands have been found to have Early Iron Age oil or wine presses.[82]

---

74 See Vita-Finzi and Higgs (1970) 1–2.

75 The clarification is made by Finkelstein (1996c).

76 Nevertheless, attempts were made, according to Meyers (1983) 500 and Davis (1982).

77 See Finkelstein (1996c). By Iron I, the cup-and-lever beam-and-weights olive press was in use according to Frankel (1997) 180), although many places were still using depression-type presses according to Dar (1986) 180.

78 See the calculations by Zertal (1987) 197; and Frankel (1997) 183.

79 See Miller (1997) 305.

80 This is the view of Rosen (1994) 342.

81 These include storage casks, etc.; see Miller (1997) 305. Examples include grape pips at Tel Hefer, noted by Chernoff (1988) 383, grapes and figs at Khirbet Seilun, described by Kislev (1993) 356, and olive pits at Afula, noted by Zaitscheck (1955) 72–74.

82 In the Tell el-Farah (North) area, Zertal (1996) 210 found a double press at the single-period Iron I site of Iraq Rajjah. Khallet esh-Sharde has five systems of Iron I

Other edible components of the economy must have included almonds (*Amygdalus common*; Zohary 1966–86:2.21), walnuts (*Juglans reg.*)—known from the Gezer calendar, the acorns of the Kermesian oak—known from Languedoc and western Iran to be consumed, and "pistachios" of *P. palestina*. Flax/linseed (*Linum*), known archaeologically from Deir Allah,[83] must have contributed as a cash crop.

In areas where wheat could be the base crop and the others secondary, a full calendric economy could be reconstructed. Where the first- or second-ranked commodities could not be supported, they can be removed from the scheme without significant changes. This presentation of the highland calendric economy would be based on the reconstructed economic strategies just presented, with information drawn from analogy,[84] although to describe such a calendar is beyond the scope of this essay.

We have thus arrived at a model of daily life in Early Iron Age Palestine. Climate, altitude, and other constants are the key to environmental zones. These are the key to finding analogous regions in the modern world. Those analogies present productivity potentials, from which can be de-

---

olive oil presses, also found by Zertal (1996) 308–9, 721–23. The first consists of two simple presses and two cups; the second of a conical cup and conical crater with a drainage hole; the third of a big basin and concavity alongside a cup and concave crater; the fourth of four elliptical basins with simple oil press; and the fifth of conical and shallow flat cups. These presses are not associated with the presses from later periods on the site. Evidence of olive oil and wine production was found at Klia in the Khirbet Tibne area by Finkelstein (1996c). Sebastiyya (Samaria) Pottery Period I/ Building Phase 0, now to be dated to the eleventh century by Stager (1990) 104; and Tappy (1992), contains a wine press 1.7 × 0.8 × 1.2 m deep on the acropolis summit—see Stager (1990) 93, an olive press three meters away using a pressing platform with two vats, four or five more olive presses north of this (in 430–450N/620–645E), another press on the north slope 4 m below the summit under the Period I robber trench, another 6 m below the summit below Wall 556–54—see Stager (1990) 94, and eleven more olive presses to the west. Most are simple-style, but there are also two circular trough presses with channels around the perimeter leading to a cup, according to Stager (1990) 95–96. Kenyon had called these presses EBI, but the simple ones cannot be dated, and the other two are typologically unlike EB in the view of Stager (1990). Farther south, there is an Iron I grape press at Tell en-Nasbeh, a two-part rectangular press with two treading basins and a cup for dregs, noted in Zorn (1993) 233, 442. This press has to be Iron I, as it is beneath an Iron II structure and an EB context would place this wine press in the middle of a cemetery, by the stratigraphy of Zorn (1993) 233.

83 Van Zeist (1985) 203.

84 Such ethnographic data would include Turkowski (1969) 27–28, 101; Moors (1989) 199; Antoun (1972) 10–12; Said (1974).

rived subsistence schemes. These can be matched with ethnographic analogies of communities engaging in those schemes, and the daily life is thus reconstructed. What has been here done for Iron I could certainly be done for other periods and other regions. It is a new way of looking at economic and ecological modeling, which shows promise for the future.

TABLE 1

ENVIRONMENTAL ZONES OF THE NORTH-CENTRAL HIGHLANDS

I. Umm el-Fahm Hills
  A. Rendzina, Terra Rosa, Mediterranean Brown Forest soils
  B. 500 mm rain per annum
  C. Evergreen Oak Forest and Maquis (q.v.)
    1. But balsam and terebinth only in higher altitudes
  D. Economy equally divided between
    1. Olive/wine horticulture
    2. Cultivation of lentils, alfalfa, fava beans, chickpeas
    3. Supplemented by hunting of red deer and hare, export of storax and mastic incense and terebinth and oak timber

II. Foothills of Samaria
  A. Rendzina, Terra Rosa, Mediterranean Brown Forest soils
  B. 500 mm rain per annum
  C. Evergreen Oak Forest and Maquis (q.v.)
  D. Economy olive/wine horticulture
    1. Supplemented by cultivation of lentils, alfalfa, flax/linseed, fava beans, chickpeas, grazing of goats and cattle, horticulture of figs, hunting of red deer and hare, and export of mastic incense and labdanum resin

III. Shephelah
  A. Brown Alluvial soil
  B. 500 mm rain
  C. Mixed Tabor Oak Forest Shrublands (q.v.)
  D. Economy of cultivation of barley, lentils, alfalfa, peas, flax/linseed, fava beans, and chickpeas
    1. Supplemented by hunting of fallow deer and export of labdanum resin and storax and mastic incense

IV. Dothan Valley
  A. Grumsols, Gley, and hydromorphic soils
  B. 500–700 mm rain

C. Natural vegetation is Heath: tamarisk, reeds, and thistles
D. Economy divided equally between
  1. Cultivation of lentils, alfalfa, fava beans, chickpeas, and flax/linseed
  2. Grazing of sheep and goats

V. Sebastiyya Arraba Massif
A. Rendzina and Grumsols, possible Terra Rosa and Mediterranean Brown Forest
B. 500–700 mm rain
C. Evergreen Oak Forest and Maquis (q.v.), except:
  1. No terebinth, due to high rainfall and altitude
D. Economy
  1. Wine on lower slopes
  2. With equal use of cultivation of lentils, alfalfa, chickpeas, and fava beans on higher slopes
  3. Supplemented by hunting of red deer and hare, export of storax incense and labdanum resin

VI. Southern Nablus Syncline
A. Rendzina and Grumsols, possible Terra Rosa and Mediterranean Brown Forest
B. 700 mm rain
C. Transitional vegetation between Mixed Tabor Oak Forest Shrublands and Aleppo Pine Forest (q.v.)
  1. terebinth only in drier areas
  2. Kermesian oak only in drier areas over 500m elevation
  3. Mt. Tabor oak and balsam on all soils except Grumsols above 500m and on north-facing slopes below 500m
D. Cereal-farming economy of wheat, barley, lentils, alfalfa, peas, chickpeas, and fava beans
  1. Especially dominant east of the longitude of modern Nablus
  2. Olive/wine horticulture only in North-central and southwestern areas
  3. Sheep and goat grazing only in southwestern corner
  4. Supplemented by nut and fig horticulture in North-central area, hunting of mountain gazelle, red and fallow deer, and export of storax incense and labdanum resin

VII. Judean Mountains
A. Rendzina soils, possibly Terra Rosa and Mediterranean Brown Forest
B. 500–700 mm rain
C. High Sparse Chaparral Maquis Brushfields (q.v.)
D. Mixed agricultural-horticultural economy

1. Cultivation of millet, lentils, alfalfa, chickpeas, and fava beans
2. Olives, wine, almonds, and walnuts on the lower slopes of the North-central and northwestern areas
3. Supplemented by hunting of red deer and hare, export of terebinth and oak timber

VIII. Northeastern Nablus Syncline
- A. Rendzina soils, possibly Terra Rosa and Mediterranean Brown Forest
- B. 500 mm rain
- C. Mixed Tabor Oak Shrublands (q.v.)
- D. Mixed economy
  1. Olives on lower slopes
  2. Elsewhere terrace farming of wheat, barley, lentils, alfalfa, peas, chickpeas, fava beans, and onions
  3. Goat herding in mountainous, eastern part
  4. Supplemented by export of oak, fig, and terebinth timber and storax incense

IX. Sanur Valley
- A. Gley and hydromorphic soils
- B. 500–700 mm rain
- C. Natural vegetation is Heath: tamarisk, willow, reeds, and leeks
- D. Mixed economy
  1. Cultivation of onions, leeks, and garlic
  2. Harvesting of lentils, alfalfa, chickpeas, fava beans, flax/linseed
  3. Sheep and goat grazing

X. Gerizim/ Ebal Massif
- A. Rendzina soils, possibly Terra Rosa and Mediterranean Brown Forest
- B. >700 mm rain
- C. Mixed Tabor Oak Forest Shrublands (q.v.), except:
  1. Rain is too high for terebinth
- D. Viticultural economy
  1. Especially wine; olives only on the lower, south slopes of Mt. Gerizim, pomegranate and figs on south and west slopes of Gerizim and west slopes of Mt. Ebal
  2. Supplemented by hunting of red and fallow deer

XI. Mikhmetat and Beit Dagon Valleys
- A. Grumsols
- B. 500 mm rain

C. Natural vegetation is Downs: willow, wild leeks and garlic, and thistles
D. Mixed economy
 1. Sheep and goat grazing
 2. Cultivation of lentils, alfalfa, chickpeas, fava beans, and flax/linseed
 3. Olives, pomegranate, and nuts

XII. Bethel Hills
A. Rendzina soils, possibly Terra Rosa and Mediterranean Brown Forest
B. 400–500 mm rain
C. Natural vegetation is a Fells, blending Mixed Tabor Oak Forest and Middle Sparse Garrigue Scrub Mattoral (q.v.)
 1. Mt. Tabor oak and balsam only where rain highest
 2. Elsewhere cypress, terebinth, etc.
D. Economy equally divided:
 1. Horticulture of wine and olives
 2. Cultivation of lentils, alfalfa, chickpeas, and fava beans
 3. Supplemented by export of timber, storax incense, and labdanum resin

XIII. The Gilboa
A. Terra Rosa, Rendzina, and Mediterranean Brown Forest soils
B. 300–500 mm rain
C. "Type B" High Dense Chaparral Maquis (q.v.)
D. Mixed economy
 1. terrace farming of wheat, barley, lentils, alfalfa, peas, chickpeas, fava beans, and onions
 2. Goat herding
 3. Supplemented by export of oak, fig, and terebinth timber and storax incense

XIV. el-Bugeia and Wadi Farah Valleys
A. Grumsols
B. 300–400 mm rain
C. Willow and thistles
D. Sheep and goat grazing dominant
 1. Supplemented by small plots of lentils, alfalfa, and flax/linseed

XV. East Samarian Hills
A. Rendzina soils, possibly Terra Rosa and Mediterranean Brown Forest
B. <300 mm rain

C. Carob-Lentisk/Carob-Mastic Maquis (q.v.)
D. Cattle and goat grazing predominant

XVI. Steppe of Samaria
A. Rendzina and Stony Light Brown soils
B. <300 mm rain
C. Steppe vegetation: oak, terebinth, almond, summer cypress, lotus, saltwort, sea blight, saltbush, glasswort, marigolds, and capers
D. Cattle and goat grazing predominant

XVII. Judean Desert
A. Loess, Grumic Dark Brown soils and vertisols, Stony Light Brown soils, Stony Serozems, and Brown and Calcareous Lithosols
B. 300–500 mm rain
C. Halophytic vegetation: almond, wormwood, date palm, ryegrass, anabasis, thistle, thorns, summer cypress, lotus, saltwort, sea blight, saltbush, glasswort, marigolds, and capers
D. Sheep grazing dominant
1. Some cultivation of lentils, rye, peas, chickpeas, fava beans, and capers
2. Supplemented by export of salt bricks (Akk. *sig*$_4$-*mun*), ashes of desert plants for use as flux in glass-making, and date-palm roofing material

XVIII. Jordan Valley
A. Desert Alluvial and Brown Desert Skeletal soils
B. <300 mm rain
C. Date palm, balsam, poplar, balm, sycamore, summer cypress, lotus, saltwort, sea blight, saltbush, glasswort, marigolds, capers, and anabasis
D. Mixed economy
1. Goats
2. Hunting of boar, oryx antelope, gazelle, ibex, duck
3. Supplemented by small plots of wheat, barley, and lentils, export of dates and date-palm roofing

TABLE 2
TYPES OF MAQUIS

I. High Dense Chaparral Maquis
    A. Carob-Lentisk/Carob-Mastic Maquis
        dense thicket of oaks, terebinth, wild olive, balsam, wild asparagus, wormwood, wild leeks and garlic
    B. "Type B"
        oaks, terebinth, carob, wild olive
    C. Humid and Sub-humid Maquis
        oaks
    D. Aleppo Pine Forest
        terebinth, olive, oaks, broomtree, boxthorn in a thicket up to 10 m high

II. High Sparse Chaparral Maquis Brushfields
    wild olive, Kermesian oak, Mt. Tabor oak, terebinth, cypress, and wild leeks

III. Garrigue Scrub Mattoral
    A. Middle Dense
        1. Evergreen Oak Forest and Maquis
            3–5m tall thicket of oak, broomtree, wormwood, olive, lilies, wild garlic and leeks, hyacinth, saffron, orchids, myrrh, peonies, wild asparagus; in higher altitudes also balsam, terebinth
        2. Savannah
            olive, terebinth, oak, acacia
        3. Thermo-Mediterranean
            olives, terebinth, oak, broomtree, myrrh
    B. Middle Sparse
        olive, terebinth, Mt. Tabor oak, myrrh, asphodel, gladiolas, thyme, lavender, rosemary
    C. Low Dense
        olive, terebinth, Mt. Tabor oak, myrrh, thyme, rosemary
    D. Low Sparse
        myrrh, juniper, thyme, lavender, rosemary, asphodel, lutea

IV. Mixed Tabor Oak Forest Shrublands
    terebinth, balsam, oak, myrrh, wild leeks and garlic – thickest on north-facing slopes under 600m elevation and on all slopes above 600 m

BIBLIOGRAPHY

Antoun, R.T. (1972) *Arab Village*. Bloomington: Indiana University Press. **Artzy, M.** (1994) Incense, Camels, and Collared Rim Jars. *Oxford Journal of Archaeology* 13: 121–47. **Aschmann, H.** (1973) Man's Impact on the Several Regions with Mediterranean Climates. Pp. 363–71 in *Mediterranean-Type Ecosystems,* ed. F. di Castri and H.A. Mooney. Ecological Studies 7. Berlin. **Aston, M.** (1985) *Interpreting the Landscape*. London. **Bornstein, A.** (1993) Precious Things of Heaven — Ancient Agriculture in Samaria. Vol. 3, pp. 87–115 in *Judea and Samaria Research Studies,* ed. Z.H. Erlich and Y. Eshel. Kedumim-Ariel: The College of Judea and Samaria Research Institute. **Borowski, O.** (1987) *Agriculture in Iron Age Israel*. Winona Lake, In. **Callaway, J.A.** (1976) Excavating 'Ai: 1964–1972. *BA* 39: 18–30. (1984) Village Subsistence. Pp. 51–66 in *The Answers Lie Below*, ed. H.O. Thompson. Lanham, Md. **Carter, C.E., and C.L. Meyers, eds.** (1996) *Community, Identity, and Ideology*. Sources for Biblical and Theological Study 6. Winona Lake, In. **Castri, F. di, D.W. Goodall, and R.L. Specht, eds.** (1981) *Mediterranean-Type Shrublands*. Ecosystems of the World 11. Amsterdam. **Chernoff, M.C.** (1988) *The Archaeological Material from Tel el Ifshar, Israel*. 2 vols. Ph.D. diss., Brandeis University, Waltham, Mass. (1992) Natural Resource Use in an Ancient Near Eastern Farming Community. *Agricultural History* 66: 213–20. **Dan, J.** (1988) The Soils of the Land of Israel. Pp. 95–128 in *The Zoogeography of Israel*, ed. Y. Yom-Tov and E. Tchernov. Monographiae Biologicae 62. Dordrecht. **Danin, A.** (1985) Paleoclimates in Israel. *BASOR* 259: 33–43. **Dar, S.** (1986) *Landscape and Pattern*. 2 vols. BARInt 308. Oxford. (1992) Samaria (Place): Archaeological Survey of the Region. Trans. M. Erez. *Anchor Bible Dictionary* 5: 926–31. Garden City. **Davis, J.B.** (1982) Availability and Use of Water Resources in Hill Country Villages in Iron Age I. Paper presented at Society of Biblical Literature Southeastern Regional meeting, March, 1982. (1984) *Hill Country Village Subsistence Strategy in the Period of the Judges*. Ph.D. diss., Southern Baptist Theological Seminary, Louisville, Ky. **Falconer, S.E.** (1987) *The Heartland of Villages*. Ph.D. diss., University of Arizona, Tucson. **Feinman, G.M., and L.M. Nicholas** (1990) Settlement and Land Use in Ancient Oaxaca. Pp. 71–114 in *Debating Oaxaca Archaeology*, ed. J. Marcus. University of Michigan Museum of Anthropology Papers 84. Ann Arbor, Mich. **Finkelstein, I.** (1985) *Izbet Sartah*. BAR International Series 299. Oxford. (1988) *The Archaeology of the Israelite Settlement*. Jerusalem. (1988–89) The Land of Ephraim Survey 1980–87, Preliminary Report. *TA* 15–16: 117–83. (1992) Ephraim (Archaeology). *Anchor Bible Dictionary* 2: 551–55. Garden City. (1995) The Great Transformation. Pp. 349–65 in *The Archaeology of Society in the Holy Land*, ed. T. Levy. London. (1996) The Emergence of the Monarchy in Israel. Pp. 377–403 in Carter and Meyers, 1996. **Finkelstein, I., S. Bunimovitz, and Z. Lederman, eds.** (1993) *Shiloh: The Archaeology of a Biblical Site*. Tel Aviv. **Flanagan, J.** (1988) *David's Social Drama*. JSOTSup 129. Sheffield. **Foxhall, L., and Forbes, H.A.** (1982) Sitrometreia. *Chiron* 12: 41–62. **Frankel, R.** (1997) Olives. *Oxford Encyclopaedia* *of the Ancient Near East* 4: 179–84. **Frick, F.** (1985) *The Formation of the State in Ancient Israel*. The Social World of Biblical Antiquity 4. Sheffield. (1987) Israelite State Formation in Iron I. Pp. 245–58 in *Archaeology and Biblical Interpretation*, ed. L.G. Perdue, L.E. Toombs, and G.L. Johnson. Atlanta. **Fritz, V.** (1996) *Die Entstehung Israels im 12. und 11. Jh. v. Chr.* Biblische Enzyklopädie 2. Stuttgart. **Gilead, I.** (1992) Farmers and Herders in Southern Israel during the Chalcolithic Period. Pp. 29–41 in Bar-Yosef and Khazanov, 1992. **Glavanis, K.** (1989) Commodization and the Small Peasant Household in Egypt. Pp. 142–62 in *The Rural Middle East*, ed. K. Glavanis and P. Glavanis. Birzeit and London. **Goffer, Z.** (1996) *Elsevier's Dictionary of Archaeological Materials and Archaeometry*. Amsterdam. **Grant, E.** (1921) *The People of Palestine*. Repr., 1976. Westport, Conn. **Harel, M.** (1984) *Journeys and Campaigns in Ancient Times*. Jerusalem. In Hebrew. **Hellwing, S., M. Sadeh, and V. Kishon** (1993) Faunal Remains. Pp. 309–50 in Finkelstein, Bunimovitz, and Lederman, 1993. **Higgs, E.S., and C. Vita-Finzi** (1972) Prehistoric Economies. Pp. 27–36 in *Papers in Economic Prehistory*, ed. E.S. Higgs. British Academy Major Research Project: The Early History of Agriculture. Cambridge. **Hopkins, D.C.** (1983) The Dynamics of Agriculture in Monarchic Israel. *SBLSP* 1983: 177–202. (1985) *The Highlands of Canaan*. Social World of Biblical Antiquity 3. Sheffield. (1997) Agriculture. *Oxford Encyclopaedia of the Ancient Near East* 1: 22–30. **Horowitz, A.** (1974) Preliminary Palynological Indications as to the Climate of Israel during the Last 6000 Years. *Paléorient* 2: 407–14. **Jarman, M.R., C. Vita-Finzi, and E.S. Higgs** (1972) Site Catchment Analysis in Archaeology. Pp. 61–66 in *Man, Settlement, and Urbanism*, ed. P.J. Ucko, R. Tringham, and G.W. Dimbleby. London. **Kislev, M.** (1993) Food Remains. Pp. 354–61 in Finkelstein, Bunimovitz, and Lederman, 1993. **Klippel, W.** (1996) Animal Harvest Profiles and the Archaeological Record. Paper presented at "Workshop on the Practical Impact of Science on Field Archaeology," October, 1996, at The Hebrew University, Jerusalem and Tel-Aviv University, Tel-Aviv. **Liphschitz, N.** (1987–89) The Carob in Israel. *Israel — People and Land* 5/6: 151–54. **Liphschitz, N., G. Biger, and Z. Mendel** (1987–89) Did Aleppo Pine Cover the Mountains of Eretz-Israel in the Past? *Israel — People and Land* 5/6: 141–50. **Lutfiyya, A.M.** (1966) *Baytin, Jordanian Village*. Studies in Social Anthropology 1. New York. **Meyers, C.L.** (1983) Procreation, Production, and Protection. *JAAR* 41: 569–93. = Pp. 489–514 in Carter and Meyers, 1996. **Miller, N.F.** (1997) Viticulture. *Oxford Encyclopaedia of the Ancient Near East* 5: 304–6. **Moors, A.** (1989) Gender Hierarchy in a Palestinian Village. Pp. 195–209 in *The Rural Middle East*, ed. K. Glavanis and P. Glavanis. Birzeit and London. **Peebles, C.S.** (1978) Determinants of Settlement Size and Location in the Moundville Phase. Pp. 369–416 in *Mississippian Settlement Patterns*, ed. B.D. Smith. Studies in Archaeology 27. New York. **Quézel, P.** (1981) The Study of Plant Groupings in the Countries Surrounding the Mediterranean. Pp. 87– 93 in di Castri, *et al.*, 1981. **Rabinovitch-Vin, A.** (1983) Influence of Nutrients on the Composition and Distribution of Plant Communities in Mediterranean-Type Ecosystems of Israel. Pp. 74–85 in *Mediterranean-Type Ecosystems*, ed. F.J. Kruger, D.T.

Mitchell, and J.U.M. Jarvis. Ecological Studies 43. Berlin. **Rosen, S.** (1993) Economy and Subsistence. Pp. 362–70 in Finkelstein, Bunimovitz, and Lederman, 1993. (1994) Subsistence Economy in Iron Age I. Pp. 337–51 in *From Nomadism to Monarchy*, ed. I. Finkelstein and N. Na'aman. Washington. **Said, M.** (1974) Letter to E.F. Campbell, Jr. Albright Institute of Archaeological Research Archives, Jerusalem. Used by permission. **Stager, L.E.** (1990) Shemer's Estate. *BASOR* 277/278: 93–107. **Stanhill, G.** (1978) The Fellah's Farm. *Agro-Ecosystems* 4: 433–48. **Steward, D., and P.J. Webber** (1981) The Plant Communities and Their Environments. Pp. 43–68 in *Resource Use by Chaparral and Matarral*, ed. P.C. Miller. Ecological Studies 39. Berlin. **Sweet, L.E.** (1957) *Tell Toqaan*. Ph.D. diss., The University of Michigan, Ann Arbor, Mich. **Tappy, R.** (1992) *The Archaeology of Israelite Samaria*. Vol. 1. Harvard Semitic Studies 44. Atlanta, Ga. **Tomaselli, R.** (1981) Main Physiognomic Types and Geographic Distribution of Shrub Systems Related to Mediterranean Climates. Pp. 95–106 in di Castri, *et al.*, 1981. **Turkowski, L.** (1969) Peasant Agriculture in the Judaean Hills. *PEQ* 101: 21–33, 101–13. **Van Zeist, W.** (1985) Past and Present Environments of the Jordan Valley. *Studies in the History and Archaeology of Jordan* 2: 199–204. **Vita-Finzi, C.** (1978) *Archaeological Sites in their Settings*. Ancient Peoples and Places 90. London. **Vita-Finzi, C., and E.S. Higgs** (1970) Prehistoric Economy in the Mount Carmel Area of Palestine. *Proceedings of the Prehistory Society* 36: 1–31. **Webley, D.** (1972) Soils and Site Location in Pre-historic Palestine. Pp. 169–80 in *Papers in Economic Prehistory*, ed. E.S. Higgs. British Academy Major Research Project: The Early History of Agriculture. Cambridge. **Wolf, E.R.** (1966) *Peasants*. Foundations of Modern Anthropology 10. Englewood Cliffs, N.J. **Wright, G.R.H.** (1997) Building Materials and Techniques: Bronze and Iron Ages. *Oxford Encyclopaedia of the Ancient Near East* 1: 363–67. **Zaitschek, D.V.** (1955) Remains of Cultivated Plants from Afula. *Atiqot* (English Series) 1: 71–74. **Zertal, A.** (1987) The Cultivation and Economics of Olives during the Iron Age in the Hill Country of Manasseh. Pp. 196–203 in *Olive Oil in Antiquity*, ed. M. Helter and D. Eitam. Haifa. (1991) Israel Enters Canaan. *BAR* 17(5): 28–49. (1996) *The Manasseh Hill Country Survey*. Vol. 2. (The Eastern Valleys and the Fringes of the Desert). Haifa. In Hebrew. **Zohary, M.** (1962) *Plant Life of Palestine*. Chronica Botanica New Series of Plant Science Books 33. New York. (1966–86) *Flora Palaestina*. 4 vols. Jerusalem. **Zorn, J.** (1993) *Tell en-Nasbeh*. 4 vols. Ph.D. diss., Pacific School of Religion, Berkeley.

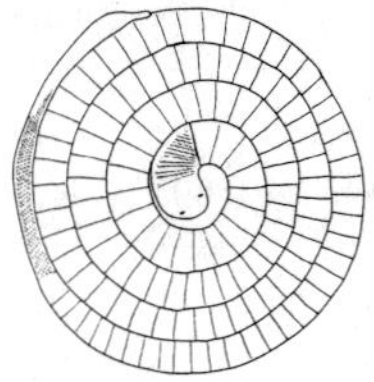

ARCHAEOLOGICAL REMAINS OF EVERYDAY ACTIVITIES

GROUND STONE TOOLS IN BRONZE AND IRON AGE PALESTINE

Jennie R. Ebeling
University of Evansville

Many artifacts represented in the archaeological record of the ancient Near East were used by its inhabitants on a daily basis. Grinding slabs, querns, handstones, mortars, pestles, palettes, pounders, and other stone objects belong to one class of such artifacts: ground stone tools. The earliest evidence for the use of ground stone tools in this region is seen in prehistoric archaeological assemblages, and ethnographic studies have documented their use in traditional Middle Eastern societies through the twentieth century. Ground stone tools play an import ant role in food processing and preparation, among other activities, and thus were critical for the daily subsistence of those who used them in antiquity.

The unchanging nature of ground stone tools excavated from sites in Palestine makes it a particularly interesting assemblage for study, as there are several lines of evidence that can be used to reconstruct grinding and pounding activities in the past in this region. This paper presents an overview of ground stone material excavated at sites in ancient Palestine and focuses specifically on Bronze and Iron Age (*ca.* 3000–586 BCE) material excavated from sites in modern Israel and the Palestinian Authority. A brief history of research of ground stone tools will highlight some recent developments in ground stone artifact analysis, and demonstrate the potential analytical techniques have for increasing our understanding of stone tool use in antiquity. Using examples of some of the more common tool types excavated from Bronze and Iron Age strata—grinding slabs and querns, handstones, mortars and bowls, and pestles—I will demonstrate how ethnographic, iconographic, and textual information can be used to help clarify the functions of these important implements in the different contexts in which they are found in archaeological excavations in Palestine.

DEFINITIONS AND HISTORY OF RESEARCH

Ground stone tools have been defined by J.L. Adams, an archaeologist working in the American Southwest, as "artifacts that are either altered by or used to alter other items through abrasion, polishing, or pecking."[1] Artifacts in this category include:

1. Artifacts used to reduce intermediate substances to a finer texture; for example, handstones, grinding slabs, mortars, and pestles, which are used to process agricultural products, pigments, clays, and tempers.
2. Artifacts used to shape other artifacts; for example, abraders, polishing stones, and hammerstones.
3. Artifacts shaped by abrasion, polishing or pecking; for example, axes, figurines, personal ornaments, and architectural pieces.[2]

Grinding technology requires a combination of knowledge, ideas, behavior, and equipment to solve problems involved in altering substances or surfaces. This is accomplished through the interaction of mechanical and chemical processes that occur when stone surfaces come into contact.[3] Understanding these technological processes involves consideration of how an artifact was designed and manufactured; an assessment of the artifact using various analytical techniques; and investigation into the archaeological context in which the object was found.[4]

The scientific investigation of ground stone artifacts is a relatively recent phenomenon the world over. Reasons for the neglect of ground stone tools from archaeological contexts are varied, although the following statement describing the situation in the American Southwest holds true for other parts of the world, including Palestine, as well:

> the analysis of ground stone artifacts has largely been neglected because they are associated with the mundane task of processing plant foods and because researchers have assumed that the uses of ground stone tools are known and well understood.[5]

Recent studies of ground stone tools have shown, however, just how much we do not know about the uses of these artifacts in the past. Use-wear and residue analyses are just two of the methods researchers working in various parts of the world have used to learn more about ground stone

---

1 Adams (1996) 2.

2 Ibid.

3 Adams (1993, 1996).

4 Adams (1996) 2.

5 Fratt and Adams (1993) 313.

tools from archaeological contexts. These studies have the potential to reveal the diverse functions of certain stone tool forms, and suggest directions future studies can take to add to our knowledge of this ancient technology.

Analyzing stone tool surfaces for evidence of use has been the focus of a number of stone tool specialists in the recent past. Such use-wear analyses allow for an understanding of ground stone tool use that goes beyond the oversimplified *form = function* equations typical of older studies. Replicative experiments have shown that processing different materials using ground stone tools produces unique wear patterns that can be identified macroscopically and microscopically.[6] J.L. Adams noticed this phenomenon when she examined the surfaces of nearly identical-looking handstones (*manos*) used for a variety of activities at the Hopi village of Walpi, in Arizona. Through a series of experiments, she was able to demonstrate how grinding soft and pliable material (in this case, animal hide) produced wear patterns distinct from those produced by grinding harder material (corn).[7] Such experimental studies allow for the creation of a baseline with which archaeological ground stone from many different contexts can be compared.

So too, analyzing organic residues on artifacts can identify organic materials processed and stored using these implements. Archaeological ceramics have been the focus of a number of residue analyses in recent years; material from the Near East and Aegean have tested positive for remains of olive oil, wine, and other substances.[8] In Palestine, the remains of opium and olive oil were detected on a sherd from a juglet found at Tel el-Ajjul (in modern Gaza) and on a sherd of unknown provenience.[9] Residue analyses performed on lithics (chipped and flaked stone tools) from archaeological sites around the world have identified remains of plants processed and animals butchered using these ancient tools.[10]

Fewer residue analyses have been performed on ground stone tools, but artifacts that have been tested suggest the potential such analyses have for our understanding of stone tool use in antiquity. Pollen samples removed from ground stone implements in the American Southwest record

---

6 Adams (1988, 1993); M.K. Wright (1993).

7 Adams (1988).

8 E.g., Badler, McGovern, and Michel (1990); Beck, Smart, and Ossenkop (1989).

9 Merrillees (1989).

10 E.g., Anderson (1980); Hyland et al. (1990); Loy and Wood (1989); Sobolik (1996).

the variety of wild plant foods processed in addition to cereals.[11] Starch grains from tuberous plants, which are notoriously elusive in the archaeological record, have been detected on grinding stones from Egypt[12] and Central America.[13] Prompted by earlier immunological analyses and numerous ethnographic accounts of the processing of animal bones and flesh in mortars and basins, researchers identified blood residues on ground stone artifacts from two archaeological sites in southern California.[14] These studies reveal the diversity of materials processed using this multi-functional equipment.

Although some of these methods have been used to analyze archaeological material from ancient Palestine, none of them has yet been methodically employed in analyses of ground stone tools from the Bronze and Iron Ages. Adopting these and other methods for use on materials from the ancient Near East can contribute greatly to our understanding of the function of this equipment in antiquity and can be used to answer specific questions about human activities in the past. The following summary of ground stone tool use in Palestine from its earliest appearance in prehistoric strata presents what we do know and suggests what we do not know about the function of these ubiquitous artifacts.

Ancient Palestine

In ancient Palestine, the earliest remains of ground stone artifacts have been found in Upper Paleolithic contexts (*ca.* 45,000–22,000 b.p.). Early in the Upper Paleolithic, small portable handstones and grinding slabs appear, many with remains of ochre.[15] Ground stone tools become more numerous in Natufian assemblages (*ca.* 12,000–10,500 b.p.). During this period a type of large, deep mortar, sometimes reaching two feet in height, appears in greater numbers; these were likely used to loosen the husks of wild cereals through pounding with a stone or wooden pestle, or used to process nuts and similarly hard substances. The increase in variety and number of plant-processing tools in the Natufian Period coincides with intensive foraging and increasing sedentism in the Levant.[16]

---

11 Greenwald (1993).

12 Jones (1989).

13 Piperno and Holst (1998).

14 Yohe, Newman, and Schneider (1991).

15 K.I. Wright (1991) 22.

16 K.I. Wright (1993) 105.

There has been great interest among prehistorians in ground stone artifacts from the Neolithic Period (*ca.* 8000–4500 BCE), when grinding implements are found in contexts of early plant domestication and permanent settlements. Excavation reports of prehistoric sites include chapters and even volumes on the ground stone artifacts uncovered in Neolithic strata.[17] An increase in the numbers of grinding tools found in Neolithic settlements corroborates the botanical evidence for the transition from foraging to farming during this period of plant domestication in the Levant.[18]

Several studies have focused on ground stone artifacts that date to the succeeding Chalcolithic and Early Bronze I periods in Palestine (*ca.* 4700–3000 BCE). These reports have focused largely on characteristic stone vessels, or mortars, which are well carved, sometimes decorated, and widespread in Chalcolithic and Early Bronze I contexts.[19] Also notable are larger basalt basins found in houses at Chalcolithic sites in the Golan Heights—the excavator suggests that they were used to process olives to make olive oil.[20] The presence of carbonized olive wood and olive pits in a number of Chalcolithic houses may support this theory, which would make this the earliest archaeological evidence for olive oil processing in Palestine.

Less is known about the ground stone assemblages of the remaining Early, Middle, and Late Bronze Ages and the Iron Age in Palestine. This is due not to the lack of such artifacts, as they are pervasive in excavations with Bronze and Iron Age remains. Although specialists in pottery, lithics, glass, and other classes of material culture have long focused on artifacts excavated from these contexts, there have emerged no real specialists in the analysis of ground stone objects from the "historic periods." As a result, there are no comprehensive studies of grinding implements from the Bronze and Iron Ages, no standard terminology for discussing them, no consistently used typology of tool forms, and no standards for published illustrations of ground stone artifacts in site reports.

The fundamental problem is the unsatisfactory way in which these artifacts are collected during the course of excavation; many archaeologists are guilty of leaving these heavy, awkward objects in the field, making

---

17 E.g., Gopher and Orrelle (1995).

18 See K.I. Wright (1991, 1993, 1994) and references therein for ground stone tools in the Levant through the Neolithic Period.

19 Amiran and Porat (1984); Braun (1990); Rowan (1998).

20 Epstein (1993) 135–35.

proper documentation, analysis, and publication impossible. Ground stone artifact collection in the field often falls victim to what S. Rosen, a lithics specialist, calls the "pretty piece syndrome," wherein poorly preserved or unidentifiable artifacts are overlooked in favor of complete, well-made, and decorated items.[21] Incomplete artifact collection results in weak ground stone reports, hinders inter-site assemblage comparisons, and renders difficult the possibility of using this data to answer specific questions about activities related to food processing during this important period.

A small number of ground stone studies (small in relation to studies of other artifact classes) focusing on ground stone assemblages that include Bronze and Iron Age material have appeared in excavation reports in recent years.[22] Many of these reports present the material in catalogue form along with other "small finds," and most, but not all, view ground stone tool morphology as the sole means of identifying function. Although these publications of often overlooked material are commendable, they are all site specific and suffer from the excavation and publication problems mentioned above.

The situation need not continue, however. The analytical methods described above can certainly be adapted to analyze comparable material in Palestine from the periods in question. Palestine and other regions in the ancient Near East are fortunate to have iconographic and textual sources describing numerous aspects of daily life, and this material can be used critically to shed further light on the function of the archaeological material. In addition, ethnographic accounts of ground stone tool use among inhabitants of Palestine in the twentieth century can help us better understand how similar implements were used in antiquity. Using these available sources, along with the scientific methods, one can reasonably reconstruct a number of aspects of this important technology.

The remainder of this paper presents an overview of some of the typical ground stone tools used in Bronze and Iron Age Palestine, using ethnographic, iconographic, and textual information to complement the picture presented by the published archaeological data. This brief review will demonstrate the diversity of stone tool use during this period and suggest ways by which future investigators might endeavor to learn more about these pervasive artifacts. In order to encourage the use of a consistent classi-

---

21 Rosen (1997) 37.

22 Ben-Tor (1987) [Tel Qiri]; Brandl (1993) [Shiloh]; Hovers (1996) [City of David, Jerusalem]; Milevski (1998) [Manaḥat, Jerusalem]; Sass (2000) [Megiddo]; Singer-Avitz (1989) [Tel Michal].

fication system and typology of Bronze and Iron Age ground stone tools, I adopt K.I. Wright's system,[23] which was developed for prehistoric assemblages in the Levant but is useful for later assemblages with some alterations and additions.

Ground Stone Tools from the Bronze and Iron Ages

Grinding Slabs, Querns, and Handstones

Known in the literature by such terms as grinding slabs, lower grinding stones, querns, saddle querns, and millstones, these implements comprise the lower, stationary half of the primary set of ground stone tools used to process agricultural materials in Bronze and Iron Age Palestine. Grinding slabs are formally differentiated from querns by the shape of their grinding surfaces; grinding slabs have a rectangular grinding surface, which indicates linear grinding motion, while querns have an oval grinding area, indicating rotary grinding.[24] Both types probably served the same general function of processing agricultural products in relatively small quantities (but see below).

The upper, hand-held components of this grinding toolkit are usually called handstones, grinders, or rubbers in the literature. Handstones appear in various shapes and sizes in the Bronze and Iron Ages, although the hand-sized "loaf"-shaped handstone seems most typical. Some handstones are nearly as long as the width of the grinding slab with which they were used, indicating operation with two hands. Others are smaller in length and were controlled with either one or both hands. It appears that the general form of grinding slabs, querns, and handstones remained essentially unchanged since their earliest appearance in the archaeological sequence of Palestine, although chronological changes in morphology might be noticed in the future with further publication and analysis.

Grinding slabs and querns are typically made of the vesicular basalt native to the Galilee, Golan Heights, and parts of modern Syria and Jordan. Experiments have shown that vesicular basalt has self-sharpening properties that make it effective for grinding hard substances. Thus they are less frequently made of other locally available materials, like flint, limestone, beachrock and sandstone, as these materials need to be pecked or deliberately roughened to create a good grinding surface. Handstones were usually made of finer-grained basalt, although examples made of limestone and other materials are known. It appears that non-vesicular hand-

---

23 K.I. Wright (1992).

24 K.I. Wright (1992) 63.

stones are preferable in grinding activities as there are few or no vesicles in the surface of the stone in which material being ground might get clogged and slow down the grinding process.

Grinding slabs and querns were operated in a sitting, kneeling, or standing position. The kneeling position is depicted in numerous "Egyptian servant statues" from Old Kingdom Egypt that show women grinding on slabs set on the floor.[25] Egyptian models and paintings provide some of the best sources of information available for agricultural practices and domestic activities common during the Pharaonic period. Several archaeological publications of sites in Palestine provide photographs of local inhabitants or excavation participants familiar with traditional grinding equipment operating the excavated stone artifacts in either a sitting[26] or kneeling[27] position. In the Western Palace at Ebla, grinding rooms were found with their grinding equipment intact and set into platforms close to the ground.[28] Although nothing in this state of preservation has yet been uncovered in Palestine, it is possible that similar rooms were in operation in the Bronze Age palaces in this area as well.

These implements were also operated from a standing position, as evidenced by intact grinding platforms excavated in Egypt and Palestine. D. Samuel, in her report on bread-making at Amarna, Egypt, conducted experiments to determine how wheat was ground into flour using typical grinding slabs and handstones from the site. The grinding slab was set into a mudbrick surface angled down and away from the person grinding. As the wheat is ground, the resulting flour is pushed forward to the front of the grinding surface by the motion of the handstone. From there, it was probably swept with a brush to the jar set beneath the grinding installation.[29] A similar quern emplacement operated from a standing position was found in an Iron Age context in Y. Shiloh's excavations in the City of David in Jerusalem; this feature was left in the field as found and can still be seen there today.[30]

Grinding slabs, querns, and handstones were used mainly to grind various grains into flour during the Bronze and Iron Ages. Based on organic remains recovered from archaeological sites and textual informa-

---

25 Breasted (1948).

26 Schumacher (1908) Fig. 81.

27 Yadin (1975) 34.

28 Postgate (1994) Fig. 12:5.

29 Samuel (1989).

30 Hovers (1996) Photo 23.

tion, barley and wheat were among the cereals cultivated in Bronze and Iron Age Palestine.[31] Other agricultural products were likely processed using grinding slabs, querns, and handstones during this period as well. There are ethnographically documented cases of similar implements being use to grind non-organic substances, such as potsherds for temper. Only by examining the damage patterns on the surfaces of this grinding equipment and/or testing it for residues can absolute conclusions about use be made.

These ground stone implements are found in many contexts in Bronze and Iron Age settlements in Palestine. M. Daviau, who has plotted the provenience of ground stone artifacts found in domestic contexts in Bronze Age sites, has shown that grinding tools are indeed found in courtyards, kitchens, and other "domestic" areas.[32] Grinding slabs, querns, and handstones are also found in Middle and Late Bronze Age and Iron Age temple complexes.[33] These tools were likely used to process grain brought to the temple as offerings, or were used by the temple functionaries to process agricultural products for their own consumption.

The Hebrew Bible provides several terms for ground stone artifacts used in everyday domestic activities, and it is apparent from the descriptions that these implements were well known to the biblical writers. The generic term for the grinding equipment pair is *rēḥayim;* according to Deut 24:6, it was forbidden to take away *rēḥayim* in pledge for a debt, as it would amount to taking away a household's means of sustenance. Samson was forced to grind grain, probably using a typical grinding slab/quern and handstone, while imprisoned in Gaza (Judg 16:21). The grinding slab or quern is called a *pelaḥ taḥtīt*, implying its lower, stationary form, whereas the handstone is called *pelaḥ rekeb* (the "rider"). A *pelaḥ rekeb* was responsible for the death of Abimelech when a woman dropped the object closest to her hand on the king's head (Judg 9:53; 2 Sam 11:21). Such anecdotes from the Hebrew Bible reveal some interesting aspects of ground stone tool use during the Iron Age in Palestine, but do not provide detailed descriptions of the form and function of these implements.

Mortars, Bowls, and Pestles

The other main group of processing equipment used in Palestine consists of mortars and pestles, which appear in a variety of shapes and sizes in the Bronze and Iron Ages. "Mortar" is the term given to the lower, stationary

---

31 Borowski (1987) 88–92.

32 Daviau (1993).

33 Mazar (1985) 17–18 [Tel Qasile]; Tufnell, Inge, and Harding (1940) Plate XXIX [Lachish].

component; used in conjunction with a pestle, various materials are pounded, pulverized, and ground into finer textures. They range from small pebble or bowl mortars used to process spices, pigments, medicines, and other materials in small quantities, to standing mortars with deep hollows, to those cut into exposed bedrock. Stone pestles are typically elongated with circular use-surfaces on either one or both of the short ends. Mortars are formally distinguished from stone bowls based on their morphology.[34]

Stone bowls, some of which may also have served as mortars, appear in various forms during this period. Three-legged bowls/mortars, which have three freestanding legs, first appeared during the Middle Bronze Age in Palestine (*ca.* 2000–1550 BCE). Tripod bowls/mortars, which have three outer legs, a leg in the center, and a horizontal central support, are characteristic of Iron Age Phoenician material culture during the tenth century BCE.[35]

Mortars and bowls are made of various types of local and imported stone, although implements made of local limestone and fine-grained basalt seem to be the most typical during the Bronze and Iron Ages. Pestles, like handstones, are made primarily of limestone and fine-grain basalt. In addition to being used with mortars, these pestles were probably used to process materials on grinding slabs, palettes, and other surfaces. Wooden pestles were probably ubiquitous during the Bronze and Iron Ages, as well. Ethnographic accounts around the world document the popularity of wooden pestles used with stone mortars—S. Avitzur relates that the bedouin used wooden pestles with stone mortars in the first half of the twentieth century in Palestine.[36]

Mortars and pestles were used to pound and pulverize various agricultural products in preparation for consumption or further grinding. Certain grains, such as glume wheats and hulled barley, require dehusking with a mortar and pestle before being ground further into flour.[37] Ethnographic accounts describe how mortars and pestles are used to process olives, nuts, fruits, seeds, toxic plants, and other edible products. G. Dalman, in his

---

34 Stone bowls, according to K.I. Wright's definition, must have "(1) a well-defined, uniform rim; (2) a well-defined base; (3) a continuous exterior surface; (4) consistent (or gradually changing) thickness of walls; (5) exterior finishing" (1992) 75.

35 Gal (1994) 21*–23*.

36 Avitzur (1976).

37 Hillman (1984).

unparalleled ethnographic work *Arbeit und Sitte in Palästina*, describes how bedouin in early twentieth-century Palestine used mortars and pestles to crush meat as well as agricultural products.[38]

Mortars, bowls, and pestles are also found in diverse contexts in Bronze and Iron Age strata in Palestine. They are known from a variety of "domestic" contexts in Bronze Age settlements,[39] and many are found in Bronze and Iron Age temples and cult sites in this region as well.[40] Those implements found in sacred contexts were likely used to process small amounts of special materials, such as pigments, for use in temple activities.

Biblical references for the use of mortars and pestles are few. Num 11:8 recounts how the Israelites used mortars, *madakah*, to pound manna during the Exodus from Egypt. Prov 27:22 uses this term for mortar figuratively ("you should crush a fool in a mortar"); another term for this implement, *makhtēsh*, is used descriptively in Judges 15:19 (referring to a "hollow place"). Again, the biblical descriptions do little to inform us about the use of these grinding tools in everyday life.

CONCLUSIONS

When investigating aspects of daily life in the ancient Near East, all available evidence must be consulted in order to present a more complete and accurate picture of the situation in antiquity. In my reading, I have encountered numerous books, articles, and encyclopedia entries on the topic of daily life in the ancient Near East that have focused primarily on the textual material (mainly from the Hebrew Bible) for evidence. Although biblical and extra-biblical texts reveal interesting anecdotal information about the use of ground stone tools in ancient Israel, the vast archaeological, ethnographic and iconographic data reveal information about the functions of these implements that cannot be seen in the textual sources alone. I feel the biblical passages and information from other textual sources should be used to *complement* the other data we are fortunate to have available to us when describing the uses of ground stone tools during the Bronze and Iron Ages.

Ground stone tools provide an excellent opportunity to study a little known, and thus largely uninterpreted, artifact assemblage in ancient Palestine. Analytical methods like use-wear and residue analyses have the

---

38 Dalman (1933).

39 Daviau (1993).

40 Mazar (1985) 17 [Tel Qasile]; Stern (1984) 27 [Tel Mevorakh]; Yadin et al. (1961) plates CCLXX; CCLXXVIII [Hazor].

potential to reveal a great deal about the function of these implements in antiquity, as can the ethnographic, iconographic, and textual information in the current state of our knowledge. The study of these tools also provides a chance to better understand food-processing technologies in antiquity and changes in the human diet through time. With more complete collection, analysis, and publication of excavated ground stone material, future scholars will be able to use these artifacts in a meaningful way to describe aspects of daily life in ancient Canaan and Israel.

Acknowledgments

This paper is based on my presentation at the "Daily Life in the Ancient Near East" conference in February 1999 and on a paper presented at the Annual Meeting of the American Schools of Oriental Research in November 1999. Research of this material was largely conducted in Jerusalem during the 1998–99 academic year, when I was a Fulbright Fellow at the Institute of Archaeology at Hebrew University. I wish to thank the Fulbright Program, as well as friends and colleagues at Hebrew University and the W.F. Albright Institute of Archaeological Research in Jerusalem, for supporting my work during that year. I also thank the Graduate and Professional Student Association at the University of Arizona for partially funding my participation in the "Daily Life" conference, and the Dorot Foundation for generously covering the cost of my attendance of the 1999 Annual Meeting of ASOR. Special thanks also go to the organizers of the "Daily Life" conference, whose kindness afforded me before, during, and after the meeting is greatly appreciated, and to Abby Limmer, Laura Mazow, and Menachem Rogel for reading a draft of this paper. Information included in this paper forms part of my doctoral dissertation for the Department of Near Eastern Studies at the University of Arizona. In the dissertation I focus on the use of ground stone tools and other utilitarian artifacts and installations in the Middle and Late Bronze Age temples in Palestine.

Bibliography

Adams, J.L. (1988) Use-Wear Analyses on Manos and Hide-Processing Stones. *Journal of Field Archaeology* 15/3: 307–15. (1993) Mechanisms of Wear of Ground Stone Surfaces. *Pacific Coast Archaeological Society Quarterly* 29/4: 61–74. (1996) *Manual for a Technological Approach to Ground Stone Analysis.* Tucson. **Amiran, R. and N. Porat** (1984) The Basalt Vessels of the Chalcolithic and Early Bronze Age. *Tel Aviv* 11/1: 11–19. **Anderson, P.** (1980) A Testimony of Prehistoric Tasks: Diagnostic Residues on Stone Tool Working Edges. *World Archaeology* 12/2: 181–94. **Avitzur, S.** (1976) *Man and His Work.* Jerusalem (Hebrew). **Badler, V.R.; P.E. McGovern; and R.H. Michel** (1990) Drink and Be Merry! Infrared Spectroscopy and Ancient Near Eastern Wine. In W.R. Biers and P.E. McGovern, eds., *Organic Contents of Ancient Vessels: Materials Analysis and Archaeological Investigation,* 25–36. MASCA Research Papers in Science and Archaeology 7. Philadelphia. **Beck, C.W.; C.J. Smart; and D.J. Ossenkop** (1989) Residues and Linings in Ancient Mediterranean Transport Amphoras. In R.O. Allen, ed., *Archaeological Chemistry IV,* 369–80. Advances in Chemistry Series 220. Washington. **Ben-Tor, A.** (1987) The Small Finds. In A. Ben-Tor and Y. Portugali, eds., *Tell Qiri – A Village in the Jezreel Valley* (Qedem 24), 236–43. Jerusalem. **Borowski, O.** (1987) *Agriculture in Iron Age Israel.* Winona Lake, Ind. **Brandl, B.** (1993) Clay, Bone, Metal and Stone Objects. In I. Finkelstein, ed., *Shiloh: The Archaeology of a Biblical Site,* 223–62. Tel Aviv. **Braun, E.** (1990) Basalt Bowls of the EB I Horizon in the Southern Levant. *Paléorient* 16/1: 87–96. **Breasted, J.H.** (1948) *Egyptian Servant Statues.* New York. **Dalman, G.** (1933) *Arbeit und Sitte in Palästina III: Von der Ernte zum Mehl.* Gutersloh. **Daviau, P.M.M.** (1993) *Houses and Their Furnishings in Bronze Age Palestine.* JSOT/ASOR Monograph Series Number 8. Sheffield. **Epstein, C.** (1993) Oil Production in the Golan Heights During the Chalcolithic Period. *Tel Aviv* 20: 133–46. **Fratt, L. and J.L. Adams** (1993) Preface. *Kiva* 58/3: 313–15. **Funk, R.W.** (1962) Mortar. In G.A. Buttrick, ed., *Interpreter's Dictionary of the Bible* 3, 439–40. Nashville, Tenn. **Gal, Z.** (1994) Basalt Tripod-Bowls and Three-Legged Bowls. *Michmanim* 7: 17*–25*. **Gopher, A. and E. Orrelle** (1995) *The Ground Stone Assemblages at Munhata, A Neolithic Site in the Jordan Valley - Israel.* Les Cahiers des Missions Archéologiques Françaises en Israël, no. 7. Publié avec le concours de la Direction Générale des Relations Culturelles, Scientifiques et Techniques du Ministère des Affaires Estrangères. **Greenwald, D.W.** (1993) Ground Stone Artifacts from La Ciudad de los Hornos. In M.L. Chenault, R.V.N. Ahlstrom, and T.N. Motsinger, eds., *In the Shadow of South Mountain: The Pre-Classic Hohokam of La Ciudad de Los Hornos, 1991–1992 Excavations, Part 1,* 317–58. Archaeological Report No. 93–30. Phoenix. **Hillman, G.C.** (1984) Traditional Husbandry and Processing of Archaic Cereals in Recent Times, Part 1: The Glume Wheats. *Bulletin on Sumerian Agriculture* 1: 114–52. **Hovers, E.** (1996) The Groundstone Industry. In A. Belfer-Cohen, A. Mazar, E. Stern, and Y. Tsafrir, eds., *City of David* (Qedem 35), 171–92. Jerusalem. **Hyland, D.C.; J.M. Adovasio; J.M. Tersak; M.I. Siegel; and K.W. Carr** (1990) Identification of the Species of Origin of Residual Blood on Lithic Material. *American Antiquity* 55: 104–12. **Jones, C.E.R.** (1989) Archaeochemistry: Fact or Fancy? In F. Wendorf, R. Schild, and A. Close, eds., *The Prehistory of Wadi Kubbaniya 2,* 260–66. Dallas. **Loy, T.H. and A.R. Wood** (1989) Blood Residue Analysis of Çayönü Tepesi, Turkey. *Journal of Field Archaeology* 16: 451–60. **Mazar, A.** (1985) *Excavations at Tell Qasile, Part II* (Qedem 20). Jerusalem. **Merrillees, R.S. (and J. Evans)** (1989) Highs and Lows in the Holy Land: Opium in Biblical Times. *Eretz Israel* 20: 148*–54*. **Milevski, I.** (1998) The Groundstone Tools. In G. Edelstein, I. Milevski, and S. Aurant, eds., *Villages, Terraces, and Stone Mounds: Excavations at Manaḥat, Jerusalem, 1987–1989*, 61–77. Jerusalem. **Piperno, D.R. and I. Holst** (1998) The Presence of Starch Grains on Prehistoric Stone Tools from the Humid Neotropics: Indications of Early Tuber Use and Agriculture in Panama. *Journal of Archaeological Science* 25: 765–76. **Postgate, J.N.** (1994) *Early Mesopotamia*. London. **Richardson, H.N.** (1962) Mill, Millstone. In G.A. Buttrick, ed., *Interpreter's Dictionary of the Bible* 3, 380–81. Nashville, Tenn. **Rosen, S.A.** (1997) *Lithics After the Stone Age*. Walnut Creek, Calif. **Rowan, Y.M.** (1998) *Ancient Distribution and Deposition of Prestige Objects: Basalt Vessels During Late Prehistory in the Southern Levant*. Unpublished Ph.D. Dissertation, University of Texas at Austin. **Samuel, D.** (1989) Their Staff of Life: Initial Investigations of Ancient Egyptian Bread Baking. In B.J. Kemp, ed., *Amarna Reports V*, 253–90. London. **Sass, B.** (2000) The Small Finds. In I. Finkelstein, D. Ussishkin, and B. Halpern, eds., *Megiddo III: The 1992–1996 Seasons*, 349–423. Tel Aviv. **Schumacher, G.** (1908) *Tell el-Mutesellim I*. Leipzig. **Singer-Avitz, L.** (1989) Stone and Clay Objects. In Z. Herzog et al., eds., *Excavations at Tel Michal, Israel*, 350–60. Minneapolis. **Sobolik, K.D.** (1996) Lithic Organic Residue Analysis: An Example from the Southwestern Archaic. *Journal of Field Archaeology* 23/3: 461–69. **Stern, E.** (1984) *Excavations at Tel Mevorakh (1973–1976), Part Two: The Bronze Age* (Qedem 18). Jerusalem. **Tufnell, O.; C.H. Inge; and L. Harding** (1940) *Lachish II: The Fosse Temple*. London: Oxford University Press. **van der Toorn, K.** (1992) Mill, Millstone. In D.N. Freedman, ed., *Anchor Bible Dictionary* 4, 831–32. New York. **Wright, K.I.** (1991) The Origins and Development of Ground Stone Assemblages in Late Pleistocene Southwest Asia. *Paléorient* 17/1:19–45. (1992) A Classification System for Ground Stone Tools from the Prehistoric Levant. *Paléorient* 18/2: 53–81. (1993) Early Holocene Ground Stone Assemblages in the Levant. *Levant* 25: 93–111. (1994) Ground-Stone Tools and Hunter-Gatherer Subsistence in Southwest Asia: Implications for the Transition to Farming. *American Antiquity* 59/2: 238–63. **Wright, M.K.** (1993) Simulated Use of Experimental Maize Grinding Tools from Southwestern Colorado. *Kiva* 58/3: 345–56. **Yadin, Y.** (1975) *Hazor: The Rediscovery of a Great Citadel of the Bible*. New York. **Yadin, Y.; Y. Aharoni; R. Amiran; T. Dothan; M. Dothan; I. Dunayevsky; and J. Perrot** (1961) *Hazor III–IV, Plates*. Jerusalem. **Yohe, R.M. III; M.E. Newman; and J.S. Schneider** (1991) Immunological Identification of Small-Mammal Proteins on Aboriginal Milling Equipment. *American Antiquity* 56/4: 659–66.

Egypt

EVERYDAY LIFE IN ANCIENT EGYPT

James K. Hoffmeier
Trinity International University

Archaeologists studying the ancient Near East have long been accused of a preoccupation with the lives of the rich and the powerful, the royal and the elite, while ignoring the world of the common folk. It might be thought that Egyptologists, like their counterparts in Western Asia, have been guilty of this same tendency. But many of the pioneers who studied ancient Egypt early on were concerned with "daily life" issues.

Sir J. Gardner Wilkinson spent ten years in Egypt studying tomb scenes from all periods of Egyptian history in preparation for his two-volume work, *The Ancient Egyptians: Their Life and Customs*, which first appeared in 1836. This seminal study dealt with a range of topics, including work and warfare, dress and hairstyles, sports and games, and diet and death. Richly illustrated with woodcut drawings, these volumes were reprinted as recently as 1988.[1]

In 1886 the distinguished Egyptologist Adolf Erman published his *Life in Ancient Egypt*, a study in excess of 500 pages. While Wilkinson's work is somewhat eclectic in nature, Erman's study is structured more logically, beginning with the land, people, and history of Egypt, before considering political and governmental institutions. Beginning with chapter 8, Erman surveys many facets of life in ancient Egypt: "Family Life," "the House, "Dress," "Recreation," "Religion," "Learning," "the Dead," "the Plastic Arts," "Agriculture," "Arts and Crafts," "Traffic and Trade," and "War."

Some areas of Near Eastern studies have only recently begun to address the role and status of women in society; this is not the case for Egyptology. Both Wilkinson and Erman devoted considerable attention to women, due to the prominent role of women in Egyptian tomb reliefs and paintings. This, in turn, has renewed interest in women's studies, resulting in the recent publication of a number of works (see bibliography).

---

1 Wilkinson (1836)

When compared to other regions of the Near East—the Levant, Syria, Anatolia, and Mesopotamia—Egypt has a cornucopia of relevant data. For our analysis of daily life in ancient Egypt we have divided the material into four areas: artistic scenes, models, miscellaneous archaeological remains, and written records.

Some Thoughts on the Egyptian Sources

John Wilson's nearly fifty-year-old statement regarding our knowledge of the people of Egypt at the dawn history still holds true: "For the first three dynasties we know little about the kings, less about the nobility, and practically nothing about the people."[2] We begin to learn about "the people" with the Fourth Dynasty and still more with the Fifth and Sixth Dynasties, as tomb scenes and texts increase in type and number. Without a doubt, tomb art is the most important source available for the investigation of daily life in ancient Egypt. A caveat is in order, however. These scenes, especially those depicting nobility, are often idealized and thus must be viewed with caution. This problem was raised a decade ago by Lisa Manniche, who, regarding "scenes of daily life," declared:

> The generally accepted interpretation that they were indeed scenes of daily life projected into eternity was not entirely satisfactory. They were far too idealized to present a true picture of the way in which inhabitants of Thebes could be expected to behave. Who would go fowling in festive outfit in a minute canoe with wife and children, and who would go hunting for a hippopotamus when the beast had long since disappeared from the area?[3]

Having issued this cautionary note, Manniche concluded that "these remarks apply to many, though not all 'scenes of daily life'."[4] Thus, we should not interpret these scenes naïvely or in an overly literal fashion, but neither should they be cavalierly dismissed. Fortunately, in addition to the scenes, artifacts often corroborate the data provided in the scenes.

Another source for the study of daily life, which provides a degree of corroboration of the scenes, are three-dimensional models. These models portray various trades and occupations and are found in tombs of the elite as early as the Fourth Dynasty. The earliest examples are carved from limestone and, in some cases, painted.[5] In contrast to the Old Kingdom,

---

2 Wilson (1951) 63.

3 Manniche (1987) 30–31.

4 Manniche (1987) 31.

5 Sameh (1964) 40.

during the First Intermediate Period painted scenes in tombs are less frequent. But more complex, painted wooden models appear, often placed on the lids of coffins.[6] Such models continue into the Middle Kingdom. Their function in the tomb was the same as the wall scenes; they tend to replicate their two-dimensional counterparts and thus do not provide us with new information.

The purpose of "daily life scenes" was not to provide glimpses of daily life for future generations or art for art's sake. But, as Richard Wilkinson has recently reminded us, "the role of representational art was closely interwoven with the religious beliefs of the ancient Egyptians and often the one cannot be understood without reference to the other."[7] Given the funerary context of "daily life scenes," the primary purpose was to show the various industries required for supporting the cult of the dead. Thus, certain scenes, such as farming and food production, are often repeated *ad nauseum* and occur in tomb after tomb, over the centuries, without much change.

The tomb was a "monument to the deceased, a medium by means of which he was able to immortalize the most important part of his life," according to Manniche.[8] This explains the appearance of some idiosyncratic elements in a tomb's artistic repertoire. And, it must be remembered, the "daily life" scenes are found in tombs of the elite—the lower social strata could hardly afford such costly burials—and thus these scenes are portrayed through the eyes of the elite. Ancient Egypt was an agrarian society; thus it is no surprise that agricultural scenes of plebeians figure prominently in tomb chapels from the Old Kingdom through the New Kingdom. Those involved in food preparation constituted the majority of the population and, not surprisingly, consisted of the lowest levels of society.

Scribes were also responsible for composing wisdom texts, such as the so-called *Satire of the Trades* and Papyrus Lansing, which ridicule the occupations of the lower classes. Dua-Khety, the author of the *Satire of the Trades*, a wisdom text that probably originated in the Middle Kingdom, has little good to say about those involved in food preparation.

---

6 Hoffmeier (1991) 70.

7 Wilkinson (1992) 9.

8 Manniche (1987) 31.

Farming

"The farmer," Dua-Khety opines, "wails more than guinea fowl; His voice is louder than a raven's; His fingers are swollen and stink to excess."[9] The gardener who carries water on a yoke to irrigate is said to "work himself to death more than all professions."[10] Clearly these were hard workers whose efforts fed the people of Egypt. Dua-Khety is indisputably biased against the uneducated, lower classes. However, his characterizations may well reflect how the elite in Egypt regarded the farmers, fishermen, and fowlers. By way of an ethnographic observation, the *fallaheen* (farmers) of Egypt are still the brunt of jokes by urban dwellers.

All aspects of farming are depicted in tomb chapels up through the New Kingdom. Irrigation was developed early on in Egypt—since rainfall was limited, once the annual inundation had subsided plants would die if not watered. The famous Scorpion mace-head (*ca.* 3100 B.C.) portrays the kings using a wooden hoe to open a channel to bring water to a field, indicating that irrigation practices had already been developed at the dawn of Egyptian history.[11] By the New Kingdom, the *shaduf*, or well sweep, was used to raise water from the Nile or canals into the fields.[12] Only with the introduction of diesel pumps in modern times has this ancient irrigating tool begun to disappear from the Egyptian countryside.

Scenes show farmers sowing seeds from cloth bags,[13] as others wielding wooden hoes and sledge hammers break up the ground to receive the seed (fig. 1).[14] Oxen drawing plows could also be used in conjunction with sowing (figs. 1 and 2).[15] The early Eighteenth-Dynasty tomb of Paheri actually has an example of four men pulling a plow, as another farmer presses the plow's handles down into the soil and his colleague tosses seed into the new furrow (fig. 2).[16] Despite the introduction of copper, and later bronze, the wooden hoe continued in use throughout Pharaonic times.

---

9 Lichtheim (1973) 187.

10 Lichtheim (1973) 187.

11 Spencer (1993) 56.

12 The tomb of Any shows a *shaduf*, with traces of a second one beside the first, irrigating a garden; cf. Davies (1927) pl. XXIX.

13 Naville (1894) pl. III; Davies (1917) pls. XVIII–XIX.

14 Davies (1917) pls. XVIII–XIX.

15 Naville (1894) pl. III; Davies (1917) pls. XVIII–XIX.

16 Naville (1894) pl. III.

Surviving hoes provide us with first-hand evidence of the principal tool of the Egyptian farmer.[17]

Harvesting the grain was a multi-faceted operation, one that is well documented in the pictorial record (figs. 1 and 3).[18] Often all phases, from the harvesting of the grain to the making of bread, are depicted on tomb chapel walls, as in the case of Hetepherakhti from the Fifth Dynasty (fig. 3). Wooden sickles with sharp lithic blades were used by Egyptian farmers from earliest times down to later periods, despite the availability of copper and bronze.[19] A threshing floor was set up in the fields and oxen were driven over the harvested ears to release the grains.[20] During the Old Kingdom, donkeys were occasionally used to thresh grain.[21] Winnowing and sifting were the final operations before the grain was taken away. From the fields, sacks of grain were taken, sometimes on donkey back, to granaries for storage. Workers carried sacks on their shoulders and dumped the grain into the silos. Scribes are ubiquitous in the agricultural scenes, their task being to record the amounts harvested.[22] One of the intricate models

Figure 1.
Norman de Garis Davies, *The Tomb of Nakht at Thebes* (New York: The Metropolitan Museum of Art, 1917) pl. XVIII.

---

17 James (1985) 96.

18 Wilson and Allen (1938) pls. 168–70.

19 Sameh (1964) 34.

20 Naville (1894) pl. III.

21 Sameh (1964) 36–37.

22 In the tomb of Paheri, for instance, a scribe is shown seated on a heap of grain recording figures, while his colleague stands to the left of the heap doing the same thing (cf. fig. 2).

from the tomb of Meket-Re portrays the entire process, while in an adjoining room a number of scribes squat on the floor, entering the amounts into their logs.[23]

From these grains, mainly barley and emmer, bread and beer were produced, staples of the Egyptian diet in all periods. Indeed, from earliest times, bread and beer are always mentioned in offering formulae on offering stelae and tombs. The Hetepherakhti reliefs depict harvest and bakery operations adjacent to each other (fig. 3). Workers are portrayed grinding the grain into flour (with querns and a mortar and pestle), kneading the dough (middle register), shaping the loaves, and tending the baking oven. An intriguing human touch in the Hetepherakhti scene is the portrayal of a worker minding the oven; he shields his face from the heat of the fire (fig. 3; middle register, right side)—a reminder of the unpleasantness of their work. The Meket-Re cache includes a model of a bakery and brewery operating side-by-side.[24]

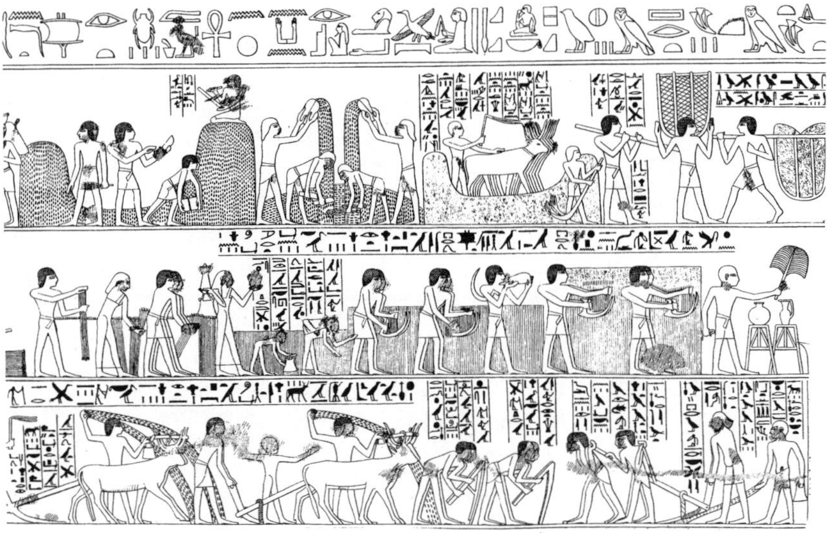

Figure 2.
Edouard Naville, *The Tomb of Paheri at El Kab* (London: Egypt Exploration Fund, 1894) pl. III.

23 Winlock (1955) fig. 20.

24 Winlock (1955) figs. 22–23.

Figure 3.
The Hetepherakhti Reliefs
(with permission of the Rijksmuseum, Leiden)

Fowling and Fishing

Egypt was blessed with a wide variety of native birds, as well as those that passed through Egypt during the annual migrations.[25] Ducks and geese were valued for their eggs and meat. Roast ducks are frequently depicted in offering scenes in all periods. As early as the Fourth Dynasty tomb of Queen Meresankh at Giza, fowlers are shown with clap nets trying to capture various waterfowl.[26] According to Dua-Khety, the fowler is said to "suffer much as he watches for birds."[27] Despite this disparaging remark, fowling with a clap net was also considered a sport. High-ranking officials, such as the Twelfth Dynasty nomarch Khnumhotep III at Beni Hasan[28] and Djehuty-hotep at Bersheh[29] are shown seated on a chair behind a blind as they tug on a rope that will snap the clap net shut, thus entrapping the birds (fig. 4). Clearly fowling had become a gentleman's sport by the Middle Kingdom.

Figure 4.
P.F. Newberry, *Beni Hasan* I
(London: Egypt Exploration Fund, 1893) pl. XXXIII.

25 Houlihan (1986).

26 Dunham and Simpson (1974) fig. 4.

27 Lichtheim (1976) 189.

28 Newberry (1893) pl. XXXIII.

29 Newberry (1895) pl. XVII.

The Nile provided Egyptians with many varieties of fish,[30] a major source of protein. Consequently, fishing was an important industry from earliest times. Fish bones, scales, and lithic hooks have been found in Paleolithic and Neolithic contexts.[31] Fishing with harpoons and spears is also attested in Pre-dynastic times throughout Egypt.[32] Also fish nets were used in Pre-dynastic times as evidenced by the discovery of a complete net at el-Omari.[33] The earliest scene depicting the use of a seine (drag) net is found on the tomb of Rahotep at Meidum, from early in the Fourth Dynasty.[34] This net required only three fishermen. Large dragnets that required teams of workers—as many as twenty-eight men—some utilizing harness straps to aid in pulling, were widely used in the Old Kingdom. Classic examples of this are carved in the mastabas of Princess Idut of the Fifth Dynasty and Mererruka of the Sixth Dynasty, where two different scenes are recorded. Teams of men—eighteen men (plus a foreman) in one scene and twenty-three in the other—are shown hauling in nets.[35] Such operations are also witnessed on a smaller scale in the Middle Kingdom (fig. 5). A model in the tomb of Meketre of the Eleventh Dynasty shows two

Figure 5.
P.E. Newberry, *Beni Hasan* I
(London: Egypt Exploration Fund, 1893) pl. XII.

30 Freidman and Brewer (1989).

31 Hoffman (1984) 75–77, 83, 176–77, 186, 188, 100–2.

32 Freidman and Brewer (1989) 21–22.

33 Freidman and Brewer (1989) 38.

34 Freidman and Brewer (1989) 38.

35 Wilson and Allen (1938) I, pls. 43 and 55.

boats pulling a seine net between them.[36] This system continued to be used into the New Kingdom.[37]

Professional fishermen operated in the marshy regions as well as in the dangerous waters of the Nile (owing to the presence of crocodiles). This reality is reflected by Dua-Khety: "I'll speak of the fisherman also, His is the worst of all jobs; He labors on the river, mingling with crocodiles."[38] While such fishermen provided most of the fish eaten by Egyptians, nevertheless, fishing was also considered a sport. Down through the New Kingdom, nomarchs and nobles were frequently shown on papyrus skiffs spear fishing in the marshes (fig. 6).[39] The tomb of Vizier Mereruka (Sixth Dynasty) contains such scenes.[40] This type of scene remained extremely popular in the Middle Kingdom, as witnessed in the tombs of Senbi and Ukh-hotep at Meir[41] and Khnumhotep at Beni Hasan.[42] The New Kingdom saw a continuation of this sport to judge from the frequency with which this motif is found in the tombs of noblemen.[43]

Although the fishing hook was known in Pre-dynastic times, during the Old Kingdom fishermen used only a line, often with multiple hooks. The fishing rod does not make its appearance in tomb scenes until the Middle Kingdom, and then continues into the New Kingdom (fig. 7).[44] The fact that the nobility of the New Kingdom fish with rods indicates that what had earlier been the tool of the lower class became the toy of the elite.[45]

Artisans and Craftsmen

Artisans played a significant role in making various utensils for domestic, temple, and funerary use. Dua-Khety's writings do not exclude craftsmen. However, these jobs were probably not as demeaning as the scribes would

---

36 Winlock (1955) fig. 52.

37 Davies (1927) pls. XXX, XXXIa, and XXXV.

38 Lichtheim (1973) 189.

39 Wilson and Allen (1938) I, pl. 9.

40 Wilson and Allen (1938) II, pl. 128.

41 Blackman (1914) pl. II; (1953) pl. XIII.

42 Newberry (1893) pl. XXXIV.

43 Manniche (1987) 36

44 Newberry (1893) pl. XXXIX; Freidman and Brewer (1989) 29–31. In the Beni Hasan scene (our Figure 6), one fisherman is shown with a rod and the other with just a line and hook.

45 Freidman and Brewer (1989) 30.

Figure 6.
P.E. Newberry, *Beni Hasan* I
(London: Egypt Exploration Fund, 1893) pl. XXXXIII.

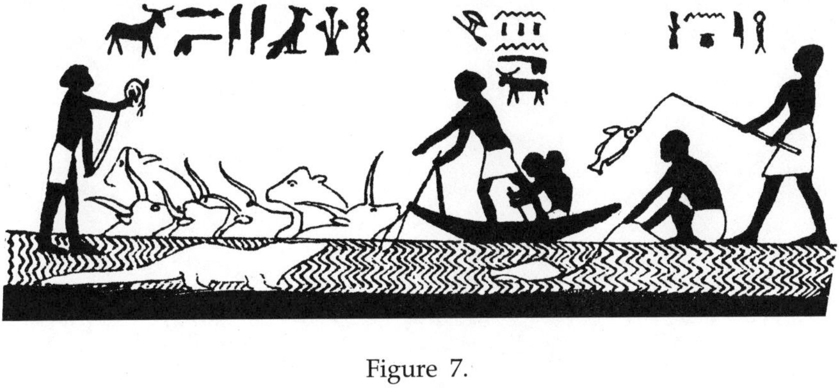

Figure 7.
P.E. Newberry, *Beni Hasan* I
(London: Egypt Exploration Fund, 1893) pl. XIX.

claim. It must be remembered that most of the New Kingdom scenes show the ablest of workers in workshops attached to temples or the royal palace. In the tomb of the vizier Rekhmire, who served under Thutmose III, we see that these workers operated under the oversight of the vizier himself. T.G.H. James points out that such scenes represent the very best workshops in Egypt,[46] and thus would seem to employ the most skilled workers, who probably received better treatment and pay. Clearly the artisans who worked for the temple and palace establishments would have been comparable to "blue collar" workers of the present day.

METALWORKERS

Metalworkers in the heat of Egypt must have suffered under difficult work conditions, a point not missed in the *Satire*: "The [stoker], his fingers are foul, their smell is that of corpses; his eyes are inflamed by much smoke."[47] The tomb of Mereruka shows metalworkers toiling over a fire, blowing on tubes to stoke the fire for melting gold and silver in order to produce electrum (*d̲ᶜm*), and then pouring the molten mass into molds (fig. 8).[48] Below this register, dwarfs are making jewelry. The smiths who worked in silver and gold were not only highly skilled craftsmen, but were probably better paid and at "the top end of the social scale," according to James.[49] Dua-Khety's description seems more fitting for copper and bronze workers.

In a Middle Kingdom scene, metalworkers are blowing through a tube to stoke a fire in a metalworking setting.[50] By the New Kingdom, however, some advancements in smelting techniques had occurred as is found in the tombs of Rekhmire and Nebamun and Ipuky in the Theban Necropolis.[51] Here, the metalworkers use foot bellows to heat the fire (fig. 9). Despite this advancement, the older mouth blowing technique is still found in the New Kingdom (fig. 10).[52]

---

46 James (1985) 182.

47 Lichtheim (1973) 186.

48 Wilson and Allen (1938) I, pl. 30

49 James (1985) 189.

50 Newberry (1893) pl. XI; Davies (1925) pl. XI.

51 Davies (1935) pl. LII, Davies (1925) pl. XI.

52 Davies (1925) pl. XI; (1922) pl. XXIII.

Figure 8.
John A. Wilson and Thomas C. Allen, eds., *The Mastaba of Mereruka* II
(Chicago: The University of Chicago Press) pl. XXX.

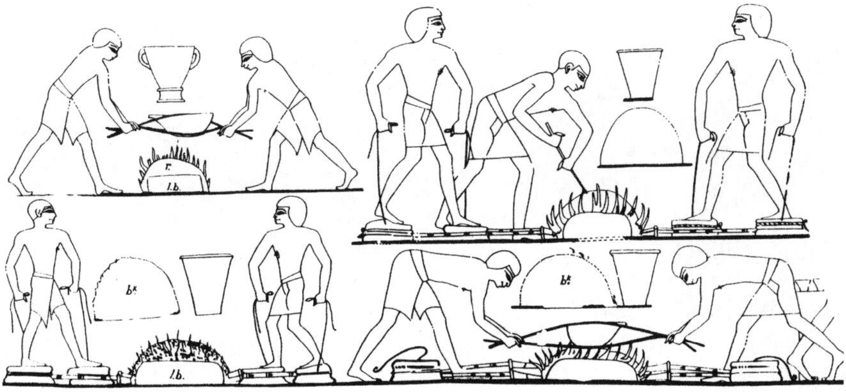

Figure 9.
Norman de Garis Davies, *The Tomb of Rekhmire*
(New York: The Metropolitan Museum of Art, 1935) pl. XI.

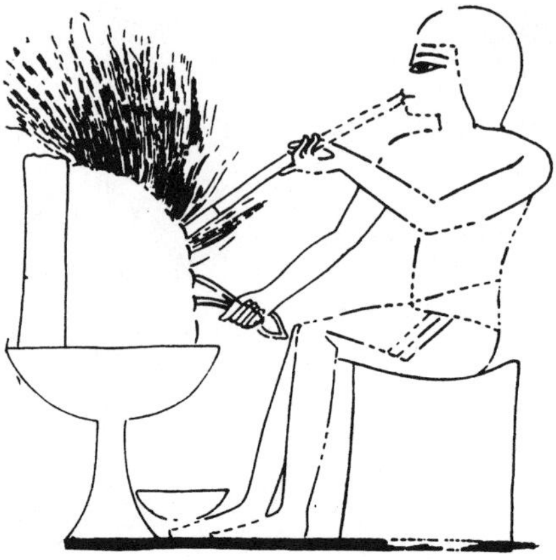

Figure 10.
Norman de Garis Davies, *The Tomb of Two Sculptors at Thebes* (New York: The Metropolitan Museum of Art, 1925) pl. XI.

POTTERS

From Neolithic times to the present day, ceramic vessels played an important role in the domestic life of the Egyptians, and the study of pottery by archaeologists serves as one of the chief mediums for understanding ancient culture. Because of the dirty nature of pottery-making, the Egyptian scribes derided the potters task: "The potter is under the soil, though as yet among the living; he grubs in the mud more than a pig in order to fire his pots. His clothes are stiff with clay."[53] Papyrus Lansing offers a similar assessment: "The maker of pots is smeared with soil, like one whose relations have died. His hands, his feet are full of clay; he is like one who lives in the bog." Workshop scenes from tombs depict the potter and his assistants at work. In the tomb of Amenemhet at Beni Hasan, four different potters are seated before a hand-turned wheel as they fashion a vessel (fig. 11).[54] In front of each potter is a small mound of clay. One worker (in front of the third potter from the right) is bending over while mixing clay, preparing it for the potter. Two different kilns are represented. Before the kiln on the left, a worker sits stoking the fire. The second kiln is

---

53 Lichtheim (1973) 186.

54 Newberry (1893) pl. XI.

Figure 11.
P.E. Newberry, *Beni Hasan* I
(London: Egypt Exploration Fund, 1893) pl. XI.

being unloaded, with one man climbing on the outside in order to remove the pots from the top, while handing a vessel to a second worker. Subsequently, another worker is shown carrying away two loads of vessels with the help of a yoke over his shoulder.

The work of the potter involved creativity and skill, however, the work of the attendants—mixing clay, loading and unloading the kiln, gathering fuel and maintaining the fire of the kiln, and carrying pots around—was difficult indeed.

CARPENTERS

Because Egypt was deprived of good quality timber, it imported various coniferous woods from Lebanon and hard woods, such as mahogany and ebony, from sub-Saharan Africa.[55] Between the higher-quality imported woods and local sycamore, Egyptian carpenters were kept busy from the Early Dynastic period on, fashioning coffins, furniture, boxes, and the like. The first step was to rip the timber to make planks and boards. Copper-toothed saws were used for this operation in Early Dynastic times (fig. 12).[56] A piece of timber was strapped to a post in the ground that served as a vise for steadying the timber during the ripping procedure.[57] In addition to producing furnishings, carpenters built boats, using the very same tools. The Sixth Dynasty mastaba of Mereruka shows carpenters busily making a boat, using hammers, a chisel, and adzes.[58] The writer of

55 Tribute scenes form the Eighteenth Dynasty frequently show Africans carrying logs of ebony and mahogany, e.g., Davies (1922) pl. XXIII.

56 Petrie (1917) 44; Moores (1991) 139–48.

57 Davies (1925) pl. XI. See also the carpenter's shop model of Meket-Re in Winlock (1955) pls. 28–29.

58 Wilson and Allen (1938) II, 152.

Papyrus Lansing commented on the hard work of the shipbuilders: "The carpenter who is in the shipyard carries the timber and stacks it. If he gives today the output of yesterday, woe to his limbs!"[59] Dua-Khety also speaks of the hard work demanded of the carpenter: "The carpenter who wields an adze, he is wearier than a field-laborer."[60] Nevertheless, carpenters worked on more intricate objects such as chariots, composite bows, and fine furniture. It would appear that such high-quality artisans were valued by their masters and remunerated accordingly. Carpenters making a bed, a chair, and a funerary shrine are included in Rekhmire's tomb (fig. 12).[61] Similarly the tomb of the Two Sculptors shows carpenters carving *djed*-pillars for a shrine.[62]

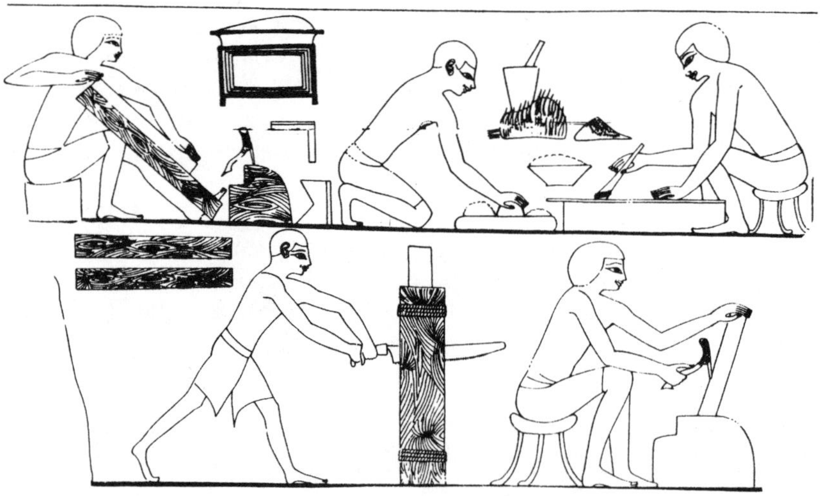

Figure 12.
Norman de Garis Davies, *The Tomb of Rekhmire*
(New York: The Metropolitan Museum of Art, 1935) pl. LII.

59 Lichtheim (1976) 170.

60 Lichtheim (1973) 186.

61 Davies (1935) pl. LII.

62 Davies (1925) pl. XI.

STONEWORKERS AND SCULPTORS

The quarry workers who obtained stone for statues, sarcophagi, and other building purposes must have endured considerable hardship since long trips were required to remote places, such as the Wadi Hamammat and Nubia. Many of the workers for such projects were conscripted from the ranks of the farmers during the inundation season, when fields were not workable. An inscription of Montuhotep IV, the last monarch of the Eleventh Dynasty, in Wadi Hammamt is dated to the "second month of the inundation." It reports that 10,000 conscripts worked on bringing the royal sarcophagus from the desert, and 3000 sailors were employed to ship the stone to Thebes from Coptos, after the blocks had been transported nearly seventy kilometers overland. Whether or not 13,000 were actually involved in this project might be debated, but it is clear that such efforts were major undertakings.

Once blocks were taken to the workshops, the sculptors (*gnwty*) set to work. Dua-Khety makes only a passing mention of sculptors by saying, "I never saw a sculptor (serve) as envoy." His more sympathetic treatment of the sculptor may be owing to the fact scribes were involved in writing out texts on the stone before they were carved and they also painted statues as the Rekhmire scene illustrates. This same scene shows sculptors standing on scaffolds in order to reach the tops of large statues. The discovery of a sculptor's workshop at Amarna illustrates that these artisans applied their craft near palace and temple.

LEATHERWORKERS

Leather was widely used in most periods in Egypt, but especially in the New Kingdom, as evidenced by surviving artifacts and workshop scenes. This industry did not escape the lampooning of our scribes. The *Satire* states: "The cobbler suffers much among his vats of oil; He is well if one's well with corpses, what he bites is leather."[63] Papyrus Lansing is equally insulting: "The cobbler mingles with vats. His odor is penetrating. His hands are red with madder, like one who is smeared with blood. He looks behind him for the kite, like one whose flesh is exposed."[64] New Kingdom workshop scenes depict the tanning process, as well as the leather goods produced, e.g., sandals, bow cases, quivers, shields, and trappings for chariots (fig. 13).[65] Dua-Khety mentions the vats in which the leather-

---

63 Lichtheim (1973) 188–89.

64 Lichtheim (1976) 170.

65 Davies (1922) pl. XXIII; Davies (1935) pl. LIV.

worker soaked and prepared the animal hides. Once again, Rekhmire's tomb provides pictorial support of this detail, depicting two workers placing hides into large jars.[66]

Figure 13.
Norman de Garis Davies, *The Tomb of Rekhmire*
(New York: The Metropolitan Museum of Art, 1935) pl. LIII.

TEXTILE INDUSTRY

Egyptian linen, perhaps the finest in the ancient Near East, was the choice material for clothing throughout Pharaonic times. The fibers that were woven into linen derive from the flax plant. The harvesting of flax entailed pulling the stalks rather than cutting them, as was done with grains. Middle and New Kingdom paintings and reliefs illustrate this pulling technique.[67] In fact, the tomb of Paheri at El-Kab contains a scene with farmers harvesting grain and flax side-by-side and the difference in harvesting methods is clear.[68] The process from the harvesting of flax to the production of linen has been studied extensively and is well understood.[69]

---

[66] Davies (1935) pls. LIII and LIV.

[67] Davies (1901) pl. XVI; Naville (1894) pl. III.

[68] Naville (1894) pl. III.

[69] Vogelsang-Eastwood (1992), see bibliography therein.

The life of the weaver is mocked by scribal elites, saying, "The weaver in the workshop, he is worse off than a woman; with knees against his chest, he cannot breathe air. If he skips a day of weaving, he is beaten fifty strokes."[70]

Whatever sexist observation is implied by being "worse off than a woman," the pictorial evidence shows that the textile industry was not the exclusive domain of men. The tomb of Khnumhotep at Beni Hasan shows a woman preparing the flax, another spinning it, and a pair of women weaving, all under the watchful eye of a corpulent male overseer (fig. 14). Among the models from the Meket-Re cache is a weaver's shop that, like the Beni Hasan scene, shows all facets of the process.[71]

It was the work of these artisans that produced the linen worn by royalty, nobility, and commoners alike.

Figure 14.
P.E. Newberry, *Beni Hasan* I
(London: Egypt Exploration Fund, 1893) pl. XXIX.

LAUNDRY WORKERS

"The washerman washes on the shore, with the crocodile as neighbor" says Dua-Khety. This form of work also merited mention in the Papyrus Lansing text from the New Kingdom: "The washerman's day is going up, going down. All his limbs are weak, from whitening his neighbor's clothes

70 Lichtheim (1973) 188.

71 Newberry (1893) pl. XXIX.

every day, from washing their linen."[72] Laundry scenes are occasionally included in funerary art.[73] At Beni Hasan, workers are shown carrying water with a yoke to a large tub where soaking and washing begin (fig. 15). Other washermen are shown beating cloth with mallets and pounding cloth against a table or stone, while others wring out cloth by twisting the material that is attached to a stake in the ground. The New Kingdom tomb of Ipuy at Deir el-Medineh contains a scene in which men are washing cloth in large vats rather than in the waters of the Nile.[74] It is doubtful the Dua-Khety implied that they washed in the Nile. Based upon my own observation of laundry work in rural Egypt in modern times, woman (not men as in ancient times) do their washing in low flat containers by the Nile or canal's edge. So the danger referred to by Dua-Khety may be in connection with going into the Nile to obtain water for the washing that took place on the bank. Gillian Vogelsang-Eastwood believes that the laundry workers depicted in the tomb scenes were professionals who worked for large estates, but that women did the laundry for small households.[75]

Figure 15.
P.E. Newberry, *Beni Hasan* I
(London: Egypt Exploration Fund, 1893) pl. XI.

Military

Since the dawn of Egyptian history, battles were fought, internally for political unification, defending Egypt's borders, and in connection with imperial designs in the New Kingdom. Throughout, soldiers and, in the empire period, charioteers played decisive roles.[76] Officers and soldiers of higher rank were men of social status and means, especially in the New

---

72 Lichtheim (1976) 169.

73 Newberry (1893) pl. XI, fifth register from the top.

74 Davies (1927) pl. XXVIII.

75 Vogelsang-Eastwood (1992) 40.

76 Concerning the organization and structure of the Egyptian army, see Schulman (1964).

Kingdom, as reflected in tomb biographies of officers such as Amenemheb, Ahmose Pa-Nekhbit, Ahmose si Abena, and Amenemheb. Si Abena traces his rise through the ranks to become a naval commander.[77] Such officers frequently included scenes of their promotions or being decorated for valor (the Horemheb Leiden relief), and they received prisoners-of-war and land from the king as rewards for faithful service. However, the life of the common foot soldier was not so romantic.

Nebmare-nakht, the scribe who authored Papyrus Lansing, offers a lengthy appraisal of the life of the soldier, recognizing the difference between officers and soldiers:

> Come, <let me tell> you the woes of the soldier, and how many are his superiors: the general, the troop-commander, the officer who leads, the standard-bearer, the lieutenant, the scribe, the commander of fifty, and the garrison-captain. They go in and out in the halls of the palace, saying: "Get laborers!" He is awakened at any hour. One is after him as (after) a donkey. He toils until the Aten sets in his darkness of night. He is hungry, his belly hurts; he is dead while yet alive. When he receives the grain-ration, having been released from duty, it is not good for grinding.
>
> He is called up for Syria. He may not rest. There are no clothes, no sandals. The weapons of war are assembled at the fortress of Sile. His march is uphill through mountains. He drinks water every third day; it is smelly and tastes of salt. His body is ravaged by illness. The enemy comes, surrounds him with missiles, and life recedes from his. ... If he comes out alive, he is worn out from marching.... Be a scribe, and be spared from soldiering![78]

It is hard to dispute these claims about the life of the soldier in ancient Egypt, especially in the Empire period (when these words were penned), since they were often on duty in remote places such as Nubia, the eastern and western frontiers, and in far-away Syria-Palestine.

Scribes

The above-quoted descriptions of various forms of work by Dua-Khety and Nebmare-nakht are clearly slanted against these trades because they were trying to persuade others of the superiority of the scribal guild. Scribes held supervisory positions, were royal emissaries, and were appointed to many administrative posts, even heading up governmental departments. While the scribes thought highly of their lot in life, their pride appears not to have been misplaced. The reason for deriding the various

---

77 Cf. Lichtheim (1976) 12–14.

78 Lichtheim (1976) 172.

forms of work in the *Satire* and Papyrus Lansing is that they were physically demanding, made one tired and weary of limb. The scribe, on the other hand, studies, writes, and uses his mind. He will be his own man! Hence Nebmare-nakht concludes:

> Set your sight on being a scribe; a fine profession that suits you. You call for one; a thousand answer you. You stride freely on the road. You will not be like a hired ox. You are in front of others.[79]

The scribes of ancient Egypt were bureaucrats who ran not only the royal court, but also the provincial capitals, the military, and temple estates. From the fine literature ancient Egypt has left us, be it literary works like *The Ship Wrecked Sailor* and *Sinuhe*, or wisdom texts and hymnody, the scribes were both authors and preservers of the tradition. While their elevated assessment of the scribal profession, as witnessed in the *Satire* and Papyrus Lansing, seems quite biased, especially since all other professions are deemed unworthy, the scribes were truly influential and played important roles in society. Nevertheless, the much ridiculed farmers, carpenters, artisans, and stoneworkers also made lasting marks on Egyptian society, some of which can still be appreciated in museum collections in the twenty-first century of our era.

Deir el-Medineh and Other Workmen's Villages

The village at Deir el-Medineh in western Thebes is a treasure of information about the "blue collar" workers of the New Kingdom. Homes, tombs, and written sources have opened up the lives of these workers like no other site in Egypt. The tomb of Kha^{c} and his wife Merit from the late Eighteenth Dynasty was discovered completely intact.[80] Its discovery was virtually obscured by Howard Carter's sensational discovery of Tutankhamun's sealed tomb two decades later. This Deir el-Medineh tomb, however, may actually be more important than its royal counterpart as a source for daily life. Presently on display at the Egyptian Museum of Turin, the tomb contents included clothes, wigs, a range of foods, herbs, spices, furniture, walking sticks, various toiletries, and much more. This tomb thus provides information on the quality of life enjoyed by the middle class during the empire period. In fairness to the sensational discoveries within Tutankhamun's tomb, hundreds of objects found in this tomb shed considerable light on daily life in as much as clothing, shoes, furniture, food stuffs, weapons, walking sticks, musical instruments, games, jewelry, etc. were

79 Lichtheim (1976) 171.

80 D'abbadie (1906) and Schiaparelli (1924–27).

included, and must be considered as valuable sources for understanding the daily life of royalty.[81]

Texts, cultic objects, and a small temple from Deir el-Medineh have served as the basis for the 1987 study, *Popular Religion in Egypt during the New Kingdom* by Ashraf Sadek.[82] This contribution by Deir el-Medineh is especially important since our knowledge of Egyptian religion is so shaped by official religion and the funerary cult. Deir el-Medineh also has provided the largest collection of *3ḫ iḳr n Rᶜ*–stelae. A thorough investigation of these stela by Robert Demarée in 1983 has revealed that there was in New Kingdom times a house-based, ancestor worship cult observed among the common folk of Egypt.[83] Consequently, Deir el-Medineh currently offers the best avenue for understanding the religious practices of the average Egyptian.

Deir el-Medineh's Middle Kingdom counterpart is the town site of Lahun, explored first by Petrie in 1889, in which the workers who built the pyramid of Senusert II lived. After the king's death they served in maintaining the cult of the king. Rosalie David's *Pyramid Builder's of Ancient Egypt* (1986) offers a helpful assessment of Petrie's discoveries. Over the past decade, Nicholas Millet of the Royal Ontario Museum has been reinvestigating this important Twelfth Dynasty site. Hence we can hope for new information about this important Middle Kingdom workmen's village.

A more recent discovery at the edge of the Giza plateau should provide new data on the common folk of the Old Kingdom. Tombs of people associated with the work force that built the Fourth Dynasty pyramids were discovered in the late 1980s by Zahi Hawass. These tombs and their contents, when published, will nicely complement the mudbrick domestic quarters for the workers discovered near the Sphinx by Hans Goedicke in the early 1970s. Mark Lehner is currently working on the southeastern part of the Giza plateau, where he has made significant discoveries from the Old Kingdom that include food-preparation areas and workshops that supported the pyramid building operations.[84]

---

81 For pictures and descriptions of many of the objects from this tomb, see Carter and Mace (1923) and Harris.

82 Sadek (1987).

83 Demarée (1983).

84 Lehner has reported on his discoveries at the ARCE meetings, but publication of this material is in process. Goedicke's excavations have yet to appear in preliminary form.

The discoveries at Deir el-Medineh, Lahun, and Giza mean that we now have domestic and funerary remains for all three kingdom periods of Egyptian history. The availability of this type of archaeological evidence will serve as a nice balance to the more idyllic tomb scenes of the nobility and the skewed perspectives of the scribes. Most of this material awaits full publication.

Because of the abundance of sources now available for the study of daily life in Egypt, coupled with renewed interest in anthropological and sociological approaches to the study of the Near East, it appears that new and creative studies will be forthcoming that will lead to a more complete picture of the life of the ancient Egyptians.

BIBLIOGRAPHY

Arnold, D. (1996) *The Royal Women of Amarna. Images of Beauty from Ancient Egypt.* New York. **Bierbrier, M.** (1982) *The Tomb-Builders of the Pharaohs.* London. **Blackman, A.M.** (1914) *The Rock Tombs of Meir I.* London. (1953) *The Rock Tombs of Meir II.* London. **Carter, H. and A.C. Mace** (1923) *The Tomb of Tutankhamen.* 3 volumes. New York. **Cerny, J.** (1973) *Community of Workmen at Thebes in the Ramesside Period.* Cairo. **D'abbadie, V.** (1906) *La Chapelle de Khâ in Deux Tombes de Deir el-Medineh.* MIFAO 58. **David, R.** (1986) *The Pyramid Builders of Ancient Egypt: A Modern Investigation of Pharaoh's Workforce.* London/Boston. **Davies, N.d.G.** (1901) *The Rock Tombs of Sheikh Saïd.* London. (1917) *The Tomb of Nakht at Thebes.* New York. (1922) *The Tomb of Puyemrê at Thebes.* New York. (1925) *The Tomb of Two Sculptors at Thebes.* New York. (1927) *Two Ramesside Tombs at Thebes.* New York. (1935) *The Tomb of Rekhmire.* New York. **Demarée, R.** (1983) *The 3ḫ iḳr n Re-Stelae on Ancestor Worship in Ancient Egypt.* Leiden. **Demarée, R.J. and A. Egerts**, eds. (1992) *Village Voices: Proceedings of the Symposium "Texts from Deir el-Medîna and Their Interpretation."* Leiden. **Demarée, R.J. and Jac. J.J. Janssen**, eds. (1982). *Gleanings from Deir el-Medina.* Leiden. **Dunham, D. and W.K. Simpson** (1974) *The Mastaba of Queen Marsyankh.* Boston. **Erman, A.** (1894/ German edition 1886) *Life in Ancient Egypt.* London. **Fischer, H.G.** (1989) *Egyptian Women of the Old Kingdom and of the Heracleopolitan Period.* New York. **Friedman, R. and D. Brewer** (1989) *Fish and Fishing in Ancient Egypt.* Cairo. **Harris, J.R.**, ed. *Tut'ankhamun's Tomb Series.* Oxford. **Hoffman, M. A.** (1984) *Egypt before the Pharaohs.* London. **Hoffmeier, J.K.** (1991) The Coffins of the Middle Kingdom: The Residence and the Regions. In S. Quirke, ed., *Middle Kingdom Studies.* Whitstable, Kent. **Houlihan, P.F.** (1986) *The Birds of Ancient Egypt.* Warminster. **James, T.G.H.** (1985) *Pharaoh's People: Scenes from Life in Imperial Egypt.* Oxford. **Lesko, B.S.** (1987) *The Remarkable Women of Ancient Egypt.* Providence, R.I. Ed. (1989) *Women's Earliest Records From Ancient Egypt and Western Asia.* Brown Judaic Studies. Atlanta, Ga. **Lesko, L.H.**, ed. (1994) *Pharaoh's Workers: The Village of Deir El*

Medina. Ithaca, N.Y. **Lichtheim, M.** (1973) *Ancient Egyptian Literature*. Vol. 1. *The Old and Middle Kingdoms*. Berkeley. (1976) *Ancient Egyptian Literature*. Vol. 2. *The New Kingdom*. Berkeley. **Mannice, L.** (1987) *City of the Dead*. Chicago. **McDowell, A.G.** (1991) *Jurisdiction in the Workmen's Community of Deir el-Medîna*. Leiden. **Mertz, B.** (1966) *Red Land Black Land: Daily in Ancient Egypt*. New York. **Moores, R.G.** (1991) Evidence of a Stone-Cutting Drag Sawing by Fourth Dynasty Egyptians. *JARCE* 28: 139–48. **Naville, E.** (1894) *The Tomb of Paheri at El Kab*. London. **Newberry, P.E.** (1893) *Beni Hassan I*. London. **Petrie, W.M.F.** (1917) *Tools and Weapons*. London. **Pomeroy, S.** (1984) *Women in Hellenistic Egypt from Alexander to Cleopatra*. New York. **Roberts, A.** (1997) *Hathor Rising. The Power of the Goddess in Ancient Egypt*. Rochester, Vt. **Robins, G.** (1993) *Women in Ancient Egypt*. Cambridge, Mass. (1995) *Reflections of Women in the New Kingdom: Ancient Egyptian Art from The British Museum*. San Antonio, Texas. **Romer, J.** (1988) *People of the Nile: Everyday Life in Ancient Egypt*. New York. **Sadek, A.** (1987) *Popular Religion in Egypt during the New Kingdom*. Hildesheimer Ägyptologische Beitrage 27. **Sameh, W.** (1964) *Daily Life in Ancient Egypt*. New York. **Schiaparelli, E.** (1924–27) *Relazione sur lavori della Missione archeologica italliana in Egitto*. **Schulman, A.R.** (1964) *Military Rank, Title and Organization in the Egyptian New Kingdom*. Münchner Ägyptologische Studien 6. Berlin. **Spencer, A.J.** (1993) *Early Egypt: The Rise of Civilisation in the Nile Valley*. Norman, Ok. **Strouhal, E.** (1992) *Life of the Ancient Egyptians*. Norman, Ok. **Trigger, B., et al.** (1982) *Ancient Egypt: A Social History*. Cambridge. **Troy, L.** (1986) *Patterns of Queenship in Ancient Egyptian Myth and History*. Uppsala. **Tyldesley, J.** (1994) *Daughters of Isis. Women of Ancient Egypt*. (1996) *Hatchepsut: The Female Pharaoh*. New York. **Vogelsang-Eastwood, G.** (1992) *The Production of Linen in Pharaonic Egypt*. Den Haag. **Watterson, B.** (1991) *Women in Ancient Egypt*. New York. **Wilfong, T.G.** (1997) *Women and Gender in Ancient Egypt from Prehistory to Late Antiquity*. Ann Arbor, Mich. **Wilson, John** (1951) *The Culture of Egypt*. Chicago: University of Chicago Press. **Wilkinson, J.G.** (1836) *The Ancient Egyptians: Their Life and Customs*. (New York; reprinted 1988). **Wilkinson, R.** (1992) *Reading Egyptian Art*. London. **Wilson, J.A. and T.G. Allen**, eds. (1938) *The Mastabas of Mereruka*. 2 volumes. Chicago. **Winlock, H.E.** (1955) *Models of Daily Life in Ancient Egypt from the Tomb of Meket-Re at Thebes*. Cambridge, Mass.

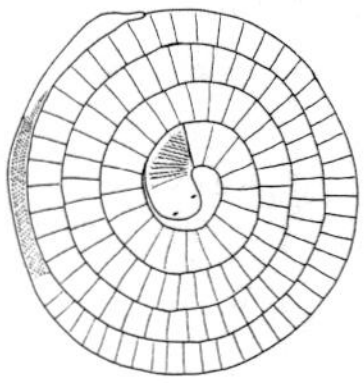

The New Testament World

DAILY LIFE IN THE NEW TESTAMENT PERIOD

Bruce J. Malina
Creighton University

The purpose of this essay is to offer a sampling of scenarios that might evoke a feeling for daily life in New Testament times. There are two general ways in which this task might be carried out. On the one hand, one might describe the daily routine of typical persons, whether a city elite, or a land-bound peasant, or a non-elite villager in the Eastern Roman Empire. Descriptions of this sort of people in their daily routine are readily recoverable from the excellent "Everyday Life…" books by Casson and Dupont to name but two.[1] For the visually oriented, there are the various archaeological films and reconstructions available on the History Channel, the Discovery Channels, and the A&E Channel.

However there is a problem with such "factual" descriptions, as indicated by the appended homilies in these "shows" about how relevant the past is to our present life. The root of the problem is that "our facts are not only already classified, they are classifications. Human data are of a conceptual order, so they are destroyed if this pre-existing order is disrespected."[2] Now whose pre-existing order do TV consultants espouse when script writers find twentieth-century relevance in first-century scenarios?

Another general way to describe segments of daily life from the distant past is to reconstruct that ancient and largely irrelevant pre-existing order that once gave meaning to daily life. In social scientific perspective, one can explain historically only if one can describe, and this one can do only if one has grasped the concepts of past societies embodied in human action and artifacts. All ancient artifacts witness to rule following activity. And because artifacts derive from human activity, each has an internal connection with the meaning embedded in the artifact by actors conceiving those meanings. Just as within a given social system, the value of any social role

---

1 Casson (1975; 1999); Dupont (1992).

2 Crick (1976) 93.

derives from all the other roles that the role in question is not,[3] so too with the values ascribed to any meaningful behavior. Access to the meanings of daily living is always rooted in social systems.

Social Systems

Social systems consist of social institutions, value sets, and person types. From the viewpoint of our own experience, all societies might be viewed as consisting of (at least) four major social institutions: kinship, politics, economics, and religion. Social institutions are fixed forms of phases of social life. They do not exist independently of each other, except in terms of abstract analysis. Institutions are the ways or means that people use to realize meaningful, human social living within a given society. Kinship is about "naturing" and nurturing people; politics is about effective collective action; economics is about provisioning society; and religion deals with the significance and meaning of human being within a given environment, including the all-embracing ultimate cosmic meaning of it all.

Meanings shared by first-century people situated around the northeast littoral of the Mediterranean were encoded in patterns of behavior deriving from various but similar social systems. Even with broad local variation, daily life in this period was daily life in the Roman Empire. Society in this segment of the Mediterranean region is best characterized as a ruralized society.[4]

Ruralized Society

What I mean by ruralized society is that great landowners set the agenda for the empire on the basis of their interests, values, and concerns. This point should be clearer from the following considerations. It is a truism among urban historians that the United States at present is an *urbanized* society.[5] Urban areas contain most of the national population, and urban agendas determine national policies. Urban concerns dominate the goals, values, and behaviors of the five percent of the population that is engaged in agricultural production. Our urbanized society is quickly developing into one with a global outreach. Before it became urbanized, the United States became an *urban* society over the period marked by the rise of indus-

---

3 Crick (1976) 116.

4 Southall (1998) also uses this designation.

5 Hays (1993).

trialization to the end of the Second World War. An *urban* society, in this perspective, is one in which a significant proportion of the population lives and works in urban centers, following an agenda quite different from rural society yet in somewhat tandem rhythms. In urban societies, urban agendas compete with rural ones in determining national policies. Urban and rural agendas foster conflicting goals, values, and behaviors. Before the waves of immigration at the end of the last century and the first quarter of this one, the United States was essentially a *rural* society, with rural agendas determining national policies and rural concerns dominating the goals, values, and behaviors of the ninety-five percent of the population living on the land and the five percent living permanently in cities.

Kinship

As is well known, such ruralized societies had two focal social institutions, realized in the spatial and architectural arrangements called the house and the city. The first, basic institution was kinship, the second was politics. Kinship is the symboling of biological processes of human reproduction and growth in terms of abiding relations, roles, statuses, and the like. Kinship is about naturing and nurturing human beings interpreted as family members (and "neighbors" in non-mobile societies). In ruralized societies, the kinship group was the economic and religious unit as well: the ancient Mediterranean knew domestic economy and domestic religion (but at the family level, no economy or religion separate from kinship). For example, domestic religion used the roles, values, and goals of the household in the articulation and expression of religion: religious functionaries of domestic religion were household personages (notably fathers and inside the household, mothers as well, oldest sons, ancestors), focus was on the deity(ies) as source of solidarity, mutual commitment, and belonging mediated through ancestors, expected to provide well-being, health, and prosperity for the kin group and its patriarchs to the benefit of family members. The house had its altars and sacred rites (focused on the family meal and the hearth as symbols of life) with father (patriarch) and mother (first in charge at home) officiating. Deities were tribal and/or household ones (e.g., lares, penates, God of Abraham, Isaac, Jacob) as well as ancestors who saw to the well-being, prosperity and fertility of the family members. There was much concern about inheritance and the legitimacy of heirs. Domestic religion sought meaning through belonging: an ultimately meaningful existence derives from belonging, e.g., to a chosen, select, holy people. In well-ordered societies, it is belonging within the proper ranking in one's well-ordered society (often called hierarchy). In societies in some disarray, it is belonging to a proper kin and/or fictive kin group.[6] In the domestic economy kinship concerns for naturing and nurturing were replicated in the production and sustenance of new life in agricultural pursuits, a family affair for non-elites. The ingroup/outgroup pattern marking kinship boundaries served as marker between families as well as between the kin group's political unit and the rest of the world.

Politics

The second, equally focal, institution in this period was politics, the symboling of social relations in terms of vertical roles, statuses and interactions. Politics was about effective collective action, the application of force to attain collective goals. The roles, statuses, entitlements and obligations of the political system were available to properly pedigreed persons from only the "best" families, hence tied up with the kinship system. The political unit was likewise an economic and religious one: the ancient Mediterranean knew political economy and political religion (at the political level, there was no economy or religion separate from politics). Political concerns for effective collective action on behalf of the ingroup were replicated in the application of force on outgroups, largely in the interest of fundamental domestic economic concerns: acquisition of more land, labor, animals and the like. Political religion, in turn, employed the roles, values, and goals of politics in the articulation and expression of religion: religious functionaries were political personages, focus was on the deity(ies) as source of power and might, expected to provide order, well-being and prosperity for the body politic and its power wielders (elites) to the benefit of subjects. In monarchic city-territories of the eastern Mediterranean, temples were political buildings, temple sacrifices were for the public good; the deity of the temple had a staff similar to the one a monarch had in the palace (major domo = high priest; officials of various ranks and grades = priests, levites; temple slaves and the like).[7] "Democratic" cities controlled by local elites altered monarchic temples into democratic ones, now owned and run by city councils or noble council members, with sacrifice offered according to the wishes of the sacrificing entity.

---

6 Malina (1986; 1994; 1996a).

7 See Elliott (1991).

City and Country

The great landowners shaped the agenda of daily life for society at large. These great landowners, the "best people" or "aristocrats," generally had two places of residence. One was a house in the countryside, on the land that provided this elite person with power and wealth. The other was a house built as part of a cluster of such houses of other landowning elites in a central (or nodal) place, the city.[8] Just as smallholders lived in houses clustered together (usually for support and protection) in towns and villages, so too the largeholders, but their housing clusters formed the center of what the ancients called a *polis, urbs, civitas,* or *ir*.

The ancient city, in fact, was a bounded, centralized set of selective kinship relationships concerned with effective collective action and expressed spatially in terms of architecture and the arrangement of places. The centralized set of social relationships among elites took on spatial dimension by means of territoriality. That is, these elites claimed dominance of their central place and its surroundings. This is simply one dimension of the effective collective action that a political institution is. Large numbers of people were required to support the elites and their concerns both in the country and in the city. Resident city support consisted of retainers that constituted the non-elite central place population.

In other words, the first-century Mediterranean *civitas* or *polis* was really a large, ruralized central place in which properly pedigreed "farmers/ ranchers" displayed and employed their unbelievable wealth in competitions for honor among each other. Largeholders thus found it in their interest to live near other largeholders in central places that likewise provided them with organized force (an army) to protect their interests from the vast masses of other persons. The elite united to promote and defend their collective honor in face of the outgroup in annual rites of war, which, if carried off successfully, brought them more land and/or the produce of that land. They equally participated in the continual, if seasonal, activity of extortion called taxation. Their honor rating rooted in kinship brought them the power that brought them further wealth.

Yet for elites, the city house was a secondary dwelling. It was not a private place like the dwellings of the city non-elite. Rather the elite city house was multifunctional, a place of constant socializing, economic, and sometimes political intercourse, and not simply a place of habitation. For these elites, living together essentially served the purpose of daily challenge-riposte interaction in the pursuit of honor.

---

8 See Rohrbaugh (1991) and Oakman (1991).

The primary elite residence was the elite country estate, a place of residence and subsistence (family plus land and buildings for production, distribution, transmission, reproduction, group identification). Non-elite farmers and tenants imagined their limited holdings in terms of the ideal, the elite country estate. These country houses were spacious, centrally heated, with a swimming bath, library, works of art, and the like. They were situated on vast agricultural estates worked by slaves in the West, and largely by tenants in the East. "At one time in the first century A.D. fully half of what is today Tunisia belonged to a mere six owners. In France archeologists have uncovered an estate that embraces twenty-five hundred acres; the farm buildings alone covered forty-five."[9]

The Eastern Mediterranean formed the outer reaches of roads that led to Rome. As is well known, Rome was a city that expanded its political web to include most other cities in the Mediterranean basin. Empire (*imperium*) and City (*urbs*) blended into a single entity, with the City at the social geographical center of the inhabited, "civilized" earth. A number of traditional features typical of ruralized society punctuated life in the city: physical violence, a sense of no control and little responsibility, endless challenges to honor with public humiliation. "Roman society demanded an uncomfortable mixture of pervasive deference to superiors and openly aggressive brutishness to inferiors, not just slaves. It was a world of deference and condescension, of curt commands and pervasive threats."[10] If our modern cities produce industrial products and information technology, what cities in antiquity essentially produced was power sanctioned by force, and what Rome attained was a monopoly on power sanctioned by force.

Power personified in the emperor or a god, reified in the central imperial city and its institutions, held full attention. If some deity resident in the sky or manifest on earth was worth its godhead, it had to be omnipotent. It is no accident that Constantine's political religion believed "in one God, the Father, the Almighty..." (Nicene Creed, 325 A.D.). The traditional cult of omnipotence can ostensibly trace its roots to the rise of the first central places serving as administrative and residential centers for elites who controlled the agrarian surround. In simpler terms, omnipotence was the focal value of "cities" from their very inception.[11] And with overarch-

---

9 Casson (1975) 27; for Palestine, see Fiensy (1991) and Hanson and Oakman (1998).

10 Hopkins (1998) 210–11; see also MacMullen (1974).

11 See Routledge (1997), and the typology in Rupp (1997).

ing value tied to omnipotence, cruelty seems to have been a necessary concomitant—albeit reserved for lower statuses and outgroups, human and non-human.

Common Daily Rhythms

The rhythms of daily life were common throughout the region. People arose at sunrise and went to bed at sunset. The period of daylight was divided into twelve hours of greater or lesser length depending on the season of the year. Noon marked the division of this daytime period. As a rule all people, whether elites, freeborn, freed persons or slaves, arose at sunrise, washed quickly, prayed to the household gods, ate a simple breakfast, and went to their occupations. Similarly, all ended their general work day shortly after noon, marked by a brief repast. The type of morning activity that persons engaged in depended on their social rank and residence. The same was true of the activity of the afternoon period. In cities, elites and non-elite free and freed persons who could afford it followed the Hellenized Roman tradition of spending the period before supper at the baths. While provision shops were open, household slaves and lower-ranking women would prepare supper. As a rule, no one "worked" in the afternoon, slaves included, unless they had to (e.g., food shop owners, farmers pressed by the weather, forced labor, seasonal requirements).[12]

Differences in daily life patterns derived almost totally from social ranking. Persons at each rank, outfitted with appropriate entitlements and obligations, engaged in rather different activities. Not only were occupations rank specific, so were the places where these occupations were pursued. Non-elites did not really work for profit, to increase their wealth, to better their social position. In popular perception it was impossible to better one's social rank by one's own efforts; all goods were limited.[13] Society was characterized by kinship groups that produced and consumed at a subsistence level. Non-elites were expected to have a "surplus" that went to elites in taxes. Elites likewise produced what they consumed at their several agricultural holdings. Given their largeholdings, their surplus was unimaginable, available for sale to wholesale merchants for cities throughout the empire. Further elite increase in wealth came from the springtime occupation of warfare and most commonly, extortion (e.g., taxation, charging interest, profits on sales, foreclosures, tenancy rates, ransom).

---

12 See Hacquard et al. (1952).

13 See Malina (1993) 94–96.

Power and City Planning

If, as previously noted, a city is in fact a bounded, centralized set of selective kinship relationships concerned with effective collective action and expressed spatially in terms of architecture and the arrangement of places, it might be of interest to consider what Rome contributes to the usual spatial arrangement. Ancient cities developed structures that were specialized dimensions of the house: the forum replicated the courtyard, the central temple with perpetual flame replicated the hearth, eating establishments replicated kitchens and dining rooms, brothels replicated bedrooms, temples replicated household shrines, public centers replicated atria, theaters replicated moral instruction sections of the house, public baths and toilets replicated the elite household equivalents of the same. Greeks added war-training facilities to their *poleis,* in the form of stadiums and hippodromes. What was distinctive of Roman cities was the amphitheater.[14]

The amphitheater was like a death-camp extermination device located in the center of the city for the pleasure of the whole populace. People came out to enjoy the torment and death of living beings, human and non-human. Such physical violence distinctively replicated the chief product of the city: power sanctioned by force. People sat in hierarchical ranks to revel in the death of others. Hopkins claims the amphitheater is the clue to understanding the Roman Empire, and I would concur. But what does amphitheater behavior tell us about Roman society and the values it spread? If a value is the quality and direction of behavior, what does institutionalized recourse to physical violence, specialized cruelty, and disregard for non-elite and outgroup well-being say about what Romans valued in their daily living?

Power and Physical Violence

Modern scholars suggest that cruelty is a process of maiming the ordinary patterns of behavior that are some living creature's way of living. Maiming makes resistance ineffectual and thus renders the victim passive. For the victimizer, what counts is power over the victim's whole life, even if exercised on a whim, with little concern.[15] And what Romans despised, as others have demonstrated, was passivity in males.[16] But how is it humanly possible to display such devotion to and public displays of physical cruelty

---

14 Auguet (1972); Hopkins (1983) 1–30 and 201–56.

15 Hallie (1982) 26 and *passim*.

16 Veyne (1998).

as those in the amphitheater and other Roman forms of punishment? Brenman suggests that for human beings

> in order that cruelty can remain unmodified various mechanisms are employed. The most important processes include the worship of omnipotence that is felt to be superior to human love and forgiveness, the clinging to omnipotence as a defense against depression, and the sanctification of grievance and revenge. In order to avoid conscious guilt, the perceptions of the mind are narrowed to give ostensible justification to the cruelty, and the obviation of redeeming features in the object.[17]

Perhaps the closest modern experience of living in a first-century Eastern Mediterranean city is living in a non-capital "city" in a Third World country.[18] For like the first-century Mediterranean, Third World countries, apart from capital cities, form ruralized society. The elite residents in these cities are large landowners, clustered together for mutual interaction and protection. The vast majority of people live on the land as peasants; elites with their retainers constituted perhaps less than ten percent of the population. And physical violence is the main way to get things done.

In the first century, the Roman elite formed a power syndicate with a network reaching out to elites in other cities of the region. These elites held a near monopoly of violence and therefore on social control throughout the empire. They not merely survived largely or wholly on extortion, but were themselves an integral part of the political system. Thus they had control over the levers of political, political economic and political religious power. While relatively modern organized crime in ruralized societies were and are part of the dominant culture like the Mafia, Camorra or L'Ndrangheta,[19] ancient Roman elites and their coopted non-Roman aristocrats were the center of dominant society. In both cases social control was based on fear, but also on a very broad consensus. The elite's function for the ingroup was to provide protection, occasionally genuine but more usually spurious protection from itself. Elites personally produced neither goods nor services and extorted quite legally since they made the laws. As the system is based on violence provided by private "armies" and the Roman military, it was highly unstable since it required personal loyalty.[20] Indi-

---

17 Brenman (1985) 280.

18 See, e.g., Breese (1966); Couglar (1996).

19 See Hess (1986); Lupsha (1986); Walston (1986); also Walters (1990).

20 See especially Taylor (1977).

vidual emperors came and went, but the system itself continued with very little change over long periods.

Life in a Ruralized Society

The city was the central administrative and residential location of the elite in the Hellenistic cultural world of the Roman *oikoumene*. Throughout the *oikoumene*, the institution serving elite interests was politics, with great social attention paid to the symbols of power that the city produced. Elites would drive, ride, or be carried in a litter to the city, where they had town houses near the city's center, in an area reserved for elite families, most often walled off from the rest of the city (*cittadella* > citadel means "little city"). On their way to the city, they would pass the tombs of the great along the highway near the city, enter through the city gate, and have their entourage make way through the teeming city streets. Upon approaching the elite quarter, the entourage would pass the city forum, splendid theaters, an amphitheater, public halls, baths, and parks. Eventually elite personages would be welcomed by yet more of their attendants at the town house, an edifice that would be almost as elegant as the country house, and largely supplied with foodstuffs by the country estate. There a swarm of clients, attended by household slaves, would be waiting to engage in another day's interaction with their noble patron.

Patronage

The only way to find salvation and survive in a society rooted in extortion and impregnated with violence as central mode of interaction was patronage.[21] Patronage is a value that characterizes patron-client relationships. It is a form of "justice" rooted in generalized reciprocity, identical with the justice meted out by relatives to each other in kinship systems. To understand it, one must begin with the patron-client relationship.[22] In Mediterranean societies of the past (as in most traditional societies), there was not the faintest trace of social equality, whether before the law or even in some ideal equality of all males. Institutionalized relationships between persons of unequal power statuses and resources were and are highly exploitative in nature. The "best" families exerted power, applied vertically as force in harsh and impersonal fashion. People of higher status sought to maximize their gains without a thought to the losses of those with whom they inter-

---

21 See Moxnes (1991); Powell (1977); Wolf (1965).

22 See Malina (1996b).

acted. To survive in some meaningful way in such societies, patronage emerged to the mutual satisfaction of both parties: clients had their needs met, especially in fortuitous and irregular situations, while patrons received grants of honor and the accolades of benefaction. Patrons were to treat clients as family members might, with both having special concern for each other's welfare, even though sometimes separated by vast differences in status and power.

The patron-client relationship is a social institutional arrangement by means of which economic, political, or religious institutional relationships are outfitted with an overarching quality of kinship or family feeling. The patron is like a father, and clients are like devoted and grateful children, no matter what their age. The client relates to his patron according to the social norms of child relations to actual parents, while the patron is expected to relate to clients as a parent would to his (more rarely, her) actual children.

Patron-client relations permeated the whole of ancient Mediterranean society. For example, Herod, the "King of the Judeans" in Matthew's infancy account (Matt 2), was a client king of his patron, Caesar Augustus. The Capernaum centurion was a patron who sent word to Jesus through some "friends," a Roman name for client (Luke 7:6). Festus the procurator acts like patron of his client chief priests and principal men of Judea by doing them a favor (Acts 25:2–3). The title "friend of Caesar" (John 19:12) was an official acknowledgment of imperial clientage. But by and large the most common form of patron client relationship would be between a landowner and *some* of his tenants. This special relationship assured the landlord of conspicuous deference and loyalty and provided the tenant with requisite favor.

A "favor" is something received on terms more advantageous than those that can be obtained from anyone else or that cannot be obtained from anyone else at all. From the client's point of view, favoritism is the main quality of such relationships. Clients seek out patrons, earthly and heavenly, essentially for obtaining favors. Often they have recourse to "brokers," persons whose task is to link clients with the patrons they need. What the inferior client lacks is assurance of aid in various emergencies and a guarantee of permanent access to resources. This lack of assurance bespeaks a lack of and need for commitment on the part of one who might do a special favor. No superior is obliged to provide such assurance and guarantee. Clients in this system know that their relation to patrons is highly unequal; patrons have much higher status, power, and resources. Patrons provide their favors and help in exchange for items of a qualitatively different sort: material for immaterial, goods for honor and praise, force for status support, and the like. On the other hand, the non-client subordinate has no social obligation to treat the superior with respect or affection or to accept any offer of abiding commitment.

Non-Elites in the City

The vast majority of city residents were non-elites: city-born plebeians, displaced peasants, and a sprinkling of capable immigrants and freed persons. In Rome, Ostia, Corinth, or Thessalonika, for example, if one were a low-ranking citizen, the day would start in a noisome tenement. Small merchants and craftsmen would live in the same building as their business, in a guild or immigrant quarter. For all there would be no central heating, possibly a charcoal brazier (chimneys had not yet been invented). There would be no running water, no in-house toilet (slop was tossed from the window—for which glass panes had yet to be invented). An oil lamp would light the room, sparsely furnished for want of coins and for fear of "wall-breakers" (as burglars were known). Ordinary tenement dwellers rose at dawn, washed their hands and prayed to the gods of the household, then donned their dirty, louse-ridden outer clothing and checked for their amulet to ward off the evil eye. Going out was to plunge down as many as six flights of stairs into the teeming mass of humanity outside, into the street.

There was a perceived opposition between the house and the street.[23] This was but another instance of that basic feature of Mediterranean cultures that dichotomized society into different social domains based on distinct interactional, ideological, hierarchical, and structural premises. Mediterranean cultures replicated their significant ingroup/outgroup boundaries with parallel social categories such as public and private, inside and outside, modesty and display, honor and shame, loyalty and betrayal. The street was a public domain of hierarchical relationships with individuals and social classes engaged in a never-ending struggle for sustenance and honor. The house, on the other hand, was a private domain of members related by blood and marriage with precise entitlements and obligations organized along age and gender.

For the tenement dwellers who just entered the street, a meal from a street vendor whose stall obstructed the press of human traffic in the street might follow, if there were time and money a wheaten cake or some fruit, maybe. Then a drink from a fountain (tea, coffee, and chocolate were as yet unknown), or a visit to the public toilets, duly adorned with statues of protective deities. Then to the day's work. For small merchants and crafts-

---

23 See Robben (1989).

men (and their family) it was in the shop. For male day laborers it might be labor in a brick works, or running errands for some dignitary or other, if they were fortunate enough to have a job currently. Women in cities took charge of child-care, cooking (fetching water, daily food acquisition), gossip in women's networks, and the like. For unemployed males the work that morning might mean to search out a patron by visiting the homes of those of the great whose arrogant slave flunkeys might let one in. Juvenal offers a scenario concerning walking on a city street:

> When the rich man has a call of social duty, the mob makes way for him as he is borne swiftly over their heads in a huge Liburnian cart. He writes or reads or sleeps inside as he goes along, for the closed window of the litter induces slumber. Yet he will arrive ahead of us. For I hurry but there is a wave ahead of me in the way, and the crowd is so dense the people behind jam against my back and sides. Someone rams me with his elbow, someone else with a pole, this fellow cracks my head with a two-by-four, that one with a ten-gallon wine-cask, my shins are plastered with mud, now I'm being trampled by somebody's big feet and there goes a soldier's hobnail firmly on my toe! (Juvenal 3.243–8 LCL).

To walk through the non-elite sections of the city required that one push through the throng, probably with running nose or hacking cough if it were winter, or feeling slightly feverish if it were summer. The noisome twisting streets between the tall tenements of the lower-ranked plebeians would give way to broader streets flanked by the windowless exteriors of the one-story houses of small merchants or the shop fronts of the two-story houses of craftsmen, clustered in guild sectors. At times, non-elites might catch a glimpse of some of the elites' imposing and important public buildings, or even amble through a portico or two. But most people would not move out of their quarter of the city: their section of fellow ethnics and guild members residing in slums as well as adjacent good residential areas, at times with well-appointed public places. Yet to venture outside one's quarter or neighborhood required vigilance, for cities were violent places, sprinkled with tough soldiers, sneaky cutpurses, and other desperate, shameless men.

If daylight had its problems with violence, nighttime was far worse. Neither cities nor towns/villages had street lighting. People had to protect themselves overnight, behind bolts and bars until dawn. Only those who could afford a retinue of slaves to light up the way with torches and to serve as bodyguard dared walk about in the dark. To go out alone was an invitation to be mugged. Again, Juvenal:

> Here is the prelude to the fighting, if it's fighting when he does all the punching and all you do is get hit. He stands in your way and orders you

> to stop, and you've got to obey; what can you do when you're being forced by someone raging mad and, what's more, stronger than you are'? "Where are you from?" he hollers, "whose beans and rotgut have you filled your belly with...? So you won't talk? You talk or get a kick in your rear...." It makes no difference whether you try to say something or retreat without a word, they beat you up all the same.... You know what the poor man's freedom amounts to? The freedom, after being punched and pounded to pieces, to beg and implore that he be allowed to go home with a few teeth left (Juvenal 3.298–301 LCL).

Such violence and cruelty permeated Roman imperial society. The sadistic enjoyment of the suffering, torment and death of animals and humans, redefined as sub-humans, served to parade the paramount position of power over every other value.[24] And those who could bully took every opportunity to do so.

Conclusion

Daily life in the Near East in New Testament times was daily life in ruralized societies under Roman domination. Everyone followed traditional values and behaviors, with elites setting trends and non-elites several generations behind. The architectural structures of the *polis* served as "wording" to articulate the significance of elite life in the aristocratic empire, largely in a political register.[25] Villages replicated the structures of the *polis* in a kinship register, while villagers emulated *polis* values. The system required a large number (by our standards) of slaves and throwaway people.

Let me conclude with an observation by Carroll Quigley:

> These Roman ruling groups were not hampered by theories or ideologies, although quick with rationalizations. They never found logical obstacles to action, because they cared nothing for logic. In fact, they had no long-range idea of what they were doing—ever. It has often been said that the Romans had no plans of world conquest and that they became rulers of the world in fits of absent-mindedness, like England acquired its empire. This may be correct, but it means nothing. The Romans had no long-range plans for world conquest because they had no long-range ideas on anything.[26]

---

24 See Carney (1975) 85–86.

25 See Kautsky (1982).

26 Quigley (1983) 374.

BIBLIOGRAPHY

Auguet, R. (1994) *Cruelty and Civilization: The Roman Games*. London. (Repr. 1972). **Breese, G.** (1966) *Urbanization in Newly Developing Countries*. Englewood Cliffs. **Brenman, E.** (1985) Cruelty and Narrowmindedness. *International Journal of Psychoanalysis* 66: 273–81. **Casson, L.** (1975) *Daily Life in Ancient Rome*. New York. Rev. ed. Baltimore. **Crick, M.R.** (1976) *Explorations in Language and Meaning: Towards a Semantic Anthropology*. London. **Duncan-Jones, R.** (1982) *The Economy of the Roman Empire: Quantitative Studies*. 2nd ed. Cambridge. **Dupont, F.** (1992) *Daily Life in Ancient Rome*. trans. Christopher Woodall. Oxford. **Elliott, J.H.** (1991) Temple versus Household in Luke-Acts: A Contrast in Social Institutions. Pp. 211–40 in J.H. Neyrey, ed., *The Social World of Luke-Acts: Models for Interpretation*. Peabody. **Fiensy, D.A.** (1991) *The Social History of Palestine in the Herodian Period: This Land Is Mind*. Lewiston. **Gugler, J., ed.** (1996) *The Urban Transformation of the Developing World*. Oxford. **Hacquard, G., with J. Dautry and O. Maisani** (1952) *Guide Romain Antique*. Paris. **Hallie, P.P.** (1982) *Cruelty*. Rev. ed. Middletown, Conn. **Hanson, K.C. and D. Oakman** (1998) *Palestine in the Time of Jesus: Social Structures and Social Conflicts*. Minneapolis. **Hays, S.P.** (1993) From the History of the City to the History of the Urbanized Society. *Journal of Urban History* 19: 3–25. **Hess, H.** (1986) The Traditional Sicilian Mafia: Organized Crime and Repressive Crime. Pp. 95–112 in R.J. Kelly, ed., *Organized Crime: A Global Perspective*. Totowa, N.J. **Hopkins, K.** (1983) *Death and Renewal* (Sociological Studies in Roman History 2) Cambridge. (Esp. Chap. 1: Murderous Games, pp. 1–30 and chap 4: Death in Rome, pp. 201–56). (1998) Christian Number and Its Implications. *Journal of Early Christian Studies* 6, 185–226. **Kautsky, J.H.** (1982) *The Politics of Aristocratic Empire*. Chapel Hill. **Lupsha, P.A.** (1986) Organized Crime in the United States. Pp. 32–57 in R.J. Kelly, ed., *Organized Crime: A Global Perspective*. Totowa, N.J. **MacMullen, R.** (1974) *Roman Social Relations: 50 B.C. to A.D. 284*. New Haven. **Malina, B.J.** (1986) Religion in the World of Paul: A Preliminary Sketch, *Biblical Theology Bulletin* 16: 92–101. (1993) *The New Testament World: Insights from Cultural Anthropology*. Rev. ed. Louisville. (1994) Religion in the Imagined New Testament World: More Social Science Lenses *Scriptura* 51:1–26. (1996a) Mediterranean Sacrifice: Dimensions of Domestic and Political Religion. *Biblical Theology Bulletin* 26: 26–44. (1996b) Patron and Client: The Analogy Behind Synoptic Theology. Pp. 143–75 in B.J. Malina, *The Social World of Jesus and the Gospels*. London and New York. **Moxnes, H.** (1991) Patron-Client Relations and the New Community in Luke-Acts. Pp. 241–71 in J.H. Neyrey, ed., *The Social World of Luke-Acts: Models for Interpretation*. Peabody. **Oakman, D.E.** (1986) *Jesus and the Economic Questions of His Day*. Lewiston. (1991) The Countryside in Luke-Acts. Pp. 151–79 in J.H. Neyrey, ed., *The Social World of Luke-Acts: Models for Interpretation*. Peabody. **Powell, J.D.** (1977) Peasant Society and Clientelistic Politics. Pp. 147–61 in S.W. Schmidt, J.C. Scott, C. Landé and L. Guasti, eds., *Friends, Followers, and Factions: A Reader in Political Clientelism*. Berkeley. **Quigley, C.** (1983) *Weapons Systems and Political*

Stability. Washington, D.C. **Rohrbaugh, R.L.** (1991) The Pre-Industrial City in Luke-Acts: Urban Social Relations. Pp. 125–49 in J.H. Neyrey, ed., *The Social World of Luke-Acts: Models for Interpretation*. Peabody. **Routledge, B.** (1997) Learning to Love the King: Urbanism and the State in Iron Age Moab. Pp 130–44 in W.E. Aufrecht, N.A. Mirau, and S.W. Gauley, eds., *Urbanism in Antiquity: From Mesopotamia to Crete*. (JSOTS 244) Sheffield. **Robben, A.C.G.M.** (1989) Habits of the Home: Spatial Hegemony and the Structuration of House and Society in Brazil, *American Anthropologist* 91: 570–88. **Rupp, D.W.** (1997) 'Metro' Nea Paphos: Suburban Sprawl in Southwestern Cyprus in the Hellenistic and Earlier Roman Periods. Pp. 236–62 in W.E. Aufrecht, N.A. Mirau, and S.W. Gauley, eds., *Urbanism in Antiquity: From Mesopotamia to Crete*. (JSOTS 244) Sheffield. **Southall, A.** (1998) *The City in Time and Space*. Cambridge. **Taylor, L.R.** (1977) Nobles, Clients and Personal Armies. Pp. 179–92 in S.W. Schmidt, J.C. Scott, C. Landé and L. Guasti, eds., *Friends, Followers, and Factions: A Reader in Political Clientelism*. Berkeley. **Terrenato, N.** (1998) Tam Firmum Municipium: The Romanization of Volaterrae and Its Cultural Implications. *Journal of Roman Studies* 88: 94–114. **Veyne, P.** (1998) Rome: Une Société d'hommes. *L'Histoire* No. 221 (May): 37. **Walston, J.** (1986) See Naples and Die: Organized Crime in Campania. Pp. 134–58 in R.J. Kelly, ed., *Organized Crime: A Global Perspective*. Totowa, N.J. **Walters, G.D.** (1990) *The Criminal Lifestyle: Patterns of Serious Criminal Conduct*. Newbury Park et alibi. **Wolf, Eric R.** (1965) Aspects of Group Relations in a Complex Society: Mexico. Pp. 85–101 in D.B. Heath and R.N. Adams, eds., *Contemporary Cultures and Societies of Latin America: A Reader in the Social Anthropology of Middle and South America and the Caribbean*. New York.

ABBREVIATIONS

LCL: The Loeb Classical Library

Reciprocity and the Poor among the First Followers of Jesus in Jerusalem

Stephan J. Joubert
University of Pretoria

Social Changes in the Ancient Mediterranean World

Social interaction in the ancient Mediterranean world was based on the minimal demand that people had to reward those who have helped them.[1] As a matter of fact, two principles, basic to most forms of social interchange, took shape at an early stage:

(a) An individual who supplied a rewarding service to another placed him/her under obligation.

(b) In order to discharge this obligation, the beneficiary had to confer a benefit on the benefactor in turn.

Any exchange of gifts or services in ancient Mediterranean societies gave rise to the constitution of specific relationships with clear patterns of superordination between the interlocutors. This imbalance of power usually established reciprocity in the exchange, since nobody wanted to be in an inferior position in social relationships, as Aristotle tells us in his *Nichomachean Ethics* (IV.3.24). Various forms of friendship, such as guest-friendships and ritualized friendships,[2] were shaped according to the principles inherent to this "reciprocity ethic." In this regard patronage, civic benefaction, and interpersonal benefaction were probably the most prominent forms of social exchange between status equals, as well as between socially disproportionate individuals and/or groups in the Mediterranean world about the first century C.E.

The exchange of services and gifts often turned into agonistic competitions for public honor among benefactors, as well as for material goods

1 Cicero (*De officiis* 1.47) writes that if obligations were incurred between any two parties, an adequate response was required: "for no duty is more imperative than that of proving one's gratitude."

2 See e.g., Herman (1987), and Fitzgerald (1997).

and services among prospective beneficiaries.[3] In these agonistic contests of gift-giving, the beneficiary who could not match the gifts or services bestowed upon him, became obliged to the benefactor, thus losing his own social standing, authority, and rank to the benefactor. Therefore, the principle of balanced reciprocity, that is, returning the same sort of gifts, or gifts of equal value for those received, was frequently stressed (e.g., Arrian, *Epictetio Dissertationes* II.9.12).

No Free Meals for the Hungry

Lenski[4] paints a grim picture of social stratification in ancient societies. According to him, only two percent of the population in these societies belonged to the ruling elite, while about eight percent comprised the so-called service class in and around the cities. The remaining ninety percent lived in villages and worked on the land to support the first two classes. However, the term "poor" did not designate social rank or economic status in the ancient Mediterranean world.[5] Poverty was rather seen as the result of "status-depriving" circumstances such as illness, debt, famine, or the death of a spouse (in the case of widows).

Shortages of basic food supplies constantly posed a threat to ancient peasant communities.[6] These shortages were caused by factors such as wars, which often led to the burning of crops and pillaging;[7] the location of cities far from sea ports;[8] the stockpiling of grain for export that denied the locals access to basic food supplies; crop failures; and damage to crops by pests.[9] Various efforts to alleviate these problems by benefactors, such as

---

3 The great Greek athletic contests provided the metaphoric framework for this agonistic Mediterranean attitude toward life. Agonistic motifs were also popular in philosophical circles; see Schwankl (1997).

4 Lenski (1966) 284.

5 Normally, financial means did not determine social status in Mediterranean societies, but birth. See in this regard the informative views of Malina (1993) 105–6.

6 From the available information we know that the Roman economy was underdeveloped affecting masses of people, mostly peasant farmers, living at or near subsistence level (Garnsey and Saller [1987] 43). The same also holds true for the Hellenistic world.

7 See Quass (1993) 231–34.

8 The locality of cities close to harbors was crucial for the transport of grain (Rickman [1980] 16).

9 These shortages were so serious that Polybius actually relates the depopulation of Greece in his day to natural disasters such as destruction of crops by bad weather, and diseases. See in this regard also Jameson (1983) 6.

officially appointed grain commissioners and grain wardens, therefore became a permanent feature of most cities.[10] However, in spite of charitable forms of assistance by benefactors to their communities, most of the benefactors used their benefactions to increase their own public honor and not to alleviate the material needs of others. In this regard Bolkestein[11] tells us that the major motivation for the bestowal of benefits in the Roman world was related to the joy of giving; the expectation of an adequate return; the striving for public honor; and political ambition.[12]

Individuals elected to public positions were expected to direct their expenditure on behalf of the community to "pleasures and public works," the so-called *voluptates* and *opera publica*.[13] Therefore, numerous public benefits, such as festivals or games, were bestowed by benefactors as part of the legal obligations associated with the holding of public positions (the so-called *euergesia ob honorem*). These benefits were always collective; they were conferred on all citizens in a specific community, not only on a few fortunate individuals.

Altruistic motives were far removed from the typical mentality of the nobles in the ancient Mediterranean world. According to Veyne: "pagan literature is full of civic or patrician pride; this harsh climate is the climate of euergetism, which gives edifices and pleasures to the citizens rather than alms to the poor."[14] In the same vein Garnsey and Saller state that the ideology of Greco-Roman euergetism was civic, not humanitarian—"very few euergetists would have described what they were doing as poor relief."[15] Whenever those who experienced severe economic hardship received material assistance in the ancient Mediterranean world, it should be understood within the framework of collective benefactions that were bestowed on communities, and not on specific individuals. Assistance to the poor was never understood as a moral obligation.

---

[10] Cf. Garnsey (1988) 15. Various inscriptions honor grain commissioners for, among others, interest-free loans to their cities and for "die von ihnen bewerkstelligten Verkäufe von Lebensmitteln zu (unter das gültige Marktniveau) gesenkten Preisen" (Quass [1993] 250).

[11] Bolkestein (1939) 317–18.

[12] The regular recipients of state grain in Rome at the time of Julius Caesar were actually a privileged group of about 150,000 people. They were not necessarily deprived of material goods (Garnsey [1988] 211ff.).

[13] Veyne (1990) 10ff.

[14] Veyne (1990) 20.

[15] Garnsey and Saller (1987) 101.

The general agonistic atmosphere of social exchange in ancient Graeco-Roman societies is very different from the early Christian world of Tertullian in the second century C.E., when he writes in his *Apologetica* (39:7) that, "instead of engaging in *euergesia,* Christians rather give to the poor, the orphans and the old people." Prell summarizes this attitude:

> Eine Armenpolitik existierte somit nicht... Ansätze altruistischen Handelns sind bei den Römern zwar sichtbar, jedoch, erkannte erst die Spätantike die Armen als soziale Kategorie, die der Hilfe anderer bedarf. Es war die Christentum, das den Armen ihren Platz innerhalb der Gesellschaft einräumte.[16]

However, the roots of this "new approach" toward the socially destitute in the earliest Christian communities should be traced back to ancient Israel. Since it is my contention that the early followers of Jesus in Jerusalem started out as a Jewish Messianic group, the views of Israel and Judaism will be used as the interpretative framework in this contribution for the early followers of Jesus' views on the poor.[17]

The Socially Destitute in Jewish Benefaction

Public bestowals of honor in the form of statues, golden crowns, honorary decrees, etc., were forbidden in Jewish societies. Flavius Josephus (*CA* II, 217), for example, tells us that those who live according to Jewish laws could not expect material rewards such as silver, gold, crowns of wild olive or parsley. The only public honor that the Jews were allowed to bestow, along the lines of Graeco-Roman benefaction, was the daily sacrifice in the temple for the Emperor's family on behalf of all Jews (*CA* II, 74–78). Other public displays of gratitude, such as the erection of statues for benefactors (*CA* II, 74f.) or funerals and monuments for the dead, were not allowed (*CA* II, 205).

In the Diaspora, where social exchange relationships such as public benefaction and patronage were operative, relatively few examples exist of Jewish participation in relationships of this nature. Rajak[18] points out that although Jews were not outside the framework of benefaction and, although they at times honored Greek and Roman officials along typical

---

16 Prell (1997) 296.

17 Textual evidence suggests that the first followers of Jesus, including Paul, were Jewish "sectarians." They broke away from the community that mothered them and were involved in the process of forming a distinct one, though "it was related in various ways to its forebear" (Witherington [1998] 88).

18 Rajak (1996) 319.

"euergetistic" lines, the absence in Jewish epigraphy "of virtually all the language in which the transactions of euergetism can be conducted" cannot be an accident. "To enter the Jewish world, as a sympathizer or proselyte, would have been to learn a new dialect of a familiar language."[19]

Although social exchange, as it was conceptualized within the ancient Graeco-Roman world, did not play a significant role in Jewish societies, this does not imply that the principles basic to social reciprocity were completely absent. On the contrary, gift exchange and the subsequent reciprocal relationships between benefactors and beneficiaries formed an important aspect of ancient Jewish societies, but then in particular forms, as indicated in the discussion below.[20]

Characteristics of Social Exchange in the Ancient Jewish World

Numerous examples in the Bible deal with the exchange of gifts or services in ancient Israel (e.g., Gen 33; Exod 2; 1 Sam; Judg 8:5–9, 35; 2 Sam 14:22; 2 Kgs 4:8–17; 2 Chr 20:10–1). In order to form a basic idea of the characteristics of these exchange relationships, the following two aspects should be taken into consideration:

> (a) *The position of the destitute.* The "poor," such as children, widows, slaves and strangers, played a significant role within ancient Israel's ethos, particularly around the second half of the seventh century B.C.E. (cf. Deut 15:1–18; 24:17–22). As part of ancient Israel's emphasis on "die Verankerung der religiösen Gesetzgebung im Alltagsleben,"[21] these groups became the focal point of ordinary Israelites' almsgiving and care. This religious duty of giving to the poor at times involved reciprocity. In Deut 15:8, for example, it is supposed that the services/gifts bestowed upon the poor are to be considered as loans that must be returned.[22]

---

19 Although some traits of benefaction were present in ancient Jewish society about the first century C.E., solid evidence for the presence of patronage only comes from Rabbinic literature from about the mid-third century C.E. onward. In *Y. Berakhot* 9, 1, for example, we read of a client who, when visiting his patron, asked his servant to inform him that he was waiting at the gate of the court. The behavior of this patron is then contrasted with that of God who not only allows petitioners into his presence, but also immediately answers those who plead their case before him.

20 In this regard I am indebted to the views of Peterman (1997) 22–50, who offers more fully documented evidence from a variety of Jewish texts, which, for obvious reasons, need not be repeated again.

21 Bultmann (1992) 37.

22 The poor in this situation were, of course, "nicht der schlechthin Mittellose,

(b) *The role of divine reward.*[23] God was soon viewed as the implicit object of the Israelites' almsgiving, particularly in wisdom literature. In Prov 19:17, for example, the wise man who is helping the poor is presented as making a loan to God. Within this context, it is not the socially destitute, but God, who actually functions as the beneficiary, since he is placed in debt to the benefactor.[24] The fact that the poor were not in a position to reciprocate the benefits they received from their benefactors obviously posed a threat to the nature of social exchange in Israelite society. However, this stumbling block was addressed by the idea of God's personal intervention in reciprocal relations. As the one who sides with the lowly and the downcast, he would personally reward their benefactors.

Within the orbit of Diaspora Judaism, the question of divine reward for good deeds remained a prominent theme, as the book of Tobit makes clear.[25] Amid Tobit's blindness, he is rewarded for his righteous deeds (which included the giving of alms) through a goat his wife received as extra payment for her work (2:11–14). However, God's response to the righteous man, who gives alms, is not only limited to material returns, but also to returns on a religious level. As a matter of fact, taking care of the needs of the destitute is considered to be such a big benefit that God replicates the benefactor with the most precious gift he himself possesses, namely forgiveness of sins and salvation (Tobit 12:9). This interpretation of ethical behavior toward the destitute is also shared by the well-known Jewish wisdom teacher, Jesus ben Sirach. He stresses that alms or good deeds toward one's father atone for sins (3:14).[26] This also holds true for almsgiving in general (3:30), since good deeds toward one's neighbor, specifically to the poor (29:8–13), leads to salvation from death.

In summary: Over against the Graeco-Roman world, where assistance to the poor was not understood as a moral obligation, the socially destitute played a significant role in the Jewish world. In the words of Klauck: "Trotz mancher Datierungsprobleme, die uns die Quellenbelege aufgeben, kann

---

sondern der in seine wirtschaftliche Existenz gefährdende Notlage Geratene" (Bultmann [1992] 82).

23 See in this regard also Peterman (1997) 23ff.

24 These ideas presuppose another well-known concept, that YHWH is on the side of the poor and the oppressed (e.g., Ps 103:6; 146:7–9).

25 See Marböck (1995) 20.

26 Cf. Sauer (1981) 14.

man ingesamt doch festhalten, daß die jüdische Armenpflege für den Bereich der vor- und außerchristlichen Antiken vorbildich war."[27] Almsgiving to the poor always signalled the start of a reciprocal relationship with God, who would personally reward the benefactors.

Benefit Exchange and the First Followers of Jesus of Nazareth

A NEW VIEW OF BENEFICIARIES

According to the Synoptic Gospels, Jesus of Nazareth viewed the poor, that is, people who were unable to maintain their inherited social status, as the objects of God's benefactions (Luke 4:18–19; 6:20). His followers were to follow in his footsteps. In their benefactions they had to shift the emphasis from the advantaged (that is, those who were worthy of receiving and also in a position to return benefits) to the poor and the lowly who could not reciprocate any favors (e.g., Matt 5:21–48; 25:31–46). At the same time it was even expected of them to bestow benefits upon people who refused to show any gratitude, such as their enemies.

The basic differentiation of status and power, as well as the expected social rewards that formed an integral part of all social exchange relationships, were given new meanings among the followers of Jesus. For them the intrinsic gratification of bestowing benefits was to be viewed as sufficient reward for their beneficent efforts. They were not to give in order to receive a return. At the same time, those who had nothing to give in return, or those who refused to offer any satisfactory return, were not to be viewed as being under obligation to them, in the sense of being placed under pressure to comply with their demands. Any bestowal of unilateral benefits in the early Christian groups did not imply that benefactors "accumulated" a capital of willing compliance on which they could draw whenever it was in their own interest.

CHRIST AS INDIRECT OBJECT OF BENEFITS

Social exchanges in antiquity had to be accompanied by a return service of some sort so as not to break off relations between the parties involved. Without reciprocity social cohesion in society was under threat. However, as already stated, the followers of Jesus were not allowed to "misuse" unilateral bestowals of benefits as opportunities to initiate and/or emphasis power differentials between them and their beneficiaries. Rather they had to consider any act of giving as sufficient and gratifying in itself. But, the very nature of reciprocity called for tangible rewards for

---

27 Klauck (1989) 170.

services rendered. Internal gratification was simply not enough. A dilemma for the first followers of Jesus? Yes, but one that was "solved" by their understanding of the resurrected Christ as the "indirect object" of their benefactions. This belief provided the main impetus for followers of Jesus to enter into reciprocal relations with beneficiaries, even in spite of the expected negative reactions from the latter. Any bestowal of benefits on their part was now to be viewed as "repayment" of their own gratitude for the eschatological benefactions of Christ. Within this context it would therefore be morally improper to break off relations with the recipients of their benefactions, whatever their response, since this would imply ungratefulness on their part for their participation in Christ's salvation.

BENEFACTORS AS SERVANTS

The role of benefactors among the early followers of Jesus took on a service-oriented character. Although individuals did attain leadership positions in their groups on account of material benefactions, such as monetary donations and provision of their houses as meeting places for the Christians, it was expected of them to use their wealth and influence to the advantage of group members and outsiders. Their "honor" within the Church was dependent upon their deeds of generosity (cf. e.g., Barnabas' surrender of his property in Acts 4:36–37), while misuse of their wealth or status in any exchange of resources was regarded as shameful behavior.[28] But, on the other hand, in terms of the demand on believers to imitate Jesus in his role as servant, pressure was placed on Christian patrons "to give in private without expecting any returns in the forms of clients or heightened status in the community."[29]

An example of an "ideal" Christian patron is presented to us in Rom 16:1–2 in Paul's reference to Phoebe as a *diakonos* as well as a *prostatis* of many, including Paul himself. Female patrons and benefactors were not a strange sight in ancient societies, fulfilling the same functions as their male counterparts, such as donating money for the building of temples and baths.[30] Therefore, the Christians in Rome would have had no difficulty in understanding Paul's reference to Phoebe as *prostatis* as an indication of her status as an influential leader of the Christian community in Cenchreae. But, at the same time, Paul's emphasis on her ministry of hospitality should also be seen in conjunction with her position as patron. The "normal"

---

28 See the discussions of Paul's refusal of material assistance from certain influential patrons and its ramifications in Corinth, by Marshall (1987) and Chow (1992).

29 Moxnes (1991) 266.

30 Cf. also Van Bremen (1983) 223–42.

power differentials embedded in patron-client relations in the ancient world were thus redefined in terms of these service-oriented functions (cf. also Matt 18:1–5; Luke 22:24–27).

The Early Followers of Jesus in Jerusalem and the Poor

THE SOCIO-ECONOMIC SITUATION IN JERUSALEM

After dealing with the first Christians' views of benefaction on a rather high level of abstraction, we now turn our attention to the views and conduct of the first followers of Jesus in Jerusalem (that is, "the Jerusalem Group") with regard to the poor. Our source of information in this regard is the book of Acts, which presents us with a secondary interpretation of the beliefs and patterns of social interaction in the Jerusalem Group.[31] According to Luke, the presumed author of Acts, this Messianic group came into existence after the outpouring of the Spirit on the day of Pentecost (Acts 2).

Luke's numerous references to poverty-related issues among the first followers of Jesus in Jerusalem (Acts 2:42, 45; 3:6; 4:32–37; 5:1–11; 6:1–6; 11:27–30; 24:17) reflect the poor socio-economic conditions in the city around 33–57 C.E. The followers of Jesus formed part of the large group of day laborers and peasant farmers who lived in and around Jerusalem. Most of these people lived beneath the sustenance level, which was calculated at about 200 *denarii* per year.[32] As a typical pre-industrial city, Jerusalem was largely dependent on the surrounding villages and on trade with neighboring territories to provide its basic needs. The cumulative impact of state and religious taxes; the underdeveloped economy; the unstable political situation in Judea; and food shortages and famines had a severe effect on most inhabitants of the city.[33] These harsh conditions made it a daily strug-

---

31 Ever since the sharp criticism of Baur (1969) of Luke's prejudiced view of the Church as "ein sehr schwaches und unklares Bild, das für die geschichtliche Betrachtung wenig sicheres darbietet," scholars have been divided into two camps on this issue. Without getting involved in the intricate debate concerning the historical reliability of Acts, I take, as my point of departure, the view of Dibelius (1957) 9, who states that "die geschichtliche Zuverlässigkeit der Apostelgeschichte aber ist von Fall zu Fall zu ermessen, jeweils nach dem Material, das Lukas verarbeitet hat."

32 Ben-David (1974) 458. He is of the opinion that the average farmer in Palestine had only about 150 *denarii* to take care of taxes and the needs of his family, usually with about four to five members (p. 298). Stegemann and Stegemann (1995) 89 come to, more or less, the same conclusion. According to them, the average net income per head during the first century was around 40 *denarii*.

33 Jewish citizens had to pay two types of tax to the Romans, namely the *tributum*

gle for many of them to survive, let alone maintain their inherited status. However, in spite of its weak infrastructures, people from all over Palestine and the Diaspora still flocked to Jerusalem because of its importance as the religious capital of the Jewish people.[34]

Poverty Relief among the Followers of Jesus in Jerusalem

STAGE ONE: SPONTANEOUS ACTS OF BENEFICENCE

The first followers of Jesus in Jerusalem did not escape the consequences of food shortages, high taxes and social unrest in Judea. However, individual benefactors soon started sharing their material means with less-privileged members of their group in spontaneous acts of generosity. For example, Luke recalls how Barnabas, who later became an influential leader in the early Christian movement (Acts 11:25–30; 12:25–15:41), sold his property in order to assist poverty-stricken believers (4:36–37). The story of Annanias and Sapphira (5:1–11) also points to the presence of other benefactors in their midst.[35] During the early stages of the Jerusalem community, assistance to the poor was not strictly organized or controlled; rather, it was the result of the spontaneous initiatives of individual benefactors.

This initial sharing of possessions among the first followers of Jesus was probably based on a "charismatisch-enthusiastischer Grundlage."[36] On the one hand, this implied a spontaneous sharing of material means along the principles as spelled out by Jesus. On the other hand, the Jerusalem Christians' actions were probably also determined by their fervent expectation of an imminent return of the resurrected Christ.

---

soli (a land tax) and the *tributum capitis* (personal tax) (Millar [1981] 92ff.), as well as a number of indirect forms of tax that were collected by the ever-present tax-collectors on the value of products or merchandise, which ranged from two to twenty-five percent. These taxes were so oppressive that many people, according to Josephus (*Ant* 18, 90), saw this as the main reason for the Jewish-Roman war.

34 Jerusalem probably also attracted a large number of peasant farmers who became day laborers in the city to avoid the high taxes, since inhabitants of cities during the reign of Herod the Great paid much less tax than the farmers. According to Oppenheimer (1977) 71, farmers had to pay about twenty-three percent of their annual income in taxes during this period.

35 According to Capper (1998) 503, this story, with its strong paraenetic force, reflects "a kind of fall of the first community from innocence." Clearly, these individual acts of beneficence in the Jerusalem group were the exception rather than the general rule; so also Jervell (1998) 194.

36 Klauck (1989b) 97.

STAGE TWO: CENTRALIZED POOR RELIEF

After a short time of spontaneous benefactions by individuals, care for the poor among the followers of Jesus was centralized. Luke's reference to a *Gütergemeinschaft*, a community of goods, in the so-called summaries in Acts (2:43–47; 4:32–27; 5:12–16) reflects a transition from individual acts of beneficence to a more organized system of poverty relief under the control of the apostles. In the second summary (4:32–37) Luke records how people placed the proceeds of the properties they sold at the apostles' feet, who then distributed it among the needy at the meetings of the believers. This points to the presence of a *gemeinsamer Kasse*,[37] a common fund, under the auspices of the apostles that was used to assist believers who, due to constant food shortages and depressing social conditions, could not provide for their own livelihood. However, this property sharing was probably voluntary. It was not strictly regulated or enforced upon all group members.

According to Luke, the followers of Jesus gathered for daily meal-fellowship at different houses in Jerusalem (2:42, 46). These meals, where the "breaking of the bread" took place, probably served as the impetus for the so-called "agape" meals (the Eucharist), which soon started taking place in the household settings of the early Church (Acts 20:7–11; 1 Cor 11:17–34; Jude 12).[38] At the daily meetings of believers during the early stages of the Jerusalem Church, the apostles distributed material means from their community's common fund to the poor whose abilities to maintain their inherited status were severely threatened.

Official forms of support to the poor by Jewish religious authorities were probably operative as early as the first century C.E. in Jerusalem. In the Mishnah tract *Peah* 8:7 reference is made to the *quppah*, a fund to which Jews had to contribute every Friday, when two officially appointed persons collected the money, which was afterwards divided among the poor by a committee of three in the form of food, money, and clothes. People who did not have enough food left for at least fourteen meals received help from the *quppah*. The *tamchui* was a fund from which food such as bread, beans, and wine was provided to strangers and the poor on a daily basis, that is, to people who did not have enough food left for at least two meals.[39] Because of a lack of sufficient historical evidence of the existence of such organized charity in Jerusalem in the Second Testament

---

37 Klauck (1989a) 171.

38 See in this regard Osiek and Balch (1997) 212; Capper (1998) 512.

39 See Shurden (1970) 73.

period, some scholars reject an early dating.[40] On the other hand, other scholars are of the opinion that such a practice did not only exist at an early stage in Jerusalem, but that it actually provided the conceptual framework for the first Christians' own system of care for the poor.[41] If the latter assumptions are correct, we may assume that the apostles replaced the individual efforts of Christian benefactors to take care of the poor with a more efficient method that was loosely based on the poverty care system of the Jewish authorities.

STAGE THREE: THE APPOINTMENT OF "OFFICIAL" HELPERS

In Acts 6:1–7 Luke refers to the appointment of the seven "official" helpers from among the ranks of the "Hellenists" (that is, Greek speaking Jews from the Diaspora) to take over the responsibility of caring for the poor within the context of the daily meal-fellowship. Due to their more critical stance toward the temple cult, believers who came from the Diaspora complained that the Judean followers of Jesus discriminated against them. Their public protest eventually led to the appointment of a number of men from their midst to take care of the poor.[42] This appointment probably represents a new, more structured phase of assistance to the poor in the Jerusalem community. The economic hardships that believers had to face, the ever-increasing numbers of the Jerusalem community, and the ideological differences between different factions in their midst, in the end forced the apostles to appoint helpers to accept responsibility for the poor.[43]

---

40 E.g. Seccombe (1978) 140–43.

41 So Jeremias (1962) 147, and Haenchen (1977) 255, 424. Against this viewpoint, Jervell (1998) 222, n. 649, and Walter (1983) 370–93 reject an independent form of poverty care among the Jerusalem Christians, because, as one of the "lose Gruppierungen innerhalb der jüdischen Tempelkultgemeinde Jerusalems" (p. 376), they still shared in the official Jewish poverty support.

42 Food shortages often led to public unrest or riots. E.g., Tacitus (*Annals* 6, 13) refers to a huge riot in Rome around 32 C.E. over excessive grain prices.

43 Hengel (1972) 41–42 bases the material neglect in the Jerusalem community in Acts 6:1–7 on the fervent eschatological expectations of the believers, which caused them to throw all forms of economical organization overboard. However, if my presupposition is correct, that Acts 6:1–7 also provides a historical glimpse into the socio-economic situation in Jerusalem during the mid-forties, this eschatological enthusiasm (which was rife from the initial stages of the Church, that is around 33/4 C.E.) was quickly tempered by the harsh realities of believers starving, falling ill, and dying because of malnutrition and severe food shortages.

STAGE FOUR: HELP FROM OUTSIDE CHRISTIAN GROUPS

Among the first followers of Jesus in Jerusalem, poverty was never idealized; it was a daily reality that stared many individuals in the face. In spite of the altruistic attitudes and beneficent deeds of believers toward each other, the daily needs of an ever-growing community could not be sufficiently met by a relatively small group of benefactors who were in a position to render material assistance. External factors such as food shortages and persecutions (cf Acts 8; 12) also posed a serious threat to the socio-economic well-being of the Jerusalem Christians. In this regard, Luke refers to a famine during the reign of Claudius (Acts 11:27–30).[44] The well-known Jewish historian, Flavius Josephus (*Ant.* 20, 51), also refers to this famine in Judea during the procuratorships of Cuspius Fadius (44–?46) and Tiberius Alexander (?46–48).[45] This famine, which could be dated somewhere between 44–46 C.E., was probably followed a few years later by yet another severe famine in Judea (Josephus, *Ant.* 3, 320). Josephus tells us that it took place during the highpriesthood of Ismael ben Phiabi, who, according to Schwartz,[46] was appointed in this position in 49 C.E.[47] From the available historical information we may deduce that during the years 44–49 the people of Jerusalem were hard hit by one or two severe food shortages.

Food crises normally led to steep increases in grain prices, which made it almost impossible for the poor to buy grain. In this regard, Josephus (*Ant.* 3, 320) reports that the price of grain was thirteen times higher than normal during the famine around 49 C.E. Although historical evidence on mortal-

---

44 However, Luke's view that the entire *imperium Romanum* was affected by this famine should probably be understood in terms of the numerous local food shortages/famines around this time in Egypt, Syria, Greece, and also in Judea. Cf. Garnsey (1988) 21, who states that between 45–47 C.E. numerous food crises affected all these territories.

45 Perhaps Flavius Josephus' reference to queen Helena of Adiabene's benefaction, which consisted of sending large quantities of figs from Cyprus and grain from Egypt to the people of Judea (*Ant* 20, 51–53), could help date this famine even more accurately. We know from information in the Tebtunis Papyrii that Egypt experienced very high grain prices due to crop failures in the spring of 45 C.E. This would imply that there would only have been excess grain in Egypt at the earliest during the spring of 46.

46 Schwartz (1992) 177–220.

47 The well-known thesis of Joachim Jeremias (1928) 98–103, that the famine, which he dates around 48 C.E., was worsened by the Sabbatical year of 47/8, is still a topic of discussion; cf. e.g., Wehnert (1997) 264.

ity rates during famines in Judea is not available,[48] we may assume that outright starvation, epidemic diseases, and death were the fate of a large number of Judeans (cf. Josephus; *Ant.* 20, 51).[49]

THE PAULINE COLLECTION FOR JERUSALEM

Luke tells us in Acts 11:27–30 that Christians in the city of Antioch came to the rescue of the Jerusalem community during the famine in the time of Claudius by sending financial aid to them. This "collection" was delivered by Paul and Barnabas in the year 48. During Paul's visit to Jerusalem, the leadership of Jerusalem also requested of him and Barnabas to take care of the poor in their midst on a more permanent basis (Gal 2:10b). In response, Paul personally undertook an imaginative "ecumenical collection" among the communities under his supervision in Galatia, Achaia, and Macedonia between the years 51/2–57 (cf. Gal 2:10b; 1 Cor 16:1–4; 2 Cor 8–9; Rom 15:25–27). This collection was aimed at enabling the followers of Jesus in Jerusalem to attain their honorable position within the early Christian movement (cf. Rom 15:25; 2 Cor 9:12). At the same time, the collection was intended to give visible expression to the bond of unity among believers.

At the beginning of 57 C.E. Paul and his companions started the journey to Jerusalem to deliver the collection.[50] Although Luke narrates Paul's meeting with James, the new leader of the Jerusalem Church in Acts 21: 17ff., he is silent about the actual delivery of the collection. As a matter of fact, his only reference to Paul's bringing of the collection to Jerusalem is to be found in the apostle's later speech before Felix in Acts 24:17, in which he

---

[48] The early Christian historian Eusebius (*Hist Eccl* 9, 8) offers a very graphic description of a famine in Palestine in 312–313 C.E., during the reign of Maximin. Due to a severe drought and a war at this time, countless people died in the cities and even more in the villages. Plagues and hunger wiped out almost the whole population. This led to people eating strange, even poisonous foods, and many women turning to shameful behavior such as begging in public.

[49] Famines also led to social dislocation, such as large-scale emigration, the selling of children, suicides, and riots against the rulers as one of the last resorts of an utterly desperate people.

[50] In Acts, Luke presents us with the specific itinerary of the apostle, from Corinth through Macedonia (20:3), via Philippi by boat to Troas (20:5). From there the party travelled to Assos (20:13), Mytilene (20:14), Samos, and Milete (20:15), and then further via Kos and Rhodos to Patara (21:1). Hereafter Paul and the delegates travelled in a southerly direction to Tyre (21:3) and then via Ptolemais (21:7) to Caesarea (21:8), which eventually brought them to Jerusalem. See the informative discussions of Paul's itinerary by R. Riesner (1998) 218–19.

is quoted as saying that the reason for his visit to Jerusalem was to bring alms to his people, and to sacrifice.[51]

Although Luke does not narrate the delivery of Paul's collection, he at least had a rudimental idea about the basic framework of Paul's final visit to Jerusalem. From the available evidence in Acts we may construct the following scenario: at Paul's meeting with the elders and James, the latter proposed a public gesture would satisfy both himself and his constituency that Paul still remained a practicing Jew, and that his "antinomian reputation among many Jews was unjustified."[52] Specifically, James expected Paul to undergo the purification rite expected of all Jews returning from pagan territory who wanted to enter the temple, as well as to pay for the Nazarite vows of four Torah-observant members of the Jerusalem community (Acts 21:23–24). Only after Paul had completed this honorable deed in the temple would the Jerusalem community "officially" accept the collection. This strategy would not only relieve the Jerusalem Christians of a heavy financial burden, but it would also safeguard them against any negative reactions from fellow Judeans.

Paul agreed to this proposal. However, he probably insisted that the costly Nazarite vows were to be paid from the collection money. Not only did his own financial position necessitate such a demand, but also his view that in the first instance the collection was intended to address the financial needs of the Jerusalem Church. In this way Paul would have ensured that Jerusalem profited from the collection funds from the onset. At the same time, this "solution" would have given concrete expression to his own role as "benefactor-servant" of this gift to Jerusalem from the side of his communities, as well as to reinforce the bond of fellowship among all believers.

This compromise, which apparently suited both James and Paul, is credited by Luke only to the leadership of the Jerusalem community. But, as Murphy-O'Connor correctly notes,[53] Paul in all probability played an active part in the finding of a solution at this meeting that would not have compromised his own interests and that of his communities. However, the solution reached at the initial meeting between James and Paul was never

---

51 On the basis of Paul's references to the collection in his letters, the majority of scholars take this expression to refer to the collection; cf. e.g., Lohse (1996) 259; Witherington (1997) 712. As to Luke's reference to the collection as a form of almsgiving in Acts 24:17, Schille (1983) 434 notes that Luke, according to his presentation of Paul as the loyal Hellenistic Jew, rightly refers to the collection as a form of almsgiving since it was intended for the poor.

52 Murphy-O'Connor (1996) 349–50.

53 Murphy-O'Connor (1996) 350–51.

concluded, because of Paul's arrest in the Temple (Acts 21). After ending up in Roman custody, the collection was out of his hands. Whether Jerusalem received the collection from the Pauline communities, we shall never know. But at least Paul briefly acted as Christian benefactor of the Jerusalem community through his paying of the Nazarite vows.

Conclusion

In the agonistic ancient Mediterranean culture, benefits were usually not bestowed out of humanitarian reasons, but rather to increase benefactors' honor. Any bestowal of a benefit signalled the start of a long-term reciprocal relationship with specific obligations linked to the role of both benefactor and beneficiary. While the former was dependent upon the positive response of his beneficiary to his gifts, it was in turn expected of the latter to show his gratitude by making an adequate return.

Among the early followers of Jesus, there was a marked difference regarding the objects of benefaction. Those who had nothing to give in return or those who refused to offer any satisfactory return were viewed as "worthy" recipients of gifts or services. However, these beneficiaries were under no moral obligation to make any returns so as to adhere to the principle of balanced reciprocity. Christians were not to give in order to receive a return. Rather, Christ himself became the indirect object of their benefactions. He would eventually reward them for their benefactions.

Among the first followers of Jesus in Jerusalem, poverty, and the consequent loss of inherited honor, was a constant problem that confronted many individuals. Through personal sacrifice, Christian benefactors initially tried to alleviate these problems. Soon afterwards, however, these efforts were centralized. During the daily meal fellowships, some material assets that were disposed to the community were redistributed among the needy by the apostles. After a while, the apostles appointed seven helpers to take responsibility for the distribution of these basic necessities to the various houses. Although these altruistic acts led to strong socio-religious integration among the followers of Jesus, in the end they had to turn to help from the outside so as to assist in alleviating their ever-growing needs. In the end, the apostle Paul had to spend a substantial amount of his time and energy to complete a collection for the Jerusalem Christians.

BIBLIOGRAPHY

Baur, F.C. (1969) *Geschichte der christlichen Kirche. I. Teil.* Leipzig. (1st edition: 1863). **Ben-David, A.** (1974) *Talmudische Ökonomie,* Hildesheim. **Bolkestein, H.W.** (1939) *Wohltätigkeit und Armenpflege im vorchristlichen Altertum.* Utrecht. **Bultmann, C.** (1992) *Der Fremde im antiken Juda. Eine Untersuchung zum sozialen Typenbegriff 'ger' und seinem Bedeutungswandel in der alttestamentlichen Gesetzgebung.* Göttingen. **Capper, B.J.** (1998) Reciprocity and the ethic of Acts. In I.H. Marshall and D. Peterson, eds., *Witness to the Gospel. The Theology of Acts.* Grand Rapids. 1998. **Chow, J.K.** (1992) *Patronage and Power. A Study of Social Networks in Corinth.* Sheffield. **Dibelius, M.** (1957) *Aufsätze zur Apostelgeschichte.* 3rd edition. Göttingen. **Fitzgerald, J.T.** (1997) Friendship in the Greek World Prior to Aristotle. In J.T. Fitzgerald, ed., *Friendship,* 13–34. Leiden. **Garnsey, P.** (1988) *Famine and Food Supply in the Graeco-Roman World: Responses to Risk and Crisis.* Cambridge. **Garnsey P. and R. Saller** (1987) *The Roman Empire. Economy, Society and Culture.* London. **Haenchen, E.** (1977) *Die Apostelgeschichte.* Kritisch-exegetischer Kommentar über das Neue Testament Band 3. 3rd edition. Göttingen. **Hengel, M.** (1972) *Eigentum und Reichtum in der frühe Kirche. Aspekte einer frühchristlichen Sozialgeschichte.* Stuttgart. **Herman, G.** (1987) *Ritualised Friendship and the Greek City.* Cambridge. **Jameson, M.** (1983), Famine in the Greek World. In P. Garnsey and C.R. Whittaker, eds., *Trade and Famine in Classical Antiquity,* 6–16. Cambridge. **Jeremias, J.** (1928) Sabbatjahr und neutestamentlich Chronologie, *Zeitschrift für Neutestamentliche Wissenschaft* 27: 98–103. (1962) *Jerusalem zur Zeit Jesu. Eine kulturgeschichtliche Untersuchung zur neutestamentlichen Zeitgeschichte.* 3rd edition. Göttingen. **Jervell, J.** (1998) *Die Apostelgeschichte.* Kritisch-exegetischer Kommentar über das Neue Testament Band 3/1. Göttingen. **Klauck, H.-J.** (1989a) Die Armut der Jünger in der Sicht des Lukas. In H.-J. Klauck. *Gemeinde, Amt, Sakrament,* 160–94. Würzburg. (1989b) Gütergemeinschaft in der klassischen Antike, in Qumran und im Neuen Testament. In H.-J. Klauck. *Gemeinde, Amt, Sakrament,* 69–100. Würzburg. **Lenski, F.** (1966) *Power and Privilege. A Theory of Social Stratification.* New York. **Lohse. E.** (1996) *Paulus. Eine Biographie.* München. **Malina, B.J.** (1993) *The New Testament World. Insights from Cultural Anthropology.* 2nd revised edition. Louisville. **Marböck, J.** (1995) *Gottes Weisheit unter uns. Zur Theologie des Buches Sirach.* Herder's Biblische Studien 6, Freiburg. **Marshall, P.** (1987) *Enmity in Corinth: Social Conventions in Paul's Relations with the Corinthians.* Wissenschaftliche Untersuchungen zum Neuen Testament 23. Tübingen. **Millar, F.** (1981) *The Roman Empire and its Neighbours.* 2nd edition. London. **Moxnes, H.** (1988) Patron-client Relations and the New Community in Luke-Acts. In J.H. Neyrey, ed., *The Social World of Luke-Acts.* Peabody. **Murphy-O'Connor, J.** (1996) *Paul: A Critical Life.* Oxford. **Oppenheimer, A.** (1975) *The Am Ha-Aretz,* Leiden. **Osiek C. and D.L. Balch** (1997) *Families in the New Testament World. Households and House Churches.* Louisville. **Peterman, G.W.** (1997) *Paul's Gift from Philippi. Conventions of Gift Exchange and Christian Giving.* Cambridge. **Prell, M.** (1997) *Armut im antiken Rom. Von den Gracchen bis Kaiser Diokletian.* Stuttgart. **Quass, F.** (1993) *Die*

Honoratiorenschicht in den Städten des griechischen Ostens. Untersuchungen zur politischer und sozialen Entwicklung in hellenistischer und römischer Zeit. Stuttgart. **Rajak, T.** (1996) Benefactors in the Greco-Jewish Diaspora. In P. Schäfer, ed., *Geschichte—Tradition - Reflexion. Band I: Judentum.* Festschrift für Martin Hengel. Tübingen. **Rickman, G.** (1980) *The Corn Supply of Ancient Rome.* Oxford. **Riesner, R.** (1998) *Paul's Early Period. Chronology, Mission Strategy, Theology.* Grand Rapids. **Sauer, G.** (1981) *Jesus Sirach, Jüdische Schriften aus hellenistisch-römischer Zeit.* Band 3. Gütersloh. **Seccombe, D.** (1975) Was there Organized Charity in Jerusalem before the Christians? *Journal of Theological Studies* 29: 140–43. **Schille, G.** (1983) *Die Apostelgeschichte des Lukas.* Theologische Handkommentar zum Neuen Testament 5. Berlin. **Schwankl, O.** (1997) "Lauft so daß ihr gewinnt" Zur Wettkampfmetaphorik in 1 Kor 9, in: *Biblische Zeitschrift* 42: 174–91. **Schwartz, D.R.** (1992) Ishmael ben Phiabi and the Chronology of Provincia Judaea. In D.R. Schwartz. *Studies in the Jewish Background of Christianity,* Wissenschaftliche Untersuchungen zum Neuen Testament I/60, Tübingen. **Shurden, S.H.** (1970) *The Christian Response to Poverty in the New Testament Era.* Michigan Microfilms International. Michigan. **Stegemann E.W. and W. Stegemann** (1995) *Urchristliche Sozialgeschichte. Die Anfänge im Judentum und die Christusgemeinden in der mediteranen Welt.* 2nd expanded edition. Stuttgart. **Van Bremen, R.** (1983) Women and Wealth. In: A. Cameron and A. Kuhrt, eds., *Images of Women in Antiquity,* 223–42. Detroit. **Veyne, P.** (1990) *Bread and Circuses. Historical Sociology and Political Pluralism.* London. **Walter, N.** (1983) Apostelgeschichte 6,1 und die Anfänge der Urgemeinde in Jerusalem, *New Testament Studies* 29: 370–93. **Wehnert, J.** (1996) *Die Reinheit des christlichen Gottesvolkes aus Juden und Heiden. Studien zur historischen und theologischen Hintergrund des soggenanten Aposteldekrets.* Göttingen. **Witherington, B., III** (1997) *Acts of the Apostles.* Grand Rapids. (1998) *The Paul Quest. The Renewed Search for the Jew of Tarsus.* Leicester.

Bishops as Brokers of Heavenly Goods: Ignatius *To the Ephesians*[*]

Ritva H. Williams
Augustana College

In his letter to the Ephesians involving the need for obedience to the bishop, Ignatius draws upon images from daily life in the Greco-Roman world, referring to musical instruments, choirs, altars, the practice of common prayer, and a tradition of Jesus' words. Interwoven with these directions, like a web in the background linking everything together, is the patron-broker-client system of social relations; in his description of the bishops in *Ephesians*, Ignatius presents these church leaders as brokers of heavenly goods.

Ignatius legitimates episcopal authority by weaving together elements from the sayings of Jesus to assert that the bishop is Christ's steward. Stewards were familiar figures in the daily life of the Greco-Roman world, frequently acting as brokers on behalf of their masters. If it is correct that Jesus proclaimed a brokerless kingdom, as J.D. Crossan suggests,[1] it is ironic that Jesus' own words are recontextualized in this way to promote the development of a system of ecclesiastical brokers.

What Is a Broker?

A broker is the intermediary or "middleman" in a patronage relationship. In the Greco-Roman world patronage was the means whereby domestic patriarchal authority was extended beyond the household and replicated

---

* This paper is an edited excerpt from my Ph.D. dissertation, "Charismatic Patronage and Brokerage: Episcopal Leadership in the Letters of Ignatius of Antioch," (University of Ottawa, Canada, 1997; supervised by Dr. Margaret Y. MacDonald; my doctoral research was made possible by a fellowship from the Social Sciences and Humanities Research Council of Canada). This paper was prepared for and presented at the Midwest Regional meeting of the Society of Biblical Literature, February 14–16, 1999 at Hebrew Union College in Cincinnati, Ohio.

Abbreviations used are: *Did.*= *Didache*; *Eph.* = Ignatius, *To the Ephesians.*

1 Crossan (1991) 227–302.

in economic, political, and religious relationships.[2] Patronage structured interactions between persons of different social status and power. The superior member of the relationship was the patron, who had control over scarce resources. These goods and services were made available to social inferiors, as favors, in exchange for public praise and other services.[3] The inferior member in the relationship was called a client or a friend depending on his or her social status.[4] Although a large number of clients was a visible sign of a person's status, power, and wealth,[5] Greco-Roman patrons "did not enter into relationships with their social inferiors indiscriminately."[6] Although preferred clients appear to have been persons with whom a patron had some prior relationship, a favor might be extended to a person with whom the patron had no previous relations, provided the prospective client was "a friend of a friend."[7] This is where the broker or intermediary came into the relationship.

Brokers were persons who had strategic contacts with those who controlled scarce goods and services. The broker knew how to get in touch with and/or influence those persons who were able to grant favors. Patron, broker, client were social roles that could be embraced alternately or in combination by the same person.[8] A good example of the interchangeability of these roles is found in Luke 7:1–10, where Jewish elders, i.e., local community patrons, become the clients of a Roman centurion who finances the building of their synagogue. When their Roman patron is in need of a healer, these same elders act as brokers in gaining the favor of Jesus.

Broker, therefore, is a name for a social role that involved connecting those who were in need with those who had the resources to meet those needs.

---

[2] Drummond (1990) 102; Pilch and Malina (1992) 133–37.

[3] Boissevain (1974) 147; Paine (1971) 15–17; Chow (1992) 31; Pilch and Malina (1992) 133–37; Eisenstadt and Roniger (1984) 213–14.

[4] Saller (1982)10–11; Saller (1990)52, 57.

[5] Wallace-Hadrill (1990) 82.

[6] Garnsey and Saller (1987) 156.

[7] Saller (1982) 108–9, 152–54, 182–84.

[8] Boissevain (1974) 147; Paine (1971) 8–9, 21; Crossan (1991) 59–60.

Brokers and Greco-Roman Religions

A close nexus existed between patronage and religion in the Greco-Roman world.[9] Relations between humans and deities replicated the patron-broker-client model of relationships between persons of differing status. The people of the Greco-Roman world inhabited a hierarchically structured universe populated by both human and nonhuman—divine and demonic—beings. A system of vertical stratification placed the ordinary person far below the level of the human and nonhuman rulers of his or her world. With respect to both earthly and heavenly resources, individuals and households faced the same difficulty: how to gain access to resources controlled by a tiny but disproportionately powerful elite.[10] The "religious problematic was one of mediation, the transportation, as it were, of goods and services"[11] between the human and divine realms. What was needed were mediators who could communicate between the two worlds, and who were capable of attracting to earth the necessary blessings of gods and goddesses.

Prosperity, good fortune, and the like were conceptualized as favors granted by the deities in exchange for human gratitude and praise,[12] and obtained through the mediation of various religious persons. The gods and goddesses of the Greco-Roman world were conceived of as divine patrons whose favors were mediated by fathers and mothers in domestic rituals and by religious officials and specialists in the political religion of the *polis*. The brokering of favors from the deities was an important power resource, which the ruling elites attempted to dominate and control.[13]

The pervasiveness of the patronage system must be taken seriously by modern readers of texts that originated in Greco-Roman societies. For Ignatius and other early Christian writers, patronage was assumed; it was implied and understood because it was part of daily life. It was the way things were done in the world. Almost all early Christian writings reflect, in some way, the system of patron-broker-client relations. Even in the *Gospel of Thomas*, which seems to reject normal social, economic and political relations, Jesus is portrayed as a broker of secret knowledge. Although

---

[9] North (1990) 52; Garland (1990) 75; Malina (1996) 28–29.

[10] Garnsey and Saller (1987)112–25; Crossan (1991) 45; Malina (1993) 90–112.

[11] Lightstone (1986) 111–12.

[12] Saller (1982) 23.

[13] Chow (1992) 70; Portefaix (1988) 43; Stowers (1995) 292–335; Shepard Kraemer (1992); van Bremen (1983); Countryman (177) 135–43; Torjesen (1992); Aune (1983) and numerous articles in Beard and North (1990).

patron-broker-client relations within the human community are criticized in the Gospel of Matthew, they continue to define interactions between humans and the deity, and Peter is appointed as Christ's steward. In the fourth Gospel the beloved disciple functions as Jesus' favored broker, while Jesus is the sole agent of access to God in heaven. In Ignatius' letters patron-broker-client relations link together all the other images from daily life.

Ignatius' Letter to the Ephesians

Ignatius begins his instructions to the Ephesians by exhorting them to be "joined in one obedience, subject to the bishop and the presbytery" (*Eph.* 2.2).[14] Obedience and submission are acts of commitment, confirming and validating the authority of these congregational leaders.[15] Such commitment is the appropriate way to honor and glorify Christ, according to Ignatius, and has the added consequence of making the Ephesian Christians holy in every respect (*Eph.* 2.2). Obedience to church leaders, as Ignatius understands it, demonstrates one's piety, one's proper attitude toward the divine authorities. His readers can be assured of acting in harmony with the purpose of God when they are in harmony with the purpose of the bishop, who is in the purpose of Jesus Christ, who in turn is the purpose of God (*Eph.* 3.2–4.1). What Ignatius spells out here is a hierarchy of mediators. God's purpose is made known through Jesus Christ (broker 1), whose purpose includes and is articulated by the bishop (broker 2). Solidarity with the bishop is a symptom or proof of unity with the divine authorities, whose purposes he represents and expresses.

Using musical imagery that would have been familiar to his audience, Ignatius spells out the benefits of being in harmony with the bishop. He begins by urging the Ephesian Christians to follow the example of their council of elders who are "attuned to the bishop like strings to a cithara." Through such concord and harmonious love Jesus Christ is made present or, as the Syrian bishop puts it, "is sung" in the midst of their congregation (*Eph.* 4.1). He assures his readers that when they "sing with one voice through Jesus Christ" the Father hears and recognizes them (*Eph.* 4.2). Again the hierarchy of mediation is stressed. In order to be recognized and to be heard by the divine patron, church members must approach him through Christ by joining their voices together with that of the bishop.

---

[14] Quotations from the letters of Ignatius come from Schoedel (1985).

[15] Overholt (1988) 71–72. An extensive discussion and bibliography on the subject of authority may be found in my unpublished Ph.D. dissertation, "Charismatic Patronage and Brokerage" (1997) 21–33. For the view that bishops in this era exercise influence and not authority see Malina (1978) 171–89.

Access to the heavenly patron, and his favors, is available through a very specific chain of mediators. Participation in the corporate rituals led by the bishop is the only proper means of approaching Jesus, who ensures access to God, as Ignatius makes even clearer in the next passage.

The Syrian bishop warns his readers, "Let no one deceive himself; if anyone is not within the altar he lacks the bread of God" (*Eph.* 5.2). In Greco-Roman religions the altar symbolized the principal point of mediation between the earthly and heavenly realms.[16] Ignatius uses the term figuratively to symbolize the venue in which the "bread of God" is made available to humans, that is, in the eucharistic gathering of the church over which the bishop presides.[17] He refers to the "bread of God" again in his final remarks to the Ephesians, where he describes it as "the medicine of immortality, the antidote preventing death" (*Eph* 20.2).[18] Thus the "bread of God" turns out to be potent stuff, indeed, which is obtainable only at the bishop's table. It represents a resource that the divine patron alone controls and dispenses through the mediation of Christ and his earthly broker the bishop.

In the Greco-Roman world, requests put to a powerful patron were much more likely to succeed when they came from and/or were supported by the commendations of those closest to the patron, members of his immediate family, friends, or employees.[19] This aspect of daily life is reflected in Ignatius' assertion that the Father hears and recognizes those who approach him in unity with the bishop (*Eph.* 4.2). It is also evident in his insistence that the corporate prayers of the "bishop and the whole church" are more powerful than those said by "one or two" (*Eph.* 5.2).[20] The

---

[16] Gordon (1990) 202.

[17] Schoedel (1985) 55.

[18] Ignatius combines Johannine, *Didachist* and Hellenistic terminology to describe the eucharist. "Bread of God" is used as a synonym for the "bread of life" in John 6:33. There too, the one who eats this bread will not die, but will live forever (John 6:50–51). The same notion occurs in *Did.* 4.8 where the eucharist is described as immortal food. "Medicine of immortality" is also the name of a legendary drug referred to in Hellenistic medical and religious literature. For further discussion, see Jefford (1995) 330–51; Aune (1972) 147 note 4; Schoedel (1985) 97.

[19] Saller (1982) 108–9, 152–53.

[20] Schoedel (1985) 55, asserts that Ignatius is here appealing to a tradition reflected in Matt. 18:19–20, but which has come to the Syrian bishop independently of Matthew. Matthew refers to the efficacy of the prayer of two together, and the presence of Jesus whenever two or three are gathered in his name. Ignatius' "prayer of one or two" is closer to *Thomas*.30 which speaks of Jesus being present with two

eucharistic gathering is an occasion not only for receiving goods from the heavenly Father but for making one's petitions known to him. Privileged access to the divine patron and those resources that he controls are the benefits of being "within the altar," of taking part in the gathering around the bishop's table.[21]

Another benefit is indicated several paragraphs later where Ignatius urges his readers to come together more frequently for "thanksgiving" and glorifying God. The Syrian bishop asserts that, when the congregation comes together in this way, the "powers of Satan are swept away and his destructiveness is brought to an end" (*Eph.* 13.1). Peace in the Christian community abolishes warfare in both the heavenly and earthly realms (*Eph.* 13.2). Similar notions are present in Ignatius' explanation of the meaning of the incarnation in *Ephesians* 19.2–3. There he asserts that the revelation of God in human form heralds the "newness of eternal life" and the destruction of the old dominion that is characterized by death, evil, bondage, and magic. Ignatius seems to conceive of the eucharistic gathering as a collective means of tapping into this power, which became active in the world at the time of Christ's birth. In doing so the church carries forward the eschatological program that was set in motion at that time.[22] The church and its members are in this way empowered and protected against the forces of evil. God's patronage thus includes access to protection, as well as to heavenly goods.

What Ignatius is describing here in his flowery and effusive style is a system of mediation in which the bishop plays the role of broker or mediator between the heavenly and earthly realms. It is the bishop who presides at the "altar," the point in time and space where communication between earth and heaven takes place. God is represented as the Father, the divine patron, who hears and recognizes those who approach him through the agency of his son, Jesus Christ, with one voice in unity with the bishop (*Eph.* 4.1–2).[23] The bishop's intermediary status is a position of power associated with control over access to God and to divine goods and services. Obedience to the bishop and participation in the eucharistic gathering over which

---

or one. This may be one of the rare points of contact between Ignatius and the *Gospel of Thomas*, and points to the Syrian bishop's opposition to Christians of that stripe.

21 Aune (1972) 165 contends that for Ignatius salvation is exclusively mediated through the cultic community.

22 Schoedel (1985) 74; Aune (1972) 142.

23 Schoedel (1985) 49, sums up Ignatius' argument as follows: "the bishop is to be obeyed because he is to Christ as Christ is to the Father."

he presides is the only means, Ignatius insists, of being heard and recognized by the Father, of receiving the "bread of God," and of securing protection against Satan and his destructive powers. Ignatius' exhortations to obey and submit to the bishop are attempts to persuade his readers to acknowledge and affirm the position of the bishop in this hierarchy of mediation.

Ignatius concludes his instructions on the subject of obedience to and solidarity with the bishop by asserting:

> And the more anyone sees a bishop keep silence, the more he should fear him. For everyone whom the householder sends into his stewardship, him must we receive as the one who sent him. Clearly, then, one must regard the bishop as the Lord himself (*Eph.* 6.1).

Numerous conjectures have been made concerning bishops who keep silence, which are beyond the scope of this paper.[24] Whatever it may entail, Ignatius argues that the bishop's silence should not result in less respect; indeed, the bishop should be looked upon as the Lord himself.

Ignatius justifies this position by weaving together two elements from sayings of Jesus. The statement about a householder sending someone into his stewardship seems to be drawn from the parable of the householder who sends servants or slaves to his vineyard. This parable is preserved in Matt 21:33–42 and Thomas 65. Ignatius' reference to householders and stewardship evokes the social institution of absentee ownership in the Greco-Roman world. Stewards or other agents of the owner were frequently put in charge of country estates as well as urban properties and businesses. A steward was the official representative of his master, exercising the authority that was delegated to him, and for which he was held accountable.[25] Such a position frequently enabled a steward to act as a broker for those seeking the patronage of his master.[26] For Ignatius, then, the bishop is like a steward managing a household in the absence of the householder. The bishop is the Lord's appointed representative and agent who functions as a broker controlling access to the divine patron and his favors.

---

[24] Discussions of silent bishops in the Ignatian correspondence can be found in Schoedel (1985) 56; Corwin (1960); Trevett (1989); von Campenhausen (1969) 97–106; Vogt (1977); Meinhold (1958).

[25] See for example Luke 12:42–48; Matt 24:45–51.

[26] The so-called parable of the "dishonest steward" in Luke 16:1–13 provides a good illustration of patron-broker-client interactions, and of how a broker might personally benefit from his activities.

The notion of receiving or welcoming the one who is sent as the "one who sent him" is preserved with variations in a number of early Christian writings. In Matt 10:40, whoever welcomes Jesus, welcomes the one who sent him. Jesus asserts, in John 13:20, that "whoever receives one whom I send receives me; and whoever receives me receives him who sent me." Paul applies the saying to himself when he commends the Galatians for receiving him as Christ Jesus (Gal 4:14). The Didache instructs its readers to receive teachers, apostles/prophets (11:1–3) and visitors as the Lord (12:1). The Didache also directs its readers to honor those who preach God's word as the Lord (4.1),[27] suggesting a movement in the direction of recognizing a ministry of the word. In marked contrast Ignatius uses the saying about receiving the one whom the householder sends to argue that a silent bishop must be regarded as the Lord himself. The bishop is the Lord's steward sent to manage God's household on earth. For Ignatius, that is a sufficient basis for recognizing him as an authoritative person in the Christian community.

Summary

Ignatius draws upon a variety of images from daily life in the Greco-Roman world to persuade his readers that they should submit to the authority of the bishop. The most important of these is the phenomenon of absentee ownership. The local congregation is analogous to a household whose owner is absent. The bishop is like a steward put in charge during the master's absence. Orders from the Lord (the householder) are relayed through the bishop (the steward) to the members of the church (the household; *Eph.* 3.2–4.1). Requests and petitions must pass through the bishop (the steward) to Christ (the absent owner). Access to God's (the householder's) resources and protection is acquired through the same means. The bishop functions in this arrangement as a broker, connecting the many on earth to the powerful elite in heaven. The bishop ensures access to Christ, who in turn is the means of access to the Father, who is the ultimate patron residing far beyond the reach of ordinary mortals.

Episcopal leadership as conceived by Ignatius is deeply rooted in the social structures of Greco-Roman society. That episcopal leadership reflected and conformed to the dominant forms of social relations in that culture is no doubt part of the reason that it became the predominant form of Christian organization. To what extent this may or may not reflect the

---

[27] Schoedel (1985) 57 contends that while this sharpens the theme of receiving someone "as the Lord" it does not change its meaning. I think that it may indeed make a significant difference, see "Charismatic Patronage and Brokerage," 66–85.

intentions or desires of Jesus is another story. Similarly the extent to which texts like these, originating in a society very different from ours should continue to shape modern ecclesiology is yet another story.

BIBLIOGRAPHY

Aune, D.E. (1972) *The Cultic Setting of Realized Eschatology in Early Christianity.* Novum Testamentum Supplement 28; Leiden. (1983) *Prophecy in Early Christianity and the Ancient Mediterranean World.* Grand Rapids, Mich. **Beard, M. and J. North**, eds. (1990) *Pagan Priests: Religion and Power in the Ancient World.* Ithaca, N.Y. **Boissevain, J.** (1974) *Friends of Friends: Networks, Manipulators and Coalitions.* Oxford. **Bremen, R. van** (1983) Women and Wealth. In A. Cameron and A. Kuhrt, eds., *Images of Women in Antiquity.* London. **Campenhausen, H. von** (1969) *Ecclesiastical Authority and Spiritual Power in the Church of the First Three Centuries.* Translated by J. A. Baker. London. **Chow, J.K.** (1992) *Patronage and Power: A Study of Social Networks in Corinth.* Sheffield. **Corwin, V.** (1960) *St. Ignatius and Christianity in Antioch.* New Haven. **Countryman, W.L.** (1977) Patrons and Officers in Club and Church. In P.J. Achtemeier, ed., *Society of Biblical Literature 1997 Seminar Papers,* 135–43. Missoula, Mt. **Crossan, J.D.** (1991) *The Historical Jesus: The Life of a Mediterranean Jewish Peasant.* San Francisco. **Drummond, A.** (1990) *Early Roman Clientes.* In A. Wallace-Hadrill, ed., *Patronage in Ancient Society,* 89–115. London. **Eisenstadt, S.N. and L. Roniger** (1984) *Patrons, Clients and Friends: Interpersonal Relations and the Structure of Trust in Society.* Cambridge. **Garland, R.** (1990) Priests and Power in Classical Athens. In M. Beard and J. North, eds., *Pagan Priests: Religion and Power in the Ancient World,* 75–91. Ithaca, N.Y. **Garnsey, P. and R. Saller** (1987) *The Roman Empire: Economy, Society and Culture.* Berkeley, Calif. **Gordon, R.** (1990) The Veil of Power: Emperors, Sacrificers and Benefactors. In M. Beard and J. North, eds., *Pagan Priests: Religion and Power in the Ancient World,* 201–31. Ithaca, N.Y. **Jefford, C.N.** (1995) Did Ignatius of Antioch Know the Didache? In C. N. Jefford, ed., *The Didache in Context: Essays on Its Text, History and Transmission,* 330–51. Novum Testamentum Supplement 77. Leiden. **Lightstone, J.** (1985) Christian Anti-Judaism in Its Judaic Mirror: The Judaic Context of Early Christianity Revisited. In S.G. Wilson, ed., *Anti-Judaism in Early Christianity.* Volume 2: Separation and Polemic, 103–32. Studies in Christianity and Judaism/2; Waterloo, Ont. **Malina, B.J.** (1978) The Social World Implied in the Letters of the Christian Bishop-Martyr (named Ignatius of Antioch). In P.J. Achetemeier, ed., *Society of Biblical Literature 1978 Seminar Papers,* 171–89. Missoula, Mt. (1993) *The New Testament World: Insights from Cultural Anthropology.* Revised Edition. Louisville, Ky. (1996) Mediterranean Sacrifice: Dimensions of Domestic and Political Religion. In *Biblical Theology Bulletin* 26/1: 26–44. **Meinhold, P.** (1958) Schweinde Bishöfe. Die Gegensätze in den kleinasiatischen Gemeinden nach den Ignatianen. In *Festgabe Joseph Lortz II: Glaube und Geschichte.* Baden-Baden. **North, J.** (1990) Diviners and Divination at Rome. In M. Beard and J. North, eds., *Pagan Priests: Religion and Power in the Ancient World,* 51–71. Ithaca, N.Y. **Overholt, T.W.** (1988) *Channels of Prophecy: The Social Dynamics of Prophetic Activity.* Minneapolis. **Paine, R.** (1971) A Theory of Patronage and Brokerage. In R. Paine, ed., *Patrons and Brokers in the East Arctic,* 8–21. Institute of Social and Economic Research, Memorial University of Newfoundland. **Pilch, J.J. and B.J. Malina** (1992) *Biblical Social Values and Their Meaning: A Handbook.* Peabody, Mass. **Portefaix, L.** (1989) *Sisters Rejoice: Paul's Letters to the Philippians and Luke-Acts as Received by First-Century Philippian Women.* Stockholm. **Saller, R.P.** (1982) *Personal Patronage under the Early Empire.* Cambridge. (1990) Patronage and Friendship in Early Imperial Rome: Drawing the Distinctions. In A. Wallace-Hadrill, ed., *Patronage in Ancient Society,* 49–62. London. **Schoedel, W.R.** (1985) *Ignatius of Antioch: A Commentary on the Letters of Ignatius of Antioch.* Hermeneia. Philadelphia. **Shepard Kraemer, R.** (1991) *Her Share of the Blessings: Women's Religions among Pagans, Jews and Christians in the Greco-Roman World.* Oxford. **Stowers, S.K.** (1995) Greeks Who Sacrifice and Those Who Do Not: Toward an Anthropology of Greek Religion. In L.M. White and O.Y. Yarbrough, eds., *The Social World of the First Christians: Essays in Honor of Wayne A. Meeks,* 293–335. Minneapolis. **Torjesen, K.J.** (1992) *When Women Were Priests: Women's Leadership in the Early Church and the Scandal of Their Subordination in the Rise of Christianity.* San Francisco. **Trevett, C.** (1989)Apocalypse, Ignatius, Montanism: Seeking the Seeds. *Vigilae Christianae* 43: 313–38. **Vogt, H. J.** (1978) Ignatius von Antiochien über den Bischöf und seine Gemeinde. *Theologische Quartalschrift* 158: 15–27. **Wallace-Hadrill, A.** (1990) Patronage in Roman Society: From Republic to Empire. In A. Wallace-Hadrill, ed., *Patronage in Ancient Society,* 63–87. London.

Special Subjects

METHODS AND DAILY LIFE

UNDERSTANDING THE USE OF ANIMALS IN DAILY LIFE IN A MULTI-DISCIPLINARY FRAMEWORK

Gerald A. Klingbeil *

Universidad Adventista del Plata

Life is all about integration. It involves integration of thoughts, actions, methods, and information. This makes the reconstruction of daily life a risky business, because in order to describe these complex relationships an integration of methods is required. Even in trying to reconstruct our present context, one needs to be aware of specific limitations. From what angle is the reconstruction undertaken: political, social, economic, cultural, or material?[1] What kind of data is utilized: written primary sources, material (i.e., archaeological) remains, artistic representations, present-day communities with a comparable social structure,[2] or specific social models?

* I would like to thank the following persons for their contributions and help in locating and accessing bibliographic references and material: Dr. Keith Clouten (Director of library services at Andrews University, U.S.); Lucien-Jean Bord (Librarian of Abbaye Ligue in France); Kurt Langguth (Scientific research assistant at the Institut für Ur- und Frühgeschichte, Abteilung für Ältere Urgeschichte und Quartärökologie at the University of Tübingen, Germany); Umberto Albarella (Department of Ancient History and Archaeology at the University of Birmingham in England); Dr. Peter Matthews (Curator at the National Museum of Ethnology in Osaka, Japan); and T. Kawami at the Arthur M. Sackler Foundation in New York.

1 It appears that Snell's (1997) very important contribution to this field is focusing upon social and economic factors influencing society. Nemet-Nejat (1998) provides a much broader introduction to the topic, focusing upon the structure of society, sciences, writing, recreation, religion, government and the economy. Her work is intended for a general audience.

2 This represents a method often utilized in anthropological work on the Old Testament, as can be found, for example, in Wright's (1987) 107–10 work on the disposal of impurity in the ancient Near East, in which he utilizes comparative material from Indian sources. Meir Malul (1990) 14 has dubbed this approach "typological comparison," whereas Talmon (1978) 322, 356 refers to it as "comparison on the grand scale." Other examples of this method can be found in Lang (1985). Compare also the contributions of O'Connor (1997), Adams (1997) and Wenke (1997) concerning the recent interdisciplinary dialogue between anthropology and Egyptology.

But the challenges do not end just with the data sets utilized; they go even further, to the basic level of terminology. In a recent study entitled *Pastoralism in the Levant*, which examines the prehistoric period, the book's editors, Ofer Bar-Yosef and Anatoly Khazanov,[3] argue for a unified terminology for their field of study. This call for a commonly accepted terminology is also true when dealing with the social dimensions of the reconstruction of daily life, especially while treading on the lesser-known territory of sociological and anthropological studies.[4] In spite of these challenges, this paper seeks to develop a workable integrated framework, set in a multidisciplinary context, which will facilitate the reconstruction of daily life in the ancient Near East during any given period by focusing upon three different sets of data: archaeological, textual, and iconographic. Recent academic discussions in many areas of ancient Near Eastern and biblical research have turned toward method, instead of focusing entirely on data (or results), as occurred in earlier discussions.[5] Recent methodological discussion does look beyond our own "chicken stall" to learn from other disciplines or geographical entities—a tendency that can be seen in the publication of a recent volume entitled *Methods in the Mediterranean. Historical and Archaeological Views on Texts and Archaeology*, published in 1995 by Brill in a series with little connection to ancient Near Eastern studies.[6] In our study, each of the data sub-sets mentioned above will be introduced. We will attempt to anchor each in the present discussion and

---

3 See here Bar-Yosef and Khazanov (1992) 2.

4 Meadow (1992) 261 maintains that this unified terminology is unfortunately non-existent because "archaeologists are inveterate categorizers and classifiers and typologists. In order to draw a picture of the past in the present many of us attempt to interpret material remains and their relationship by defining patterns and then trying to fit those patterns into an existing categorization—chiefdom, state, sedentary, nomadic, agricultural, pastoral—in an attempt to place what we think we see into a broader socioeconomic framework."

5 See here Herion (1992). One extreme outgrowth of this tendency is the danger of concerning oneself exclusively with methodological issues while neglecting to interpret the assembled facts in an intelligent manner. Stern (1987) 32 makes mention of this in his remarks concerning the controversy between biblical and Syro-Palestinian archaeology, which he terms as a "purely American controversy." Compare also Small (1995a) 9, who stresses the need for a fuller discussion of the role of archaeology and texts in Mediterranean studies. He writes: "With few exceptions, works to date have dealt with general concepts or correlation, rather than focusing on specific issues and methods."

6 Compare also Small (1995b) 143–76; Hitscher (1995) 124–42; and Kosso (1995) 177–96.

show possible contributions, as well as possible pitfalls. Finally, a concise application of this multi-disciplinary approach will be utilized to study the use of the mule in the daily life of ancient Israel (and, to a certain degree, its neighbors).

CONTRIBUTIONS AND LIMITATIONS OF ARCHAEOLOGY

Syro-Palestinian archaeology has shifted away from a predominant focus upon the Bible toward a more integrated reading of the past.[7] A good example of this tendency can be found in paleozoology and the function and role of fauna in the cultural processes of sedentarization, domestication, and nomadization, which has been a mainstay of general anthropological research. However, only during the past thirty to thirty-five years[8] has the realization of the importance of the systematic study of animal bones from a specific site made an impact on ancient Near Eastern archaeology, providing valuable insights into the economic, religious, and material culture of a given society.[9] More and more studies appear that seek to integrate the thousands and thousands of bones and bone frag-

---

[7] For a recent review including ample references to the relevant literature, see Bartlett (1997) 1–10.

[8] Compare Borowski (1998) 29 and Meyers (1983) 576.

[9] See the important articles by Firmage (1992) and Gilbert (1995). Concerning the shift in archaeological focus (especially in ancient Near Eastern archaeology), see LaBianca (1995) for a discussion of the method in the context of the Hesban expedition and Hole (1995) and Maisels (1990) 1–15 in a more general context. Wapnish (1993) and Hesse and Wapnish (1997a) provide a good introduction to the relatively new field of "archaeozoology" or "paleozoology." A good introduction to the importance of bone work in connection with archaeological field projects can be found in Rackham (1994). Another important resource are the studies found in Meadow and Zeder (1978), which, although a bit dated, still provide a good introduction to the pertinent issues in the field. For an appreciation of the integration of this data in "everyday" archaeological research, see Fritz (1994) 61–64 and Mazar (1992) 27, although Mazar, in his brief introduction, focuses mainly on different stratigraphical methods and mentions the importance of paleozoology in only one sentence. For the territory of Jordan compare also the collection of essays edited by Hadidi (1985), which includes studies concerning climate changes, environmental pressures, food procuring strategies, etc., and which does emphasize the new focus upon the environment instead of just concentrating upon architectural, epigraphical, or ceramic remains. A good introduction to the field of interaction between humans, plants, and animals can also be found in Hansen's (1997) 200–1 introductory article on "Paleobotany," (with more references provided there) and in Hesse's (1995) and (1997a) entries on "animal husbandry." For a synthesis of this material and the application to a specific region see LaBianca (1990).

ments that come to light during an excavation into our still fragmented knowledge of the history of Palestine and the ancient Near East.[10] The study of the fauna of a specific site or region is not only helpful for a reconstruction of social or economical realities, but also provides an important window into religious realities.[11]

When assessing the helpfulness of archaeology for the reconstruction of daily life in the ancient Near East and focusing upon the use of animals, the following limitations should be kept in mind. (1) Due to the very fragmentary nature of the data, results should be considered preliminary that need to be integrated into the larger emerging picture of ancient Near Eastern culture and society.[12] (2) Survey data, which seems to provide the backbone for most recent overarching theories in Syro-Palestinian archaeology,[13] although useful, must be treated with caution, since the data is subject to the same destructive processes of distortion and abstraction as are other material artifacts.[14] Furthermore, the methodology as to how the data is acquired also determines, to a certain degree, the results obtained.[15] E. Banning[16] suggests differing survey layouts for differing geographical

---

10 I profited especially from Wapnish (1996), who studied the faunal remains of Tell Jemmeh and related them to Assyrian military policies. See also her earlier discussion concerning this point in Wapnish (1993). An interesting example of the lack of integration of the faunal remains into archaeological and (by extension) historiographical reconstruction can be found in Ahlström's (1993) monumental *History of Ancient Palestine.* While his introduction emphasizes the predominance of "material" data (= archaeological data) over textual (= biblical/literary data), I could not find any reference to the study of paleozoology or paleobotany in his extensive introduction nor were references to specific animals or processes of domestication listed in the indices.

11 See here, for example, my comments on "animal participants" during the ritual of ordination as found in Lev 8 in relation to established ratios from other lists and archaeological sites in Klingbeil (1998) 216–19.

12 Compare Jerricke's (1997) 1–24 poignant critique of recent settlement or conquest models of early Israel.

13 See here Finkelstein's (1988) contribution concerning the archaeology of the Israelite settlement or his study of the archaeology and history of the Negev, Sinai, and neighboring regions in the Bronze and Iron Ages (1995).

14 This is based upon Harrison's (1997) 1–3 fitting observations.

15 Harrison (1997) 2 rightly points to the adoption of differing chronological schemes (without proper indication in the survey design) as one of the limiting factors for the usefulness of surveys.

16 Banning (1996) 25–45.

regions, namely, highlands and lowlands. And even more challenging is the fact that there is still a general discussion going on as to the usefulness of the surface data for the suggested reconstruction of the history of a specific site.[17] (3) Concerning the paleozoological data available through the systematic excavation of specific sites, the fragmentary nature of the bone evidence and its often tentative identification should be kept in mind. For example, one of the main problems in the identification of mules is the morphology of the skeletal remains of horses, donkeys, and mules in the archaeological record. Based upon personal communications with Kurt Langguth, scientific assistant to Prof. H.-P. Uerpmann of the University of Tübingen, recent research on equids is focusing upon techniques and technology to differentiate between the different species[18]—it appears that one important source of a more secure identification of mules is its dentition or dental characteristics.[19] Finally, the purpose and contribution of archaeological research should be kept in mind: it is not *l'art pour l'art*, but needs to serve a rationally comprehensible research agenda or, as has been suggested by some researchers, including William Dever,[20] archaeology will make itself obsolete. The gap that was created between so-called Syro-Palestinian archaeology and biblical archaeology must be bridged, as it is a gap about history and focus, not method.[21]

CONTRIBUTIONS AND LIMITATIONS OF WRITTEN MATERIAL

Written material has always played a significant role in the reconstruction of history or cultural realities, because it was precisely the invention of writing that provided a clearer perspective on ancient life and culture, separating prehistory from protohistory.[22] However, when one looks at

---

17 Compare Harrison (1997) 2–3.

18 See especially the helpful discussion of mule remains from archaeological digs of the Roman period in Germany in Uerpmann and Uerpmann (1994) 353–57.

19 Compare also Hesse (1995) 216, who writes: "A particular problem is the difficulty zooarchaeologists find in assigning fragmentary osteological remains to taxonomic categories more precise than 'equid'." See also Davies (1980) and his discussion of Late Pleistocene and Holocene equid remains from Israel.

20 I remember a memorable lecture by Dever during the 1996 season to the participants of the Madaba Plains Project excavation project in which he suggested that the archaeologists either look for other work or connect archaeological research with real-world historical (including biblical) questions.

21 Writes Drinkard (1989) 607: "As archaeology has moved away from history it has simultaneously moved more and more into the sphere of anthropology."

22 See here Hallo's (1971) 27–28 pertinent remarks. Both Dalley (1998) 9–12 and

current "thought leadership" concerning the relationship between archaeology and textual data (as found in the Hebrew Bible, for example), the current paradigm favors a predominance of artifact and architecture over text.[23] The main arguments include the often cited "fact" that most of the Hebrew Bible is (a) elitist; (b) late, i.e., written just before, during, or immediately after the Persian conquest;[24] and (c) eclectic, i.e., it had an agenda—something that can be said for most twentieth-century scholars as well.[25] In recent years William Dever[26] seems to have toned down a bit regarding the preeminence of artifact over text in view of the rampant "minimalist" virus that is plaguing Biblical Studies.[27] Thus, it appears to be of the utmost importance to include both textual as well as material remains in order to be able to reconstruct any aspect of a culture hundreds or thousands of years removed from ours.

Textual sources can be roughly divided into two main categories:[28] (1) official texts (including monumental, public, and religious texts) and (2) private texts (such as invoices, accounts, messages) or, in other words, texts

---

Nemet-Nejat (1998) 47–49 point to the fact that writing appears to have been developed principally as part of a drive to get a better grip on the economics of human society (namely as a means of accounting)—although the larger sociocultural dimensions of that intention should not be forgotten and included the beginning processes of urbanization, accumulation of capital, hierarchical societal structures, and technological advances. Concerning the multifaceted approach to complex societies in ancient times, see also recently Stone (1999) 203–6.

23 See here Dever's (1990) 3–11 influential essay on the Hebrew Bible as an "artifact"; compare also Ahlström's (1993) 10–11 preface to his monumental history of ancient Palestine and the review of the works of van Seters and representatives of the minimalist (or Copenhagen/Sheffield) school of thought in Yamauchi's (1994) introductory essay on the current state of Old Testament historiography.

24 What is peculiar, however, is the fact that most Hebrew literature is projected into a historical period of which very little is known. See here Klingbeil (1992) and also Eph'al (1988) and (1998), who comments that the history of Syria-Palestine in the Persian period "is extremely difficult to reconstruct, primarily because of the paucity of our information concerning the region" (1988) 141. Stern (1982) xv comes to a similar conclusion.

25 Compare here also Lemche (1996) 19–33.

26 See, for example, his remarks in (1997).

27 Halpern (1997) is here also of great importance. Compare also Chavalas (1995), a review on recent trends in the study of Israelite historiography.

28 This categorization is useful for the purpose of this study, distinguishing between official texts and private texts. Hallo (1971) 154–56 has suggested a tripartite division of genres found in the ancient Near East, namely archival texts,

that were not intended to be kept or even read by other people apart from the original recipients. Starting with official texts, Gary Knoppers has provided a convenient review of recent scholarship on the United Monarchy during the tenth century B.C.[29] It appears that this period—as well as other periods of the biblical period, such as the patriarchal era—is systematically discredited on the basis of the very nature of the biblical text, which is characterized as being "ideological"[30] or "fictitious."[31] Both ideology and fiction describe the depiction of reality with a certain "strategy" or bent. Michelle Marcus has defined ideology as the "way in which signs, meanings, and values help to reproduce a dominant social power."[32] It is clear that ancient texts partially took part in this enterprise. So, if modern research on everyday life wants to utilize monumental or literary texts from ancient times, it has to be aware of these tendencies without discrediting the entire textual corpus *per se*.[33] Or, in other words, it needs to take into consideration the literary artistry of ancient historians in depicting their reality[34] and their own hidden or open agendas.

Turning now to the second category of written material that often comes to light during excavations, namely private texts (including accounts, incidental messages, lists). Since they were not intended for safekeeping and thus were not considered as "tradition-building," they are often regarded as being free of slants and bents. However, care should be taken as well when reading these texts, since their sole use (without referencing them to public texts, material remains, or iconographic data) would lead to distortion or plain lack of information. I have demonstrated the importance of the study of this type of material in my research concerning Aramaic inscriptions, written on hard surfaces and found in Syro-Palestine, during the Persian period.[35] Specifically for this period—the formative period of the biblical text for most critical scholars—very little source

---

monumental texts, and canonical texts. For a discussion of these divisions, see Klingbeil (1998) 335–36.

29 Knoppers (1997) 19–44.

30 Lemche (1996) 19–47 calls these narratives "stories" (in German: "Erzählungen") that have very little or nothing to say about the time they purport to describe.

31 Halpern (1988) 68 writes that "history ... is all fictionalized, and yet history."

32 Marcus (1995) 2487.

33 A very balanced treatment of the subject is provided by Long (1994) 58–87.

34 See especially Long (1994) 73–76.

35 See Klingbeil (1992).

material from Palestine is available.[36] Due to a lack of material and its often fragmentary nature, the usefulness of the material is limited to onomastic studies (with its bearing on ethnicity),[37] genre identification based on semantic domains,[38] socioeconomic realities (usually based upon a very limited data set), and the odd historical, political, or religious piece of information contained in them.

CONTRIBUTIONS AND LIMITATIONS OF ICONOGRAPHIC DATA

Twentieth-century scholarship has discovered the importance of iconographical primary sources in conjunction with textual sources and archaeological data. Othmar Keel, the don of modern iconographical studies from the University of Fribourg in Switzerland, has formulated iconography's contribution: "Ancient Near Eastern iconography is suitable for the illustration of the typical and the institutional, but not for that of the individual person or the historical event."[39] Iconographical research has been integrated into studies illustrating the biblical text,[40] into historical research,[41] into cultural research seeking to establish a specific motif history of a partic-

---

36 In my 1992 study only 104 inscriptions could be included. Recently, however, the corpus has been greatly expanded with the publication of some 400 ostraca from Idumea, written in Aramaic and dated to the fourth century B.C. Compare here Eph'al and Naveh (1996) and also Eph'al (1998) 108.

37 Klingbeil (1993) and also Eph'al (1998) 110–11 and Hess (1998). However, the issue of ethnicity cannot be solved solely by looking to onomastics; it is also a "hot issue" in archaeology. See here, for example, the discussions of Esse (1992), Arnold (1995), and Dever (1995), all of whom consider ceramics to be one of the major indicators of ethnicity, while Finkelstein (1996a) would rather look at settlement patterns. Another important study in this area has been presented by London (1989), who investigated the distinct material culture of the highlands and lowlands of Canaan during the second millennium B.C. She suggests that the traditional indication of two differing ethnic groups should be reconsidered, since the differences could also be explained in terms of different geographic and economic factors. Recently, Kletter (1999) has studied distinct material features (such as figurine types) and their connection to political units, which—he claims—are easier to distinguish than ethnic units.

38 As demonstrated by Klingbeil (1997).

39 Keel (1992a) 361.

40 See here Keel (1996)—originally published in German in 1972.

41 See, for example Pitard (1988), who suggests that, based upon iconographical and textual affinities, the author of the Melqart stela should not be connected to any of the Damascus dynasties, but rather was the lord of an "Aram" in northern Syria, which was not associated with Damascus.

ular site or region,[42] and more recently it has also been used to understand better the religious cosmos of the ancients.[43] Thus, iconographic research should be broadly included in the comparative method and its comparison is a comparison of thoughts and motifs expressed in pictures and images, whereas texts are just another vehicle of expression.[44] Recent iconographic research has begun to provide a more systematic approach to the field in order to avoid the subjectivity that is often associated with iconographical studies. Keel suggests three important points regarding the methodological issues in iconography:[45] (1) each picture has to be evaluated on its own right without the reception bias of Judeo-Christian exegesis before it can be linked exegetically to a given text; (2) Image and Word are complementary and not dichotic; and (3) pictures can be interpreted with the help of other pictorial material without necessarily resorting to textual sources.

However, even taking into considerations Keel's (rather recent) methodological affirmations, one of the major problems of iconographic research is its often criticized subjectivity.[46] How can one know exactly how a certain motif was utilized and understood some three thousand years ago? Jürg Eggler[47] has provided a very helpful three-step approach to iconography based upon Panovsky's work, in which he distinguished between three levels that must be included in legitimate iconographic research: (1) pre-iconographical description that demands familiarity with objects and events; (2) iconographical analysis, which looks at themes and concepts; and (3) iconological interpretation that seeks to integrate the knowledge gained via the first two steps and formulate the "Weltanschauung" of the specific group/people as expressed by their art. See figure 1 for

42 Leinwand (1992) has studied regional and urban glyptic styles of the seal impressions of level II at Kültepe.

43 Compare here Uehlinger (1996) and Keel and Uehlinger (1995), a work that was originally published in 1992 and is now also available in English. Uehlinger (1996) was studying the stamp seals that would illustrate not necessarily official religion, but rather "persönliche Frömmigkeit" (personal piety). See also Strange (1985), who studied the Old Testament idea of the afterlife from the perspective of the iconography of Solomon's temple.

44 See Keel (1992a) 372. For a good review of past tendencies and present reality in iconographic research, see M.G. Klingbeil (1999) 158–60 and the references provided there.

45 Keel (1992b) xi–xiii.

46 Compare, for example, the criticism found in Barkay (1988) and Haran (1985).

47 Eggler (1992) 22–28.

a helpful illustration in which I introduce three main categories in iconographic research: (a) motifs, (b) scenes, and (c) images.[48]

In spite of recent methodological considerations, iconographic data should be evaluated critically in view of the following challenges:

(1) A large amount of published iconographic material is taken from monumental art and thus represents "official" viewpoints. When utilizing this material, the issue of ideology in art should be taken into consideration. This has also been emphasized by Michelle Marcus, who writes:

> Visual materials have a unique role in expressions of ideology. Material culture can take on the responsibility of carrying certain messages that a culture cannot entrust to language. The ability of art and other material goods to carry messages nonverbally makes them an especially subtle and stealthy means for communicating certain potentially controversial political messages.[49]

Figure 1. Three main categories of iconographic research according to M. Klingbeil (1999)

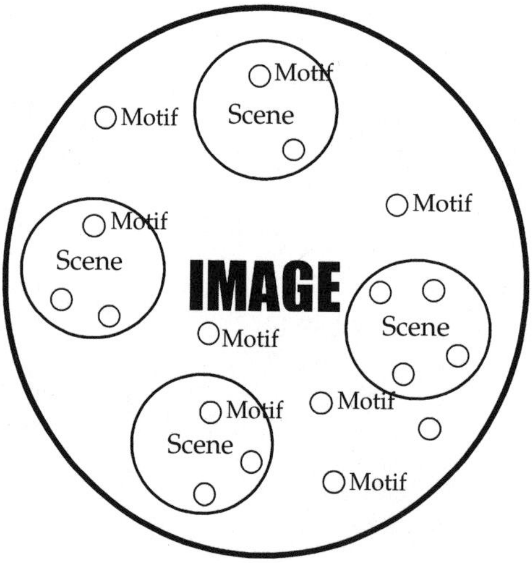

LARGE CIRCLE = the whole image.

INNER CIRCLES = the scenes that contribute to the whole image.

SMALLEST CIRCLES = the motifs that are the elements of the individual scenes and/or the whole image.

48 This figure first appeared in Klingbeil (1999) 162–65.

49 Marcus (1995) 2487.

However, the comprehensive publication project of Keel and his team of the stamp-seal amulets of Palestine/Israel (and in the near future of the Transjordanian material as well)[50] should provide a welcome counterbalance to this problem, inasmuch as it presents miniature art that was predominantly utilized in private contexts, but that was at the same time stylistically influenced by official art. It is here that Keel's corpus will make a significant contribution as it provides the researcher with the primary material to study motifs, scenes, and images from both an official and a private perspective.

(2) The very act of producing an image in ancient times was a laborious and costly process, involving specialized artists. Therefore, only significant events and important symbols were reproduced, making its value for the reconstruction of mundane "daily life" rather doubtful.

In spite of the reservations and issues mentioned above, iconography makes a contribution to the study of daily life in ancient times. Besides being thousands of years closer to the actual event than the "more objective" twentieth-first-century scholar, it also helps us to see ancient perspectives and designs of their art. Understanding a specific artistic perspective and design is often more meaningful and information-laden than taking a "mere snapshot" of an event.

Reconstructing Daily Life Archaeologically: The Case of the Mule

Paleobiologists differentiate among three key classifications in regards to the economic value of a given animal: (a) wild, (b) managed, and (c) domesticated.[51] Of these, domesticated animals obviously had the most impact on human society because they affected not only the "tamer" but also the society to which he belonged.[52] Domestication has been defined as "the

---

50 Namely Keel (1995) and (1997). In a private communication, Dr. Jürg Eggler, assistant to Prof. Keel at the Institute in Fribourg, confirmed the plans to publish the stamp seal material from Transjordan in the near future, following a similar layout.

51 See Hesse (1995) 203.

52 See here the insightful essay of Clutton-Brock (1994), in which she discusses the impact of domestication in terms of a natural stage in the development of relations between animals and humankind. Compare also Schwabe's (1994) 37 discussion of the differing social contexts in connection with the role of animals in folk-, agrarian-, and industrial-type societies. Recently Janowski, Neumann-Gorsolke, and Glessmer (1993) have edited and republished important essays concerning the role, function, relationship, and interaction of animals and humans in

integration of living animals into human society"[53] with reasons ranging from (a) a need for reliable meat provision,[54] (b) the need for significant offerings in the religious context,[55] (c) as social indicators, since "it not only produces domestic animals, [but] encourages the adoption of different values and social organizations by the societies that employ it,"[56] (d) as beasts of burden,[57] (e) as provider of secondary (recyclable) benefits, such as fiber, wool, and milk, and finally, (f) as draft animals.[58] Table I provides a synopsis of the current suggested timetable concerning the domestication of the major mammalian types in the ancient Near East.

Two main tendencies can be observed in regards to the domestication of the major mammals in the ancient Near East:[59] (1) primary-products domestication focused predominantly upon the primary usage of the

---

the Old Testament. The interesting essays for the present study include Henry (1993), Westermann (1993), de Pury (1993), and Keel (1993).

53 This definition has been taken from Hesse (1997a) 141. For a more nuanced (but not necessarily clearer) definition, see Borowski (1998) 24–29. Pierre Ducos (1978) 54 defined domestication more in terms of utilitarianism when he suggests that "domestication can be said to exist when living animals are integrated as objects into the socioeconomic organization of the human group…"

54 However, this does not appear to have been the main motive for domestication. See here the convincing case built by Hesse (1995) 206–7. Against this Borowski (1998) 23–24, who bases his conclusions on the work of Clutton-Brock (1981).

55 A good example can be found in the use of the domesticated ass (*Equus asinus*) in the Uruk IV levels at Warka and the late-Uruk deposits at Tel Rubeidheh in the Jebel Hamrin area, where partial skeletons (and not fragmented bones) were found. In conjunction with textual evidence of this period, it is reasonable to argue that these donkeys were used in a ritual context as part of a special (and obviously very costly) offering during a covenant-making process. See here Hesse (1995) 207. Often domesticated animals were included as burial offerings in graves. Donkeys were also used in Egyptian burials, as has been indicated by Osborn and Osbornová (1998) 135 and Houlihan (1996) 29.

56 This quote was taken from Hesse (1997a) 141. He continues: "An increased sense of property becomes a measure of social status."

57 See here Sauer's (1995) 40–41 important comments concerning this result of the process of domestication, which also influenced patterns of human settlement and trade. This function is obviously connected to travel as described by Dorsey (1991).

58 This has also been described as being part of the "secondary products revolution." See Hesse (1997a) 142. The draft function included agricultural as well as military aspects.

59 Compare here also Firmage (1992) 1115–16.

animals in terms of their meat and possibly milk production and included sheep, goats, pigs, and cattle; (2) the secondary-products revolution focused more upon additional usage of these domesticated animals (and newly domesticated ones as well), such as wool and fiber production, draft usage, and as transport medium. Animals that were introduced during this period include the donkey, the horse, hybrid equids (including mule and hinny), and the camel. It should be noted that ritual use of the animals in a religious context can be documented throughout most of the process of domestication.[60] It appears that animal ownership during the Chalcolithic and Neolithic periods did not focus so much on status but rather on necessity. After the secondary products revolution, status appears to have been of more concern to the ancients.[61] However, when looking specifically at mule remains, the difficulty of distinguishing among the different types of equids should be kept in mind. As it appears, recent methods of morphologically distinguishing between horse, mule, and donkey need to be developed further.

Reconstructing Daily Life Textually: The Case of the Mule

Two corpora of texts will be included in this textual study, namely the Hebrew Bible and extra-biblical texts—predominantly from Mesopotamia. In the Hebrew Bible I will apply a synchronic reading[62] of the occurrences of the nouns *pered* (and its feminine form *pirdâ*) because, firstly, I do not subscribe to the philosophical and methodological presuppositions of

60 See here also recently Malamat (1995) 226–29 and his discussion of two recent letters (A. 1056 and A. 2226) by Ibal-Il, Zimri-Lim's representative in Ida-Madras, who mentions the replacement of puppies, calves, and goats by asses for sacrifices in peace treaties at Mari.

61 One should consider only the type of animals introduced during this period, i.e., horse, mule/hinny and, much later, the camel. These were expensive animals whose primary purpose had nothing to do with survival, but rather with getting from point A to point B or with indicating the importance of its owner(s).

62 Compare here the interesting remarks of Barr (1995) 1–14, who suggests that both synchronic and diachronic approaches are intrinsically historical approaches. I tend to agree with Barr inasmuch as one defines synchronic as a model that describes the "as is"—in a specific historical context. However, the fact that the synchronic method is historical *per se*, does not nullify its inherent critique of the historical-critical (or diachronic) method. Compare also the discussion of Sprinkle (1989) 299–310 and Ryken (1990) 3–15.

TABLE I

Animal	*Date Introduced*	*Function*	*Reference in Literature*
Sheep (*Ovis aries*)	c. 8000 B.C.	Meat production. Around 3000 B.C. secondary products revolution focusing on the secondary use of fiber and dairy products. See Hesse (1997) 142.	Hesse (1995) 213 and Zeder (1997) 24
Goat (*Capra hircus*)	c. 7500 B.C.	Meat production, milk production. Around 3000 B.C. secondary products revolution focusing on the secondary use of fiber and dairy products. See Hesse (1997a) 142.	Hesse (1995) 213–14 and Zeder (1997) 24
Cattle (*Bos taurus* and *Bos indicus*)	c. 6000–5000 B.C.[a]	Meat production (although only 10–15% of the carcasses at ancient sites are cattle). From 4000 B.C. onwards dairy production and use as draft animal. See Hesse (1997b) 442.	Hesse (1995) 214 and Hesse (1997b) 442–43
Pig (*Sus scrofa*)	c. 8500–8000 B.C., although generally accepted 6000 B.C.[b]	Meat production and later on as urban scavengers	Hesse (1995) 214–16 and Hesse (1997c) 347–48
Donkey (*Equus asinus*)	c. 3500–3000 B.C.	Part of the secondary products revolution valued for labor; ritual context	Hesse (1995) 216; Firmage (1992) 1137; Wapnish and Hesse (1997) 255–56
Horse (*Equus caballus*)	c. 3500–3000 B.C.[c]	Minor role in economy of ANE; indicator of status; military use; transport; ritual activity	Hesse (1995) 216, Firmage (1992) 1136–37; Wapnish and Hesse (1997) 255–56

Mule (fem. *E. caballus X* masc. *E. asinus*)	c. 2200 B.C.[d]	Minor role in economy of ANE; indicator of status; transport; ritual activity	Hesse (1995) 216; Clutton-Brock (1981) 95–97; Wapnish and Hesse (1997) 255–56; Clutton-Brock (1992) 43–44 Hesse
Hinny (masc. *E. caballus X* fem *E. asinus*)	c. 2500 B.C.	Minor role in economy of ANE; indicator of status; transport; ritual activity[e]	Borowski (1998) 108–10
Camel (*Camelus dromedarius*)	c. 2600 B.C.[f]	Milk and fiber production; used as pack and riding animals from 1500 B.C. onwards	Sauer (1995) 41–42; Zarins (1989) 127–55; Hesse (1995) 217; Wapnish (1997) 407–8

a. The evidence from Çatal Höyük for the sixth millennium B.C. is ambiguous because the animal seems to have been employed primarily in a ritual context. According to Hesse (1997b) 442, the morphology of cattle—based upon size diminution—clearly points to its domestication by 5000 B.C.

b. See Hesse (1997c) 348, who cites new evidence from Hallan Cemi in southeastern Turkey based upon morphological changes and mortality patterns. In an earlier article Hesse (1995) 216 argued for a date of domestication c. 6000 B.C. Compare also Firmage (1992) 1115.

c. Clutton-Brock (1992) 38, 53 date it to c. 4000 B.C. Compare also the discussion of Borowski (1998) 100, note 24.

d. One of the main problems in the identification of mules is the morphology of the skeletal remains of horses, donkeys, and mules in the archaeological record. As has been indicated above, recent paleozoological research on equids is focusing on the techniques and technology to differentiate among the various species. See especially the helpful discussion of mule remains from archaeological digs of the Roman period in Germany in Uerpmann and Uerpmann (1994) 353–57. On the role of the mule in Roman times and more specifically in Britain, see Armitage and Chapman (1979) 339–59. One important source for a more secure identification of mules is its dentition or dental characteristics. Compare also Hesse (1995) 216: "A particular problem is the difficulty zooarchaeologists find in assigning fragmentary osteological remains to taxonomic categories more precise than 'equid'."

e. Borowski (1998) 109—based upon Clutton-Brock (1992) 45—has suggested that during Sumerian times "more hinnies were bred because a rare imported stallion could produce a whole herd of hybrids in the time it would take one mare to produce a mule."

f. Wapnish (1997) 407 argues that the famous Umm an-Nar camel-bone collection (c. 2600 B.C.) does not represent the skeletal remains of a domesticated camel, but rather a hunted camel.

the historical-critical method[63] and, secondly, I try to take seriously the inherent historical assertions of the Old Testament in their ancient Near Eastern context.

The noun *pered* occurs fourteen times in the Old Testament in its masculine form,[64] whereas *pirdâ* (the feminine form, indicating "she-mule" or, more technically, "hinny") appears only three times.[65] Looking at the usage of the two forms of the root *pered* in their purported historical context one will immediately discern the concentration of occurrences during the tenth and ninth centuries B.C. (see fig. 2).

Apparently mules were important indicators of social status during the time of the united and the early part of the divided monarchy. Absalom—in his unsuccessful bid for the crown—is caught on a mule (2 Sam 18:9). The king's sons are all provided with mules as their preferred means of transport (2 Sam 13:29). During the coronation of David, food is transported by mules and camels—both very costly animals—in order to emphasize the importance of the event for the Davidic dynasty (1 Chr 12:41)—a literary strategy that is in tune with the general tendency or "theological reading" of Israel's past by the Chronicler.[66] Solomon is put upon King David's own hinny during his coronation (1 Kgs 1:33, 38, 44) and when "all the world" comes to pay homage to his wisdom, they bring mules among the choicest presents (1 Kgs 10:25; 2 Chr 9:24). A century later, during the ninth century B.C., Ahab demands that his captain Obadiah water the royal horses and mules during a time of extreme drought (1 Kgs 18:5), a fact that expresses social realities. While mules always were considered a costly item (in the lists in Ezek 27:14 and in Ezra 2:66 they occur right after horses and before camels), it would seem that they were more common and also frequently utilized as pack animals in later periods. The prophetic passages

---

63 See here also recently the relevant remarks of Brueggemann (1997) 726–29 concerning the philosophical basis of the historical-critical method.

64 Namely in 2 Sam 13:29, 18:9 (3x); 1 Kgs 10:25, 18:5; 2 Kgs 5:17; 1 Chr 12:41; 2 Chr 9:24; Ps 32:9; Isa 66:20; Ezek 27:14; Ezra 2:66; and Zech 14:15. Note that Even-Shoshan (1985) 959, as well as Maiberger (1989) 738, erroneously suggests fifteen occurrences, including Neh 7:68 (which is a parallel to Ezra 2:66). BHS has there *ḥamōrîm*, "donkeys" with no variant reading of "mules." The LXX does not read the customary ἡμιόνος, "mule" either, but rather ὄνος, "donkey." Compare also Moore and Brown (1997) 675.

65 See here 1 Kgs 1:33, 38 and 44 in Even-Shoshan (1985) 959.

66 This appears to be in line with the general tendency of the Chronicler, who, according to Fouts (1997) 387, "examines the history of Israel with emphasis on King David." Compare also the comments in Japhet (1993) 48–49.

Figure 2.
Graphical Indications of Time Periods when *pered* and *pirdâ* Are Utilized

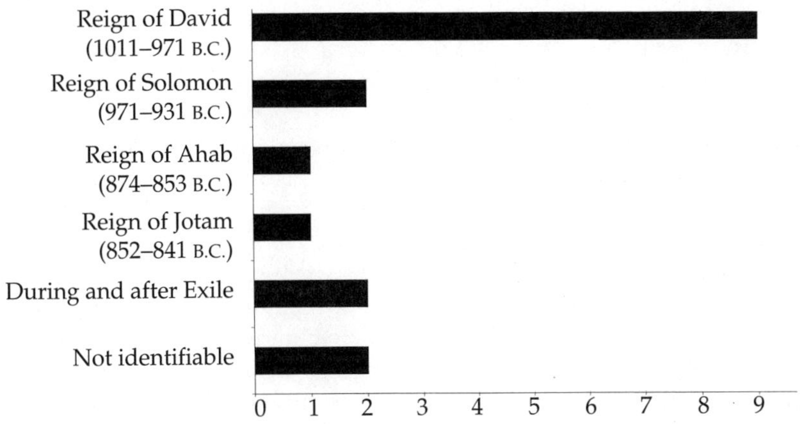

in Isa 66:20 and Zech 14:15 describe the Messianic age and by including mules in the list, draw attention to the importance of the related events.

Why was a mule so special in the tenth century B.C. (or earlier) in the ancient Near East, while in modern times it is often connected to insults in colloquial language? Firstly, mules were hybrids and in view of Lev 19:19 it has been argued that mules were not bred directly in Israel.[67] This raised the price of a mule considerably, because it was imported ware and could not be "copied" locally. Secondly, mules being hybrids that had to be imported, were very costly and could not reproduce themselves.[68] Therefore, besides the transport use, the mule was dead capital and could not produce on a utilitarian level. Thus it was an animal for rich people who could afford to have "dead capital" standing around. The breeding problems connected with the mule are reflected in its high price. The prices paid for mules in the surrounding cultures during different historical periods show that this was not just a typical "Israelite" problem. In ED III texts from the third millennium B.C. the price of a mule ranges from twenty to thirty

---

67 See here, for example, Borowski (1998) 110; Mayoral (1995) 345; and Harrison (1986) 430.

68 No hybrid can successfully reproduce itself, as has been pointed out by Zarins (1986) 185.

shekels or seven times the amount paid for an ordinary donkey. At Ebla the average price for a mule was sixty shekels and the highest bid ever found in a text there for a mule was a staggering three hundred shekels.[69] Hittite records show that while the price of an ox was ten sheep (= ten shekels) and that of a horse twenty shekels, a mule cost sixty shekels.[70] Juris Zarins has suggested that these costly hybrids (although not always exactly "mules") were most probably present in the "royal graves" as funerary gifts.[71] Thirdly, it appears that its very hardy nature made the mule attractive to their ancient masters. Mules are sure-footed, faster than a donkey, and can pull or carry more weight than a horse.[72] In sum, they are the ideal 4x4 utility van—fancy, gleaming, expensive, but rugged.

Looking outside the Hebrew Bible toward Egypt, very little material concerning the mule can be found. Although Kenneth Kitchen suggested in 1974 that Egyptian *p-t-r* (which he obviously derived from Hebrew *pered*) meant "mule" in New Kingdom Egyptian,[73] this suggestion has not been universally accepted. Alessandra Nibbi vehemently disagrees with Kitchen, on the basis of biological ("mules do not just 'happen' and they do not appear in herds") and iconographical arguments—albeit not on philological.[74] However, the fact remains, that even if Kitchen's suggestion proves to be true, it represents a rare occurrence of the lexeme in a huge base of textual data and thus points to the fact that the mule either played a very limited role (Kitchen) or no role whatsoever (Nibbi) in Egyptian culture.[75]

In Sumerian the composite term ANŠE.BAR.AN appears to have been used in the ED III period with the possible connotation of a hybrid or

---

69 Compare Zarins (1986) 185–87.

70 See here Dent (1972) 62 and Borowski (1998) 109 and the sources cited therein.

71 Zarins (1986) 164.

72 Compare here Zarins (1978) 11; Dent (1972) 62–63; and Nibbi (1979) 167.

73 He based his suggestion on a list of domestic animals in an ostracon (Gardiner 86) from the period of Ramses II, where a so-far unidentified *p-t-r* (group written and with no clear vocalization) is mentioned among goats, sheep, donkeys, and pigs. Kitchen argues for the meaning "mule" of that lexeme because of its close association with "donkey" (preceding) and because of the possibility that it represents a Semitic loanword. Compare Kitchen (1974) 17–20.

74 Nibbi (1979) 166–68.

75 Compare here Störk (1978) 1248–49 and his discussion of the possible use of mules during the eighteenth and twenty-fifth dynasties, based upon iconographic material. The pictorial distinction between mule, donkey, horse, and regarding hybrids such as horse and onager is at best difficult—if not impossible.

mule.[76] Other possible terms include ANŠE.ŠÚ.MUL, whose Akkadian equivalent is *parû*, which has been translated as "mule" or "onager," although the evidence is not clear-cut.[77] Zarins[78] has suggested that ANŠE.ŠÚ.MUL should be understood as "mule" or "hybrid," at least starting from the fourteenth century B.C. with the term ANŠE.ŠÚ.AN as the connecting link between ANŠE.BAR.AN in the third millennium B.C. and ANŠE.ŠÚ.MUL in the first millennium B.C.[79] Among some Sumerian proverbs written during the early Old Babylonian period is:

> O, mule, do you know your ancestors,
> and do you know your mother?[80]

Other less important terms in Akkadian include *damdammu(m)*, "eine Art Maultier,"[81] *kudanu(m)*, "Maultier, -esel,"[82] and *agālu*,[83] "hybrid, mule," which in earlier references seems to indicate a draft animal and in later booty lists a hybrid, although not necessarily a mule since it often occurs together with *parû*.[84] It appears that *damdammu*-mules were considered very elegant draft animals, as their mention before horses and their use for the procession at the *akītu*-festival show.[85]

In an intriguing quote from Mari, the court official Bakhdi-Lim, prefect of the palace at Mari, pleads with King Zimri-Lim not to utilize a horse but rather mount a mule:

> I told my lord the following, "Now that the land of Yakhdun-Lim has reverted to my lord and because this land is wearing Akkadian garb,[86]

---

76 See here Littauer and Crouwel (1979) 42; Zarins (1978) 11–12; Gordon (1958) 46; and also Postgate (1986) 195–98.

77 See here von Soden (1965–81) 837. It is possible that von Soden included this term here understanding it as a loanword from West Semitic sources.

78 Zarins (1978) 12.

79 Compare here Zarins (1978) 13 and Postgate (1986) 195–96.

80 Alster (1997) 307.

81 von Soden (1965–81) 157.

82 von Soden (1965–81) 498–99.

83 At Ebla *ag-lum* has been found in a lexical list in MEE 4, no. 116. Sjöberg (1996) 9–10 suggests here the translation "equid," since no further identification can be made.

84 See here *CAD*, A, 141.

85 *CAD*, D, 64; and also Cohen (1993) 417.

86 Nicolas Vanderrosts of Brussels Free University brought the following new

> my lord should give majesty honor. Since you are king of the Khana tribesmen and you are, secondly, king of Akkad (land), my lord ought not to ride horses; rather, it is upon a palanquin or on mules that my lord ought to ride, and in this way he could give honor to his majesty. This is what I told my lord.[87]

In later, Neo-Assyrian sources from the eighth to the sixth centuries B.C. mules were part and parcel of the transport routes,[88] connecting the great Mesopotamian centers with the outside world. A team of mules sold for eight minas during this period,[89] although it appears that both sides were not always happy with their bargain:

> After he gave us eight minas for a team of mules, and after we brought a team of mules, he said. "They're no good." The king will return and say: "The silver—where is it?" He won't consent. He'll say, "Bring me fine mules and give (them) to me."[90]

In another letter[91] several high-ranking officials were involved in a dispute over the distribution of three fine teams of mules. It appears that mules were still considered a prized possession, but the fact that they were sold in teams indicates that they were used as draft or transport animals, instead of being used for riding purposes.[92]

In a building inscription the Neo-Assyrian king Tiglath-Pileser III mentions mules as part of the booty from his campaigns against Syria and

---

reading of this text by Durand (1998) 485, note 103 to my attention: "Aujourd'hui, le pays benjaminite t'est livré." Or "ce pays-ci est revêtu de l'habit akkadien."

[87] Sasson (1995) 1204; also Kupper (1963) 191.

[88] Cole (1996) 21.

[89] This can be seen in several letters from the Governor's palace in Nippur, e.g., letters 56–59. The recipient of the letter is the *šandabakku* of Nippur who—according to Cole (1996) 50—"was an influential political figure in the mid-eighth century who often governed independently of the crown, joined in political alliances with the tribal chiefs around him, and ruled a city whose economic ties reached to the middle Euphrates, Assyria, the Zagros highlands, and to Uruk and the Chaldeans near the Persian Gulf."

[90] Cole (1996) 98–99.

[91] Namely in letter 57; see Cole (1996) 99.

[92] However, in letter 59 one can find the request for a single mule for the king. The texts reads as follows: "Every day my lord keeps writing, saying: 'send me a mule'. Now I have sent to my lord a mule after my lord's own heart" Compare Cole (1996) 100.

Palestine.[93] Mules were often referred to in tribute payment sections in Neo-Assyrian texts—perhaps representing something costly and precious.[94] In the so-called Taylor Prism, describing the siege of Jerusalem by Sennacherib in 701 B.C., the Neo-Assyrian king claims to have taken 200,150 inhabitants and "horses, mules, donkeys, camels, big and small cattle beyond counting" from Judah.[95]

In summary, according to Mesopotamian usage, apparently mules not only held religious significance (the *akītu*-festival, mentioned above),[96] but were among the costliest of animals and thus an indicator of social status. With improvements in breeding techniques, mules became synonymous with "great booty," valuable possessions won by war or as tribute payments. Also, beginning in the ninth century B.C., mules were used ever more frequently as a means of transport.

RECONSTRUCTING DAILY LIFE ICONOGRAPHICALLY: THE CASE OF THE MULE

When studying the iconographic data concerning the question of the status and function of the mule in the ancient Near East, one major issue should be kept in mind: while it is difficult to distinguish among the physical osteological remains found in fragments of equid bones, their artistic rendering is even more complex to distinguish.[97] This is partly due to perspectives of the artist and also to the hybrid nature of the animals, which might appear either as a horse or a donkey.

Figure 3, copied from the palace in Nineveh of the Neo-Assyrian king Ashurbanipal, depicts a mule performing transport work. It should be dated around 645 B.C. The mule is laden with hunting gear and is accompanied by one driver and three attendants, who apparently are carrying other hunting gear.[98] Since the hybrid's head and front resemble the sire's

---

[93] Pritchard (1969) 282.

[94] Compare Pritchard (1969) 283 in an annalistic record from Tiglath-Pileser's ninth year.

[95] See Pritchard (1969) 288.

[96] See further Cohen (1993) 417. This reference comes from a text from Mari in a letter from Šamši-Adad to his son Yasmah-Adad: "As to the [...]-ceremony, let your teams of *damdammu*-mules and horses come here to the New Year's festival."

[97] This can be illustrated in the discussion of Perkins, Daly, and Hesse (1972) concerning the depiction (and identification) of a stag on a bronze mold from Mari, which does have a direct bearing upon the question of domestication.

[98] The illustration was taken from Clutton-Brock (1981) 97. The original is housed in the British Museum.

Figure 3.
Mule transporting hunting gear; found in Ashurbanipal's palace in Nineveh and dated to 645 B.C.
Courtesy Trustees of the British Museum.

head and front, while the hindquarters are like those of the dam, it would appear that we have, indeed, a mule in this depiction, with its front part resembling the horse connection and its hindquarters being closer to the donkey dam.

Thomas Staubli, in his study on the image of the nomads in ancient Israel and in the iconography of its neighbors, sees a mule in the imposing bronze gate of Shalmaneser III from Balawat, in which the prisoners of a north-Syrian city are being led away by an Assyrian officer, who is followed by two dromedaries that are being led by another Assyrian soldier (fig. 4).[99] Next to the second Assyrian soldier is a mule, which is then followed by another soldier and four female prisoners. Unfortunately the illustration included in his study is incomplete and thus a secure identification as a mule cannot be guaranteed. It appears that Staubli does not differentiate between a mule and a donkey, since he treats all Hebrew terms denoting these equids in the same breath.[100] Staubli does, however, point out the importance of this class of mammals as the decisive factor for the pluralistic development of nomadism in the ancient Near East.[101]

99 Compare Staubli (1991) 79.

100 Staubli (1991) 179–84.

101 Staubli (1991) 179. Figure 4 was taken from Staubli (1991), figure 57.

Figure 4.
Drawing of a train of prisoners and booty from the bronze gate of Shalmaneser III from Balawat.

Figure 5 was taken from Dent[102] and represents an Assyrian mule team drawing a heavy wagon. Dent does not include further information as to the provenance of the drawing, but the characteristics of the animals clearly point to their identification as mules, especially in view of the low hind quarters and the raised neck/head. This is typical of a mule since it generally exhibits the characteristics of both parents, neatly divided into front and hind quarters.

Figure 6 depicts a rare Egyptian example from a tomb painting of the scribe Nebamun from Thebes (to be dated around 1400 B.C.) and shows in the upper part a pair of horses drawing a chariot. The equids in the lower painting are more difficult to identify but they could be hinnies. The fact that they have a strongly marked shoulder stripe that is not part of the harness precludes their being domesticated onagers.[103] According to Clutton-Brock, this is the only ancient picture of a hybrid from Egypt.[104]

---

102 Dent (1972) 60.

103 The illustration was taken from Clutton-Brock (1981) 96. The original is housed in the British Museum.

104 See Clutton-Brock (1981) 96. The figure has been taken from Houlihan (1996) 38 and can also be found in Osborn and Osbornová (1998) 136.

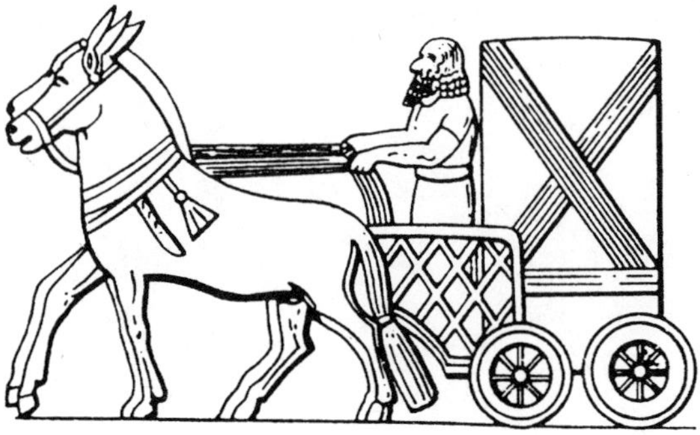

Figure 5.
Assyrian mule team drawing a heavy wagon.

Figure 6.
Possible mule from Egyptian tomb painting from Thebes ca. 1400 B.C.
(from the tomb of the scribe Nabamun, eighteenth dynasty)

MULES AND DAILY LIFE – CONCLUSION

Recent contributions by leading archaeologists have suggested a radical re-dating of the generally accepted stratigraphy[105] of major Israelite sites (including Megiddo), resulting in the disappearance of the tenth century B.C.[106] Israel Finkelstein's and David Ussishkin's contention has to do with the dating of stratum VA–IVB, which they propose to date to the ninth century B.C.[107] This is of the utmost importance in light of the fact that Megiddo is a crucial "index" site from which other sites can be dated (in terms of material characteristics, for example). Their re-dating of the stratigraphy is based upon a small base of data from their Jezreel excavation close by Megiddo that Mazar (in a defense of the traditional stratigraphy)[108] calls "flimsical." Among archaeologists, Finkelstein and Ussishkin seem to be alone so far, although they are known to be meticulous, albeit vocal, experts. Amihai Mazar[109] has strongly argued against the disappearance of the tenth century B.C. on archaeological grounds—the debatable re-dating of Myc IIIC pottery beyond the end of the Egyptian presence in Canaan. He has called for a more "detailed typological and if possible, quantitative study"[110] of the Jezreel material where local features should not be ignored. Other recent hotbeds of discussion concerning the tenth century B.C. include David's Jerusalem, which some suggest is a fiction of the biblical authors.[111] It appears that this development goes hand in hand with the systematic discrediting of the historical period of the United Monarchy under David and Solomon in historiographical research.[112]

After having scrutinized occurrences of the terms *pered* and *pirdâ* synchronically in their Old Testament context, one notes immediately the concentration during the tenth and early-ninth centuries B.C. This seems to coincide with the usage documented in the surrounding nations, especially in Mesopotamia, that refer to the mule in terms of its status function. This

---

105 A good example can be found, for example, in Dever (1982).

106 See here specifically Finkelstein (1996b).

107 See here also Shanks (1998) for a summary of the arguments.

108 Mazar (1997) 160.

109 Mazar (1997).

110 Mazar (1997) 161.

111 See the relevant references in Na'aman (1996) and (1998).

112 Neumann (1997) and the full bibliography provided by Knoppers (1997); see also recently Dever (1998). The work of the minimalist Copenhagen school comes here also to mind.

function seems to have somewhat diminished by the seventh/sixth century B.C., when mules were predominantly utilized as draft animals. This change in status and use can also be documented in the biblical material where mules appear to be more common in lists of useful domesticated animals—although close to the highly regarded horse. While ancient Near Eastern societies were intrinsically conservative about their values and status institutions,[113] one can nevertheless detect and pinpoint certain developments—especially when connected to technological advances.[114]

If David and/or Solomon had not existed, how was their chronicler able to utilize with an innate sense of security the socially correct terms, phrases, and status animals peculiar to the tenth century B.C.—and not—as commonly argued—those of the post-exilic community?[115] One might even go a little further in arguing that the mule as a status symbol represented a conscious snub or affront to the still powerful Egyptian neighbor—especially in view of the fact that mules did not appear to have had this function in Egypt. Theologically and politically, Egypt was always the "house of slavery," the oppressor from the South, and it is possible to find David (and later also Solomon) copying the closer Syrian or Mesopotamian practices.[116] Thus, it would seem that the stubborn mule, digging in his status-loaded heels, has helped us not to loose sight of David and Solomon's tenth century B.C. and points us toward the value of an integrated approach to investigations into the everyday life in the ancient Near East. In other words: the mundane and common that might be unearthed while

113 Pilch and Malina (1993) xv: "Roles and statuses are replicated throughout a social system because their dimensions distinguish one individual person not only from another person but also from nature, space, time and... God."

114 Or, perhaps, in the case of the mule, advanced breeding techniques.

115 See also here my article on an obscure Hebrew term in the Book of Esther, which has now also been documented in a contemporary Aramaic ostracon from Arad and which seems to point to the fact that the author of Esther was more at home in Persian court circles than in Hellenistic or even Maccabean circles several hundred years later (Klingbeil [1995] 301–3).

116 This underlying anti-Egyptian feeling would lead to the flight of Jeroboam to Egypt, his state-sponsored asylum on the other side of the Sinai (1 Kgs 11:26–40), and the later incursion of Pharaoh Shishak against Judah and Israel (1 Kgs 14:25; 2 Chr 12:2). Malamat (1982) 197 has poignantly pointed out that one of the titles of Solomon, as the builder of the temple, was *melek rāb*, "the great king" (Ps 48:3 [ET 48:2]), which should be connected to the Mesopotamian title *šarru rabû*, "great king, emperor." His reconstruction of Israel's relationship with Egypt (Malamat [1982] 198–204) also seems to reaffirm conscious anti-Egyptian sentiments during the tenth century B.C., which included even different prestige objects.

studying features of everyday life might be able to tell us more about the pattern of the specific and historical. This is indeed an important point of departure for future studies seeking to understand ancient life, history, religion, economics, and thought.

BIBLIOGRAPHY

Adams, W.Y. (1997) Anthropology and Egyptology: Divorce and Remarriage? In J. Lustig, ed., *Anthropology and Egyptology. A Developing Dialogue*, 25–32. Monographs in Mediterranean Archaeology 8. Sheffield. **Ahlström, G.W.** (1993) *The History of Ancient Palestine from the Palaeolithic Period to Alexander's Conquest*, with a contribution by G.O. Rollefson, ed. by D. Edelman. JSOTSS 146. Sheffield. **Alster, B.** (1997) *Proverbs of Ancient Sumer*. Bethesda. **Armitage, P. and Chapman, H.** (1979) Roman Mules. *The London Archaeologist* 3: 339–59. **Arnold, P.J.** (1995) Ethnicity, Pottery, and the Gulf Olmec of Ancient Veracruz, Mexico. *Biblical Archaeologist* 58: 191–99. **Banning, E.B.** (1996) Highlands and Lowlands: Problems and Survey Frameworks for Rural Archaeology in the Near East. *Bulletin of the American Schools of Oriental Research* 301: 25–45. **Barkay, G.** (1988) Burial Headrests as a Return to the Womb – a Reevaluation. *Biblical Archaeology Review* 14: 48–50. **Barr, J.** (1995) The Synchronic, the Diachronic and the Historical: a Triangular Relationship? In J.C. De Moor, ed., *Synchronic or Diachronic? A Debate on Method in Old Testament Exegesis. Papers Read at the Ninth Joint Meeting of Het Oudtestamentisch Werkgeselschap in Nederland en Belgie and The Society for Old Testament Study*, 1–14. Oudtestamentische Studiën 34. Leiden/New York/Köln. **Bartlett, J.R.** (1997) What has Archaeology to do with the Bible – or Vice Versa? In J.R. Bartlett, ed., *Archaeology and Biblical Interpretation*, 1–19. London. **Bar-Yosef, O. and Khazanov, A.** (1992) Introduction. In O. Bar-Yosef and A. Khazanov, eds., *Pastoralism in the Levant. Archaeological Materials in Anthropological Perspectives*, 1–9. Monographs in World Archaeology 10. Madison. **Borowski, O.** (1998) *Every Living Thing. Daily Use of Animals in Ancient Israel*. Walnut Creek/London/New Delhi. **Brueggemann, W.** (1997) *Theology of the Old Testament. Testimony, Dispute, Advocacy*. Minneapolis. **Chavalas, M.W.** (1995) Recent Trends in the Study of Israelite Historiography. *Journal of the Evangelical Theological Society* 38: 161–69. **Clutton-Brock, J.** (1981) *Domesticated Animals from Early Times*. Austin/London. (1992) *Horse Power: A History of the Horse and Donkey in Human Societies*. Cambridge. (1994) The Unnatural World: Behavioural Aspects of Humans and Animals in the Process of Domestication. In A. Manning and A. Serpell, eds., *Animals and Human Society. Changing Perspectives*, 23–35. London. **Cohen, M.E.** (1993) *The Cultic Calendars of the Ancient Near East*. Bethesda. **Cole, S.W.** (1996) *Nippur in Late Assyrian Times (c. 755–612 BC)*. SAAS 4. Helsinki. **Dalley, S.** (1998) Occasions and Opportunities. 1. To the Persian Conquest. In S. Dalley, ed., *The Legacy of Mesopotamia*, 9–33. Oxford. **Davies, S. J.** (1980) Late Pleistocene and Holocene

Equid Remains from Israel. *Zoological Journal of the Linnean Society* 70: 289–312. **Dent, A.** (1972) *Donkey. The Story of the Ass from East to West.* London/Toronto/Wellington/Sydney. **de Pury, A.** (1993) Gemeinschaft und Differenz. Aspekte der Mensch-Tier-Beziehung im alten Israel. In B. Janowski et al., eds., *Gefährten und Feinde des Menschen. Das Tier in der Lebenswelt des alten Israels,* 112–49. Originally published in French in 1984. Neukirchen-Vlyun. **Dever, W.G.** (1982) Monumental Architecture in Ancient Israel in the Period of the United Monarchy. In T. Ishida, ed., *Studies in the Period of David and Solomon and Other Essays. Papers Read at the International Symposium for Biblical Studies, Tokyo, 5–7 December, 1979,* 269–306. Winona Lake. (1990) *Recent Archaeological Discoveries and Biblical Research.* Seattle and London. (1995) Ceramics, Ethnicity, and the Question of Israel's Origin. *Biblical Archaeologist* 58: 200–13. (1997) Philology, Theology, and Archaeology: What Kind of History of Israel Do We Want, and What Is Possible? In N.A. Silberman and D. Small, eds., *The Archaeology of Israel. Constructing the Past, Interpreting the Present,* 290–310. JSOTSS 237. Sheffield. (1998) Archaeology, Ideology, and the Quest for an 'Ancient' or 'Biblical' Israel. *Near Eastern Archaeology* 61: 39–52. **Dorsey, D.A.** (1991) *The Roads and Highways of Ancient Israel.* ASOR Library of Biblical and Near Eastern Archaeology. Baltimore/London. **Drinkard, J. F.** (1989) The Position of Biblical Archaeology within Biblical Studies. *Review and Expositor* 86: 603–15. **Ducos, P.** (1978) "Domestication" Defined and Methodological Approaches to Its Recognition in Faunal Assemblages. In R.H. Meadow and M.A. Zeder, eds., *Approaches to Faunal Analysis in the Middle East,* 53–56. Peabody Museum Bulletin 2. Cambridge. **Durand, J.-M.** (1998) *Documents épistolaires du palais de Mari. Tome II.* LAPO 17. Paris. **Eggler, J.** (1992) *Scarabs from Excavations in Palestine/Transjordan from Iron Age I (c. 1200–1000 B.C.),* M.A. thesis. University of Stellenbosch, South Africa. **Eph'al, I.** (1988) Syria-Palestine under Achaemenid Rule. *CAH* 4: 139–64. (1998) Changes in Palestine during the Persian Period in Light of Epigraphic Sources. *Israel Exploration Journal* 48: 106–19. **Eph'al, I. and Naveh, J.** (1996) *Aramaic Ostraca of the Fourth Century BC from Idumaea.* Jerusalem. **Esse, D.L.** (1992) The Collared Pithos at Megiddo: Ceramic Distribution and Ethnicity. *Journal of Near Eastern Studies* 51: 81–103. **Even-Shoshan, A.** (1985) *A New Concordance of the Bible.* Jerusalem. **Finkelstein, I.** (1988) *The Archaeology of the Israelite Settlement.* Jerusalem. (1995) *Living on the Fringe. The Archaeology and History of the Negev, Sinai and Neighbouring Regions in the Bronze and Iron Ages.* Monographs in Mediterranean Archaeology 6. Sheffield. (1996a) Ethnicity and the Origin of the Iron I Settlers in the Highlands of Canaan: Can the Real Israel Stand Up? *Biblical Archaeologist* 59: 198–212. (1996b) The Archaeology of the United Monarchy: An Alternative View. *Levant* 28: 177–87. **Firmage, E.** (1992) Zoology. *ABD* 6: 1109–67. **Fouts, D.M.** (1997) A Defense of the Hyperbolic Interpretation of Large Numbers in the Old Testament. *Journal of the Evangelical Theological Society* 40: 377–87. **Fritz, V.** (1994) *An Introduction to Biblical Archaeology.* JSOTSS 172. Sheffield. **Gilbert, A.S.** (1995) The Flora and Fauna of the Ancient Near East. *CANE* 1: 153–74. **Gordon, E.I.** (1958) Sumerian Animal Proverbs and Fables: "Collection Five". *Journal of Cuneiform Studies* 12: 1–75. **Hadidi, A.**, ed. (1985) *Studies in the History and Archaeology of Jordan II.* Amman. **Hallo, W.W.** (1971) Mesopotamia and the Asiatic Near East. In W.W. Hallo and W.K. Simpson, eds., *The Ancient Near East. A History,* 1–183. New York. **Halpern, B.** (1988) *The First Historians. The Hebrew Bible and History.* San Francisco. (1997) Texts and Artifacts: Two Monologues? In N.A. Silberman and D. Small, eds., *The Archaeology of Israel. Constructing the Past, Interpreting the Present,* 311–41. JSOTSS 237. Sheffield. **Hansen, J.** (1997) Paleobotany. *OEANE* 4: 200–1. **Haran, M.** (1985) Das Böcklein in der Milch seiner Mutter und das säugende Muttertier. *Theologische Zeitschrift* 41: 135–59. **Harrison, R.K.** (1986) Mule. *ISBE* 3: 430–31. **Harrison, T.P.** (1997) Shifting Patterns of Settlement in the Highlands of Central Jordan during the Early Bronze Age. *Bulletin of the American Schools of Oriental Research* 306: 1–37. **Henry, M.L.** (1993) Das Tier im religiösen Bewußtsein des alttestamentlichen Menschen. In B. Janowski et al., eds., *Gefährten und Feinde des Menschen. Das Tier in der Lebenswelt des alten Israels,* 20–61. Originally published in 1958. Neukirchen-Vlyun. **Herion, G.A.** (1992) Introduction. *ABD* 1: xxxvii–xliii. **Hess, R.S.** (1998) Issues in the Study of Personal Names in the Hebrew Bible. *Currents in Research/Biblical Studies* 6: 169–92. **Hesse, B.** (1995) Animal Husbandry and Human Diet in the Ancient Near East. *CANE* 1: 203–22. (1997a) Animal Husbandry. *OEANE* 1: 140–43. (1997b) Cattle and Oxen. *OEANE* 1: 442–43. (1997c) Pigs. *OEANE* 4: 347–48. **Hesse, B. and Wapnish, P.** (1997a) Palaeozoology. *OEANE* 4: 206–7. (1997b) Equids. *OEANE* 2: 255–56. **Hitschner, R.B.** (1995) Historical Text and Archaeological Context in Roman North Africa: The Albertini Tablets and Kasserine Survey. Pp. 124–42 In D.B. Small, ed., *Methods in the Mediterranean. Historical and Archaeological Views on Texts and Archaeology,* 124–42. Mnemosyne: Biblioteca Classica Batava Supplementum 135. Leiden/New York/Köln. **Hole, F.** (1995) Assessing the Past through Anthropological Archaeology. *CANE* 4: 2715–27. **Houlihan, R.F.** (1996) *The Animal World of the Pharaohs.* London. **Janowski, B., Neumann-Gorsolke, U. and Glessmer, U.**, eds. (1993) *Gefährten und Feinde des Menschen. Das Tier in der Lebenswelt des alten Israels.* Neukirchen-Vlyun. **Japhet, S.** (1993) *I & II Chronicles.* OTL. Louisville. **Jerricke, D.** (1997) *Die Landnahme im Negev. Protoisraelitische Gruppen im Süden Palästinas. Eine archäologische und exegetische Studie.* Abhandlungen des Deutschen Palästina-Vereins 20. Wiesbaden. **Keel, O.** (1992a) Iconography and the Bible. *ABD* 3: 358–74. (1992b) *Das Recht der Bilder gesehen zu werden. Drei Fallstudien zur Methode der Interpretation altorientalischer Bilder.* OBO 122. Fribourg/Göttingen. (1993) Allgegenwärtige Tiere. Einige Weisen ihrer Wahrnehmung in der hebräischen Bibel. In B. Janowski et al., eds., *Gefährten und Feinde des Menschen. Das Tier in der Lebenswelt des alten Israels,* 155–93. Neukirchen-Vlyun. (1995) *Corpus der Stempelsiegel-Amulette aus Palästina/Israel. Von den Anfängen bis zur Perserzeit. Einleitung.* OBO.SA 10. Fribourg/Göttingen. (1996) *Die Welt der altorientalischen Bildsymbolik und das Alte Testament.* 5th edition. Göttingen. (1997) *Corpus der Stempelsiegel-Amulette aus Palästina/Israel. Von den Anfängen bis zur Perserzeit. Katalog*

Band I: Von Tell Abu Farag bis 'Atlit. OBO.SA 13. Fribourg/Göttingen. **Keel, O. and Uehlinger, C.** (1995) *Göttingen, Götter und Gottessymbole. Neue Erkenntnisse zur Religionsgeschichte Kanaans und Israels aufgrund bislang unerschlossener ikonographischer Quellen.* 3rd edition. QD 134. Freiburg/Basel/Wien. **Kitchen, K.A.** (1974) *Prd > Ptr* = 'Mule' in New Kingdom Egypt? *Göttinger Miszellen* 13: 17–20. **Kletter, R.** (1999) Pots and Politics: Material Remains of Late Iron Age Judah in Relation to its Political Borders. *Bulletin of the American Schools of Oriental Research* 314: 19–54. **Klingbeil, G.A.** (1992) *The Aramaic Epigraphical Material of Syria-Palestine during the Persian Period with Reference to the History of the Jews,* M.A. thesis, University of Stellenbosch, South Africa. (1993) The Onomasticon of the Aramaic Inscriptions of Syria-Palestine during the Persian period. *Journal of Northwest Semitic Languages* 18: 67–94. (1995) "*rkš* in Esther 8,10.14: A Semantic Note" *Zeitschrift für die alttestamentliche Wissenschaft* 107: 301–3. (1997) A Semantic Analysis of the Aramaic Epigraphical Material of Syria-Palestine during the Persian Period. *Andrews University Seminary Studies* 35: 33–46. (1998) *A Comparative Study of the Ritual of Ordination as found in Leviticus 8 and Emar 369.* Lewiston/Queenston/Lampeter. **Klingbeil, M.G.** (1999) *Yahweh Fighting from Heaven. God as Warrior and as God of Heaven in the Hebrew Psalter and Ancient Near Eastern Iconography.* OBO 169. Fribourg/Göttingen. **Knoppers, G.N.** (1997) The Vanishing Solomon: The Disappearance of the United Monarchy from Recent Histories of Ancient Israel. *Journal of Biblical Literature* 116: 19–44. **Kosso, P.** (1995) Epistemic Independence between Textual and Material Evidence. 177–96 In D.B. Small, ed., *Methods in the Mediterranean. Historical and Archaeological Views on Texts and Archaeology,* 177–96. Mnemosyne: Biblioteca Classica Batava Supplementum 135. Leiden/New York/Köln. **Kupper, J.R.** (1963) L'Opinion puplique a Mari (A Summary). *Iraq* 25: 190–91. **LaBianca, Ø.S.** (1990) *Sedentarization and Nomadization: Food System Cycles at Hesban and Vicinity in Transjordan. Hesban 1.* Berrien Springs. (1995) The Development of the Bone Work on the Heshbon Expedition. In Ø. S. LaBianca and A. von den Driesch, eds., *Faunal Remains. Hesban 13,* 3–14. Berrien Springs. **Lang, B.** (1985) Introduction: Anthropology as a New Model for Biblical Studies. In B. Lang, ed., *Anthropological Approaches to the Old Testament,* 1–20. Issues in Religion and Theology 8. Philadelphia/London. **Leinwand, N.** (1992) Regional Characteristics in the Styles and Iconography of the Seal Impressions of Level II at Kültepe. *Journal of Near Eastern Studies* 21: 141–72. **Lemche, N.P.** (1996) *Die Vorgeschichte Israels. Von den Anfängen bis zum Ausgang des 13. Jahrhunderts v. Chr.* Biblische Enzyklopädie 1. Stuttgart/Berlin/Köln. **Littauer, M.A. and Crouwel, J. H.** (1979) *Wheeled Vehicles and Ridden Animals in the Ancient Near East.* Handbuch der Orientalistik 7/1. Leiden/Köln. **London, G.** (1989) A Comparison of Two Contemporaneous Lifestyles of the Late Second Millennium B.C. *Bulletin of the American Schools of Oriental Research* 273: 37–55. **Long, V.P.** (1994) *The Art of Biblical History.* Foundations of Contemporary Interpretation 5. Leicester. **Maiberger, P.** (1989) *pered.* In G.J. Botterweck, H. Ringgren and H.-J. Fabry, eds., *Theologisches Wörterbuch zum Alten Testament,* 10 vols., 6: 738–39. Stuttgart/Berlin/Köln. **Maisels, C.K.** (1990) *The Emergence of Civilization. From Hunting and Gathering to Agriculture, Cities, and the State in the Near East.* London/New York. **Malamat, A.** (1982) A Political Look at the Kingdom of David and Solomon and Its Relations with Egypt. In T. Ishida, ed., *Studies in the Period of David and Solomon and other essays. Papers Read at the International Symposium for Biblical Studies, Tokyo, 5–7 December, 1979,* 189–204. Winona Lake. (1995) A Note on the Ritual of Treaty-Making in Mari and the Bible. *Israel Exploration Journal* 45: 226–29. **Malul, M.** (1990) *The Comparative Method in Ancient Near Eastern and Biblical Legal Studies.* AOAT 227. Neukirchen-Vluyn. **Marcus, M.I.** (1995) Art and Ideology in Ancient Western Asia. *CANE* 4: 2487–505. **Mayoral, J.A.** (1995) El uso de los animales en los profetas. *Estudios Bíblicos* 53: 317–63. **Mazar, A.** (1992) *Archaeology of the Land of the Bible. 10000–586 B.C.E.* New York. (1997) Iron Age Chronology: A Reply to I. Finkelstein. *Levant* 29: 157–67. **Meadow, R.H.** (1992) Inconclusive Remarks on Pastoralism, Nomadism, and Other Animal-Related Matters. In: O. Bar-Yosef and A. Khazanov, eds., *Pastoralism in the Levant. Archaeological Materials in Anthropological Perspectives,* 261–69. Monographs in World Archaeology 10. Madison. **Meadow, R.H. and Zeder, M.A.** (1978) Preface. In R.H. Meadow and M.A. Zeder, eds., *Approaches to Faunal Analysis in the Middle East,* xiii–xv. Peabody Museum Bulletin 2. Cambridge. **Meyers, C.L.** (1983) Procreation, Production, and Protection: Male-Female Balance in Early Israel. *Journal of the American Academy of Religion* 51: 569–93. **Moore, M.S. and Brown, M.L.** (1997) *pered. NIDOTTE* 3: 675–76. **Na'aman, N.** (1996) The Contribution of the Amarna Letters to the Debate on Jerusalem's Political Position in the Tenth Century B.C.E. *Bulletin of the American Schools of Oriental Research* 304: 17–27. (1997) Cow Town or Royal Capital? Evidence for Iron Age Jerusalem. *Biblical Archaeology Review* 23: 43–47, 67. **Nemet-Nejat, K.R.** (1998) *Daily Life in Ancient Mesopotamia.* The Greenwood Press "Daily Life Through History" Series. Westport/London. **Neumann, J.** (1997) *Der historische David. Legende und Wirklichkeit in der Geschichte Israels und Judas von der Frühzeit bis zur Dynastie Omri.* Radebeul. **Nibbi, A.** (1979) Some Remarks on Ass and Horse in Ancient Egypt and the Absence of the Mule. *Zeitschrift für Ägyptische Sprache und Altertumskunde* 106: 148–68. **O'Connor, D.** (1997) Ancient Egypt: Egyptological and Anthropological Perspectives. In J. Lustig, ed., *Anthropology and Egyptology. A Developing Dialogue,* 13–24. Monographs in Mediterranean Archaeology 8. Sheffield. **Osborn, D.J. and Osbornová, J.** (1998) *The Mammals of Ancient Egypt.* The Natural History of Egypt 4. Warminster. **Perkins, D., Jr., Daly, P. and Hesse, B.C.** (1972) Animal Domestication and Species Identification: Inferences from Ancient Art. *Journal of the Ancient Near Eastern Society of Columbia University* 4: 20–32. **Pilch, J.J. and Malina, B.J.**, eds. (1993) *Biblical Social Values and their Meaning. A Handbook.* Peabody. **Pitard, W.T.** (1988) The Identity of Bir-Hadad of the Melqart Stela. *Bulletin of the American Schools of Oriental Research* 272: 3–21. **Postgate, J.N.** (1986) The Equids of Sumer, Again. In R. H. Meadow and H.-P. Uerpmann, eds., *Equids in the Ancient World,* 194–206. Beihefte zum Tübinger Atlas des Vorderen Orients, Reihe A, Naturwissenschaften 19/1. Wiesbaden. **Pritchard, J.B.**, ed. (1969) *Ancient Near Eastern Texts relating to the Old Testament.* 3rd edition with supplement. Princeton. **Rackham, J.** (1994) *Animal Bones.* Interpreting the Past. Berkeley/London. **Ryken, L.** (1990) The Bible as Literature – Part 1: "Words of Delight." The Bible as Literature. *Bibliotheca Sacra* 147: 3–15. **Sasson, J.M.** (1995) Official Correspondence from the Mari Archives. *CANE* 2: 1204. **Sauer, J.A.** (1995) Artistic and Faunal Evidence for the Influence of the Domestication of Donkeys and Camels on the Archaeological History of Jordan and Arabia. In K. 'Amr et al., eds., *Studies in the History and Archaeology of Jordan. V: Art and Technology throughout the Ages,* 39–48. Amman. **Schwabe, C.W.** (1994) Animals in the Ancient World. In A. Manning and A. Serpell, eds., *Animals and Human Society. Changing Perspectives,* 36–58. London. **Shanks, H.** (1998) Where is the Tenth Century? *Biblical Archaeology Review* 24: 56–60. **Sjöberg, Å.W.** (1996) The Ebla List of Animals MEE 4, no. 116. *Welt des Orients* 27: 9–24. **Small, D.B.** (1995a) Introduction. In D.B. Small, ed., *Methods in the Mediterranean. Historical and Archaeological Views on Texts* and *Archaeology,* 1–22. Mnemosyne: Biblioteca Classica Batava Supplementum 135. Leiden/New York/Köln. (1995b) Monuments, Laws, and Analysis: Combining Archaeology and Text in Ancient Athens. Pp. 143–76 In D.B. Small, ed., *Methods in the Mediterranean. Historical and Archaeological Views on Texts and Archaeology,* 143–76. Mnemosyne: Biblioteca Classica Batava Supplementum 135. Leiden/New York/Köln. **Snell, D.C.** (1997) *Life in the Ancient Near East. 3100–332 B.C.E.* New Haven/London. **Sprinkle, J.M.** (1989) Literary Approaches to the Old Testament: A Survey of recent Scholarship. *Journal of the Evangelical Theological Society* 32: 299–310. **Staubli, T.** (1991) *Das Image der Nomaden im Alten Israel und in der Ikonographie seiner sesshaften Nachbarn.* OBO 107. Fribourg/Göttingen. **Stern, E.** (1982) *Material Culture of the Land of the Bible in the Persian Period.* Transl. from Hebrew by E. Cindorf. Warminster. (1987) The Bible and Israeli Archaeology. In L. Perdue, L.E. Toombs and G.L. Johnson, eds., *Archaeology and Biblical Interpretation. Essays in Memory of D. Glenn Rose,* 31–40. Atlanta. **Stone, E.C.** (1999) The Constraints on State and Urban Form in Ancient Mesopotamia. In M. Hudson and B. A. Levine, eds., *Urbanization and Land Ownership in the Ancient Near East,* 203–27. Peabody Museum Bulletin 7. Cambridge. **Störk, L.** (1978) Maultier. In W. Helck, E. Otto and W. Westendorf, eds., *Lexikon der Ägyptologie.* 6 vols., 3: 1248–49. Wiesbaden. **Strange, J.** (1985) The idea of afterlife in Ancient Israel: Some Remarks on the Iconography of Solomon's Temple. *Palestine Exploration Quarterly* 117: 35–40. **Talmon, S.** (1978) The Comparative Method in Biblical Interpretation – Principles and Problems. In *Congress Volume: Göttingen 1977,* 320–56. VTS 29. Leiden. **Uerpmann, H.-P. and Uerpmann, M.** (1994) Maultiere in der römischen Armee zur Zeit der Eroberungsfeldzüge in Germanien. In: M. Kokabi and J. Wahl, eds., *Beiträge zur Archäozoologie und Prähistorischen Anthropologie. 8. Arbeitstreffen der Osteologen Konstanz 1993 im Andenken an Joachim Boessneck.* Forschungen und Berichte zur Vor- und Frühgeschichte in Baden Württemberg. Stuttgart. **Uehlinger, C.** (1996) Die Sammlung ägyptischer Siegelamulette. In O. Keel and C. Uehlinger, eds., *Altorientalische Miniaturkunst,* 58–86. 2nd edition. Fribourg/Göttingen. **von Soden, W.** (1965–81) *Akkadisches Handwörterbuch.* 3 vols. Wiesbaden. **Wapnish, P.** (1993) Archaeozoology: The Integration of Faunal Data with Biblical Archaeology. In A. Biran, and J. Aviram, eds., *Biblical Archaeology Today, 1990. Proceedings of the Second International Congress on Biblical Archaeology, Jerusalem, June–July 1990,* 426–42. Jerusalem. (1996) Is *ṣēnī ana lā māni* an Accurate Description or a Royal Boast? In J.D. Seger, ed., *Retrieving the Past. Essays on Archaeological Research and Methodology in Honor of Gus W. van Beek,* 285–96. Winona Lake. (1997) Camels. *OEANE* 1: 407–8. **Wapnish, P. and Hesse, B.** (1997) Equids. *OEANE* 2: 255–56. **Wenke, R.J.** (1997) Anthropology, Egyptology and the Concept of Cultural Change. In J. Lustig, ed., *Anthropology and Egyptology. A Developing Dialogue,* 117–36. Monographs in Mediterranean Archaeology 8. Sheffield. **Westermann, C.** (1993) Mensch, Tier und Pflanze in der Bibel. Pp. 90–106 In B. Janowski et al., eds., *Gefährten und Feinde des Menschen. Das Tier in der Lebenswelt des alten Israels,* 90–106. Originally published in 1984. Neukirchen-Vlyun. **Wright, D.P.** (1987) *The Disposal of Impurity. Elimination Rites in the Bible and in Hittite and Mesopotamian Literature.* SBLDS 101. Atlanta. **Yamauchi, E.M.** (1994) The Current State of Old Testament Historiography. In: A.R. Millard, J.K. Hoffmeier and D.W. Baker, eds., *Faith, Tradition, and History. Old Testament Historiography in its Near Eastern Context,* 1–36. Winona Lake. **Zarins, J.** (1978) The Domesticated Equids of Third Millennium B.C. Mesopotamia. *Journal of Cuneiform Studies* 30: 3–17. (1986) Equids Associated with Human Burials in Third Millennium B.C. Mesopotamia: Two Complementary Facets. In R.H. Meadow and H.-P. Uerpmann, eds., *Equids in the Ancient World,* 164–93. Beihefte zum Tübinger Atlas des Vorderen Orients, Reihe A, Naturwissenschaften 19/1. Wiesbaden. (1989) Pastoralism in Southwest Asia: The Second Millennium BC. In J. Clutton-Brock, ed., *The Walking Larder,* 127–55. London. **Zeder, M.A.** (1997) Sheep and Goats. *OEANE* 5: 23–25.

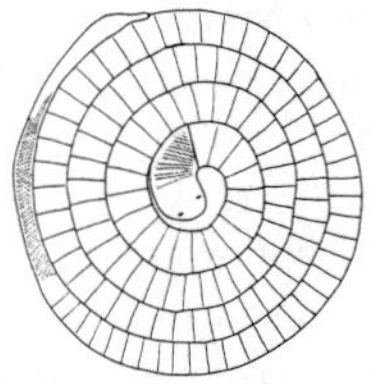

ANCIENT AND MEDIEVAL SOURCES AND MECHANISM OF THE CALENDRICAL PRACTICE OF *YOM TOV SHENI SHEL GALUYYOT*

Leo Depuydt
Brown University

> In the Diaspora an extra day...is added to each of the biblical festival days, except for *ḥol ha-moᶜed* and the Day of Atonement. The practice originated because of the uncertainty in the Diaspora of the day on which the Sanhedrin announced the New Moon. Later, when astronomical calculations were relied upon, the sages declared that the custom should nevertheless be accepted as permanent.[1]

This calendrical practice is not just about doubling feast days. It affects the goings-about of daily life. This specialized topic has, therefore, some claim to a place in this volume. Quite in general, calendars have always played key roles in the daily lives of people in all periods of history.

In the course of a larger investigation provisionally entitled *Time and the Moon in Egypt and the Ancient World*, the property of the Hebrew liturgical calendar called Yom Tov Sheni Shel Galuyyot "Second Feast Day of the Diaspora (Dispersion)" emerged as an important and unique facet of lunar time-reckoning in the ancient Near East. The comparative study of the calendrical customs of different nations is fertile. But to allow inclusion of Yom Tov Sheni Shel Galuyyot into the comparison, presenting an accessible survey of this calendrical practice seemed a necessary prerequisite and a worthwhile challenge. In fact, what follows may well be the first in-depth analysis of the anatomy and basic structure of this calendrical phenomenon.

Yom Tov Sheni Shel Galuyyot involves a distinction between the Galuyyot or Diaspora (Jewish residence outside the Holy Land) and Israel. The phenomenon will henceforth be referred to in abbreviated form as YTSheni. A feast is celebrated just one day in Israel but two successive days

---

ABBREVIATIONS: B.T. = Babylonian Talmud; YTSheni = Yom Tov Sheni ("Second Feast Day") Shel Galuyyot ("of the Diaspora").

1 *Encyclopaedia Judaica*, vol. 6 (Jerusalem, 1972) 1244.

in the Diaspora. The second feast day of the Diaspora *follows* the single day celebrated in Israel. But as will be seen below, before the institution of the Hebrew fixed lunar calendar in the late first millennium C.E., the second feast day of the Diaspora could presumably either *follow* or *precede* the sole feast day celebrated in Israel, even if the sources do not positively confirm this. The later Hebrew lunar calendar is fixed because its lunar months are synchronized with the lunar phases through calculation and not through observation of the moon.

Rosh Hashanah is a case apart. It too is celebrated for two days. But the feast is doubled both in the Diaspora and in Israel. Obviously, the doubling of Rosh Hashanah could not be an instance of Yom Tov Sheni *Shel Galuyyot*. The second feast day of Rosh Hashanah might be called a Yom Tov Sheni "second feast day," without the extension Shel Galuyyot "of the Diaspora." But there is no tradition of calling it that. The doubling of Rosh Hashanah is intriguingly similar to YTSheni. It therefore deserves to be included in an analysis of YTSheni as an associated phenomenon. It is sometimes even assumed that the second feast day of Rosh Hashanah has the same origin as YTSheni. True, both phenomena exhibit a connection with the moon. But their anatomies differ. The special case of Rosh Hashanah is analyzed in section 3 below.

A small number of ancient historians have always gravitated toward technical subjects such as calendars and chronology. A more serious commitment to these subjects involves some measure of acquaintance with all the calendrical systems of the ancient world. This includes the Hebrew calendar. One is reminded of the relevant chapters in milestones of chronology such as J.J. Scaliger's *De emendatione temporum* of 1583, D. Petavius' *De doctrina temporum* of 1627, and the two great handbooks by Ideler and Ginzel, published in 1825–26 and 1906–14. The following investigation is inspired by this long-standing tradition.[2]

---

2 When I read an abbreviated version of this paper at the joint SBL/AOS/ASOR meeting held at the Hebrew Union College, Jewish Institute of Religion in Cincinnati on 14–16 February 1999, the choice of venue was not unintentional. It was there, in 1981–82, that, as a student of Egyptology devoting a year of study to Semitic languages, I first became acquainted with the tradition of celebrating a Jewish holy day twice on two successive days, as opposed to just once in Israel. Two weeks into the academic year, the College went into recess for the High Holidays. I have fond memories of this festive occasion in its sunny and bright Indian summer setting. It appeared that the doubling of feast days somehow related to the moon. The little I knew then about this celestial body, sung by many great poets, in its capacity as a tool of time-reckoning did not afford insight into this calendrical practice. A feeling of dissatisfaction lingered with me ever since. In recent years, I developed a re-

Introductory Remark on Sources and the Historical Method

This is an analysis of a calendrical practice. But it is as much an analysis of the sources describing this practice. By far the two most important sources on the calendrical structure of YTSheni are the tractate *Rosh Hashanah* of the Babylonian Talmud and Maimonides (1135–1204 C.E.) (see 1.3 below). From perusing the standard works on Hebrew chronology, I am not aware of any other significant sources. Scouring a wide range of sources dating to Late Antiquity and the Middle Ages in search of information on YTSheni remains desirable. Perhaps someone with the requisite expertise in rabbinic literature, which I lack, will feel called upon to take this matter further, even if only to confirm that nothing of relevance is to be found.

Three properties of the sources complicate the study of this topic as they do of any topic of ancient history. First, the problems pertaining to the sources go far beyond the topic's narrow focus. This involves limitations as to what can be done here. In general, the study of calendars and chronology is characterized by a sharp contrast between the narrow focus of the subject and the wide range of possibly relevant sources. For example, one source for YTSheni is the Talmud. Like other great religious texts, such as the Bible and the Qur'an, the Talmud has had a long history. This history is indirectly relevant to the present investigation. Yet, it will be readily understood that shouldering the weight of this complex history is an effort that exceeds the present investigation.

Second, the sources are mostly not facts but facts reported and transmitted by human beings. Science is about observable and reproducible facts. History is not a science in this narrow sense. To keep asking what role the human factor plays in the surviving sources is crucial to the historical method. Consider the other principal source for YTSheni, Maimonides. Maimonides was an inveterate rationalist, defender of שלטון השׂכל "the rule of reason." This is a good state of mind to be in when writing about calendars. What is more, Maimonides was as versed in Ptolemaic astron-

---

search interest in calendars and chronology. I was pleased, therefore, to return to this eminent institution and to the oldest Jewish seminary in the Americas to finally tie up this loose end to a fine education.

In preparing the final version of the following text, I gratefully benefitted from comments and corrections received from the editorial board of the *Hebrew Union College Annual*, communicated to me by E.P. Goldman, the Editor, in a letter of 8 June 1999. I am also grateful to David Weisberg for pushing me to present certain points more clearly, including the doubling of Rosh Hashanah. I thank Keter Publishing for granting permission to reproduce the calendar of holy days in Figure 1 from *Encyclopaedia Judaica*.

omy as any. This is a rare asset. It adds much to his reliability in technical matters such as the calendar. On the other hand, Maimonides knew YTSheni, not as an active calendrical mechanism, but as a set of vestiges of this mechanism in the Hebrew fixed calendar. Indeed, a distinction is made below (1.1) between the earlier and the later YTSheni. Maimonides was not an eyewitness to the earlier YTSheni, this paper's primary focus. He was, therefore, just as dependent on reports as we are. To ask what it means that a source is not contemporary with an event is also part of the historical method.

A third property of the sources, especially of ancient sources, is their paucity. The present topic is no exception. The earlier YTSheni is not portrayed as fully as is desired in the available sources. This will affect the organization of the following account. When the sources are a sorry few, the temptation arises to make them say more than they do. A historian of the ancient period may often find it necessary to affirm explicitly what *cannot* be inferred from the sources. No field has otherwise over the centuries been more the victim of unfounded speculation than ancient chronology.

1. *Preliminary Definition and Delimitation of Yom Tov Sheni*

YTSheni is the calendrical practice of doubling certain holy days by celebrating them on two successive days. Before proceeding with an analysis in section 2, it will be useful to begin by adding focus to the topic. Where in the universe of past events is YTSheni located? Three modes of sharpening focus are distinguishing between two types (1.1), dating the two types (1.2), and identifying the two principal sources (1.3).

1.1. *Earlier Yom Tov Sheni and Later Yom Tov Sheni*

If distinctions are the stuff of which knowledge is made, there is not one YTSheni but two, an earlier and a later one. The earlier YTSheni dates to the time when the beginnings of Hebrew lunar months were still determined by observation of the moon. As a descendant, or a reflection, or a vestige of the earlier YTSheni, the later one is part of the fixed Hebrew calendar. This calendar is called fixed because it relies no longer on observation but on computation to establish the beginnings of lunar months. The natural primary focus of a paper dealing with ancient Near Eastern calendrical practices involving the moon is the earlier YTSheni. But this analysis also should include the later YTSheni. The two stages elucidate one another. But there is a hierarchy. The earlier YTSheni can ultimately be understood fully without making reference to the later one. But the later YTSheni cannot be understood without the earlier one.

What follows illustrates the difference between the two. In the earlier YTSheni, the sole day celebrated in Palestine could presumably be either the *first* or the *second* of the two days observed elsewhere. In the later YTSheni, the sole day celebrated in Israel is always the *first* of the two days observed elsewhere. Therefore, in the later YTSheni, Sheni means "second" not only in the sense of "additional" but also in the sense of "posterior" in time.

The earlier and later YTSheni serve different causes: the earlier one, practical exigency; the later one, tradition. The later one consists of vestiges of the earlier one. The vestiges have been preserved in deference to tradition. Maimonides states about the later YTSheni,

> The Sages, however, have seen fit to decree that the Jewish communities adhere to what had been the custom of their ancestors. (Maimonides, *Laws for the Sanctification of the New Moon*, 5:5)[3]

Everyone has always agreed that the function for which YTSheni was created became obsolete with the introduction of the fixed Hebrew calendar. Observing the moon plays a crucial role in the original YTSheni. But the later fixed Hebrew calendar does not rely on observation. Thus, YTSheni turned from an active calendrical practice into vestiges of that practice. These vestiges do not interact as parts of an active system. No amount of historical analysis will change this fact. For almost a millennium now, there has been an ongoing debate about the role of YTSheni as a tradition. The religious significance of YTSheni as a tradition falls outside the narrow scope of this paper. This investigation is part of a larger survey and analysis of ancient calendrical practices of the lunar kind. Many issues pertaining to YTSheni as a tradition are discussed in detail in a set of contributions to *Conservative Judaism* 24 (1970) 21–59, namely, "Introductory Comments" by B.Z. Kreitman (pp. 21–22), "A Responsum on Yom Tov Sheni Shel Galuyot" by Ph. Sigal and A.J. Ehrlich (pp. 22–33), "Response to a Responsum" by W. Schuchat (pp. 33–45), "The Challenge of Yom Tov Sheni" by A.H. Blumenthal (pp. 45–47), and "Second Thoughts about the Second Day" by J.J. Petuchowski (pp. 48–59).

Some calendrical features of the later and modern YTSheni are better known than others. Probably the best-known feature is the celebration of five holy days in the Diaspora in addition to those celebrated in Israel. They are, in the order in which they occur in the calendar:

---

3 For the Hebrew original, see the edition by Mahler (1889) 29. The English translation is taken from Gandz, Obermann, and Neugebauer (1956) 23.

(1) Day 2 of Tabernacles or Sukkot on 16 Tishri (that is, Month 1 of the liturgical year);
(2) Day 2 of Shemini Atzeret (Simḥat Torah) on 23 Tishri (Month 1);
(3) + (4) Days 2 and 8 of Passover or Pesach on 16 and 22 Nisan (Month 7 of the liturgical year, or Month 8 in an intercalated year with a Second Adar as Month 7);
(5) Day 2 of Pentecost or Shavuot on 7 Sivan (Month 9, or Month 10 in an intercalated year).

These feasts can be located in the calendar in Figure 1, reproduced here for the reader's convenience. As one can see, the doubling applies to the three great pilgrimage festivals, Sukkot, Pesach, and Shavuot.

Other vestiges are less known to the general public but equally fascinating to the student of ancient calendars. One such vestige concerns the term ראש ח(ו)דש "beginning of the month." Lunar months have 29 or 30 days. Day 1 is always named Rosh Ḥodesh. But in addition, Day 30 in 30-day months is also named so. Thus, what is undeniably the last day of the month is named as if it were the first of the following month. This remarkable circumstance results from the survival of features of a calendar in which Day 1 of the month is not known beforehand into a calendar in which it is.[4]

1.2. *Dating the Earlier and the Later YTSheni*

The end of the earlier YTSheni coincides with the beginning of the later YTSheni. The beginning of the later YTSheni and the transition between the two also coincide with the introduction of the fixed calendar. It follows

---

4 A somewhat similar phenomenon occurs in ancient Egypt's calendar of daily life, the Egyptian civil calendar, a non-lunar calendar consisting of 12 months of 30 days plus five added days, for a fixed total of 365. Its twelfth or *last* month could be called *wp rnpt* "opener of the year" or *mswt* r^{c} (Mesore) "birth of Re." Both these terms otherwise denote New Year's Day, the quintessential calendrical *beginning*. I have proposed a comprehensive explanation for this peculiar circumstance in Depuydt (1997), with additional clarification of the theory's structure in Depuydt (1999).

The Egyptian and Hebrew phenomena have in common that a name denoting a beginning refers to an end. The similarity is tantalizing but superficial. The Egyptian phenomenon pertains to the names of *months* and the beginnings of *years;* the Hebrew phenomenon, to the names of *days* and the beginnings of *months*. The ultimate cause of the Egyptian phenomenon is a transfer of names from lunar months to civil months. (Lunar time-reckoning was used for religious purposes in Egypt.) The ultimate cause of the Hebrew phenomenon is the transformation of an observational lunar calendar into a fixed one.

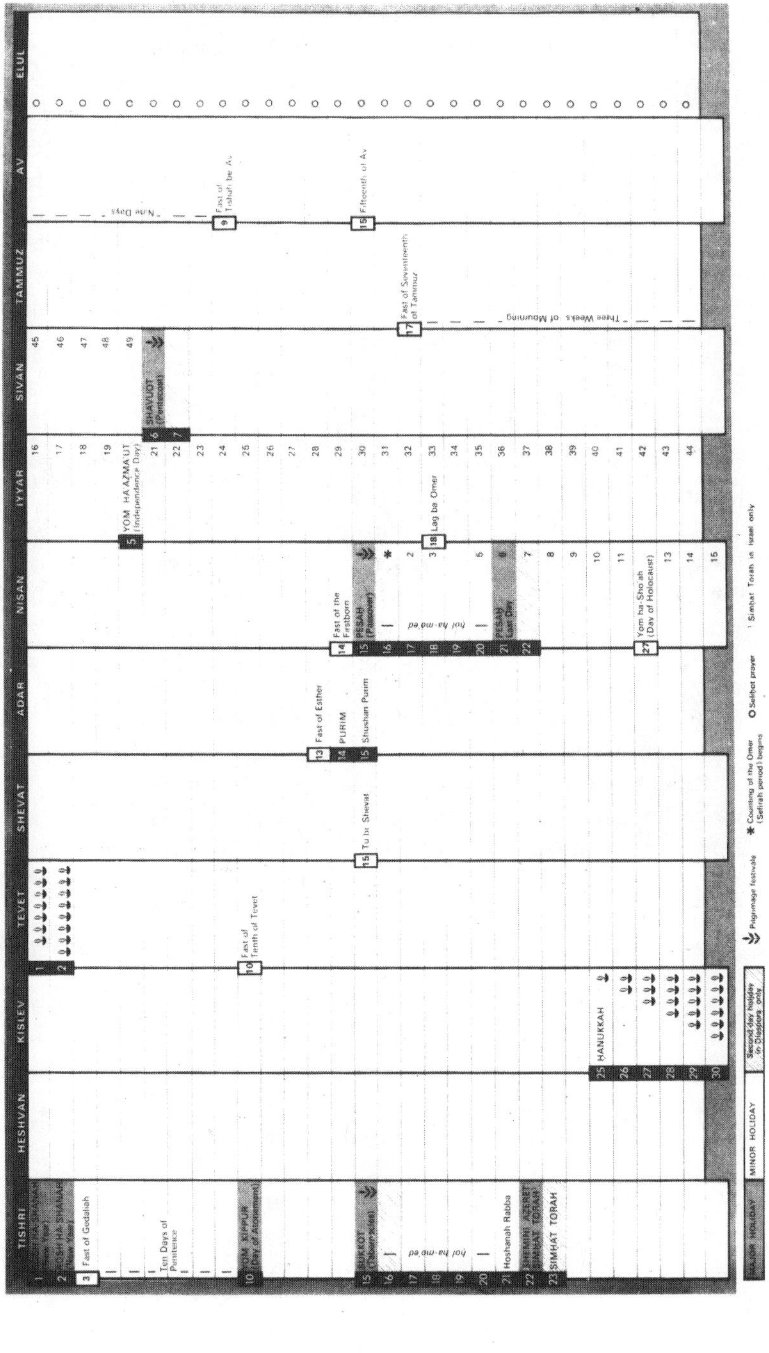

Figure 1: The Liturgical Year
(reprinted from *Encyclopaedia Judaica*, vol. 6, 1239, with permission)

logically that two events require dating: the beginning of the earlier YTSheni and the beginning of the later YTSheni and the fixed calendar. However, the sources do not allow precise dating. Furthermore, the two forms of YTSheni cannot have appeared instantly and everywhere simultaneously in their full-sized proportions. Yet, one likes to believe that there must have been this one single time in history when the very first instance of celebrating a certain holy day two days in a row occurred somewhere as a result of reckoning time by the moon. The decision to repeat a holy day is discrete enough that assuming a first-time-ever seems reasonable. Moreover, such a first time may be assumed for both the earlier and the later YTSheni. However, the sources do not allow us to establish when those days occurred, even if assuming their existence is necessary.

First is the beginning of the earlier YTSheni. The phenomenon of YTSheni is intimately associated with that of the Diaspora. Dating the beginning and the dissemination of the earlier YTSheni therefore overlaps considerably with dating the beginning and the rise of the Diaspora. Tracing the Diaspora's history from its beginning exceeds the scope of this paper. The circumstances, fortunate and less fortunate, in which Jewish communities were established in Babylonia and in Egypt, and later throughout the Roman Empire and beyond, are well known in outline, even if much information is forever lost. Let it suffice to state that it is reasonable to assume that the practice of YTSheni must have expanded considerably in the Second Temple period (*ca.* sixth to first centuries B.C.E.). The Talmud is the chief historical source for this period. But again, the complex problem of the Talmudic strata, which may span a period of as much as a millennium, cannot be addressed here. What the Talmud says about time-reckoning was compiled conveniently by Zuckermann more than a century ago.[5] This sparse information does not allow a precise statement about every aspect of how YTSheni was observed in the time period covered by the Talmud.

That much for the beginning of the earlier YTSheni. Its end coincides with the beginning of the later YTSheni. The transition from one to the other cannot have happened all at once in every place. A period of transition has to be assumed. The later YTSheni is part of the fixed lunar calendar. Dating the beginning of the later YTSheni, therefore, means more or less the same as dating the beginning of the fixed calendar.

In the fixed lunar calendar, the beginnings of the months are not determined by observation of the moon. Yet, this calendar follows the moon just as much. Only, the beginnings of the months are fixed beforehand by

---

5 Zuckermann (1882).

computation. Consistent harmony with the moon is achieved because a very accurate value of the average lunar month is used. This value will be adequate for thousands and thousands of years. It amounts to 29 days, 12 hours, and 793 *ḥ^alāqīm* (חלקים), that is, 29 days, 12 hours, 44 minutes, and 3⅓ seconds. There are 1080 *ḥ^alāqīm* in an hour. Each *ḥeleq* lasts 3⅓ seconds. 793 *ḥ^alāqīm* amount to 44 minutes and 3⅓ seconds.

I have elsewhere described the origins of this value for the mean lunar month in detail.[6] It is a tale that spans almost two thousand years. What matters here is that this tale involves the date of the institution of the fixed lunar calendar. This date coincides with the institution of the later YTSheni, which is a component of the fixed calendar. The traditional date for the institution of this calendar is the fourth century C.E., the time of Hillel II, patriarch of Palestine. This date most commonly appears in general works. But it is obvious that most everyone who, in light of all the sources, has studied the matter in more detail dates the full enactment of the fixed lunar calendar several centuries later, to the late first millennium C.E., perhaps as late as the tenth century, though not after that. For example, Albiruni (973 to after 1050 C.E.) describes the Hebrew fixed calendar in detail in his epochal *Al-ʾāṯāru l-bāqiya ʿani l-qurūni l-ḵāliya* "Monuments Remaining from Past Centuries," a work compiled about 1000 C.E.[7] There is wide consensus now that the fixed lunar calendar came about in the wake of the rise of Arabic astronomy, promoted by Muslims and others, from the late eighth century C.E. onward. In the twentieth century, authorities such as U. Cassuto and J. Obermann have defended this thesis.

The earlier YTSheni was discontinued as the fixed calendar was gradually introduced, one assumes late in the first millennium C.E. The later YTSheni is a set of vestiges of the earlier YTSheni. These vestiges cannot be studied as parts of an active mechanism. They do not interact as parts of an organic whole. They are monuments to tradition. They can ultimately be understood only in light of the earlier YTSheni.

1.3. *The Two Principal Sources*

As for the *later* YTSheni, its structure does not need to be retrieved from the sources. It is part of the modern fixed calendar. Few master all the details of this calendar, but the details are available when needed. The oldest detailed account is Albiruni's in Arabic, mentioned above and dat-

---

6 Depuydt (2002a).

7 For the Arabic original, see Sachau (1878) ١٤٤–٢٠٤. For an English translation, see Sachau (1879) 141–85.

ing to about 1000 C.E. The oldest description of the fixed calendar in Hebrew is Abraham bar Ḥiyya ha-Nasi's ספר העבור "Book of Intercalation," composed *ca.* 1122–23 C.E.[8] Abraham "Judaeus" resided most of his life in Barcelona. He is also called Savasorda, a Spanish-Latin form of Arabic *ṣāḥib aš-šurṭa* "lord of the royal suite (or the like)."

As for the *earlier* YTSheni, no complete account exists in modern surveys or ancient sources. Nor is there an account of how exactly the later YTSheni was derived from it. There are two principal sources for the earlier YTSheni. They are reproduced for the sake of convenience in Appendix I and Appendix II.

The first source consists of a couple of passages in B.T. *Rosh Hashanah,* namely 20b–21a (Gemara) and 30b (Mishnah).[9]

The other source comprises two sections, namely 3:11–13 and 5:4–12, in Maimonides' הלכות קדוש החדש *Hilkhot Qidduš ha-Ḥodeš* "Laws for the Sanctification of the New Moon." This calendrical treatise is part of Maimonides' Code, the *Mishneh Torah.*

Neither source provides a systematic account of YTSheni. Both are rich in details concerning all the various problems that are related to the observation of the practice. As historical sources, both have a drawback. The Talmud is contemporary to the earlier YTSheni. But its design is not to be a work of history narrowly speaking. Maimonides' treatise, on the other hand, is not a religious work but an analytical study of the calendar. But it was written when the earlier YTSheni was no longer practiced. Maimonides relies in great part on the aforementioned passages of the Talmud.

2. *Calendrical Structure of the Earlier YTSheni*

No complete picture of the calendrical practice of YTSheni emerges from the sources. The following mode of description is therefore proposed. The point of departure is a fundamental assumption: the practice of YTSheni must have worked. It is then necessary to show *how* it must have worked, without making any reference to any of the sources. The result is a theoretical model of a calendrical system that should have worked flawlessly. Only then do we turn to the sources to seek either lack of contradiction or positive confirmation.

---

8 For the Hebrew original, see Filipowski (1851).

9 The Mishnah is the Talmud's smaller and older portion, written in Hebrew, compiled about 200 C.E. The Talmud's Gemara is a commentary on the Mishnah written in Aramaic.

This procedure may seem like putting the cart before the horse. But it appears necessary because of the nature of the evidence. The procedure also serves clarity. The model YTSheni is theoretical. But it consists of structural features—people, places, things, and events—whose existence can be considered certain. To the extent that the existence of these features is problematic, the theory is also weakened. Each of the following sections is devoted to an essential ingredient of the calendrical practice of YTSheni.

2.1. *First Feature: The Moon and the Lunar Cycle as a Unit of Time*

First is the moon. The lunar cycle, from new moon to full moon and back, readily impresses itself on the senses. It is not surprising that the cycle was used as a principal time unit of daily life just about everywhere in the ancient world except in ancient Egypt, where lunar time-reckoning was restricted to the religious domain.

2.2. *Second Feature: Determining the Beginnings of Lunar Months*

In most lunar calendars, the lunar months begin around new moon, that is, the moment in time when the moon is right between the sun and the earth and therefore invisible from the earth. Before the institution of the fixed Hebrew lunar calendar in the late first millennium C.E., observing the moon in the night sky played a crucial role in determining the beginnings of lunar months. The fixed calendar rendered observation of the moon superfluous. It is certain that observing the moon played some role before the fixed lunar calendar. But it is by no means certain what that role was.

It is commonly assumed that sighting the first crescent was the determining factor for beginning a new lunar month. The first crescent can be seen one evening shortly after sunset in the western horizon one to two days after new moon. The thin sliver of the first crescent then soon sets after the sun. Kepler regarded the computation of the crescent as impossible.[10] First crescent sighting is not an astronomical event, but an astronomical event *observed by people* located on the earth's surface. Astronomers can calculate with high probability by which evening the first crescent should have been visible.[11] But this does not mean, historically speaking, that the crescent was indeed seen at that time.

---

10 My source is Schoch in Langdon, Fotheringham, and Schoch (1928) 98.

11 Some recent studies on the scientific aspects of computing first crescent visibility, ordered by author or first co-author and date, are as follows: Bruin (1977); Caldwell and Young (1997); Doggett and Schaefer (1994); Ilyas (1988), (1994a), and (1994b); Pepin (1996); Schaefer (1988), (1991), and (1996); and Schaefer, Ahmad, and Doggett (1993).

By the assumption of first crescent visibility, observers were peering out soon after sunset in the evenings following new moon to sight the first crescent. Presumably, as soon as the first crescent was spotted, it was decided to designate the daylight period beginning the next morning as daylight of Day 1 of the lunar month. Such is the neat and tidy method that is inferred, though hardly ever explicitly stated, in handbooks on chronology. It appears, however, that the requirement of first crescent visibility is one of the most overrated assumptions, not only of Hebrew chronology, but also of ancient chronology in general. It may take some effort to wean ancient history from this universal assumption.

The fact is that the sources do not support the existence of first crescent sighting. There are two exceptions. The first is the Muslim religious calendar. The second seeming exception (more on this elsewhere) is practice followed in Babylonian astronomical texts dating from the eighth century B.C.E. to the first century C.E. and documenting what may well be the longest-lasting unified research project in history. But in both these cases, first crescent visibility was or is strictly supervised by a highly centralized authority, either a council of clerics or an academy of scholars. In neither case can one speak of a calendar that has naturally and intuitively arisen from popular usage.

Outside of these two exceptions that have done much to keep the universal assumption of first crescent sighting in antiquity alive, there are many unambiguous indications in the sources that point to methods other than first crescent visibility, even if it is not entirely clear what these methods are. I have assembled this evidence elsewhere and discussed it at length.[12] Suffice it to note here that there is no need for a neat and tidy method for lunar calendars to be perfectly functional. All peoples using lunar calendars must sooner or later have realized that lunar months are 29 or 30 days long. The lunar phases impress themselves to such a degree on the senses that it is difficult for lunar Day 1 to stray all that far from conjunction or new moon, that is, the time when the moon is between the sun and the earth and therefore invisible. Suppose that the first crescent is seen a little too early or a little too late, that is, before 29 days have passed or three to four days after conjunction. Those deciding for village, town, or country could easily correct the problem by their specific choices of 29-day or 30-day months. By the most simple of manipulations, lunar Day 1 can easily be prevented from wandering far away from conjunction. An untidy system does not need to be an ineffective system. In an untidy system, watching the

---

12 See Depuydt (2002b).

crescent still fulfills a function. It serves as a check that new moon and lunar Day 1 have not drifted apart more than a day or two.

True, the Talmudic treatise Rosh Hashanah discusses in detail how witnesses testifying about sighting the crescent need to be interrogated in order to ascertain that their sighting is bona fide. Adequate testimony allows sanctifying the new crescent, declaring it to be מקודש "sanctified!" Maimonides wrote a treatise on the matter, namely his הלכות קדוש החדש *Laws for the Sanctification of the New Moon*. However, handbooks on chronology assume that sanctification had a *calendrical* function, namely to identify Day 1 of the month. But the Talmud nowhere says so. In fact, there are clear indications that the sanctification of the new moon was at least in some cases liturgical and not calendrical. A more detailed discussion is found in the aforementioned forthcoming paper.

In sum, the present paper makes no assumptions about how exactly the beginnings of lunar months were determined. We do not know precisely. However, such an assumption is not necessary for treating the problem at hand.

2.3. *Third Feature: The Length of Calendrical Lunar Months Is either 29 or 30 Days*

The length of astronomical lunar months ranges from about 29.27 days to about 29.83 days. The average is about 29.53059 days. Calendrical lunar months were therefore almost always—and from some point onwards always—29 or 30 full days long.

2.4. *Fourth Feature:* בזמנו *bi-z^{e}mānō?*

In Chapter One of his *Laws for the Sanctification of the New Moon*, Maimonides assigns a role to the concept of sighting the first crescent בזמנו in the transition from one lunar month to the other. בזמנו literally means "in its time." "Its" clearly refers to the moon, more specifically to the first crescent. Maimonides explains בזמנו as follows. Because lunar months have 29 or 30 days, one needs to watch for the crescent just one evening, the evening at the end of daylight of Day 29. If the crescent is seen at that time, one takes the next morning as the beginning of daylight of Day 1. If the crescent is not seen, the next morning is considered Day 30. There is no need to watch the next evening at the end of daylight of Day 30 because the day after Day 30 must be Day 1 anyhow, lunar months lasting no longer than 30 days. By this method, the evening at the end of daylight of Day 29 is called זמנו "its time," that is, the same time slot assigned every month to watching the moon. It is the time when you either see it or you do not. No other time is assigned to watching for it. בזמנו is often translated as "in its *proper* time." But strictly speaking, there is nothing proper or improper about the time slot in question. The monthly watch at the end of Day 29, that is, בזמנו, seems wonderfully tidy. But there is no trace of it in the Talmud. It is therefore not clear at which stage in the long evolution of the Hebrew calendar the above mechanism was applied. Maimonides wrote in the twelfth century C.E. The fixed calendar had already become well established. בזמנו plays no role in this fixed calendar. בזמנו is adduced here to illustrate the frustrating problems that students of Hebrew chronology predating the fixed calendar face. There must have been much variation in calendrical practice over time and from place to place. But information about all this variation largely ceased being transmitted in the sources with the institution of the fixed calendar in the late first millennium C.E. This calendar fixes every last detail of the religious calendar beforehand for many thousands of years. It is a calendar-maker's dream. But it has turned into a historian's nightmare by causing the obliteration from the surviving record of most information about the structure and evolution of the earlier Hebrew calendar. This needs to be kept in mind. The present remarks on YTSheni are therefore based on a historical record that is very incomplete.

2.5. *Fifth Feature: Central Place of Declaring the Beginning of the Month*

A crucial structural feature of YTSheni is the central place where the beginning of the month is declared, in this case a court in Jerusalem. The sources provide more details about this central place. The fact of the location's centrality suffices for the present argument. Maimonides conveys this centrality of Jerusalem in the context of a discussion of the Hebrew calendar by citing Isa 2:3:

> For out of Zion shall go forth the Law and the word of the Lord from Jerusalem. (Isa 2:3, cited by Maimonides, *Laws for the Sanctification of the New Moon*, 1:8)[13]

2.6. *Sixth Feature: Distance between Jerusalem where the Beginning of the Month Is Decreed and Any Places where the Jerusalem Calendar Is Followed*

A second crucial feature of YTSheni is the distance between Jerusalem where the beginning of the month is decreed and any places in the Diaspora where the Jerusalem calendar is followed.

The relevance of a second type of distance is not clear. It is the distance between Jerusalem and any places where observers have seen the first crescent in order to testify about its visibility before the religious court in Jerusalem. However, because the role of the first crescent in determining

13 For the Hebrew original, see Mahler (1889) 5. For an English translation, see Gandz, Obermann, and Neugebauer (1956) 5.

the beginnings of months is not clear from the sources (see 2.2), contrary to what the accounts in all the handbooks of chronology suggest, the relevance of this second type of distance is not certain.

2.7. *Seventh Feature: Principle of Celebrating Feasts Everywhere Simultaneously*

What motivates this principle falls outside this paper's scope. But the emotional value and sense of solidarity attached to the knowledge that one is celebrating a feast at the same time as in Jerusalem appear obvious.

2.8. *Eighth Feature: Compulsory Delay in Beginning the Monthly Day Count, with a Margin of Uncertainty of One Day Only*

People living far from Jerusalem could not immediately know when a lunar month had begun in the Holy City. However, well into the month, news must have arrived as to which day had been Day 1. The count of days could then be picked up in synchrony with Jerusalem. But soon, that month too came to a close. It could not be known immediately whether the day following Day 29 had been Day 30 or Day 1 in Jerusalem. Only these two possibilities exist. The margin of uncertainty amounts to a single day only. This is because lunar months are always either 29 or 30 days long.

As a consequence, for a number of days in the early part of the month, the days are not counted. The day count is in limbo, as it were. Maintaining the two possible day counts simultaneously is hardly practical. There is no evidence or any report in the sources that such a double count was ever practiced.

In modern life, the absence of a day count is unthinkable. But a number of factors made this absence acceptable in the case of the Hebrew calendar. First, calendars were not as central in antiquity as they are now. Second, the Hebrew calendar is a religious calendar. Its main purpose is to fix a limited number of feast days. Third, for much of the business of daily life, the Jewish Diaspora observed local civil calendars. A case in point is the large Jewish community in Ptolemaic Alexandria (last three centuries B.C.E.), which no doubt used the Egyptian calendar. Fourth, the week was important for the observation of the Sabbath and other purposes, but counting week days is independent from counting the days of the month.

The details of how communities outside Jerusalem were informed about the beginning of the month fall outside the scope of this paper. The two main sources for the original Hebrew calendar (see 1.3) describe at least two ways in more detail, lighting fires on mountain tops and sending messengers. There is hardly any detail, though, about what is of great interest to the present argument: the speed with which different places were reached according to these methods.

2.9. *Ninth Feature: The Assumption of Synchrony by Month's End*

The system of doubling feast days described in the Talmud and by Maimonides makes the unstated assumption that the month preceding the one in which feasts are doubled has been synchronized with Jerusalem by month's end. The description then pertains to the uncertainty of what happens in the transition from that synchronized lunar month to the next one and beyond. It is assumed that the situation will again be synchronized by the end of that next month. The scenario of uncertainty then repeats itself.

2.10. *Tenth Feature: Aspects of the Uncertainty Resulting from Lack of Knowing When the Month Began in Jerusalem*

There are different ways of looking at the uncertainty of what happens when the month ends. It is this complexity that makes it difficult to describe the custom of doubling feasts with brevity. The complexity has several facets that all have to be made explicit. A clear and analytic understanding of the phenomenon requires looking at the uncertainty from different angles.

The first angle is the identity of the day following Day 29: it could be either Day 30 or Day 1. The second is the location of Day 1: it could be either the first day or the second day following Day 29. The third is the extent of the period in which Day 1 can fall: it is a block of two successive days immediately following Day 29. And the fourth angle is the identity of the two days in the block of two successive days immediately following Day 29: it is either Days 30 and 1 or Days 1 and 2.

It is also possible to look at the days of the lunar month after Day 1 from the same four angles for as long as it remains unknown when the month began in Jerusalem. The margin of uncertainty is always just one day. As said, this is ultimately an outcome of the fact that the margin of variation in the length of the lunar month is just one day: lunar months are either 29 or 30 days long.

2.11. *Eleventh Feature: The Point in Time Marking the End of Certainty and the Beginning of Uncertainty (End of Day 29)*

This point in time plays a crucial role in the structure of YTSheni. It is listed here as a separate feature because of its importance.

2.12. *Twelfth Feature: Counting from the Beginning of Uncertainty (End of Day 29)*

The problem of YTSheni has much to do with counting days in succession. The most conspicuous count is obviously that of the days of the month. The days of the month derive their identity from the ordinal number that relates them to the other days of the month.

But there is another count that is also crucial to YTSheni. It is an implicit one. It is the count of days that begins with the time of the beginning of uncertainty at the end of Day 29. By this count, the day after Day 29 is always the first, the day after that is always the second, and so on. This count from the end of Day 29 is crucial. It explains why the second feast day added in the Diaspora always *follows* the feast day celebrated in Israel and never precedes it in the later YTSheni (see below).

Feast days are associated with a certain day of the month. That day is identified by its ordinal number. The count from the end of Day 29 onward plays no role in dating feasts. A possible exception from Mesopotamia, reported in Babylonian tablet NCBT 58, is discussed below.

2.13. *Thirteenth Feature: Doubling Feast Days to Address the Uncertainty as to When They Were Celebrated in Jerusalem*

The practice of YTSheni implies that, by Day 29 at the latest, months were synchronized with Jerusalem time. The problem that YTSheni is supposed to solve is the uncertainty in communities far from Jerusalem whether the next day was called Day 30 or Day 1 in Jerusalem. As long as this was not known, a feast day could fall on either of two successive days. The remedy was to celebrate the feast on both days. As noted earlier, either the first or the second day could have been the one celebrated in Jerusalem. By contrast, in the later and modern YTSheni, the one celebrated in Jerusalem is always the first. This difference is explained below.

2.14. *Fourteenth Feature: Factors of Diversity and Harmony*

The available sources do not allow us to establish to what extent the earlier YTSheni was celebrated in certain places and at certain times. For example, the Talmud states:

> There are the six new moons to report which messengers go forth (from Jerusalem to the Diaspora):
>
> (The new moon) of Nisan on account of Passover,
> of Av on account of the Fast (of the ninth),
> of Elul on account of the new year,
> of Tishri for the adjustment of the festivals,
> of Kislev on account of Chanukah, and
> of Adar on account of Purim.
>
> (B.T. *Rosh Hashanah* 18a [Mishnah])[14]

---

14 Translation according to Simon (1938) 73.

The feasts and their dates can conveniently be located in Figure 1. There is no way of knowing to which degree the prescribed practice was implemented. If one considers all the variables, mounds of information would be necessary to obtain a clear picture. First of all, each community lives at a different distance from Jerusalem, requiring a different travel-time for messengers to arrive there from Jerusalem. Second, each feast falls a different number of days after the end of Day 29 of the previous month. For example, Yom Kippur falls 10 or 11 days after the point in time that is the beginning of uncertainty, the end of Day 29 of the previous month. As for Sukkot, that number is 15 or 16. Furthermore, it seems obvious that messengers could not have been sent to every single small community.

There are many factors such as those indicated above that tend to create diversity in the observation of YTSheni. On the other hand, the very same motive that created the practice of YTSheni, namely the desire to observe in unison with Jerusalem, also worked to make the practice of YTSheni the same everywhere. Feasts were doubled even if one knew with certainty beforehand when they were going to be celebrated. The following statement from Maimonides' *Laws for the Sanctification of the New Moon* documents this harmonization of YTSheni. There is no reason to doubt the statement's veracity. But again, we do not know exactly, and probably will never know, how widespread the practice expressed in this statement was at different times and in different places.

> There were places which the Nisan messengers could reach in time, while the Tishri messengers could not.[15] By law the people of these places should have observed the Passover feast (Pesach) one day only, since the messengers had reached them in time and they knew which day was declared New Moon Day (Day 1 of the month); whereas they should have observed the feast of Tabernacles (Sukkot) for two days, because the messengers had not reached them in good time. However, in order not to make a distinction between the festivals, a law was enacted by the Sages that in all places which could not be reached by the Tishri messengers, the people should observe all the holidays, including even the feast of Pentecost, for two days. (Maimonides, *Laws for the Sanctification of the New Moon*, 3:12)[16]

---

[15] As Maimonides explains in the next section (3:13), messengers have two fewer days to travel in Tishri, Day 1 because of Rosh Hashanah and Day 10 because of Yom Kippur.

[16] For the Hebrew original, see Mahler (1889) 17. The English translation is Gandz' in Gandz, Obermann, and Neugebauer (1956) 13–14.

An example in which a feast day is doubled even though the day on which it is celebrated in Jerusalem is always known is Shavuot (Pentecost). Shavuot by definition falls 50 days after Pesach. It is the 51st day, counting Pesach as the first. Exigency is no cause to practice YTSheni in this case. A sense of harmony is.

3. *The Related Case of Day Two of Rosh Hashanah*

3.1. *Similarities Between YTSheni and Day Two of Rosh Hashanah*

As far as the sources allow us to see, day two of Rosh Hashanah is not a case of YTSheni. But a number of factors make it very tempting to associate the two. In fact, the two have been associated with one another here and there in writing. This fact suggests that an understanding of day two of Rosh Hashanah is important for an understanding of YTSheni itself. At least four factors make it tempting to associate day two of Rosh Hashanah with YTSheni. It will appear, however, that none of these factors is binding.

First, both YTSheni and day two of Rosh Hashanah are discussed in the Talmudic treatise *Rosh Hashanah*. But then, the treatise's title is merely an instance of *pars pro toto*. The treatise deals with all kinds of aspects of the calendar.

Second, both Rosh Hashanah and YTSheni involve a celebration on two successive days, in the case of Rosh Hashanah on 1 Tishri and 2 Tishri. But then, Rosh Hashanah is doubled also in Jerusalem. The second day in Jerusalem by definition cannot be an instance of Yom Tov Sheni Shel Galuyyot. It would fit the description Yom Tov Sheni "second feast day," without Shel Galuyyot. But the concept of YTSheni *tout court* is nowhere articulated in the sources. Shel Galuyyot is always presented as indispensable to the concept of YTSheni.

Third, day two of Rosh Hashanah exhibits two features of YTSheni: (1) distance from Jerusalem; (2) observation of the moon. But then, these two features seem to play a different role (see below).

Fourth, the inability of messengers to reach certain communities in the Diaspora in time to announce on which of two possible days the new lunar month had begun in Jerusalem is a key characteristic of YTSheni. At first sight, this element makes Rosh Hashanah a prime candidate for YTSheni. Rosh Hashanah falls at the beginning of the month. In fact, it is the only holiday to fall at or even near the beginning of the month (see Figure 1). Messengers sent from Jerusalem could hardly have reached any community of the Diaspora in time to announce the beginning of the month.

3.2. *Day Two of Rosh Hashanah in Israel (Jerusalem)*

It appears from 3.1 that the potential for conceptual entanglement of day two of Rosh Hashanah and YTSheni is great. The main task at hand is therefore to disentangle the two as clearly as possible. For that purpose, it will be useful to begin by making a distinction between two cases: Rosh Hashanah in the Diaspora and Rosh Hashanah in Jerusalem. It is logically desirable to begin with the case that clearly disqualifies day two of Rosh Hashanah as an instance of YTSheni, namely Rosh Hashanah in Jerusalem.

A key element of YTSheni was uncertainty as to when the lunar month had begun in Jerusalem. This uncertainty was itself a consequence of the geographical distance between Jerusalem and the Diaspora. But with the celebration of Rosh Hashanah in Jerusalem, there was no distance and there could therefore have been no uncertainty. The very motive for practicing YTSheni is wanting.

The question arises: Why then was Rosh Hashanah doubled in Jerusalem? Once again, the surviving sources do not provide a complete picture. But a partial answer may be obtained from the following passage in the Talmud.

> Originally they used to accept testimony with regard to the new moon during the whole of the day. On one occasion the witnesses were late in arriving, and the Levites went wrong in the daily hymn. It was therefore ordained that testimony should be accepted (on new year) only until the afternoon sacrifice, and that if witnesses came after the afternoon sacrifice that day should be kept as holy and also the next day. (B.T. *Rosh Hashanah* 30b [Mishnah]; also cited in Appendix I)[17]

This scenario is not YTSheni. But the passage does refer to two elements that one also finds in YTSheni: (1) distance from Jerusalem and (2) observation of the moon. However, the elements do not play the same role as in YTSheni. As for (1), YTSheni involves sending messengers out *from* Jerusalem. The above passage concerns witnesses coming *to* Jerusalem. As for (2), the concern with the moon in YTSheni is calendrical. The need is for knowing when the lunar month has begun in Jerusalem. In the above passage, the concern is with sanctifying the first crescent in Jerusalem.

It is clearly stated in the passage that the month of Tishri is already in its first day. This statement seems to imply that lunar Tishri had begun without observation of the first crescent, even if the moon must always play some role in beginning lunar months. The above passage can therefore be used as an argument in favor of the following two-part theory (for other

---

17 Translation according to Simon (1938) 143–44.

arguments, see 2.2 above). First, the first crescent did not directly mark the beginning of the month (contrary to the currently prevailing assumption that daylight of Day 1 of the lunar month had to follow visibility of the first crescent in the previous evening). Second, the role of the first crescent was liturgical and not calendrical. There was a desire to confirm the sighting of the first crescent ceremoniously, declaring it "sanctified!" The fact remains that the month began close to first crescent visibility.

The above passage is not fully explicit. But it does seem to transmit a desire to sanctify the first crescent on New Year's Day. For that purpose, New Year's Day was extended by a day in order to allow ample time for reports of first crescent sighting to reach Jerusalem during the holiday. It is not said what happened when no reports of the first crescent sighting arrived even on the second day of Rosh Hashanah. What matters for the present line of argument is that the practice of doubling Rosh Hashanah in Jerusalem differs from YTSheni. Clearly, day two of Rosh Hashanah in Jerusalem is not YTSheni. But what about the Diaspora?

3.3. *Day Two of Rosh Hashanah in the Diaspora*

There is no reason why Rosh Hashanah could not have been doubled in the Diaspora for the same reasons as in Jerusalem. The practice could simply have been adopted. The surviving sources do not transmit any explicit information on this point, however. But what matters here is that the adoption of the Jerusalem practice in the Diaspora would not be an instance of YTSheni.

Celebrating two days in Jerusalem and, in imitation of Jerusalem, also in the Diaspora is one thing. Synchronizing Jerusalem and the Diaspora is another. Yet, there must have been a desire in the Diaspora to celebrate in synchrony with Jerusalem. And since two days were celebrated in Jerusalem, there may even have been a desire to celebrate both days in synchrony.

As it happens, the sources provide indications of a procedure that would allow exactly that, celebrate both 1 and 2 Tishri on the same day in the Diaspora as in Jerusalem. The procedure consists of two precepts.

First precept. B.T. *Rosh Hashanah* 18a (cited in 2.14 above) states that messengers went out to announce when Elul had begun for the sake of Rosh Hashanah, which falls on Day 1 of the next month, Tishri. This precept still does not eliminate the uncertainty at the end of Elul, which might be 29 or 30 days long. But, at least, the uncertainty is reduced to a margin of one day. What is more, the remaining uncertainty could be eliminated by a second precept also reported in the Talmud.

Second precept. B.T. *Rosh Hashanah* 19b (Gemara) transmits a tradition that Elul always had 29 days from the days of Ezra, while granting that there were exceptions to this practice.

It is an undeniable fact that, together, the two precepts described in *Rosh Hashanah* 18a and 19b would allow communities in the Diaspora to determine many days beforehand exactly on which days Day 1 and Day 2 of Tishri would fall in Jerusalem. What the sources do not tell us is to which extent these precepts were heeded at various times and in various places.

YTSheni guarantees that there will be no day of celebration in the Diaspora that is not also a day of celebration in Jerusalem. Full synchrony is guaranteed. The special problem with Rosh Hashanah is that there are *two* days of celebration in Jerusalem. It is tempting to assume that the procedure described above was designed specifically to guarantee full synchrony. It is not clear from the sources to which extent this procedure was actually practiced. The institution of the fixed calendar made this earlier procedure superfluous and therefore obliterated traces of it in the sources that would otherwise have survived.

In sum, the doubling of Rosh Hashanah itself is not an instance of YTSheni, either in Jerusalem or in the Diaspora. Its aim is not synchrony. On the other hand, the doubling of Rosh Hashanah seems to have spawned the two precepts described above that do have synchrony as their aim and are therefore similar in design to YTSheni. Such is the nature of the entanglement: Rosh Hashanah itself is not YTSheni, but some of its offshoots are very similar to it.

In the absence of the two said precepts, the margin of uncertainty in the Diaspora about the beginning of Tishri in Jerusalem is two days at least. The first precept alone reduces the margin to one day. By combining the first precept with the practice of YTSheni, communities in the Diaspora could at least guarantee synchrony with one of the two days of Rosh Hashanah. But that is still not satisfying and the sources do not document this specific theoretical combination. Finally, the two precepts together completely eliminate the uncertainty.

4. *A Related Calendrical Practice in Babylonia?*

All ancient nations except Egypt had lunar calendars. Synchronizing a lunar calendar in every city and hamlet of a single nation is not easy. But then, calendars did not have nearly the central role in life that they have nowadays. If two cities were at a fair distance from one another, their economies would probably have been little intertwined. Each city also tended to have its own gods and its own cult calendar. Messengers and other travelers may have transported information about which day in the month it was in their calendar to other places. But it is not clear how a difference of one or two days in the day-count would negatively affect commerce and communication between those places.

The Hebrew calendar uses doubling of feast days to ensure synchrony with celebrations in Jerusalem. No evidence of a similar practice is known to me from any other civilizations using lunar calendars.[18] The practice may well never have existed elsewhere.

It is difficult to let distant towns know soon whether the day following Day 29 is Day 30, still in the same month, or Day 1 in the next month. The resulting problem is that feasts might not be synchronized with celebrations in the capital. YTSheni is designed to solve this problem. Doubling feast days is the remedy. However, there is another way in which the problem might conceivably be solved. An imaginary example may illustrate this method. Yom Kippur falls on Day 10 of Tishri. Suppose that the calendars are synchronized everywhere by Day 29 of the previous month, in this case Elul. This is an assumption on which also YTSheni is based. In order to ensure synchrony, one might decide to celebrate Yom Kippur always 10 days after the end of Day 29 of Elul. Accordingly, if Elul had 29 days, Yom Kippur would be celebrated on 10 Tishri in Jerusalem. If Elul had 30 days, it would be celebrated on 9 Tishri because an extra day, Day 30 of Elul, intervenes. The distance from 29 Elul would in both cases be 10 days. The day date would not yet be known in the distant diaspora. The day number would be one higher if the previous month had only had 29 days.

This practice may seem adequate. But it poses problems. First, feasts are associated with a certain day of the month and the days of the month are named after their number. This would tend to establish a strong connection between a day number and a feast, for example, between the number 10 and Yom Kippur. However, in the alternative practice described above, that connection would be ruptured. Yom Kippur is never doubled, but the day on which Yom Kippur is celebrated would shift back and forth between 9 Tishri and 10 Tishri. Second, the day number would shift in Jerusalem for the benefit of the Diaspora. Jerusalem would surrender its centrality, as it were.

No evidence for this alternative practice exists in relation to Jewish feasts. This practice is mentioned here because something structurally

---

18 A standard treatment of similarities and differences in the lunar time-reckoning described by rabbinic and cuneiform sources is Wacholder and Weisberg (1976). For a comprehensive survey of ancient Near Eastern calendars, see Cohen (1993).

close to it has been identified "tentatively (and speculatively)" in a Neo-Babylonian tablet (NCBT 58) from the archive of the Eanna temple at Uruk dated to the sixth century B.C.E.[19] This identification is part of a large and interesting study of lunar calendrical practices in Babylonia. The main problem with the identification is that the practice in question is not known from elsewhere. Also, the source, NCBT 58, is ambiguous at best. It is one thing to identify an ambiguous instance of a well-established phenomenon in a source. It is another thing to establish the very existence of a phenomenon on the basis of an ambiguous source. In fact, realizing this, the author does urge caution.[20]

The practice is postulated on the basis of the following two statements in NCBT 58:

> We heard the report concerning the "turning back" of the day. Šamaš will be clothed on the 15th day.

The expression "turning back" conveys that the previous month had had 29 days.[21] By the proposed theory, the feast of Šamaš would be celebrated on Day 14 if the previous month was 30 days long. Thus, 14 days would always separate the feast from Day 29, regardless of whether the previous month had had 29 or 30 days. To use a modern analogy, this is as if a feast celebrated on 15 March in non-leap years would be celebrated on 14 March in a leap year, which has a 29th day in February.

The source in question explicitly notes that Šamaš will be clothed on the 15th. However, there is no compelling reason to assume that this statement implies that it is celebrated on the 14th after a 30-day month. The reminder could simply serve to indicate either when the clothing is going to take place or that the clothing would be a day earlier because the previous month had only had 29 days and not 30 days. The letter is one of several "requests made of the authorities of the Eanna (temple at Uruk) to send supplies of various commodities and paraphernalia for cultic performances at Larsa."[22] Commodities would need to arrive a day earlier if the clothing of the 15th occurs after a 29-day month. This could have served as the motive for the reminder.

Why keep the distance to Day 29 of the previous month the same, regardless of whether there is a Day 30 or not? After all, this also changes

19 Beaulieu (1993), especially 76–80.

20 Ibid., 81 n. 36.

21 Ibid., 68–69.

22 Ibid., 77.

the distances in time to feasts that *follow*. Celebrating a feast in synchrony with a central location does not seem the motive, as it is with YTSheni. What added benefit is there to keeping the distance the same in relation to Day 29 rather than to Day 1? The days in the month are counted and feasts are associated with a certain day number for organizational purposes. What satisfaction is derived from keeping the same distance to Day 29 in order to override this orderly principle?

Then again, NCBT 58 does exhibit some kind of synchronizing. In that sense, there is a similarity with YTSheni. Larsa is clearly following Uruk. However, it is one thing to listen to Uruk to ensure that a feast celebrated at Larsa will occur on Uruk Day 15. It is another thing to shift a feast in date between Day 14 and Day 15.

5. *Vestiges of the Earlier YTSheni in the Later One*

The later YTSheni is a set of vestiges of the earlier one. The fixing of the Hebrew lunar calendar overrides the need to double feast days. However, vestiges of the doubling are retained in deference to tradition. These vestiges do not interact as parts of an active system. A complete treatment of every aspect of the later YTSheni will not be attempted here. What follows is limited to attempts to answer three technical questions.

5.1. *Why Does the Feast Day Celebrated Everywhere Always Precede the One Celebrated Only in the Diaspora?*

In the later YTSheni, the extra feast day observed only in the Diaspora falls undeniably after, not before, the one observed everywhere, which is also the sole one observed in Israel. The earlier YTSheni differed. The sole day observed in Jerusalem could have been either the first or the second of the two days celebrated elsewhere (cf. 1.1). This is not stated anywhere explicitly in the sources, but it may be inferred from the following passage in the Talmud:

> Rabbah was accustomed to fast two days (on Yom Kippur). Once he was found to be right. (B.T. *Rosh Hashanah* 21a [Gemara]; also cited in Appendix I)[23]

The probable interpretation is as follows. Rabbah added a second day of fasting. Afterwards, it was found out that Yom Kippur had been observed in Jerusalem on the second day. Rabbah was thus "found to be right" because he had fasted in synchrony with Jerusalem.

---

23 Translation according to Simon (1938) 87.

Why did the makers of the fixed calendar place the sole feast day observed in Jerusalem on the first of the two days observed in the Diaspora? First of all, they could not have it both ways. A choice imposed itself. Perhaps the choice was inspired by some sense that time added to another time period tends to be thought of as *following* that other time period.

However, I believe that there may be an organic and systemic reason why YTSheni follows, and does not precede, the feast observed in Israel. Consider Sukkot (Tabernacles), which begins on 15 Tishri. In the later YTSheni, the first day of Sukkot is celebrated on both Days 15 and 16 of Tishri. What role do the numbers 15 and 16 play in the earlier YTSheni? They are the days counted from the time of uncertainty, that is, the end of Day 29 of the previous month (see 2.11). If one celebrates the 15th day and the 16th day after the moment of uncertainty of Day 29 without knowing on which day the month had begun in Jerusalem and therefore on which day 15 Tishri would fall, then overlap with the observation of the sole feast day in Jerusalem is guaranteed. Indeed, if the previous month had had 29 days, the 15th day would coincide with 15 Tishri. If the previous month had had 30 days, the 16th day would coincide with 15 Tishri.

This manner of counting from Day 29 as what I would call the time of uncertainty is not stated anywhere explicitly in the sources. Yet it is the only method that guarantees overlap with Jerusalem. I believe that it is implicit in the following passage from the Talmud:

> Rabbi Zera said in the name of Rabbi Naḥman: Wherever (a second feast day is kept) out of doubt, we make it the succeeding day. This means to say that we keep (Passover and Tabernacles) on the 15th and 16th (day) but not on the 14th. (B.T. *Rosh Hashanah* 20b [Gemara])[24]

The numbers 15 and 16 in this passage can have validity, that is, make YTSheni work, only if they are counted from the end of Day 29, not from the beginning of the month, which the Diaspora is not supposed to know yet. But the text does not explicitly state that this is how the count was made.

The base number is 15. Numerically speaking, why is the second number 16 and not, say, 14? This results from how two counts relate to one another, the count from the end of Day 29 and the count from Day 1. The base number 15 expresses the distance from Sukkot back to the beginning of the month, Day 1. However, the count from the end of Day 29 was either the same, 15, if the previous month had had 29 days, or one more, 16, if the previous month had had 30 days. The extra Day 30 adds one to the count.

---

[24] Translation according to Simon (1938) 86.

The count from the end of Day 29 is a feature of the earlier YTSheni. The count fluctuates depending on whether the month is 29 or 30 days long. This count could not survive into the later YTSheni, in which everything is fixed as part of the fixed calendar, including the lengths of the months. By necessity, there was only one point of departure left to count 15 and 16 days from, namely the beginning of the month, Day 1. Therefore, in the transition from the observational calendar to the fixed calendar and from the earlier YTSheni to the later YTSheni, the counting of the 15th and 16th days by necessity had to be disconnected from Day 29 and attached to the beginning of the month.

But one might object that the question is moot. Indeed, in the fixed calendar, all the months in which doubled feast days fall are preceded by months of 29 days (see Figure 1). Counting from Day 29 is therefore *in effect* always the same as counting from Day 1 of the month. Why then postulate a *shift* or *change* with regard to day-from-which-to-count from the earlier to the later YTSheni if the two ways of counting are the same?

First, the fact that counting from the end of Day 29 and counting from the beginning of Day 1 happen to coincide *in effect* does not mean that the two counts are the same from the points of view of concept and intention. It cannot be denied that, in the earlier YTSheni, one could not count from Day 1 in the Diaspora because it was not certain on which day Day 1 had fallen. Nor can it be denied, conversely, that, in the later YTSheni, there was no need at all to count from Day 29 (as the last day whose location is known with certainty) because the calendar became fully fixed. For these reasons, *conceptually* speaking, one had to count from Day 29 in the earlier YTSheni but from Day 1 in the later YTSheni, even if the two manners of counting are *in effect* the same.

Second, there is in fact one case in which counting from Day 29 and from Day 1 do indeed differ *in effect*. It is at the same time clear that, in this case, the count is always from Day 1 in the later YTSheni and must always have been from Day 29 in the earlier YTSheni. In the Hebrew calendar, 7 out of 19 years have 13 lunar months (specifically, years 3, 6, 8, 11, 14, 17, 19). The other 12 years have 12 months. The intercalary 13th month is called Second Adar. In the fixed calendar, Adar Sheni is always 30 days long. By contrast, Adar itself is always 29 days long. Consequently, the following month, Nisan, in which Passover is celebrated, can be preceded either by a 29-day or a 30-day month. Now suppose that the aforementioned counting of the 15th and the 16th day to obtain the two days of Passover started from the preceding Day 29. Obviously, the two days of Passover in the Diaspora would coincide with the Jerusalem dates of 15 Nisan and 16 Nisan after Adar, but with 14 and 15 Nisan after Second Adar. In fact, this is what must have happened in the earlier YTSheni. One of the two days always overlaps with 15 Nisan. But in the fixed calendar and the later YTSheni, the two days of Passover always fall on 15 and 16 Nisan. Two conclusions are patent. First, the count was in effect always from Day 1 in the later YTSheni. Second, the existence of a shift from the earlier YTSheni to the later YTSheni is proven.

5.2. *Why is Day 30 Called Rosh Ḥodesh, "Beginning of the Month"?*

In the fixed religious calendar, Rosh Ḥodesh "beginning of the month" not only designates Day 1 of every lunar month, but also Day 30 of 30-day months. As a result, at the end of a 30-day month, two days called Rosh Ḥodesh follow one another in succession, namely Day 30 of that month and Day 1 of the next month.

Calling Day 30 Rosh Ḥodesh has no apparent function in the fixed calendar. In fact, it seems to make little sense to associate a day in name with the beginning of the lunar month if it is in fact Day 30 or the last day of the month. The logical inference is that calling Day 30 Rosh Ḥodesh must be a feature of the earlier, observational, calendar that was preserved in the later, fixed, calendar in deference to tradition.

No explanation of Rosh Ḥodesh is preserved in the surviving sources. In this case too, the rise to absolute dominance of the fixed calendar has erased most traces of earlier calendrical practice from the historical record. It will therefore be necessary to propose a theoretical explanation.

The main reason for discussing Rosh Ḥodesh here is a certain similarity with YTSheni. Like YTSheni, Rosh Ḥodesh involves the doubling of a feast day. However, the two cases of doubling appear to have different causes. At the origin of YTSheni lies the relation between the Diaspora and Jerusalem. That relation seems to play no role in the doubling of Rosh Ḥodesh. In other words, even if there had been no Diaspora, there would still have been instances of two days called Rosh Ḥodesh following one another in succession. Rosh Ḥodesh therefore does not strictly belong to the subject matter of this paper.

It seems natural to relate the double Rosh Ḥodesh to the ambiguous status of the day that follows Day 29 of the month in a lunar calendar. It can be either Day 30 or Day 1. In that sense, that day is at the very least a candidate for being the first of the new month even if it ends up being identified as Day 30 of the old month. In fact, the sources suggest that the status of the day following Day 29 was sometimes held in suspense even during the day itself. In such a case, after Day 29 the cycle of lunar months would enter a kind of limbo stage during which the beginning of the month was being decided. It should be stressed that the sources, primarily the Talmud, do not allow an explanation that can be verified in every detail. I refrain from further speculation on the problem of Rosh Ḥodesh at this time.

5.3. *Why Is Yom Kippur Never Doubled Anywhere in the Later YTSheni?*

There is some evidence in the Talmud that Yom Kippur could be doubled in the earlier YTSheni (see B.T. *Rosh Hashanah* 21a [Gemara]; the fifth paragraph in Appendix I, from "Rabbah was accustomed..."). But this evidence also suggests that it was not the norm. There is also some evidence that fasting two days was considered a great hardship (see B.T. *Rosh Hashanah* 21a [Gemara]; the sixth paragraph in Appendix I, from "Rabbi Naḥman had once fasted..."). I suspect that observing Yom Kippur for two days was rare. This must be the reason it is not doubled anywhere in the fixed calendar.

Appendix I

The Babylonian Talmud on Yom Tov Sheni Shel Galuyyot

The reader may find it convenient to have ready access in this appendix and the next to the two principal sources on YTSheni Shel Galuyyot. They may well be the only two sources dealing explicitly with the calendrical structure of YTSheni.

What follows in this appendix is M. Simon's translation of the two relevant passages of the tractate *Rosh Hashanah* in the Babylonian Talmud.[25] The first passage is part of the Aramaic Gemara or commentary on the Hebrew Mishnah (compiled mainly from about 200–500 C.E.), the second is part of the Hebrew Mishnah itself (compiled around 200 C.E.). The language of the Talmud is compact. In the following translation, portions placed between parentheses or square brackets are not in the original. They are taken from Simon's main text, derived from his footnotes, or otherwise added for clarification. Words between parentheses flesh out the original text. Square brackets encompass explanatory notes.

I. *B.T. Rosh Hashanah 20b–21a (Gemara)*

Rabbi Zera in the name of Rabbi Naḥman: Wherever (a second feast day is kept) out of doubt, we make it the following day. This means to say that we keep (Passover and Tabernacles) on the 15th and 16th (day) but not on the fourteenth. But should not the 14th also be kept, in case both Av and Elul have been declared short [that is, have 29 days]? [21a] If two (successive) months are declared short, the matter becomes known.

Levi once arrived (from the west) in Babylon on the eleventh of Tishri. [Apparently, he arrived in the evening just as Yom Kippur or 10 Tishri was coming to an end and the fast was being lifted. By his reckoning, 10 Tishri or Yom Kippur was just beginning. This is because the previous month had 30 days in the west but 29 in the east.] He said (to the people there): How good and sweet is the dish of the Babylonians on the great day of the West [that is, Yom Kippur]. [This remark is made in jest because Levi assumes that the fast of Yom Kippur should begin, yet his hosts are getting ready to eat.] They said to him, Testify (that 10 Tishri is now just beginning). He replied: I did not (personally) hear the Beth din (in Jerusalem proclaim the month) "sanctified."

Rabbi Joḥanan issued a proclamation: In all those places which can be reached by the messengers sent out in Nisan (on account of Passover on Day 15) but not by those sent out in Tishri (on account of Sukkot on Day 15),

25 Simon (1938) 86–88, 143–44.

two days should be kept (on Passover), Nisan being included so that there should be no mistake as to Tishri. [The messengers have two days less to travel in Tishri because of Rosh Hashanah on Day 1 and Yom Kippur on Day 10. It is recommended that the feast be also doubled in Nisan, lest people celebrate also just one day in Tishri out of habit and by analogy with Nisan even if no messengers announcing which day had been the month's first have arrived.]

Rabbi Aibu ben Nagri and Rabbi Ḥiyya ben Abba once arrived at a certain place which had been reached by the messengers sent out in Nisan but not by those sent out in Tishri, and though the inhabitants kept only one day (of Passover) they did not reprove them. When Rabbi Joḥanan heard this he was annoyed and said to them: Did I not tell you that in places which have been reached by the messengers sent out in Nisan but not by those sent out in Tishri they should keep two days, Nisan being included so that no mistake should be made in Tishri?

Rabbah was accustomed to fast two days (on Yom Kippur). Once he was found to be right. [In other words, if he had fasted just the first day, his fasting would not have been in synchrony with Jerusalem where Yom Kippur fell on the next day. Rabbah would have been wrong in the sense of fasting on the wrong day.]

Rabbi Naḥman had once fasted the whole of Yom Kippur, when in the evening a man came and told him, Tomorrow is the great day of the West [that is, Yom Kippur]. (Rabbi Naḥman) said to (the man): Where are you from? (The man) replied: From Damharia. (Rabbi Naḥman) exclaimed: Blood will be his latter end. [This is an untranslatable pun on the name Damharia.] To himself he applied the verse: "Swift were our pursuers" (Lam 4:19).

II. *B.T. Rosh Hashanah 30b (Mishnah)*

Originally they used to accept testimony with regard to the new moon during the whole of the day (of new year). On one occasion the witnesses were late in arriving, and the Levites went wrong in the daily hymn. It was therefore ordained that testimony should be accepted (on new year) only until the afternoon sacrifice, and that if witnesses came after the afternoon sacrifice that day should be kept as holy and also the next day. After the destruction of the temple Rabban Joḥanan b. Zaccai ordained that testimony with regard to the new moon should be received during the whole of the day.

Appendix II

MAIMONIDES ON YOM TOV SHENI SHEL GALUYYOT

What follows is Gandz' translation of the two passages in which Maimonides discusses YTSheni in his הלכות קדוש החדש *Hilkhot Qidduš ha-Ḥodeš* "Laws for the Sanctification of the New Moon" (compiled around 1180 C.E.).[26] This treatise is part of his Code, the *Mishneh Torah*.

I. *Hilkhot Qidduš ha-Ḥodeš, Chapter 3: Sections 11–13*

11. In places that the messengers could reach in good time, each of the (annual) holidays was observed one day only, as prescribed in the Law. In remote places, however, which the messengers could not reach in time, it was customary to observe the holidays for two days, since the people were in doubt as to the exact day (the 29th or the 30th) which the court had declared as New Moon Day.

12. There were places which the Nisan messengers could reach in time, while the Tishri messengers could not. By law the people of these places should have observed the Passover feast one day only, since the messengers had reached them in time and they knew which day was declared as New Moon Day; whereas they should have observed the feast of Tabernacles for two days, because the messengers had not reached them in good time. However, in order not to make a distinction between the festivals, a law was enacted by the Sages that in all places which could not be reached by the Tishri messengers, the people should observe all the holidays, including even the feast of Pentecost, for two days.

13. The difference in traveling time between the messengers of Nisan and those of Tishri is two days; for the messengers of Tishri could not travel on the first day of Tishri, because it's New Year's Day, nor on the tenth, because it is the Day of Atonement.

II. *Hilkhot Qidduš ha-Ḥodeš, Chapter 5: Sections 4–12*

4. In the time of the Synedrium, when New Moon Days were determined by observation, the rule was as follows: The people in Palestine and in places that could be reached in ample time by the messengers of Tishri, celebrated (each of) the holidays one day only; while those living in more distant places that could not be reached in time by the messengers of Tishri used to celebrate the holidays for two days, because they were in doubt,

---

[26] Gandz, Obermann, and Neugebauer (1956) 11–13, 23–26.

inasmuch as they did not know which day the Palestinian court had declared as New Moon Day.

5. But in our times, when no Synedrium exists and the Palestinian court itself determines the calendar by calculation, it might seem proper that the Jews of all countries, even the more distant countries of the Dispersion, need celebrate the holidays one day only, just as the Jews of Palestine do—seeing that all follow the same method in determining the calendar. The Sages, however, have seen fit to decree that the Jewish communities adhere to what had been the custom of their ancestors.

6. Accordingly, the rule is as follows: Those places that could not be reached in time by the messengers of Tishri, in the days when messengers used to be sent out, must observe (each of) the holidays for two days, even in our times, just as they had been wont to do in the time when the Palestinian courts used to determine the calendar on the basis of visual observation. On the other hand, the present-day people of Palestine should continue to celebrate the holidays only one day (each), according to their custom of old, for they had never celebrated two days. We thus see that the second day of the holidays, as we celebrate it now in the Diaspora, is based merely on an ordinance of the Scribes.

7. Even in the days when the calendar depended on observation of the new crescent, the majority of the Palestinian Jews, too, were wont to celebrate the New Year's holiday for two days, because they were in doubt as to which day had been declared by the court as New Moon Day, seeing that the messengers could not travel on a holiday (which in the case of New Year's coincides with the first day of the month).

8. Moreover, even in Jerusalem itself, which was the seat of the court, it often happened that the people had to observe the New Year's holiday for two days. For if witnesses did not arrive on the 30th day (of Elul), they were wont to celebrate this day as the (New Year's) holiday, while waiting for witnesses to arrive, as well as the following day. Now inasmuch as they used to celebrate this holiday for two days, even in the time when the (ancient) method of observation had been in use, custom required that the Palestinian Jews, too, should continue to celebrate it for two days—even down to our time when the calendar is determined by calculation. You thus realize that at present even the observance of the second New Year's Day is based on the authority of the Scribes only.

9. The observance of the second day of the other holidays in a given locale does not depend upon its proximity (to Jerusalem). For example: A locality at a distance of five days' journey or less from Jerusalem could certainly have been reached in time by the messengers; yet it cannot be said

that the people living in this place should celebrate only one-day holidays; for we do not know whether (in former times) any messengers used to be sent out to this particular place at all. Possibly no messengers were ever sent thither: either because (in those times) there were no Jews settled there, and after the courts began to determine the calendar by calculation the place was settled by Jews upon whom the observance of two-day holidays had been incumbent (by their previous custom), or because no travel was possible between Jerusalem and that locality on account of war, as was the case in the war between Judea and Galilee in the days of the Sages of the Mishnah; or because Cutheans, living along the road, would not let the messengers pass through the area.

10. Were this matter of observance of a second holiday dependent upon the proximity to Jerusalem, all the Jews of Egypt would have to observe only one day, since the messengers of Tishri could have reached them in time. For the journey from Jerusalem to Egypt by way of Ascalon takes only eight days, or less. And the same is true of most of the localities of Syria. Hence it should be clear that the matter does not depend upon the proximity of a locale (to Jerusalem).

11. Therefore, the main principle governing the observance of a second day of the holidays is as follows: The inhabitants of any place situated at a distance of more than ten full days from Jerusalem should always observe two days in conformity with their age-old custom. For, as a rule, the messengers of Tishri could reach in time only those places which were located at a distance of ten days or less from Jerusalem. As for places which are situated at a distance of exactly ten days, or less, from Jerusalem, one has to take into consideration the following circumstances: If the place is in Palestine and Jews used to live there after the Second Conquest, when the calendar was (still) being regulated by visual observation—such as the towns of Usha, Shefaraam, Luz, Jamnia, Nob, Tiberias, and others—the people of such a locality need observe only one day. If the place is in Syria, e.g., Tyre, Damascus, Ascalon, and the like, or if it is outside of Palestine, as in Egypt, Ammon, Moab, and similar countries, the people there must continue to adhere to the old custom of their ancestors: If the custom has been to observe the holidays only one day, they should observe one day; if the custom has been to observe the holiday two days, they should observe two days.

12. If the place is situated in Syria or elsewhere outside of Palestine at a distance from Jerusalem of ten days or less and the people there have no tradition (concerning the observance of a second day), or if it is a new city built in the uninhabited part of Palestine, or if it is a place in which (there

was no Jewish settlement previously): the people are obliged to observe two days, according to the usage of the majority of Jewish communities throughout the world. However, the observance of a second day, even in the case of the second day of New Year's, which is universally kept in our time, is based only on an ordinance of the Scribes.

BIBLIOGRAPHY

Beaulieu, P.-A. (1993) The Impact of Month-lengths on the Neo-Babylonian Cultic Calendar. *Zeitschrift für Assyriologie und Vorderasiatische Archäologie* 83: 66–87. **Bruin, F.** (1977) The First Visibility of the Lunar Crescent. *Vistas in Astronomy* 21: 331–58. **Caldwell, J., and L.D. Young** (1997) *Crescent Visibility Predictions for 1997 (Islamic 1417/1418)*. South African Astronomical Observatory. **Cohen, M.E.** (1993) *The Cultic Calendars of the Ancient Near East*. Bethesda, Md. **Depuydt, L.** (1997) *Civil Calendar and Lunar Calendar in Ancient Egypt*. Orientalia Lovaniensia Analecta 77. Leuven. (1999) The Two Problems of the Month Names. *Revue d'Égyptologie* 50: 107–33. (2002a) History of the *ḥeleq*. To appear in the series AOAT as part of the acts of "Under One Sky," a conference on ancient astronomy held at the British Museum in June 2001. (2002b) The Date of Death of Jesus of Nazareth (forthcoming in the *Journal of the American Oriental Society*). **Doggett, L.E., and B.E. Schaefer** (1994) Lunar Crescent Visibility. *Icarus* 107: 388–403. **Filipowski, H.** (1851) *Abraham bar Chyiah, the Prince, who Flourished in Spain in the 11th century, on the Mathematical and Technical Chronology of the Hebrews, Nazarites, Mahommetans, etc.* London. (Hebrew text, no translation.) **Gandz, S., J. Obermann, and O. Neugebauer** (1956) *The Code of Maimonides, Book Three, Treatise Eight: Sanctification of the New Moon*. Yale Judaica Series 11. New Haven. (English translation with detailed commentary.) **Ginzel, F.K.** (1906–14) *Handbuch der mathematischen und technischen Chronologie*. 3 vols. Leipzig. **Ideler, L.** (1825–26) *Handbuch der mathematischen und technischen Chronologie*. 2 vols. Berlin. **Ilyas, M.** (1988) Limiting Altitude Separation in the Moon's First Visibility Criterion. *Astron. Astrophys.* 206: 133–35. (1994a) *New Moon's Visibility and International Islamic Calendar (for the Asia-Pacific Region 1407H–1421H)*. Malaysia. (1994b) Lunar Crescent Visibility and Islamic Calendar. *Q.J.R. Astr. Soc.* 35: 425–61. **Langdon, M.A., J.K. Fotheringham, and C. Schoch** (1928) *The Venus Tablets of Ammizaduga: A Solution of Babylonian Chronology by means of the Venus Observations of the First Dynasty*. With Tables for Computation by Carl Schoch. Oxford. **Mahler, E.** (1889) *Maimonides' Kiddusch Hachodesh* (הלכות קדוש החדש). Vienna. (Hebrew text with German translation.) **Pepin, M.B.** (1996) In Quest of the Youngest Moon. *Sky & Telescope*. December 1996: 104–6. **Sachau, E.** (1878) *Chronologie orientalischer Völker von Alberuni*. Leipzig. (Arabic text.) (1879) *The Chronology of Ancient Nations*. London. (Albiruni's work on chronology in English translation.) **Schaefer, B.E.** (1988) Visibility of Lunar Crescent. *Q.J.R. Astr. Soc.* 29: 511–23. (1991) Length of the Lunar Crescent. *Q.J.R. Astr. Soc.* 32: 265–77. (1996) Lunar Crescent Visibility. *Q.J.R. Astr. Soc.* 37: 759–68. **Schaefer, B.E., I.A. Ahmad, and L.E. Doggett** (1993) Records for Moon Sightings. *Q.J.R. Astr. Soc.* 34: 53–56. **Simon, M.** (1938) *The Babylonian Talmud: Rosh Hashanah.* Translated under the editorship of I. Epstein. London. (English translation annotated.) **Wacholder, B.Z., and D.B. Weisberg** (1976) Visibility of the New Moon in Cuneiform and Rabbinic Sources. In Wacholder, *Essays on Jewish Chronology and Chronography*, 59–74. New York. This article first appeared in *Hebrew Union College Annual* 42 (1971). **Zuckermann, B.** (1882) *Materialien zur Entwickelung der altjüdischen Zeitrechnung im Talmud.* Jahres-Bericht des jüdisch-theologischen Seminars "Fraenckel'scher Stiftung." Breslau.

GAMES PEOPLE PLAYED

BOARD GAMES IN THE ANCIENT NEAR EAST

Alfred J. Hoerth
Wheaton College

To see the ancient world more completely it is necessary to move beyond the monuments of the past. Preserved texts allow us a glimpse of how people viewed the world around them and how they interacted with their contemporaries. Games were part of that interaction, and they provide another avenue by which we can identify with ancient life.

Several games are known only from one or two preserved examples of their boards.[1] A board found in a Pre-dynastic cemetery at El-Mahasna in Egypt, cited as the oldest preserved gameboard, dates to the last centuries of the fourth millennium.[2] It is small, only eight inches long, made of clay, and poorly preserved. Kendall sees it as an early example of *Senet*,[3] discussed below, but it carries none of the expected markings and it is doubtful that it was ever sufficiently long to have all thirty squares required for a Senet board.[4]

MEHEN

Mehen is the oldest game for which several boards are definitely attested.[5] The examples range in date from Pre-dynastic to the Old Kingdom. The

---

1 See, for example, Mariette (1889) 16–17, and Quibell (1913) 20–21, pl. xi. The designation "gameboard" is as much overused as the term "cult object." Any series of squares or holes may, indeed, have been used for the playing of a game, but they could as well have served such purposes as counting boards, calendars, or guidelines. The archaeological literature has long been sprinkled with alleged game boards. For fairly recent additions to this questionable category, see Bar-Yosef (1982) 10–11, Richard and Boraas (1984) 83, and Swiny (1989) 186.

2 Ayrton and Loat (1911) 30, pl. xvii(1,4).

3 Kendall (1978) 7.

4 Needler (1953) 63, n. 1, examined this board and concluded it could not be a *Senet* board.

5 Finkel (1997) no pagination. Finkel relates that "about fifteen...boards have survived."

boards for this Egyptian game are flat disks, usually stone, with the representation of a coiled snake on the upper surface (see fig. 1). The cross-lines that segment the body vary greatly in number from board to board. Although most boards were set on a low stand, more than one example has a pierced projection that could have been used to hang the board when not in use. Not surprisingly, the name *mehen* means "serpent."[6]

Early studies of the game focused on a relief from the tomb of Hesy-Re (Dynasty 3) that depicted the board together with an equipment box containing "marbles" and animal figurines.[7] No gaming equipment was recovered with any of the preserved boards, but another relief shows marbles being used to play the game.[8] Various attempts have been made to recover the rules for this game. For example, an early study concluded that as many as six people could play together, and that the figurines advanced along the segments of the snake on the basis of how well a player guessed the number and color of the marbles held by an opponent.[9]

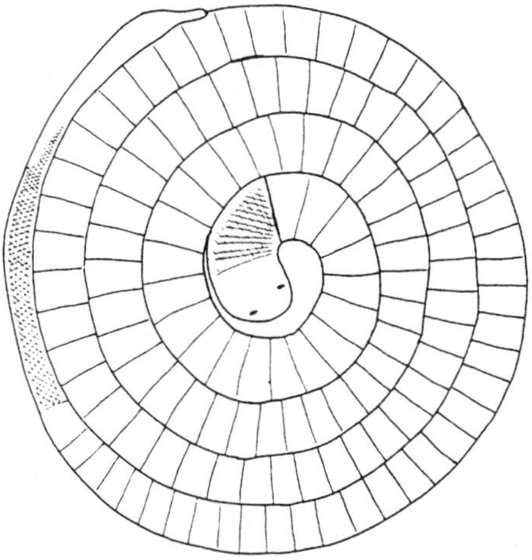

Figure 1.

[6] It was Ranke (1920) who first established this as the correct ancient name for the game.

[7] Quibell (1913) pls. xi, xvi.

[8] Lepsius (1849–56) pl. lxi(a).

[9] Quibell (1913) 20. For a recent attempt to provide rules for the game, see Finkel (1997).

SENET

More examples of the Egyptian boardgame *Senet* are known than for any other boardgame found in the ancient Near East. Dozens of gameboards, as well as texts and numerous reliefs, provide evidence of this game. Its popularity extends from the Old Kingdom down, perhaps as late as the Greco-Roman period.[10] *Senet* was played on a board that was divided into three rows of ten squares each (see fig. 2). The name of this "3 × 10" board means "passing."[11]

In the tomb relief of Hesy-Re mentioned above, a *Senet* board is shown with a separate equipment box containing two sets of seven playing pieces and four casting sticks (a form of counting device). The preserved games are often fitted with a drawer for storing the gaming equipment. Game equipment found with several boards suggests that, by New Kingdom times, the number of playing pieces to a side had been reduced to five. The reliefs sometimes carry short utterances from the players as the game was in progress: "I make a three in *Senet*," "carrying of two threes in *Senet*," or "playing six."[12] Due to the large number of boards found, along with the many tomb depictions of the game being played, the Egyptians must have found great delight in the game. Indeed, its obvious popularity led Kendall

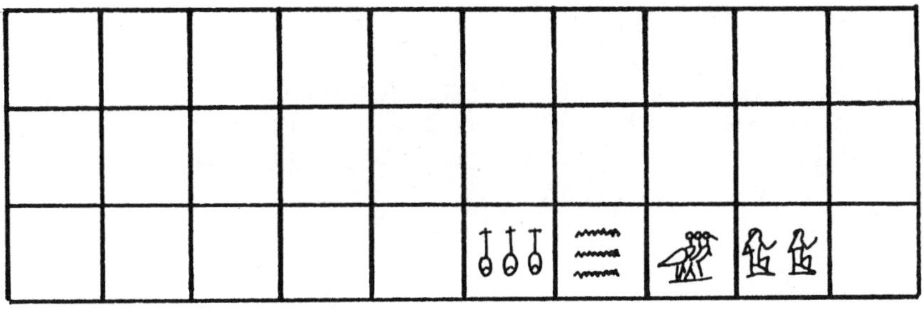

Figure 2.

10 See Needler (1953) 73–75 for a sample catalogue of boards and Pusch (1979) for a more comprehensive gathering of the data.

11 See Kendall (1978) for a well-illustrated introduction to all aspects of this game.

12 Petrie (1927) 51–52.

to call it a "true national pastime."[13] But it is also clear that within the New Kingdom *Senet* became increasingly connected with religion and funerary ritual.[14]

Figure 2 shows a typically marked board. In a few examples none of the squares seems to have been marked; in three examples all the squares are marked. The corner square is frequently blank, as here, but it can sometimes contain a falcon or the sun. The next square generally carries two strokes, gods, or men. The third square normally has three strokes, men, gods, or birds. The fourth square contains an X, *mw* ("water"), or a scene connected with water. The fifth square holds one or three *nefer* ("good")-signs. The consensus is that the fourth square represents a barrier and that the fifth square is lucky, perhaps even the goal of the game.

A back and forth routing across three squares has been suggested for the playing pieces,[15] but it is generally assumed to have been along the length of the board. Bell suggests a game of position,[16] whereas Kendall believes the pieces progressed along the board and were borne off. Kendall reasons that "the goal of the players was the mastery of the five final squares [the bottom right in fig. 2], and the winner of the game was doubtless he who first brought all of his pieces successfully through the course and off the board."[17] With regard to the marked squares, he sees square 26 [*nefer*] as

> clearly the primary goal of the players, while square 27 marked ominously "X" ("difficulties" or "encounters") [the water square] was a square to be avoided....Presumably one's object was to land on "good," pass beyond "X" to "3" or "2," and to remove his pieces safely from the board by an exact count [using the casting sticks or some other form of counting device] before his opponent did so.[18]

---

13 Kendall (1978) 4.

14 Kendall (1978) 28–33, 44–58. See also Piccione (1994) 197–204.

15 Petrie (1927) 52.

16 Bell (1983) 83.

17 Kendall (1978) 5.

18 Kendall (1978) 18.

TJAU (TAU, TWENTY SQUARES)

When Woolley excavated the Royal Cemetery at Ur, he discovered six elaborately decorated gameboards.[19] Unlike the two boardgames discussed above, this game spread over much of the Near East and dozens of examples are known from sites across the region.[20] The recovered boards range in date from the mid-third millennium B.C. to almost the midpoint of the first millennium B.C.

In its original form twenty squares were arranged into 3 × 4 and 2 × 3 rectangles connected by a bridge of two squares (see fig. 3, top). In subsequent twenty-square boards the 2 × 3 rectangle is unwrapped as in Figure 3, bottom.[21]

Various attempts have been made to discover the ancient name for the game. Birch seems to have been the first to identify the twenty-square board with *Tau*, an Egyptian word that he translated "thieves" or

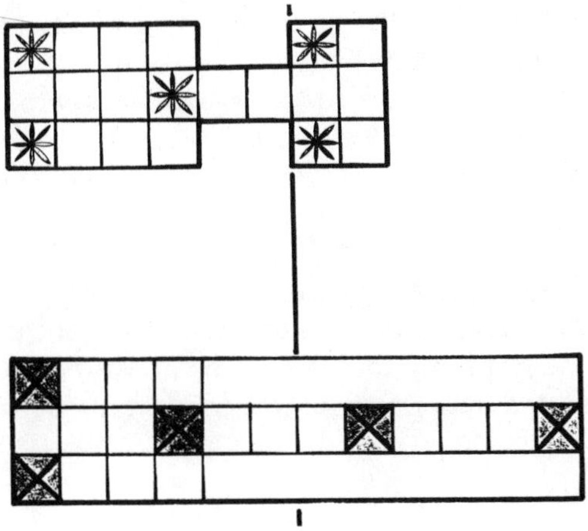

Figure 3.

[19] Woolley (1934) 149, 275–78, 534, 540, 548, 557, 559, pls. xcv–xcvii, xcix, ccxxi. Not all are complete.

[20] Boards have been found not only in Mesopotamia, but also in Syria-Palestine, Egypt, Iran, and Cyprus. I have catalogued over seventy examples.

[21] Another option was to have the squares extending from the 3 × 4 rectangle loop back toward the rectangle, rather than extend straight out from it. See, e.g., Grant (1934) 34, fig. 4, pl. xx.

"robbers." Texts listing the games of *Senet* and *Mehen* mention a game of *Tau* also. Noting that the game of *Mehen* was played on a circular board, correctly reasoning that a thirty-square board was used for the game of *Senet*, and finding a twenty-square board on the reverse of one example of a thirty-square board, he surmised that a twenty-square board "might be intended for the game of Tau."[22] Birch's identification is supported by the fact that the game of *Tau* (now usually rendered *Tjau*) does not appear in Egyptian inscriptions until the New Kingdom, that is, at about the same time that the twenty-square board reached Egypt. Additionally, the reconstructed rules of the game (see below) provide good reason for calling it by the name "Robbers." Thus the identification seems justifiable. However, "Robbers" may not have been the original Mesopotamian name.

Two of the boards from Ur were found with fourteen playing pieces divided into two sets of seven. Both casting sticks and small pipped pyramids recovered with the boards would have served as counting devices, but it is uncertain whether any complete set was found.

One Palestinian board that retained its equipment possesses five playing pieces to a side, and has one teetotum-shaped die, numbered one to four.[23] Most of the Egyptian boards were "double boards," that is, a *Senet* board was on the other side. Four boards have sets of five playing pieces as in the Palestinian example. These four boards also contain two knucklebones (another form of counting device). Casting sticks in sets of three are also known from Egyptian boards.

The evidence suggests that the game was originally played with seven playing pieces on a side, but later with five. The pieces on a given side are identical, implying that there was no difference in their value. Moves were directed by counters whose totals ranged from one to four.[24]

---

22 Birch (1870) 267–69. Pusch (1979) 211–12 favors "twenty squares" as the name of the game.

23 Albright (1938) 49, pl. xxxvii(a). A similar die was found in Egypt together with a fragmented double gameboard (Dunham [1978] 72–73, pl. LIX).

24 This is obvious with the die, and is also the expected range for three sticks or pyramids. Casting sticks were marked on one of their two faces. The count is determined by the number of marked faces turned up after a toss unless none is turned up, in which case the highest count is awarded (Kendall [1978] 62). With three sticks cast the count would be 1, 2, or 3 if marked faces appear and 4 when all marked faces are down. The small pyramids are pipped on two of their four corners. In essence then, like the casting sticks, they have two faces. How counts were obtained using knucklebones has been variously suggested; compare Petrie (1927) 52 with Kendall (1978) 66–67, but they too can produce a 1 to 4 range.

Over half the boards I have studied have marked squares. Except for those from Ur no more than five squares are marked on any one complete board.[25] A good proportion of the complete boards is marked in squares 8, 12, 16—and in squares 4 and 4' when five squares are marked (see fig. 4).[26]

It is natural to assume that the goal of the game was on the board.[27] The numbering of the squares in Figure 4 assumes the game was played by two people starting in squares 1 and 1', proceeding through their respective side columns, and then up the center row toward square 16. This route allows the players to start individually, then mix in the central column, and finish at a common goal. In support of this path, one board not only widens as it proceeds along the "tail," but also has rosettes that become increasingly large, culminating in square 16.[28]

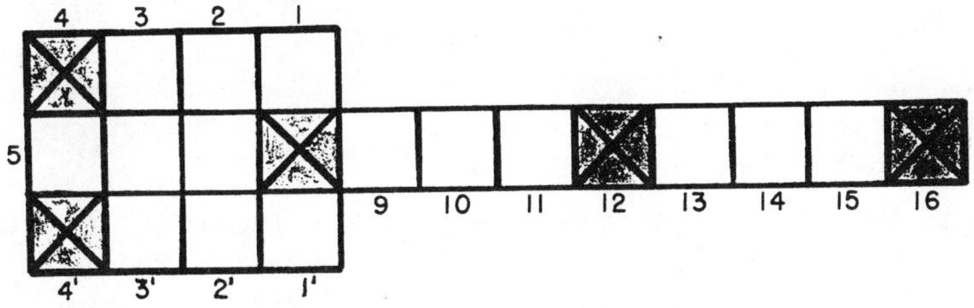

Figure 4.

[25] All the squares are decorated on the Ur boards, which led Van Buren (1937) 14 and others to assign a special meaning to each square. However, all subsequent examples make it clear that only five marked squares were meaningful; the others were merely decorative.

[26] The lack of markings on some of the boards could be due to their being incomplete. In other plain boards the marking may have faded away. Also, since most Egyptian boards were found among tomb furnishings, perhaps it was not always thought necessary to make them fully functional. This same explanation could also account for the unmarked *Senet* boards.

[27] Austin (1940) 259 divides board games into three groups: the battle, the hunt, and the race. The battle is one of position, the hunt of tracking down a quarry, and the race of being the first to reach a certain objective. The number of playing pieces (10 or 14) in comparison to the number of squares (20) leaves little opportunity for *Tjau* to be a game of position. Nor does it seem to be a game of hunt, because of the equal number of playing pieces to a side and all the playing pieces on a side being alike. However, the board and the playing pieces are well suited for a race.

[28] Petrie (1930) 12, pl. xxxiv (188). Curiously, more than one scholar has studied the Ur boards without relation to the game's subsequent configuration, and argued for routes of play impossible on later examples. See Burrett and van Splunteren (1989) 22–24; Finkel (1997).

The special squares are normally marked alike on a board, e.g., all rosettes, all crosses. Assuming square 16 is the goal, its marking—as well as the other similarly marked squares—should have a positive connotation and be advantageous to the player whose pieces land there. In the literature, "lucky" marks are often thought to have awarded the player another turn, that is, another throw of the counting devices. This suggestion is both simple and plausible, and, in the case of *Tjau*, makes for a very interesting game.

If the method of entering the board is by casting a certain number, it seems that this cast should entitle the playing piece to enter the board but not to move forward. There are three reasons for this conclusion:

1. Any entering number but the number 1 would result in one or more of the squares never being used. And the number 1 cannot be thrown with two knucklebones.
2. If the entering number was 4, each time a playing piece entered the board it would land on the first marked square and automatically be granted an additional move.
3. If the "entering cast" (other than 4) was counted out on the squares, the player would not have a chance to land on the first special square with a throw of four and would be deprived of the possibility, however remote, of casting a series of fours and moving to the goal in a single turn.

In conclusion then, a player won permission to enter the board by throwing a certain number. This number was immediately followed by an additional cast to determine how far the playing piece moved onto the board.

I suggest the following set of rules for the game of *Tjau*. These rules result in a game that is based largely on luck but still requires some thought in the choice of moves.

Rules for Playing Tjau©

1. There are five playing pieces on a side. All five are identical.
2. The counting devices have a range of 1 to 4, and are thrown to determine who has the first move; high count goes first. (It was necessary to invent this rule so that the game could begin!)
3. A throw of two is required for admission to the board. When a two is used to start a new playing piece, a second throw is immediately taken to determine how many squares the entering playing piece is to move. This number must be used to move the new playing piece.

4. A player is entitled to an extra turn when his or her playing piece lands on a marked square, including the goal square 16.
5. A playing piece can only be borne off when an exact count is thrown to reach square 16. That is, a playing piece on square 15 cannot be borne off until a 1 has been thrown. (In case knucklebones are used, the player has the option of throwing only one knucklebone.) Counts must be used to move a single playing piece. Moves can be forfeited only if no move is possible.
6. Players may pass over their own or their opponent's playing piece. When a playing piece lands on a square already occupied by another, the latter is removed from the board and must start again, even if it is the player's own playing piece.[29]
7. The game is won by the first person whose playing pieces have all touched and been borne off square 16.

A Variant of Tjau (Twenty Squares)
Banks illustrated a game consisting of two 3 × 4 rectangles joined by a bridge of seven squares that he saw in a Baghdad shop (fig. 5, top).[30] A Twentieth Dynasty papyrus containing an elaborate version of *Senet* also depicts a gameboard laid out almost exactly like that drawn by Banks. The only difference between the two is that the Egyptian version is rosetted rather than crossed in its special squares and has markings in squares 4 and 4' (fig. 5, center).[31]

A faience board in the Cairo Museum provides a third example of a "joined board" (fig. 5, bottom).[32] The Turin papyrus provides a tentative date for the other two examples.[33] It is interesting that the genuineness, as

---

29 Of the other possible alternatives the one offered here is not only the most reasonable, but the most entertaining solution. This rule adds the element of frustration, for one's playing pieces can be made to start over when they are all but "home." Here, the name "Robbers" becomes meaningful. This rule also addresses the problem of what to do when a playing piece is in line to occupy an already filled square.

30 Banks (1912) 355–56.

31 Turin Papyrus 1.775. See Seyffarth (1833) pl. iii for an early illustration.

32 Squares 8, 12, and 16 would be expected to carry rosettes, but the poor condition of the board surface makes it difficult to tell whether this was originally the case. According to the museum register, this board (J.E.88006) was taken from a dealer "in exchange" and is reported to have come from the delta area. The large rosette at one end of this board is only decorative.

33 Pusch (1977) 199–212 cites both the papyrus and Cairo Museum board. He

well as the probable date, of the Baghdad board is established by a papyrus and board(s) from Egypt.[34]

This version of *Tjau* may have been played by four people—either individually or in teams—with the marked squares at each end of the bridge serving as either the 8th or the 16th square. It is surprising that so little evidence of this variation exists. The fact that it has been found in such widely separated places as Egypt and Mesopotamia demands the conclusion that this is not a unique or isolated alteration.

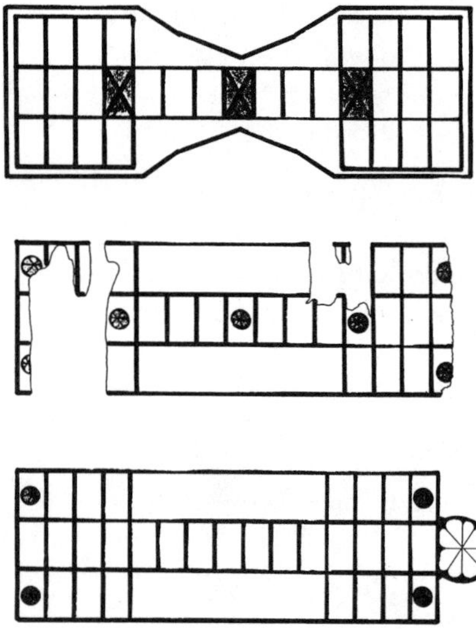

Figure 5.

further identifies a badly charred board in the British Museum (BM38429) as an additional example of this variant. Pusch's figure 2 shows a bit more of the bridge squares than was apparent to me when I closely examined this board. He also shows traces of a second rectangle at the opposite end of the board, something I was not convinced I could see. Still, the length of the board is nearly perfect for it to have been a fourth example. Also in favor of this identification is that its opposite face carries a *Senet* board marked much like that in the Turin papyrus.

34 The whereabouts of the Baghdad board is unknown.

HOUNDS AND JACKALS (58-HOLE GAMEBOARD)[35]

In 1890 Petrie published a roughly made pottery gameboard from Kahun in Egypt. In commenting on this board, Petrie stated that "no such game is known in Egypt as yet."[36] In fact, a drawing of this gameboard appears on the Turin papyrus mentioned earlier, which was published in 1833. It was there, however, incorrectly restored.[37] Presently there are over forty known examples of this game and, like *Tjau*, they were found over much of the Near East.[38] The game originated in Egypt approximately 2100 B.C. and the last known example dates to the sixth century B.C.

Typically the playing surface carries two central rows of either ten or eleven holes each, plus two outer rows of nineteen holes each. In addition, there is a larger hole at one end of the board. Figure 6 shows the basic

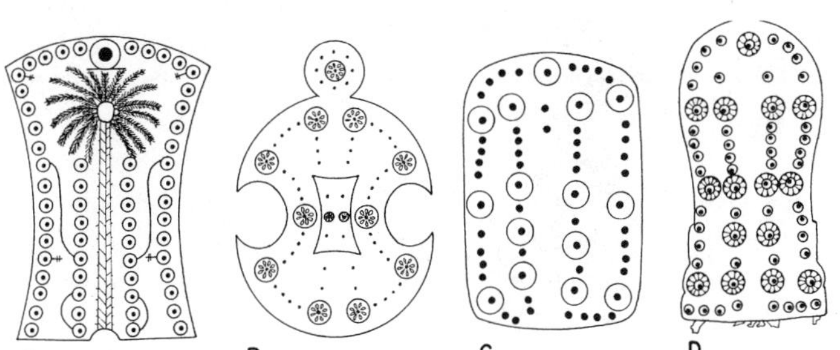

A B C D

Figure 6.

[35] In 1990 a colloquium titled "Board Games of the Ancient World" was held at the British Museum. I presented a paper on this game at the meeting, and Finkel is editor for "Board Games in Perspective," which is an outgrowth of that gathering. The publication, including my more detailed study of this game, continues to be "forthcoming."

[36] Petrie (1890) 30, pl. 16.

[37] Seyffarth (1833) pl. 3.

[38] In addition to Egypt, boards have been found in Palestine, Anatolia, Mesopotamia, and Iran. A board excavated at Gezer was initially identified as an "ashtoreth plaque" (Macalister [1912] 416). This misidentification seems responsible for subsequent allusions to an anthropological shape and religious implications for the violin-shaped boards (B in Figure 6). Not everyone has recognized this misidentification; see Dessel (1988) 59. This misunderstanding might also account for Burrett and van Splunteren (1989) 24 saying that "Academic opinion was divided as to whether or not it [the Gezer example] was used as a game board."

shapes and patternings of the board as it appeared in Egypt (A), Palestine (B), and Mesopotamia (C and D).[39]

The ancient name for the game is unknown, but Carter called it "Hounds contra Jackals" on the basis of the two sets of five pegs associated with the board he excavated at Thebes.[40] Petrie was the first to use the term "58-hole gameboard,"[41] but Carter's "Hounds and Jackals" suggestion, as his phrase has usually been rendered, has more image appeal.

A board from Nippur is the only other example to have definitely retained any of its equipment. This board was found together with three disks that could have functioned like the casting sticks and pipped pyramids mentioned earlier.[42]

Holes have been given numbers in Figure 7 to facilitate discussion of their markings and the play of the game. In the figure, holes 6 and 20, and 8 and 10, are linked by lines. Holes 15 and 25 are marked by *nefer*-signs. The linking lines are absent in almost all subsequent examples of the board (cf. fig. 6, B–D). Rather, those special holes are brought close together on the board and/or are given special markings. For someone familiar with the game, the proximity of special holes to each other, and/or the marking of special holes, would render the connecting lines unnecessary.[43]

Carter made the first serious attempt to understand the game. He began by "presuming the Shen sign, which forms a large centre hole at the top to be the goal" (fig. 6A and 30 in fig. 7).[44] There has been little objection

---

39 A, from Thebes, dates c. 1800 B.C.; see Carnarvon (1912) 58. B, from Megiddo, dates within the Late Bronze period; see Loud (1939) 19, pl. 48. C, from Ur, is contemporary with B; see Gadd (1934) 45–50, pl. viii(b). D, also from Ur, illustrates the later Assyrian-period boards; see Woolley (1932) 246–47, pl. xlii(2). The boards are not to scale and are restored as needed.

40 Carnarvon (1912) 58.

41 Petrie (1927) 55.

42 McCown, Haines, and Hansen (1967) pl. 32:3. Similar disks were in the Megiddo ivory horde and could have been for use with the boards found there (Loud [1939] 19, pls. 52–53).

43 An anomaly of the Palestinian-type boards is that hole 10, but not hole 8, is given a special marking. Since the 8 and 10 linkage reappears in almost all subsequent examples the probability is that this minor element in the play of the game was sacrificed to maintain symmetry in the design of the playing surface. The desire for symmetry could also be responsible for the special marking of hole 1 in these boards. This marked first-hole feature is found on some Mesopotamian boards; cf. Figure 6C and D.

44 Carnarvon (1912) 58.

to this conclusion.[45] Bell seemingly stands alone in suggesting that the large hole is the starting point for the game.[46]

Carter believed that his Theban board was divided into two identical sets of twenty-nine holes, running from the goal-end down the central rows and then up the outer rows of the board. He numbered each set from 1 to 29 with '30' as the common goal.[47] Ghirshman reversed the route of play. Ghirshman would start at the goal-end of the outer row, descend, and then go up the central row to the goal.[48] The layout of several boards shows the improbability of this route. For example, on Carter's board the last hole

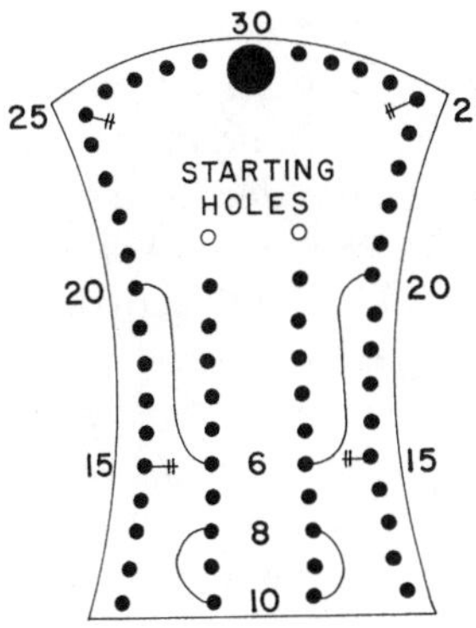

Figure 7.

would then be separated from the goal by the foliage of the palm tree, while what will be identified as "starting holes" would likewise intrude between the last hole and the goal. Moreover, in the route of play suggested by Carter, the last hole on most boards is nearest, or at least as near as any other functional hole, to the goal.

Bell follows Ghirshman's routing except that, for him, there is no goal. As already noted, Bell interprets the large hole at the "goal-end" of the

---

45 In a pamphlet accompanying a Metropolitan Museum reproduction of the Theban board Kendall notes that to an Egyptian this sign would mean "completion of the circuit." Such a designation would nicely fit Carter's route of play to the goal, and the large hole makes a convenient repository for borne-off pegs.

46 Bell (1983) 45.

47 Carnarvon (1912) 57–58.

48 Ghirshman (1939) 42–43.

board to be the starting point of the game. For him, the game ends when a player assembles the pegs in holes 1 to 5, Bell's last holes.[49] This reconstruction answers the "foliage" objection of Carter's board, but does not explain the "starting holes."[50]

Carter noted that holes 15 and 25 on his board are marked with a *nefer*-sign. He assumed that these "holes marked 'good' incur a gain" and suggested that a peg landing in such a hole received another turn.[51] Petrie, however, considered these marked holes to be set off "evidently for the sake of counting."[52] Here Petrie could be correct, since the *nefer*, as well as the other special markings, certainly can serve to visually segment the board; every fifth hole of the outer row is normally marked in some way. But this segmenting function need not preclude Carter's interpretation of the *nefer*-signs, and it has been generally accepted that a peg landing in such a marked hole should be awarded another turn.

Carter also dealt with the curved lines that link hole 6 with 20, and hole 8 with 10 in the early Egyptian examples. As he had assumed that the *nefer*-signs signify a gain, he thought it followed that the holes connected by lines "incur a loss."[53] Bell seems to reason that the lines only provide a forward jump.[54] Petrie's inference has won the most support: the connecting lines mean a jump either forward or backward, depending on the end of the line at which the peg stops.[55] His suggestion introduces both gain (expectation) and loss (frustration), and makes for a more entertaining game.

Carter started the game with the pegs lined up in holes 1 to 5 "the only place where five playing pieces aside could be placed without clashing with the obstacles (i.e., holes incurring gain or loss)."[56] This setup of the board has won general acceptance, but it fails to account for the additional hole found near hole 1 on over half the examples in which this portion of the board is preserved. Since these holes are found throughout the game's popularity, the holes must have served a useful but not absolutely neces-

---

49 Bell (1983) 45.

50 For other even less probable routes of play, see Petrie and Brunton (1924) 7; Murray (1952) 15.

51 Carnarvon (1912) 58.

52 Petrie and Brunton (1924) 7.

53 Carnarvon (1912) 58.

54 Bell (1983) 45.

55 Petrie (1927) 55.

56 Carnarvon (1912) 58.

sary function. As they are invariably near the first holes of the route of play, it is most plausible that they served as "starting holes."[57] The pegs were not lined up in holes 1 to 5 prior to the start of the game; rather, each player placed a peg in a starting hole and then proceeded to race that peg along the board as the throws of the counting devices indicated.

In Carter's study of the game he posits a 1 to 6 range for the counting devices.[58] Such a range would explain why hole 5 is not made special to continue the 10, 15, 20, 25, 30 segmenting of the playing surface. With hole 6 made special and a counting range of 1 to 6, a player would have the hope of casting the highest number in the first turn, landing in hole 6, and jumping ahead to hole 20.[59] The following rules are suggested for the game:

Rules for Hounds and Jackals©

1. Each player has five pegs.
2. Each player places one peg in his or her starting hole. If the board is not outfitted with starting holes, the player holds the peg until the counting devices determine how many holes to move into the board.
3. The counting devices have a range of 1 to 6, and are thrown to determine the first player. High count goes first.
4. Pegs landing in hole 6 move forward to hole 20. Pegs landing in hole 20 move back to hole 6.
5. On boards with holes 8 and 10 marked, pegs landing in hole 8 move forward to hole 10. Pegs landing in hole 10 move back to hole 8.
6. Play alternates between the two players except when a peg lands in marked holes 15 or 25; then the player is awarded another turn. On boards in which these holes are not marked, no extra turn is awarded.

---

57 Drioton (1940) 189. Drioton speaks of "postes de depart" but seems to think their presence or absence was dependent on the number of pegs used in the game. Nevertheless, he must be credited with being the first to move toward correctly understanding the nature of these additional holes.

58 Carnarvon (1912) 58–59.

59 Linked holes 8 and 10 would constitute a consolation jump forward or a minor impediment. A 1 to 6 range can be thrown with the various counting devices then in use. Six-sided dice are known from Palestine as early as the Middle Bronze II period, and cubed dice dating to the third millennium B.C. have been found in Mesopotamia. Cubed dice are reported from Egypt at least by the New Kingdom; perhaps the marking of hole 6 implies they were in use in Egypt earlier than that date.

7. The turn is forfeited when pegs are too near the goal to be moved the full total thrown by the counting devices.
8. When one player's peg has entered the goal, the player who has lost that race returns his or her peg to the starting hole and takes the first turn of the next race. The winning player fields a new peg.
9. The game is won by the first player to reach the goal with all five pegs.

THE HISTORY OF BOARDGAMES IN THE ANCIENT NEAR EAST

A variety of games were invented and played in the ancient Near East, but few gained wide acceptance. *Mehen* seems to have been the earliest game to win some popularity, but it did not spread beyond Egypt or outlive that country's Old Kingdom.[60] The great variation in the number of segments into which the board's playing surface was divided might indicate that the game died out even before it had been formalized.

Evidence for the game of *Senet* extends far beyond the Old Kingdom, and the game board changed little over the centuries. Despite Egypt's interaction with the outside world, *Senet*'s popularity was limited to that country. Perhaps the game's increasing connection with Egyptian religion prevented it from gaining acceptance elsewhere.

The history of Hounds and Jackals is more complex. This third Egyptian game first appeared at the end of the First Intermediate period and continued into the Middle Kingdom. For many years the next dated board was thought to come from Nuzi, in Mesopotamia, some three centuries later. Drioton tried to account for this hiatus as well as for the appearance of the game outside Egypt, but he had little evidence to support his suggestions.[61] More recently, Buchanan dated a board fragment to the Old Babylonian period, thus making it contemporary to the Egyptian boards, and bridging the time gap.[62]

In Palestine, all currently known examples of the game date to the Late Bronze period. Even if Buchanan's dating is correct, Syria-Palestine was probably the conduit through which the game moved to the other end of

---

[60] A seventh-century B.C. relief depicts the game of *Mehen*, but it was copied from an Old Kingdom tomb (Ranke [1920] 13–14).

[61] Drioton (1940) 200.

[62] Ellis and Buchanan (1966) 201. A consequence of this dating is that Ellis thinks five fragmentary examples from Susa in Iran must be pushed back from their originally assigned date of c. 1150 B.C. to this same time period (199).

the Fertile Crescent. In Palestine the board has a "violin shape" (cf. fig. 6B). This shape is also evident in three boards found in Egypt. Their similarity with Palestinian board design and the absence of any Egyptian boards from the Second Intermediate period may indicate that the boardgame died out in Egypt, only to be briefly reintroduced into that country during the New Kingdom. But pegs similar to, or reminiscent of, those found with the Theban board (Figure 6A) have been dated to the Second Intermediate, Empire, and Third Intermediate periods.[63] If correctly identified as board pegs, they are evidence of a continuity not yet borne out by the gameboards themselves.[64] A uniquely shaped board from Anatolia also has certain affinities with the violin-shaped boards and is contemporary to them.[65]

Five boards from Mesopotamia are contemporary, or nearly contemporary, to the violin-shaped boards found in Palestine and Egypt, but they are comparatively simple in design (fig. 6C). Then, after a gap of some four centuries in our evidence, a dozen or more boards appear during the Assyrian period (cf. fig. 6D). With that the game of Hounds and Jackals seems to have finally expired.[66]

The game of *Tjau* spread as widely as Hounds and Jackals. The earliest examples, from Ur, date to approximately 2500 B.C.[67] There is a gap of several centuries in our evidence before boards appear, c. the eighteenth century, at Mari. By this time the tail had been unwound, as is typical throughout the game's future. It is shortly after the appearance of the game at Mari that *Tjau* boards are found in both Palestine (Middle Bronze IIB) and Egypt (end of the Second Intermediate period). In Egypt, *Tjau* was almost always coupled with the game of *Senet* on double boards. Toward the end of the New Kingdom, when the game of *Tjau* began to die out in Egypt, certain variations appeared there, as well as in other areas of the Near East. The most noteworthy variation was the melding together of two *Tjau* boards so that the game could be played by four people. At the same time, isolated examples of the game appear in Cyprus and Iran. Then the

---

63 Hayes (1959) 38, 200; Dunham (1950) pl. 36.

64 It could also be argued that the game resurfaced in modified form during Egypt's New Kingdom and that this form then found its way to Palestine.

65 Bittel (1937) 22–23, pl. 14.13.

66 Drioton (1940) 177–206 would like to see the game live on in a Coptic form. See also Decker (1992) 134–35.

67 Kainlis (1942–44) 31 used an incomplete board to argue that there must have been forerunners to these examples; but the board does not really support such a conclusion.

game lingered on in Mesopotamia and Palestine until it died out in approximately the seventh century B.C.[68]

Ancient boardgames show that "fun and games" is not of recent origin. Two of the games above swept across the Near East and continued to be played for many centuries. Boards have been found in both large and pocket-size editions. They have been found crudely made of clay and finely crafted with costly inlays. They have been found in tombs of commoners and kings. Clearly, their popularity cut across all segments of society. It also follows that the games must have been entertaining to have experienced such popularity and longevity.

The rules provided here for two of the games allow us to experience that entertainment. Importantly, both games can be played by young and old alike; parents and children can compete on equal terms.

BIBLIOGRAPHY

Albright, W. F. (1938) *The Excavation of Tell Beit Mirsim, Vol. II.* AASOR XVII. New Haven. **Austin, R.** (1940) Greek Board-games. *Antiquity* XIV:257–71. **Ayrton, E. and Loat, W.** (1911) *Pre-dynastic Cemetery at El Mahasna.* EEF XXXI. London. **Banks, E.** (1912) *Bismya; or, The Lost City of Adab.* New York. **Bar-Yosef, O.** (1982) Pre-Pottery Neolithic Sites in Southern Sinai. *BA* 45: 9–12. **Bell, R.** (1983) *The Boardgame Book.* New York. **Birch, S.** (1870) Rhampsinitus, and the Game of Draughts. *TRSL* Second Series, IX:256–70. **Bittel, K.** (1937) *Bogazköy, die Kleinfunde der Grabungen, 1906–1912. Band I.* WVDOG LX. Leipzig. **Burrett, T. and van Splunteren, C.** (1989) *The World of Games.* New York. **Carnarvon, G.** (1912) *Five Years' Explorations at Thebes.* London. **Decker, W.** (1992) *Sports and Games of Ancient Egypt.* New Haven. **Dessel, J.** (1988) An Iron Age Figurine from Tel Halif. *BASOR* 269:59–64. **Drioton, É.** (1940) Un ancien Jeu Copte. *BSAC* VI:177–206. **Dunham, D.** (1950) *El Kurru: The Royal Cemeteries of Kush.* Vol. I. Cambridge. (1978) *Zawiyet El-Aryan.* Boston. **Ellis, R. and Buchanan, B.** (1966) An Old Babylonian Gameboard With Sculptured Decoration. *JNES* XXV:192–201. **Finkel, I.** (1997) *Ancient Board Games.* New York. (forthcoming) ed. *Board Games in Perspective.* London. **Gadd, C.** (1934) An Egyptian Game in Assyria. *Iraq* I:45–50. **Ghirshman, R.** (1939) *Fouilles de Sialk.* Tome II. Paris. **Grant, E.** (1934) *Rumeileh.* Part III. Haverford. **Hayes, W.** (1959) *The Scepter of Egypt.* Part II. Cambridge. **Kainlis, A.** (1942–44) Un jeu assyrien du Musée du Louvre. *RA* XXXIX:19–34. **Kendall, T.** (1978) Passing through the Netherworld: The Meaning and Play of Senet. An Ancient Egyptian Funerary

[68] In the 1990 colloquium at the British Museum, Finkel used a second-century B.C. cuneiform text and a boardgame from southern India to argue for the continued existence of the game.

Game. (Booklet distributed with a reproduction of a Senet board by the Kirk Game Company, Inc.). **Lepsius, R.** (1949–56) *Denkmaeler aus Aegypten und Aethiopien.* Band III. Berlin. **Loud, G.** (1939) *The Megiddo Ivories. OIP LII.* Chicago. **Macalister, R.** (1912) The Excavation of Gezer. Vols. II–III. London. **Mariette, A.** (1889) *Monuments divers recueillis en Égypte et en Nubie.* Paris. **McCown, D., Haines, R., and Hansen, D.** (1967) *Nippur I. OIP LXXVIII.* Chicago. **Murray, H.** (1952) *A History of Board-Games Other than Chess.* Oxford. **Needler, W.** (1953) A Thirty-square Draught-board in the Royal Ontario Museum. JEA XXXIX:60–75. **Petrie, W. M. F.** (1890) *Kahun, Gurob, and Hawara.* London. (1927) *Objects of Daily Use.* Egyptian Research Account and British School of Archaeology in Egypt. Vol. XLII. London. (1930) *Beth-pelet (Tell Fara).* Vol. I. Egyptian Research Account and British School of Archaeology in Egypt. Vol. XLVIII. London. **Petrie, W. M. F., and Brunton, G.** (1930) *Sedment.* Vol. I. British School of Archaeology in Egypt and Egyptian Research Account. Vol. XXXIV. London. **Piccione, P.** (1994) The Gaming Episode in the Tale of Setne Khamwas as Religious Metaphor. *SAOC* 55:197–204. **Pusch, E.** (1977) Eine Unbeachtet Brettspielart. *SAK* 5:199–212. (1979) Das Senet-Brettspiel im Alten Ägypten. Münchner Ägyptologische Studien 38. Munich. **Quibell, J.** (1913) *Excavations at Saqqara 1911–1912.* Cairo. **Ranke, H.** (1920) *Das altägyptische Schlangenspiel.* Heidelberg. **Richard, S. and Borass, R.** (1984) Preliminary Report of the 1981–82 Seasons of the Expedition to Khirbet Iskander and Its Vicinity. *BASOR* 254:63–87. **Seyffarth, G.** (1833) *Beiträge zur Kenntniss der Literatur, Kunst, Mythologie und Geschichte des Alten Aegypten.* Vols. II–V. Leipzig. **Swiny, S.** (1989) Prehistoric Cyprus: A Current Perspective. *BA* 52:178–89. **Van Buren, E.** (1937) A Gaming-board from Tall Halaf. *Iraq* IV:1–15, pl. vi. **Woolley, C. L.** (1932) Excavations at Ur. *UPMJ* XXIII, No. 3:193–248. (1934) *The Royal Cemetery.* Vol. II. London.

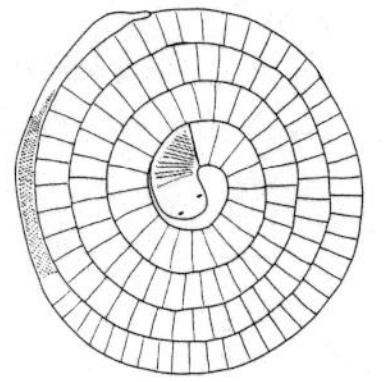

ATHLETICS IN THE ANCIENT NEAR EAST

Edwin M. Yamauchi
Miami University, Ohio

Athletics and Sports

According to Webster's *New Collegiate Dictionary* an athlete is "one who is trained or skilled in exercises, sports, or games requiring physical strength, agility, or stamina." We normally do not associate athletics and sports with the Ancient Near East. The word "athletics" is derived from Greek *athleuein,* "to contend for a prize," and is thus associated with the contests developed by the Greeks in such activities as running, boxing, and wrestling for "crowns," i.e., wreaths at Olympia. On the other hand, the word "sport" is derived from the Latin *disportare* "to remove from labor, i.e., to amuse oneself" by physical endeavors.

Athletics in Mesopotamia

Whereas there are a number of monographs on sports in ancient Egypt,[1] most of the treatments of daily life in Mesopotamia do not devote any space to this subject.[2] H.W.F. Saggs does devote one page to the wrestling between Gilgamesh and Enkidu, with an illustration of Sumerians engaged in belt-wrestling.[3] If we delve further, however, we find that there are more than a few intriguing references and artistic representations of "athletics" in the Ancient Near East.

We have considerable evidence of running, boxing, and wrestling in Mesopotamia from artistic representations and texts (royal and epic). In *The Curse of Agade* the destructive Naram-Sîn is described according to Samuel Noah Kramer's translation:

---

1 Touny and Wenig (1969); El Habashi (1972); Decker (1992).

2 Contenau (1959); Snell (1997); Nemet-Nejat (1998).

3 Saggs (1965) 88.

Like a might man *accustomed* to high-handed (action),
He put a restraining hand on the Ekur.
Like a runner *contemptuous* of (his body's) strength,
He treated the *giguna* like thirty shekels.[4]

According to another translation, the first line could be rendered: "Like an athlete coming into the great courtyard, he clasped his hands in triumph over Ekur."[5]

If Professor Kramer had been more interested in athletics (he did play tennis even at an advanced age), he might have added another chapter to his readable account of Sumerian "firsts" in history[6]—"The First All-Around Athlete." This would have been Shulgi (2093–2046 B.C.E.), the second king of the Ur III Dynasty. Kramer chose to highlight the king's boasts and achievements about his prosperity, buildings, and learning.[7] But in the extraordinary self-laudatory hymn, which Kramer titled *The King of the Road*, Shulgi boasted about his running.[8]

I, the runner, rose in my strength, *all set* for the course,
(And) from Nippur to Ur,[9]
I resolved to traverse as if it were (but a distance) of one *danna*.
Like a lion that wearies not of its virility, I arose,
Put a *girdle* about my loins,
I swing (my) arms like a dove feverishly fleeing a snake,
I spread wide the knees like the *anzu*-bird that has lifted (its) eye toward the mountain.

Another translation of the first few lines reads: "I, the runner, arose in my strength, (and) in order to test(?) (my speed) in running. From Nippur to the brickwork of Ur. My heart prompted me to traverse, as if it were (a distance) of 'one mile'."[10] That is, Shulgi boasted of having run from Ur to Nippur and back in one day—about 90 miles each way—in order to celebrate the lunar festival on the same day.[11] He also bragged about his

4 Kramer (1969b) 648.

5 Cooper (1983) 55.

6 Kramer (1959).

7 Kramer (1971) 68–69.

8 Kramer (1969a); Frayne (1983).

9 The distance was about 100 miles.

10 Klein (1981) 193; Vermaak (1993) 12.

11 Hallo (1996) 79.

speed, "Whenever I run, I can pass by/catch a gazelle." Even after running such a great distance, he had lots of energy left.

> As a donkey colt in its running, my strength never fades away. When I come back from the race, my knees never feel tired. Without any rest, as I am of strong complexion, I can still dance and prance.[12]

In another part of the same hymn, Shulgi boasted of his other athletic abilities, as an archer/hunter and a hurler of the lance.

> In Dabrum, the place where bows skills were instructed, I proved to be an expert in shooting with the bow. Its speed was that of light(ning) sent from on high. Whatever I hit did not raise its head from the spot.[13]
>
> The projectiles thrown by my arm could go as far as the arrow of my bow.[14]

A later king, Ishme-Dagan of the First Dynasty of Isin, set up a royal runner statue of Shulgi at Nippur, but claimed that he only ran one way between Nippur and Ur. A prayer relates, "It is in your power, Ishtar (to grant) speed in a footrace, attainment of what one strives for."

There are several representations of boxing from the third millennium B.C.E., including a limestone votive tablet from Khafaje and another tablet from the Diyala River.[15] Two boxers with bound wrists are depicted on an object from Tell Asmar (c. 2000 B.C.E.) and Larsa (Sinkara).[16]

Judging from both the numerous representations and the frequent textual references, it appears that the most popular sport in ancient Mesopotamia was wrestling. Ur III tablets list clothes and rations for wrestlers and athletes. The earliest representation comes from a stela from Badra (2900 B.C.E.). A plaque from Khafaje depicts pairs of wrestlers, one of whom is taking hold of his opponent's ankle. From Tel Agrab the copper

---

12 Vermaak (1993) 13.

13 Vermaak (1993) 14.

14 Vermaak (1993) 15.

15 Strommenger (1964) fig. 46.

16 A remarkable fresco (c. 1600 B.C.E.) from Akrotiri on Thera (Santorini) depicts two young boys with boxing gloves on their right hands; a Minoan rhyton (c. 1500 B.C.E.) from Hagia Triada on Crete depicts boxers with gloves. See Parke (1987). Among the Greeks the gloves were leather thongs; the Romans added metal studs on their gloves. See Papalas (1984); Scanlon (1982–83).

model of a pair of wrestlers with jars on their heads, who are grasping each other's belts, may have been a trophy.[17]

According to the *Gilgamesh Epic* the gods sent a wild-man, Enkidu, to wrestle and subdue Gilgamesh, who had been oppressing the city of Uruk. A ferocious fight ensued. According to Å. Sjöberg's translation:

> Enkidu barred the gate with his foot. They seized each other,
> they bent down like expert [wrestlers],
> they destroyed the doorpost,
> the wall shook. Gilgamesh and Enkidu were holding each other,
> like expert [wrestlers] they bent down,
> they destroyed the doorpost, the wall shook
> Gilgamesh bent [his one knee], with the [other] foot on the ground.[18]

After this fierce context, the rivals became fast friends. A text of the first millennium B.C.E., *Astrolabe B*, describes the month of Ab as: "Month of Gilgamesh. For nine days young men contest in wrestling and athletics in their (city) quarters."[19] *The Death of Gilgamesh* relates: "When before him wrestling and athletics are conducted, in the month of Ab...."

Shulgi also boasted that he was a nonpareil wrestler in international contests. Wrestling was part of the athletic entertainment at the sacred-marriage ceremony at Mari. Shamshi-Addu complained to his son Yasmah-Addu, king of Mari, about the way he was directing the war against his enemies: "You and the enemy continually devise stratagems for killing each other just like wrestlers, one seeking stratagems against the other."[20] At Nuzi a text reports the use of belt wrestling as an ordeal to decide a legal case.[21]

Athletics among the Hittites

Hittite texts (thirteenth century B.C.E.) indicate that a variety of athletic contests were held at religious festivals, including wrestling, weight lifting, and shot putting.[22] The great men of the realm competed in races for the

---

17 Strommenger (1964) fig. 48; Offner (1962) 38.

18 Sjöberg (1985) 7.

19 Tigay (1982) 186.

20 Rollinger (1994) 14–15.

21 Gordon (1952) 134–35.

22 Carter (1988).

honorary office of "holder of the reins of the royal chariot." One scholar has even seen such games as "prefigurations" of the later Greek games.[23]

Athletics in Syro-Palestine

A passage dealing with the combat between Baal and Mot (Death) in the Ugaritic myth of Baal (VI 16b–22a) reads as follows:

> (16) *yt*^{c}*nn km gmrm*
> (17) *mt* ^{c}*z b*^{c}*l* ^{c}*z*
> *yngḫn* (18) *k rumm*
> *mt* ^{c}*z b*^{c}*l* (19) ^{c}*z*
> *ynṯkn k bṯnm*
> (20) *mt* ^{c}*z b*^{c}*l* ^{c}*z*
> *ymṣḫn* (21) *k lsmm*
> *mt ql* (22) *b*^{c}*l ql*

Translators have usually compared the combatants with fierce animals. G.R. Driver translated the passage as:

> They attacked one another with might and main. Mot did gather strength, Baal did gather strength; they butted like wild oxen. Mot did gather strength, Baal did gather strength; they bit like serpents. Mot did gather strength, Baal did gather strength; they kicked (?) like chargers. Mot fell down, Baal fell down on top (of him).[24]

Cyrus H. Gordon rendered the passage as:

> They *glare at* each other like *champions*
> Mot is strong, Baal is strong.
> They gore like buffaloes
> Mot is strong, Baal is strong.
> They bite like serpents
> Mot is strong, Baal is strong.
> They kick like racing beasts
> Mot is down, Baal is down.[25]

M. Dietrich and O. Loretz have persuasively argued that the text should be translated in terms of the athletic imagery of wrestling and running.

---

23 Puhvel (1988).

24 Driver (1956) 114–15.

25 Gordon (1977) 116.

They grasp each other like two wrestlers:
Mot is strong, Baal is strong!
They push each other like wild beasts:
Mot is strong, Baal is strong!
They bite each other like serpents:[26]
Mot is strong, Baal is strong!
They push each other like runners.
Mot is fallen, Baal is fallen![27]

Athletics as such are not attested in the Old Testament. Jacob wrestled with an angel, who caused a hip injury (Gen 32:24–32). Against the earlier "athletic" interpretation of 2 Sam 2:14ff., Yigael Sukenik (later Yadin) argued that this should be interpreted as an armed combat between chosen warriors on the basis of a relief from Tell Halaf, which shows two combatants grasping each other's heads and plunging their daggers into each other.[28] Cyrus H. Gordon, on the other hand, saw in the proposed contest between Joab's men and Abner's men (2 Sam 2:14) "Let's have some of the young men get up and fight hand to hand in front of us" a possible allusion to a belt-wrestling contest.[29] (It is probably not without significance that Gordon as a young man was a wrestler himself.)[30] Jack Sasson has noted a Mari text that relates what the queen of Mari told her husband, Zimrilim, about a diviner's report concerning his conflict with an enemy: "My lord has lifted the *ḫumašu* for the *ḫumašu*(-match) with Ishme-Dagan, saying: 'In the *ḫumašu*(-match) I will overpower you. Come on, wrestle and I will overpower in wrestling'."[31] Sasson suggests that this may lend support to the translation of the Hebrew word *ḥomeš* (which occurs four times only in 2 Sam 2:23, 3:27, 4:6, 20:10) as a "wrestling belt" or "warrior's belt."[32]

---

26 In the violent pancration, which was a combination of boxing and wrestling popular among the Greeks, some contestants like Alcibiades were known to bite, though this was against the rules.

27 Dietrich and Loretz (1987) 20.

28 Sukenik (1948); cf. Yadin (1963) 267.

29 Gordon (1952).

30 Gordon (1957) 39: "After working hours I used to wrestle on an extra tent flap with our sturdy photographer."

31 Sasson (1974) 406. Malamat (1994), on the basis of this Egyptian text, suggests that Jer 12:5 may also be an allusion to a race and the collapse of a runner.

32 Sasson (1974).

Athletics in Egypt

From Egypt we have an abundance of royal texts and images that illustrate the athletic feats of the pharaohs and the sporting activities that entertained them. The king performed on the thirtieth year of his reign and every three years thereafter a ritual called the Heb Sed festival. He demonstrated his physical vigor by running around a courtyard as illustrated by the relief of Djoser (Third Dynasty) at the pavilion of his stepped pyramid at Saqqarah.

A remarkable stone monument of Taharqa, a king of the Twenty-fifth dynasty (690–664 B.C.E.), who is mentioned in Isa 37:9, relates the king's running prowess as he encouraged his soldiers on their daily run from Memphis to Faiyum and back.[33]

> His Majesty commanded that [a stela] be erected [at] the back of the western desert to the west of the palace and that its title be "Running Practice of the Army of the Son of the Sun Taharqa, may he live forever," His Majesty commanded that his army, raised upon on his behalf, daily run [in] its five [sections].
>
> The king himself was in his chariot to inspire the running of his army. He ran with them at the back of the desert of Memphis in the hour "She has Given Satisfaction." They reached Fayum in the hour "Sunrise." They returned to the palace in the hour "She defends her Master." He distinguished the first among them to arrive and arranged for him to eat and drink with his bodyguard. [He] distinguished those others who were just behind him and rewarded them with all manner of things.[34]

That is, the runners ran the first stretch of 100 kilometers or 60 miles in the coolness of the night; then, after a two-hour pause, they went back to Memphis. Total elapsed time, including the rest, was nine hours.[35]

Contestants sometimes fought with sticks, as depicted from a tomb at Amarna. A relief from Kheruef of Thebes (ca. 1365), an official of Amenophis III, depicts men fencing with papyrus stalks. His tomb also has a rare illustration of twelve boxers.

In the New Kingdom, pharaohs, such as Tuthmosis III and his son Amenophis II, boasted about their skill in archery. An inscription from Medamud relates how the latter challenged nobles to match his superb

---

33 Altenmüller and Moussa (1981).

34 Decker (1992) 62–63.

35 In 1978 Don Ritchie covered 100 kilometers in 6 hours, 10 minutes, and 30 seconds.

bowshot. The royal archers are depicted shooting at copper targets, sometimes on horseback.[36]

The Egyptians often had bulls fighting other bulls.[37] A recent discovery by Manfred Bietak at the Egyptian Delta site of Téll ed-Daba'a revealed a Minoan-style fresco of a bull-jumping scene.[38] The bull is shown *en face*, with a leaper grasping the bull around his neck. This does not mean that such events took place in Egypt, but rather reflects an athletic practice that was unique to the Minoans. The practice of bull-jumping involved both young men and women, who faced a rampaging bull, leaped, and then somersaulted onto the bull's back![39] In some depictions the athletes gained leverage by grasping the horns of the bull. This sport, which is depicted on frescoes and in sculpture, was probably performed in the large central courtyards of the great Minoan palaces at Knossos, Mallia, and Phaistos. Needless to say, the dangers of such a hazardous enterprise were so great that no one other than the Minoans attempted such sport.

The best-attested sport in Egypt is wrestling. Old Kingdom reliefs (2400 B.C.E.) from Ptahhotep depict naked youths wrestling. The most extraordinarily detailed illustrations of wrestling come from Middle Kingdom (2050–1930) paintings from Beni Hasan, Deir el-Bersheh, and other sites. The great "Wrestling Ground" from the tomb of Baqti III depicts 219 pairs of wrestlers, the tomb of Prince Kheti depicts 122 pairs, and the tomb of Amenemhat depicts 59 pairs. About every possible wrestling position is shown, including belt grips, leg pick-ups, knee pick-ups, and double body holds.

An exhibition match between Egyptians and foreigners, who always seem to lose, is depicted in the temple of Ramesses III at Medinet Habu. Inscriptions have the referee saying, "Take care! You are in the presence of the Pharaoh: Life, Prosperity and Health!" and "Woe to you, O Negro enemy! I will make you take a helpless fall in the presence of the Pharaoh."

One of my doctoral students, Scott Carroll, who was a champion wrestler in high school, published an interesting article in which he compared the scenes of ancient wrestling in Nubia represented in the Egyptian reliefs with the custom of wrestling among the present-day Nuba of Kordofan in the Sudan.[40] He illustrated his article with photos of the Nuba taken by the

---

36 Yadin (1963) 200–1.

37 Galán (1994).

38 Bietak (1996) 73–74; cf. Morgan (1995).

39 Younger (1976).

40 Carroll (1988).

famous German cinematographer Leni Riefenstahl, who filmed the Berlin Olympics.[41] A recent *Life* magazine (September, 1999) issue also featured these Nuba wrestlers, who also engage in stick fighting.[42]

The ancient Olympic games were held every four years from 776 B.C.E. for over a thousand years without interruption until the Christian emperor Theodosius I ended such pagan festivities in A.D. 393.[43] Even during wars between city-states a truce was called to allow athletes to participate. It is even more remarkable that even during the recent violent civil war in the Sudan the Nuba are still maintaining their tradition of championship wrestling, a tradition that goes back over three millennia!

BIBLIOGRAPHY

Altenmüller, H. and Moussa, A.M. (1981) Die Inschriften auf der Taharkastele von der Dahshurstrasse. *Studien zur altägyptischen Kultur* 9: 57–84. **Bietak, M.** (1996) Avaris: *The Capital of the Hyksos.* London. **Carroll, S.C.** (1988) Wrestling in Ancient Nubia. *Journal of Sport History* 15: 121–37. **Carter, C.** (1988) Athletic Contests in Hittite Religious Festivals. *JNES* 47: 185–86. **Contenau, G.** (1959) *Everyday Life in Babylon and Assyria.* London. **Cooper, J.** (1983) *The Curse of Agade.* Baltimore. **Decker, W.** (1984) Die Lauf-Stele des Königs Taharka. *Kölner Beiträge zur Sportwissenschaft* 13: 7–37. (1991) *Sports and Games of Ancient Egypt.* New Haven. (1991) Sport im alten Ägypten. In. S. Schoske, ed. *Akten des vierten internationalen Ägyptologen Kongresses.* Munich. (1985) IV 35–45 Hamburg. **Dietrich, M. and Loretz, O.** (1987) Ringen und Laufen als Sport in Ugarit (KTU 1.6 VI 6b–22a). *UF* 19: 19–21. **Driver, G.R.** (1956) *Canaanite Myths and Legends.* Edinburgh. **El Habashi, Z.** (1972) *Tutankhamun and the Sporting Traditions.* New York. **Finley, M. and Pleket, H.W.** (1976)*The Olympic Games: The First Thousand Years.* New York. **Frayne, D.R.** (1983) Šulgi, the Runner. *JAOS* 103: 739–48. **Galán, J.M.** (1994) Bullfight Scenes in Ancient Egyptian Tombs. *JEA* 80: 81–96. **Gordon, C.H.** (1952) Belt-Wrestling in the Bible World. *HUCA* 23: 131–36. (1957) *Adventures in the Nearest East.* London. (1977) Poetic Legends and Myths from Ugarit. *Berytus* 25: 5–133. **Hallo, W.W.** (1996) *Origins: The Ancient Near Eastern Background of Some Modern Western Institutions.* Leiden. **Klein, J.** (1981) *Three Šulgi Hymns.* Ramat Gan. **Kramer, S.N.** (1959) *History Begins at Sumer.* Garden City, N.Y. (1969a) The King of the Road. In J.B. Pritchard, ed., *The Ancient Near East.* 584–86. Princeton. (1969b) The Curse of Agade: The Ekur Avenged. In J.B. Pritchard, ed., *The Ancient Near East.* 646–51. Princeton. (1971) *The Sumerians: Their History, Culture, and Character.* Chi-

41 Riefenstahl (1973); cf. Luz (1966).

42 Nadel (1947) 231.

43 Finley and Pleket (1976).

cago. **Luz, O. and H.** (1966) Proud Primitives, the Nuba People. *National Geographic* 130.5: 673–99. **Malamat, Abraham** (1994) Foot-Runners in Israel and Egypt in the Third Intermediate Period. *Bibliothèque d'Étude* 106: 100–201. **Morgan, L.** (1995) Minoan Painting and Egypt: The Case of Tell el-Dab'a. In W.V. Davies and L. Schofield, ed., *Egypt, the Aegean and the Levant.* 29–53. London. **Nadel, S.F.** (1947) *The Nuba.* **Nemet-Nejat, K.R.** (1998) *Daily Life in Ancient Mesopotamia.* Westport/London. **Offner, G.** (1962) Jeux corporels en Sumer: documents relatifs à la compétition athlétique. *RA* 56: 31–38. **Papalas, A.** (1984) The Development of Greek Boxing. *Ancient World* 9.3–4: 67–76. **Parke, H.W.** (1987) A Note on the Fresco of the Boxing Boys at Akrotiri. *Journal of Prehistoric Religion* 1: 35–38. **Puhvel, J.** (1988) Hittite Athletics as Prefigurations of Ancient Greek Games. In W.J. Raschke, *The Archaeology of the Olympics.* 26–31. Madison. **Riefenstahl, L.** (1973) *The Last of the Nuba.* New York. **Rollinger, R.** (1994) Aspekte des Sports im alten Sumer. *Nikephoros* 7: 7–64. **Saggs, H.W.F.** (1965) *Everyday Life in Babylonia and Assyria.* New York. **Sasson, J.M.** (1974) Reflections on an Unusual Practice Reported in ARM X:4. *Or* NS 43: 404–10. **Scanlon, T.F.** (1982–83) Greek Boxing Gloves: Terminology and Evolution. *Stadion* 8–9: 31–45. **Sjöberg, Å.W.** (1985) Trials of Strength: Athletics in Mesopotamia. *Expedition* 27.2: 7–9. **Snell, D.C.** (1997) *Life in the Ancient Near East.* New Haven. **Strommenger, E.** (1964) *5000 Years of the Art of Mesopotamia.* New York. **Sukenik, Y.** (1948) "Let the Young Men, I Pray Thee, Arise and Play before Us." *JPOS* 21: 110–16. **Tigay, J.H.** (1982) *The Evolution of the Gilgamesh Epic.* Philadelphia. **Touny, A.D., and Wenig, S.** (1969) *Sport in Ancient Egypt.* Leipzig/Amsterdam. **Vermaak, P.S.** (1993) Šulgi as Sportsman in the Sumerian Self-Laudatory Royal Hymns. *Nikephoros* 6: 7–21. **Yadin, Y.** (1963) *The Art of Warfare in Biblical Lands.* **Younger, J.G.** (1976) Bronze Age Representations of Aegean Bull-Leaping. *AJA* 80: 125–37.